A

ONE WEEK LOAN

A History of
The British Army

BY

THE HON. J. W. FORTESCUE

VOL. XIII

1852–1870

The Naval & Military Press Ltd

Reproduced by kind permission of the Central Library,
Royal Military Academy, Sandhurst

Published by

The Naval & Military Press Ltd

Unit 10, Ridgewood Industrial Park,

Uckfield, East Sussex,

TN22 5QE England

Tel: +44 (0) 1825 749494

Fax: +44 (0) 1825 765701

www.naval-military-press.com

© The Naval & Military Press Ltd 2004

PREFACE

At last, just thirty years after the publication of the first volume, I offer the final volume of this history to the public. Saving for the war I should have finished it long ago; but the war interrupted my work, as it did that of every man; and, since the peace, heavy taxation has made it difficult for me to find leisure for unremunerative work, such as this history inevitably must be.

The close of my long task has been shadowed by sadness owing to the loss, almost at the last moment, of my invaluable map-maker, Mr. Herbert Cribb, who had worked with me from the beginning. I had made over to him, as usual, the material for this volume's maps, and he had actually drawn some of them; but he died in May last before he could complete more than a few. I cannot overstate the debt which I owe to him.

No one without actual experience can have any conception of the difficulty of producing even approximately accurate maps for bygone campaigns. The science of surveying is of comparatively recent growth; and, even if surveys be for the time exact, they may not so continue for long. Rivers alter their courses or are canalised, coast lines are upheaved or submerged, marshes are drained, forests are felled, land is reclaimed from the sea or abandoned to it, villages are absorbed into towns or altogether deserted. There is literally no end to the changes on the face of the earth thus continually wrought by nature or by man.

So far as a slender purse permitted, I tried to

visit the scene of every European campaign which I described; but I could not accomplish this wholly, and was obliged to leave America, Asia and Africa unseen. Happily I had travelled up the Nile. I knew some of the West Indian islands well and had spent four years in New Zealand; but in general I could only make good my local ignorance of many places far beyond sea by buying every map of them that I could find, and heaping the whole mass of these upon Mr. Cribb. Then by comparison of old maps with (when obtainable) modern surveys he contrived to produce the beautiful maps which adorn this history.

The difficulties which he had to overcome were enormous. Of Haiti, for instance, none but the crudest maps were to be found. Of the British West Indies the maps could not be trusted, and I could not always help him by my local knowledge. The staff-map of Portugal though good is on a very small scale. The best maps of Spain are very erratic. Of the Franco-Spanish frontier the Spanish map is chaotic, and the French map, which is on a small scale, by no means too accurate. There was nothing to help us but the rather rough sketches of Wellington's staff, and such very rude scribbles as, with no knowledge of surveying, I could set down myself. Yet Mr. Cribb contrived somehow to turn this unpromising material to good account. I found, too, that the maps even of battle-fields were very imperfect. On the field of Vitoria, for instance, I discovered a sheer cliff, mentioned by no writer, shown on no plan, which materially influenced the tactical movements of the British. I tremble to think of the number of errors which may exist in plans of fields which I have not seen.

One of the most troublesome spheres of operations was fortunately close at hand—North Holland. I began by walking eleven miles along a sandy shore to find the place of Abercromby's disembarkation. Then came the awful work of ascertaining the exact

state and position of the dykes (which for centuries
have been and are still constantly changing), as they
were in 1799. The very names of former hamlets
had disappeared; but luckily the most important of
them for my purpose was still retained by a wretched
hovel, which I ran to ground after hours of hard searching and walking. Then I returned to Mr. Cribb laden
with maps. He sought out yet more, and by comparison of six centuries of maps he finally wrought
out that which is attached to my fourth volume.

We always checked maps and text by reading aloud
twice, I reading and he checking the first time, and
he reading and I checking the second time. I cannot
say how often we read and checked the North Holland
campaign. But Buenos Aires was almost worse.
With immense difficulty I got hold of three or four
plans and charts of the city and worked out all the
details of the attack. We had read and checked it
already at four distinct stages, when Mr. Cribb produced
a quite new survey, and told me, " The orientation
of all your plans is wrong; what you have called
north should be east." Altogether we checked that
wretched attack on seven different occasions, making
fourteen times in all, before we could pass it.

The reader may now understand how great is the
strain upon a military historian when, after endless
documentary research, he settles down finally to
wrestle with his maps, and how invaluable to him
must be such a coadjutor as Mr. Cribb. His geo-
graphic knowledge was immense; his craftsmanship
masterly; his draughtsmanship superb; his patience
never-ending; his industry and ingenuity unwearied;
and finally—an invaluable quality to me—his enthusiasm for the history of the Army was unquenchable.
Never had historian a more able, conscientious and
unselfish colleague.

Against the irreparable loss of Mr. Cribb I can
fortunately set the survival of many who have shared
in my work from the outset. The three partners of

Messrs. Macmillan who entrusted my task to me in 1896 are all still living as I write, and I am happy in being able to express my obligations to them. By the encouragement which they gave to Mr. Cribb they have mightily raised the cartographical standard of our military literature.

Messrs. R. & R. Clark have printed the thirteen volumes with unvarying excellence. The care and vigilance of their readers have been of the greatest service to me; and to them and to the compositors I return my cordial thanks.

In the preparation of this final volume I have for the first time employed a " devil." My brother, Brigadier-General Charles Fortescue, toiled for months among the Archives both at Paris and in London to procure me material for the Crimean war, and further drew me out an analysis of the New Zealand campaign. If I had searched the world I could not have found a better " devil," his military experience and peculiar knowledge of French military terms being most valuable. I gratefully acknowledge my indebtedness to him.

I must thank also Miss Ann Macleod for her generous service in voluntarily transcribing and indexing for me this and the preceding volume.

There are yet two without whose stay the shouldering of this last load would have been a heavy task indeed, and whose aid cannot be repaid with mere thanks. However wearied by his own work, however harassed by his own cares, my friend Dr. John Vance has during the past three years been always ready with help, counsel and encouragement, with great stores of knowledge, stimulating criticism and inspiring suggestion.

And there is she, nearest of all to me, who, in defiance of pain and sickness, has fought incessantly to win me the leisure for completion of my task, and by sheer courage and resolution has prevailed. I had not the presumption when I began this history to inscribe it to anyone, illustrious or obscure. I could not have inscribed it to her, for she was then a child of whose existence I was for many years to remain unaware. But, now that it is done, I dedicate it with loving thankfulness to my wife.

J. W. F.

October 1929.

CONTENTS

BOOK XVI—*Continued*

CHAPTER XLI

AFFAIRS AT HOME, 1840–1852

CHAPTER XLII

THE CRIMEAN WAR

CONTENTS

CHAPTER XLIII

THE CRIMEAN WAR

CHAPTER XLIV

THE CRIMEAN WAR

b

CHAPTER XLV

THE CRIMEAN WAR

CHAPTER XLVI

THE CRIMEAN WAR

CONTENTS

CHAPTER XLVII

THE CRIMEAN WAR

CHAPTER XLVIII

THE PERSIAN WAR AND THE INDIAN MUTINY

CHAPTER XLIX

THE INDIAN MUTINY

CONTENTS

CHAPTER L

THE INDIAN MUTINY

CHAPTER LI

THE INDIAN MUTINY

CHAPTER LII

THE INDIAN MUTINY

CONTENTS

CHAPTER LIII

THE INDIAN MUTINY

CHAPTER LIV

THE INDIAN MUTINY

CHAPTER LV

THE CAMPAIGN IN CHINA

CHAPTER LVI

THE AMBELA CAMPAIGN

CHAPTER LVII

THE ABYSSINIAN CAMPAIGN

CHAPTER LVIII

THE WARS IN NEW ZEALAND

CONTENTS

CHAPTER LIX

AFFAIRS AT HOME, 1856–1870

CONTENTS

CHAPTER LX

A SKETCH OF THE NEW ARMY, 1870–1914

LIST OF MAPS

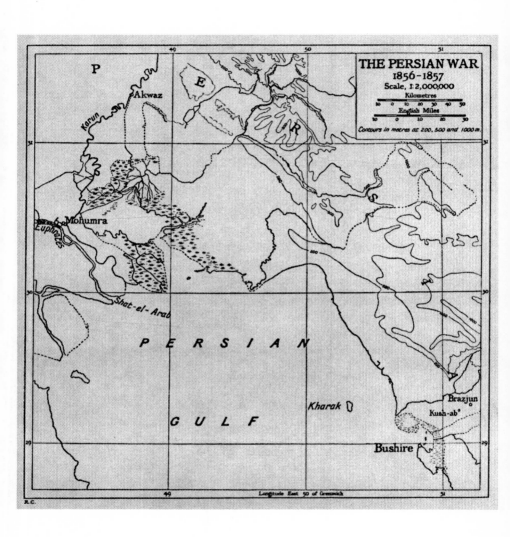

THE PERSIAN WAR
1856–1857
Scale, 1:2,000,000

Kilometres

English Miles

Contours in metres at 200, 500 and 1000 m.

P

E

R

Akwaz

Karun

Mohumra

Euphrates

Shat-el-Arab

P E R S I A N

G U L F

Kharak

Brazjun

Kush-ab

Bushire

Longitude East 50 of Greenwich

R.C.

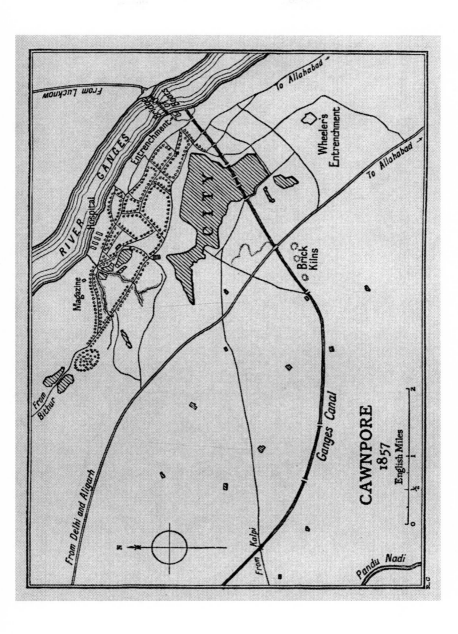

CAWNPORE
1857
English Miles

THE ADVANCE TO PEKIN, 1860

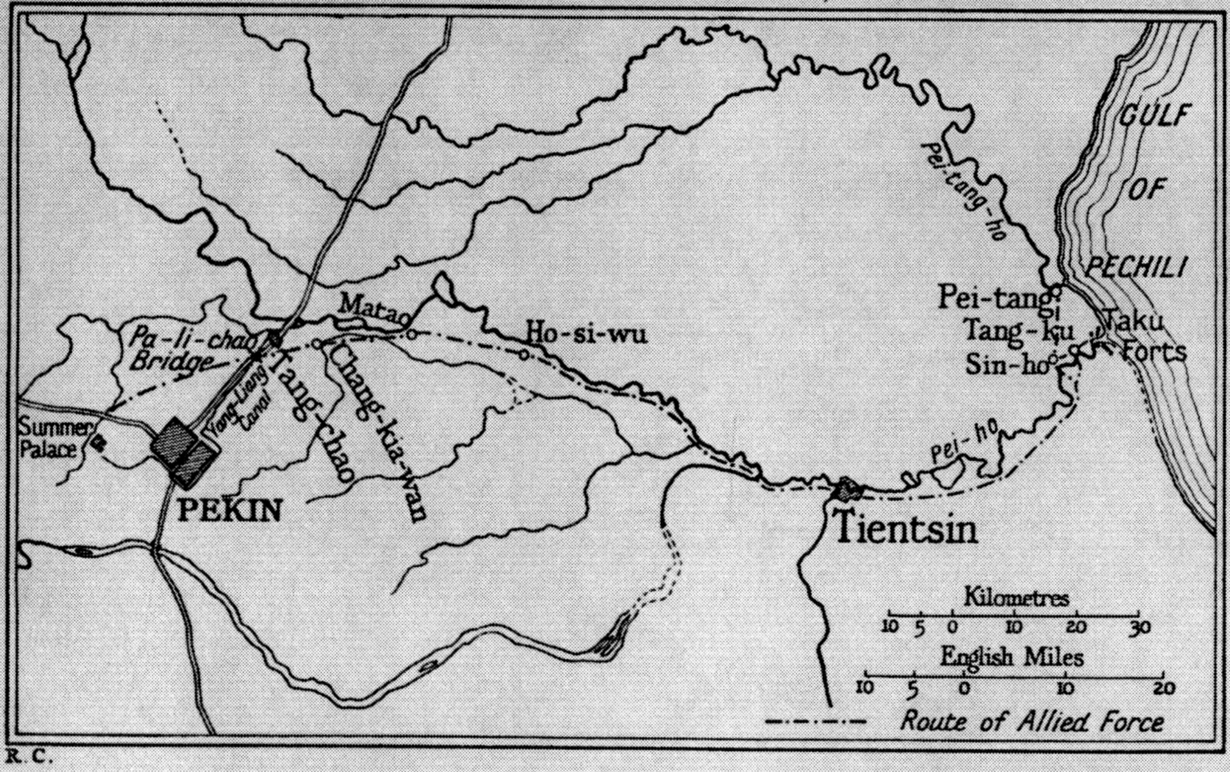

GULF OF PECHILI

Pei-tang-ho

Pei-tang
Tang-ku
Taku Forts
Sin-ho

pei-ho

Tientsin

Ho-si-wu

Matao
Chang-kia-wan
Tang-chao

Yang-liang canal

Pa-li-chao Bridge

PEKIN

Summer Palace

Kilometres
10 5 0 10 20 30

English Miles
10 5 0 10 20

———— Route of Allied Force

R. C.

ERRATA

P. 458—Line 16 from top, *for* " by the end of the year matters were greatly improving " *read* " before the end of the year matters were already improving."

P. 459—Line 12 from top, *for* " but one pier had been completed. Moreover, one condenser had been set up," etc., *read* " but, though only one pier had been completed, one condenser had been set up," etc.

CHAPTER XLI

THE reader has now been occupied with many chapters concerning operations undertaken for the consolidation of the Empire; and he can hardly have failed to notice that these campaigns, in one quarter or another, form an almost unbroken series. Before Waterloo has been fought, there is the expedition to Nepal, and then follow quickly the Pindari war, the deadly operations in Ceylon, Burma and the west coast of Africa, the siege and capture of Bhurtpore, the first Kaffir war, the Afghan war, the first China war, the campaigns in Sind and the Punjab, the troubles in New Zealand, and fresh wars both in Cape Colony and in Burma. In fact, the work imposed upon the British Army was endless, and was accompanied, as has been seen, very frequently by peculiar dangers and hardships. It is now time to see what manner of treatment it received from its masters at home.

The story has already been carried as far as the year 1840, when Lord Melbourne's Ministry was still in power; and in that year the introduction of the Army estimates fell to the lot of Thomas Babington Macaulay, the historian, who, strangely enough, found the work not uncongenial. He announced an increase of the Army from one hundred and ten thousand to one hundred and twenty thousand men, which was to be effected by raising the strength of battalions at home to nine hundred, and of battalions in India to eleven hundred apiece, and by adding five hundred to the establishment of the First West India Regiment

for garrisons in the tropics.   There was the usual
carping at the augmentation by fanatics; but Lord
Howick, a good friend to the Army, declared that he
considered it to be insufficient; and Sir Henry Hardinge
pointed out, not for the first time, that of the twenty
battalions in Great Britain not one had been there for
more than four years, and that in fact there were not
troops enough to furnish the necessary colonial reliefs.
1841. In the following year, 1841, the case was even worse.
There were seventy-eight battalions in the Colonies
and India, six on passage, making eighty-four abroad
altogether, and only nineteen at home, of which eight
had returned in the previous year, and only eleven were
fit, from a military point of view, for service.   Hardinge
gave as a particular instance the fate of the Twenty-
second, which, after serving for ten years in Jamaica,
had remained for less than four years in the British
Isles, and had then been shipped off to India.   Since
this hard treatment brought the Twenty-second under
Charles Napier's command at Miani and Hyderabad,
the regiment had its consolation; but the fact did not
invalidate Hardinge's argument that the battalions
of the line were practically condemned to perpetual
banishment.[1]

It does not appear that Parliament was in the least
moved by this statement; and indeed members took
little more interest in the Army estimates then than in
the Indian Budget now.   It was only the British soldier
who was concerned, and he always did as he was
bidden, and accomplished the tasks that were set to
him.   It was a matter of small moment to politicians
whether he were condemned to continuous exile, so
long as they remained at home and could share in the
delights of faction.   For there were two great agitations,
as they were called, in full play, for repeal of the union
with Ireland and for the reversal of England's old
commercial policy; and it cannot be denied that both

[1] Hansard : Debates on Army Estimates, Mar. 9, 1840; Mar. 5,
1841.

questions were of the first importance. Moreover, 1841.
Parliament could flatter itself that lately it had acted
not ungenerously by the British soldier. In 1840 it
had actually voted the sum of £3500—no less—for
schoolmistresses to educate the ten thousand children
who hung on to the skirts of all regiments at home and
abroad. Moreover, it had given its sanction to the
establishment of regimental savings-banks and regimental libraries in 1841; and Hardinge's scheme of
good-conduct pay, which had cost the country no
additional expense, was working well. It seems never
to have occurred to members that these latter reforms
had been painfully thought out by regimental and other
officers who were almost at their wits' end to keep the
Army—or rather the collection of regiments which
composed the Army—efficient and, so far as might be,
contented.

In September 1841 the wheel of faction turned.
Sir Robert Peel came into power, and Hardinge
succeeded Macaulay as Secretary at War. Hardinge 1842.
dared not augment the Army by more than fifteen
hundred men, but he wrestled manfully with the
problem of colonial garrisons. First, he carried out a
project, initiated by Macaulay, for the formation of a
Royal Canadian Corps, eleven hundred strong, which
was raised by volunteers from the nineteen regiments
then in Canada and was practically a veteran battalion,
no man having fewer than fifteen years' service. Next
he raised a local corps of four hundred men for St.
Helena, and, by further strengthening of a West Indian
regiment, he enabled the white garrison of Jamaica to
be reduced to two British battalions, a part of which
were to be quartered in the healthy mountains instead
of on the poisonous low ground. Lastly, he increased
six of the depôt-battalions of the Line from four companies to six, each one hundred strong, and arranged
that these should be sent to healthy foreign stations
such as Bermuda, Halifax, Quebec or the Mediterranean. Through this expedient he reckoned that he

1842. could increase the twenty-five battalions at home to thirty-one, and slightly forward thereby the relief of the seventy-eight battalions which were abroad. The cost he estimated at £63,000, and to meet it he reduced fifty battalions which were serving in other foreign stations than India and Canada, by six men apiece. To all intent, therefore, the change was one of organisation only, fifty battalions being submitted to a petty paring in order to augment six battalions—a number which was presently reduced to three—from ten companies to twelve. However, the fact explains the unexpected appearance of " reserve-battalions " on active service at the Cape in the second Kaffir War. It was thoroughly characteristic of Parliament to compel reserve-battalions to do the work of the first line.[1]

The disaster in Afghanistan caused some little stir at Westminster, but more attention was given to the political than to the military side of the question; and the close of the war, added to the pacification of 1843. Canada, compelled Hardinge, in 1843, to reduce the numbers of the establishment by nearly six thousand men. This was accomplished once again by scraping fragments from fifty-nine battalions; so that there was no reduction of active units. But the battalions at home were already weak. They numbered, exclusive of the Guards, only twenty-three, and of these only one had been at home for more than three years. Regiments returning from hot climates were almost invariably mere skeletons, since the men before their departure were encouraged to join other regiments on the spot and thus to make good their casualties without the expense of transporting drafts. It so happened that there was a good deal of disorder in rural England owing to what were called the Rebecca riots in 1842 and 1843; and consequently there was a demand for troops to do the duty of police which was only with difficulty met. In fact Hardinge, in August 1843, was obliged to bring in a bill empowering the govern-

[1] *H.D.*, Debate on Army Estimates, Mar. 17, 1842.

ment to summon out-pensioners of Chelsea Hospital 1843. to act, armed, in aid of the civil power. The bill was strongly opposed by a small group of members under the leadership of Cobden and Bright. The out-pensioners numbered seventy-six thousand; and these members dreaded, or professed to dread, a measure which would enable the government to call out what seemed to them an unlimited host. All the objections which had been urged against a standing army for over a century, and had been repeated against the establishment of the police-force, were brought forward anew; and the meaningless word " unconstitutional " was as usual very prominent. There could be no doubt of the zeal of Cobden and his followers for peace. They never ceased to preach it in and out of season; but how peace could be promoted by denying to the government the means for suppressing disorder they did not explain. On the other hand, they heeded not the hardship to the pensioners of being suddenly wrenched away from their homes upon no stronger legal plea than that, having been enlisted for life in the first instance, they remained subject to the Sovereign's command until death excused them from further service. But then the cost of a militiaman, if employed in aid of the civil power, would have been seven shillings a day, whereas that of a pensioner did not exceed two shillings. If Parliament had done its duty in maintaining a force adequate to the needs of the country and the Empire, there would have been no occasion either for militiamen or pensioners. How-ever, Hardinge, by consenting not to enrol more than ten thousand pensioners, steered his bill successfully through the Commons, and in due course it became law.[1]

    In the following year Hardinge maintained the 1844. same numbers for the establishment of the Army—roughly speaking, one hundred thousand men for

[1] *H.D.*, Debate on Army Estimates, Feb. 27; on the Chelsea Out-pensioners Bill, Aug. 10, 1843.

1844. home and the Colonies, and thirty thousand for India. Once again he denounced the hardship of keeping regiments in exile, pointing out that of those in India fourteen battalions had been there for fifteen years, one, the Thirteenth, for twenty years, and one, the Fifty-fifth, then at Hong-kong, for twenty-two years. The House seems to have taken no notice; and the only suggestion of help came from Lord Howick, who, having sent two battalions of Guards to Canada during the alarm of the rebellion, pleaded that, since they had now returned, they, or some two battalions of the Guards, should always be quartered in the Mediterranean. But this expedient, though it might have eased the difficulty of relieving troops abroad, could have done so only at the expense of weakening the home-garrison, and was really no solution of the problem. Parliament, it is abundantly evident, would not face the question of the defence of the Empire, and indeed, if pressed, was not unprepared to get rid of it by renouncing the Empire itself.

1845.   In 1845 the political dissensions at home were brought to a crisis by a famine in Ireland, which in-
1846. duced Sir Robert Peel in the following year to repeal the Corn Laws and initiate the policy of what is called Free Trade. This signified disaster to British agriculture, which, after staggering along with uncertainty for a generation, collapsed with the calamitous season of 1879, and, despite of occasional appearance of revival, has never since held up its head. The upholders of Free Trade of course repudiated the possibility of any such result; but sensible men, who looked to plain facts and refused to be deluded by talk, predicted it to be inevitable; and they were right. Beyond all question the leaders of the movement acted from the purest motives. They were indeed very jealous of the country gentlemen who had for so long ruled England, and pined to overthrow them in the name of liberty; but it would be unjust to trace their action consciously to this source. On the other hand, among their followers

were a vast body of self-seeking men who desired cheap 1846.
food in order that they might obtain cheap labour and
make large profits; and these formed the majority which
imposed Free Trade upon the nation. The military
significance of the measure was threefold. First, it
released the Army from the duties of the preventive
service, which had absorbed a great part of its energies
at home ever since 1662. This was of great advantage,
though little was said about it. Secondly, there was
the military danger of leaving the country unable to
feed itself without importing corn. Of this no account
was taken. The logical outcome of the policy, from a
military point of view, should have been an immediate
increase of the Navy and special attention to naval
matters in order to secure safe transport of food from
oversea. The fleet had, as a matter of fact, been
allowed in the generation that followed Waterloo to
sink to dangerous weakness; and the peril was the
greater inasmuch as railways had destroyed the coasting
trade and thus cut off the supply of seamen upon which
the Queen's ships had hitherto depended.[1] But little
heed was paid to any such warnings, for the leaders of
the Free Traders had prophesied that the whole world
would presently follow England's example, and that
the result would be universal free exchange and universal peace. In effect, Sir Robert Peel's celebrated
measure of 1846 was in the nature of an act of disarmament, for what is called a tariff-war is as truly a
war as any that goes by the same name. A commercial policy may even be aggressive, as in the case of
our own Acts of Trade and Navigation, which were
aimed specially at the Dutch and served their purpose.
In such a case it is of no great moment to the defeated
party whether its great commercial cities fall to pieces
because they are no longer supported by trade, or
whether they are knocked to pieces by shot and shell.
The essential consequence, desolation, remains the

[1] *H.D.*, May 16, 1845. Debate on Mr. Berkeley's motion for
manning the Navy.

1846. same.   From a sentimental point of view, therefore, the policy of free exchange in 1846 may seem to deserve commendation as a generous act of voluntary disarmament, though assuredly it would not have been adopted without the hope of solid gain.   But disarmament is a dangerous game to play unless all powerful neighbours take part in it.   The Free Traders were not only absurdly sanguine; they were not only sublimely ignorant of history and of human nature; but they had utterly misconceived the nature of war.   They imagined it to be a matter of red coats and guns and bayonets, whereas its root lies in the competitive instinct of every human heart and human brain.

Another result of Free Trade in England, and one of the greatest military importance, was also ignored in 1846, namely, the depopulation of the rural districts and the attraction of the peasantry into the towns. Thence have followed many mischiefs, the most serious of which from a military point of view (with which alone this work is concerned) have been the physical deterioration of the men bred in towns and the steady fall in the supply of rustic recruits.   Throughout this history, so far as we have followed it, all officers without exception had declared these recruits to be preferable to any.[1]   They were not, as a rule, so keen-witted as those drawn from the towns, but they were, generally speaking, strong, healthy, docile, steady, stable and trustworthy, and blessed moreover with good eyesight and alert observation.   The countryman is generally supposed to see nothing because he says nothing; but a hundred signs of sky and trees and beasts and birds mean something to him, though nothing to the townsman, and this knowledge is of no small value to him on active service.   These things were either hidden from men's eyes or, as is more likely, contemptuously rejected from consideration by the greedy rank and file who followed Bright and Cobden.   These folk have

[1] The proportion of agricultural recruits in 1847 was 628 per 1000. *H.D.*, Mar. 30, 1847, vol. xci. p. 695.

left their mark deep upon the urban districts of Eng- 1846.
land; and it is a very hideous and repulsive mark.[1]

Meanwhile at the end of 1845 began the first Sikh
War with its critical actions and heavy casualties in the
British regiments; and in 1846 there came a more
serious event in Europe. This was the rupture of the
good understanding which had for some years sub-
sisted between France and England, owing to the
deceitful behaviour of King Louis Philippe over the
affair of what was known as the Spanish marriages.
Hence in the estimates of 1847 the number of men 1847.
provided for was close upon one hundred and thirty-
nine thousand for the British Isles and the Colonies,
including thirty thousand for India; and there was a
further increase of the Artillery by twelve hundred
men, raising the strength of the Royal Regiment to
nine thousand five hundred. The fact was that in
1845 Palmerston had sounded the alarm of a French
invasion and had recommended the balloting and training of the Militia; to which Peel had answered that the
country would not endure a large standing army and
that he had therefore set apart a million for the fortifications of arsenals and dockyards.[2] The works had
accordingly been taken in hand at fourteen different
stations at home and abroad, with the natural result
that, all remaining in the elementary stage, none were
of the slightest value. Then, none too soon, it occurred
to someone that fortifications and guns were of little
worth without gunners. The authorities were helped
to this conclusion by the criticism of a military veteran,

---

[1] That the meaner sort of Free Traders were well understood at
the time is apparent from the following extract of a speech by a Mr.
Drummond upon Disraeli's motion concerning agricultural distress in
1849 (*H.D.*, Feb. 19, 1849). "You think you have settled the
question of free trade. I tell you it is now but the first skirmish of
the battle. The struggle is yet to come between capital and labour,
between wealth and life. You [the Manchester School] are the
advocates for money and capital, *coute que coute*, but I say the labourer
shall also have the right to exist."

[2] *H.D.*, July 21, 1845.

1847. Sir Howard Douglas, who pointed out in the Commons that he knew of one fort of three hundred and thirty-nine and another of one hundred and seventy-five guns for which the allowance was only half a man to each gun.   He also quoted the case of a foreign station, mounting three hundred and thirty-five guns, in which the whole garrison mustered less than half that number of men.   No doubt Parliament, when voting the money for the new defences, had not considered the possibility of this unfortunate complication.   But there was an argument in favour of the defensive works which at the moment was formidable, namely, that the French could in a very short time have collected from one hundred thousand to one hundred and fifty thousand men on the coast within a few hours' steam of the English shore, and that the English could not have brought thirty thousand men into the field to meet them.

Towards the end of 1846 Sir John Burgoyne, the veteran Engineer of the Peninsula, drew up a memorandum as to the defencelessness of England and sent it to the Duke of Wellington.   To this the Duke replied at length, deploring the situation with as lively a sense of its danger as Burgoyne himself; and, by a fortunate indiscretion, though greatly to the Duke's annoyance, this letter found its way into the press. Then at length the public began to take the alarm, and to feel that something must be done.   It was time that such an awakening should come.   That in the dire distress which followed upon the close of the long war of the French Revolution and Empire our forefathers should have shrunk from the burden of large military and naval establishments, was natural enough.   For a time it was, perhaps, fairly safe for them to cut down Navy and Army to the lowest dimensions, while other nations were as exhausted as themselves.   But it was shameful that they should have required, as they did, excessive work from the Army, while continuing to neglect it and refusing to augment it to a proper strength.   And it was sheer madness in the electorate to suppose that, because they wanted to make money, the world would remain at peace in order to accommodate them. Yet this was precisely what the petty shopkeepers, enfranchised by the Reform Act of 1832, did believe, and were encouraged to believe by the leaders of what was called the Manchester School. They forgot that a new generation had sprung up since Waterloo, a generation which knew the stress of war only as a legend and, in France, was by no means unready to try once again the fortune of arms. The French love making money at least as well as any other people, but until the war of 1870 finally and cruelly disillusioned them, they were still fascinated by the will-of-the-wisp which they call glory.

Therefore it was that not only were the estimates of 1847 rather higher than they had been for many years, but that a bill was introduced to alter the term of service in the Army with a view to the building up a reserve. This measure was introduced by Mr. Fox Maule, the future Lord Panmure, who had succeeded to the War Office upon the coming of Lord John Russell's Administration in the latter months of 1846; and his handling of this particular matter revealed him at once to be no great genius. The bill provided that no man should be enlisted in the infantry for more than ten, or in the cavalry for more than fourteen years, upon the expiration of which term he could, with his superior's approval, re-engage himself for a further period of eleven years in the infantry and of twelve in the cavalry and artillery. The original idea was to form a reserve by offering a deferred pension of sixpence a day to men who should take their discharge at the end of the first period and enrol themselves for another twenty-two years, doing twelve days' exercise annually for what may be called militia-service. But this provision disappeared from the bill and is not to be found in the final Act. " You might just as well tell a man," said Sir Howard Douglas, " that having taken the best ten years' service out of him and enrolled

1847. him for twenty-two years more, you would engage in
the end to pay his funeral expenses."

This criticism appears to have been fatal to the
scheme of deferred pensions. But the sharpest
opposition to the measure was provoked by recollec-
tion of the difficulties which had attended Windham's
plan of short service during the great war, when
soldiers nearing the end of their term had frequently
become insubordinate, and could only be persuaded
to re-enlist by a large bounty. The old Peninsular
officers almost with one voice uncompromisingly
condemned the whole project; and indeed the bill
seems from the first to have been improvidently
and carelessly prepared. In its original form it had
been applicable to men already enlisted as well
as to future recruits; but this provision had been
withdrawn upon the discovery that it would enable
twenty-seven thousand men to take their discharge on
the spot. The great theme of the older officers was
the value of old soldiers. To this Mr. Sidney Herbert
replied that unlimited service hardly existed in practice, nearly all of the men taking their discharge after
fifteen years' service. He added the curious statistics
that, of twelve thousand men who left the Army every
year, three thousand bought their discharge, three
thousand more retired on pension, and six thousand
made their escape by fraud. But there were at least
two officers who warmly supported the bill, the more
prominent of whom, General de Lacy Evans, boldly
maintained in the teeth of his comrades that young
battalions of three or four years' service were as good
as any. The final word upon the whole subject of
course lay with the Duke of Wellington, who delivered
himself with his usual decision and clearness. First
laying it down that old soldiers were absolutely essential to train and discipline the young, he gave his
opinion that the bill would not attract a better class of
recruit, but that the men whom it did attract would
re-enlist, and that consequently there need be no

apprehension of a dearth of old soldiers. This was 1847. sufficient; and the bill became law.

Except that it marked a stage in advance towards really short service, this Act is of very little significance, for none of its details had been properly considered. The measure actually reached the House of Lords before it was pointed out that no free passage home was guaranteed to men who took their discharge abroad, and that without such a free passage discharge was a mockery. Again, it was originally provided that a commanding officer might detain a man for two years after expiration of his term of service in case of war. " What," asked Lord Stanley, very pertinently, " *is* war?"; and the question was evaded by enacting that the power of extending a man's service for two years in any foreign station should be vested in the commanding officer in that station; the point, whether an enemy's territory could be construed as a foreign station or not, being judiciously left in doubt. Lastly, and principally, the scheme of building up a reserve, which was the professed object of the bill, was practically abandoned; and here again Lord Stanley put the case with epigrammatic force. The Duke of Wellington had pronounced old soldiers to be essential; but if there were old soldiers there would be no reserve, and if there were a reserve, there would be no old soldiers. From such a dilemma there was no escape except by the sacrifice of the reserve, unless indeed the Militia, which at this time consisted only of a few officers and non-commissioned officers, kept in permanent pay upon the regimental staffs, should be revived. Lord Ellenborough actually proposed resort to the Militia at this very time, though he admitted that it was a question, not of reviving but of re-creating the force. But his wise counsel received at the moment no attention.[1]

---

[1] The debates on the Army Service Bill are in Hansard, vol. xci. of 1847. *Commons*, Mar. 22, 29, 30; April 13. *Lords*, April 26. Lord Ellenborough's speech is on the Militia Ballot Suspension Bill, *Lords*, July 13, 1847.

1847.   It need hardly be said that, since the government pinned its faith to the regular Army, altogether ignoring the Militia, the debate on the Army Service Bill called forth endless suggestions for making a military career more attractive, and incidentally brought to light a good many abuses. The overcrowding of barracks, the hardships of the purchase-system, the evils of the existing regulations as to canteens, and the question of flogging, were subjects that were freely ventilated in the Commons in the years 1846 and 1847, and not without good results. Good barracks could not be substituted for bad in a day, but the necessity for change was at least recognised. As to purchase, the system, though full of glaring injustices, saved the country so much money in pensions that no politician could yet venture to propose its abolition. But a decided step forward was taken in this same year in the matter of canteens by an order that, at the termination of the contracts of the existing licensees, spirits should no longer be sold in barracks. Flogging Wellington refused to abolish, deeming it still absolutely necessary to the maintenance of discipline; but in 1846 he reduced the number of lashes that could be inflicted by the sentence of any court to fifty, and never ceased to express his hope and belief that in due time the lash might be dispensed with altogether. But, he added significantly, it was not punishment that rendered the army unpopular, but the regularity and strictness of the discipline and the hardships of long service in the Colonies. The truth is that Parliament first created discontent in the Army by condemning it to perpetual exile, and then blamed the officers for keeping that discontent within bounds.[1]

1848.   In the year 1848 the establishment of the Army

[1] As to purchase, see *H.D.*, Aug. 19, 1846; Mar. 5, 1847. As to barracks, *ibid.*, speeches of Col. Reid, Aug. 7, 1846; de Lacy Evans and Col. Lindsay, April 12, 1847. As to canteens; speeches of Col. Lindsay, Fox Maule, Sir Howard Douglas and de Lacy Evans, Mar. 5, 1847, and of Fox Maule, Feb. 8, 1848. As to flogging, *ibid.*, speeches of Wellington, Aug. 11, 1846; April 26, 1847.

was slightly raised, the number of men being fixed at 1848.
one hundred and fourteen thousand, exclusive of the
usual thirty thousand for India. Fox Maule, as befitted
a Whig minister, was extremely apologetic in propos-
ing the maintenance of so mighty an armament, and
could only plead that Bermuda, having been turned
into a convict station, now required a larger garrison,
while the military business of the United Kingdom
could not be carried on with fewer than fifty-six
thousand men. One of the government's supporters,
Sir William Molesworth, was heavily defeated in a
motion to reduce the number by five thousand, but
returned to his project later in the session, and showed
how the Colonial garrisons might be reduced from
twenty-two thousand to ten thousand men. His
methods were very simple. He proposed to give up
the Ionian Islands, the West African settlements and
the West Indies altogether, to yield up the Falkland
Islands to the Argentine Republic, and to transfer
Ceylon to the East India Company. This done, he
would have given self-government to Canada and free
institutions to the Cape Colony and to Mauritius; and
he then calculated that four thousand men would
suffice for Bermuda, the Cape, Mauritius and Hong-
kong, which, added to six thousand more for Malta
and Gibraltar, would make a round ten thousand in
all. The gist of his argument went to prove that the
Colonies were a great expense and did not yield a
profit, which was thoroughly characteristic of the time
in which he lived, of the political school to which he
belonged, and of the electorate by which the House
of Commons was at that time returned. Petty shopkeepers would naturally think of the Empire in terms
of " turnover " and " overhead expenses." By a
strange irony the discovery of gold in Australia was
within two years to fulfil their basest dreams, and,
added to a like discovery in California, to satisfy their
longing for higher prices; while lapse of time has,
without any such heroic measure as the cutting adrift

1848. of the Colonies, practically accomplished Sir William Molesworth's wishes as to Colonial garrisons. Well did the younger Pitt say that the first quality required of a statesman is patience.[1]

In this year the revolutionary spirit broke out for the third time since Waterloo, and with greater violence than ever. In the spring the Ministry was much terrified by a threatened demonstration of poor folk, discontented owing to real distress, who called themselves Chartists; and the Duke of Wellington, now in his eightieth year, was called in to provide for the security of London. With great content he returned to his old work for a few days and did it admirably, securing every important point without showing a single red-coat. By the enrolment of many tens of thousands of special constables the demonstrators were overawed, and the danger passed away harmlessly. In the country no fewer than twenty-two towns applied for military assistance, but here again the law was upheld with no great effort. There was further a silly semblance of a rebellion in Ireland, which was subdued without difficulty. But on the Continent of Europe there were revolutions in every direction. In February Louis Philippe was driven by a rising in Paris to take refuge in England; and in December, after a brief interval of wild folly and stern repression, Louis Napoleon, nephew of the Great Emperor, was elected President of the French Republic. Immediately afterwards followed outbreaks in Italy, Sicily, Spain, Austria, Germany and Poland. Everywhere there was sharp fighting, not always to the advantage of the established authorities, and much granting of constitutions. The Emperor of Austria was twice compelled to fly from Vienna in the course of the year, and finally in December resigned his throne to his nephew Francis Joseph. He in turn found himself immediately involved in a Hungarian revolt which was only put down by the intervention of Russia. The

[1] *H.D.*, July 25, 1848.

disturbances, and the serious military operations which 1848. sprang out of them, were prolonged until the end of 1849, and practically spared no important part of Europe except England and Russia. For the moment, however, the most weighty consideration to England was that France, our only dangerous neighbour and rival at sea, had passed under a new ruler who might or might not be less unfriendly than the last.

Upon this subject the government appeared to be 1849. wholly at its ease, for the Army estimates provided for a reduction of five thousand men. The Minister, indeed, annnounced that the number would have been ten thousand, but that five regiments were needed in India for the Second Sikh War. In 1850 a further 1850. four thousand men were dispensed with; and Cobden and his followers seized the opportunity to press for a decrease of officers rather than of rank and file. It seems, indeed, that from this moment was started the mendacious agitation against the Army as being a mere pasturing ground where an idle aristocracy could obtain easy subsistence at the expense of the country. The lie was easily refuted, as indeed it was by Fox Maule on this occasion, who pointed out that the net pay of a lieutenant-colonel, after deducting income-tax and interest on the price which he had paid for his commission, amounted to the magnificent sum of one hundred and seven pounds annually. Fox Maule added, with perfect truth, that British military officers were the hardest worked and worst paid of public servants; but there was no convincing such men as Cobden, Bright, and their following. They were very ignorant of the world; they were wholly lacking in imagination, and they were blinded by jealousy of the country gentlemen, from whose families for the most part came the officers of the Army. Another insinuation was that regiments existed only to furnish speculative adventures for the colonels. Now undoubtedly the system of paying general officers by inviting them to make a profit out of the clothing of the men

1850. was, though of great antiquity, vicious in principle and liable to abuse. In these days, indeed, it appears beyond measure scandalous. But the remedy lay with the House of Commons. They had only to place the clothing of the soldier in the hands of the War Department, and pay compensation to the generals, as was subsequently done, and the problem was solved. But this would have cost money, which was the very last thing which the House was willing to furnish. The meanness and improvidence of the Commons were incredible. They would not supply money enough for good-conduct medals to permit a medal to be given to every man who had earned it. They allowed men who had earned good-conduct badges to pay three shillings apiece for them; so that, practically, the better a man behaved the more heavily was he fined. Moreover, they withdrew good-conduct pay from private soldiers upon their promotion to be serjeants and serjeant-majors. The House did not, of course, lay down regulations to this effect, but, by its niggardliness in the matter of military expenditure, forced such regulations upon the War Department. Then, of course, as it would not become those who called themselves radicals, philanthropists, democrats, what not, to grudge benefits to the labouring man, they insinuated that it was the pampered officer, the son of the tyrannical squire, who ran away with all the money. And the calumny died hard, lasting for some forty years before it finally vanished from the area of faction. By that time the country squire, his market for corn having been destroyed by free trade, and his market for timber by the use of iron in shipbuilding, was well-nigh extinct; and the lie, having lost its sustenance, perished from inanition.[1]

---

[1] *H.D.*, Mar. 19, 1849; Mar. 11, 1850; speeches of Fox Maule, Cobden, Hume and Molesworth. As to good-conduct medals, etc., speeches of Col. Chatterton, *ibid.*, and on July 26, 1850. An egregious publication of about 1880 called the Liberal Reform Almanack was, so far as I know, the last attempt to represent the Army as a means of

On the other hand, there were details in which the 1850. intervention of Cobden and his followers did good. In 1850 was first put forward the bill, passed in the following year, for the government of the Australian colonies, which conceded to them representative institutions and launched them on the way to their present status of practical independence. Cobden thereupon urged that, since the bill granted to these Colonies all the land in their vast area, it should include a clause binding them to defray their own military and naval expenditure. The proposal was premature, particularly as regards the naval side, but the principle was sound and, so far as defence by land was concerned, was in due time adopted. In granting self-government to the Colonies, indeed, at this time, Liberal statesmen hardly concealed their expectation, almost their hope, of taking leave of them presently upon friendly terms. The lesson of the American Colonies had sunk very deeply into the hearts of all thinking Englishmen; and, since the Whigs had done their utmost to bring the coercion of the seceding settlements to naught and had contributed chiefly to its ultimate failure, their descendants were naturally anxious to deliver themselves from any possible chance of having to deal with a secession of Australia. Naval stations Liberal statesmen understood and accepted as a necessary evil, but they were accustomed to think of them in terms of Malta and Gibraltar; and thus Hong-kong, though hideously unhealthy, was considered comparatively unobjectionable. But that Wellington, Auckland and Akaroa could not be held

---

endowment for idle aristocrats. It followed the very crude method of registering the name of anyone bearing a title, by courtesy or otherwise, who held a commission in the Army, Navy, or Reserve Forces, with the amount of his pay over against it ; not a word being said of the work that he did or of the expense that he incurred in virtue of his commission. It was, of course, no worse in its way than similar publications on the other side. Party government, from its nature, lives at best upon half-truths and, when these fail, upon lies.

1850. without taking over both islands of New Zealand, was most galling; and the complaints of Lord Grey, during the Kaffir War, that England wanted only Simon's Bay and was weary to death of the rest of South Africa, were positively pathetic.[1]

The question of withdrawing troops from Australia was raised again on the Army Estimates of 1851, when Fox Maule answered that the Colonies always raised an outcry if troops were taken away. And this was undoubtedly true. Tradesmen in colonial capitals loved the money which was spent by English garrisons; and if they alone had been consulted, there would have been no end to Kaffir and Maori wars. But Cobden's principle was unquestionably right. Communities which clamour to govern themselves must also defend themselves.[2]

In yet another province the eternal nagging of Hume and Cobden produced good results by drawing from the Horse Guards in this same year, 1850, an order that ensigns and lieutenants should undergo an examination before receiving promotion. The subjects named were euclid, algebra, logarithms, mensuration, trigonometry, geography and history, a terrifying list for a generation which, at the public schools, had been brought up chiefly upon Latin verses. It seems probable, however, that it was inspired by the Duke of Wellington himself, who, when directing the education of his own sons for the Army, insisted strongly upon mathematics, with the addition, "of course," of perfect knowledge of geography and modern history. The matter was brought up in the House of Commons by a colonel who elicited that the examination of ensigns would begin at once, but that that of lieutenants would be deferred for two years; and further, that some allowance should be made and some discretion used in the

[1] There has been a curious survival of this feeling in our own day, when a British Government has renounced its rule over the whole of southern Ireland except the naval station of Cork.
[2] H.D., Cobden's speech on Army Estimates, Mar. 11, 1850.

case of officers who had risen from the ranks.   But one 1850. great difficulty was for the moment overlooked, namely, that in the Colonies and India no books could be procured except from England, and no teachers could be found at all; and that consequently it was unfair to officers to require them to pass examinations for which they could not possibly prepare themselves.   It was therefore presently provided that an extra captain, without a company, should be attached to each battalion for purposes of instruction; but it may be conjectured with tolerable certainty that both the teaching and the examination were for some time very much of a farce. The incident throws light upon the reaction of prolonged exile upon the efficiency of the Army.[1]

Unfortunately the estimates for 1851 showed that 1851. Cobden's worst work had wrought powerfully with the Ministry.   The actual diminution in the number of the establishment was trifling—a mere four hundred—and the strength of the Army was maintained practically at its existing figure of sixty thousand at home, forty thousand in the Colonies, and thirty thousand in India. But of the four hundred reduced, one-fourth were officers; and this was a great blunder.   Looking back over the records of the Army in the field, one may say with some confidence that it has often inclined the scale to victory instead of defeat by the fact that it possessed a larger proportion of officers than any other force in Europe; and this was an advantage not lightly to be thrown away.   Moreover, it must be remembered that the Army was England's sole fighting force.   There was no second line.   In the Lords another effort had been made in 1850 to bring about the re-creation of the Militia, but to no purpose.   The year 1851, it must be remembered, was that of the first International Exhibition.   The building known as the Crystal Palace was erected in Hyde Park, and foreigners from all quarters swarmed into London.   The world was beginning to

[1] *H.D.*, Speeches of Col. Reid and Fox Maule, June 21, 1850; of Fox Maule, Mar. 28, 1851.

1851. feel the benefit of the gold produced from California and Ballarat. The recent revolutions all over Europe had brought about a plentiful crop of constitutions on the English model, which was thought to be the last word in political wisdom. Everywhere there was talk of the brotherhood of man and of universal and perpetual peace.

In December there came an unpleasant shock. Louis Napoleon by armed force seized his principal political opponents, shot down their adherents in Paris, and established what was practically a military despotism in France. A vote of the whole nation confirmed him as supreme magistrate; and there was once again a Bonaparte, not yet for a year titular emperor with the title of Napoleon the Third, but actually wielding imperial power and controlling all the might of the French nation. Then at last England bethought herself that it was time to set her military house in order. More than once in the past ten years she had been in danger of a rupture with France, first in 1843 over an outrage to the British Consul in Tahiti, and more recently in 1850 over wrong done to a British subject in Athens. The French government supported the Greeks, and not until the French ambassador had been withdrawn from London did the British Ministry, which had been led into error by Palmerston, yield up its pretensions and so restore friendly relations. Had war ensued, there would not have been forty thousand men at hand to resist an invasion, nor more than five properly manned ships of the line ready to meet twenty of the 1852. French. Accordingly in February 1852, the Whig government increased the cavalry and infantry by four thousand and the artillery by one thousand; and further, brought in a bill to form a local militia of seventy thousand men, which was to be increased in the course of two years to one hundred and thirty thousand. The bill was opposed by Palmerston, who contended for a national rather than a local militia, and carried his point in the House of Commons. Thereupon the

Whig Ministry resigned, and Lord Derby, who had 1852. succeeded to the leadership of the Tory party since the death of Peel, became Prime Minister in February 1852, with Lord Hardinge for Master-General of the Ordnance.

The new administration held office for only ten months, but within that short time did great national service. A new Militia Bill was brought in and passed, with the warm support of Palmerston from the Whig benches. It provided for the embodiment of eighty thousand men in England, who were to be enlisted voluntarily or, if that expedient failed, chosen by ballot, and were to receive twenty-one days' training annually. It was bitterly resisted by Cobden, Bright, and their followers, and by all who called themselves " radicals," the soldier de Lacy Evans, who should have known better, among them. These persons in the Commons mustered nearly one hundred and fifty; but in the Lords, where history apparently was better known and human nature certainly better understood, the measure was carried without opposition. The Duke of Wellington used his last important speech in Parliament to give it his strongest support and to utter at the same time a few home-truths. " We have never up to the present moment," he said, " maintained a proper peace establishment; and we are now in the position that we can no longer carry out that system. You have been carrying on war in all parts of the globe by means of your peace establishment, yet in that establishment you have never had more men than are necessary to relieve the sentries and regiments on foreign service, some of which have been twenty-five years abroad." Later in the year, in spite of violent denunciations from the preachers of peace, six thousand men were voted for the Navy, as a basis for the formation of a Channel Fleet, and an additional thousand men, with two thousand horses, for the artillery. This latter arm had been discovered by Lord Hardinge to be in a deplorable condition. There were not more than forty field-pieces

1852. and siege-guns in the whole of Great Britain ; and even of these the carriages were unserviceable. Only by extreme exertion was the deficiency in some measure made good by the end of the year. Before that time the Government had been driven from office; but there was at least some restoration of security by sea and land.

Yet, amid all the troubles and difficulties thrown upon the Military Department by the intemperance of fanatics in Parliament, the Board of Ordnance had been considering the re-armament of the infantry, and had sent out, as we have seen, a certain number of Minié rifles for trial in active service in South Africa. This weapon, the first of its kind ever issued to the whole Army, had three grooves with a spiral twist of one inch in seventy-two inches, to give rotation to a conical bullet. The bore being very wide—seven-tenths of an inch—the bullet was heavy and had what is called great smashing power. It was sighted up to nine hundred yards, at which range it was only fairly accurate; but none the less, though a muzzle-loader, it was a great advance upon the old smooth-bore musket. Moreover, being a long rifle, it was effective with the fixed bayonet. The Duke of Wellington himself went down to witness some of the experimental trials of the Minié and gave it his warm approval, stipulating only that it should not be called a rifle lest the whole of the infantry should clamour to be clothed in green. Men might say that the Duke was old-fashioned, difficult and obstructive, but he had still a mind open enough to welcome a new-fashioned weapon, and though past eighty had not forgotten the whims of the Army.

This acceptance of the Minié must have been his last important administrative decision as Commander-in-chief, as his speech on the Militia Bill was his last Parliamentary utterance. On the 1st of May, as the guest of the Royal Academy, he had spoken of the discipline of the men in the *Birkenhead* with all his old strong sense, and for some months later he appeared to be in his usual health ; but in truth he had for some time been failing. The secrets of the Horse Guards were loyally kept; but it was whispered that he was often difficult and impracticable, and that he would drop off to sleep, as old men will, in the middle of business. Possibly, had he possessed any other military secretary than his old staff-officer, Lord Fitzroy Somerset, there might have been more openly expressed discontent. But no one could resist Lord Fitzroy, gentlest and most lovable of men, who was as accessible to the ensign of eighteen as to the veteran of eighty, and showed precisely the same courtesy to both. The Duke, therefore, had lost no hold of the public respect when he retired as usual to Walmer Castle after the session; and it came as a shock to the nation when he died there suddenly on the 14th of September 1852. He was buried with great pomp at St. Paul's Cathedral on the 18th of November, being followed to the grave by detachments of every regiment in the Army and by the whole of his own two regiments, the Thirty-third, still known as the Duke's, and the Rifle Brigade. The pall-bearers were Lord Londonderry, sometime his Adjutant-general in the Peninsula; the most brilliant of his pupils, John Colborne, ennobled as Lord Seaton for his services in Canada; Gough, Combermere, Charles Napier, William Napier and Harry Smith. And so hard by the tomb of Nelson the Duke was laid to his rest.

Of his military life enough has already been told, and little remains to say of his career after his final return to England when the army of occupation had been withdrawn. As a leading politician in England he certainly failed. With his peculiar qualities he could not have succeeded. The mob broke the windows of his house in 1831 when the Duchess was lying dead within it ; but as the virulence of factious feeling died down, the people returned to their allegiance, and during his latter years everyone saluted him and everyone called him " Sir," as if he had been a royal personage. Moreover, if he failed as a politician

1852. he stood as a departmental administrator in the very
first rank. His insight was swift, his common sense
transcendent, his decision prompt, and his orders terse
and clear. It has been reproached against him that he
neglected the Army during the years of his prosperity;
that he might have saved it from many injustices
and sufferings; and that, in brief, he kicked away the
ladder by which he had risen to eminence. This is not,
I think, borne out by facts. The periods of his actual
tenure of office were brief, and after 1830 the Tories
were in power for barely six years out of the twenty-two
which intervened before the Duke's death. It was
while Sir Henry Hardinge, a Tory, was Secretary at
War that the only measures for the real benefit of the
British soldier were taken; and it cannot be doubted
that they had the warm approval of the Duke, being
quite possibly initiated at his instance. While the
Whigs were supreme it was not possible for him to
exert any influence. They hated him because his
victories had kept the Tories for so long in power. It
was their custom to belittle him and to insinuate that
he owed his success to others; and they betrayed
acute vexation when the publication of the Duke's
despatches proved that every detail of his work was
done by himself. " When are you going to publish
another of your damned volumes ? " asked Brougham
in high dudgeon of Colonel Gurwood. The question
gives us a strange glimpse of the infinitely little.

It was too much to expect that a proud and self-
respecting man should abase himself by pleading the
cause of the Army to such men as Lord Grey and
Lord John Russell. Lord Grey had used information,
treacherously furnished by Wellington's chief staff-
officer, Willoughby Gordon, to damage him in Parliament. Lord John Russell had so sublime a conceit
of himself that, as Sydney Smith said, he would
cheerfully have undertaken to command the Channel
Fleet or to perform an operation for stone; and it was
not for one of Wellington's stature to court rebuff

from such comparative pigmies. Moreover, the 1852.
Whigs treated him with studious contempt and almost
with insult.   It might have been thought that so great
a soldier was worth consulting before the issue of a
new drill-book, if not for the value of his judgement, at
least as a mark of respect; but such was not the way
of the Whigs.   On the other hand, they were glad
enough to call him into counsel during the threatened
revolution of 1848; and he heaped coals of fire upon
their heads by giving them his very best work.   Beyond
doubt the knowledge that the safety of the capital had
been committed to his guardianship inspired law-
abiding citizens with that confidence which brought
the schemes of the Chartists to naught.   Nothing
could have been more characteristic of a man who put
his duty to his country before all things.

It is curious to contrast his fame with that of the
political opponents who triumphed over him.   He was
what is called a High Tory.   He had no faith in the
virtues of a low suffrage, nor of secular education, nor
of free trade.   He did not believe at the time of the
dispute over the boundary of Maine that " without a
regiment or a line-of-battle ship, without bombarding
any town whatever, free trade will conquer the Oregon
territory for us and will conquer the United States
for us also."   And time has amply justified him.
The great majority of men are stupid, unable to grasp
many facts, and incapable of forming any judgement
upon them; and the possession of a vote has not
changed their nature.   It was hoped at least that what
is called democracy would quench the revolutionary
spirit; but it has entirely failed to do so.   It was
hoped that education would make men good, but it
has left them no better than before.   It was hoped that
free trade, as shown by the extravagant quotation
above given, would be everywhere imitated and would
bring universal peace, whereas it has been practically
everywhere rejected; nor would war have ceased if it
had been accepted.   Wellington, believing in none of

1852. these things, shared none of these hopes, and therein
he showed his essential sanity. In political as in
artistic life there seem to be periods when men are disposed to take leave of their senses, and to welcome
obvious foolishness. " It is a principle," wrote a very
acute literary critic, " that if we put down a healthy
instinctive aversion, nature avenges itself by creating
an unhealthy, insane attraction." And hence arise,
in the domain of art, schools which worship ugliness
and absurdity. Something of the same description
seems to take place when men, in the face of all the
evidence of their senses, force themselves to believe
such doctrines as that all men are equal and that human
nature is perfectible, and endeavour to reconstruct
human society upon these treacherous foundations.
Their enthusiasm and their persistence of assertion
carry away with them the majority of their fellows;
and the few that remain unconvinced are treated with
contempt or with hatred according to their intellectual
powers. These few may not always be very clever;
they may not be very receptive of new ideas; but they
are at least sane, and they refuse to entertain any idea
which is obviously repugnant to common sense.

Thus though the names of Cobden and Bright are
still honoured—for both were eminently good, earnest
and conscientious men—it is not in virtue of their
prophecies. It may indeed not be long before they
are set down as teachers who with the best intentions
led England woefully astray. However that may be,
it is certain that for ten years, by their unwearied
condemnation of armaments, they placed their country
in very deadly peril. It may be pleaded for them that
at least they denounced war and praised the beauties
of peace. But what is war? And what is peace?
The gradations whereby the state of what is called
internal peace may pass into the state of what is called
civil war are far too subtle and delicate to be accurately
traced. For all practical purposes Cobden and Bright
simply reiterated the old song of the Hebrew poet:

" Mercy and truth have met together; righteousness and peace have kissed each other." Yet mercy and peace were waiting in vain for their partners long before the days of that poet, are waiting still, and must continue to wait.

The fame of Wellington is of a very different nature. During his lifetime some thought it in excess of his merits, but time has done little to diminish it. A plain, simple soldier, he dealt with the world as he found it, and not as he would have had it to be; and he conceived that he could best serve it by faithful and enlightened service to his own country. And the field of that service was wide, embracing diplomatic besides military and political work, all of which he did to the best of his ability and according to the dictates of his transcendent common sense. He lacked the personal charm of Marlborough, and was never beloved as had been Corporal John; yet his name alone is worthy to stand with Marlborough's in the military annals of England. Let the Army never abate one jot of its pride in Wellington. Let them examine his campaigns critically, failing not to mark his faults whether as general or as an individual. But let them never forget that, apart from all other services, he raised the standard of public duty and of discipline among all ranks of his countrymen, thereby approving himself not a great soldier only but a great man.

CHAPTER XLII

1853. In the year 1853 there was tried, for the first time during a period of peace, the experiment of forming a camp of exercise. In June, three brigades of infantry and one of cavalry, with artillery, engineers and a pontoon-train—altogether from eight to ten thousand men—were assembled at Chobham under the command of Lord Seaton. After a month's training these were replaced by a smaller force of two brigades of infantry and one of cavalry; and towards the end of August the camp was broken up. The novelty of the proceeding excited great interest. Hitherto there had been but one quarter in the United Kingdom— Dublin—where men enough could be collected for the manœuvring even of a brigade; which was the necessary consequence of scattering the Army about in small detachments for purposes of the preventive service and of police. It was in the course of the manœuvres at Chobham that were laid bare the defects which Hardinge had endeavoured to make good in the artillery. Neither gunners nor drivers had been trained to their work; and three years later Lord Panmure confessed that but for the camp at Chobham it was doubtful whether the Royal Regiment could in 1854 have produced six batteries fit for service in the field.[1] Unfortunately there were other shortcomings which were not corrected.

For the day of reckoning for all the follies—they might almost be called crimes—of Parliament during

[1] *H.D.*, Speech of Panmure on Army Estimates, June 16, 1856.

the past forty years was now close at hand. There had 1853.
arisen a dispute in the East which was assuming a
threatening aspect. It arose originally out of a
seemingly petty matter, the custody of the Holy
Sepulchre, which was in contest between the Greek
Church, under the protection of Russia, and the Latin
Church, under the protection of France. By a treaty
of 1740 France had gained certain privileges for the
Latin Church in this sacred duty, but had allowed them
to lapse until 1850, when she suddenly revived them
and pressed the Turkish government for them with
such diligence that in December 1852 they were
finally conceded to her. Thereupon the Emperor
Nicholas, as champion of the Greek Church, waxed
very indignant; and, Turkish troops being at the time
employed in repressing a rebellion in Christian
Montenegro, Nicholas called upon the Porte to withdraw them on pain of war. The Porte complied; and
Nicholas then required of it a treaty which should
place the Greek Church in Turkey under the protection
of Russia. The Porte in panic begged for the British
fleet to be sent up to Constantinople, which request
was refused, though the French fleet moved up as near
to the Dardanelles as Salamis. The dispute about the
Holy Places was presently settled by Lord Stratford
de Redcliffe, the British Ambassador at Constantinople,
through a compromise; but he steadily supported the
Sultan in rejection of the further demands of Russia,
announcing that, if necessary, he had authority to
summon the British fleet to the Bosporus. Thus by
slow and imperceptible degrees the British ministers
allowed England to drift, practically, into a defensive
alliance with Turkey, a proceeding which, as a single
and deliberate act, they certainly would not have
sanctioned.

Greatly irritated, Nicholas, on the 2nd of July
1853, marched troops into the Danubian principalities
of Moldavia and Wallachia, and announced that he
should occupy them as security for Turkey's compli-

1853. ance with his demands. Here he made a false step, provoking strong objections not only from France and England, but from Austria and Prussia also. The concert of the four Powers was not, however, too perfect, for Louis Napoleon, now become the Emperor Napoleon the Third, was anxious to settle matters in alliance with England only. However, representatives of the four met in conference at Vienna and approved a draft note which should be forwarded by the Porte to Russia through Austrian mediation. The Porte, nevertheless, rejected the note and required the Tsar to withdraw his troops from the principalities within fifteen days. Nicholas was then inclined to be conciliatory; but England and France, which held their fleets in hand at the mouth of the Dardanelles, ordered them to proceed on the 22nd of October to the Bosporus; and on the 23rd Turkey declared war. Nicholas, greatly incensed, retaliated by attacking and destroying the Turkish fleet at Sinope on the 7th of November. This perfectly legitimate stroke was bitterly resented by public opinion both in France and England; and the English Cabinet, yielding to the Emperor Napoleon, joined him in declaring that any act of Russian aggression against Turkish territory or the Turkish flag should be repelled by force. Thereupon the Tsar recalled his ambassadors from Paris and London, and England and France withdrew theirs from St. Petersburg. Russia bestirred herself to gather forces for the invasion of Turkey; and France and England not only despatched each a skilled engineer—Sir John Burgoyne was the English officer—to aid the Turkish armies with their counsel, but agreed to send a small body of troops to the Levant.

1854. In February 1854 accordingly the first British soldiers sailed to Malta, and with them went a correspondent of the *Times* newspaper, who carefully chronicled the arrival of each regiment, adding very often an exact account of its strength, for the edifica-

tion of the British public and the benefit of the Russian 1854.
staff. But beyond the dispatch of these battalions no
preparations were made for a campaign; and their
arrival in the Mediterranean could well be construed
as a mere demonstration in support of diplomacy.
There were many members of the Government, above
all the Prime Minister, Lord Aberdeen, who loathed
the very name of war; and, after all, the business of
compelling the Russians to evacuate the principalities
lay much more with the Central Powers of Europe, and
particularly with Austria, than with England. But
forty years had passed since Waterloo; and that seems
to be almost the extreme period for which men can
abstain from flying at each other's throats. A generation had sprung up in England, as in France, which
knew nothing of war and desired to try its mettle by
experience. The Government having begun, through
its diplomacy, to drift into threats of active hostility
against Russia, was hurried upon its perilous way by
popular clamour. Instead of waiting until Austria
and Prussia should join them in putting irresistible
pressure upon Nicholas, France and England sent to
him an ultimatum requiring him to withdraw his
troops from the principalities by the 30th of April, and
intimating that his refusal to do so would be regarded
as a declaration of war. On the 19th of March the
Tsar declined to send any answer to this appeal, and on
the 28th war against Russia was finally proclaimed. It Mar. 28.
remained only for France and England to enter into a
covenant of alliance with each other and into a treaty
engaging to defend Turkey. These objects were
accomplished by the 10th of April; and on that same April 10.
day Lord Raglan—formerly Lord Fitzroy Somerset,
the veteran of Wellington's staff in the Peninsula and
at Waterloo, and since then for years his right-hand
man at the Horse Guards—received his letter of service
as Commander-in-chief of the British Army in the East.
    How that army was to be employed was fully set
forth. Its first duty was to prevent a Russian advance

1854. upon Constantinople; and, as a counter-offensive
April. movement, it was stated that no stroke could be so
effective as the capture of Sevastopol. But the government had no information as to the strength of the place,
nor of the Russian forces in the Crimea, and Lord
Raglan was instructed to make good this ignorance.
For the rest, the government went no further than to
admit that a siege of Sevastopol would be " a serious
matter," which is not uncommonly the case with
military operations. However, the defence of Constantinople being the first consideration, the French
had sent in March two generals of high rank with a
couple of light battalions and some engineers to
Gallipoli, to throw up entrenchments about Bulair.
Thereupon the English thought it advisable to do likewise; and Sir George Brown was dispatched thither
May. with a due number of battalions. By the end of May
the greater part of the British infantry had been brought
from Malta either to Gallipoli or to Scutari, at which
latter place there were luckily barracks, for the troops
stationed in the Mediterranean had not been provided
with tents. At the beginning of May Raglan began
to contemplate the transfer of his troops to Varna,
where they would be nearer at hand to support the
Turks against the Russian invasion; but the Commissariat Department was so deficient in the number
of its officers that the Commissary-general doubted his
ability to feed the army in Bulgaria. This was no
fault of the Treasury, but ascribable directly to the
false economy of previous Administrations. Sir Charles
Trevelyan, Secretary to the Treasury, had in 1850
protested earnestly against the fatal policy of keeping
no reserve of trained Commissariat officers. "An
army," he had written, " is quite as helpless without a
properly trained Commissariat as without ammunition." His wise counsel was ignored by the Whig
Cabinet. This was the first symptom of a trouble that
was to haunt the entire campaign, and was aggravated
by the indecision of the British government, which had

moved a force into the Levant without any clear notion 1854.
what they should next do with it.

Meanwhile the public in England, hungry for
exciting news, was regularly fed with camp-gossip by
the correspondent of the *Times*, who criticised with
easy superiority the sites of camps, the hardship of
making the men shave, and above all, the use of the
leathern stocks which the soldiers wore round their
necks.   These two last topics were of great service to
one whose duty it was to fill many columns of a newspaper; but they were only details.   The stocks did
undoubtedly choke the men during a hot march, but
Raglan had always allowed them to be dispensed with
at such times; and, in the matter of shaving, he made the
shrewd remark that it was the first notion of cleanliness
among the lower classes in England.   Moreover, the
country swarmed with vermin, for which long hair
furnished the best of harbours.   The fact was that the
French, fresh from their campaigns in Africa, were
bearded, and that English officers, with nothing in
particular to occupy their thoughts, wished to imitate
them.   Raglan was not inclined to give way to this fancy.
" I am old fashioned," he wrote, " and I cling to the
desire that an Englishman should look like an Englishman, though the French endeavour to make themselves
look like Africans, Turks and infidels."

Incidentally the correspondent had made the discovery, long since patent to the officers and men who
had served in Kaffirland, that the dress of the Army,
a legacy from the Prince Regent, was absolutely unfitted for work in the field.   Officers with hardly a
pocket in which to stow even a handkerchief in uniform,
assumed the dress of civilians directly they came off
duty; and the traditions of Wellington in the Peninsula
by no means bore against the practice.   There can be
no question that, in spite of its campaigns in every
quarter of the globe since 1815, the Army, as a whole,
knew little of its business except on the parade-ground.
Raglan was no doubt aware of it, but he had more

1854. serious matters to think of. For one thing, his infantry
May. was actually in process of re-armament. The brigade
of Guards started with two hundred Minié rifles and
six hundred and fifty percussion-muskets in each
battalion. Lord Hardinge had sent out more rifles;
and as a matter of fact the Guards were armed completely with the Minié by the end of May, though
ammunition was still deficient. On the whole, Raglan,
when the Secretary of State brought to his notice the
strictures of the press, was justified in answering: " I
am surprised that any statesman should have thought
it his duty to notice such verbiage and idle gossip." [1]
    The time was now coming for the concert of action
between the allied commanders. The French Commander-in-chief, Marshal St. Arnaud, had gained his
high place by paving the way for Napoleon the Third's
ascent to the throne. He was a man with a strange past.
He had joined the Army originally in 1816, but had
been obliged to leave it, and indeed to quit France,
owing to his wild life. He had rejoined it in 1830, but
had made no way until in 1836 he became a lieutenant
in the Foreign Legion and fought in Algeria. Very
brave, dashing and unscrupulous, he then advanced
rapidly and deserved advancement; and finally after
December 1852 he emerged as a Marshal of France.
Being master of several languages, English among
them, he was in one way well fitted for his place; but
he was in bad health, which subjected him to disabling attacks of pain, and, with unquestionable
military gifts, he was quite unfit for the command of
a large force against a disciplined enemy. Indeed this
was recognised by Napoleon, who had attached to him
a special officer, Colonel Trochu, to make good his
defects. St. Arnaud was not on that account without
assurance, for he attempted to gain the command
first of the Turkish troops and next of the entire allied
army; but though he was easily foiled, he bore no
malice. Altogether, he seems to have been a flighty,

[1] *Raglan MSS.*, Raglan to Newcastle, May 14, 15, 1854.

but not a formidable person. Omar Pasha, the Turkish 1854.
Commander-in-chief, was a capable and loyal soldier
who was perpetually harassed by the intrigues of rivals
at court, but was most anxious to work cordially with
his allies.   He immediately gained Raglan's liking
and respect.   As to Raglan himself, his qualities will
unfold themselves in the course of the narrative.   His
position was most difficult; but having shrewd insight,
a sense of the ridiculous and a strong will, and being,
moreover, an English gentleman in the highest sense
of the term, he could work even with so strange a
yoke-fellow as St. Arnaud.

The three commanders met at Varna, a port on the
Black Sea, about fifty leagues north of Constantinople.
The Russians had established a bridge over the
Danube below Silistria and invested that place; and
the immediate military question was that of its relief.
Omar Pasha's main army and headquarters were at
Shumla, fifty miles west of Varna, and there the three
commanders met again on the 23rd of May, when it May 23.
was agreed that Raglan and St. Arnaud should assemble
all the troops that they could in Bulgaria in order to
make a demonstration.   Both armies were as yet practically without cavalry, and were also deficient in artillery,
owing to lack of horses; while the provision of land-
transport had so far offered insuperable difficulties.
Nevertheless St. Arnaud talked big of carrying out
the project immediately.   Raglan thereupon gave his
orders for the embarkation of two divisions for Varna,
and was disagreeably surprised when Trochu came to
tell him two days later that the French army, owing May 25.
to backwardness in its preparations—supplies, shoes
and even ammunition being scanty—was quite unfit
to move, as had been arranged.   However, Raglan
did not alter his own dispositions; and a few days
later, on the 4th of June, St. Arnaud came forward June 4.
with a new suggestion that the allied armies should
take up a line south of the Balkans, with their right on
the sea at Burgas and their left, which was to be the

1854. station of the British division, thirty miles to west at Karnabat. On this project Raglan firmly set his foot; and finally it was settled that the entire allied army should move to Varna, one French division going by land, the remainder by sea. Thus the idea of a joint demonstration for the relief of Silistria vanished into air.[1]

Happily no such operation was needed. The Russians, thanks to the energy of two young English officers, Captain Butler of the Ceylon Rifles and Lieutenant Nasmyth of the Indian artillery, did not prosper before Silistria. Elsewhere on the line of the Danube Omar Pasha attacked them more than once or June 22. twice with success; and on the night of the 22nd of June the Russians raised the siege and fell back in disorderly retirement. By the end of the month the whole of the British, excepting one-third of its little force of July. cavalry, was at Varna, and on the 4th of July Omar Pasha came to the British headquarters and asked the British to join him in pressing the Russian retreat. But there was no need to press it. The Russians abandoned the Dobrudscha and recrossed the Danube. They tried to make a stand at Giurgevo, opposite Rustchuk, on the north side of the river, but were driven out by the Turks and forced in the middle of July to retire towards Bucharest. The victorious Turks (for the story may as well be ended at once) followed them up and reached Bucharest on the 8th of August; the Russians having by that time withdrawn in some confusion to the Pruth. But now another Power stepped in. Austria on the 14th of June had come to an agreement with the Porte, by which she undertook to make Russia evacuate Moldavia and Wallachia, and to occupy them herself while hostilities lasted. Biding her time carefully until the issue in the field had been Aug. 20. decided by the victory of the Turks, she on the 20th of August sent her troops into the principalities, in

[1] *Raglan MSS.*, Raglan to Newcastle, May 25, 29; June 5, 8, 10, 1854.

pursuance of the above convention, thereby covering 1854.
the retreat of the Russians to the Crimea. However,
the main point for the Allies was that Russia had
evacuated the Danubian principalities, which was the
object for which France and England had taken up
arms.

Meanwhile, the Allies continued inactive at Varna. July.
The French sent up a division, indeed, to the Dobrudscha which in a few weeks was half destroyed by
sickness, and Lord Cardigan, who commanded the
British Light Cavalry Brigade, at the beginning of
July made a short reconnaissance in the same direction;
but otherwise nothing was done. In the middle of
July, however, St. Arnaud received a rebuke from Paris
for not attacking or preparing to attack the Crimea.
The name of Sevastopol was not mentioned, though it
was hinted at by the suggestion that the army should
leave Varna by sea. Raglan, knowing that the French
siege-train had not yet left Toulon, was amazed; but
at precisely the same time he was informed by the
Secretary of State that the Cabinet favoured the siege
of Sevastopol, supposing the Allied armies to be
sufficiently prepared for the task. Had this been all,
no great harm might have come of it, but, with the
private letter came a secret despatch which practically
contained definite orders to attack Sevastopol.[1] Raglan
answered privately that the question was a very serious
one, and the more so since neither he nor St. Arnaud
had been able to obtain the slightest information about
the Crimea. Moreover, not only was the French
battering train still in France, but his own was incomplete, and he could not expect it to be supplemented
until November. He could only sound the Turks
cautiously as to the possibility of obtaining heavy pieces
from them, because the design must be kept a profound
secret.[2]

There was a sad irony about this last remark. In

---

[1] It is printed in full in Kinglake, chap. xvi.
[2] *Raglan MSS.*, Raglan to Newcastle, July 14, 1854.

1854.
July.
two violent leading articles of the 15th and 22nd of June the *Times* had declared that "the political and military objects of the war could not be attained as long as Sevastopol and the Russian fleet were in existence." It proclaimed that the fortress was the centre of Russian power in the south, and that with its annihilation the whole fabric must fall to the ground. As a natural consequence the blind public seized upon the name, never troubling themselves to ask whether their guide might not be equally blind; and a campaign against Sevastopol became the talk in every mouth. The English had worked themselves up into eagerness for a fight; and irresponsible individuals, so innocent of war as to scorn all ideas of secrecy, boldly dictated where the struggle should take place. This bare fact should have compelled Ministers to shift the scene of operations to any place but the Crimea. The clamour for the siege of Sevastopol could have been turned to excellent account by any man who understood war; but the Ministry had not the remotest understanding of it. Weak, ignorant, dismayed at the results of their own mismanagement, they knew not what to do, and submitted themselves to be governed by popular outcry.

Meanwhile, they had received from without a warning through a private letter written by a Peninsular veteran, which had been forwarded to them by the recipient. An attack on Sevastopol, said Major-general Shaw-Kennedy in effect, was so desperate and reckless an adventure that no Commander-in-chief would attempt it. The place was invulnerable on the side of the sea; to force the line of defence on the side of the land would be very difficult; and the besieging force would be exposed to attack by all the forces in the south of Russia. Of all operations this appeared to Shaw-Kennedy the most absurd and the most dangerous. He himself favoured attack from the eastern shore of the Black Sea upon the territory to south of the Caucasus, where the Turks, generally called by the generic name of

Circassians, still maintained their independence against all the efforts of Russia. With the sea denied to the enemy, such a campaign could hardly have failed of success. The Russians might have been expelled from the south of the Caucasus; and their advance upon India, which would have been a reason, if not an excuse, for war, might have been for long delayed. Ministers did send, or announced their intention of sending, an emissary to stir up the Circassians, but they seem never to have dreamed of turning the expedition to that quarter. Governments which drift into war are apt to drift also to their theatre of operations.

This letter had been sent to Raglan in May, but he needed no such help to open his eyes about Sevastopol. He called into council one of his divisional commanders, Sir George Brown, who declared that Wellington would not have accepted the responsibility for such an enterprise, but that the English government had evidently made up its mind and, if Raglan refused to attack Sevastopol, would recall him and send out some more pliant instrument. Beyond all question Brown's judgement upon this point was sound; though it can hardly be supposed that the same thing had not occurred to Raglan also. He was in as cruel a position as was Abercromby when Henry Dundas sent him to North Holland without any transport, and to Egypt with the prospect of having no water, except that which could be carried in the fleet, until he had captured Alexandria. His chief naval colleague, Vice-admiral Dundas, openly disapproved of the whole enterprise, doubting his ability, not to land the military forces, but to supply them when landed and to re-embark them in case of mishap. But Raglan was not a man to shelter himself behind the opinions of others. He accepted the task obediently as had Abercromby, abstaining even from Abercromby's comment, " There are risks in a British warfare unknown in any other service."

Moreover, having come to this decision, Raglan resolved that he would make another army, of far

1854. greater reputation than the British, share all its hazards with him. It is true that the French Emperor had already ordered St. Arnaud to attack the Crimea; but French generals do not as a rule so readily yield to civilians as English when military operations are in July 18. question. On the 18th of July Raglan met St. Arnaud in conference, the chiefs and seconds in command of both fleets being also present, and the details of disembarkation in the Crimea were discussed; but at a second July 28. conference on the 28th, when Trochu and two more French generals attended, as well as St. Arnaud, the French urged the abandonment of the enterprise on the ground that Turkey was not yet safe from invasion. The fact was that, with perfectly sound military judgement, they abhorred the whole project. But, though they were absolutely in the right, they had not the courage, in the face of the Emperor's orders, to ground their objection upon military foundations; and Raglan, who had correctly gauged the full significance of the Russian retreat from the Danube, had little difficulty in demolishing the feeble protest advanced by the French generals. Accordingly, orders were given for reconnaissance of the Crimean coast; and the preparation of flat-bottomed boats and other facilities for disembarkation went forward with all possible activity.

The troops so far sent out from England were probably as fine a lot of men, for their numbers, as ever were put into the field. Three battalions of Guards and twenty-five of the line with sixteen squadrons of cavalry had been the force originally assigned to Raglan, the battalions being eight hundred and fifty strong. But these numbers had only been attained by drafting volunteers from other battalions ruthlessly into those selected for service; and even the regiments of cavalry, though reduced to but two squadrons, had not been completed without resort to the same device. As a body, therefore, the men were healthy and strong, though the Guards, exposed constantly to the temptations and diseases of great cities, were, as was natural, less sound physically than the rest.   Six regiments only 1854. of the twenty-five of the line had seen active service within the previous thirty years, namely, the Thirty-eighth and Forty-seventh, which had fought in Burma in 1826; the Forty-fourth, which had been annihilated in the retreat from Kabul; the Forty-ninth and Fifty-fifth, which had been with Gough in China in 1842; and the Fiftieth, which had covered itself with glory in the first Sikh War of 1843.   There were, therefore, not many regimental officers and men who had any previous experience of war; and few had any knowledge of their work beyond that of the barrack-yard.

In the matter of armament three out of the four divisions had been furnished with the Minié rifle by the middle of June, and measures had been taken to equip the fourth also.   A special instructor in the use of the new weapon had been attached to Raglan's staff. Another reserve division of infantry was preparing to leave England; and Raglan was anxious that it should have its due allowance of artillery—two batteries— which apparently had not at first been thought of at home.   Four more squadrons of cavalry were also on their way, but these were not nearly sufficient to make good the deficiency in that arm.   Moreover, a good many horses had been lost on the voyage, and a fire upon one transport had caused the death of two officers, sixteen men and fifty-seven horses of the Inniskilling Dragoons.   The remedy recommended in England was the raising of a body of Turkish irregular horse, to be commanded by Colonel Beatson, an Indian officer of great reputation; but Raglan had a horror of half-disciplined troops.   He remembered the enormous difficulty with which Wellington had brought his army to abstain from plunder and to deal justly and honestly with the inhabitants of a hostile country; and he dreaded the power of irregular levies for mischief, in provoking the enmity of the native villagers and in sapping, by example, the discipline of his own men. Many thought that herein he was narrow-minded, and

1854. quoted the good service done by irregular horse in India; but there is a wide difference between a campaign in Sind and a campaign in the Crimea.

In the matter of transport and supply, matters were still very backward. The Chief Commissary, Mr. Filder, was an able man who laboured from morning till night, but his department was still undermanned, and few of his subordinates had the slightest idea of their business. Raglan himself had told a committee of the House of Commons a few years before that the work of the Commissariat in peace was no training for its duties in war. It was not a very difficult thing to make contracts to feed garrisons, but a totally different matter to bring food to the mouths of an army in the field. Yet the wisdom of Parliament had never been able to grasp this simple fact, and all military endeavours to save a few troops of the Waggon-Train, as a nucleus for a land-transport corps, had been fruitless. The Commissariat had been much blamed by all and sundry ever since the first disembarkation of the troops at Gallipoli. " We are all disposed to throw a stone at it," wrote Raglan to Newcastle; but he knew that it was idle to blame unfortunate men because God had not granted them the gift of doing at a moment's notice work which can only be learned by years of careful training. He took the far more practical step, in June 1854, of asking the government to organise a land-transport corps and send it out to him. But the Ministers could see no occasion for anything of the kind. It was not that they lacked goodwill, but that they had no knowledge of war; and the army was destined to pay dearly for their ignorance.

In the matter of a staff Raglan had for his Quarter-master-general an exceptionally able man in General Richard Airey. The training of Airey's later days had been singular, for he had been called from a desk at the Horse Guards to take charge of a vast territory, bequeathed to him by a relative, in the backwoods of Canada. There he had for three or four years lived

the rough life of a settler, working hard with his own 1854.
hands and directing the work of others—no bad school
in foresight for needs ahead and in skill towards turning
primitive resources to the best account. The Duke
of Wellington had so high an opinion of Airey as an
officer that he arranged for his return to the Army as
soon as the work in Canada should have been completed; and, though Airey had at first declined the
post of Quartermaster-general, preferring the command
of a brigade, he accepted it when it fell vacant at Varna
owing to the sickness of Lord de Ros, who had at
first held the appointment. Of Raglan's divisional
generals the most prominent was Sir George Brown,
a veteran of the Peninsula and an old rifleman, who had
commanded a battalion of the Rifle Brigade for seventeen years. He knew his profession, but, like Raglan
himself, had spent his later years at the Horse Guards.
General de Lacy Evans was also a Peninsular veteran,
and had seen more recent service with the unfortunate
British Legion in Spain.

Of the naval commanders the chief, Vice-admiral
Dundas, had, for many years previously, spent his life
in political and official business; but, being a Whig,
he had been appointed to the command of the Mediterranean fleet and so found himself involved in the
operations. His second in command, Sir Edmund
Lyons, had been much employed in diplomatic work
in the Levant, but as a naval officer was of inexhaustible
energy and enterprise.

All things considered, therefore, the force, in spite
of many very serious deficiencies, might have been in
worse case considering the long neglect of the Army
since the peace of 1815. Certainly it was very greatly
superior to that entrusted to the Duke of York in
1793. But now, just when active work was in immediate prospect, a new and formidable enemy
appeared. Until June colonels reported less sickness among their men than there would have been at
home, justifying Omar Pasha's testimony as to the

1854. salubrity of Bulgaria.   But, as the summer advanced,
July-Aug. the men began to suffer from the climate; dysentery,
typhus and ague became frequent; and the sick increased so rapidly that the resources of the medical
department were quickly over-strained.   Hence it was
impossible in many cases to give the sufferers better
shelter than a bell-tent, which a blazing sun made
unbearably hot; and consequently there were many
deaths.   Moreover, it was not only those who were
actually stricken by disease, but all the soldiers who were
brought low.   They were weak, pallid, gloomy and
depressed, losing all taste for food and even for tobacco.
In July cholera appeared, seemingly brought from
Marseilles in a French transport, and in a week there
were two cases, not fatal, among the British troops.
Then after a few days it flew upon the Light Division,
the healthiest of all the troops, killing sixteen men
within forty-eight hours; and thenceforward it raged
terribly.   Within the next fortnight there were over
six hundred deaths among the British troops, and over
one hundred in Admiral Dundas's flagship.   Even so,
however, these losses were trifling compared to those
of the French, who had as many as ten thousand men
in hospital.

Towards the end of August matters improved
somewhat; but every commanding officer reported
that his men, whether on the sick-list or not, were
unfit for great exertion.   The Coldstream Guards,
marching less than fourteen miles from their camp into
Varna, could not accomplish the distance in less than
three days, and even so were unable to carry their packs.
And they were no worse in this respect than many other
battalions.[1]   In the circumstances it might well have
seemed doubtful whether the invasion of the Crimea
should be undertaken at all; but it was thought that
the voyage, the change to fresh ground, and above

---

[1] *Raglan MSS.*, Raglan to Newcastle, June 20, July 14, 19, 24,
Aug. 9, 14, 24, 1854. Ross, *History of the Coldstream Guards*,
pp. 152-153.

all, active service, would be the best cure for the 1854.
general debilitation of the men.   All things considered,
there was probably nothing better to be done, unless
operations were to be abandoned until the following
spring.   Already in the first week of August [1] Raglan
was anxious about the quarters of the troops for the
winter.   Even if Sevastopol should be taken, he saw
difficulties in putting the whole of the troops under
cover.   Bulgaria would be useless, for the villages
were wretched, and there could be no communication
between them for want of roads.   If, therefore, the
enterprise against Sevastopol had been given up, the
army could hardly have found any resting-places
nearer than Malta and Corfu; and, in the state of the
British public's expectations, such a step would have
meant the downfall of the Ministry, the recall of Raglan,
and a strain, which might have very dangerous consequences, upon our relations with France.   Such are
the perils of thoughtless adventure in war.

Accordingly on the 24th of August the embarkation Aug. 24.
was begun under the direction of Lyons; and notwithstanding bad weather which delayed the shipping of
the horses, the entire force, thanks to the admirable
work of the Navy, was got on board without the loss
of a man.   The French having not enough steamers
to carry their troops, nor even to tow their sailing
vessels, set sail on the 5th of September; the British
weighed anchor on the morning of the 7th, and over- Sept.
taking the French on the following day, passed through
them.   But, while the two fleets were near one another,
St. Arnaud sent a message begging Raglan and Dundas
to meet him in conference on the French man-of-war
Ville de Paris; and since Raglan, with his one arm, could
not easily board a ship in rough weather, a second
conference was held on board his ship, the *Caradoc*.
The proposal broached by the French was that the
landing should be made, not, as had been agreed, just
to north of Sevastopol, but at Kaffa, a hundred miles

[1] *Raglan MSS.*, Raglan to Newcastle, Aug. 8, 1854.

1854. distant from it, on the eastern coast of the Crimean peninsula. Practically this signified the abandonment of all operations against Sevastopol until the spring, and it was rather a clever way of combining nominal obedience to the Emperor's orders with avoidance of the perilous enterprise whereof the execution had, to all intent, been already begun. Such a wile was not likely to commend itself to Raglan. St. Arnaud, who appears to have been too ill to take any part in the discussion, threw the whole burden of decision upon his English colleague; the French officers present, one after another, disclaimed any individual responsibility for the proposal; and the result of the conference was to leave matters exactly as they stood. The incident is interesting as proof that the leading French officers thought so ill of the contemplated operations as to attempt even at the eleventh hour by some means to avert them. A stronger man than St. Arnaud might have asserted these opinions, which were perfectly sound, two months earlier.

Sept. 10. On the 10th, Raglan, with some of his own and some of the French generals, made a personal reconnaissance of the western coast of the Crimean peninsula from Sevastopol northward to Eupatoria; and, after examining in succession the inlets formed by the rivers Belbek, Katscha, Alma and Bulganak, he rejected the whole of them in favour of a strip of open beach, known as Old Fort Bay, six miles to north of the Bulganak. General Canrobert favoured the Katscha, which was certainly nearer to Sevastopol; but Raglan objected to it, first because it was too narrow and lay between perpendicular cliffs on either side, and secondly because the English press had been for weeks trumpeting its advantages as a landing-place far and wide; and Canrobert gave way. Light breezes delayed the arrival of the French
Sept. 13. fleet until the 13th, when Eupatoria was summoned to surrender; and the united fleets, British, French and Turkish, anchored before Old Fort Bay. Cholera had not forsaken the Allied armies at sea, and many

a dead man was thrown overboard during the voyage; 1854.
but the French suffered more than the English, being
terribly overcrowded, not only in their transports but
on their men-of-war.   Until the last moment it had
never been suspected that the French had not steam-
power enough to move the whole of their fleet; and
the delay caused by their journeying under sail was by
no means a trifling matter.

It was arranged that on the night of the 13th a
buoy should be placed in the centre of the bay appointed for the landing-place, and that the French,
who justly claimed the right of the line, should land
their troops to the south and the English to the north
of it.   Lyons, steaming in at daylight of the 14th in Sept. 14.
his flagship, the *Agamemnon*, found that the buoy had
been deposited by a French naval officer at the extreme
northern end, thus claiming the whole length of the
shore for the French army.   The result was confusion
and delay, for the English troopships, following close
upon the *Agamemnon*, became mixed up with the
French.   With great patience and good sense Lyons
made no protest, but quietly turned away to the bay
next to northward and began the disembarkation there.
It was carried out according to the immortal model
established by Abercromby in Aboukir Bay; and, the
weather being fine during the forenoon, both armies
succeeded in landing the whole of their infantry.   But
at noon the wind rose, and before sunset the surf made
the disembarkation of guns and horses very difficult.
Rain fell heavily all night, and all ranks, being without
shelter of any kind, suffered considerable discomfort.
Men were still dying of cholera, and such a night was
not favourable to the weakly.   The surf was so high
on the 15th as to forbid further progress until the Sept. 15.
afternoon, when the landing of the horses was carried
on with some difficulty and risk but with no appreciable
loss.   The French, having practically no cavalry and
not even their full complement of artillery-teams, and
being further less hampered by the surf, completed

1854. their disembarkation with comparative ease; but it was
Sept. 18. not until the 18th that the whole of the English were
ashore. Save for the zeal, resource and indefatigable
industry of the Navy the work could hardly have been
accomplished, as it was, within five days.

So there the allied armies were in an enemy's
country, the British about twenty-six thousand strong
with sixty-six guns, the French about thirty thousand
with seventy guns, and a small contingent of between
four and five thousand Turkish infantry with no guns.[1]
They had no base except the floating base of the fleet,
with which bad weather might at any moment sever
their communication. They had no land-transport, and
the men were too weak to carry even their packs. The
English had no ambulances, for the ambulance-waggons
had been left behind, presumably from want of animals
to draw them or from want of tonnage to carry the animals.
The Allies were twenty miles from their objective, and

[1] CAVALRY DIVISION: Earl of Lucan.
  Heavy Brigade: Scarlett—2 squadrons each, 2nd D.G.,
          4th D.G., 5th D.G., 1st D., 6th D.
          (These regiments had not yet arrived.)
  Light „   Cardigan—2 squadrons each, 4th Hrs., 8th
          Hrs., 11th Hrs., 13th L.D., 17th Lrs.
  1 Horse-artillery battery.
INFANTRY:
  1*st Division*: Duke of Cambridge.
    Guards Brigade: Bentinck—3/Gren. Guards, 1/Coldstream,
          1 Scots Fusr. Guards.
    Highland „   Campbell—42nd, 79th, 93rd.
  2*nd Division*: Sir de Lacy Evans.
    Left Brigade: Pennefather—30th, 55th, 95th.
    Right „   Adams—41st, 47th, 49th.
  3*rd Division*: Sir R. England.
    Right Brigade: Sir J. Campbell—1st, 28th, 38th.
    Left „   Eyre—44th, 50th, 60th.
  4*th Division*: Sir George Cathcart.
    Right Brigade: —20th, 21st, 63rd.
    Left „   —46th, 57th, 1/R.B.
  Light Division: Sir George Brown.
    Right Brigade: Codrington—7th, 23rd, 33rd.
    Left „   Buller—19th, 77th, 88th, 2/R.B.
  10 Field batteries.

they had no information whatever as to the strength 1854.
or dispositions of the enemy. Airey, dispersing parties
in every direction, managed to collect, during the days
of disembarkation, some three hundred native carts
with their teams and drivers, otherwise it is difficult to
see how the English could have moved at all. But the
mere representation of the conditions under which the
expedition stood, when first it set foot on the enemy's
territory, shows the insane risk of the entire enterprise.

The actual Russian force in the Crimean peninsula
at the time of the Allies' landing seems to have been
about eighty thousand soldiers, seamen, marines and
local levies, of which number fifty thousand belonged
to the active regular army. Their commander, Prince
Mentschikoff, had early intelligence by semaphore
telegraph of the approach of the allied fleet on the
13th; and, having given orders for strengthening the
defence of the north side of Sevastopol, he assembled
a force of nearly forty thousand men, close upon one-
tenth of them cavalry, with ninety-six guns, on the
heights of the river Alma, some fifteen miles to north
of the fortress. Some of these troops must have been
in or near the ground when Raglan reconnoitred the
coast from the sea, for he had observed large camps in
the valleys both of the Alma and the Katscha. Beyond
their presence and that of small parties of Cossacks,
which had been observed hovering about the army
after the disembarkation, nothing was known to the
Allies of the enemy.

When, therefore, the allied armies marched south- Sept. 19.
ward on the morning of the 19th of September, they
moved off in an order which permitted of speedy
deployment in case of action. The French, having
their right flank protected by the sea, arrayed their
four divisions in a cruciform shape, with their baggage
and reserve-artillery in the centre of the cross. The
divisions moved in two columns, consisting each of a
brigade with the divisional artillery between them. The
English were massed in close columns, two divisions

1854. in first line, two more in second line, and the in-
Sept. 19. complete Fourth division in third line on the exposed
flank, with the encumbrances on its right. The ten
squadrons of cavalry, with detachments of the Rifle
Brigade in support, were pushed out to cover front,
flanks and rear. The day was hot and, before the
march had lasted for an hour, the men, though they
were not carrying their packs, began to fall out, some
writhing in the agony of cholera, more from sheer
weakness and thirst; and, when the halting-place was
reached at the river Bulganak early in the afternoon,
the stragglers were so many that it was necessary to
send back a force to bring them in. Meanwhile the
advanced cavalry, pushing on beyond the river, caught
sight of a body of some two thousand Russian horse
a few hundred yards ahead, and halted. The Russians
thereupon advanced for a short distance, and threw
out skirmishers, who opened a straggling and useless
fire from their saddles. Then the flicker of the sun
on bayonets was seen in the hollow, and Raglan realised
that the enemy was in his front with a force of all three
arms. Anxious for the safety of his precious cavalry,
for he had present but one thousand in all to serve
the whole of the allied armies, he called up the Eighth
Hussars, the Seventeenth Lancers, his two leading
infantry divisions and two field-batteries, and deploying
the infantry, ordered the advanced squadrons to retire.
As they did so, Russian guns, hitherto unseen, galloped
up, unlimbered and opened fire, but were quickly
driven back by the English field-batteries; whereupon
the Russian commander, perceiving the red-coats to be
deployed, withdrew his force and disappeared. It was
discovered later that the Russian force present numbered about six thousand infantry, a brigade of regular
cavalry, nine squadrons of Cossacks and two batteries
of artillery. Had their leader been a man of any
enterprise he could at least have manoeuvred his horse
about the flanks and rear of the British line of march
until Raglan's handful of cavalry was worn out, doubled

the fatigue of Raglan's infantry by compelling constant 1854. deployments or counter-movements and delaying their access to water, and swept up some hundreds of stragglers. Fortunately he did none of these things; and the British cavalry escaped with only two men and half a dozen horses wounded.

The two allied armies had fallen a mile asunder in the course of the day's march, and Raglan made his troops bivouac in two sides of a square with the Bulganak river at their backs, so as to be able to deploy rapidly to front or left flank. Cathcart's battalions and the Fourth Light Dragoons watched the rear from the north side of the stream, and the left division of the French drew nearer to secure the right flank. The night, however, passed quietly; dawn revealed no sign Sept. 20. of an enemy; and it was now practically certain that the Russians were awaiting attack in a position which could only be that on the heights of the Alma. This had been carefully reconnoitred, so far as was possible, by French naval officers from the sea; and it was clear that for a mile up the river from its mouth the heights upon its southern side were precipitous, though they then became gradually less steep. St. Arnaud, who for the moment had regained his health, in the course of the night had brought to Raglan a neat but vague plan for turning both flanks of the position, the French on the right, the British on the left; but as the enemy's strength and distribution of his forces was not yet known, Raglan could only assure him in general terms of his hearty co-operation. Since the coast south of the Alma trended away to south-west, it was agreed that General Bosquet's division, which was on the extreme right, should march at five o'clock and that the remainder of the allied armies should follow them two hours later. The whole were to get under arms in silence without sound of trumpet or drum.

The position of the Alma, from the sea to the Russian right, occupied a front of nearly six miles. For the first mile, up to the village of Almatamack, it is pro-

1854. tected by more or less sheer cliff. Opposite Alma-
Sept. 20. tamack a road wound up the heights; and from this
point eastward the acclivity becomes so much less
precipitous as to be easily accessible to men and not
impossible for country carts. Yet another mile to
eastward, from a point marked by a house known as
the White Homestead, on the north bank of the river,
the northern face of the heights ceases to be uniform;
being broken up into ridges, hollows and ravines for
yet another mile eastward to the village of Burliuk,
and beyond it to the main road to Sevastopol,
which was carried across the river by a strong wooden
bridge. From this bridge the course of the Alma,
following it up-stream, bends from east to north-east,
and here for more than two thousand yards the southern
bank of the stream presents first a short but steep
ascent from the water, then a terrace of easier acclivity
some eight hundred yards wide, then a hollow, and
finally a commanding height known as Kourgane Hill.
The summit from the sea to a point known as Telegraph Hill, nearly opposite the White Homestead, is
one flat plateau, but from thence eastward is broken
into knolls and spurs. In rear of the position the
ground rolls southward in ridges which for some
distance rise higher and higher, offering many facilities
for a rearguard action.

The position was far too much extended for
Mentschikoff's numbers, but he got over the difficulty
by treating the plateau from the sea to Telegraph Hill
as inaccessible from the north; and this assumption
was the more convenient since the summit could be
swept by the guns of the allied fleets. But there was
a rugged path by which the cliffs could be ascended
close to the sea; and even if this were overlooked, the
road, practicable for artillery, that climbed the heights
above Almatamack, had been neither broken up nor
prepared for defence. The only Russian troops on
the plateau were a single battalion and a half-battery
stationed at the village of Ulukul Acles, overlooking

the sea, quite a mile and a half south of the river.
Mentschikoff's left flank, in fact, rested on the lower
slopes of Telegraph Hill; and for defence of the ground
between these points he had assigned thirteen battalions,
four of them inferior troops of the second line, and ten
guns, under command of General Kiriakoff. The road
itself was committed to four battalions of light infantry
with a detachment of rifles; and eighteen guns were posted
on a ledge six hundred yards above the river to sweep
both road and bridge.   In rear there was stationed on
the east side of the road the main reserve, consisting
of seven battalions and two field-batteries.   East of the
road, upon the terrace already described, Mentschikoff
had thrown up an earthwork, mounting twelve guns,
which commanded both the river in front and the road
on the left.   This work was miscalled by the British
the Great Redoubt, and it was connected with the
sixteen guns on the road by eight more guns.   At
right angles to this first earthwork and a thousand
yards to east of it was another small breastwork armed
with a battery of field-guns, which was known as the
Lesser Redoubt.   For the defence of this, the key of
the position, Mentschikoff had further assigned four
field-batteries and sixteen battalions, twelve of them
on the flanks of the redoubts and four higher up on
Kourgane Hill.   Finally, the array was closed by a
mass of cavalry, sixteen squadrons of regular horse and
eleven of Cossacks, which was drawn up in a curve
from his extreme right flank to his right rear.

Early on the morning of the 20th General Bosquet,
a young general and an active officer, rode forward
and satisfied himself by personal reconnaissance that
infantry could not only cross the river at its mouth
but could find their way up the cliff beyond it.   He
accordingly decided to send one brigade of his division,
together with the Turks, by this route, and to lead the
other with the whole of his artillery up the road by the
village of Almatamack.   By half-past five all of his
men were in motion; and the remainder of the French

1854. army was likewise ready to move off at the appointed
Sept. 20. hour. But the British lagged behind. They had
first to uncoil themselves from the constrained position
in which they were bivouacked, then to take ground to
their right to fill up the intervals between their own
right and the French left, and lastly they had to clear
the ground before them of Cossacks and make provision for the safety of their left flank. All of this
took time; and the delay was prolonged further by
misapprehension of some of Raglan's orders. It was
necessary to suspend the advance of Bosquet; and, as
the hours dragged on, the French army at nine o'clock
came to a halt and cooked their coffee. Not until ten
was the entire host under way, and not until half-past
eleven was the British right level and in contact with
the French left. The British marched in the same
formation as on the previous day, in double column of
companies from the centre of divisions, the Second and
Light divisions, right and left respectively, leading, the
Third and First divisions following them, and the
three battalions, which were all that were present of
the Fourth division, in rear of the First. The day
was cloudless, windless and hot, and the way for two
hours lay over rolling grassy downs, until the last
ridge was topped, and the armies halted at the head of a
plain which sloped down gently for a mile to the waters
of the Alma.

Raglan and St. Arnaud then met and, after some
scrutiny of the Russian position, St. Arnaud asked his
colleague if he were prepared to turn the enemy's right.
He had evidently no ideas beyond the vague scheme,
founded upon a total misconception of the enemy's
dispositions, that he had laid before his colleague on
the previous night. Raglan replied that looking to the
great force of cavalry displayed by the Russians on
their extreme right, he should not attempt to turn the
position; and therewith all plans for concerted action
seem to have come to an end. Division of command
had already produced many evil consequences, and

they did not cease even in the immediate presence of the enemy. The two commanders, or at any rate Raglan, were so afraid of friction between their two armies and of the resulting injury to the Alliance, that they sacrificed unity of design lest the attempt to arrive at it should engender disunion.   At about one o'clock the advance was sounded and the entire host moved steadily forward.

On the extreme right, and far ahead of the rest, Bosquet had distributed his division into two columns; Bonat's brigade, followed by the Turks, making for the mouth of the river, and Autemarre's, accompanied by Bosquet in person, for Almatamack.   On the left of Bosquet, but far in rear, came in succession, upon the same alignment, Canrobert's and Prince Napoleon's divisions, each in two lines with the leading brigade deployed into line of columns.   Forey's division followed in reserve;   and immediately on Prince Napoleon's left came in succession the British Second Division and Light Division, in first line, with the Third and First. Divisions in support.   The three battalions of Cathcart's division were echeloned. in the left rear of the First Division, and the front, left flank and rear were covered by the two battalions of the Rifle Brigade,[1] in extended order, and by the cavalry.

Just before half-past one the French war-steamers opened fire upon the village of Ulukul Acles, and even threw a shot or two upon Telegraph Hill and the ground below it, with the result that the six Russian battalions alongside the river to west of Burliuk fell back for some distance up the hill.   Meanwhile the Rifles, in advance of the British, had engaged the Russian skirmishers in the vineyards and enclosures which covered the right bank of the Alma for a full quarter of a mile.   Bullets began to fall near the Light

[1] Raglan had complained in June of his want of light infantry (Raglan to Newcastle, June 17, 1854) and had asked for the 43rd and 52nd. The 1/ Rifle Brigade was sent out to join the 2/ Rifle Brigade in July.

1854. Division, and the Russian gunners on the left bank
Sept. 20. fired ranging shots. The Second and Light Divisions
therefore deployed into line, but were soon in difficulties. All the morning the British columns had
been edging to their right to fill the gap between them
and the French; but, when the French deployed, they
jostled the right of the Second Division and forced it
to take ground to its left, whereby it jostled in turn the
right of the Light Division and edged that likewise
leftward. Unfortunately Sir George Brown had not
taken nearly ground enough to eastward, and thus,
when the two divisions deployed, Brown's right-hand
battalion was overlapped by two battalions of Evans's
left brigade. It was then too late to correct the blunder,
for the fire of the Russian artillery now became brisk,
and began even to reach the First Division. The
Duke of Cambridge therefore deployed it, and taking
plenty of ground, extended his battalions until its right
covered the left of the Second Division, and its left—
the Highland Brigade—was completely clear of the
Light Division, and practically stood in first line.
Raglan, observing that the Third Division had no
space to deploy, ordered it to act as support to the
Guards; and the whole then halted and lay down,
except the Riflemen, who pressed forward actively into
the vineyards and were soon steadily engaged. Raglan
meanwhile rode up and down with his staff in front of
the line, attracting much attention from the Russian
gunners, who, failing to drive him away with round
shot, burst shell after shell over his head, but hurt no
one. Possibly, knowing how high is the trial for
troops to remain passive under ricochet round shot,
Raglan, like Gough at Ferozeshah, deliberately set
himself to draw the enemy's fire.

During this time Bosquet's two columns were
pushing on; and Bonat's brigade having, as Bosquet
had anticipated, found a path up the cliff by the sea,
had begun the ascent and was toiling up with such
speed as was possible on a very steep and narrow way.

Bosquet himself with Autemarre's brigade advanced rapidly upon Almatamack, covered by a cloud of skirmishers who threaded the vineyards by the river, firing diligently at the hill-side where no enemy was. Soon after two o'clock the head of the column forded the river and the guns began the ascent of the hill by the road, while the Zouaves with incredible rapidity swarmed up the heights by rougher paths and formed at the summit. The four Russian guns at Ulukul Acles had moved five hundred yards eastward to Ulukul Tinets and now opened fire, but could not check at so long a range Bosquet's steady, though necessarily slow, progress on the plateau. Practically Bosquet had no other enemy to meet, for Kiriakoff thought himself unwarranted without superior authority in doing more to meet the turning movement than to send two battalions to a point opposite the White Homestead and some guns to the eastern end of Telegraph Hill. Mentschikoff, however, when he realised the situation, galloped off himself to the left of the line, directing seven battalions and two batteries, drawn from his general reserve and his left wing, to follow him. The batteries arrived first and engaged Bosquet at long range, but, just as the battalions were reaching their appointed place, Mentschikoff ordered them back, and the guns alone were left to stop the advance of Bosquet. Nevertheless Bosquet's situation was unpleasant, for he had only one brigade, and no other troops within a mile of him; and in this isolated position he hesitated to commit himself further.

However, St. Arnaud, observing his progress, had ordered Canrobert and Prince Napoleon to advance; and their artillery coming forward opened fire on the battalions which Kiriakoff had withdrawn from the low ground to the higher slopes. Covered by skirmishers, Canrobert's battalions rapidly crossed the river and began the ascent opposite the White Homestead, meeting with little opposition, for Mentschikoff had withdrawn one if not both of the battalions which

Kiriakoff had moved to that quarter.   But, finding it
impossible to bring up his guns by the same route as
his infantry, Canrobert sent them to take the road up
the heights by Almatamack, and meanwhile halted his
infantry in the dead ground under the crest of the
heights.   Prince Napoleon's division, less fortunate
than Canrobert's, had before them seven battalions and
the Russian batteries on Telegraph Hill, which could
fire over the heads of their own men into the thick of
the French ranks.   Prince Napoleon's batteries made
little progress; some of them did not even cross the
river, and all hung back, though hesitation did not
make them the safer from the Russian cannon-shot.   St.
Arnaud made matters worse by pushing one brigade
of Forey's division behind Canrobert's division and
the other behind Prince Napoleon's, for this only
brought more men uselessly under the fire of the
Russian artillery, without propelling the front of the
divisions forward.   The attack, in fact, came to a
standstill, for Bosquet was waiting for someone to join
him to right or left, so that he might bring up his right
shoulder and wheel upon the Russian flank.   But no
one came.

Throughout this time, fully an hour and a half, the
British had been lying down under the fire of the
Russian batteries, quite passive, for the English guns
could not reach the Russian pieces on the high ground,
and suffering appreciable loss.   A French aide-de-
camp now came to Raglan and told him plainly that
unless Bosquet received support he would retreat.
Thereupon, though the bulk of the Russian array lay
in his and not in the French front, Raglan gave the
order to advance.   The first line rose to its feet,
dressed its ranks, and with a front of two miles began
its march down the slope.   Thereupon Raglan, who at
the moment was on the extreme right of his own army,
cantered down, followed by his staff, into the valley
east of Burliuk, forded the river, passed through the
French skirmishers who were engaged in a blind fight

with the Russians in the vineyards and, hardly pausing 1854.
to order Adams's brigade to come up with all possible Sept. 20.
speed, ascended a sunken lane which led up the hill.
Looking to his left to see how affairs were progressing,
he found himself on the flank of the Russian batteries,
and hastened to the summit.   There on a commanding
knoll he took his stand midway between the Russian
centre and the Russian left, well in rear of the enemy's
front line and on the flank of their batteries and reserves
by the Sevastopol road.   At once he sent for a couple
of guns; and from his vantage point he watched the
long lines of his army stretching eastward up the
valley as they advanced to the attack.   Never did
Commander-in-chief take up a more amazing station
from which to fight a battle.

On the extreme right of the British line the Russians
had earlier in the day set fire to the village of Burliuk,
which, being filled with coarse hay, burned fiercely with
clouds of smoke and practically forbade access to quite
half a mile of ground.   Brown, as has been told, had
already formed the Light Division too far to the right,
and the conflagration so greatly straitened the space
left for the Second Division that, though Evans had
drawn up his division in two lines, each of a brigade,
his left still overlapped the right of the Light Division.
He now broke up his force anew, sending the Forty-
first and Forty-ninth together with Turner's battery
to the western side of the village, and leaving the four
remaining batteries, with Franklin's battery, on the
eastern side.   While moving thus to the right, Turner
received Raglan's order to bring up two guns, and
taking charge of them himself, hurried them on,
despite of all difficulties, with extraordinary speed.
But in the meantime Evans had a heavy task before
him, for the ground near the river was blind with
vineyards and bushes and small enclosures, among
which a swarm of Russian skirmishers maintained an
obstinate fight; and it was swept not only by the
sixteen guns on either side of the Sevastopol road but

1854. by another battery of eight guns to west of them and
Sept. 20. by the heavy cannon of the Great Redoubt.   All
regular formation was lost, and Evans's four battalions struggled forward as best they might, not without
severe loss.   The Forty-seventh, on the extreme
right, passing the water well below the bridge, was
sheltered from the worst of the fire.   The Thirtieth,
next to them, worked its way across the stream, and
taking cover in the dead ground on the south bank,
opened a steady fire on the batteries athwart the road;
the Ninety-fifth also struggled forward from shelter to
shelter, and the Fifty-fifth, advancing in line over open
ground, was met by such a blast from the Russian
guns that it wavered, but recovering itself, advanced
once more and on reaching cover lay down.   The
whole attack of Pennefather's brigade seems to have
conducted itself according to the principles of the
twentieth rather than of the nineteenth century.

On the left of Evans the Light Division had to
endure nearly as severe a trial, having the twelve heavy
guns of the Great Redoubt and of a field-battery
higher up the hill in its front, those of the Lesser
Redoubt on one flank, and eight guns to east of the
Sevastopol road on the other.   The Rifle Brigade had
already cleared most of the Russian skirmishers from
the vineyards and enclosures by the river ; and as the
line advanced, Colonel Norcott, of the second battalion, extended the four companies which he had in
hand, before the front of Buller's, the left, brigade.[1]
Then the division plunged into the maze of vineyards
and enclosures, carrying with it some men of Pennefather's brigade.   Buller's brigade, having somewhat
clearer and easier ground before them, were first across

---

[1] This is not according to Kinglake, but it is according to a letter
written by Norcott to Kinglake, dated Mar. 17, 1863, and published
in the *Times*, of which a copy was sent to me in 1924 by Colonel
Norcott himself.   Kinglake, a very vain man, declined to notice
Colonel Norcott's correction, presumably because accuracy would have
marred one of his purple patches.

the water; and Buller, re-forming them, halted two of 1854. his battalions, the Seventy-seventh and Eighty-eighth, Sept. 20. and made them lie down under cover, ready to parry any stroke that might be threatened by the Russian cavalry on his left flank. Norcott, seeing that Codrington's front was uncovered by riflemen, now extended his men eastward to make good the want. Codrington's brigade reached the south bank of the river, as was inevitable, in much disorder, and though there was a small space of dead ground, the men were so much overcrowded and the battalions so much intermixed, that he judged it hopeless to re-form them. So, putting his horse at the steep bank which rose beyond the river, he scrambled up to the top, while the word to advance was passed up and down the line; and the men surged after him on to the natural glacis, some five hundred yards in extent, which separated them from the Great Redoubt.

As they emerged into the open, two dense Russian columns, each of two battalions, one on either flank of the Great Redoubt, came marching down to meet them. That on the eastern flank was raked at once by a party of Riflemen which had taken cover in a homestead; and when the Nineteenth, other of the Riflemen and the Twenty-third all opened fire upon it, the hostile mass fell back, and left these regiments free to advance upon the Great Redoubt. The other Russian column was engaged at first by the Seventh Fusiliers, Codrington's right-hand battalion, only. This body of the enemy, which had a front of only one company, came to a halt and did not deploy, though swarms of skirmishers were continually running out from both flanks, firing and running back again. Lacy Yea, the colonel of the Seventh and the most detested commanding officer in the army, saw his advantage. Riding in among the thickest clusters of his men, he contrived by main force and hard swearing to extend them into a line which overlapped the Russian column, and tore its front and

1854. flanks with fire.[1] He was thus busily employed when
Sept. 20. the remainder of Codrington's brigade, half of the
Ninety-fifth which had become mixed up with it, the
Rifles and the Nineteenth, converged, for the most part
in irregular groups, upon the Great Redoubt. Then
the Russian heavy guns opened a murderous fire of
round shot, grape and canister, seconded by another
battery farther up the hill. Great gaps were torn in
the ragged advancing line, but the survivors closed
up and went on, pressing hard after Codrington,
who led them steadily forward. Then suddenly the
guns fell silent, and through the rising bank of smoke
the Russian teams were seen withdrawing their heavy
cannon from the redoubt in all haste. It seems that
the Emperor Nicholas, believing that Wellington had
never lost a gun,[2] had laid it down that the loss of a
piece of artillery was an unforgivable sin. A final rush
carried the mob of British battalions into the earthwork; two guns were taken; and the men, wildly
cheering, imagined that their work was done.

Codrington knew better, and, dismounting, tried to
establish a line of defence by lining the parapet with
rifles. But the battalions were all intermingled.
Officers could not find their men, nor men their officers.
A great many officers had fallen, and the survivors,
through lack of experience and training, did not realise
the old truth that the climax of a successful attack is
a moment of extreme peril. The second line should
have been at hand to make good the success of the first,

---

[1] One of Lacy Yea's subalterns told me this story of him at the
Alma. The subaltern had been shot through the ankle and was lying
on the ground faint with pain and unable to stand, when Yea
came up storming: " Come on! Why the hell don't you come on! "
" I am very sorry, Colonel, but I'm shot through the ankle and can't
walk." " Why, damn your eyes," answered Yea, " I've got a bullet
through my guts, and I'm going on ! " He had been struck by a spent
bullet on the belt and imagined that the shot had gone through him.

[2] This is not a fact. Four Portuguese guns were abandoned on
July 25, 1813 (see Vol. IX. of this History, p. 262) and Wellington
was greatly annoyed at (to use modern slang) the spoiling of his record.

but the Commander-in-chief was not on the spot to 1854.
ensure that it should be.   The Duke of Cambridge, it Sept. 20.
is true, had orders in general terms to support the
Light Division; and to some men, though probably to
very few in the British army at that time,[1] this would
have been sufficient.   He had brought his division
down to the edge of the enclosures and there halted it,
not without suffering occasional casualties from cannon-
shot.   Airey, marking this from his station more than
a mile away, galloped up to the Duke and requested
him to push on at once.   Evans, who could see in
what disorder the Light Division was advancing, also
urged the need for supporting it without delay; and
then at last the First Division plunged into the enclosures.

Meanwhile the Russian battery on Kourgane Hill
began to play upon the British within the redoubt, and
drove them out of it to take cover on the lower side of
the parapet.   But these British could see great masses
of infantry on either flank, and of cavalry also on their
left flank, which did not inspire confidence; and now a
huge Russian column of four battalions came out of
a hollow on their front and bore steadily down upon
them without firing a shot.   The Light Division, disordered though it was, might have shattered its front
and flanks, but someone cried out that the column
was French, giving word not to fire; and an officer who
tried to correct the blunder was shot dead before he
could do so.   The order to "cease fire" passed along
the line and was emphasised by the sounding of the
"cease fire" by a bugler of the Nineteenth.   Then, in

---

[1] It might almost be said at any time.   Wellington was always
complaining of the lack of initiative among his divisional commanders.
Yet there seems to have been a feeling among the divisional commanders in 1854 that, even after they had received their orders, they
must wait for a final word to execute them.   Sir George Brown had
orders to march at 7 A.M. on the 20th and was ready to do so, but waited
for the final word before he would move (Kinglake, iii. 29).   Possibly
Airey had not realised this, being himself a man with plenty of
initiative.

some mysterious fashion, as at Ferozeshah, through the agency of some officer who had lost his senses, the command to retire was given, was sounded by a bugler of the Nineteenth, and was repeated by the regimental buglers from left to right. Neither officers nor men were disposed to obey, for they felt that there must be some mistake; and they knew also that they would be far more exposed to fire on the glacis behind them than under the parapet where they lay. But a repetition of the call "Retire" set their doubts at rest, and they began to fall back in swarms as they had advanced, though without unseemly haste, carrying their wounded with them. One party, chiefly men of the Twenty-third and Ninety-fifth, even turned to fire at the infantry of the Russian column, which by this time was entering the redoubt.

At this moment the Scots Fusilier Guards, who were the centre battalion of the Guards Brigade, emerged from the enclosures on the south side of the river and, re-forming hastily and imperfectly, advanced alone up the glacis towards the redoubt. It seems that Codrington had sent an urgent message asking for their help, seeing them immediately in his rear, and hoping that they might prevent the retirement of the Light Division. They came instantly under a heavy fire; and presently the Russians, having lined the parapet of the redoubt, poured a shower of bullets into the disordered mass of the Light Division which, as above mentioned, had lingered behind to fire. These last gave way and carried with them three or four companies which formed the left of the Scots Fusilier Guards, though the right wing went on almost to the foot of the parapet. Then they too fell back upon the command, authorised or unauthorised, "Fusiliers retire," and the whole battalion receded to the foot of the slope, followed up by the Russian column. The mishap was only momentary. The Grenadiers and Coldstream, on the right and left flank of the Fusilier Guards, threw out markers after they had crossed the river and, declining to be hurried,

re-formed their line with all the precision of the parade-
ground.   Two companies of the Fusilier Guards rallied
at once, and scattered parties of the Light Division,
likewise forming up, helped them in some degree to
fill the gap between the Grenadiers and the Coldstream.
The calm deliberation of these two battalions evidently
had a steadying effect.

On the Russian side the situation had changed
since the attack of the Light Division.   Prince Mentschikoff had handed over to Kiriakoff the seven battalions, now increased to eight, with which he had
wandered backwards and forwards over the field; and
Kiriakoff, moving them to his left over against the
front of Canrobert, held him and his division in check.
But the two guns of Turner's battery had meanwhile
arrived, and after a few shots against the Russian
batteries on either side of the Sevastopol road, they
compelled these to limber up and retire farther up
the hill, whence their fire could indeed still reach the
river but was far less destructive.   Then turning his
pieces upon the remaining battalions of the main
Russian reserve, Turner constrained them also to withdraw, though in good order, higher up the slope.
Thereby the pressure upon Evans's front was greatly
relieved; and he was able not only to push forward the
Thirtieth, Fifty-fifth and Forty-seventh, but to bring up
his own batteries and those of the Third Division which
General England had placed at his disposal.   The
Fifty-fifth, seeing the Seventh on its left still engaged
with a Russian column, brought up its right shoulder,
and harrying the column in flank, drove it off in disorder.   Thus the right of the Guards was by this time
covered; the Russian guns on their right flank had
been withdrawn, and the heavy pieces in the Great Redoubt had also fallen back.   None the less the Guards
had on their right front the two battalions of the Kazan
regiment, which had been driven back by the Seventh
Fusiliers, but had rallied and again come forward,
and in their direct front one Russian column of two

1854. Vladimir battalions before the Redoubt, another of the
Sept. 20. same regiment and strength in rear of it, and yet another
to the right rear of the last, making eight battalions in
all.   Farther to the left Campbell was confronted by
two more columns, each of two battalions, with a third,
of four battalions, in reserve; while on the left of all
still stood from two to three thousand Russian cavalry.

The Grenadiers and Coldstream, with the gap
between them still unfilled, marched up the glacis as
if on parade, and Colonel Hood, finding directly
before him the two half-beaten Kazan battalions and
two Vladimir battalions on his left front, wheeled the
Grenadiers obliquely to the left and engaged them
both.   For five minutes there was an unequal duel of
musketry, of one battalion against four, to state the
matter in one way, but of perhaps seven hundred Minié
rifles against four hundred muskets, to state it in
another.   Then the Russians gave way, and Hood,
handling his battalion to admiration, continued his
advance, still riddling them with bullets.   The Coldstream, who were covered from artillery fire by the
ground, dealt even more summarily with the two
remaining Vladimir battalions; and the Highlanders,
equally untroubled by artillery, had the less difficulty
in repelling the rest, since the Russians, slow and unwieldy, came forward to meet them.   One column,
indeed, which attempted to assail Campbell's centre
regiment, the Ninety-third, in flank, was itself caught
in flank by the Seventy-ninth, the left-hand battalion
of Campbell's echelon, and torn to pieces by its fire.
The four Russian battalions in reserve strove to stay
the flight of their comrades, but in vain.   Six guns of
Lucan's horse-artillery came upon Campbell's right to
complete their discomfiture; and the Russians were
presently in full retreat, while the British batteries,
following them up under escort of the cavalry, poured
shot mercilessly into the retiring masses.

It should seem indeed that after the defeat of the
Vladimir and Kazan battalions by the Grenadier

Guards, if not earlier, the Russian generals abandoned
all hope, and not without reason. Not only were the
batteries of the Second and Third Divisions coming up
rapidly to the knoll where Raglan stood, and worrying
the Russian right wing with flanking fire, but the French
had really come into action. After long delay their
artillery had at last ascended the plateau. Advancing
eastward unseen up a hollow, they came within range
of Kiriakoff's huge column of eight battalions and had
the whole mass at its mercy. Kiriakoff drew off his
unfortunate men as best he could. They behaved
nobly, with shot and shell tearing great gaps in them,
until he was out of range. The French infantry, meanwhile, made no attempt to prevent him, and he had
reached the Telegraph and unlimbered his two batteries
to cover his retreat before the heads of Canrobert's
and Prince Napoleon's divisions at last got into motion
and struck southward over the plateau. This was just
at the moment when the Grenadier Guards began their
march up the slope; and the natural inference would
be that the French were in a favourable position at
a favourable moment to strike full upon the flank of
the retreating Russian right wing. They had nothing
before them but a handful of riflemen, who had been
left behind and became an easy prey; and, having
really taken little part in the battle so far, it was
reasonable to suppose that they would be eager to press
on. Moreover, it was evident from the direction of
the retreating army that a great part of it was throwing
itself into a single road through a gorge which must
impede its movements and, in case of pursuit, might
bring it into hopeless confusion.

Nevertheless the French infantry halted at Telegraph Hill, content, apparently, though it was barely
five o'clock, to have done nothing. An aide-de-camp
from Raglan arrived and asked the general in command
of the leading French brigade to continue his advance.
The French officer willingly assented, but remained
at the halt. Another messenger also preferred the

same request to St. Arnaud, but the Marshal refused,
upon the ground that his troops had left their packs in
the valley below. Airey then proposed that the whole
of the British cavalry, one division of British infantry
and such French troops as the Marshal might think
fit to spare, should press upon the enemy; but he was
told that any further advance of the French was impossible. Meanwhile Lord Lucan had ridden forward
with a portion of the cavalry and had already captured
a certain number of Russian stragglers, when he was
stopped by Raglan, who was unwilling to risk possibly
heavy losses among his small force of cavalry. As a
matter of fact, Kiriakoff did face about with some
squadrons of horse and about thirty guns at a point
about two miles from the battle-field; but this was the
last effort of the Russians. They had suffered a loss of
some six thousand killed and wounded; though half of
the casualties had fallen upon sixteen battalions only,
and there were many which had been but slightly engaged. Before they had retreated far, however, they
were seized with panic, and when they reached the
valley of the Katscha, nine miles away, the confusion
and disorder were such that they could not be stopped.
The troops strayed all over the country in the darkness
and, even when the bulk of them had been assembled
at midnight about the Katscha, the panic was renewed
two hours later, and the whole streamed away into
Sevastopol. Such was the chance, though of course he
could not have divined it, which St. Arnaud threw
away; and dearly the Allies were to pay for his
incompetence.

As to the action itself, it partook on all sides of the
insanity which marked the whole campaign. First
there was Mentschikoff, occupying half of a position
and pretending that the other half was inaccessible;
then when his blunder was revealed to him, straying
away with eight battalions to the threatened point and
walking them backwards and forwards, like d'Erlon
on the day of Ligny and Quatre Bras, but never

attempting, apparently, to grasp the problem of the 1854.
battle as a whole; and, worst of all, making absolutely Sept. 20.
no use of his formidable cavalry.   Then there was
St. Arnaud, sending three divisions to the brink of the
plateau, where at first there was nothing, and later only
eight battalions and two batteries, to stop him, and
keeping them there for hours without the slightest
effort to go further.   And lastly, there was Raglan,
impatient—perhaps excusably—at the hesitation of
the French, launching his infantry straight at superior
numbers of foot and on partially entrenched artillery;
then taking his stand in the middle of the enemy's line
and carrying out a little flank-attack upon his own
account, at first with his staff and a section of a battery,[1]
and later with two battalions.   It is true that from his
vantage-point he had a good view of his own troops
in profile, and could and did send orders to them; but
if the Russian cavalry had even menaced his left flank,
he would not have been in a good position to counter
such a threat.

It is a more serious question whether he should not
have waited longer for the French movements to take
effect; but here we strike the essential weakness of a
divided command.   A single commander in control of
the entire allied force could easily have turned the
action of the Alma into a great Russian disaster, and
even the two commanders working well together, like
Marlborough and Eugene, would hardly have accomplished less.   But St. Arnaud was an impossible colleague.   It may justly be pleaded that he was a dying
man, but, living or dying, he was unfit to command the
French army, because he could exert no authority over
it.   Some at least of his divisional commanders made
no secret of their contempt for him, and it is evident
that he inspired no confidence.   It was a pitiable thing
—but for unimpeachable evidence it would be past

---

[1] Kinglake gives the interesting detail, which he witnessed, that one
gun was laid by the C.R.A., Colonel Dickson, himself, the guns having
outstripped the gunners.

1854.
Sept. 20.
belief—that a French staff-officer should have come panting to Raglan for reinforcements because the entire French army found itself confronted by eight Russian battalions. But it was very plain evidence that the English Commander-in-chief was better trusted by the French themselves than was St. Arnaud.

Only thus can the long hesitation of the French troops to appear on the plateau be accounted for. They were called upon to attack—the work which the French soldier always by instinct prefers and in which he especially shines—but never did they show less of their vaunted *élan*. Some account for this astounding fact by the plea that the French infantry would never attack without the support of artillery, and that the nature of the ground long delayed the advent of their guns. Undoubtedly the Napoleonic tradition was that French infantry should be employed mainly for shock-action, the missile action being committed to the artillery; and this was partly a legacy from the tumultuary levies of the Revolution, partly the result of Napoleon's extravagance in squandering men, for the leaven of recruits in his ranks was so large that he could only use them when packed into dense bodies. Yet French officers, who trusted their chief, would never have hesitated to throw such tradition to the winds when so favourable an opportunity presented itself as at the Alma. It would be not only unjust but ridiculous to judge of the French army by its proceedings on the 20th of September; but it must be confessed that it cut a very poor figure upon that day. Moreover, they were fully aware of it. Their officers knew perfectly well that, properly handled, they could have done brilliant things, and above all they were conscious that, if St. Arnaud had permitted them to advance, they could have captured many prisoners and dispersed the Russian army. Excusably sore over their humiliation, they tried to soothe themselves by other methods. They returned a casualty-list of sixteen hundred which Raglan, after quiet inquiry among the

French medical officers, reduced to sixty killed and 1854. five hundred or fewer wounded.[1] They set up a pillar Sept. 20. on the heights to commemorate their victory, and they sent a gun-team—though fruitlessly—to filch away one of the two guns captured by the British. Too much should not be made of these little petulancies of wounded vanity. No soldiers, least of all the French, can endure to be fooled by their commander.

Given all these difficult conditions in the allied army with which he was working, Raglan can hardly be blamed for taking the brunt of the day's work upon himself, for otherwise there was no prospect that it would be done at all. It was of course hazardous to make a frontal attack upon a strong position defended by thirty-six battalions, some three thousand horse and a superior artillery, with twenty-seven battalions and a thousand horse; but Raglan seemed to divine by intuition that the Russians were not really very formidable. The action of the Alma, indeed, had a good deal in common with Gough's battles in the Punjab, the vineyards and enclosures representing the jungle that generally covered the front of a Sikh position, and the two earthworks the Sikh entrenchments. Raglan hurled his infantry straight at the Russian batteries very much after the manner of Gough, and the Russians saved them the trouble of spiking the guns by withdrawing them. It must be confessed that the attack was not well managed, for the Light Division was overcrowded and therefore unable to re-form in the dead ground on the south side of the river. Nor was their onslaught properly supported, for the First Division was slow to follow them, and the Scots Fusilier Guards were hurried into the attack while still in disorder and ahead of the rest of the brigade. Such blunders occur in every battle; but it seems likely that, if the Light Division had advanced in the perfect order of the Grenadier and Coldstream Guards, they would have been able to check the Russian

[1] Raglan to Newcastle, Sept. 24, 1854.

1854.   counter-attack until the First Division, although belated,
Sept. 20. came up to their help.   For the Russian columns were
made up of brave but over-drilled men, and were so
heavy and cumbrous that they fell an easy prey to the
supple British line.   Moreover, the British infantry
had a superior weapon, and a single smashing Minié
bullet must frequently have disabled more than one
man in the Russian masses.   Lastly, it seems certain
that, when the First Division attacked, the flanking
movement of the French had made itself very dis-
tinctly felt, and that the Russians were already out of
heart.   The missile tactics of the British infantry
must also have had a discouraging effect upon the
Russian columns, which were formed for shock-action,
for it was noticed that the Russians in the heart of their
columns fired into the air rather than not fire at all.   In
brief, the Russians were very hardly treated by their
commander.

Raglan's casualties amounted almost exactly to two
thousand.   Of these more than one-half fell upon the
four battalions which stormed the Great Redoubt and
upon the Seventh Fusiliers, which covered their right.
The Thirty-third counted two hundred and fifty killed
and wounded, the Seventh and Nineteenth both of
them over two hundred, and the Twenty-third and
Ninety-fifth over one hundred and ninety, the fallen
officers of the latter numbering eighteen.   Pennefather's brigade, the Grenadier Guards and the Scots
Fusilier Guards, contributed the greater part of the
balance.   The entire Highland brigade had not as
many casualties as the Grenadier Guards.   The truth
is that little damage was done by the Russian infantry,
though a good deal by the Russian artillery.   Therefore, considering the numerical odds against them, the
British casualties were light, and the gain would have
been well worth the sacrifice if St. Arnaud had taken
up the pursuit of the Russians.   It was he who
wrecked the day's work from beginning to end.

CHAPTER XLIII

THE Allies bivouacked on the battlefield, much en- 1854. cumbered not only by their own wounded, but also by some five hundred Russians who had been left helpless and suffering upon the ground. Raglan was eager to advance on the following day to the Belbek and assault Sept. 21. the northern forts of Sevastopol. This was in accordance with the whole spirit of the campaign, the object of which was the seizure of Sevastopol by a sudden stroke. It involved formidable hazards, no doubt, but the entire enterprise, imposed upon the commanders by ignorant civilians in Paris and London, was of such a nature as to demand imperatively the running of extraordinary risks. It is now practically certain that if Raglan's advice had been taken, the Allies could have occupied the northern side of Sevastopol without resistance. There was no serious obstacle in the way but the Star Fort, an octagon earthwork not yet fully armed, which was commanded from the heights by which the Allies would approach it and could further be reached by the fire of the ships. Moreover, the Russian troops were so greatly demoralised that Mentschikoff actually renounced all idea of defending the northern side of the place; and the possession of the north side of the roadstead would have enabled the Allies to destroy the Russian fleet and the naval establishments of Sevastopol, which were the ostensible objects of the whole campaign. Lastly, the Allies, by operating against the north side, could, without dangerous dispersion to eastward, seize the line

1854. of the enemy's communications with the rest of the Crimean peninsula, and certainly shorten—possibly accomplish at a blow—the reduction of the south side of the fortress.

But once again St. Arnaud, though twice eagerly pressed by Raglan, refused to move, alleging in excuse Sept. 22. the fatigue of his troops.   On the 22nd Raglan once more urged the same project upon the Marshal, and was answered by him that the Allies could not afford the losses that would attend the storming of the Russian works on the north side.   Raglan was in a difficult position.   It was impossible for him to divine how far he could count upon St. Arnaud's co-operation in any enterprise; and meanwhile he had no base save an open beach.   If Sevastopol were taken, this defect would be made good; but who could count, with such a colleague, upon getting anything done?   And meanwhile it was certain that every day was adding to the strength of the north side of Sevastopol.   There was no suitable harbour north of the fortress on the west coast of the Crimea, but there were small harbours just to south of it.   As a general proposition, without reference to the circumstances of the moment, Raglan, when considering in England the possibility of operations against Sevastopol, had favoured attack upon the southern side; and herein he was supported by the high authority of Sir John Burgoyne, who, writing actually on the heights of the Alma on the day after the battle, declared himself emphatically for immediate movement to the south side without attempting an assault from the north.   In the general uncertainty Raglan seems to have decided that at least he must free the army of all encumbrances and embark the whole of his sick and wounded before he went further; and this was a long and tedious business.   The French being close to the sea and having fewer patients to take on board, finished their part of the work on the 21st, but the English having many more than they—some sixteen hundred in all—and twice as far to go, could not pro-

ceed so rapidly. Every disabled man—and cholera 1854.
was still striking down scores of soldiers a day—had to
be carried by hand for three or four miles; and only
through the unselfish devotion of the officers and men
of the Navy was the task accomplished even in two
days. This was another little matter which had been
overlooked by the Cabinet that put the army ashore on
the Crimea without land-transport.

At last on the morning of the 23rd the allied armies Sept. 23.
resumed their advance, and after a march of six to
eight miles bivouacked in the valley of the Katscha,
where the Scots Greys and the Fifty-seventh Foot
joined Raglan's army. The cavalry division on this
day pushed on to the Belbek and bivouacked at the
village of Duvankoi for the night, having met with no
enemy, and seen none except in the distance to south
and south-west. On the morning of the 24th the Sept. 24.
troops were about to pursue their way against the north
side of the fortress when St. Arnaud sent a message
begging that Raglan would delay the march for some
hours. Intelligence had reached him that the Russians
had thrown up a battery which commanded both the
line of the French advance and the mouth of the
Belbek, where their siege-material must be landed, and
had further closed the entrance to the port of Sevastopol
by sinking five ships of war across it. Raglan of course
consented, and the armies did not move until ten, when
after climbing the ridge between the Katscha and the
Belbek, they inclined to their left, so as to avoid the new
battery, and crossing the Belbek, encamped upon the
heights to south of it. Raglan was anxious to push on,
according to his original plan, and assault the works
upon the north side, but St. Arnaud refused to attack
the Star Fort without regular siege-operations; and
his decision practically put an end to all projects of
onslaught upon Sevastopol from the north. He had
already, after some hesitation, agreed provisionally to
Burgoyne's plan of marching round to the south side
of the fortress; and so without further parley it was

1854. understood that this should be the next movement. As a matter of fact there was nothing else to be done unless the Allies should retreat; for by leaving the works at the mouth of the Belbek untouched, they suffered the enemy to sever their communication with their only base, the fleet.

Meanwhile, though much shaken by his defeat at the Alma, Mentschikoff had taken a momentous resolution; namely, to close the entrance of the harbour by sinking ships across it, to commit the defence of Sevastopol to the thousands of seamen thus released for service ashore, and to withdraw the whole of his army, with the exception of some six thousand men, mostly troops of the second line, in a northerly direction so as to maintain his communication with the interior of Russia by Baktchi Serai. In reply to all protests he answered that the Allies would never dare to attack the northern fortifications in great force, with his own army on their flank and rear; and he insisted that his orders should be carried out. On the night of the 22nd the ships were sunk, and at dawn of the 23rd only the masts were visible of five line-of-battle ships

Sept. 23. and seven frigates. On that same day Kiriakoff was sent northward with twelve battalions, twenty guns and four hundred Cossacks; and late in the afternoon he caught sight of Lucan's cavalry on the Belbek, whereupon he fell back south-eastward to the main

Sept. 24. road from Sevastopol to Baktchi Serai. On the night of the 24th the main Russian army moved out of Sevastopol by way of the hills known as the Mackenzie Heights upon that same main road to Baktchi Serai.

Sept. 25. Mentschikoff himself followed on the morning of the 25th and took up his quarters for some hours at the village of Otarkoi on the upper waters of the Belbek, not above six miles from the Allied bivouac.

These things for the most part were hidden from the Allied commanders, but the most important of them—the closing of the entrance to the harbour—became known to them, as we have seen, on the morning of the

24th.   St. Arnaud based his refusal to attack the
northern fortifications upon the ground that they had
been greatly strengthened, above all by the new battery
which commanded the mouth of the Belbek.   The
Russian engineer, Colonel Todleben, had indeed done
all that was possible in a few days to improve these
defences, throwing up earthworks upon each flank of
the Star Fort, and connecting it by trenches with two
more batteries, farther to the north-west, which he had
designed to keep the Allied ships at a distance.   These
last works it was that had scared St. Arnaud, because
they threatened also his line of advance along the coast;
but at the time that St. Arnaud first raised his objection, they had, as Sir Edmund Lyons ascertained by
personal reconnaissance, no guns yet mounted in them.
The fact when reported to St. Arnaud did not in the
least shake his decision; and by the morning of the
25th the defect had been made good.   In all, by the
25th, Todleben had mounted twenty-nine guns on the
northern earthworks and could bring eleven thousand
seamen, many of them armed with inferior weapons, to
defend a mile of front.   Whether he could have held
this mile of front with this force against fifty thousand
men of the Allies, seconded by the heavy guns of their
fleet, is a question which cannot be profitably debated.
The fairest opportunity for capturing Sevastopol was
lost when St. Arnaud refused to advance on the evening
of the battle of the Alma.

Moreover, it may well be doubted whether an
assault upon the northern side on the 24th or 25th
would have been then worth the sacrifice of lives, for,
even if successful, it would still have left the Allies
without a base.   The closing of the harbour was in
fact a master-stroke, sufficient to redeem many faults
in Mentschikoff.   If the northern fortifications had
been taken, the capture of those on the south side of
the harbour might not have taken long, but, until these
were reduced, it would have been impossible even to
begin to work at the removal of the sunken ships,

How much time would have been needed then to re-
open the harbour and make it an effective base for a
force of fifty thousand men is not an easy question to
answer; but until it was done, the Allies must certainly have sought another base, or other bases, probably where they ultimately found them, to south of
Sevastopol. In all the circumstances it might well
seem better to move to the south side of the fortress at
once. Already valuable time had been wasted owing
to the conflict of opinions between the Commanders-in-
chief, and the armies had approached the north side
to no purpose; whereas if Burgoyne's advice was to be
followed, it would have been much better to act upon it
at once and to strike south-westward instead of due
southward straight from the heights of the Alma.

On the morning of the 25th St. Arnaud was too
prostrate to attend to any business, but, since the
general movement of the Allies lay leftward and
Raglan had the left of the line, it was obvious that the
British must lead the way. A flank-march is always a
difficult and dangerous operation, and this was one of
peculiar peril, for the ground was no longer open, but
densely wooded, difficult and blind. It was only
possible to traverse it in long columns of route, which
must rely upon the compass for guidance; the direction being chosen so as to strike the road from Sevastopol to Baktchi Serai at a building called Mackenzie's
Farm. Cathcart with his division was left on the Belbek to maintain communication with the Katscha for
the time and to convey thither the sick. Lord Lucan
with the cavalry, a battery of horse-artillery and a battalion of Rifles, moved in advance, but missed his way;
and so it fell out that Raglan and his staff, having taken
the right track, were the first to emerge from the forest,
where they came upon a battalion of Russian infantry
and a few waggons, being the extreme rearguard of
Mentschikoff's army. Raglan quietly waited for a
few minutes until some of his cavalry came up, when
the Russians moved off rapidly. Maude's horse-

artillery battery fired a few shots after them, and the 1854.
enemy presently disappeared, leaving behind them a Sept. 25.
few prisoners and one or two waggons. Had the
Russian infantry by chance entered the wood, they
would have found at their mercy the Commander-in-
chief and his staff, a long train of thirty guns without supports, and the rest of the army in hopeless
disorder. The men, in the graphic words of one
who was with them, were like a mob of beaters making
their way through thick covert. They could hardly see
their neighbours to right or left; and they struggled on
with hands uplifted to guard their faces, while briers
and thorns almost tore the clothes off their backs. The
heat was intense; not a breath of air was stirring, and
the number of stragglers through exhaustion and the
ever-present cholera was very great. A single battalion of sharpshooters, skilled in forest fighting and
with knowledge of the country, could have made havoc
of them.

However, eventually they all emerged upon the
appointed place where Raglan had first sighted the
enemy, Mackenzie's Farm, and marched down a steep
chalky hill past the head of Sevastopol harbour over
chalky plains to the valley of the Tchernaya, where
water and rest were found at last. The foremost of
the troops did not reach the halting-place till nightfall;
many did not come in till midnight, and some not until
next day. The French halted for the night at Mackenzie's Farm, where they suffered much from want of
water. Many were the opportunities offered to Mentschikoff upon that day, but fortunately he seized none
of them.

On the morrow Raglan again rode forward in ad- Sept. 26.
vance of everyone, and striking south passed through
the village of Kadikoi, where he caught sight of what
seemed to be an inland lake, between lofty hills on
either side. A few shots were fired from an old fortification upon one of them; but the Light Division,
ascending the heights, found only a tiny garrison of

1854. militia whose commander at once surrendered. Rid-
Sept. 26. ing on, Raglan saw the inland lake expand into a little
landlocked harbour some six furlongs long by one
furlong broad; and, while he watched, a small British
vessel glided in to take soundings. Not long afterwards Lyons's flagship, the *Agamemnon*, steamed in and
dropped her anchor. A base had been found in the
harbour of Balaclava, and communication had been
re-established with the fleet. It is easy to imagine
what must have been Raglan's relief.

Meanwhile St. Arnaud had resigned his command
to General Canrobert. When Canrobert marched in
on the 26th he had at the very outset a difficult
question to settle, namely, whether Balaclava should be
the base for the English or for the French, for its situation bound it to be the port for the army on the right
of the line, which place of honour had hitherto been
held by the French. With great tact and delicacy he
gave Raglan his choice of harbours, only stipulating
that, if he should select Balaclava, the British must hold
the right of the line. After consultation with Lyons,
Raglan decided that he would take Balaclava, which
was as a matter of fact far too small for its purpose;
abandoning to the French the far more spacious and
convenient bays of Kamiesh and Kazatch, some ten or
eleven miles further west. This was a great and far-
reaching blunder, for it threw upon the English the
heaviest of the work and the greatest of the danger, with
the least facility, owing to the minute size of Balaclava,
for meeting either. The responsibility for it rests
with the naval officer Lyons.

The Allied armies having now reached their objective, it is time to examine more minutely the field
of operations. The Crimean peninsula itself is of the
shape of a diamond, measuring, from the extremi-
ties, roughly one hundred and thirty miles north and
south by nearly two hundred east and west. It is
joined to the mainland at its most northerly point by
the isthmus of Perekop; and at its eastern extremity

the strait of Kertch gives access by water from the
Black Sea to the sea of Azov and to the mouth of the
Don.   By the seizure of these two points and the
maintenance of a naval force in the sea of Azov, therefore, it was possible for the Allies to sever communication between the Crimea and the rest of Russia.   Sevastopol itself lies on a peninsula immediately to westward
of the most southerly point of the diamond.   This
peninsula, named the Khersonese, has the shape of a
Norman heraldic shield, with its point, Cape Kherson,
to the west.   To the north it is bounded by the great
harbour of Sevastopol, an inlet which runs inland from
west to east for some three and a half miles, with an
average breadth of three-quarters of a mile.   It was
defended at its mouth by fortifications which defied any
attack by ships alone, and, as has been told, had since
been barred by a line of sunken vessels.   At a point
rather less than a mile within the entrance there runs
southward from this harbour a deep creek, which was
known as Dockyard Creek or Man-of-War harbour—
names that explain themselves—and about a mile to
east of this again is a second creek, called the Careenage
Creek.   The line of the land-defences of Sevastopol
ran from a height just to east of Careenage Creek south-
westward to the head of Man-of-War harbour, and
thence north-westward to the forts that guarded the
entrance to the main haven from the southern shore.
The lines of defence, which shall be more minutely
described later, thus formed, roughly speaking, an
isosceles triangle with sides rather less than two miles
long, and a base, along the southern shore of the harbour, of nearly three miles.

The Khersonese itself is a plateau, with an extreme
length from east to west of about eleven miles and an
extreme width from north to south of eight miles,
sloping down gradually from east to west.   Its eastern
boundary is a steep ridge which rises abruptly to a
height of seven to eight hundred feet above the plain,
and runs almost continuously from the head of the

1854. Great Harbour by the heights above Balaclava to the
Sept. 26. sea, the only break being at a point called the Pass of
Balaclava, some two and a half miles to north of the
southern coast line. The name of this ridge is Mount
Sapouné, and it was this natural fortification which
alone made it possible for the Allies to attack Sevastopol at all, presenting as it did a practically impregnable
bulwark towards the mainland.

To the east Mount Sapouné descends into the
valley of the Tchernaya, the general course of which
is from south-east to north-west, until it flows into the
head of the Great Harbour. There is a bridge—
Inkerman bridge—about half a mile above its mouth.
Some three miles above this bridge the valley is divided
in twain by an oval mass of low heights, called the
Fedukhine Heights, about two miles east and west by
a mile north and south, which are broken towards the
eastern extremity by a shallow depression. To north
of this depression is the Traktir Bridge over the
Tchernaya, and it was over this bridge and through
this gap in the heights that Raglan marched to Balaclava. Half a mile to south of the Fedukhine Heights
there traverses the plain a long slender ridge, known
to the English as the Causeway Heights, which runs
out for some three miles from the higher hills to eastward until it nearly bridges over the plain between
those hills and the Sapouné Heights. Along this ridge
ran, in a direction from south-east to north-west, the
Woronzoff road, a good metalled way, which was the
main line of communication between Sevastopol and
the east. Roughly speaking, therefore, the position
was this. The Allies held the plateau of the Khersonese, excepting the little triangle defined by the
fortifications of Sevastopol, and had secured their
communication with the sea, while their fleets, with a
base at Constantinople, dominated the Black Sea. On
the other hand, the Russian garrison had free communication through the north with all the resources of
Russia, but by land only; and this was the salvation

of the Allies. Just as every French soldier of Napoleon 1854. had been obliged to walk from France into Spain upon Sept. 26. his own feet, so likewise must every Russian soldier of Nicholas march over hundreds of miles to reach the Crimea.

In the course of the flank-march Sir John Burgoyne suggested that a summons should be sent to the garrison of Sevastopol to surrender. This was not done, probably because St. Arnaud was at the time incapable of giving any orders, and such a summons must of course have been authorised by him as well as by Raglan. On the 26th Sir George Cathcart, who had just come in, sent a letter to Burgoyne, saying that the defences opposite him at the extreme north-eastern angle of the fortress were so slight as to be negligible, and that, if a few additional guns were given to him, he could secure them with his own division alone. The letter did not reach Burgoyne until late in the evening, head-quarters having meanwhile been shifted to Balaclava. But Burgoyne was of opinion that a great opportunity had been lost on the 26th; and he was right, for on that day not only were many of the defences weak, but there were no men in them, the great mass of the Russians being all still on the north side of the harbour. The fortress, therefore, would probably have surrendered upon summons, and, if not, could have been taken and occupied with little difficulty or loss.[1] Had the Allied armies been subject to a single commander Sevastopol would have fallen on that day.

During the night of the 26th - 27th Admiral Sept. 27. Kornilov, with extraordinary energy, ferried practically the entire Russian army from the north to the south side, and, when the Allied commanders reconnoitred the place on the morning of the 27th, the works were swarming with Russians. It was then too late for an assault. In the English front there was a large semi-

[1] See *Royal Engineers Journal*, April 1906; *The Siege of Sevastopol*, by Major-gen. Hon. G. Wrottesley.

1854.   circular tower — the Malakoff Tower — mounting
Sept. 27.   several guns. On the French front the dockyard was
surrounded by a crenellated wall. Before these
defences of masonry were earthworks armed with
heavy guns; and no general in his senses could dream
of throwing his troops against fortifications so formidable until they had been first battered with heavy
artillery. Still there was as yet no idea of a regular
siege. Burgoyne—and the Russian engineer Todleben
agreed with him—reckoned the earthworks in their
existing state to be of small account. The Malakoff
Tower was then the only serious obstacle to an assault,
and if that could be overpowered, there would be
little difficulty. It was therefore decided to go to
work after the fashion of Wellington in the Peninsula
—to erect batteries to subdue the fire of the place and
then without further ado to assault.[1] Upon this
decision, it remained for the Allies to make their
dispositions alike for this object and for protection
against the enemy outside Sevastopol. In Marlborough's wars we are accustomed to the terms
" besieging army " and " covering army "; and the
Allied forces had to supply both. Canrobert accordingly assigned two of his four divisions, under General
Forey, to do the work of the siege, reserving the other
two, under General Bosquet, to guard them while
engaged upon it. Forey encamped with his left on
Streleska Bay, an inlet two miles west of the mouth of
the Great Harbour, and his right opposite the head
of Dockyard Creek. Bosquet occupied the southern
portion of the Sapouné Heights, and, neglecting no
precaution, fortified not only the entrance to the
Balaclava Pass, but the whole line of the eminence that
was under his charge. It is to be noticed that Forey
was placed upon comparatively easy ground, that his
rear was secured by the sea, and that the distance from
his camp to his base at Kamiesch was not above three
miles.

[1] *Royal Engineers Journal, ut supra.*

The situation of the English was very different.
Their base at Balaclava, though in itself easily defen-
sible, lay just outside the protective line of the Sapouné
Heights and was accessible both from north and east.
Over and above the detachment of marines furnished
by the Navy, Raglan assigned to Balaclava a battalion
and a battery, placing Colin Campbell in charge of the
whole, while the cavalry were encamped about the
entrance to it by the village of Kadikoi, with orders to
patrol the plain northward to the Tchernaya.   Moreover, it was projected to throw up a chain of redoubts
along the Causeway Heights as an outer protection,
which should be manned by some three thousand
Turks, lately placed at Raglan's disposal.   From the
head of Balaclava harbour to the British camp on the
northern half of the Sapouné Heights was a distance
of from seven to eight miles; and the ground occupied
by the army was seamed by a succession of ravines
running from south-east to north-west, which practically divided it into three distinct parts.   The most
easterly of these ran down to the Careenage Creek
and was called by its name; the next to westward was called the Karabel Ravine, because it de-
bouched upon the Karabel suburb of Sevastopol; the
next was the Woronzoff Ravine, up which ran the
Woronzoff road; the next, christened by our men the
Valley of the Shadow of Death, was a tributary to the
fifth, called the Great Ravine.   These last three converged northward till they united at the head of the
Dockyard Creek.   Wide, steep and profound, they
were very serious obstacles to all lateral communication, not only on the plateau but within Sevastopol
itself; and in fact it was easier to go round their heads
on the immediate summit of the Sapouné Heights than
to cross them.   But this was not the only trouble.   The
triangular section, cut off by the Dockyard Creek
Ravine, at the north-eastern angle of the plateau, was
the most dangerous point in the whole position.   In the
first place, it was practically isolated by the Careenage

1854. Ravine from the ground to westward, the only
Sept. 27. access to it from that side being a neck of land six
hundred yards broad at the ravine's head; in the
second, its lower features to northward were held by
the enemy; and in the third it was threatened both
in flank and rear by Mentschikoff's army from the
Mackenzie Heights. Many saw the danger, and
urged that defensive works should be thrown up on
Mount Inkerman, as the English (incorrectly) named
this triangle. Burgoyne, in particular, pressed urgently
for keeping a strong reserve in an advanced position
within it, with the double object of securing it against
attack and of throwing up batteries to flank the eastward line of the enemy's defences. It is incredible
that Raglan himself should have failed to realise the
perils that beset his army; and yet nothing was done.

The truth is that those who enter upon a campaign
of this kind must be eternally drawing and renewing
bills upon fortune; and fortune is an usurious goddess.
The whole expedition had been one huge gamble, and
it seems that, though Raglan realised it from the first
to be such, the French commanders either did not
or would not. Raglan had been eager repeatedly to
stake everything upon a single throw, but had been
hindered by his partner. Now once again it was
necessary to hazard all for one great object—to assault
and capture Sevastopol after the cannonade for which
he was now landing his siege-train. But meanwhile
his resources were dwindling, for cholera was still
at work, and sickness, already very prevalent, was
Oct. 3. steadily increasing. On the 3rd of October he wrote
that he had but sixteen thousand men under arms,
which, after deducting the garrison of Balaclava, can
have left little more than fourteen thousand for active
work. It was ridiculous to think of dividing such a
force into a besieging army and a covering army.
Doubtless, if the entire body of the Allies had been
under a single command, one of Bosquet's divisions
could have been moved to Mount Inkerman, as Bur-

goyne desired; but, as matters stood, such a measure 1854.
would have endangered the Alliance. The British Oct.
soldiers could of course have been employed in fortifying Mount Inkerman, but there were not enough of
them for both offensive and defensive work; and,
whereas the latter certainly could not bring about the
speedy fall of Sevastopol, the former possibly might.
Even for offensive operations the British army was too
small, for there was still practically no land-transport,
and the work of bringing up guns and ammunition had
consequently to be done by men. Perhaps Raglan's
small contingent of Turks might have been usefully
employed on Mount Inkerman instead of outside
Balaclava, but Raglan did not wish Turkish soldiers
to be mixed up with his army, and his army did not
wish it either. In Bulgaria the men had observed how
the Bulgarian peasants, who sold them provisions, were
insolently waylaid and robbed by the Turks of the
money that had been paid to them; and they were
very indignant.[1] There would thus have been always
a possibility of a free fight between British and Turks,
if thrown together; and this consideration may very
likely have strengthened Raglan's prejudice against the
Turks. But undoubtedly the motive which wrought
most powerfully with Raglan for throwing all his
strength into the offensive operations of the siege was
the dread of wintering upon the plateau.

From the nature of the case—the cramped accommodation of Balaclava, its long distance from the camp
and the dearth of transport-animals—the work of
preparation for the siege took time, and every day's
delay raised the moral spirit of the garrison of Sevastopol. The seamen had a fine leader in Admiral
Kornilov; and the chief engineer, Colonel Todleben,
was not only an officer of great skill but of indefatigable
industry and inexhaustible resource. Moreover, he had
abundance of workmen, and a whole arsenal of guns
and ammunition. The garrison was further heartened

[1] Raglan to Newcastle, July 19, 1854.

1854. by the fact that early in October Mentschikoff added
Oct. to it from his field-army some eighteen battalions,
raising the full strength of its fighting men to nearly
fifty-four thousand.   This he could the better afford
to do since he had already received some reinforcements
and was expecting more; and indeed so much increased was his confidence that he not only reoccupied
the Mackenzie Heights, but pushed large parties of
cavalry down into the valley of the Tchernaya into
actual contact with the British patrols.   Evidently he
was beginning to realise, what was actually the fact,
that his field-army and the garrison of Sevastopol,
taken together, outnumbered the Allies.

Meanwhile the engineers of the Allied armies had
agreed upon their plan of attack, namely, that the
French should assail the western and the British the
eastern side of the triangular defences of Sevastopol,
the guns of both converging upon the Flagstaff bastion,
which formed the apex of the triangle.   The conditions
under which the two armies laboured were, however,
widely different.   On the French side there was
abundant depth of soil within reasonable range of
the western defences; and accordingly the French
engineers, being able to work in the conventional
fashion, threw up their batteries upon the commanding
height of Mount Rudolph within a thousand yards of the
Central bastion and thirteen hundred of the Flagstaff.
The English, on the other hand, had nothing but bare
rock beneath them and were obliged to establish their
main batteries on either side of the Woronzoff Ravine,
at a distance of from fourteen to fifteen hundred yards
from their objectives; while two batteries of Lancaster
guns—weapons of extraordinarily long range, according
to the standard of the time—were established some five
hundred yards in rear again of these.   The fire of the
whole was designed to demolish the eastern flank of
the Flagstaff bastion, the Redan and the Malakoff
Tower, which last Burgoyne had from the first desig-
nated as the key to Sevastopol.

The French were the first to break ground on the 1854. night of the 9th of October; and in the course of the Oct. 9. next week they erected a chain of batteries, mounting in all fifty-three guns. From the first Todleben annoyed them with constant cannonade and frequent sallies, while he set himself to erect counter-batteries and make other dispositions so as to meet the French fifty-three pieces with sixty-four. He could not, or at any rate did not, make equal efforts to contend with the British, because they were out of his reach. The English did not open their trenches until the 10th, Oct. 10. when they began to throw up one battery, of forty-one guns, called Chapman's battery, on an eminence known as Green Hill to west of the Woronzoff Ravine, and another, Gordon's battery, of thirty-six pieces, on the Woronzoff Height to east of the ravine. It was arranged that fire should be opened on the morning of the 17th, and that at the same hour the naval forces should attack the fortifications of the harbour from the sea. Before daylight parties of British sharpshooters— ten from each battalion—stole down to within range of the Russian gunners, and at half-past six at a given signal Oct. 17. the cannonade began. It was carried on for some four hours with great effect until a French magazine was blown up by a Russian shell. The casualties from the accident did not exceed fifty, but its moral effect was great, and the battery ceased firing. A second explosion of an ammunition-waggon heightened the discouragement of the French, and at half-past ten the whole of their guns fell silent. The British batteries meanwhile continued to pour in shot and shell, utterly wrecking the Redan, which was finally reduced to ruins by the explosion of a magazine at three o'clock, and silencing the Malakoff. Every gun had been dismounted or disabled, and Todleben, giving up the fortress for lost, put on all his orders so that his corpse might be recognised. The Russians had massed infantry in rear of their works to be ready to meet an attack, and these, exposed for long to a heavy fire of

1854. artillery while themselves perforce inactive, had been—
Oct. 17. very pardonably—much shaken. An assault would
almost certainly have succeeded; and had the Allied
army been homogeneous and subject to a single commander, French or English, Sevastopol would probably
have been taken that day. But an assault by the
English upon the Redan had never been contemplated
apart from an assault of the French on the Flagstaff
bastion, and Raglan, to the bitter disappointment of
Burgoyne, abstained from launching his own men alone
against the breach made by his artillery.[1] Once again
every advantage gained was sacrificed to the safety of
the Alliance. No blame can be attached to Raglan.
Any auspicious work done by his army in which the
French did not share might have set the Allied hosts
fighting each other, even as the armies of Ney and Soult
came near to a pitched battle in June 1809. The
safety of the Alliance was a deity that, Saturn-like,
devoured its own children.

The naval attack had no influence whatever upon
the day's work, though it had been hoped that it might
have distracted some of the defenders from the land-
batteries. It was, in fact, an utter failure. At the last
moment the French Admiral changed both the hour
and the plan of attack, and though many brave deeds
were done, ships both French and English were badly
damaged and over five hundred sailors were killed and
wounded, there was nothing to show for it except the
destruction of a battery which was not casemated.
The action showed only the futility—which needed no
showing—of matching wooden ships against six feet of
masonry; and it calls for mention only because it marks
the beginning and end of all offensive naval efforts
against Sevastopol.

The casualties of the Allies in the cannonade of the
17th were small, those of the French, including the
men injured by the explosion, not exceeding ninety-
six, nor those of the British one hundred and forty-

---

[1] *Royal Engineers Journal, ut supra.*

four.   In fact, the readiness of the French to cease fire
is difficult to account for; but they began on the 18th
to erect new batteries and to proceed by regular
approaches against the Flagstaff bastion, while the
British maintained a steady fire all day which once again
reduced the Redan to ruin.   On the 19th it was hoped
that the French might so damage the Flagstaff bastion
as to enable them to assault; but Todleben's counter-
measures once more brought their efforts to naught.
In two of the French batteries magazines were exploded,
a third was silenced early, and by three o'clock in the
afternoon their fire had ceased.   The British, who had
been held ready for the storming of the Redan, were
not sent forward to the attack; and from this day
forward it should be seen that the idea of a speedy
assault was abandoned.   The cannonade was continued for another week, but the Russian casualties,
which had amounted to over two thousand in the first
three days, soon dwindled to an average of no more than
two hundred and fifty a day.   Moreover, through the
energy and devotion of their working parties not only
was all damage done by day repaired by night, but the
general power of the defences was steadily increased.
It must be said, in common fairness, that the British
had fulfilled their part with ability and success; but the
misfortune was that the Russians needed only to foil one
half of the Allied army in order to paralyse the whole.

The situation now became most anxious and
difficult.   The British troops were rapidly wearing out
from overwork, and sorely needed rest; and it was too
evident that the cream of the entire Army had been
skimmed in order to fill the ranks of the regiments
originally dispatched to the East.   Some drafts had
been received at Varna in July, but these had been
imperfectly trained, and in many cases had been composed not of men but of boys under eighteen years of
age.   To send out these striplings to such a service
was simply murder, and Raglan entreated that they
should be weeded out and that only men should be

1854. sent to him "strong enough for a campaign where shelter is unknown." From the very first Raglan had been anxious about the winter, and he now received warning from Mr. Calvert, an Englishman who knew the Crimea well, that bitter cold was to be expected on the plateau. It can hardly be supposed that this was news to Raglan, but he sent Calvert's information to England to bring home to Ministers the urgency of the danger.

And now it began to appear that, even if the Allies should decide to abandon the attack upon Sevastopol and evacuate the Crimea, the operation would be one of extreme difficulty and peril. On the 18th a Russian force of all arms was seen marching eastward upon Tchorgun, where it established itself as the nucleus of a field-army which was evidently designed to threaten the British communications with Balaclava, little more Oct. 24. than five miles distant. By the 24th of October this force had swelled to twenty-five battalions, thirty-five squadrons and seventy-eight guns, perhaps twenty-five thousand men, under General Liprandi. Meanwhile the Causeway Heights had been fortified by a chain of six weakly constructed redoubts, numbered consecutively from east to west, which were held by some three thousand Turks with nine twelve-pounder guns, three of these being mounted in the most easterly redoubt, Number One, and two each on Numbers Two, Three and Four. The Turkish commander, Rustam Pasha, a vigilant officer, was informed by a spy on the evening of the 24th that Liprandi had prepared an attack for the morrow; and this intelligence was at once passed on by Lucan and Colin Campbell to Raglan's headquarters. A similar report, however, a few days before had caused a detachment of the Fourth Division to be marched down to the plain and back again to no purpose; and Raglan, alive to the moral not less than the physical results of such fruitless marches upon exhausted troops, decided to take no steps until further information should reach him,

Before dawn of the 25th the British cavalry were
standing to their horses and Lucan with his staff was
riding out towards Number One redoubt, when he
perceived on the flagstaff the signal which announced
a Russian advance and almost immediately afterwards
heard the guns of the redoubt open fire.   Liprandi had
in fact moved off at 5 A.M., directing two columns with
a joint strength of eight battalions, a squadron and
twenty guns, against Number One redoubt, a third of
three battalions and ten guns against Number Two,
and a fourth of four battalions, three squadrons and a
field-battery against Number Three; supporting the
whole with the mass of his cavalry and horse-artillery,
and holding the remainder of his force in reserve on
the Fedukhine Hills.   Lucan at once mounted his
cavalry division—too grand an appellation for fifteen
hundred sabres and lances—and manœuvred upon the
flank of the advancing Russians, bringing his horse-
battery into action, though with no great effect for a
time, but abstaining from any attack.   Excepting the
Ninety-third Highlanders his was the only force which
lay between the Russians, if they should carry the
Causeway Heights, and Balaclava; and he husbanded
it against the peril of a Russian advance across the
plain upon Kadikoi.   Herein beyond question he
evinced sound judgement.

With a superiority in numbers of ten to one both
men and in guns, the Russians had little difficulty in
mastering Number One redoubt, though the Turks
made a most gallant defence.   The garrison was
driven out with very heavy loss, and therewith the little
isolated bodies in the remaining redoubts, seeing the
fate that threatened them, made haste to evacuate them
and fly towards Kadikoi.   The Cossacks pursued until
checked by Lucan's cavalry.   The Russians then
occupied Redoubts Numbers One, Two and Three,
and Lucan fell back westward and took up a position
to threaten the flank of any advance towards Balaclava.
Raglan, who had been early informed of Liprandi's

1854.
Oct. 25.
movement, had watched the proceedings from the summit of the plateau and ordered the First and Fourth Divisions to move down to the defence of Balaclava, while Canrobert, joining him, likewise bade two brigades of infantry and two regiments of cavalry to descend into the plain. Raglan further directed Lucan to fall back to the foot of the plateau till the course of the action should be further developed. Meanwhile, until the First and Fourth Divisions should come up, which could hardly be for a couple of hours, nothing stood between Liprandi and the mouth of the Balaclava gorge but the Ninety-third Highlanders, a handful of invalid soldiers, and two battalions of Turks.

The Russian general, however, whether from failure to perceive his advantage or from set purpose, remained inactive for a time, until at last he set his cavalry in motion westward up the valley to north of the Causeway Heights. The Russian artillery also opened upon Campbell, who had posted the Ninety-third, with a Turkish battalion upon either flank, upon an eminence north-east of Kadikoi. Campbell thereupon withdrew his troops to the reverse slope of the hill, a movement which had the effect of sending the two Turkish battalions flying in panic to Balaclava. A detachment of five or six Russian squadrons presently wheeled southward directly upon Kadikoi, whereupon Campbell brought the Ninety-third again to the summit, in line, and opened fire upon this detachment at long range, with the result that the Russian horse turned away and, after a feeble demonstration against Campbell's right flank, retired in some disorder, some of the guns in position for defence of Balaclava adding materially to their discomfiture.

Meanwhile the main body of the Russian cavalry, with over thirty guns, moved at a trot up the valley until it was checked by two cannon-shots fired from the batteries on the plateau. Thereupon, after some hesitation, it wheeled to the left and began to cross the Causeway Heights, lending its flank to the British

Light Brigade. The ground was undulating and 1854.
broken by occasional orchards, and it should seem that Oct. 25.
the Russian commander had thrown out no scouts and
Lucan no vedettes, so that each force was unconscious
of the other's vicinity. It happened, however, that
Raglan, observing the unsteadiness of the Turks on
the flanks of the Ninety-third, had ordered eight
squadrons of the Heavy Brigade to their support;
and Brigadier-general Scarlett accordingly trotted off
south-eastward with the six squadrons of the Fifth
Dragoon Guards, Greys and Inniskillings, ordering
the Fourth Dragoon Guards to follow. This movement necessarily took him straight across the front of
the advancing Russian cavalry; but Scarlett's eyes were
bent upon the Turks on his right, and it was his aide-
de-camp who called his attention to the huge mass
bearing down upon his left, only a few hundred yards
distant. Thereupon Scarlett gave the order to wheel
into line, but, finding himself cramped for space, owing
to an enclosure, he broke again into column of troops
to take further ground towards the east. He was still
in this formation when Lucan, being informed of the
situation, galloped up and ordered him to wheel into
line and attack at once.

By this time the bulk of the Russian cavalry had
reached the summit of the Causeway Heights, when
General Ryjoff, who was in command, moved the whole
mass further to the east—a manoeuvre which was
accomplished with admirable precision—and then
resumed the original direction of the advance to southward. Scarlett, on his side, was in difficulties. He
imagined that his six squadrons had followed him in a
single column of troops, but as a matter of fact they
had broken themselves into two columns, one of the
Greys and a single squadron of the Inniskillings, which
was nearest to the enemy, and the other of the three
remaining squadrons which were further to the south;
and some little time was necessary to get them into
order. But to the general amazement Ryjoff halted

1854. his whole body of horse, offering a chance too favour-
Oct. 25. able to be missed; and Lucan was so impatient to
take advantage of it that more than once he ordered
his trumpeter to sound the charge.   At last, however,
Scarlett's array was formed, the three squadrons afore-
said in first line, a squadron of the Inniskillings
echeloned to the right rear, and the two squadrons of
the Fifth Dragoon Guards to the left rear.   The odds
against him were very heavy, at least three—perhaps
five—to one.   The dense mass of the Russians not only
seemed to be impenetrable in depth but actually overlapped his line widely upon both flanks, for in the
front of the column the Russian commander had thrown
out two shallow wings to right and left.   Finally the
approach to the enemy lay uphill.   Nevertheless the
Russians remained stationary, perhaps five hundred
yards away, and that was sufficient.   Scarlett placed
himself at the head of the leading squadrons and
sounded the charge.

The Greys, having to advance over the edge of
their camping-ground, could not immediately move at
any speed, but, once clear of obstacles, they rapidly
gathered way.   Scarlett, his staff and his trumpeter
galloped straight into the Russian array fifty yards
ahead of the first line, and a second or two later the
three squadrons crashed headlong into the standing
mass and to all appearance were swallowed up.   The
great Russian column heaved and swayed but did not
break up; and the two shallow wings began to wheel
inward as if to cut off the retreat of the three leading
British squadrons.   The manœuvre was still in progress
when in quick succession the remaining squadron of
the Inniskillings galloped into the left or south-eastern
angle of the Russian column; the Royals, who had
come forward without orders, sprang upon the south-
western angle, and the Fifth Dragoon Guards burst in
to the left of the entry made by the Greys.   Under
this succession of shocks the huge Russian column
reeled backwards up the hill; and then the Fourth

Dragoon Guards, by Lucan's direction, rode up the
right flank of the Russian mass in column of troops,
wheeled into line and bore down headlong upon it
at right angles to the attack of Scarlett's three leading squadrons. This onslaught was decisive. The
Fourth Dragoon Guards went straight through the
Russian column from flank to flank, and the enemy
broke up in disorder and fled northward up the hill,
more than three thousand men utterly dispersed by
seven or eight hundred.

Scattered parties of the heavy dragoons pursued,
but were speedily checked by their officers, who
naturally were urgent first to rally and re-form the
squadrons. Lucan's horse-artillery battery fired a few
rounds at the retreating enemy; and therewith the
action came for the moment to an end. Brilliant
though it had been, it was sadly incomplete. Throughout its duration the Light Brigade had remained
drawn up full upon the Russian right flank and not
more than five hundred yards distant from it; yet
Cardigan had not attempted to move. It is true that
he was swearing and chafing with impatience at being
left out of the fight, but it never occurred to him of
his own initiative to take part in it. Had he done
so, the cavalry-action of Balaclava might have taken its
place as a classic in military literature, and the host of
the Russian horse might have suffered a discomfiture
with few parallels in the annals of war. But Cardigan
was a soldier by drill-book only. No officer in England
could handle a brigade more deftly at a field-day; but
he had none of the instincts of a leader of cavalry.

The success of Scarlett's brigade within a few
minutes changed the whole aspect of the action; and
Raglan, who had watched it from the plateau, saw that
this was the moment for recovering the Causeway
Heights. The First Division was already well on its
way—apparently on the crest of the plateau—but the
Fourth was lagging; Cathcart, according to one
account, being very unwilling to lay further work upon

1854. his men, who had only just returned from duty in the
Oct. 25. trenches.[1] In the circumstances Raglan ordered
Lucan to advance his cavalry and take advantage of
any opportunity to recover the heights, adding that he
should be supported by infantry. Lucan accordingly
moved the Light Brigade to the valley north of the
Causeway Heights, and there halted. It should seem
that the First and Fourth Divisions then reached their
appointed positions in the plain, the former aligning
itself to left of the Ninety-third Highlanders with its
front to the north, while the latter advanced eastward
along the Causeway Heights as far as Redoubt Number
Four, but no further. After the lapse of forty or fifty
minutes Raglan's staff observed Russian artillery-teams
approaching the captured redoubts with the apparent
intention of carrying off the guns ; and Raglan sent
a second order to Lucan directing the cavalry to advance
rapidly to the front and prevent the removal of those
pieces, adding that he might take his horse-artillery
battery with him, and that the French cavalry was on
his left. The message was in writing, and was carried
by one of Airey's aide-de-camps, Captain Nolan of the
Fifteenth Hussars, an officer who had written a book
about cavalry and was an enthusiast concerning the
powers of that particular arm. Lucan after reading
the order. decided at once that its execution was impracticable and would lead to serious losses for no
purpose.

It must be remembered that Lucan was on the low
ground and could not survey, as could Raglan from the
plateau, the whole field of action, nor perceive the
Russian teams approaching the redoubts. But, though
from the spot where the message reached him he could
see nothing, he could have shifted his ground and,
observing for himself the Russian dispositions, as he
should have done upon receiving Raglan's first order,
might better have divined the wishes of his chief. Lip-

[1] See Kinglake's account, *Invasion of the Crimea*, cabinet edn.,
v. 67 *seq.*

randi's troops were distributed somewhat in the form of 1854
the merrythought bone of a chicken. On the Fedukhine Oct. 25.
Heights to north, which formed, so to speak, the longer
shank of the bone, were drawn up eight battalions, four
squadrons and fourteen guns facing south. On the
Causeway Heights, which represent the shorter shank,
were the remainder of his battalions about the captured
redoubts, Numbers One, Two and Three, with a
general front to the south. Between the two shanks
ran what is called by English writers the Northern
Valley, with an average breadth of a thousand yards;
near the point of their junction were six squadrons of
lancers, three on either side of the valley; and at the
point of junction were the horsemen lately defeated by
the British Heavy Brigade, drawn up in three lines
across the valley, with twelve guns unlimbered before
them, the whole facing to the east. For six or seven
hundred lances and sabres to attack four or more
battalions in position with a battery in support might
at the first blush have appeared to Lucan an unreasonable order; but he was not directed to attack,
only to advance. Nor was he limited to any particular
ground for this movement. He could do so either
north or south of the Causeway Heights, or along the
heights themselves. Raglan, who had a remarkably
shrewd intuition into the moral state of troops on
a battle-field, evidently judged that Liprandi's entire
army had been shaken by the audacious charge of the
Heavy Brigade and that the Russians would withdraw
from the Causeway Heights if threatened by the terrible
British horse. After events seem to prove that he was
right.

Lucan, however, quarrelled with the order, not only
inwardly but openly before the aide-de-camp Nolan,
and at length he asked impatiently what he was expected to do. Thereupon Nolan seems to have lost
his temper, and waving his hand dramatically and, as
Lucan averred, insultingly, to eastward, he said,
" There, my lord, is your enemy and there are your

guns ! " After this Lucan said no more, but rode across to the Light Brigade and passed on the order to Cardigan, bidding him advance steadily with four squadrons, keeping the remainder in hand. Cardigan understood him to mean that he was to attack the Russians at the extreme western end of the valley, which was a mile and a half distant, and pointed out that there were Russian batteries in his front and on both flanks. Lucan assented, but added that these were Raglan's orders; and, before he left, he narrowed Cardigan's front line down from six squadrons to four. Cardigan then gave the word for the entire brigade to advance, and placed himself at its head.

The brigade moved off at a trot, in three lines. In the first, from right to left, were the Thirteenth Light Dragoons and the Seventeenth Lancers, in the second the Eleventh Hussars only, covering the Seventeenth, and in the third the Fourth Light Dragoons and the Eighth Hussars, the latter having only a squadron and a half present instead of two squadrons. They had not advanced more than a hundred yards when Nolan came galloping diagonally across its front from northwest to south-east, shouting and gesticulating as if to make the brigade change direction to half-right. A moment later he was struck dead by a fragment of shell and the purport of his action died with him. The brigade continued to advance down the valley in beautiful order, and the four Russian battalions, which occupied redoubt Number Three, thereupon withdrew from the work and, retiring to eastward of redoubt Number Two, threw themselves into squares as if expecting attack. But meanwhile batteries and riflemen on both flanks opened fire upon the devoted squadrons, and men and officers began to fall fast. Instinctively the speed of the advance was quickened, in spite of Cardigan's efforts to control it. The officers still looked to the order and dressing of their men; discipline never failed; and, though riderless horses crowding in upon the still mounted men caused

embarrassment, they did not bring about confusion. 1854.
Very soon the foremost line came within range of the Oct. 25.
twelve guns at the end of the valley. It was torn to
pieces by shot and thinned to a mere remnant; and
then the men instinctively opened out, leaving vacant
the spaces where the flashes of fire through the smoke
showed the actual position of each gun;[1] and thus it
was that the first line seems to have outflanked the
Russian battery both to right and left. On the extreme left Colonel Morris of the Seventeenth, finding
Russian hussars before him, called to the handful of
men that were behind him, and charged, killing the
Russian leader with his own hand. The hussars,
remaining at the halt, were utterly broken, and Morris's
men were pressing on in pursuit when they were
checked by a body of Cossacks coming down upon
their flank. On the right the Thirteenth Light
Dragoons rode into the Russian batteries and joined
parties of the Seventeenth in cutting and thrusting at
the Russian gunners. The Eleventh Hussars of the
second line, under Colonel Douglas, encountering a
body of Russian lancers on the south flank of the guns,
rode straight at them; but the enemy did not await
the shock, and fled away with the Eleventh in pursuit.
The Fourth Light Dragoons, having secured absolute
mastery of every Russian gun, rode off to join the
Eleventh. The Eighth Hussars coming up a minute
or two later, and seeing not a sign of any formed body
of English horse, was halted for a few minutes by its
colonel, who, having rallied a few men of other regiments upon it, presently resumed his advance. In
truth, the whole body of Ryjoff's cavalry, already cowed
by the charge of the Heavy Brigade, was in panic
retreat; and actually two of Liprandi's reserve bat-

[1] This detail was told me by Colonel John Brown, who, either as
a private or a trumpeter (I forget which) in the 17th Lancers, rode
with his regiment in this action. On his authority I assert with
confidence that the only trumpet-signal given to the Light Brigade was
the one note that signifies " March." The " charge " was never
sounded at all.

talions, far in rear, threw themselves into squares, lest the worst might come. Given speedy support, it seemed that the attack of the Light Brigade might achieve great results.

Lucan had, as a matter of fact, followed Cardigan with the Heavy Brigade, himself riding far ahead so as to keep in touch with him. While thus engaged he was struck in the leg by a musket ball, his horse was hurt in two places, one of his staff was wounded, another was killed, and the third had his horse shot under him. Looking back he found that the men of the Heavy Brigade were falling fast, wherefore, still retaining command, he withdrew it out of range so as to be able to protect the Light Brigade against pursuit. And meanwhile a regiment of French Chasseurs d'Afrique, fresh from service in Algeria, showed him, too late, how to do what Raglan had desired by attacking the Russians on the western spurs of the Fedukhine Heights. Their objective was a battery supported by two battalions, and the French advanced in two bodies each of two squadrons, the first upon the flank of the battery, the second biding its time to assail the infantry. The ground was rough and broken and the skirts of the hill were covered with Russian skirmishers; but the two leading squadrons galloped through these in loose formation; and, before the actual attack could be delivered, the Russian batteries limbered up and the two battalions likewise retired. Thereupon the French commanding officer sounded the recall, having accomplished his object at a cost of fewer than forty casualties.

No support, therefore, was forthcoming for the Light Brigade, though it was now assured of deliverance from artillery-fire on its northern flank when it should retire; and soon it became evident that it must retire. Its remnants were broken up into two principal bodies under Colonels Shewell and Douglas, with no central direction, for Cardigan could not be found. He had ridden into the Russian battery practically

alone, well ahead of his squadrons, and having lost all 1854.
touch with them in the smoke had extricated himself Oct. 25.
in some miraculous fashion from the midst of a horde
of Cossacks and was riding back up the valley. Shewell,
after hunting for him in vain, looked back and saw three
squadrons of Russian lancers forming across the valley,
a furlong in his rear. Wheeling about, he charged
them without hesitation, with odds of from four to
one against him, broke through them and, seeing no
supports approaching, continued his retreat under the
fire of the guns from the Causeway Heights. Douglas,
likewise, finding his pursuit checked by overwhelming
numbers, turned about and was presently joined by the
Fourth Light Dragoons. The Russians, gathering
courage, followed them up, but the handful of British
troopers, still preserving their discipline, wheeled about
to face them, and the Russians came to a stand. Now,
however, a body of Russian lancers formed up in the
valley to cut off their retreat, so that they were threatened both in front and rear. In these trying circumstances Lord George Paget, who was the senior officer,
gave the order " Threes about," and the party resumed
its way up the valley, rear rank in front and officers in
rear. The Russians, from five to six squadrons strong,
were formed in double column of squadrons, facing
south, evidently designing to attack Paget in flank.
The fate of the party seemed sealed, for their horses
were wearied out and they could no longer preserve
much order; but the Russians, just when they should
have borne down upon them irresistibly, suddenly
halted, and the British brushed across their front,
parrying lance-thrusts as they passed. They thus
continued their retreat with little further trouble.
Scattered men, wounded and unwounded, also strag-
gled back to their own lines, and the whole being
mustered were found to amount to one hundred and
ninety-five mounted men where half an hour before
there had been six hundred and seventy-five.
    Liprandi thereupon brought back his infantry once

1854. more to Number Three redoubt, increasing the bat-
Oct. 25. talions there from four to eight. Cathcart had made
no attempt to occupy the redoubt while it was evacuated;
but there were now troops enough to drive the Russians
from the Causeway Heights, and it should seem that
Raglan wished to do so. But Canrobert objected;
alleging, not without force, that looking to the urgent
need for an early capture of Sevastopol, the Allies
could not afford troops to occupy the Causeway
Heights. Liprandi was therefore left in possession
of the three most easterly of the redoubts, while the
Turks reoccupied the three to westward. Therewith
at about four in the afternoon the action came to an end,
leaving the Russians with the very solid advantage of
controlling the Woronzoff road—the only metalled
way between Balaclava and the British camp.

The action of Balaclava is remembered, not, as it
should be, for its very serious result mentioned just
above, but for the exploits of the British cavalry, and
chiefly, though wrongly, for those of the Light Brigade.
In reality the charge of the Heavy Brigade was the finer
incident, for it was brilliantly successful and seems to
me to be one of the great feats of cavalry against
cavalry in the history of Europe. Of course the
Russian horse were miserably handled. I do not know
where to find a parallel for Ryjkoff's action in manœuvring such large numbers in so dense and unwieldy a
mass and actually keeping them halted when threatened with attack. But no common spirit and discipline
are needed to make seven hundred men attack thirty-
five hundred, even when the latter are stationary; and
no praise can be too high for the five regiments of the
Heavy Brigade. Not the least striking detail in the
engagement is the fact that the adjutant of the Greys
rallied his men while still surrounded on all sides by
the wavering but not yet broken ranks of the Russian
regiments. It indicates an astounding moral ascendancy; for it does not seem that the British dragoons
could do the Russians any great physical harm. They

had been taught to use their unwieldy sabres chiefly 1854.
to cut, and even if they had been fine swordsmen, Oct. 25.
which few of them were, they could make little impression upon the thick greatcoats worn by the enemy.
Probably, as is the way of Englishmen, they handled
their swords as bludgeons, and so inflicted little damage.
It was the fearless crashing of the red-coats into the
midst of them that dismayed the Russians, as well it
might. The losses of the Heavy Brigade were, in the
circumstances, singularly light, not exceeding seventy-
eight killed and wounded. Altogether the charge was
a very fine feat of arms, and the credit of launching it
belongs to Lucan.

The advance of the Light Brigade into artillery-fire
upon three sides was of course a grand but pitiful
blunder. The really remarkable thing is, not that the
squadrons should have ridden through such a fire
without flinching, but that the remnant left at the end
should still have been under perfect control, ready to
charge bodies of five times their strength both after
the capture of the battery and during their retreat.
This is indeed worthy of commemoration, being an
example of discipline which every recruit in the five
regiments should be taught to remember and to revere.
The losses of the Light Brigade were, however, grievous. Cardigan himself was wounded, and of his staff
one was killed, another wounded, and a third had his
horse shot under him. In the Fourth Light Dragoons
four out of eleven officers present were killed or
wounded; in the Eighth Hussars four out of ten; in
the Eleventh Hussars three out of six; in the Thirteenth Light Dragoons three out of seven; and in the
Seventeenth Lancers seven out of ten. Altogether the
Brigade lost one hundred and thirteen of all ranks
killed, one hundred and thirty-four wounded, and four
hundred and seventy-five horses killed; a loss for
which practically nothing was gained except a great
tradition nobly won for the British cavalry.

Raglan held Lucan responsible for the destruction

1854. of the Light Brigade, and it should seem with justice.
Oct. 25. In a private letter to the Duke of Newcastle he pointed
out truly that Lucan had taken no steps to watch the
Russians nor to discern their dispositions, that he had
not brought up his horse-artillery, that he had not
invited the co-operation of the French cavalry, and that
he had made no use of the Heavy Brigade. Looking
to the hasty retreat of the Russians before the attack
of four French squadrons on the Fedukhine Heights,
it seems hardly questionable that a simultaneous
advance of the French horse against the Fedukhine
and of the British against the Causeway Heights
would have caused Liprandi to withdraw the whole of
the troops from both of those positions. Why Lucan
was guilty of this perversity it is impossible to explain.
He was no fool, but, on the contrary, above the average
of ability. He had served not without distinction as
a volunteer in the Russo-Turkish War of 1828–1829;
he had made the Seventeenth Lancers so smart in every
way while he commanded them that they were known
as "Bingham's Dandies"; and thus he had done his
best to learn his business not only on the parade-
ground but on active service. Lastly, he was a man
of vigorous health and fine physique,[1] very young for
his fifty-four years and, by the admission even of his
many enemies, extraordinarily cool and self-possessed
under fire. But he was difficult and cantankerous, and
not the man to inspire his subordinates with the fire
that is the essence of the true cavalry-leader. It is
possible, indeed, that he was unfortunate in his
brigadiers. Cardigan seems to have been only a better
kind of serjeant-major, while Scarlett threw out no
flanking parties to watch the enemy when leading his
brigade towards Kadikoi, and apparently could not

---

[1] He was born in 1800 and died in 1888. I have still a vision of
him riding down St. James's Street when past eighty—rather stout
but perfectly dressed, sitting bolt upright in the saddle with his body
swaying to every movement of his horse, and (with his whiskers dyed)
looking little more than fifty.

move six squadrons in open column of troops without 1854.
allowing half of them to form themselves into a separate Oct. 25.
column.   In any case, whether Scarlett were to blame
or Lucan, it is certain that Lucan took an active personal share in directing the attack of the Heavy
Brigade, whereas his right place would have seemed
to be rather with his reserve—the Light Brigade—
when once he had given Scarlett his orders.   Then he
might in person have directed Cardigan against the
flank of Ryjoff's massive column and practically have
destroyed it.

Altogether, despite of the devotion and courage of
the British cavalry and the brilliant achievement of the
Chasseurs d'Afrique, the day's work was thoroughly
unsatisfactory; and the principal reason was that the
British cavalry had, as a whole, been unhappily handled.
Raglan, already far too deficient in infantry, was evidently unwilling to venture it in any important operation
apart from the siege, and Canrobert was apprehensive,
not unreasonably, that Liprandi's movement was simply
a feint to give the garrison of Sevastopol the chance of
an effective sortie.   Both were therefore unwilling to
commit their battalions very deeply on the low ground,
and Cathcart was evidently even more reluctant than
they to engage his division in any serious combat for the
Causeway Heights.   Beyond question Lucan and Cathcart did not work kindly for Raglan upon this day, the
one seeming to think that the men in the plains were
not concerned with the men on the plateau, and the
other that the men on the plateau had nothing to do
with the men on the plains.   Neither was destined to
see fully what evil they had wrought.   Cathcart had
just eleven more days to live, and Lucan was recalled
in January 1855.   Meanwhile the consequences of
their conduct were far-reaching.   Raglan was obliged,
owing to the destruction of the Light Cavalry, to give
Campbell the entire Highland Brigade, instead of one
battalion only, at Balaclava; and above all, the Woronzoff road was lost.   The sequel showed that it would

1854. have been truer economy for the Allies to fall upon Liprandi and beat him handsomely at once and possibly for all. Had Raglan been in command of a homogeneous army he would almost certainly have done so; but always in the way of every progressive operation stood that fatal obstacle, the alliance.

CHAPTER XLIV

The menace to Balaclava was now become a permanent 1854. diversion in favour of the Russians, and they lost no time in turning the advantage to account. The northeastern angle of the plateau, called by the English Inkerman Ridge, was, as has been explained, virtually in Russian possession, the greater part of it lying under fire from the powerful guns of the fortress or of men-of-war anchored at the head of the great harbour. It lies between the marshes of the Tchernaya on the north and the Careenage Ravine on the south, both of them practically impassable; but near the mouth of the Tchernaya a causeway and a bridge—Inkerman bridge —gave access to Sevastopol from the north, while about half way up the Careenage Ravine there was a track leading along a lateral hollow from the Inkerman Ridge across the ravine to the Victoria Ridge next to southward. The Inkerman Ridge from its foot, where it abuts on the Careenage Creek, to its summit, rises from west to east in a gradual acclivity of about three miles to a height of over six hundred feet. As it ascends it broadens out from a width of about five hundred yards at its base to about twenty-five hundred yards at the point where the head of the Careenage Ravine becomes merged in the plateau. Its comb or spine, frequently contracted by lateral hollows on either side, expands, about a mile and a half upward from its foot, into something more or less resembling a little plain, with an extreme width north and south of about fourteen hundred yards. In the midst of this plain rises a slight eminence,

1854. nearly six hundred feet high, called by the English
Oct. Shell Hill, the name really embracing the whole of the
level ground about it. Shell Hill marked the limit of the
British outposts; and, as surely as two or three British
soldiers showed themselves on its seaward slope, the
Russian ships in the harbour, apprised by signal, opened
fire with shot and shell. From Shell Hill upward the
comb again contracts for another seven hundred yards
until it gradually widens, close to the summit, into what
was called Home Ridge, where stood the camp of the
Second Division.

The whole of the Inkerman Ridge was covered with
scrubby oak, but that on the comb was so sparse and
stunted, owing to the thin layer of earth on the rock below and the play of wind and salt above, as to be negligible. In the hollows, where more soil had been washed
down and there was shelter from the wind, this brushwood varied from the height of a man's waist to that of
twice his stature. While, therefore, even heavy cannon
could move easily along the open ground of the comb,
they could hardly travel through the hollows without a
road. But there were good metalled ways leading on to
the lower slopes of the comb both from Sevastopol itself and, by a slight detour, from Inkerman bridge; and
this latter road passing up the Tchernaya valley sent off
a branch, known as the Post Road, up a hollow, known
as the Quarry Ravine, and so led straight upon the
Home Ridge, the camp of the Second Division being
pitched in fact astride it. In the neighbourhood of the
camp much of the brushwood had been uprooted for
fuel, but no effort had been made to clear it for purposes
of security.

The general disposition of the Allies was as follows:
The Second Division on the extreme right was posted
as above described. Fourteen hundred yards to south
of them stood the Guards Brigade[1] of the First Division
on a height called Windmill Hill at the head of the

[1] The Highland Brigade of this Division was, it will be remembered, at Balaclava.

Careenage Ravine.   About the same distance to south-   1854.
west on the ridge—Victoria Ridge—next to westward   Oct.
of the Careenage Ravine, lay Codrington's brigade of
the Light Division, astride the track that led to Victoria
Ridge from Inkerman Ridge.   These troops may be
styled the British covering army, being charged with
the protection of the besieging army on its right flank
and rear.   This besieging army, consisting of Buller's
brigade of the Light Division and the Fourth and Third
Divisions, in succession from right to left, was separated
from Codrington by the westward ravine which bounds
Victoria Ridge.   Its rear was protected by Bosquet's
division, which was aligned along the edge of the plateau
from the Woronzoff road to the *col*, or pass, at its
south-eastern corner.   On the left of the British besieging force stood that of the French—Forey's division—
with its rear and left flank secured by the sea and its
right by the British cavalry, by a body of Turks and by
Vinoy's brigade of French infantry, which carried the
line along the plain from the *col* till it joined that of
Colin Campbell, which covered Balaclava.

About noon on the 26th there was seen moving   Oct. 26.
out from the east of the fortress a Russian force, which
was later found to be a column of six battalions with
four light guns—perhaps four thousand men.   Making
its way eastward, along the lower slopes of Shell Hill
almost to the road which led to the Tchernaya, this
column wheeled into line to the north, and attacked.
Its right was covered by a second column, apparently
of a single battalion, which moved up the Careenage
Ravine; and the object seems to have been to ascertain
the feasibility of overwhelming the Second Division,
whose strength was then of about twenty-six hundred
bayonets.   The Russian movements were observed
early from the Victoria Ridge, but the picquet of the
Forty-ninth alone sustained the first shock of the
onslaught, contesting every inch of ground stub-
bornly, and retiring slowly to the support of three more
companies of their regiment.   The Russians could

1854. only force these back by turning their flanks, and
Oct. 26. meanwhile Evans had got his division with its artillery
into position on the upper slopes before his camp,
resolving to accept battle there.   The Russians gained
the crest of Shell Hill, but the Forty-ninth still held
them in check until the enemy's foremost line, having
been strongly reinforced, at length came under the
fire of Evans's three batteries. This was too destructive
for the Russian battalions to endure it for long, and
they gave way, harassed at every step by the British
skirmishers, and further harried not only by the flanking
fire of three guns on Victoria Ridge but by a Lancaster
gun from the naval battery on the same ridge.   In the
Careenage Ravine the Russians were early checked
by sixty sharpshooters of the Guards under Captain
Goodlake of the Coldstream, and were held back until
finally dispersed by a picquet of the Rifle Brigade.
Altogether this was a creditable little affair, the English
casualties not exceeding eighty-nine, while the Russians
acknowledged (probably with under-statement) a loss
of two hundred and seventy killed and wounded in
addition to one hundred prisoners.   There could be
no question of the enormous moral superiority of the
British over the Russian infantry, heightened as it was
by the possession of a more efficient fire-arm.

In the days that followed, the French pressed the
advance of their siege-works against the Flagstaff
Nov. 4. bastion with such energy that on the 4th of November
Raglan and Canrobert appointed a meeting for the 5th
to arrange for an assault.   But large Russian reinforcements had reached Mentschikoff on the 2nd and
3rd; and by the 4th he had under his hand, within
Sevastopol and without, at least one hundred thousand
men.   Against these the Allies could oppose no more
than forty thousand French and twenty-two thousand
British, of all three arms, besides ten thousand Turkish
infantry, or seventy-two thousand in all.   The Allied
commanders had some, though imperfect, intelligence
of the storm that was gathering about them; and

Raglan, feeling nervous about the situation on Inker- 1854.
man Ridge, begged Canrobert to lend him troops to
reinforce the Second Division and Guards. The
French general, however, was unwilling to spare them;
and there the matter rested.[1] Mentschikoff, anxious
to avert the peril to the Flagstaff bastion, laid his plans
for a general attack at daylight of the 5th as follows:

Three thousand men with four guns under General
Timoviev were to make a sortie from the southern
angle of the fortress so as to hold Forey's division to
its ground.

Twenty-two thousand men with eighty-eight guns
under Prince Gortschakoff, who had taken over the
command from Liprandi at Tchorgun, were to threaten
and contain Bosquet's division, endeavouring further
to obtain a footing on the plateau. The main body of
the garrison of Sevastopol was to act in his support.

Forty thousand men with one hundred and thirty-
five guns under General Dannenberg were to assail
Inkerman Ridge from the fortress in front and from
the Tchernaya valley in flank, and, rolling up the
Allied line from right to left, to drive it into the arms of
Gortschakoff.

Rain had fallen from an early hour on the morning
of the 4th, and the night and the early hours of the 5th Nov. 5.
were damp and misty. Gortschakoff moved out before
daylight, and drew up his men in a line five miles long,
extending from the village of Kamara, about two miles
and a half east and north of Balaclava, across the
Fedukhine Heights to the lower valley of the Tchernaya,
where he posted a strong body of cavalry in readiness,
apparently, to ascend to the plateau by the Quarry
Ravine. In this position he threatened Balaclava,
Bosquet and the Brigade of Guards, and, though he
had only received his orders at five on the previous
evening, he seems to have been upon his ground in
good time.

For the true attack Dannenberg's troops consisted

[1] *Raglan MSS.*, Raglan to Newcastle, Nov. 3, 1854.

1854. of two divisions, Soimonoff's of nineteen thousand men
Nov. 5. and thirty-eight guns, which was to move direct from
the Karabel suburb of Sevastopol, and Pavloff's of
thirty-one thousand men and ninety-seven guns, which,
being stationed on the old city heights to north of the
Tchernaya, had before them of necessity a long defile
across the Causeway and over Inkerman bridge before
they could reach the road which gave them access to
Inkerman Ridge.   Dannenberg had endeavoured to
modify Mentschikoff's orders by directing that
Soimonoff should attack Victoria Ridge and that
Pavloff alone should deal with Inkerman Ridge; but
Soimonoff disregarded this change of instructions, and
the original plan was adhered to.   According to this,
Soimonoff was to lead the direct attack up the comb
of the ridge, while Pavloff, on reaching the road on
the western bank of the Tchernaya, was to send six
thousand men along it up the valley.   These were to
ascend the ridge by the Quarry Ravine, or any other
lateral approach that might offer itself; while the
remainder, with the guns, should follow the road in
the opposite direction to the foot of the ridge and
ascend it in support of Soimonoff.

At 5 A.M. Soimonoff marched out of the Karabel
suburb, and by 6 A.M. was well on his way up the ridge,
his front covered by a cloud of riflemen, and the main
body marching in company-columns.   It was not,
apparently, the habit of the British picquets on Shell
Hill to send out patrols to their front, but a roving
body of about thirty picked marksmen of the Guards
under Colonel Goodlake, doing that duty for them,
encountered the head of Soimonoff's force when it had
advanced about a mile up the ridge.   It was difficult
to see anything clearly through the darkness and mist,
but Goodlake satisfied himself at least that Russian
infantry was advancing, and sent a man back to give
warning in the camp.   This man lost his way and
was intercepted and captured; but Goodlake's party,
engaging the enemy, caused firing which set the

British on the alert. A staff-officer from head-
quarters had ridden round the British lines between
four and five o'clock and found all quiet. The Second
Division having stood to arms, as usual, before daylight, had been dismissed to fetch wood and water; and
General Codrington, who had ridden down to his
picquets at the same time, found likewise all quiet,
and allowed the relieved picquets to proceed on their
return to camp. A few minutes later he heard the
patter of Goodlake's musketry and, after bidding the
relieved picquets to return, galloped back to call his
brigade under arms. On his way he met the staff-
officer from head-quarters, and sent him straight back
to Raglan. Then Gortschakoff opened fire along the
whole length of his line, and Bosquet's guns answered
him from the plateau. The Duke of Cambridge
moved two of his battalions of Guards likewise to the
edge of the plateau. Raglan was in the saddle in a
few minutes and, heedless of the din which encom-
passed him on every side, rode with true instinct
straight to Inkerman Ridge.

Soimonoff meanwhile pushed steadily and silently
on. Owing to the mist and drizzling rain the line of
British sentries thrown out from Shell Hill was drawn
in closer than usual to enable the men to keep each other
in sight; and, since the troops on both sides wore their
grey greatcoats, it was not easy to distinguish friend
from foe. The light had just come when the first
Russian columns struck against the picquets on Shell
Hill, which at once engaged them, fighting continuously as they fell back, while the Russians, pressing
steadily forward, brought up their guns. By half-past
six they had unlimbered all their pieces, twenty-two
of them twelve-pounders of long range, and opened
fire, giving such elevation, whether through accident
or design, that their shot all flew high into the British
camp, doing much damage to tents and dealing great
slaughter among the picketed draft-horses, but otherwise working little harm. For the Second Division

1854. was already under arms, and its twelve guns were
Nov. 5. drawn up on the Home Ridge, whence they opened
fire blindly on the flashes of the Russian cannon.

De Lacy Evans, as we have seen, had on the 26th
deliberately chosen the front of the Home Ridge as the
spot where he would accept battle; but little had been
done to strengthen the position by field-works. Indeed
this would have been no easy matter, for the rock was
so close to the surface that to dig trenches was out
of the question. On Home Ridge itself an embankment had been thrown up, fairly thick in places but
nowhere more than two feet high, to give some protection to artillery. Five hundred yards to north of
the camp a wall of loose stones hardly breast-high,
known as the Barrier, had been built up astride the
Post Road, to afford shelter to the main picquet; and
a trench had been dug across the road itself further
down to hinder the passage of guns. Five hundred
yards to the east of the Barrier and on the right front
of the camp was a dismantled work called the Sandbag
battery, which had been raised for heavy pieces to
silence Russian cannon on the old city heights; but
the guns had been withdrawn, and the work, being
ten feet high except at the embrasures and lacking a
banquette, was useless to infantry. In any case Evans
was on the sick-list, and the division, no more than three
thousand strong, was under the command of Pennefather. The attack was very evidently a serious one,
but, in the fog and drizzle, would be difficult to control.
There was little to be seen, but the picquets were
plainly making a lively resistance, and Pennefather,
the "swearing general," was a fighting man, who
objected to yielding up a foot of ground. He resolved,
therefore, to support the picquets by small bodies;
and thus it was that the battle of Inkerman resolved
itself into a series of little detached combats. Raglan
made no attempt to interfere with Pennefather, only
telling him that he should have all the help that he
asked for; but of his own motion he ordered two

eighteen-pounder guns of the siege-train to be brought
to Home Ridge immediately.

Meanwhile Soimonoff, having gained an excellent position for his artillery, kept back the bulk of his force until he should see the effect of the lateral advance of Pavloff's six thousand men from the Tchernaya by the Quarry Ravine. During the time necessary to bring his guns forward he pushed on two battalions against Pennefather's left flank and rear. One party of these came up the Careenage Ravine, having apparently strayed to the bottom of it; and here it surprised one of Codrington's picquets and captured an officer and a few men. It then left the ravine and turned into another hollow, called the Wellway, which led to the left rear of Pennefather's camp. Here being caught in flank by the fire of a company of the Grenadier Guards which was on picquet-duty, it was driven back and pursued for some distance, when it disappeared, leaving a few prisoners behind it. The next column, a complete battalion, followed a spur next to north of the Wellway, announcing its approach by wild and high firing. It was met by a wing—three hundred men—of the Forty-seventh in line, who advanced to within eighty yards of it, riddled its front and flanks with fire, and sent it reeling back in confusion. A third party, advancing rather further to the north, encountered a wing—two hundred and fifty men—of the Forty-ninth under Major Grant, who gave it one volley and then charged, hunting the fugitives, with the British bayonets in their backs, to the very line of the Russian batteries. Then rallying his men, Grant withdrew and took post at the foot of Shell Hill.

Satisfied apparently that Pavloff's division was by this time sufficiently well forward to take part in the attack, Soimonoff now bestirred himself in earnest, and set twelve battalions—some nine thousand men—in motion to advance up the comb of the ridge upon the left front of Pennefather's main position; while

1854. simultaneously Pavloff's six thousand, having passed
Nov. 5. up to the ridge by a hollow a little further down the
Tchernaya valley than the Quarry Ravine, moved upon
its centre and right.   The first enemy that Soimonoff's
columns had to deal with was Grant, who fell back
slowly towards his original station, worrying them with
continual destructive fire and suffering little punishment in return.   Whether misled by the course of his
retirement or shrinking from the flashes of the British
guns, Soimonoff's troops bore away to their right, that
is to say, to westward.   He and they alike were unfamiliar with the ground; and in the fog there was
some excuse for confusion.   His first line of columns,
groping its way forward, can have moved but slowly,
for three of the four battalions of his second line came
up on the right of the first line, while the fourth strayed
off eastward and joined Pavloff.   Edged down from
the comb of the hill into lower ground, which was encumbered not only by oak-scrub but by boulders, the
Russians could not by any possibility preserve any regular formation; and meanwhile British reinforcements
were advancing to meet them—Townsend's battery,
four companies of the Eighty-eighth and as many of
the Seventy-seventh, the eight companies numbering
some five hundred and fifty men in all.   The Eighty-
eighth came into action first, being directed by Pennefather westward to meet the menace against his left
flank.   Advancing in line they were met by a wedge of
Russians which cut them in two.   The two right-hand
companies were driven back at once, but the two left-
hand companies fired a volley, charged and pursued
until, encountering overwhelming force, they fell back
in turn, closely followed by the enemy.   Retreating
towards the western end of Home Ridge they came
upon three guns of Townsend's battery, which had
groped their way forward through the fog and had just
been unlimbered.   Passing these by they left the pieces
to their fate.   The gunners, after a short but gallant
resistance, were overpowered; and the Russians

pressed on, triumphant, against Pennefather's left 1854.
flank.

There was nothing to stop them but the four
companies of the Seventy-seventh, which had just
arrived, and which now came forward in line to meet
the attack. Their commander, Colonel Egerton, can
have had no conception of the numbers opposed to
him, but he was vaguely conscious of a deep column
in his front and of a straggling irregular column
turning his left flank. His left-hand company turned
to its left and charged straight through the turning
column, while the three other companies halted, fired
a volley to their front, and charged. The Russians
gave way and, with the English often in their midst
rather than at their backs, ran back to Shell Hill, at the
foot of which Egerton rallied his men, and made them
lie down. Thus Egerton, with two hundred and
sixty men, had disposed of two Russian battalions;
and two more battalions on the immediate left of
these conformed to their movement and fell back,
abandoning their three captured guns of Townsend's
battery. These were presently secured by the advance
of rallied men of the Forty-seventh and Eighty-eighth.

Further to the east, that is to say, in Soimonoff's
centre and left, six more Russian battalions advanced
more directly upon Pennefather's left front, driving the
British picquets before them. They were thus exposed
to three guns of Turner's battery at the western end
of Home Ridge; but these dared not fire until the
British picquets, which maintained a running fight,
could be induced to lie down, by which time the
Russians had come within range of case-shot. Two
rounds sufficed to turn back the foremost of them;
the remainder wavered; and the picquets, rising to
their feet, hunted the whole of them back to Shell Hill.
The retreating masses passed just within sight of
Egerton's men, who, however, mistaking them for
British troops advancing, made no attempt to molest
them. Another isolated Russian battalion was routed,

1854.
Nov. 5.
without the firing of a shot, by a bayonet charge of three companies of the Forty-ninth.   Thus Soimonoff's attack, after one brief moment of success, had been completely repulsed by mere handfuls of detached British troops.   He himself had been killed, and most of his senior officers had fallen, wounded or slain.   But his reserves had not yet been brought up; and the defeated troops could rally on these in preparation for a further effort.

On the other hand, the British had suffered also. Of the two batteries belonging to the Second Division which had been originally unlimbered on Home Ridge, Pennycuick's on the left or western end had been silenced by the heavier guns of the Russians on Shell Hill.   Moreover, the picquets and their supports had all of them exhausted their ammunition and were swarming back in no kind of formation and with regiments all intermixed.   For, though Soimonoff had been driven back, Pavloff had come on, and his nine battalions were now drawn up in company-columns from the Post Road to the Sandbag redoubt.   Two of these battalions now advanced along the line of the Post Road.   There was nothing to meet them but a wing of the Thirtieth, little more than two hundred strong; and when these attempted to open fire, it was found that their rifles were so wet that the charges would not explode.   Thereupon their colonel, Mauleverer, led his men straight down to the Barrier wall and made them lie down behind it. Waiting until the Russians were within a few yards he and his officers sprang over the wall and into the midst of them.   The men followed him with the bayonet, and the two battalions, utterly surprised, gave way at once and were hunted away to Shell Hill, while the two remaining battalions of the same regiment, which had come up the Quarry Ravine, turned about and began to descend it again.

Meanwhile General Adams had advanced with seven companies of the Forty-first—for once some approach to a complete battalion—to attack the Russians about

the Sandbag battery. He had something over five 1854.
hundred men; the enemy had over four thousand. But Nov. 5.
as Adams marched down boldly in line the enemy became unsteady at the very sight of him. At his first
volley the foremost company-columns turned, and, as
he pressed on, they dissolved in confusion and ran down
the steep declivity in their rear, carrying away with them
the battalion in support. Adams, far too wary to pursue
them into rough, densely wooded ground, plied them
with fire so long as any of them remained in sight; and
thus they were free to recover themselves, if they would,
in the dead ground of the valley.

It was now eight o'clock; and both the Duke of
Cambridge and Bosquet had realised that Gortschakoff's
menace was no more than a feint. The Duke had
drawn off two of his battalions towards the scene of
conflict; and Bosquet, meeting Sir George Brown and
Sir George Cathcart, offered his assistance, saying that
he had already ordered infantry and artillery to march
to Inkerman Ridge and was prepared to send more
troops if required. Brown and Cathcart, apparently
from sheer insular pride, declared that the British had
plenty of reserves in hand and asked Bosquet rather to
watch the plain in their rear; whereupon Bosquet
naturally countermanded the movements which, with
a juster appreciation of the true state of things, he had
initiated, and directed troops to take up the station suggested by Cathcart and Brown. But Dannenberg now
took matters into his hand; for by this time the remainder of Pavloff's division—over ten thousand men
—had ascended the Inkerman Ridge from its foot and,
joined to Soimonoff's reserves which had not yet been
engaged, gave him not far short of twenty thousand
fresh troops. Bringing into position additional artillery
which raised the number of pieces on Shell Hill to
over ninety, Dannenberg pushed forward the ten
thousand of Pavloff's men against the British centre
and right.

On the British side most of the troops that had been

1854. engaged so far on the British left were still much
Nov. 5. scattered; the regiments were mixed up, the men were
greatly exhausted, and, with their officers, in search of
ammunition.   Of the rest Adams with the Forty-first
and three companies of the Forty-ninth remained by the
Sandbag battery, and the remnant of Mauleverer's
party of the Thirtieth were near the Barrier.   These
together might number seven hundred men.   On the
reverse, or southern, slope of the Home Ridge were a
few of the Fifty-fifth, most of whom had been absorbed
by the original picquets, three companies of the Forty-
seventh, and the Ninety-fifth, together about another
seven hundred of all ranks.   Close at hand were two
more field-batteries, two battalions of Guards, with the
third not far behind, and two thousand men brought
up by Cathcart from the Fourth Division.   These
amounted to some thirty-two hundred infantry, in
addition to which two French battalions, together sixteen hundred strong, had also been set on march by
Bosquet at Raglan's request.   Owing to the fog it was
not yet realised that the Russians were attacking in
great force, and that this was no affair of outposts but a
pitched battle.

Adams had hardly repelled the first onslaught of
Pavloff's troops when he found himself menaced again
either by them or by Dannenberg's fresh battalions or by
both.   Having ascertained that the Duke of Cambridge
was ready to come to his support with two battalions
of Guards, he engaged the enemy without hesitation,
seven hundred against four thousand, pouring in a most
destructive fire.   But the Russians took their punishment without flinching.   Though the front ranks fell,
the rear ranks pushed on, and threatened Adams not
only in front but on both flanks.   Gradually his line,
broken up by the brushwood, was forced back, contesting every foot of ground, and in places closing to a bitter
fight hand to hand.   Four young officers of the Forty-
first actually sprang alone into the enemy's ranks and
were all of them killed.   But by sheer weight the

battalion was pressed back and back until by a supreme 1854.
effort it disengaged itself and retired towards the eastern Nov. 5.
end of Home Ridge, carrying its wounded with it.
Meanwhile three guns under Captain Hamley had
come up and, unlimbering under shelter from the
Russian cannon on Shell Hill, opened fire with round
shot upon the Russian supporting battalions and broke
them up. The troops that had engaged Adams made
little attempt to advance further, and such as ventured
to come closer were promptly checked by case-shot
from Hamley's guns. There was in fact a lull, in the
course of which Adams fell mortally wounded, while
the Russians apparently gathered themselves up for
their next effort.

Then the Brigade of Guards, responding to Adams's
summons, came up, Grenadiers in first line, Scots
Fusilier Guards in support. Finding that the enemy
had just possessed themselves of the Sandbag battery,
the Grenadiers charged them, drove them out and then
formed line, with their centre in the battery, their right
flank thrown back, lining the ridge that overlooks the
plain of the Tchernaya, and their left likewise thrown
back to confront the main Russian advance. The Scots
Fusiliers aligned themselves on the left of the Grenadiers
—the two battalions together not exceeding seven hundred men—and there began a desperate struggle with
the mass of the Russian columns. Again and again
these advanced from the dead ground of the ravines and
strove to rush across the small level plateau upon which
the battery stood, and again and again they were thrown
back with fire, with the bayonet, with the butt, with
stones, with any missile or weapon which came to hand.
Sometimes they attempted to turn one flank of the
Guards, sometimes the other; and the combat swayed
to and fro from the battery to the edge of the plateau
and from side to side as each fresh menace was flung
back. At last a determined effort of the enemy
against the right flank caused the Grenadiers to retire
steadily, always fighting, when the Coldstream came

1854. up, recovered the lost ground, carried the line forward
Nov. 5. once more, and regained the lost battery after a violent
struggle hand to hand.   In the midst of the turmoil
the quartermaster-sergeant of the Grenadiers, knowing
that the men had not breakfasted, appeared with a
huge load of provisions upon his back; ready to feed
the fight in one sense, while two detached companies
of the Grenadiers arrived from the outlying picquets
to feed it in another.   And so the struggle went on,
with the three battalions of Guards all intermixed and
a leaven of linesmen from the original picquets among
them, fighting in small groups among the brushwood,
each group for itself, and every man shouting himself
hoarse.

During this time two French battalions had come
forward to the reverse slope of the Home Ridge, but
would move no further, their commanders declining
to take orders except from their own chiefs. Seventeen
hundred men of the Twentieth, Twenty-first, Fifty-
seventh, Sixty-third and Rifle Brigade had also arrived,
and had been thrown by Cathcart in driblets into
various positions.   Half of the Twentieth and Rifle
Brigade, with half of the Ninety-fifth from the Second
Division, were pushed forward to the left of the Guards,
half of the Twenty-first were sent to strengthen the
extreme left, where Soimonoff had attacked, and the
remainder were distributed about the main position
on the Home Ridge.   It seems to have been intended
that the troops sent to the left of the Guards should
occupy the ground between them and the Home Ridge,
but such a handful of men—not more than five hundred
in all—was naturally drawn into the struggle about the
Sandbag battery, and they were soon distributed along
the whole length of the Guards' line.   There remained
four hundred men more — two companies of the
Forty-sixth and four of the Sixty-eighth—which Raglan
instructed Cathcart to place on the left of the Guards,
so as to fill the gap between them and the main position.
Cathcart, however, thinking that he knew better,

determined to take them along the edge of the plateau 1854.
and attack the left flank of the Russians who were Nov. 5.
engaged with the Guards. Off he marched accordingly,
and drove the Russians before him with ease, while
his men eagerly followed them down the steep sides
of the ravine beyond. Therewith, despite of the Duke
of Cambridge's remonstrances, the bulk of the troops
about the Sandbag battery seem to have caught the
infection of the offensive, and leaping forward into the
depths of the brushwood they hunted the Russians
before them like sheep. Some went so far that they
found themselves engaged with Gortschakoff's skirmishers in the valley of the Tchernaya. About the
Sandbag battery, as it seems, only the colours and a
few score men of the Grenadiers remained, though to
their left rear there were still small parties of the Coldstream and Scots.

Very soon Cathcart discovered his mistake. Plung-
ing down into the brushwood he found himself under
fire from his left rear, and realised that Russian columns
from the Quarry Ravine were marching eastward
across his rear upon the Sandbag battery. Collecting
a few scattered men he led them upon the flank of the
nearest column, and was shot dead, whereupon Colonel
Maitland, his staff-officer, though very severely
wounded, drew off such men as he could collect eastward. Other officers assembled other parties and made
their way back, mostly under the eastern ledge of the
plateau and so unseen, to the right rear of the Home
Ridge; but one party of the Ninety-fifth at least was
left in isolation near the foot of the slope.

It should seem that Dannenberg, unaware, or possibly without heed, of what had just passed, had already
organised a fresh attack from the Quarry Ravine by
one body upon the Sandbag battery, and by another
upon the main position upon Home Ridge. The latter
were the first to disengage themselves and advance;
whereupon the remnant of the Coldstream and Scots
Fusiliers, seeing the menace to their left flank, took

1854. ground to their left by fours, and then fell back steadily
Nov. 5. to the right of Home Ridge.   The troops in the
Sandbag battery, unable to see what was going on,
stood fast, until they found themselves again assailed
in front, and with another body of Russians, who had
turned about on catching sight of the Grenadiers'
colours, coming down upon their rear.   Facing about,
they charged the column which stood between them
and the Home Ridge and broke through it, though
with heavy loss, when the 6th French battalion of the
Line came forward, drove the Russians off, and reoccupied the Sandbag battery.

Throughout this struggle on the British right front
the Russians had delivered attack upon attack upon the
Barrier, all of which were fended off, first by the little
party of the Thirtieth, and when these, quite exhausted,
had been withdrawn to the main position, by a handful
of the Rifle Brigade.   The Russians then made an
attempt to strike at the extreme British left of the main
position, but here there were actually six hundred men,
one-third of them of the Twenty-first and the remainder
of the Sixty-third, who fired a volley, charged, and
hunted them back in the old style.   Then two Russian
battalions fell upon the other extreme of the line.   A
detachment of the Twentieth, fewer than two hundred,
promptly engaged them with musketry — for the
Fourth Division had not yet received the Minié rifle
— and charging, drove them down into the Quarry
Ravine.   The remainder were dealt with in like manner
by two hundred men of the Fifty-seventh; and altogether the enemy on this side made no progress
whatever.

But the great attack now initiated by Dannenberg
was far more serious.   Covering their advance with a
furious fire of artillery he now launched some six
thousand men in echelon from his right against the
British left; and this time Pennefather was unable to
prevent it from striking home.   To meet the onslaught
he had about one thousand French and six hundred

British on the Home Ridge itself, and fourteen hundred 1854.
more British—all of course in small detachments— Nov. 5.
ranged along the western flank of the enemy's advance.
These last harassed and worried the parties of Russians
which covered this flank but could not arrest the progress of the main body, the foremost battalion of which
made straight for three guns which were unlimbered
at the western extremity of the Home Ridge, and
taking them in flank, overpowered them directly.
They had not, however, been in possession of them for
five minutes before they were driven from them with
the bayonet by a small party of Zouaves. Farther to
their left another body of Russians, being mistaken by
the British opposed to them for their own comrades,
were allowed to approach the main position on the Home
Ridge unmolested; and these swarmed in an irregular
line over the crest, driving a little party of the Fifty-
fifth before them. On the reverse slope of the ridge
the French 7th Light Infantry was drawn up in line,
but these, being young soldiers, gave way and fell
back; and the position seemed to be at the mercy of
the enemy.

Throughout the attack shot and shell from the Russian batteries had fallen thick upon the Home Ridge,
sparing neither friend nor foe; great numbers of them
skimming low with commendable accuracy just over
the crest. Exposed to the full blast of this fire stood
Raglan and his staff; and here General Strangways, the
veteran of Leipzig and Waterloo, who commanded the
artillery, was mortally wounded by a round shot, while
simultaneously a shell killed many horses of the staff.
Through all this Raglan sat perfectly unperturbed,
though he could not repress an angry exclamation when
he saw the French retire. Seeing, however, that the
little party of the Fifty-fifth had rallied, Raglan
ordered them to counter-attack, which they promptly
did. Four companies of the Seventy-seventh came up
from the British left. The French 7th Light, having
been re-formed in company columns, advanced stoutly

1854. to their support; and the foremost attacking column
Nov. 5. of the Russians, much harassed by the fire of their own
guns, abandoned the Home Ridge and fell back.

The second and far more formidable column was
meanwhile moving up slowly and resolutely, and the
first brunt of its onslaught fell upon the French 7th
Light. This battalion deployed into line with great
steadiness and poured in so deadly a fire as brought
the masses before them to a standstill. The order to
charge at this moment would probably have carried
the 7th Light forward with irresistible impetus; but
the word was not given. The battalion began to waver
and retire, and the Russians exultingly pressed on.
Thereupon Colonel Daubeney with thirty men of the
Fifty-fifth ran down along the western flank of the
Russian column, charged the battalion next to rear
when in the act of deployment, crashed straight through
it and emerged on the other flank, himself and half of
his men unhurt. The sound of tumult in their rear
arrested the advance of the foremost of the Russians.
The French 7th Light quickly recovered themselves
and, with small parties of British intermixed among
them, they counter-attacked the main Russian column
and drove it slowly down the hill. The Russian troops
disposed to protect the flanks of this column during its
advance had meanwhile strayed away from it, both to
east and west. Those on the east—the Russian left—
were driven back with heavy loss by the British guns
on the right of the Home Ridge. Those on the
Russian right were met by six hundred men of the
Twenty-first and Sixty-third, who easily overmatched
them in the first fire-fight among the brushwood, and
hunted them back in a diagonal line from the British
left towards the Quarry Ravine. The course of the
chase brought them upon the retreating masses of
the main Russian column; and two French horse-
artillery batteries, which had come up to the Home
Ridge, galloped down most gallantly to aid in its
overthrow, but lost so many horses from the enfilading

fire of the Russian guns on Shell Hill that they were 1854.
perforce checked.   The Twenty-first and Sixty-third, Nov. 5.
however, succeeded in forcing the enemy back; and
the foremost of the pursuers, by this time much
scattered, took post at the head of the Quarry Ravine.

Thus again a great Russian attack had been repelled,
though not routed; but the enemy had still nine
thousand fresh troops on the ground, whereas Raglan
had not so much as another battalion to throw into the
fight, whether to press an advantage or avert a catastrophe.   However, the scene of the struggle had once
again been moved down from the main position on the
Home Ridge to the old ground between the Barrier
and the Sandbag battery; and additional French troops
under General Bosquet were near at hand.   The
Russians without delay resumed the offensive, and a
column assailing the French 6th Light, which had for
some time remained unmolested on the eastern bank
of the Quarry Ravine, compelled it to fall back.
General Bourbaki thereupon recalled the 7th Light
from among the British further to the west, so that the
two battalions might act together; but the Russians
did not follow up their advantage, and a French battery
coming forward, drove back another column which was
advancing to reoccupy the Sandbag battery.   Nevertheless these Russian troops on the east of the Quarry
Ravine threatened to turn the right of the British, and
another column presently emerged to threaten their
left.   General Goldie, who had succeeded to the command of the Fourth Division, withdrew the British
troops—a mingled body of many regiments—to the
Barrier, formed them up behind it and in the brushwood on either flank, and posted under some accidental
cover on the left a party to maintain a carefully aimed
fire at the Russian batteries on Shell Hill.   Presently
a dense Russian column advanced against the Barrier
and was thrown back by the terrible fire of the defenders;
but the enemy now threw out riflemen to engage the
British skirmishers in the brushwood, and between

1854. their fire and that of the Russian artillery Goldie's men
Nov. 5. began to fall fast.   Two companies, one of the Forty-
sixth and another of the Seventy-seventh, reinforced him
from the rear, and stray parties from many regiments,
drifting to the Barrier, helped to maintain the fight.
Goldie himself was killed, but Colonel Haines of the
Twenty-first, taking his place, continued to repel attack
after attack on his centre and right with success.
Nevertheless this little band of men was alone and
unsupported and, under the full blast of the Russian
artillery, could not hold their own for ever.

At this moment, however—apparently at about 9.30
—the two eighteen-pounder siege-guns, summoned by
Raglan at the beginning of the action, at last came up,
dragged by one hundred and fifty gunners, and were
placed behind the embankment at the western end of
Home Ridge.   The fog was by this time clearing off;
the gunners quickly found the range; and the Russian
batteries at once turned their full strength upon the
newly arrived cannon.   Seventeen British gunners
were killed or disabled in the first fifteen minutes, and
then the eighteen-pounders gained the upper hand and,
with little further annoyance, tore the Russian batteries
to pieces.   Twelve French heavy guns had also opened
fire a little to north of the eighteen-pounders; and the
moment seemed to be approaching for a great counter-
offensive.   Bosquet, however, on coming up, found a
state of things belonging rather to the twentieth than
the nineteenth century—a battle-field with no troops,
or at least no English troops, to be seen, a sound of
firing and clouds of smoke about the Barrier, and in
rear of it Bourbaki's two battalions.   Moreover, Bourbaki, or one of his staff for him, had sent Bosquet an
alarming message about the danger of his position;
wherefore Bosquet, without consulting Raglan, decided
to move the battery and two battalions and a half that
he had with him to a ridge overlooking the eastern
bank of the Quarry Ravine, where he formed them on
Bourbaki's right, facing nearly due west.   He had not

been long there before, more by accident than design, 1854. one Russian column came up out of the dead ground Nov. 5. upon his left front and flank, while another toiled up to the next ridge, on which stood the Sandbag battery. A battalion of Zouaves, facing about, sprang against these last and brought them to a halt; and, ere the Russians could realise the position, Bosquet had extricated his men and brought them back to the shelter of a ridge before the right front of the Second Division. He left one gun, which was afterwards recovered, in the enemy's hands. The 6th of the Line and the 7th Light, conforming to his movement, retired likewise; a regiment of Chasseurs d'Afrique, which had followed in support of the French infantry, with the wreck of the British Light Cavalry Brigade in their rear, also fell back; and the fragmentary British infantry was left to continue the fight about the Barrier alone.

Presently, however, three more French battalions arrived, and Bosquet, leaving them in reserve, advanced again with the same troops as before upon his former assailants, who now occupied the Sandbag battery and ground upon either flank of it. As the French marched down, the little party of the Coldstream, which had encountered Gortschakoff's skirmishers and was working its way back through the scrub on the eastern ledge of the plateau, joined themselves to their right and went on with them. According to an officer with the party of the Coldstream,[1] the Russians were already retiring when the two French battalions came into action; but be that as it may, they were very soon driven into retreat by the French attack and hunted down into the valley of the Tchernaya.

It was now 11 A.M. Three more French battalions had by this time reached the field, giving Canrobert a total of some seven thousand infantry. He made no further use of them; but his artillery continued to fight on, though suffering generally, and the twelve heavy guns in particular, heavy losses. Haines,

[1] Ross of Bladensburg, *History of the Coldstream Guards*, p. 219.

1854. however, perceiving that the attacks on the Barrier
Nov. 5. were growing weaker, made preparations to attack the
batteries on Shell Hill.   He was anticipated by Lord
West, second-in-command of the Twenty-first, who
from his place on the left front of Home Ridge instructed Lieutenant Acton of the Seventy-seventh to
take his own company and two companies of the Twenty-
first and to attack one group of guns.   Dividing his
little party into three, so as to assail the front and both
flanks, Acton made a rush, and the Russian officers,
hastily limbering up, carried off their pieces.   Other
parties from Haines's force at the Barrier joined Acton;
and Dannenberg decided at 12.45 to retreat.   To
cover the withdrawal of his guns he brought forward
four battalions, which suffered cruelly from the two
British eighteen-pounder guns, but were not otherwise
molested, Canrobert being unwilling to employ any
part of his infantry against them.   By 3 P.M. the last
Russian gun had been limbered up, and half an hour
later Canrobert sent two battalions and a battery to the
northern spur of Shell Hill.   But these, coming under
the fire of the Russian war-vessels at the head of the
harbour, presently retired; and the battle of Inkerman
was over.

Nowhere did the Russians use their strength effectively to support their operations upon Inkerman Ridge.
Gortschakoff, whether in obedience to instructions or
not, did nothing with his twenty thousand men.   Timoviev made his sortie against Forey with great spirit,
broke into the French batteries, spiked eight or ten
guns, and drew upon himself the whole of Forey's force
before he fell back into the fortress.   But he did not
move at all until 9.30, which was two hours too late.
The Russians over against the British siege-batteries
kept up a lively fire, but made no attempt at a sortie,
though, pursuant to orders, masses of men were held
ready to attack and seize the British batteries if confusion should be observed in them.   Yet some kind of
diversion at this point would have been easy.   The two

roads by the mouth of the Careenage Ravine were so 1854.
steep that part of the Russian reserves and ammunition- Nov. 5.
trains were sent by a track which runs south-eastward
from the Malakoff Tower into the Middle Ravine,
whence it doubles back northward into the Careenage
Ravine. This brought them full on the flank of the
most important British battery, the guards of which
were insufficient to protect it both in front and flank.
Six of the guns were therefore run back, so as to fire
along the flank; spikes were issued for disabling the
whole of the twenty-one guns in the battery, and the
men were instructed as to their line of retreat. These
apprehensions, of course, proved to be groundless; and
the tail of the Russian column, coming to a halt owing
to some obstruction in front, was ravaged unmercifully
by the guns of the battery, at a range of eleven hundred
yards, until it broke up.[1] Still these facts suffice to
show how much might have been effected by a little
activity on the part of the garrison. As things were,
we have seen that Cathcart drew away two-thirds of his
division to the main fight, while England did not hesi-
tate to move half of his division eastward to take the
place of Cathcart's troops in support of Codrington.
Even Codrington, posted in a vitally important position
on Victoria Ridge with but eleven hundred infantry
and no guns, thought only of sending every man that
he could spare to feed the main fight upon Inkerman
Ridge. In brief, the British commanders, one and all,
were prepared to take every risk at all points for one
main object, and the Russian commanders, except on
the actual field of conflict, were prepared to take none.

Apart from these failings there seems to be little
doubt that the plan of the principal Russian attack was
in itself faulty, and that it would have been better if
Soimonoff had, as Dannenberg desired, attacked the
Victoria Ridge and left Pavloff to deal with Inkerman
Ridge. Soimonoff, as has been pointed out,[2] could

[1] Evelyn Wood, *From Midshipman to Field-Marshal*, i. 51.
[2] Evelyn Wood, *The Crimea in 1854 and 1894*, p. 159.

1854. have sent up his heavy guns to Shell Hill with three
Nov. 5. thousand infantry to guard them and still have had sixteen thousand men and his field-batteries for an advance
up Victoria Ridge.   It is true that the British Twenty-
one gun battery of the right attack would have
threatened his left as he marched; but, moving at night
and under cover of darkness and fog, he could have
passed upward to a point, afterwards marked by the
Victoria Redoubt, which would have brought him, in
turn, upon the flank of the Twenty-one gun battery.
The comb of the Victoria Ridge is, up to this point,
half a mile wide, so that he could have advanced on a
broad front and with comparative rapidity; and it is
obvious also that he could have been helped by a powerful demonstration of the garrison against the British
battery.   Codrington's handful of men could not long
have withstood him; and then, while Pavloff, under the
fire of the guns on Shell Hill, assailed the Second
Division in front, Soimonoff could have crossed the
Careenage Ravine near its head and fallen upon Raglan's
left flank and rear. The massing of forty thousand men
on to the Inkerman Ridge gave them no chance.   The
narrowness of the comb, the depth of the lateral hollows,
the obstacles presented by boulders and by the scrub,
which grew steadily denser as the ground descended
—all these conditions were against the profitable
handling of a vast crowd of men, brave and resolute
indeed but unintelligent, over-drilled, and unused to
manœuvre except in heavy cumbrous formations.

It is none the less a marvel that, even so, they failed.
That there were skulkers among the scrub and the low
ground is likely enough, but the Russian officers set a
noble example of courage and devotion and their men
followed them most loyally.   Yet in spite of all their
sacrifices they were beaten off with very heavy loss and,
if Canrobert had consented to harass their retreat,
might have been brought not merely to defeat but to
humiliation.   It is not easy to explain except in very
general terms how this came about.

The entire action remains, as encounters under such 1854. conditions always must remain, very much of a mystery. Nov. 5. The principal historian of the war, with great industry, devoted a whole volume to details of the various groups, and even individuals, which were engaged on both sides at stated times and stated places; and it may be accepted that some such groups and individuals did do some such things at some such places at some uncertain time. But the sequence of events cannot be surely determined. In no battle can men see what is going forward except in their own little section of the field. In this particular battle they could, owing to the fog, see next to nothing, and inevitably gave false values to such glimpses as they could catch when the fog at odd moments lifted. As to the British units engaged, weak though they were, hardly any, if indeed any, came into action complete, while all alike, after they had been in action an hour, were dispersed and for the most part mixed up with others. The Russian units being larger— four battalions to a regiment—may perhaps be more accurately specified, but they also must have been much intermingled; and their officers, being unfamiliar with the ground and lost in the fog, must frequently have been quite unable to say where they were or what was opposed to them.[1] There is therefore little more certainty as to their proceedings than as to those of the British; and comment can proceed only on the broadest lines.

The first and central fact is that the Russians succeeded in placing thirty-eight guns in battery within thirteen hundred yards of the British camp unobserved and unmolested. The British had been in the field against the Russians for two months and still had not

[1] Colonel Ross observes with much force that it is hard to accept Kinglake's theory that 15,000 Russians (Soimonoff's) were dispersed into space after an hour's fight with 700 or 800 British, never to appear again, whereas 10,000 more Russians (Pavloff's) were only with difficulty defeated after a fight of three and a half hours by 4700 British, aided at first by 1600 and later by 4000 French. See *History of the Coldstream Guards*, p. 215, *n.*

1854.
Nov. 5.

learned to push a strong patrol well forward in the enemy's direction before daylight. Another piece of neglect was that the ground round the camp had not been cleared; the space of seven hundred yards from the right flank of the Second Division's camp to the Sandbag battery in particular being a confused mass of brushwood and trees which, by the exercise of a little method, might have been cleared away for fuel.[1] Pennefather had taken command only five days before the action, so the main responsibility for these failings must rest upon Evans, and it lies the more heavily upon him since it was his policy, if attacked, to fall back at once to the main position. Pennefather, on the contrary, determined to defend every inch of ground; and it should seem that, in the peculiar circumstances, his plan was certainly the better. For, apart from any question of mere tactics, Pennefather's resolution fired the British with the aggressive spirit which was their most striking characteristic in the action. That the result might have been different if the British had realised how many, and the Russians had realised how few, were the forces arrayed against them, is possible; but we have to deal with facts and not with possibilities. Under the conditions which actually prevailed, the moral ascendancy of the British was astonishing. They met every attack virtually with a counter-offensive, and hesitated not to encounter any numbers whether with bullet, bayonet or butt. There never was a fight in which small parties of scores, tens, and even individuals, showed greater audacity or achieved more surprising results. They never lost heart nor, by all accounts, cheerfulness. The enemy might be in front, flanks or rear, or at all three points together: it mattered not. They flew at them quite undismayed and bored their way out. The military instinct of the French soldier warned him against any such desperate exploits; but the slower-witted Briton accepted them all as a natural part of the day's work. The British suffered heavy losses, of

[1] Hamilton, *History of the Grenadier Guards*, iii. 222-223.

course, and not from bullet and bayonet only. It must 1854.
be remembered that the camp of the Second Division Nov. 5.
and all the ground before it was swept by the Russian
guns, and that an advance through enfilading fire of
artillery was the preliminary to going into action at all.
But, whether from their extreme dispersion or from
what cause soever, the British seemed not to feel these
losses. Moreover, the struggle was so fast and furious
that the men appear to have accepted gladly the
leadership of any officer, and to have fought as heartily
alongside comrades of other regiments as of their own.
Never have the fighting qualities of the British been
seen to greater advantage than at Inkerman. But it
was wrong to call Inkerman, as it was styled, a soldiers'
battle. It was a regimental officers' battle, and to the
regimental officer belongs the credit.

At the same time Pennefather's plan disclosed one
very serious flaw in the execution. He had overlooked the need for the replenishment of ammunition.
Hence the rear of the British was covered with a
swarm of straggling men in search of cartridges.
During the fight about the Sandbag battery the Guards
depended greatly on the pouches of dead or disabled
men; but frequently they economised their supply by
working together in pairs, one man loading while the
other fired.[1] There were other dangers in the distribution of a force of three or four thousand men to
engage in indiscriminate combats over a front of a mile
and a half. The first was that they might waste their
strength upon some irrelevant object, as they actually
did over this same Sandbag battery. But in a fight
against a sluggish and unenterprising enemy, such as
the Russians, in the confusion of a fog, this did not
greatly signify. So long as the British struck them
hard and continued to strike them, the quarter in
which the blow was delivered proved not to be of

---

[1] An old Crimean officer of the Scots Fusilier Guards told me
that two serjeants of his worked thus together. They had 30 rounds
apiece and were quite confident that they had knocked over 60 Russians.

1854. great moment; and the Sandbag battery became one
Nov. 5. of these strange centres of contention which called
forth the utmost powers of British tenacity. It is said
to have changed hands six or seven times—the exact
number is unimportant—but it certainly cost the
Russians many more men than the British.

More serious was the tendency of little victorious
bodies to press the pursuit too far and to break up into
knots of lost and masterless men. The most flagrant
instance of this was when the Guards and the troops
brought up by Cathcart dashed into the wooded hollows
below the Sandbag battery; many officers, to use the
words of Colonel Hamilton of the Grenadiers, "only
fearing that they would not be the first to enter
Sevastopol." The fog no doubt helped to propagate
this blunder, but it was serious, for the Brigade of
Guards—and thirteen hundred men constitute an
appreciable fraction of four or five thousand—was not
collected again until the action was practically over.[1]
They did not cease fighting, but they had ceased to be
an organised body; and the like may be said of practically every battalion present. The units, as has been
told, were in the first instance miserably weak; they
were decanted into action by driblets; they were still
further thinned by casualties. Small wonder that the
remnant of the organised was minute.

Nevertheless, it was a fine and creditable fight,
which enormously impressed the French with the
prowess of their allies; and it deserves the name of a
general action, though on the British side it was

[1] See Ross, *History of the Coldstream Guards*, p. 225, *n.* Kinglake
took great pains to make inquiry of all officers of all regiments upon
all details. I suspect that he had the experience which is common to
such inquirers, namely, that he found 90 per cent of the officers
reticent and inarticulate, and 10 per cent forthcoming and voluble,
with the natural result that his narrative is built upon the utterances
of the voluble. I have heard old officers of the Guards who were
present at Inkerman discuss with much amusement Kinglake's account
of the Brigade in that action, knowing well the individual from whom
he derived most of his information. His name may easily be guessed
from perusal of Kinglake's narrative.

handled from first to last by a Brigadier-general.
Pennefather had commanded the Twenty-second at
Miani and was known both as a swearing and a fighting
general. For so stubborn and confused a struggle he
was the very man, with just one idea in his head, a
personal bravery which was eminent even on a day
conspicuous for valiant deeds, and a vocabulary lurid
enough to pierce even the fog upon Inkerman Ridge.
By some miracle he escaped untouched, though always
at the spot where shot and bullets were flying thickest.
So also did Raglan, albeit almost equally exposed.
But of the head-quarters staff, General Strangways was
killed; of the three divisional commanders present,
Cathcart was slain and Sir George Brown wounded,
and of the brigade-commanders Goldie, Adams and
Torrens were mortally, and Bentinck of the Guards
slightly, wounded. The Duke of Cambridge, and
Pennefather, had each a horse, and Buller two horses,
shot under them. The commanders of battalions and
detachments suffered as heavily. Of seventeen who
were engaged on Inkerman Ridge six were killed, nine
were wounded, and the two that remained unhurt had
their horses killed under them. Mounted officers, in
the peculiar circumstances of the fight, enjoyed advantages of vision, but paid for them very dearly.
Altogether the casualties of the British on the 5th of
November amounted to close upon twenty-six hundred.[1]
The greater number of them fell on Inkerman Ridge,
where from first to last not more than eight thousand
men were engaged; the casualties of Codrington, who
from Victoria Ridge had some little skirmishes with
Russian parties in the Careenage Ravine, falling under
two hundred. Roughly speaking, then, the British on
Inkerman Ridge sacrificed a third of their numbers.
The Brigade of Guards, out of a total strength of rather
more than thirteen hundred of all ranks, lost just over

---

[1] Actual figures, 635 killed, 1938 wounded; total, 2573. The
casualties among officers were 47 killed or mortally hurt, and 97
wounded.

1854. six hundred, the Grenadiers, which were the strongest
Nov. 5. of the three battalions, suffering most in the matter of
men, while the Coldstream, by some strange fatality,
had no fewer than eight officers killed and five wounded
out of seventeen present. The Twentieth had over
one hundred and seventy casualties, the Forty-ninth
one hundred and fifty, the Twenty-first, Thirtieth,
Forty-first, Eighty-eighth, Ninety-fifth, and first battalion of the Rifle Brigade, each over one hundred; and
it must be borne in mind that one and all of these
battalions were miserably weak in numbers.

The casualties of the French on Inkerman Ridge
slightly exceeded nine hundred, which number Forey's
engagement outside the Flagstaff bastion increased to
exactly eighteen hundred.

The losses of the Russians on the 5th of November
in killed, wounded and prisoners were admitted to be
just below twelve thousand, of which total close upon
eleven thousand were incurred upon Inkerman Ridge.[1]
It appears that the casualties were pretty equally
distributed between Soimonoff's corps and that of
Pavloff, though Pavloff's were, proportionately, rather
higher; but, since the reserves were never really brought
into action, it seems certain that of thirteen thousand
Russians actually engaged there fell or were taken
rather more than one-third, three generals being killed
and as many wounded, besides two hundred and fifty
more officers. And, according to Russian accounts,
this havoc was wrought almost entirely by rifle-fire.
It is said that a single Minié bullet sometimes killed
or disabled as many as six or seven men among the
densely packed Russian masses, and it may be difficult
to limit the destructive power of so heavy a projectile

---

[1] Raglan reckoned their loss at 20,000. The Turks and English
buried just over 4000. The French buried an uncertain number;
500 were still unburied a fortnight after the battle (Campbell,
Letters from Sevastopol, p. 25). Raglan's figures are different, but
make the same total—5000 killed. Allowing three wounded to one
killed (a low estimate), the casualties would be 20,000 killed and
wounded besides 2000 prisoners.

at close range.   But be this as it may, here is only one 1854.
more testimony to the coolness and steadiness of the Nov. 5.
British infantry.

At the close of the action the British fell to the
ground utterly exhausted, and unable to speak.   For
some reason—possibly the fog, possibly the wild
excitement of a game which continued long at the
highest pressure with the issue ever in doubt, possibly
the dismal howl of the Russians—every officer and
man had shouted unceasingly while in action, and few
had any voice left to them.   The reaction was sharp
after such a strain, and the miserably attenuated ranks
of the battalions that had passed through the fire
struck some officers with dismay.   Evans, who had
left his sick-bed on board ship and had reached the
field in time to see the numbers of the Russians, urged
that the siege should be immediately raised.   He was
at once and firmly put down by Raglan, for indeed
the only alternative to prosecution of the siege was
re-embarkation;   and how re-embarkation could be
accomplished without the sacrifice of at least half of
the Allied armies, it was difficult to see.   The
situation was not really much worse than it had been
for three weeks past.   Perhaps it was even rather
better, for the enemy, though reinforced, had received
a staggering blow.   But even so it was such as to
heighten immensely Raglan's anxieties.   Already on
the 23rd of October he had pressed upon the Secretary
for War the urgent need of rest for the troops.
Between sickness, casualties in action and overwork
the British Army was dwindling with dangerous
swiftness, and any further heavy blow would virtually
annihilate it altogether.[1]

[1] Even before Inkerman convalescents at Constantinople were
asked to volunteer for the front (Campbell, *Letters from Sevastopol*,
p. 11).

CHAPTER XLV

1854. AFTER witnessing the numbers of the Russians at
Nov. Inkerman Canrobert abandoned all idea of an assault
upon the Flagstaff bastion, and he and Raglan agreed
to stand for the present on the defensive. The situation
of the two commanders was widely different, for
Canrobert was receiving a steady flow of reinforcements,
whereas Raglan could count at best only on driblets.
The main body of the Forty-sixth, of which parties
had been present since the beginning of the campaign,
arrived on the 8th of November, seven hundred strong,
and the Sixty-second landed a few days later; but these
could do little to make good the losses at Inkerman.
Raglan endeavoured to persuade Canrobert to take
over some of his ground and siege-works on the
extreme right of the position; but the French general,
while not absolutely refusing, delayed compliance,
though he consented to spare a division to help in
entrenching and guarding Inkerman Ridge. However, both commanders were resolved that they must
spend the winter before Sevastopol, and indeed they
had no alternative. On the 7th Raglan wrote home
to ask for the immediate dispatch of a field-battery;
and meanwhile he arranged for the collection of tools
—not at that time part of the equipment of the Army—
so that parties of Turks might take in hand the metal-
ling of the road that led from Balaclava through the
col on to the plateau. The work had just been begun
when it was abruptly and violently stopped.

Since the end of October the weather had broken
up, and from the 10th of November onward there was

constant rain, which reduced both trenches and roads 1854.
to beds of sticky mud and made the work of bringing Nov.
up provisions very difficult. The men had received
no fresh clothing since they had landed in Bulgaria.
Some effort had been made to recover their knap-
sacks, which had been left on board ship when the
troops disembarked in the Crimea, but, it seems, with
indifferent success, probably owing to the congestion
in the port of Balaclava. The result was that from
continual wear day and night the men's garments were
threadbare and ragged, while even the officers were
insufficiently clothed. The cold nights in October
had alone caused great increase of sickness,[1] and this
was aggravated by the rations of salt pork and biscuit
which were the fare of all ranks. The Englishman
generally is deplorably helpless as a cook, and the
British soldier is the most helpless of all. Camp-
kettles in the proportion of one to every five men had
been issued when the troops landed in Old Fort Bay,
but had been dropped or thrown away on the subsequent marches. It was not until Wellington had conducted three campaigns in the Peninsula that he could
trust his men to carry their camp-kettles; and it will
be remembered that the battalions which disembarked
at Old Fort Bay were too weak to bear their packs.
The camp-kettles, therefore, quickly vanished, and the
men were reduced to their mess-tins, which would not
hold sufficient water to extract the brine from the salt
meat. Fuel was not easily procured in many places,
the engineers having taken all trees for the platforms
of their batteries; and soldiers, shivering with cold,
used such wood as they could get to roast their coffee-
berries and make themselves hot drink. This was
not too easy, for the coffee was issued in the green
berry,[2] and needed first to be roasted and pounded,

---

[1] *E.g.* the Coldstream Guards sent 190 more men to hospital in
October than in September (Ross, p. 201).
[2] How this came to be I know not. Green coffee had been issued
with great success in one of the Kaffir wars. Probably the example

1854. frequently in a fragment of a Russian shell. But the
Nov. general result was that the men ate their salt pork raw,
if they ate it at all, and that this diet, added to constant
cold and exposure in the trenches, induced diarrhœa
and dysentery. The greater the number of men who
succumbed, the fewer were left to do their work, and
the greater was the burden laid upon those few. These
had therefore the less energy to toil through the mud
in the search for fuel, and gradually succumbed in
their turn. This vicious circle was in full turn while
the winter was only threatening, when a great catastrophe
aggravated its evil an hundredfold.

Nov. 14.   On the 14th a circular storm of unusual violence[1]
broke over the plateau, beginning from the south-west
with heavy rain, and veering round to west with sleet
and snow. At 4 A.M. it was blowing hard in heavy
gusts. Within an hour it had freshened to a gale, and
by 6 A.M. it had reached its full force. The hospital
marquees, with their great spread of canvas, were torn
down early; and by daylight there were not a dozen
tents of any kind standing, many having the poles
broken and several having been uplifted, pole and all,
and blown clean away. Waggons were overturned,
drums and every kind of object came rolling and
whirling before the blast; and hapless terrified horses
pulled their picketing pegs out of the soaking ground
and galloped away with their picket-ropes into the
darkness. No man, not even a mounted man, could
stand up against the storm at the height of its fury.
The sick, the sound, the vigorous, the prostrate, all
alike cowered before it. The men in the trenches
suffered perhaps even more than those in the open.

had been set by the Boers and copied by our Commissaries with good
results. But the conditions at the Cape of Good Hope and in the
Crimea were very different.
    [1] Kinglake quotes a French authority to the effect that its speed
was 52 miles an hour. In that case it was no worse than we encounter
every year in England; but, to judge from the effects of the storm,
this estimate seems too low.

One party of one hundred and fifty of the Forty-sixth 1854.
started at eight o'clock that evening, having been Nov. 14.
relieved after twenty-four hours at duty, upon a march
of five miles to their camp. Seven men were left
behind, two of them unconscious, the other five unfit
to march. The remainder toiled on with the gale and
driving snow in their teeth; and it was only by threatening that any man who fell out should be left to die where
he lay, that their officer at last brought them in, utterly
exhausted, after four hours spent on the way. They
found their comrades shivering under the lee of their
fallen tents. One hundred and seventy of them, who
had been taken sick that day, were huddled under
the sodden canvas of the fallen hospital-tent. Ten of
them died that night, and this was but one example of
what was passing all over the plateau.[1]

At sea the tempest was equally destructive. Twenty-
one British vessels were wrecked off Balaclava, including
the *Prince*, which was laden with warm clothing and
stores, the *Resolute*, with which went down ten million
rounds of ammunition, mostly for the Minié rifle, and
ships containing twenty days' supply of forage. Many
more vessels were badly damaged, for the merchant-
captains with one accord raced for the scanty shelter
of Balaclava harbour, which was crammed with shipping. The French also lost several transports and a
line-of-battle ship, and the Turks a line-of-battle ship
off Eupatoria. Some hundreds of seamen perished;
and now became manifest the awful hazard which the
French and British Governments had accepted when
they ordered a joint naval and military expedition to
a sea proverbially tempestuous, without any adequate
harbour upon the scene of operations. But this detail
was lost sight of in the desolation that overtook the
Army on shore.

The storm of the 14th of November naturally
intensified suddenly and abruptly all the troubles that
had been slowly increasing throughout October. The

[1] Campbell, *Letters from Sevastopol*, pp. 20-22.

1854.
Nov.
track from Balaclava to the British camp became a sea
of mud, knee-deep; and the task of bringing food (to
say nothing of clothing and stores of war) from the
depôt or the ship to the soldier became desperate.
There was nothing in the least surprising in this. It
was simply a repetition of the old story which Sir Ralph
Abercromby had tried in vain to din into the ears of
Dundas in 1799: "An army cannot move without
horses and waggons," and Abercromby should have
added, drivers. The Crimean Army had never been
a movable army, even in Bulgaria. There had been
the greatest difficulty in collecting waggons there in
spite of liberal payments; nor could any convoy
proceed without a guard of infantry, not to protect
it against an enemy, but to prevent the drivers from
running away with their teams and leaving the
waggons high and dry. Even when the animals were
purchased, the drivers were perforce hired, and, if they
did not desert, they so disgracefully neglected their
beasts as to wear them out very quickly with lameness
and sore backs.[1] Raglan, as has been already told,
had begged for the formation of a land-transport corps
in June; but nothing had been done. The French,
knowing the business of war, had a complete military
department for transport and supply. The English
had none. The House of Commons had deliberately
destroyed the last vestige of a waggon-train many years
before; and the Ministry, as ignorant as the House of
Commons, could see no greater necessity for such a
thing in war than in peace.

There was great clamour at the time because no
road was made from Balaclava to the camp. Three
separate inquiries by three different authorities established the fact that the construction of such a road was
impossible from sheer want of men. But even a road
would have been useless without transport-animals, and
not only were these far too few for the wants of the
Army, but it was useless to procure more from want of

[1] Stanmore, *Life of Lord Herbert of Lea*, i. 285-286.

forage.   The only forage obtainable near the spot was 1854. chopped straw, which was inconveniently bulky, and Nov. the Commissary had accordingly applied to the Treasury, before the Army landed in the Crimea, for two thousand tons of hay; but little more than a tenth of that quantity arrived before the end of the year. The loss of twenty days' forage in the storm of the 14th of November was, of course, a piece of bad luck, but, if the authorities at home had had any idea of the conduct of a campaign, such a misfortune should not have brought the Army, as it did, to the verge of starvation. There was no ill-will among the officials at home; on the contrary, there were honest zeal and devotion. But there was also abysmal and, seemingly, invincible ignorance, with a lordly disdain for all past experience. What they could not understand was that, while a very slender intelligence may suffice to fill a depôt, a very elaborate organisation is needed to bring food and clothing to the body.   The distance from England to Balaclava by sea was called three thousand miles, but the distance to the camp was three thousand and eight; and it was just the eight odd miles that made the difference.

Not that the shipping arrangements were faultless. There was carelessness in the stowage of cargoes and in noting the nature of the cargoes themselves, so that ships sometimes returned from the Crimea without unloading valuable stores, either because no one knew that they were on board, or because they were buried under a heap of stuff that was not urgently required. These failings will always recur, unless proper precautions be taken, and have not been unknown even in the last twenty years.[1]   Then at Balaclava itself the cramped space of the tiny harbour made both the landing and the transhipment of burdens most difficult.   The wharves erected by the overworked

[1] It will be remembered that Sir Ian Hamilton in 1915 had to order all his ships to Alexandria for re-stowage and rearrangement before he could attempt his landing at Gallipoli.

1854. engineers for landing the requirements of twenty-six
Nov. thousand men had a frontage of seventy-five feet only.
The place itself was tiny.   The ingress to it was along
one narrow road " with a steep rocky hill on one side
and the muddy end of the harbour on the other." [1]
The port was under the charge of the Navy; and an
energetic naval officer, with military assistance, did his
utmost to keep it in order—no easy matter in a place
swarming with English, French, Turks and the scum
of the Levant.   Yet through this bottle-neck every
pound of supplies and stores had to pass.   In Airey's
picturesque phrase, it was the needle's eye through
which the rich man struggled to penetrate.

The inevitable result was that the British troops
between November 1854 and February 1855 simply
perished of exposure and starvation.   Had they been
encamped on a bleak hillside in England during those
same months, the ground would inevitably have become
a sea of mud, and there would have been many cases
of sickness,[2] despite of abundant food and fuel, warm
clothing and good shelter, at any rate, for the ailing.
But in the Crimea there were none of these things.
The work of the siege practically came to an end on
the British side; but it was still necessary to man the
trenches for purposes of security.   So men and officers
went down, drenched, ragged and hungry, to crouch
on the wet ground or stand knee-deep in water, did
their twelve hours of duty and returned to the sodden
soil under their dripping tents to find, at best, a ration
of salt pork and biscuit without the means of cooking
it, and at worst nothing at all.   There was shelter,
in the shape of planks for huts, plenty of food and plenty
of warm clothing at Balaclava, but these things might
almost as well have been at Constantinople.   Eight

[1] See General Estcourt's letter (Stanmore, *Life of Lord Herbert
of Lea*, i. 298).
[2] This is amply proved by the instance of the division which,
for some reason or no reason, was encamped on the hills outside Win-
chester during the winter of 1914–15.

miles does not sound a great distance, but let any 1854
Londoner picture himself returning to camp on Hamp- Nov.–
stead Heath after a bitter night in trenches on its Dec.
northern slope, to find that food and clothing can only
be obtained by walking through a sea of mud, knee-
deep, to Vauxhall Bridge and back again.

Yet the men of the old long-service army, to their
eternal honour, passed through this ordeal without a
murmur. They died by scores and hundreds daily of
cholera, dysentery, diarrhœa and sheer hardship, but
they stuck to their work and did not complain. The
same soldiers were on duty in the trenches at least four
days, and sometimes five or even six days, out of seven,
but so long as they could move, they obeyed orders
and waited patiently for relief by death. The weather
varied. There were bright days, when the camp dried
a little; there were frosty days, when the ground
hardened a little; there were days of constant rain and
snow and bitter cold when nature seemed resolved to
do her worst, and frost-bite was added to all other evils.
As usual, it was the better disciplined battalions that
suffered least.[1] There were commanding officers who,
by impressing the horses or ponies of all under them
and taking advantage of a favourable day, managed to
bring up clothing from Balaclava by some means. But
speaking generally, the animals, from starvation and
exposure, were so weak that they died by hundreds
under their loads, while those of the artillery and
cavalry, after gnawing the spokes of the wheels away
from hunger, dropped down and died. Wheeled
traffic was impossible; and the poor creatures, being
unfitted with pack-saddles, were simply burdened as
best they could be and driven along by exhausted
soldiers until one or both sank down in the mire, too
often to rise no more.

Most tragical of all, perhaps, was the fate of the

---

[1] Readers may remember the first trouble with " trench-feet " in
Flanders in the winter of 1914–15. Very soon it was said that immunity from trench-feet was simply a matter of discipline.

1854. troops landed during the winter. The Forty-sixth
Nov.– landed on the 8th of November seven hundred strong;
Dec. by the 27th it had buried ten per cent and could
show only three hundred men on parade.[1] The Ninth
and Ninety-seventh disembarked in November, and
by the 13th of December the former regiment had
buried eighty men and could not produce three hundred
fit for duty. The Ninetieth arrived in the first week
of December, and the Seventeenth and Eighty-ninth
later in the same month. Drafts also had come in, and
on the 18th of December Raglan returned his reinforcements, exclusive of the Seventeenth and Eighty-
ninth, at just under seventy-three hundred, adding
that over five hundred of these were already dead, and
over a thousand on the sick-list.[2] There was nothing
to marvel at herein, seeing that most of the drafts were
boys of sixteen, or even immaturer years, who were
simply transported three thousand miles over sea to
die. It was not the first time that such a thing had
happened, nor is it likely to be the last; but at that
moment the disembarkation of some thousands of
children in the Crimea was particularly unfortunate.

The arrangements for the sick were in part inevitably and in part condemnably defective. The field-
hospitals on the plateau were little better than the tents
from which the sick men had been removed. That,
in the circumstances, could hardly be helped. The
removal of the disabled, when once wheeled traffic became impossible, could never have been effected without the help of the French, who generously and freely
lent their mule-litters or *cacolets* for the purpose. Indeed, the field of Inkerman could hardly have been
cleared of the British wounded without this same assistance from our Allies. But the sick or wounded soldier's

[1] Campbell, *Letters from Sevastopol*, p. 28.
[2] *Raglan MS.*, Raglan to Newcastle, Dec. 18, 1854 (two letters).
Raglan mentions that one of his guard appeared to be only fourteen
years old, but adds, with his usual gentleness and consideration, that
he knows Newcastle has no older men to send.

miseries only began upon his departure from the field-
hospital. At Balaclava, owing to want of space, want
of shelter and the constant tide of traffic setting landward, there were long delays and much suffering; while
the ships wherein the invalids were transported over the
three hundred miles to Constantinople were ill-fitted and
ill-adapted to their purpose. There was so little provision
for the comfort and the care of the patients that during
December and January from eighty to ninety in every
thousand of them died and were buried at sea in the
course of the passage. Arrived at Scutari they were
borne ashore with brutal roughness and callousness
by Turkish carriers and finally deposited in hospital,
where, for a time, they were not always much better off
than before.

It does not appear that the doctors received fair
treatment at the outset. In May 1854 the Director-
General of the Medical Department sent in plans for
the preparation of hospital-ships, both for the transport and reception of patients, and for the establishment of hospitals at suitable points on land. The result
was that a Turkish military hospital at Scutari was
made over to the British, and by the exertions of a good
military surgeon was reduced early to good order and
system. But the recommendations as to the ships
seem to have been ignored, possibly because the actual
sphere of operations was then still uncertain, more
probably because the whole business of shipping was
turned over to the Admiralty. There was then a
difficulty about hospital orderlies. The Director-
general asked for able-bodied soldiers. Lord Hardinge
firmly refused. The ranks of the army were thin
enough already without taking fighting men out of
them to do the work of nurses; and he would allow
none but pensioners for the hospitals. This was hard
upon the doctors, but no fault of Hardinge's. The
House of Commons, by its deliberate destruction of
all auxiliary services, was to blame in this matter as in
that of land-transport.

The General Hospital would admit only one thousand patients; and it was necessary after the action in the Alma to establish more hospitals. The most famous of these was known as the Barrack Hospital, where matters did not go as smoothly as in the first-named. There was no one co-ordinating head to organise it. The various medical departments would only work according to the system of routine in which they had been trained; and scores of men died while requisitions were made and initialled and passed through endless hands before the simplest stores and medicines could be procured. There was no lack of goodwill among the medical men, but they dreaded responsibility and would take no initiative, having been most carefully taught to avoid both the one and the other. They were strangled by what is called "red tape," and red tape is in its inception no more than precaution against human rascality. Embezzlement of stores is an evil to be found wherever anything is stored, and there had been plenty of it in the Medical Department during the last great war. There was consequently general helplessness, with the result that the condition of the hospital became unspeakable. The commonest appliances were wanting, and foul chaos reigned everywhere, breeding torture and death.

Such a state of things was not new in the history of the Army, but in the Crimea there were correspondents of newspapers who brought them before the eye of the public. The Duke of Newcastle had delegated the business of hospitals to the Secretary at War, Mr. Sidney Herbert, who had the courage to take an entirely new departure, and to send out a party of female nurses under the charge of Miss Florence Nightingale. Arriving at the Barrack Hospital on the 4th of November she found nothing but confusion and was almost immediately inundated with the wounded of Inkerman. The situation would have struck most people of either sex with despair. The atmosphere of any hospital in the days of septically

healing wounds was almost unbearable, and that of the 1854–
Barrack Hospital was quite beyond description. The 1855.
building stood, after the careless Oriental manner, in Nov.–
a sea of sewage; there was no proper ventilation, and Feb.
it was shockingly overcrowded. The patients had no
clothes except the rags that they brought into hospital,
often soaked with blood; and there were no others
for them. The hospital orderlies had mostly died of
cholera or delirium tremens. The simplest medical
and surgical necessaries, to say nothing of comforts,
were often wanting, and there were no facilities for
cooking and washing. The doctors were hopelessly
overworked and not all of them friendly. Some of
Miss Nightingale's own nurses proved to be useless
and mutinous. Above all, the terror of responsibility
and of departure from routine paralysed the store-
departments. The unfortunate storekeepers dared
think of nothing but saving expense, lest they should
find themselves ruined.[1]

With all these difficulties this extraordinary woman,
not less masterful than competent, grappled instantly
and with dauntless courage. Strong not only in the
assured support but in the intelligent sympathy of
Sidney Herbert, and fortified further by resources
placed at her disposal by private individuals,[2] she beat
down official barriers and not only obtained speedily
all that she wanted but became a dispenser of necessities to others. Possessing administrative gifts of the
highest order, a resolute will and a keen sense of the
ridiculous, she raised herself practically to the supreme
direction not only of her own department but of
others. She had naturally to battle against much
prejudice, not all of it unreasonable, from medical
men and also from other officers. For the experiment

---

[1] Wreford, Purveyor-General, said: " This is the first time that
I have had it in *writing* that I am not to spare expense. I never knew
that I might not be thrown over " (*Life of Lord Herbert of Lea*, i. 361).

[2] Notably Mr. Macdonald, the Administrator of the Public Fund
raised under the auspices of the *Times* newspaper.

1854–
1855.
Nov.–
Feb.
of bringing a number of women into a military camp was new and hazardous. She had her difficulties even with the little band of women which she took out with her; and she positively refused at first to have anything to do with a second batch which was sent out after them.[1] But her outbreaks of impatience, very pardonable in a woman naturally of a combative temperament and at the moment overwhelmed by work, were not misinterpreted by the gentle and sympathetic understanding of Sidney Herbert, who made light of any mortification to himself, in his devotion to the cause of the sick and wounded soldiers.

Formidable as Miss Nightingale might be in her righteous wrath, her tenderness and attention to her patients passed into a proverb. The old long-service soldier was identified in the public mind with a rough, hard-drinking, hard-swearing fellow, who had his merits as a fighting man but no others. It was always the worst member of a family who enlisted, and even then the poorest parents, who possessed self-respect, would pinch themselves to buy him out. The women-nurses now discovered that, as one great lady put it, the soldier was a Christian and a gentleman, courteous, respectful of goodness and purity, grateful for the slightest care, and infinitely patient. Miss Nightingale's first efforts were the more heart-breaking because the insanitary state of the Barrack Hospital almost invited the omnipresence of death. At one time the average number of patients who died was forty-two in a hundred, nor was this materially abated until the building was taken in hand by a sanitary engineer, when the rate of mortality gradually shrank from forty-two to two only. Nevertheless it may be said that from the very day when Miss Nightingale landed the conditions of the hospitals began to improve. Voluntary helpers, male as well as female, placed themselves gladly under her command, and worked with unsparing devotion; while others, seeking to make

[1] *Life of Lord Herbert of Lea*, i. 370-371.

good the failings of the Commissariat, sent out clothing
and delicacies in a private yacht, and, providing for
their own transport and their own porterage, contrived
by some means to distribute them to the Army.

All these alleviations, however, came a little late. By the end of December most of the troops at the front had received warm clothing, but the difficulties of transport were not yet overcome, and the work thereby thrown upon the men was still excessive. A certain number of them were employed in repairing the road, which they had little strength to do, but the bulk had to struggle into Balaclava and bring back on their shoulders the food which alone saved them from starvation, and the munitions which alone could secure them against hostile attack. On Christmas Day, despite of the arrival of at least eight thousand reinforcements and drafts since the action of Inkerman, fewer than eighteen thousand men were fit for duty.[1] Cholera, dysentery, diarrhœa and, latterly, scurvy, were all doing their deadly work. Two days later the Eighteenth was disembarked, and on the 14th of January 1855 the Thirty-ninth. The latter regiment was about to land in the clothing which it had worn at Gibraltar, when the surgeon begged the administrator[2] of one of the private funds to supply it with warm under-garments, which that gentleman promptly did by purchase at Constantinople. This was fortunate, for on the 16th of January there was a heavy storm which covered the plateau with three feet of snow, with drifts four times as deep; and there was naturally an increase of sickness, and especially of frost-bite. On the 20th of January the Fourteenth Foot landed, and the effective strength rose slightly for a moment; but the sick list rose steadily from something under eight thousand at the end of November to over twelve thousand at the end of January; and though a certain number of huts had been brought up, the plague was by no means

---

[1] *Raglan MSS.*, Raglan to Newcastle, Dec. 23, 1854.
[2] Once again Mr. Macdonald.

1855.   abated.   On the 4th of February the Seventy-first
Jan.-Feb. landed, but by the end of the month the sick list had
reached the figure of thirteen thousand six hundred,
and the effective strength had dwindled to little over
seventeen thousand, leaving only eleven thousand infantry upon the heights above Sevastopol.   Between
the beginning of November and the end of February
the deaths in hospital amounted to close upon nine
thousand.   Yet still the remnant stuck to their duty,
and with indomitable patience and courage worked on
all day and for four or five nights out of seven.   There
could be no finer tribute to their own discipline and to
the silent influence exerted by their chief.

    It must be repeated that such a record of misery and
death was not new in the history of the Army.   Tobias
Smollett had written down in burning words the far
more horrible scenes at Carthagena in 1741, but these
had been forgotten.   The body of the English people
knew nothing of what the troops had endured at
Quebec in the winter of 1759–60, and at Havana in
1762.   They had signified their resentment against the
squandering of life in the West Indies between 1794
and 1797 by dumb refusal to supply any more recruits
for service in that quarter, but they realised little of the
whole truth.   They had caught a glimpse of the sufferings of the Duke of York's army in Flanders in 1794,
when the sick and wounded, laid on the open deck,
came into some of the channel-ports and stirred all
hearts to compassion; but they had no knowledge of
the horrors of the retreat to the Ems, which was worse
than anything in the Crimea.   They had fifteen years
later been shocked by the arrival of Moore's army from
Coruña, with all the stains of war fresh and thick upon
it.   But the vision in every case was confined to a few,
and there was not then the means to reveal it to the
multitude.   Now, however, in the Crimea there were
correspondents of newspapers at the front, men with
eyes to see and pens to write, privileged men who, by
the government's orders, received rations of food to

maintain them on the spot. These sent home vivid 1855
descriptions of all that was passing, not omitting many Jan.–Feb.
details of obvious value to the enemy; and the chiefs of
their newspapers at home at once became not only indignant, as was their undoubted right, but hysterical,
which was contrary to reason. Had they possessed the
slightest knowledge of war, these able editors, instead
of pressing the governments to undertake this mad
Crimean campaign, would have condemned it from the
first as impracticable. Had they gathered even an
inkling of the history of the Army, they would have
insisted, as the first step of all, upon the formation of
a land-transport corps and upon provision against the
possibility of a winter campaign. However, if they
were incapable of giving wise counsel, they could at
any rate with vehement iteration bring abuses, defects
and positive evils to light, and by so doing they did on
the whole more good than harm. It was when they
attempted to apportion the responsibility for these failings that they went grievously astray.

The natural target for the nation's wrath is at all
times of mishap the government, and among its
members the person held chiefly responsible was naturally the Secretary for War. The Duke of Newcastle
was a painstaking, industrious man, by no means lacking in ability, and anxious to do his best both for his
country and for Lord Raglan. It must be noted that,
as soon as he realised the difficulty of communication
between Balaclava and the British camp, he in the first
days of December contracted for the construction of a
tramway, which in March 1855 took the completer
form of a railway. One very competent judge, Sir
John Burgoyne, did indeed opine that the money would
have been better spent in making an ordinary road and
providing more horses and waggons, which could have
been used wherever they were most wanted, whereas
the railway was serviceable only on the ground where it
lay.[1] This opinion, however, was based upon fore-

[1] *Military Opinions of Sir John Burgoyne*, p. 209.

1855. thought, long knowledge of war and some power of
Jan.-Feb. imagination, endowments which were absolutely wanting in the Duke of Newcastle; so it is only just that he
should receive credit for his railway.

But the Duke was unfortunately deficient also in
nerve.   Not the war - correspondents only but the
relatives of officers at the front showered upon him
letters of anger and complaint.   A powerful newspaper had selected Lord Raglan and the staff at his
head-quarters as the scapegoats for every miscarriage;
and in a weak moment—if it were not a weak, it was a
very evil moment—Newcastle turned against them
likewise.   Lord Raglan, with his vast experience of
British military administration both in war and in
peace, knew the difficulties of Ministers and was
studiously gentle and lenient towards them.   He had
seen all the auxiliary services of the Army deliberately
sacrificed one after another after Waterloo, and, as he
said, had never known the time when a Minister could
propose the maintenance of such establishments, nor
even the cadres of them in time of peace.[1]   But that
was the fault of the House of Commons, and he would
not in justice blame any Minister for it.   He therefore, while frankly revealing plain facts or figures,
never drew harrowing pictures, never complained and
never lamented.   He failed not to invite attention to
the morning-states, which told their own tale, but he
trusted Ministers to do their best for him, and gave
ample proof that he was doing his best for them.
Never was Secretary for War more loyally served by a
general than was Newcastle by Raglan, and never did
one prove himself less worthy of such loyalty.

On the 18th of December Newcastle began a series
of letters to Raglan which gathered vehemence as they
progressed.   He condemned the Adjutant-general and
Quartermaster-general for carelessness and inefficiency
in the discharge of their duties, upon the evidence of
private letters received from the front, and pressed

[1] *Raglan MSS.*, Raglan to Newcastle, Jan. 15, 1854.

with increasing urgency that Raglan should consent 1855.
to the removal of those officers.   The whole proceeding Jan.–Feb
was characteristic of the not uncommon type of man
who tries to veil weakness and fright under an outburst
of spasmodic violence.   Raglan was the very last man
to be moved by so deplorable an exhibition of administrative futility and bad taste.   With perfect dignity
and self-restraint he prostrated Newcastle with a few
crushing sentences.   " It is with the deepest concern
that I observe that, upon the authority of private letters,
you condemn Generals Airey and Estcourt without
reference to me. . . . I have been conversant with
public business nearly half a century, and I have never
yet known an instance of it before.   The officers above
named are perfectly efficient. . . . I consider myself
most fortunate in having General Airey in the situation of quartermaster-general.   Am I or the writers
of private letters in the better position to pronounce
upon his merits? . . . You must pardon me for
adding that I can only regard your adoption of the
imputations against my officers as an indirect reflection
upon myself."[1]

It soon became apparent that Airey was the man
whom the Press, and therefore Newcastle, desired to be
thrown to the wolves; and Newcastle presently suggested that Airey should receive the command of a
division.   Raglan replied flatly that he could not get
on without Airey, who was a very able and invaluable
man, and that he intended to keep him as quartermaster-general.   Meanwhile, Newcastle received
Raglan's first letter above quoted and, instead of feeling
ashamed and apologising for his lapse in condemning,
unheard, men of whose competence he was quite un-
qualified to judge, he plunged still deeper into official
indecency.   He actually wrote that " he felt great
concern at the unequivocal terms in which Lord
Raglan had expressed his entire approval of the
quartermaster-general's department."   Raglan saw

[1] *Raglan MSS.*, Raglan to Newcastle, Jan. 15, 1855.

1855.
Jan.-Feb.
his opportunity at once. " I cannot conceive," he wrote, "why you should feel this concern. I should have thought that you would have been happy to learn from the man best qualified to give a just opinion and form a correct judgement that I was ably assisted by Major-general Airey." This delicate sarcasm, with its touch of compassionate contempt, was unanswerable. The government realised that Raglan would die sooner than sacrifice his staff to save Ministers from the consequences of their own shortcomings. The only resource left to them was to recall him, but that they dared not do, for they could think of no one who, in the peculiar circumstances, could take his place. Nothing, therefore, remained to them but to take all responsibility upon themselves, which, after all, was what they were paid and expected to do. It was perhaps a little hard on them, for it fell to them to bear the sins of all the Administrations which had for forty years past neglected and overworked the Army. On the other hand, they, and no others, were answerable for the war and for the dangerous plan of campaign which they had thrust upon Raglan; and it must be sorrowfully acknowledged that their attempt to transfer the odium of its miscarriage to Raglan's staff suggests a very mean form of cowardice.

Their fate was not long in suspense. On the 23rd of January 1855 Parliament met, and a motion for a Committee of the Commons to inquire into the condition of the Army and the conduct of the war by the various departments was carried by a large majority. Thereupon the government resigned. The only Ministers actually displaced, however, were the Prime Minister, Lord Aberdeen, whose place was taken by Lord Palmerston, and the Duke of Newcastle, who accordingly vanishes, not in the sweetest of savour, from these pages. He was succeeded by Lord Panmure, who as Mr. Fox Maule had been Secretary at War under Lord John Russell in 1847. He had begun life as an officer of scanty means in the Seventy-ninth

Highlanders, where he may have acquired some military knowledge but had certainly failed to learn good
manners.   Howbeit, though a boor, he seems not
really to have been a bad-hearted man, and his industry
and power of work were stupendous.

The new government began by recalling Sir John
Burgoyne and giving the command of the siege-
operations to Sir Harry Jones.   Next they entrusted
to Colonel McMurdo the organisation of a land-
transport corps; appointed two Commissioners, Sir
John McNeill, a doctor, and Colonel Tulloch, to
inquire on the spot into the working of the commis-
sariat-system in the Crimea; took steps to improve the
hospitals and the transport of the wounded by sea;
dispatched a Sanitary Commission, with considerable
powers, to improve the sanitary conditions of both
camps and hospitals; and bestirred themselves to furnish an adequate supply of forage.   Most of these
measures had been initiated by the late Administration; but the credit for them—whatever it may have
been—was, as usually happens in such cases, appropriated by the new government.   A Parliamentary
Committee of eleven members, after some deplorable
scenes of lamentation and despair in the House of
Commons, was duly appointed, and entered upon its
work of inquiry with ardour.   Any expedient was
clutched at to meet the emergency of the moment, for
there seems to have been something very like a panic
among the politicians at this time.

There was some talk of raising a regiment of Irish
Guards from the ranks of the Irish Constabulary, and,
as an alternative to drawing upon this magnificent
body of men, to enlist criminals who were on ticket of
leave.   Neither of these projects was smiled upon by
Raglan.[1]   More practical was the passing of an Act
to permit militia regiments to volunteer for service
abroad, and so to liberate regular battalions from foreign

[1] *Raglan MSS.*, Panmure to Raglan, Feb. 26; Raglan to Panmure,
June 1.

1855. garrisons for work in the field.   A second Act enabling
Jan.-Feb. recruits to be enlisted for two or three years would, it
was hoped, attract grown men instead of boys to the
ranks.   But meanwhile, without any statutory warrant,
militiamen also were encouraged to enlist in the
regular Army; and it cannot have been a judicious
measure to use the militia simultaneously as garrisons
over sea and as a recruiting depôt for the Army.   The
establishment of a reserve of drafts at Malta, however,
showed that the realities of war were at last receiving
recognition.

These plain measures, however, could not silence
the clamour of the Press for a scapegoat, and the new
Ministers took early steps to divert that clamour from
themselves.   On the 12th of February Panmure,
taking his cue from Newcastle, began writing to Raglan
a series of attacks, almost incredible in their coarse
vulgarity, upon that general and his staff.   Without
taking the trouble to read Raglan's letters to Newcastle,
he accused him of giving the government no information either of his operations or of the sufferings of his
army.   He hoped Raglan's chivalrous feelings would
not lead him to extend too much protection to Estcourt
and Airey.   He did not believe that Airey or any of his
department had ever been to Balaclava.   If Estcourt
and Airey would not accept command of a division or
resign, even greater difficulties would arise.   He was
sending out General Simpson to report on the efficiency
of Raglan's staff at large, as the only alternative to the
peremptory removal of Estcourt.   Something must
be done to satisfy the House of Commons, and he
hoped Raglan would give way to the current of public
opinon in some degree.   As a climax he insinuated that
Raglan seldom visited his camp, and that neither he
nor his staff knew the condition of his " gallant men."[1]

Raglan was deeply hurt.   He had known Panmure
possibly as an obscure regimental officer; he had
known him certainly when Fox Maule was Secretary

[1] *Raglan MSS.*, Panmure to Raglan, Feb. 12, 19, 1855.

at War, and doubtless had noted in his shrewd way 1855.
the rough crust which covered a not very valuable Jan.-Feb.
kernel. But to be accused of indifference to the condition of his men—he, Raglan, whose heart was torn
by their sufferings—was an inexcusable insult. Pub-
licity, to use the modern phrase, had never been to
Raglan's taste. When he visited the camp and the
field-hospitals he rode with a single aide-de-camp,
unlike Canrobert, who was always the centre of a
prancing cavalcade. Yet because they did their duty
with zeal though without ostentation, he and his staff
were to be condemned, unheard, on the evidence of
grumbling officers and ignorant correspondents. With
perfect dignity but not without vigorous protest he
refuted the charges against him categorically; and
positively refused to part with Airey or with any
member of his staff. He was rewarded by a characteristic answer from the Secretary for War. Panmure
now averred that he had written his disagreeable
despatches only in order to elicit an indignant statement
of facts, adding that the government, if only it had
received such particulars before, would have had more
heart and ground to defend Raglan and his officers.
He had evidently no idea that it was his duty, as a
master, to be the champion of a loyal servant, until
that servant had been proved to have failed him.

Five weeks later he passed once again from this
uncouth wheedling to open threats. Everyone at
home, he wrote, looked upon Estcourt and Airey as
the sources of the sufferings of the Army during the
winter; and, if anything should happen in the field
which could be traced to them, there would be such
a storm of indignation as would lead to the ruin of
their professional prospects; wherefore Raglan must
consider carefully before keeping them on his staff. It
is needless to say that Raglan was totally unmoved by
this contemptible artifice; but it is not surprising that
Panmure should have thought it necessary a month
later to assure Raglan that Raglan would find him

1855. " strictly honest " in taking all his own responsibility in
Jan.-Feb. his support. Finally, General Simpson having reported
that better men could not have been found for the
purpose than the actual members of Raglan's staff,
and that he wished to see not one of them removed,
Panmure abandoned his persecution. " You shall hear
no more from me about your staff," he wrote; " I
have told my colleagues that I acquiesce in your
reasons for not submitting to a change and that I will
press it no further." He may not have been quite so
mean and vulgar at heart as his language suggests;
but the bare fact that he did his utmost to break up
the staff of a general in face of the enemy at a very
dangerous moment, ignoring that general's protests
and yielding only to the shrieks of idle chatterers and
irresponsible editors—this is most damning proof of
Panmure's utter unfitness for his office. He actually
risked disaster in the field rather than brave popular
clamour. There are few more striking examples of
the peril of setting a moral coward in high place.[1]

It may be convenient in this place to state briefly
the results of all the inquiries set on foot in the early
weeks of 1855 by a frightened government and an
hysterical House of Commons. The Parliamentary
Committee, after examining many witnesses and asking
tens of thousands of questions, finally came to the conclusion that the " expedition, planned and undertaken
without sufficient information, was conducted without
sufficient care and forethought," with the corollary,
" that this conduct on the part of the Administration
was the first and chief cause of the calamities that befell
the Army." Any similar inquiry into any one of the
campaigns initiated between 1793 and 1805 would
have resulted inevitably in the same verdict. There was
nothing new in the misconduct of war by British
administrations, nor in their efforts to shift the blame
for it on to the military. Had anyone in Parliament

---

[1] *Raglan MSS.*, Raglan to Panmure, Mar. 3 ; Panmure to Raglan,
Mar. 16, May 21, June 1, 1855.

or any writer in the Press possessed any knowledge
of British military history, they would have guessed
directly where to seek for the primary cause of all
miscarriages and might have saved a great deal of
trouble and expense.   Howbeit, many interesting
details were brought to light; and it was better that
the civil authorities should be judicially damned by
a tribunal composed in the main of their fellows, than
that they should be merely ousted from power by the
prejudice and reaction of party.   Meanwhile they paid
no penalty, nor does it appear that anyone required
the lives of ten thousand British soldiers at their
hands; and this was logical, for a nation which had
overlooked the sins of an older Newcastle, of the second
Pitt and of Henry Dundas, could hardly be extreme
to mark what was done amiss by an Aberdeen and a
younger Newcastle.   Moreover, it must be repeated
that the chief sinner was really the House of Commons,
which even after two centuries still remembered that
the one man who from beginning to end of its career
had really called it summarily to account had been a
soldier.

The Sanitary Commission did good work in the
hospitals and elsewhere, which need not further occupy
us, though the stimulus which it gave to the improvement of military hygiene was of inestimable value.
Sir John Macneill and Colonel Tulloch made an
exhaustive inquiry into the work of the Commissariat,
and reported not altogether in favour of Mr. Filder,
the Chief Commissary.   Unfortunately they did not
end their functions there, but took occasion to pass
censure upon certain other officers, General Airey
among them.   The Press instantly seized the opportunity to renew its vindictive attacks.   The officers
demanded an inquiry, and in February 1856, only a
month before the signature of the treaty of peace, a
Board of seven general officers, under the presidency
of John Colborne, Lord Seaton, was convened to
conduct it.   The result was most ludicrous.   McNeill

1855.
Jan.-Feb.
prudently refused to appear at all in defence of his report, and left Tulloch to do the work single-handed. Tulloch had to meet five different men, every one of them his superior on their own ground, and Airey his superior upon any common ground. He fought manfully for a month until Airey read his opening address, perhaps the best review of the whole subject which is to be found in a small compass—simple, dignified, untainted by a touch of bitterness, though not unenlightened by humour, but absolutely crushing. Then Tulloch took to his bed and appeared before the Court no more. The seven generals continued their inquiry as they had begun it, in grave silence, and after reviewing the vast mass of evidence laid before the House of Commons' Committee, in addition to that which had come before themselves, they with reasoned judgement pronounced that the sufferings of the Army during the winter of 1854–55 were due mainly to want of land-transport, that the want of land-transport was due to want of forage, and that the want of forage was due to the neglect of the Treasury in London.

Thus the long effort of the government and of the Press to saddle upon Raglan's staff and commissary-general the blame for the government's own shortcomings was finally and triumphantly baffled. The Army was intensely amused at the discomfiture of McNeill and Tulloch; and indeed it is difficult to understand why two men, who knew nothing whatever of war, should have been selected to examine one of the most difficult problems in the conduct of a campaign. It is true that Panmure considered that Tulloch would make a good field-commissary and gave Raglan leave to employ him as such;[1] so it is possible that some job was at the bottom of his appointment. But since Raglan resisted the temptation to test Tulloch's talents in this line, nothing more need be said of it. The real evil, however, lay less in the government's choice of

[1] Panmure to Raglan, April 23, 1855.

instruments than in the purpose for which they chose them. It was not the fault of Newcastle or Panmure that Airey escaped the fate of Admiral Byng; and Airey could never forget it. He served later on the Head-quarters Staff at the Horse Guards with all his old ability and diligence, but without enthusiasm.[1] There is no greater administrative evil than disloyal mastership.

These various committees, with their inevitably tardy reports, were designed of course principally as sedatives for the public irritation; but the government also seized the opportunity to make sweeping administrative changes. The first concerned the clothing of the men. Upon the outbreak of war the establishment of many regiments was at once increased, and the off-reckonings [2] for the clothing of the additional men were accordingly granted to the colonels. Since, however, the whole of the additional men were not always (through no fault of the colonel) forthcoming, it necessarily followed that the public was paying money for the clothing of soldiers that did not exist. Mr. Sidney Herbert, therefore, in June 1854 abolished off-reckonings and gave the colonels a fixed sum in lieu of any profits upon clothing, leaving them, however, still free to appoint their own clothiers and responsible to the public for the raiment of their men. Such a system could not long endure, and its disappearance was hastened by far more sweeping administrative reforms, which must be briefly recounted in order.

The first, which was effected by a Treasury Minute of 22nd December 1854, was the transfer of the Commissariat from the control of the Treasury to that of the War Office. It could not of course take effect until after many months had passed—practically not

---

[1] Wolseley, *Story of a Soldier's Life*, iii. 246-247.
[2] The deduction made from the soldier's pay and handed over to the colonel to provide for his clothing. See Vol. I. p. 318 of this History.

1855. until the principal business of the war was over—but
Jan.–Feb. it was of the first importance, since it recognised the
Commissariat as a military and not a civil department.
In February 1855 the office of the Secretary at War
was merged in that of the Secretary of State for War,
and in March all business connected with the militia
was transferred from the Home Department to the
War Department.   Finally in May 1855 the powers
of the Board of Ordnance were vested likewise in the
Secretary of State for War, and the Commander-in-
chief took over from the Master-general of the Ordnance the supreme command of the Royal Engineers
and Royal Artillery.   By this last reform two different
classes of soldier, regulated by two totally different
systems, were brought under a single head—the engineers and artillery, whose officers were chosen by educa-
tional qualification and whose men were clothed by
contract, and the infantry and cavalry, whose officers
bought their commissions for money and whose men
were clothed by the colonels.   From that moment
" purchase " and " clothing colonels " were doomed,
but the government dared not yet attack the citadel
of purchase.   They decided, however, to make an end
of " clothing colonels " at once, and to dress the
entire army by contract.   A Clothing Department was
therefore established to superintend this particular
business, and an officer who had lost both legs at
Inkerman, Sir Thomas Troubridge, was appointed the
first Director.   Lastly in the same fateful year was
established the Small Arms Factory at Enfield.   Since
the eighteenth century the Army had depended for its
muskets principally upon private factories at Birmingham, though Government factories had indeed been tried
at Lewisham in 1808 and at Enfield in 1811.   But the
latter had relapsed into insignificance after Waterloo,
the House of Commons grudging the money, and had
not revived until the introduction of percussion-
muskets in 1839.   Even then its production was
trifling; but during the Parliamentary session of 1854,

the Birmingham workmen showing symptoms of a desire to make profit out of the country's necessity, a committee was appointed to inquire into the whole matter. American factories for the production of small-arms by machinery were quoted as examples and were visited by officers of the Royal Arsenal. Raglan, in his capacity of Master-general of the Ordnance, reported strongly in favour of a government factory. The work of extending the buildings at Enfield was begun at the end of 1854, and in February 1855, though the machinery was not yet installed, there was appointed the first Superintendent of the Royal Small Arms Factories.

1855.
Jan.–Feb.

Thus within a space of six months the old administration of the Army was transformed by sudden and violent revolution. The reader may ask whether such a subject does not rightly demand the dignity of a separate chapter. But such treatment would imply that these reforms were the result of plans carefully thought out and prepared; and they were nothing of the kind. They were the headlong expedients of a Cabinet of terrified men, anxious to still popular clamour and eager to show that they were doing something. The middle of a serious war is hardly the time for turning everything upside-down; and indeed it is ridiculous to suppose that any number of Royal Warrants and Treasury Minutes can materially have altered the existing system within the space of months or even of years. The transfer of the Commissariat and of the Ordnance Corps to the War Office, indeed, awakened much opposition. Wellington, as narrated in a former volume of this history, had been adverse to it, and so now were both Hardinge and Raglan, while civilian sticklers for constitutional control of military expenditure were more acrid even than military critics.[1] But the objectors spoke to deaf ears. Panmure met Raglan's comments on the possible

[1] See, *e.g.*, Clode, *Military Forces of the Crown*, xi. 239-251, and the whole of the chapters xix. and xxix.

1855.
Jan.–Feb.
disadvantage that might accrue from the abolition of the Board of Ordnance by the unanswerable argument, " every man's tongue was against the Department." [1] There were probably not twenty men in England who were competent to give an opinion on so difficult a subject; and it is quite possible that Wellington, Hardinge, Raglan and others were, for all their intimate knowledge, contracted in their views and mistaken in their judgement. But the government thought this no time for weighing opinions. " Every man's tongue was against the Department." Nothing could be more conclusive.

Nevertheless it would be unfair to blame Palmerston's or any other British administration for launching all of these changes suddenly and hastily when the tide of public opinion was in riotous flood. It is only thus that military reforms can be accomplished at all. Civil not less than military administrators wait for what is called a " war-scare " in order to fasten this or that improvement upon a reluctant nation; and actual war serves their purpose still better. During the first half of the nineteenth century Parliament refused to pay for an army large enough even for the requirements of the Empire, much less large enough for hostilities against an European power. It was well that the House of Commons should be shocked out of all moderation, even though it might still refuse to acknowledge its own blameworthiness. There exists a vast mass of printed matter all tending to show that the new system of military administration would be less efficient and more costly than the old. Very likely it was so for a time. Administrative changes generally cost money at the outset. But it was a great gain to have placed the whole of the military forces under one head instead of under four different departments of War Office, Board of Ordnance, Treasury and Home Office, with the Admiralty frequently added for purposes of marine-

---

[1] *Raglan MSS.*, Raglan to Panmure, May 21; Panmure to Raglan, June 4, 1855.

transport and victualling.   The reforms were of course 1855.
quite incomplete, and needed more than forty years for Jan.–Feb.
full achievement.   It is possible, indeed probable, that
Palmerston and Panmure knew not what they did, but
they need not plead to us for forgiveness.

CHAPTER XLVI

1855. THE practical impotence of the British Army after the
Jan.–Feb. storm of the 14th of November 1854 could not but
affect powerfully the operations of the Allies at large.
The French Army since October had been receiving
reinforcements at the rate of ten thousand a month,
raising its total in December to sixty-five thousand
men; but there was much sickness among them, their
tiny shelter-tents, little higher or larger than a dog-
kennel, affording small protection from the weather
and from frost-bite. At the beginning of December
their chief engineer, General Bizot, had still some idea
of delivering an assault, but, realising that the British
could give little or no assistance, was fain to abandon it.
There was no bitterness of feeling at the French head-
quarters against their allies. They spoke with the
highest respect and admiration of their fighting
qualities, but they reflected justly upon their imperfect
organisation, their lack of means, their inexperience,
their dislike, traditional for two centuries, of work
with the spade,[1] and their neglect of precaution.
Happily, England had given France very substantial
help in tonnage, which alone enabled the French reinforcements to be transported to the Crimea, and
Canrobert repaid this by freely lending his mule-litters

[1] Two men only, until recent times, seem to have been able to
make the British dig with cheerfulness, Marlborough and Charles
Stuart. But as Napier says of the French before Gerona, " the
soldiers, as they will be found to do in protracted operations, become
careless and disinclined to the labour of the trenches " (*Peninsular
War*, iii. 51).

for removing the British sick, and teams (though he 1855.
too had lost many horses) for drawing their guns.   But Jan.–Feb.
he could not, in justice to his own army, make good
the defects of an ally which was always and permanently
behindhand.[1]

The British and, indeed, the allied armies had also
an excellent friend in the French Minister for War,
General Vaillant.   He, remembering the Peninsular
War, did full justice to the red-coats as fighters, and
willingly granted a request made by Lord Cowley,
British Ambassador in Paris, that British officers should
come over and study the organisation of the French
army.   For weeks he waited, but no one came; and
on the 26th of December Cowley sought out Vaillant
and confessed with despairing lamentations that the
British government was helpless to succour its Army
in the Crimea.   " Well," said Vaillant, " if they cannot
send a few officers from London to Paris in two months,
they will never get the organisation of their army
accomplished within any reasonable time.   Now I will
take a great responsibility on myself.   We have large
magazines at Constantinople with every kind of supplies.   I offer to throw them open to you and we will
share as brothers."   Cowley, hardly able to believe his
ears, asked if Canrobert would actually comply with
Raglan's requisition for anything that he wanted, supposing that Canrobert had it and could spare it.   " Yes,"
answered Vaillant, " you will repay us in money, and we
will do our best to keep our supplies up to your requirements."   Cowley, " with tears in eyes and voice,"
shook Vaillant warmly by both hands, and departed
overjoyed for London.   Vaillant obtained the emperor's sanction next day, and wrote at once accordingly to Canrobert with orders to apprise Raglan.   It
was of course understood that the needs of the French
army should come first; and it was discovered at once
that not a scrap of forage, for one important item, could

[1] Canrobert to Vaillant, Dec. 8, 22, 28; Trochu to same, Dec. 12,
1854.   Canrobert's phrase is, " en état de retard permanent."

1855. be spared.   Nevertheless, the offer, though it might in
Jan.-Feb. actual fact amount to little more than fair words, was
made in a generous and helpful spirit and should be
gratefully remembered.[1]

Before Sevastopol the situation became increasingly
difficult.   Not only was the British army melting away
and was Raglan calling upon Canrobert to take over
more ground from him, but Sir John Burgoyne was
pressing strongly for a change in the whole system of
operations.   He had always looked upon the Malakoff
Tower as the key of the Russian defences, but, so long
as the plateau of Inkerman had been left in possession
of the Russians, he had recognised attack upon it to be
impracticable.   Since the battle of Inkerman, however,
the plateau had been fortified, and not only was onslaught upon the Malakoff feasible, but the extension of
the siege-works would close the valley of the Tchernaya
to the enemy and forbid the entry of his reinforcements
into Sevastopol except from the north, across the harbour.   As Burgoyne was fain to admit, however, this
new project could only be carried out by the French,[2]
who were not very favourably disposed to it.   Their
points of attack, the Central bastion in the western
front, and the Flagstaff battery at the south-western
angle, being close to their naval base, suited them very
well.   If they were to take over the attack of the Malakoff, they would have to occupy the Inkerman plateau
and the ridge next to west of the Careenage Ravine, and

[1] Vaillant to Canrobert, Dec. 20, 28, 1854; Jan. 2, 1855.   Canrobert to Vaillant, Jan. 22, 1855.

It may be added that Vaillant complained of the incessant obstruction of Lord Stratford de Redcliffe to all French proposals to the
Turkish government, and of his attitude to France, "smacking rather
of 1815 than 1855"; but he was careful to add that he alluded only to
the British diplomats, not to the soldiers who were fighting alongside
the French (Vaillant to Canrobert, Jan. 20, 1855).

[2] It seems that Burgoyne suggested that the French should take
over the British left attack, over against the Redan, and leave the
British to deal with the Malakoff.   Canrobert, however, refused to do
so (very wisely from his own point of view), but consented to take over
the right attack (Kinglake, cabinet edn., viii. 23).

they would have a taste, which was by no means to be 1855. relished, of the difficulty of feeding their troops at those Jan.–Feb. remote points.   Canrobert and Bizot, therefore, naturally combated the proposal, though they could not deny that the extension of the attack along a wider front was important.   But on the 26th of January Vaillant sent to Canrobert the Emperor's positive orders that the new plan was to be accepted, and so the matter was settled.   Thenceforward, therefore, the French were, as Canrobert with some justice complained, divided in twain, half of them taking charge of the two ridges on either side of the Careenage Ravine, and the other half remaining on their old ground opposite the western front and the south-western angle, while the British lay midway betwixt them on either side of the Woronzoff Ravine.   This was gradually accomplished in the course of February.[1]

This month was the period in which the British strength sank to its lowest, whereas that of the French rose to close upon ninety thousand men.   But the French also had a terrible sick list—over two thousand cases of frost-bite, over four hundred of cholera and as many of scurvy, besides five thousand cases of fever, in January alone.   In March the British began slowly to recover, but their impotence still caused delay, for they could not fulfil their part, and the sacredness of the Alliance forbade the French to move too far without them.   Canrobert at the beginning of March wrote to Vaillant his opinion that the Malakoff could be taken by a *coup de main*.   But on the very same day his chief engineer, General Bizot, declared to Burgoyne that it would be hazardous to attempt the Malakoff without first mastering a hill in advance of it, known as the Mamelon, the capture of which would remove all objections on the part of the English to their pushing

---

[1] Bizot to Vaillant, Dec. 12, 27, 28, 1854; Jan. 14, Feb. 16, 1855.   Canrobert to Vaillant, Dec. 12, 17, 1854; Jan. 8, 9, 12, 19; Feb. 5, 10; to the Emperor, Jan. 5, 1855.   Vaillant to Canrobert, Jan. 26, 1855.

1855. their approaches towards the Redan and assaulting that
Jan.–Feb. part of the work.   Now, as a matter of fact the British
engineers from the first condemned an assault upon the
Redan.   The nature of the soil forbade them to push
their trenches within less than four hundred yards of it;
and they judged that the Russian fire, not only from
the Redan itself but from the works on either flank,
would prevent any troops from advancing over so wide
a space of open ground.   But this was a detail which
did not at once become prominent.   It was the impotence of the British, owing to the melting away of the
army, that simply paralysed operations; and the astute
and energetic Colonel Todleben took prompt advantage of the paralysis.   Whether from good intelligence
or from sheer penetration, he readily divined the change
in the allied plans which was transferring their energies
to the north-eastern front of the fortifications, and he
initiated in the last week of February a system of throwing up new defences in advance of them.   He had
thousands of workers ready to his hand, abundance of
tools and mechanical appliances, and a practically inexhaustible supply of guns.   He began by erecting three
new redoubts at the foot of the Inkerman Ridge.   The
Feb. French attacked these in the night of the 23rd-24th of
23-24. February; but though they met with initial success,
they were, after an hour's fighting, repulsed with a loss
of nearly three hundred men.   The affair was in itself
trifling, but the reverse came at an unfortunate
moment.
Mar. 6.   On the 6th of March news reached the allied commanders of the death of the Tsar Nicholas, and it was
thought that the depression, which the intelligence would
throw upon the Russians in Sevastopol, offered a favourable moment for an attack upon the Mamelon.   On
Mar. 9. the 9th Sir Harry Jones gladdened the hearts of the
French engineers by undertaking to push forward the
approaches against the Redan; and everything pointed
to the seizure of the Mamelon by the French on the
following day.   The measure was actually proposed by

General Bizot but rejected by Canrobert,[1] and on the 1855.
night of the 11th Todleben began the construction of a Mar. 11.
new advanced work, known as the Kamtchatka lunette,
upon the Mamelon itself. Day after day the Russians
made steady progress with it; and on the 14th, Raglan, Mar. 14.
at the instance of Sir Harry Jones, pressed urgently
that the enemy should be driven from it, but in vain.
Bizot, however, pushed forward his approaches vigorously against the new work; and on the 22nd, Todleben Mar. 22.
directed two powerful sorties from the Kamtchatka
redoubt—one of some five thousand men against the
French trenches, and another against the right flank of
the English trenches before the Redan. Both, after
slight initial success, were repulsed with a total loss to
the enemy of thirteen hundred casualties, whereas those
of the French did not exceed six hundred nor those of
the British seventy. The affair was on the whole profitable to the Allies, for the British troops behaved very
well, and the French were thus reassured that the red-
coats were prepared to take their share in the operations.

Throughout this period Canrobert was a much harassed man. On the 27th of January General Niel, aide-
de-camp to the Emperor Napoleon, had appeared on the
scene with powers to inquire and report to his master and,
to a great extent, to take charge of the operations. It
was the Emperor's idea that Sevastopol could not be
taken unless really invested and closed in upon all sides.
There was nothing original nor unsound herein; but
when the Emperor proposed to take personal command
of the force for completing the investment, the matter
assumed a very different aspect. Such, however, was
Louis Napoleon's project; and arrangements for the
concentration of additional French troops at Constantinople were begun in February. By the 2nd of
February Canrobert was converted to the new plan,
though Bizot did not accept it until the 24th of March;[2]

[1] So says Niel, Kinglake viii. 80 (cabinet edn.), but Canrobert
in a despatch of the same day says nothing of it.
[2] Niel to Vaillant, Feb. 2, 12; Bizot to Vaillant, Mar. 24, 1855.

1855. but Raglan was from the first opposed to it. Another
Feb.- detail of this plan was that twenty thousand of Omar
Mar. Pasha's Turks should be moved to Sevastopol to take
part in the siege. Upon the abandonment by the
Russians of their campaign in Bulgaria, several Turkish
battalions had been carried over to Eupatoria in
English transports; and by the middle of February
there were twenty-three thousand Turks there under
Omar Pasha's personal command. On the 17th a
Russian force, which had long held the place under
blockade by land, attacked him there and, being without
difficulty repulsed, withdrew. Canrobert then proposed that a garrison should be brought from Egypt
to hold Eupatoria, so as to release Omar for work at
Sevastopol. Raglan did not favour the idea. He
thought that the Turkish army would be more useful
at Eupatoria, where, only forty miles west of Simpheropol, it would threaten the flank of any hostile
force marching from Russia to Sevastopol. But being
now at the mercy of the French army, which outnumbered his own by two or three to one, and finding
that Omar was inclined to come to Sevastopol himself,
Raglan could not persist in his objections. Accord-
April. ingly at the beginning of April the Turkish troops
arrived, to the number of some twenty thousand men
with thirty guns.[1]

At this same time—the 6th of April—Panmure
wrote to Raglan that another ally was about to take the
field with him. Count Cavour, already laying his
plans for an united Italy under the rule of the House
of Carignan, had persuaded King Victor Emanuel of
Sardinia to declare war against Russia, so that he might
be represented, on behalf of Italy, in the European
Congress which would inevitably come at the close of
the war. This, as he astutely judged, would be what

---

[1] The last shipment, 10,000 men, arrived on April 5 (Canrobert
to Bosquet, April 6, 1855). The Egyptian Division had embarked
from Constantinople for Eupatoria on April 4 (General Larchey to
Vaillant, April 5, 1855).

is called in commercial circles a good advertisement; and accordingly fifteen thousand Sardinian troops were dispatched to the seat of war under General de la Marmora, with orders to place himself at the disposal of the British Commander-in-chief. The French, as Panmure was careful to emphasise, were to have nothing to do with them. With the arrival of these, together with the Buffs, Forty-eighth and Seventy-second from the Mediterranean garrisons, Raglan by May was more on a par with his French colleague.

During the first three months of 1855, however, Raglan was in a most difficult position. He, and indeed the whole of his army, put so brave and stoical a face upon their misfortunes that the French hardly realised to the full that the English were helpless rather from want of food to eat and of clothes and shelter to cover them, than from lack of goodwill. Inwardly Canrobert and Bizot fretted not a little at the constant delay in the bringing up of English guns and ammunition for a new cannonade, when for weeks they had themselves been ready to open fire. It needed all their forbearance and all of Raglan's tact and patience to prevent friction between them; and, apart from this, there was always at work the secret influence from Paris. Niel, the Emperor's emissary, was labouring sedulously to forward the Emperor's schemes, and interfering with everything, while the unhappy Canrobert, never a strong man, had not the courage firmly to suppress him, and was consequently worried beyond endurance. It was not until Balaclava had been reduced to order by the able and energetic Admiral Boxer, and the railway had, in the course of March, been completed from the port to the camp, that the British were at last in a position to take their full share in the coming attack. Meanwhile Canrobert was fain to admit that the English, when they did get to work, had pushed their approaches towards the Redan with remarkable speed.[1]

[1] " Avec une rapidité singulière "; Canrobert to Bosquet, April 8, 1855.

1855.   At last on the 9th of April the bombardment was
April 9. opened.   The British batteries were even then still
incomplete. The foremost of them, within seven hundred yards of the Great Redan, had not yet received
their guns, so that on the British left attack—that is to
say, on the Dockyard Ridge—only the old batteries,
fourteen hundred yards distant from their target, were
ready.   This was due to no slackness nor negligence,
but to the sheer physical difficulty of moving the heavy
guns into position.   In all, the Allies had five hundred
pieces mounted, those of the French numbering three-
quarters of the whole, though those of the British were
not very much lighter, taken in the aggregate, in weight
of metal.   The great bulk of the French ordnance was
directed against the Flagstaff bastion and the works of
the western front, while those of the British engaged
the forts along the southern front, namely (taking them
in succession from the Flagstaff bastion eastward), the
Barrack battery, Redan, Mamelon and Malakoff.   All
through the day of the 8th the rain had poured down
incessantly, and the morning of the 9th broke with
sheets of rain and mist still driving before a heavy
southerly wind.   With the first light the guns opened
fire; gunners and blue-jackets standing in a sea of mud
and water, and drenched to the skin by the downpour.
The Russian reply was feeble, for, though the fact was
not known, they were for the moment short of powder;
and before nightfall one face of the Redan was in ruins,
every gun being silenced.   On the western front likewise the Central and Flagstaff bastions received terrific
damage.   With darkness the guns fell silent, but the
mortars continued their fire, playing havoc among
the Russian working parties which, with admirable
discipline and devotion, toiled all night to repair the
mischief wrought by day.

    For the next ten days the bombardment was con-
tinued with the like havoc to the enemy, and not
without loss to the besiegers.   All seemed to be going
well; but the French showed unusual irritation over

the fact that the most advanced British battery before 1855.
the Redan had not yet been armed. Bosquet com- April.
plained to Canrobert, and Canrobert sent remonstrance
after remonstrance to Raglan, who could only answer
that he was doing his utmost in the face of great
difficulties.[1]   On the night of the 10th a great effort April 10.
was made to drag six thirty-two pounders, each
weighing nearly three tons, into position; but three
hundred men failed to move them through the deep
mud. The Russians, hearing a hubbub, opened fire, and
a shot disabled one of the six pieces by knocking off its
muzzle.   However, in the course of the 11th and 12th
four guns were got into battery, and on the 13th these April 13.
opened fire.   The open space in front was riddled
with rifle-pits, from which the Russian sharpshooters
poured an accurate stream of bullets into the embrasures;   and   the   battery,   being   opposite   to   the
re-entrant angle at the head of the Dockyard crest, was
exposed to the concentric fire of five different works,
all situated on higher and commanding ground, in
front and flanks.   None the less Captain Oldershaw of
the artillery, who was in command, though under the
full blast of at least twenty heavy cannon, silenced
one battery over against him, and maintained the contest for five hours.   Three of his guns were disabled
and the parapet of sandbags was blown away, but he
continued firing with his one surviving gun until he
received orders to withdraw, by which time forty-four
out of sixty-five men with him had fallen.   It was a
trifling incident in the siege, though very honourable
to the Royal Regiment;[2] but why the French should
have laid such stress on the arming of these advanced
batteries is not very clear.

For, although the Russian works had suffered
terribly and the Flagstaff bastion in particular had been

---

[1] Canrobert to Bosquet, April 9, 10, 11; Raglan to Canrobert,
April 10, 1855.
[2] The incident is briefly narrated by Hamley, and at length by
Kinglake, viii. 144 (cabinet edn.).

1855.   reduced to ruins faster than Todleben could repair it,
April.   yet the French delivered no assault.   The Russians
were kept under arms in constant expectation of such an
event.   They had suffered cruelly in consequence,
losing thousands [1] where the Allies had lost hundreds;
and the capture of the Flagstaff bastion must inevitably
have led to the fall of Sevastopol.   The British became
extremely impatient.   The French had been very
urgent with them to begin; and to what end was this
intense labour thrown upon the gunners [2] and this
vast expenditure of ammunition if there were to be no
assault?   It is true that Canrobert and most of his
generals wished to discontinue the bombardment on
the 14th, but were persuaded by Raglan to prosecute it,
which could only be for some definite purpose.   And
April 16.   in fact on the 16th Canrobert, Raglan and Omar Pasha
met, and decided that, upon some day to be fixed, troops
from all three armies should storm the three new
Russian redoubts on the Inkerman Ridge.   But on
approaching Canrobert upon the subject three days
later, Raglan found the French general was indifferent
to the project.[3]   The truth was that the Emperor
wished the campaign to be prolonged until he himself
should appear upon the scene, and desired that the
French arms should be weakened by as few casualties
as possible meanwhile.   He had charged Canrobert
not to commit himself; and Niel, now more powerful
than ever since General Bizot, the French chief engineer
and an excellent officer, had died on the 17th of wounds
received a few days before, was working energetically
on his side.   On that very day Niel wrote to the
Emperor that the bombardment had produced little
effect; that the capture of the Kamtchatka redoubt on
the Mamelon had become objectless; that the English

[1] Their casualties were over 6000.
[2] The gunners spent an hour going down to the batteries, eight
hours with their guns, and an hour in returning to camp, making
altogether ten hours on their legs.   Their feet became so sore that they
could hardly do their work (Hamley, p. 214).
[3] Raglan to Panmure, April 16, 21, 1855.

did indeed declare themselves ready to storm the
Redan across seven hundred yards of open ground,
but that on consideration they would probably think
better of it; and that finally a complete investment of
Sevastopol was the only solution of the problem.

Though Niel's estimate of the damage done by the
bombardment was very different from Todleben's, his
opinion as to the futility of an assault, unless the
besiegers had sapped their way very close to the
enemy's works, was perfectly sound.   But the Flagstaff bastion had been reduced to such ruin that
Todleben had given it up for lost on the 15th; and on
the 21st the French, by joining together three mine-
craters, had established themselves within a hundred
yards of the counterscarp.   On the 23rd a conference
of the chief engineer and artillery officers of both armies
was held, as the outcome of which Canrobert visited
Raglan on the same evening and proposed an assault
upon Sevastopol.   Raglan was a little astonished, for
Canrobert had shown hitherto disinclination to take
any risks.   However, he readily agreed; and it was
arranged that the guns should renew their fire for
forty-eight hours and that the assault should be
delivered on the 28th.   On the 25th, however,
Canrobert and the French generals reversed their
previous decision, on the ground that the French
reserve-corps at Constantinople would be ready to
begin operations on the 10th of May, and that it would
be more prudent to postpone the assault until later.
Once again Raglan acquiesced, though with increased
surprise at this second sudden change of views in the
French generals.   It has been suggested that they
counted on Raglan's shrinking at the last moment from
the idea of an assault, and hoped to lay the responsibility
for rejecting the venture upon him.   This is possible,
but, as it seems to me, unlikely, for Raglan had made
no secret of his anxiety for more energetic action.
The cause is rather to be sought in the weakness of
Canrobert's resistance to the pressure of Niel.   The

1855. unhappy Commander-in-chief seemed to be unable to
April. come to any determination, or to refrain from regretting
even previous decisions. He now lamented that he
had been so eager and had urged the British so strongly
to open the bombardment; which is hardly wonderful
if he intended to take no advantage of it.[1]

Throughout this period of Canrobert's inaction
Todleben continued strenuously to cover the old works
of Sevastopol with an outer chain of new entrenchments,
thereby, of course, converting any apparent progress of
the siege into retrogression. Canrobert and Niel contemplated the growth of these new works with apathy.
Not so did Raglan and the British engineers; and
happily there was one French officer who thought with
them. This was General Pélissier, who had taken over
from General Forey the command of the troops employed against the western front, and had no idea of
idly watching Todleben's measures of counter-aggres-
sion. Whether with or without Canrobert's consent,
he as early as the 10th of April began a series of attacks
upon the Russian outworks within his own sphere of
command, captured them one after another, and turned
some of them to his own account. The British did the
like with an outwork opposite their right attack on the
19th of April; and on the 20th Raglan sent Canrobert
a memorandum from Sir Harry Jones strongly advo-
cating pursuance of this policy in principle. The
Kamtchatka lunette was already a serious obstacle on
the Mamelon, while in advance of the salient of the
Redan the Russians were busy with an outwork called
by the English the Quarries. Jones urged that these
should be assaulted simultaneously and at once; but
Canrobert did nothing. He was paralysed by a
stronger hand in Paris.[2]

[1] See authorities in Kinglake, viii. 228-236 (cabinet edn.); also
Raglan to Panmure, April 24; Canrobert to Vaillant, April 24, 28,
1855.
[2] Kinglake (cabinet edn.), viii. 220-240; Raglan to Canrobert,
April 30, enclosing Jones' memo. of April 29, 1855.

The Emperor Napoleon, indeed, had been very
busy during April.   On the 16th he and the Empress
arrived in England on a visit of state to Queen
Victoria, and in a Council of War [1] held at Windsor
Castle he put forward his own proposals.   He purposed to divide the forces in the Crimea into four
armies.   Of these, one, made up of thirty thousand
Turks and Egyptians, was to occupy Eupatoria, and a
second, consisting of thirty thousand French and as
many Turks, was to hold the trenches before Sevastopol
and the posts occupied by the Allies.   The other two
were to be " armies of operation."   Of these the first
was to consist of twenty-five thousand British, five
thousand French, fifteen thousand Sardinians and, if
possible, ten thousand Turks, under the supreme command of Raglan.   Its function would be to drive the
Russians from the Mackenzie Heights and advance
northward upon Simpheropol.   The second, of seventy
thousand men, composed in part of French troops
drawn from before Sevastopol and in part of the
reserve at Constantinople, was to go by sea to Aloushta,
on the eastern shore of the Crimean Peninsula, move
thence some thirty-five miles — half of the distance
lying over very rugged and mountainous country—
upon Simpheropol, join hands in some unexplained
fashion with Raglan there or thereabouts, and then, turning southward, drive the Russians either into the sea
or into Sevastopol and invest the place completely.[2]

Every one present at the Council condemned the
idea of the Emperor's proceeding to the Crimea, and
even Panmure at once dismissed the projected operations as absurd.   To divide a compact force into four,
acting on exterior lines, was, in the first place, to invite
defeat of them in detail.   Next, the Russians had so

---

[1] Those present were the Emperor, Prince Albert, Lord Clarendon,
Lord Palmerston, Lord Cowley, Lord Panmure, Count Walewski,
Hardinge, Burgoyne and Vaillant.   Of these ten the last three alone
can have known what they were talking about.
[2] Panmure to Raglan, April 20, 1855.

1855.
April.
strongly fortified their position on the Mackenzie Heights that it was deemed impregnable. Lastly, the Emperor proposed to land at Aloushta, without forming there a base of operations and without land-transport, loading his men with eight days' rations, and trusting apparently to meet with further supplies from the west. No further words need be wasted upon this childish project; but the Emperor remained wedded to it. The most dangerous detail in the whole of it—that he should proceed to the Crimea and take command—he reluctantly abandoned; but, if he could not give the French nation a little glory in person, he was determined to do so vicariously. So far his campaign had not been very glorious, although his losses had, principally through sickness, been very heavy. It had, in fact, been something like his uncle's Polish campaign without the victory of Friedland. What he now meditated, apparently, was a bold stroke in the style of Marengo.

Meanwhile the completion of the railway and the organisation of the British land-transport service by Colonel McMurdo, a very energetic officer, were by this time working great improvement in the condition of the British army. Hence at the instance of Admiral Sir Edmund Lyons, Raglan proposed to send a small expedition to seize the straits at the eastern end of the Crimean peninsula, which give access to the Sea of Azov, and so to cut off the marine communications between the mainland of Russia and the seat of war. At the narrowest point in these straits the opposite shores of the Crimea to west and of Circassia to east were within artillery-range of each other, and on the Crimean shore the Russians had erected seven powerful batteries to command the passage. Their troops on the spot numbered about six thousand infantry, mostly of poor quality, and three thousand cavalry under General Wrangel. His position, however, was very difficult. The Straits, called, from the principal town, the Straits of Kertch, lie at the end of a peninsula

measuring some sixty miles from west to east, which 1855.
about Arabat is no wider than ten miles from north to April.
south, though it broadens out, as it trends eastward,
to from thirty to forty miles.   An enemy of superior
strength at sea, as were the Allies, could therefore land
a superior force on this narrow neck—there was a
convenient bay at Theodosia on the southern shore—
cut off his communications and fall upon him from the
rear.   Raglan was eager to undertake this enterprise,
and after some pressure Canrobert on the 29th of
April reluctantly agreed to [1] an arrangement whereby
twelve thousand men, three-fourths of them French
and the remainder British, under Sir George Brown,
should sail without delay for Kertch.

In those very days, as it chanced, a submarine
cable, newly laid from Varna to the allied quarters in
the Crimea, came into working order, the first message from Paris arriving on the 2nd of May.   It was May.
an order from the Emperor empowering Canrobert
to transport the French reserve-corps from Constantinople to the Crimea; and this was the more
welcome, since it banished any anxiety that might have
arisen through the detachment of troops to Kertch.
The expedition designed for that place accordingly
embarked on the 3rd of May and set sail, steering first,
as a feint, north-westward, as if for Odessa, but taking
up the true course as soon as darkness fell.   Late on
that same night Canrobert came to Raglan's head-
quarters with a telegram from the Emperor, ordering
him to send at once every ship that he could lay hands
on to bring the reserve-corps immediately from Constantinople; to despatch a division, as soon as these
arrived, to Aloushta; to take Raglan under his orders,
and to enter upon a confused offensive movement
to northward.   Raglan pointed out that this would
involve recalling the expedition that was on its way to
Kertch; and after more than two hours' discussion he

---

[1] Canrobert (to Vaillant, May 5, 1855) says that he was always
adverse to this expedition.

1855. persuaded Canrobert to go to his quarters and leave
May. things alone, saying that Canrobert might charge the
responsibility upon him. Within an hour a French
staff-officer came to Raglan with another telegram
from the Emperor urging an immediate offensive, and
with a letter from Canrobert saying that he could not
now allow his detachment to proceed to Kertch and
had sent a despatch-boat to recall it. Raglan thereupon wrote to Brown giving him discretion to go on
with the enterprise single-handed; but neither Lyons
nor Brown thought this expedient; and the entire
expedition, though arrived within thirty miles of
Kertch, returned. Men and officers, whether French
or British, were both angry and sore; Raglan for once
seems to have shown something like temper; and
Panmure declared Canrobert's conduct to be quite
inexcusable.[1]   Considering that the expedition had
proceeded far enough to make clear to the Russians its
intended destination, Panmure's epithet seems to be
fully justified.

This mischievous step taken by Canrobert, Niel on
the very same day submitted the Emperor's latest plan
to Raglan, who, with his usual tact, excused himself
from discussing it, but stated to Panmure in very plain
terms the manifold objections to it. On the follow-
May 5. ing day, Pélissier addressed a letter to Canrobert
insisting that, until the garrison of Sevastopol had
been reduced to a strictly limited defensive, it was
unwise to contemplate other operations, and that to
this end the siege must be pressed with the utmost
vigour, the first requisite being to make an end of
Todleben's counter-offensive works. Raglan and Sir
Harry Jones continued to press for an early assault on
the Quarries and the Mamelon, and General Dalesme,

---

[1] " Mon instance à ce sujet (the recall of the expedition), a vive-
ment préoccupé et contrarié Lord Raglan "; Canrobert to Vaillant,
May 5, 1855. Raglan wrote to Panmure (May 5) that Canrobert,
having never liked the enterprise, made the Emperor's telegram an
excuse for recalling it; Panmure to Raglan, May 7, 1855.

who had succeeded Bizot, fully agreed in principle, 1855.
provided that the siege were to be continued and the May.
proposed complete investment of the place were not to
be carried out.[1] Once again, therefore, the Emperor's
plans stood in the way of decided action. Those plans
were duly discussed by Canrobert, Raglan and Omar
Pasha, when it appeared that the very essential object
of defending the siege-works could not be attained
unless the whole of the British troops were left in the
trenches. Neither Canrobert nor Omar Pasha would
undertake to fulfil that duty for them, and thus the
whole project collapsed. On the 16th Canrobert
resigned the chief command to General Pélissier, for
whom he held a dormant commission, reverting, at his
own request, to his old charge of the 1st French
division. He had taken a true measure of his own
capacity.

The change of commanders made itself felt at once,
for Pélissier immediately and absolutely reversed the
policy of his predecessor. On the 21st the expedition
to Kertch, three thousand British, seven thousand
French and five thousand Turks, started again, and on
the 24th landed unopposed at Kamish Burun, seven
miles south of the Narrows. Wrangel, the Russian
commander, thereupon destroyed his coast-batteries
and withdrew westward on the main road to Russia,
after burning vast quantities of supplies. The Admiral
commanding the Russian squadron in the bay of
Kertch, finding his retreat threatened by the British
flotilla, burned ten of his fourteen vessels and escaped
into the sea of Azov with the remaining four. The troops
then advanced unopposed to Yeni Kale, the northern
mouth of the Straits, where they and the flotilla captured huge quantities of corn and coal and several
merchant vessels, without the loss of a man. The
flotilla then passed into the sea of Azov, drove the
Russian Admiral to destroy his four remaining ships,

[1] Raglan to Canrobert, May 7, 10; General Dalesme to Canrobert, May 13, 1855.

1855. coasted along the northern shore, capturing and
May. destroying, to the mouth of the Don, and finally, picking
up a few troops, pursued its raids along the south coast
of Circassia. Altogether within twenty days the Allies,
besides other damage, made away with over three
hundred Russian guns and five hundred ships belonging to the Russian supply-service, all at a cost of two
men wounded. Leaving five thousand Turks, a
thousand French and as many British to guard the
Straits of Kertch, the expedition returned to the Crimea.
Apart from its material success, it had a good moral
effect upon the allied forces and, as Pélissier had
intended, restored the good feeling between French
and British which had been impaired by the recall of
the original expedition.[1]

But the activity of the Allies was not confined to
distant points. On the night following the departure
of the armament for Kertch the Russians began the
construction of two additional works in advance of the
Central bastion, and Pélissier determined that they
should make no progress. On the night of the 22nd he
attacked, when after very sharp fighting—the French
having five times captured one work and as often been
driven from it—he finally mastered it by a sixth onslaught, and on the night of the 23rd converted it into a
new parallel in a commanding position. The affair cost
the Russians three thousand casualties and the French
twenty-three hundred, figures which sufficiently attest
the stubbornness of the struggle upon both sides. Three
May 25. days later, by agreement between the three commanders,
the Russian advanced posts on the Tchernaya were
thrust back; a French division, with twenty squadrons
of cavalry, was pushed forward to the Fedukhine
Heights; and the construction of a bridge-head to the
Traktir bridge was begun at once. On the right of
the French were encamped the Sardinians, who had
landed on the 8th of May, holding the ground for
some two miles higher up the river. Thus the Allies

[1] Pélissier to Vaillant, May 22, 1855.

gained greater space, and by fortification of the heights 1855. on the south bank of the Tchernaya held the enemy's field-army at greater distance.

Perhaps the greatest change of all was that Pélissier, abjuring all ideas of investment and of exterior operations, supported Raglan steadily in pressing the siege, and insisted upon having his own way. Niel, attempting to expound his own views, as had been his custom with Canrobert, was peremptorily bidden to hold his tongue;[1] and another French general, who offered a mild remark, was silenced with a roughness that brought tears to his eyes. Pélissier might be right or he might be wrong, but he meant to be master in his own house. On the 1st of June Raglan forwarded to Pélissier another memorandum from Sir Harry Jones, urging speedy attack upon the Quarries and the Mamelon; the French engineers agreed with it in principle; and the ground was cleared for a decisive assault upon the Mamelon and the Redan.[2] The first operation was fixed for the 7th of June, and Pélissier announced his intention by telegram to Paris on the 5th. On that same day the Emperor sent him, likewise by telegram, positive orders to undertake no vigorous siege-operations until Sevastopol had been completely invested. Whether either message reached its destination until two or three days later seems doubtful, for the cable between Varna and Balaclava had for the time broken down;[3] but however that may be, Pélissier was determined to go his own way.

At three o'clock in the afternoon of the 6th of June June 6. the allied batteries opened fire from nearly six hundred pieces with terrible effect; the cannon, as usual, ceasing at sunset, but the mortars continuing throughout the night. On the morning of the 7th the whole reopened June 7.

[1] " Il m'a imposé silence avec une dureté inqualifiable"; Niel to Vaillant, May 29, 1855.
[2] Raglan to Pélissier, June 1; Niel to Vaillant, June 2; Memo. of Generals Frossard, Dalesme and Niel, June 2; Niel to Pélissier, June 3, 1855.
[3] Niel to Pélissier, June 5, 1855.

1855. once more, and from three in the afternoon every
June 7. possible piece was turned upon the southern front.
By six o'clock the redoubts on the northern spur of the
Inkerman Ridge, the Kamtchatka lunette and the
Quarries had been grievously damaged; and at half-
past six a rocket gave the signal for the assault.   Two
French brigades at once dashed out against the redoubts
on the Inkerman Ridge, crossed a quarter of a mile of
open ground under heavy fire, mastered them after a
short struggle, and repulsed a feeble counter-attack
without difficulty.   On their left another French
brigade rushed over five hundred yards of open ground
against the Kamtchatka lunette, carried it in the face of
all difficulties and losses, and, excited by their success,
pushed on to the assault of the Malakoff itself.   Here
they encountered the Russian reserves, which not only
drove them back, but, counter-attacking, swept them
out of the lunette.   General Bosquet, however, having
still three brigades in hand, turned his guns once more
upon the lunette, and then launching his assaulting
columns afresh, recaptured the work and held it.   On
the left of Bosquet the British assailed the flanks of the
Quarries in two columns, each two hundred strong,
made up of detachments from the Second and Light
divisions, while three hundred more fell upon the col-
lateral works; the whole being supported by six hundred more men.   The enemy was swept out by the
first rush of the storming columns; and then some of
the British, making the same mistake as the French,
pursued almost up to the ditch of the Redan.   The
Russians counter-attacked and drove them back, recovering even the Quarries for a moment, till the red-
coats rallied and recaptured the lost ground.

Then the working parties turned to their real business
of throwing up shelter against the fire of the guns from
the Redan; but they were obliged constantly to throw
down their tools and take up their arms; and this
double duty wore them out.   Somewhat later a second
Russian counter-attack was repulsed, but the labour of

reversing the parapet and of connecting the Quarries 1855.
with the outlying works and with the British trenches June 7.
made slow progress.   The rock was so near the surface
that there was little earth, and it was necessary to build
up some kind of a parapet with half-filled gabions, piles
of stones, and even bodies of dead Russians.   The
working parties, much thinned by casualties, were too
weak; and towards dawn the men dropped down from
sheer fatigue, fell asleep, and could not be roused.
Just before daylight a heavy Russian column came
down to a third counter-attack with loud cries.   Such
of the British as were still on foot answered with all the
noise that they could make.   Colonel Campbell of the
Ninetieth, who commanded one of the two storming
columns, kept his bugler blowing every kind of call
furiously; the officers shouted and emptied their revolvers into the advancing mass; and the Russians,
when they were within ten paces, wavered and halted.
Their officers tried to drag them forward, but they
shrank back and presently retired, leaving the British
in possession of their captures.[1]

The loss of the Russians in these affairs (apart from
the casualties inflicted by the bombardment) were five
thousand killed and wounded, those of the French five
thousand five hundred, and those of the British six
hundred and seventy.   It was the wild attack upon the
Malakoff[2] which seems to have cost the French so dear,
but, according to Colonel Todleben, the Malakoff
really lay at their mercy had they been supported, and
might easily have been taken.   In the case of the
British it should seem that the small numbers employed
and the neglect to push up supports seriously imperilled
the success of the assault.   In fact, the affair was imperfectly prepared and badly managed.   Nor indeed was
it necessary to attack the Quarries at all if the Mamelon
were mastered, since the Mamelon took in reverse the
whole of the trench by which the Russians communi-

---

[1] Wolseley, *Story of a Soldier's Life*, i. pp. 156-162.
[2] Bosquet returned his losses at 97 officers and 2051 other ranks.

1855. cated with the Quarries. This had been pointed out by Raglan to Canrobert a month earlier, yet the exigencies of the alliance appear to have required that French and British should at least, in semblance, share all work equally. But the most serious aspect of the whole affair lay in the heavy price which the Allies had to pay for allowing the Russians to push forward their counterworks without hindrance; and for this, as it should seem, they had to thank the Emperor Napoleon.[1]

The bombardment was resumed on the 8th, and on June 9. the 9th Raglan urged Pélissier to press the operations of the siege with all possible energy. Pélissier readily agreed; but the Emperor was cold and discouraging in his reception of the news of the capture of the Mamelon; and Pélissier, greatly irritated, became difficult and ill-tempered. The French and British engineers had agreed that the new attack should embrace assaults upon the Flagstaff and Central bastions, as well as upon the south front; but, though Raglan supported them, Pélissier insisted upon assailing the south front only. Bosquet maintained that it was hazardous to fall upon the south front until the approaches had been pushed much nearer to the Russian works; whereupon Pélissier removed him from his command and transferred him to that of the force in the valley of the Tchernaya. Bosquet, whose opinion was perfectly sound, was naturally much hurt; Canrobert declared his regret that he should ever have made way for such a chief as Pélissier; and the higher commanders of both armies June 16. were seriously upset.[2] Finally on the 16th Pélissier telegraphed to the Emperor requesting that he might either have a free hand or be allowed to resign. Such a sign of Pélissier's masterful character commands respect; and it was a pity that he should have allowed himself to visit his worries also upon his subordinates.

[1] Raglan to Canrobert, May 10, 1855; Campbell, *Letters from Sevastopol*, pp. 242, 247.
[2] Niel to Vaillant, June 16, 1855.

However, it was decided that on the 18th of June 1855. the French should assault the Malakoff, and that, as soon as they had mastered it, the British should fall on the Redan.   At daybreak on the 17th the batteries of June 17. the Allies opened another—the fourth—great bombardment, the fire of two hundred and eighty pieces being turned upon the southern front alone.   The Russian works on that side were terribly damaged; the Malakoff was silenced; and the Russian troops, which were drawn up ready to resist an assault, suffered four thousand casualties.   Pélissier, much encouraged by the comparative weakness of the enemy's fire, informed Raglan that he should re-open fire at daybreak for a couple of hours, in order to destroy any reparation made by the enemy during the night, and should assault at five o'clock or a little later.   Raglan, cordially approving, undertook that his own batteries should re-open fire at the same hour, though, with Pélissier's consent, he reserved to himself the time for storming the Redan.   In both armies there were high hopes that the morrow would see the fall of Sevastopol.

Then suddenly in the evening Pélissier, without a word to Raglan, announced to Sir Harry Jones that he had changed his plans and that he would assault at daybreak without previous preparation by artillery. He conveyed this decision as unalterable, and, when Jones transmitted it to Raglan, the English general could only accept it and prepare, though with misgiving, to act in loyal conformity with it.

All night the Russians worked strenuously to repair their ruined entrenchments.   Before daybreak their infantry was crowded behind the parapets, and several field-guns were in position along the ramparts of the Malakoff.   Whether the Russian commander had inner intelligence of the projected attack or not, he could see and hear without difficulty in the summer night the movements of the allied columns to their appointed places.   Pélissier's plans were as follows: On the extreme right of the Allies, General May-

1855.
June 18.

ran's division was to assault the flank of the Russian battery, called the Point battery, overlooking Careenage Bay, and turning to its left, take the next battery—the Little Redan—in rear.

Next on Mayran's left, General Brunet's division was to assail the curtain between the Little Redan and the Malakoff, turn to his left, and attack the Malakoff from the north side.

Next on Brunet's left General Autemarre's division was to fall upon the curtain of the Gervais battery from the Dockyard Ravine, and, having carried it, to turn to its right upon the south side of the Malakoff.[1]

The three attacks were to be made simultaneously; and as a general reserve the division of the Imperial Guard was drawn up in rear of the Victoria redoubt, between the Careenage Ravine and the Dockyard Ravine and near the heads of both. As this position seemed to be somewhat far in rear Pélissier summoned also two additional brigades, Faucheux's and Monteynard's from the Second Corps and Reserve Corps, to take up ground somewhat in advance of the Imperial Guard. The signal for the onslaught was to be a bouquet of rockets sent up near the Victoria redoubt by the personal order of Pélissier.

Matters began to go amiss early. Mayran, a nervous, anxious man, mistook a shell thrown from the Mamelon for the signal, and launched his division forward prematurely. His columns were met by a devastating fire from the ramparts and from six men-of-war off the head of the Careenage Ravine. Three several efforts could carry them no farther than to the edge of the outermost defences. Mayran was killed, and the wreck of the division eventually took shelter in dead ground, being a " spent force."

In due time Pélissier made his signal, but there

---

[1] Mayran's division was the 3rd of the *II* Corps; Brunet's the 5th of the *II* Corps; Autemarre's the 1st of the *I* Corps. Faucheux's brigade belonged to the 4th Division of the *I* Corps; Monteynard's to the 2nd Division of the Reserve.

was considerable delay before it produced any result. 1855.
Brunet's men, when passing down the trenches to their June 18.
appointed starting-point, had found them still obstructed by d'Autemarre's troops, which had not yet
filed out of them.   At length the two divisions rushed
out together to the assault.   Brunet's was cut to
pieces by the Russian fire, and the foremost men could
approach no nearer than within a hundred yards of the
curtain.   Brunet himself was killed, and all the efforts
of his officers failed to get the men forward.   D'Autemarre was for a moment more successful.   One of his
battalions broke into the curtain south of the Malakoff,
and another party mastered the Gervais battery; but
the supporting columns were stopped by the fire from
the Malakoff and from the eastern face of the Redan;
and the French battalion, left in isolation, was after a
stubborn fight driven out by the counter-attack of two
Russian battalions.   Raglan, seeing that the entire
enterprise was going to wreck, gave the signal for
assault on the Redan as the only chance of saving the
day.

It had been arranged that the Redan should be
attacked in three columns, each led by an advanced party
of a hundred riflemen, followed by a few engineers and
some two hundred soldiers and sailors carrying ladders
and wool-packs, and closed by a storming party of four
hundred, with a reserve of eight hundred.   The right
and left of these three were to attack the eastern and
western faces of the Redan respectively, and the centre
column was a little later to fall upon the salient.   The
distance to be traversed from the British to the Russian
trenches was nearly five hundred yards, the ground
being covered with long rank grass and seamed with
shell-holes, rifle-pits and disused gravel-pits; and it was
swept by the guns not only of the Redan itself in
front, but by those of the Barrack and Garden batteries
on the western and by those of the Malakoff on the
eastern flank.   About one hundred yards in advance of
the ditch of the Redan was an abatis about four feet wide

1855.
June 18.
and from four to five feet high; the ditch itself was eleven feet deep and about fifteen feet broad, and beyond it the parapet rose from fifteen to seventeen feet above the surface of the level ground. Altogether there were a good many obstacles to be overcome.

No proper means of scaling the parapet had been prepared, so, upon the order to attack, the men scrambled over as best they could. In the left column, which was commanded by General Sir John Campbell, some of them, owing to the crowded state of the trenches, filed away to the left and gained the open in that way. One and all were met by such a storm of grape and musketry, steady and prolonged, as that even Raglan had never seen the like. Campbell led the storming party, which was formed of the Fifty-seventh, most gallantly, and was found lying dead with many men round him within twenty yards of the abatis; and one man only, a private of the Rifle Brigade, reached the edge of the ditch before he was shot down. The right column fared no better. The ladder-carriers were shot down almost as soon as they emerged from shelter, and the storming party was swept away in ranks. The supports were brought up very promptly by Colonel Lysons; but a detachment of the Seventh Fusiliers alone advanced, the remainder being stopped by order of Sir George Brown, who saw the hopelessness of the venture. Colonel Yea of the Seventh, who, as acting brigadier, commanded the support, was killed, and a very valuable officer was lost. Many men made their way as far as the abatis, and there lay down in such cover as they could find from the blast of bullets which tore up the whole surface of the ground. Modern machine-guns could have poured in no more destructive fire.

At the main point of attack, therefore, the onslaught was a hopeless failure. On the extreme British left, however, General Eyre had been directed to move down the Dockyard Ravine with his brigade[1] and attack some

---

[1] 9th, 18th, 28th, 38th, 44th.

advanced Russian works in a cemetery at the head of the Dockyard Creek. At 2 A.M. his brigade was in action. The position was strong, the ground being covered by stone enclosures, with fortified houses in rear; but Eyre stormed it, despite of all difficulties, out of hand, and occupied the houses. He seems, however, to have pushed on too far, the buildings being within close range of the battery, known as the Garden battery, adjoining the Flagstaff bastion; but he held his own until five o'clock in the evening, when, having made over such ground as was worth holding to the engineers, he obeyed the order which recalled him. Out of two thousand men with him five hundred and sixty had been killed and wounded. Among the latter was Eyre himself, but though he retained his command throughout the day, he was shortly afterwards obliged by his wound to relinquish it. He was the officer whom we have already seen working his troops by sound of bugle through the wooded mazes of the Waterkloof.

Altogether the assault of the 18th of June was a disastrous miscarriage, for which Pélissier must be held chiefly responsible. His first great blunder was his limitation of the attack to the western front only; his second and greater was the alteration of all plans at the last moment; and the third and greatest was the countermand of the preliminary cannonade before launching the infantry at the Russian works. Mayran's mistake in not waiting for the signal was a contributory cause; but this was only an incident due in great measure, apparently, to the general unrest which Pélissier's somewhat violent and arbitrary measures had awakened in the French army. The excitement of a contest with the Emperor, in which his whole future was at stake, seems to have disturbed his mental balance for a time rather seriously.

As to Raglan, never was commander placed in a more cruel position. He was forced against his better judgement into operations which he would never

1855.
June 18.

1855. willingly have undertaken, and compelled to share to
June 18. the uttermost the burden of their failure. " I am
quite certain," he wrote,[1] " that if the troops had
remained in our trenches, the French would have
attributed their non-success to our refusal to participate
in the operation." If the situation had been reversed,
Englishmen would no doubt have laid blame in the
like fashion upon the French. There would have
been angry recrimination by the ignorant of both
nations, for which the natural vent would have been
the public Press. When, therefore, Raglan saw how
stoutly the Russians resisted the French, he felt it his
duty to throw his own troops at the Redan, and he
did so with the full concurrence of Sir George Brown
and Sir Harry Jones. But after witnessing the failure
of the first two columns, he refused to sacrifice more
men. Good judges who shared in the attack held that
even the army which fought at the Alma would have
failed on the 18th of June; and that army had perished
and given place to soldiers of inevitably inferior quality.
Lastly, as Raglan well knew, the Redan could not have
been held, even if carried, so long as the Malakoff
remained in the enemy's hands; and the futility of the
whole proceeding must have been painfully evident to
him.[2]

At the same time there were faults in the execution
of the British attack. The covering parties of riflemen,
true to their training, took the first shelter that they
could find and from thence opened fire; whereas they
would have been twice as effective if they had received
orders to run out at once to the abatis and not pull a
trigger until they had reached it. They would have
obeyed such orders, but none were given to them.
Many of them and of the storming party remained at
the abatis for hours, unable to advance or retreat, until an

---

[1] To Panmure, June 19, 1855.
[2] Evelyn Wood, *The Crimea in 1854 and 1894*, p. 331; Wolseley,
Story of a Soldier's Life, i. 167, 169; Campbell, *Letters from
Sevastopol*, pp. 185, 250, 257, 286.

opportune sand-storm gave them concealment enough 1855.
to retire.   Again, there were not facilities enough pre- June 18.
pared to enable the stormers to surmount or pass
through the parapet quickly and in large numbers;
and the occasion was one for wave upon wave of
attackers following in quick succession.   Lastly, the
numbers employed were far too small for the appointed
task, so that success, even in the most favourable circumstances, would have been doubtful.

The casualties of the English, including the losses
of Eyre's brigade, just exceeded fifteen hundred.
Many valuable officers were slain, and Colonel Tylden
of the Engineers was grievously wounded; but he was
only one of a very gallant company of that corps.   Sir
Harry Jones, while looking over the parapet from one
of the trenches by Lord Raglan's side, received a nasty
scalp-wound from a grapeshot which disabled him for
a month.   Two lieutenants, Gerald Graham and
Charles Gordon, who were later to become conspicuous,
were greatly distinguished.   None, however, perhaps,
behaved so superbly as a little party of bluejackets
which acted as ladder-carriers to the right column.
Their leader, Captain Peel, was a proverb throughout
the siege for heroic courage, and a young midshipman
named Evelyn Wood, who was destined to become a
field-marshal, fell little behind him.   Both were
wounded, and they lost half of their men.   If any
fighters could have reached the ditch of the Redan, it
was this tiny group from the sister service; and as a
matter of fact, the only man who actually crossed the
ditch and was found dead in an embrasure of the Redan
was a bluejacket.[1]

The casualties of the French were about thirty-five
hundred[2] and those of the Russians, including four
thousand inflicted through the bombardment of the

---

[1] Evelyn Wood, *From Midshipman to Field-Marshal*, i. 97.
[2] But Colonel Beville (who was no friend to Pélissier) stated the
French loss at 5387 killed, wounded and missing.   Beville to Napoleon,
July 14, 1855.

1855.   17th, nearly fifty-five hundred.   If the cannonade had
June 18. been continued, as originally arranged on the 18th, its
havoc among the Russians crowded in the trenches
might have ensured success.

Looking to the nature of the operation the losses of
the British cannot be considered unduly heavy.   The
army, though disappointed, was not cast down; but
Raglan, though outwardly calm, was stricken to the
heart.   He had hoped that Waterloo Day might have
set a period to his troubles and anxieties, yet, through
no fault of his own, they promised to be multiplied.
The Emperor would now feel justified in binding
Pélissier by positive orders, if he did not remove him
from the command; and then there would be controversies and doubts and delays and all the weary
struggle of cross-purposes which had already paralysed
the operations for weeks.   Moreover, cholera had returned, and the Sardinians had already lost forty to fifty
officers and eight hundred men.   However, Raglan
transacted all business with his usual care and industry,
and on the 21st sent a memorandum to Pélissier repeat-
ing his old advice that the next assault should be general
on both the southern and western fronts, but urging
abandonment of attack on the Redan as hopeless, and
asking where the British should, in that case, be employed.   On that same day General Estcourt, the Adjutant-general, a man beloved by all and particularly by
Raglan, was stricken by cholera; and in three days he
was dead.   Raglan, who had been slightly ailing since
the 23rd, was so much overcome that he could not trust
himself to attend Estcourt's funeral.   He continued
his work until the evening of the 26th, when he suddenly
collapsed.   He rallied somewhat on the 27th, but in
June 28. the afternoon of the 28th he gradually sank and at sunset he died.

It is expedient that one man should die for the
people; and rarely has a nobler victim for the British
nation been found than Raglan.   By a strange irony
it fell to him to expiate the sins of improvidence, mis-

named economy, wherewith the British Parliament had 1855.
for forty years visited a starved and over-worked army,
and to atone for the vulgarity, half sentimental, half
aggressive, which, preached noisily to the country
through the Press, had plunged her unnecessarily into
war.   Nothing was wanting to fill the cup of his bitterness.   He was forced into a campaign which he knew
to be unsound if not insane; he saw the scourge of
cholera descend upon his army; he trembled in early
autumn for its existence during the winter; but no
words and no warnings could move the incompetent
Government at home.   He realised that he must take
great risks, but at the critical moment could never prevail with his colleagues of France to share them.   St.
Arnaud was unfit, even had he not been mortally
stricken, to command an army; Canrobert was timid
and irresolute; Pélissier, though a strong and cordial
co-operator, lost his head and upset plans at the last
moment.   Then, as if these were not troubles enough,
there were infamous slanders published by anonymous
writers in London, which were countenanced rather
than repelled by Raglan's craven and disloyal masters
in the Cabinet.   There was, in fact, a conspiracy, alike
of the irresponsible and the responsible, to shift the
burden of their shortcomings upon the army, and to
sacrifice, if not Raglan himself, then those who had
most faithfully served both him and them.   This was
unutterably mean in itself, but it was even worse when
the conspirators invited—even strove to exact—Raglan's participation in their meanness.   There are few
more shameful pages in the history of the Cabinet's
dealings with the army.

And amid all this skulking and shuffling of scared
politicians Raglan stood unmoved, too great a man to
be infected with their panic, too great a gentleman even
to pour scorn upon their trepidation, resolute only to
do his duty to the army and to his country.   His ex-
quisite tact and courtesy have veiled the greatest of his
qualities, his moral strength and his moral courage.   It

1855. is an amazing tribute to him that he kept his army together at all during the winter, and that, though reduced
to a shadow by cold, sickness and starvation, it remained
a body of disciplined men, facing all hardships with ex-
emplary patience and doing all the duty that its strength
permitted. We can picture the stream of officers resorting to him one after another with tales of misery
and despair; but it is not so easy to picture the calm,
much-enduring old chief who by his own mysterious
power endued them at least with his own courage and
his own endurance. " He threw upon those who con-
versed with him," said Airey in his noble tribute to his
beloved chief, " the spell of his own undaunted nature.
Men came to him anxious and perturbed. They went
away firm." Raglan possessed very high qualities as
a commander.

As a general he is commonly dismissed with the
compassionate comment that he was too old. He was
indeed past his sixty-fifth year, but he was younger
than most men of his age. The excellent quality of
his writing, whether in French or in English, together
with his long service at the Horse Guards, might
suggest that he was only efficient in an office; but
though an admirable man of business, he was by no
means one who was glued to his desk, being active in
body and much happier in the saddle (as befitted a son
of Badminton) than in a writing chair. As to his
conduct of the campaign at large, the absurdity of the
whole enterprise entrusted to him and the division of
command make criticism practically impossible. As
to details I cannot but think that, though a Commander-
in-chief has other things to look to besides outposts,
the army would not have been surprised at Inkerman
had Lord Seaton or Sir Harry Smith, pupils of Moore
and Craufurd, stood in Raglan's place. But Raglan
had not done a day's regimental duty for forty-five
years. It is somewhat curious that both at the Alma
and at Inkerman his chief share in the action should
have been the bringing up of a couple of guns. But

the two cases were widely different. At Inkerman, a 1855. magnified affair of outposts, he was no doubt right to leave a free hand to Pennefather in the handling of the infantry, while his intervention had the very important result of driving the massed Russian batteries from the field. He must, therefore, have possessed a quick tactical instinct as well as a swift intuition, doubtless gained by long service with Wellington, as to the moral condition of the enemy's forces opposed to him in the open field. For the rest he exposed himself so freely that it is wonderful that he should have escaped unhurt. Once when he was sitting in the trenches of the Naval Brigade a shot cut through the parapet six inches above his head, smothering him with stones and dirt. He stood up to shake the rubbish off his neck, remarking with undisturbed calm, " Quite close enough."[1] Nothing could fluster him, whether in the field or in his quarters.

But it is chiefly as a public servant that his character deserves to be held up as an example to the British Army. No commander was ever worse treated; but maltreatment only evoked from him the greater loyalty and the higher standard of duty. Thereby he saved not only his staff from abominable injustice but ministers from the consequences of their own panic. If Raglan had lost his head it is difficult to see where the trouble would have ended. There might well have been confusion and disaster both in Downing Street and in the Crimea. His constancy, his courage and his uprightness alone for a time held the tottering fabric erect, until he had shamed ministers into sharing something of his own undaunted spirit. This was no common achievement and could be wrought by no common man. Ignoble writers sneered at his great descent, misled by the fact that his every action involuntarily showed grace and breeding.[2] But it was

[1] Evelyn Wood, *From Midshipman to Field-Marshal*, i. 69.

[2] Wolseley, *op. cit.* i. 170; and see Evelyn Wood's account of Raglan's reception of " a very dirty midshipman."

1855. not for nothing that Raglan had for ancestors old John of Gaunt, his "bold son" Henry Hereford, and that Lord Worcester who for four years held Raglan Castle for Charles the First, and poured out all his vast riches for the King's cause. He summed up in himself the essence of all true aristocracy, self-reverence, self-control, loyal mastership and loyal service.

CHAPTER XLVII

Upon the death of Raglan General Simpson took over 1855. the command of the British Army. He was a Grenadier Guardsman who had served with his regiment in the Peninsula and in the Waterloo campaign, and had, in 1845, been Sir Charles Napier's second in command in some punitive operations in Sind. He was a shrewd, sound, sensible soldier, but not a striking personality and hardly young enough for his post. In the first days of July he was warned from London of an impending attack by the Russians on Balaclava, and prepared dispositions for the defence of his base. Pélissier did not share his apprehensions, but gave such orders as were necessary to his own troops to second Simpson's movements. In a week or ten days Simpson's anxieties proved to be groundless, but meanwhile little progress was made by the British in the prosecution of the siege. In fact, the change of command, the temporary disability of Sir Harry Jones, and the absence of Colonel Tylden, added to a general discouragement felt by the divisional generals after the repulse of the 18th of June, seem to have caused some slackness for a time; and the British working parties, always averse from the spade and often not encouraged by their officers to labour heartily with the engineers, did not fail to show that they felt it.[1]

On the 12th of July Simpson and Jones again July 12.

[1] Pélissier to the Emperor, June 29; to Vailant, July 6, 7, 10; to Gen. Morris, July 9, 1855. Simpson to Pélissier, July 3, 1855. Campbell, *Letters from Sevastopol*, p. 275.

1855. brought forward the question of renouncing any
July. further assault on the Redan, and there followed the
usual exchange of memoranda between the chief
engineers. Then succeeded conferences, in which
not only this problem but those of an attack upon the
Russian field-army, and of a general assault upon the
whole of the Russian works, were again brought up,
discussed and re-discussed. During these weeks of
July and August the allied forces steadily increased.
The French had a strength of about one hundred and
twenty thousand men and the British close upon fifty
thousand of all ranks.[1]   On the other hand, in consequence of a Russian movement against Kars in Asia
Minor, Omar Pasha on the 12th of July pressed for
permission[2] to take his army thither, which proposal,
after long delay, was finally rejected. The general
resolution, after all the debates, was that the siege
should be continued as heretofore, and that another
assault should be delivered before long without any
preliminary complete investment of the fortress or any
previous engagement with the Russian field-army.[3]

Aug. 16.   On the 16th of August that army set this last
question at rest by advancing at daybreak against the
French and Sardinian positions on the south side of the
Tchernaya with some six thousand cavalry, five divisions
of infantry and over one hundred guns.   The Russian
infantry forded the river and carried the bridge-head
constructed by the French, but, meeting the main body
of the French infantry, after a short struggle turned
and fled.   By eight o'clock the fight was over and
the enemy in retreat.   Their losses amounted to at

---

[1] Gen. Torrens to Vaillant, July 30, 1855.   The regiments that
arrived in 1855 were: January, the 14th and 89th; February, the 71st;
April, the 3rd and 48th; May, the 72nd; June, the 13th; July, the
56th.
[2] Omar Pasha to Pélissier, July 12, 1855; Napoleon III. to Vaillant,
Aug. 23, 1855.
[3] Simpson to Pélissier, July 12, 30, Aug. 2; Niel to Pélissier,
July 13; Memo. of Jones and Niel, Aug. 1, of C.R.A.'s and C.R.E.'s,
Aug. 5, 7; Pélissier to Vaillant, Aug. 3, 8; Niel to Vaillant, Aug. 4, 11.

least five thousand men, whereas those of the French 1855.
and Sardinians did not amount to one thousand. Aug. 16.
Altogether it was a brilliant little affair for our
Allies, and brought the decisive moment perceptibly
nearer.

Ever since the 18th of June the French had been
pushing their approaches to the Malakoff sedulously
forward; and by the date of the battle of the Tchernaya
they had brought them within fifty yards of the
Russian trenches and had armed their works in the
Mamelon with scores of cannon of one description and
another.[1] On the 17th August the Allies opened a new Aug. 17.
bombardment from eight hundred pieces of ordnance,
which wrought appalling damage; but the British had
been by no means so energetic as the French, and no
assault followed. The British engineers were still
strongly opposed to an assault on the Redan and would
make no great effort towards that end; and this
attitude appears to have continued—or was, in the
opinion of the French, continued—until the 25th of
August. In those very days, however, the British
resumed their sapping up to the Redan and the construction of new batteries. The daily losses of both
French and English in the trenches—the former
suffering far more than the latter—made so steady
a drain upon them that the expediency of a general
assault became increasingly evident. Some delay was
caused by the explosion of a large French magazine
on the Mamelon on the 27th, which did much damage Aug. 27.
and caused a hundred and fifty casualties; but on the
3rd of September the chiefs of engineers and artillery Sept. 3.
met in conference and agreed upon the details. There
was to be a preliminary bombardment of three days,
and the first assault would be directed against the
Malakoff, the little Redan to north of it, and the works
between the two. When the Malakoff had fallen, the
French at a given signal would storm the south front

[1] Campbell, *Letters from Sevastopol*, p. 288; Niel to Vaillant,
Aug. 25, 1855.

1855. and the British the Great Redan.[1]   Thus the British,
Sept. though their engineers still considered it foolish,[2] were
after all committed to a second attempt upon the Great
Redan.   But, on the other hand, Pélissier had yielded
to them in agreeing to attack the south front, and it was
therefore hardly possible for them not to make this
concession.   By this time the French approaches were
within twenty-five yards of the Malakoff and no further
from the Little Redan; but the British were still two
hundred yards from the Great Redan, and the intervening ground was mostly solid rock.

The French preparations were admirably complete,
General Bosquet having after the 18th of June been
restored to his old command.   Every precaution was
taken to make access to the trenches easy, to conceal
large bodies of troops, and to make broad cuts, hidden
for the time by gabions, which would allow of the
advance of supporting columns in formed bodies, and
even of the passage of field-artillery.   The day was
fixed for the 8th of September, and the time for noon;
for it had been ascertained that at that hour the
Russians relieved the guards in their trenches, and
that, owing to the intricacy of the traverses and other
defensive works, it had become the habit for the old
guard to march out before the new guard marched in.
The troops appointed for the assault were one division
in advance, with another division and an additional
brigade in support, for the Malakoff; a third division,
with four regiments in support, for the intervening
curtains; and yet a fourth division, with a brigade and
a battalion in support, for the Little Redan.   Pélissier
was rightly taking no risks of a second failure.

The British arrangements, on the other hand, were
very imperfect.   The troops selected were from the
Second and Light Divisions, which had been before the
Redan for months, knew the ground well, and were
therefore thought to have earned the honour of storm-

---

[1] Niel to Vaillant, Sept. 3, 1855.
[2] Campbell, *Letters from Sevastopol*, p. 307.

ing the work. This was an initial blunder, though 1855. dictated by consideration for regimental pride. These two divisions had suffered cruelly and had been filled up with raw young recruits who, moreover, had for months been taught, not without much difficulty and hard language, to duck and dodge and take shelter from the Russian fire. The engineer officers realised that such training must necessarily take all dash out of the men;[1] and many thought that the assault should have been entrusted to the Highland Brigade, which had hardly been in action since the Alma, had lost few men in any engagement, and had spent most of their time comfortably near Balaclava while their comrades were perishing in the trenches and on the plateau. The Highland Brigade was therefore still composed of fine old soldiers, and for this very reason there was a tendency, by no means checked by Sir Colin Campbell,[2] to exalt it; though Simpson evidently thought it would be unfair to give them the final glory when they had done little of the hard work. The incident is a good example of the evil that could be wrought by the time-honoured British policy of maintaining not an army but a collection of regiments.

The detailed arrangements for the assault were much the same in principle as on the 18th of June. It was to be led by a covering party of two hundred men, to keep down the fire from the Russian embrasures; armed ladder-parties of three hundred and twenty men were to come next; then the main storming column, one thousand in all; then an armed working party of two hundred men; then the supports, fifteen hundred men; then the reserve, about three thousand strong, made up of the remainder of the Second and Light

---

[1] Hamley, p. 306. An officer of the 7th Fusiliers, who took part in the attack of June 18, laid great stress upon this point to me in conversation many years afterwards.

[2] For Sir Colin's schemes to gain glory for the Highlanders in India, see Wolseley, i. 308, 309, 315.

1855. Divisions.   And here a second blunder was committed, for each of these several groups was composed in equal numbers of the Second and Light Divisions; and more than this, in each division no fewer than five different units were employed to make up the fourteen hundred men who were to go forward in advance of the supports.   The stormers were therefore bound to lack cohesion.   The crowning mistake of all was that the British engineers, untaught by the experience of the 18th of June, made no wide way through their trenches for a rapid advance of the assaulting parties and of their supports on a broad front, thereby compelling all the troops to crawl in single file through miles of narrow trenches to the attack.

Sept. 5.   On the 5th of September the final bombardment was opened and continued, with terrible loss to the Sept. 8. garrison, until the 8th; but on that morning the Russian defences were all manned, the guns loaded with case-shot, and the reserves drawn up close at hand. Upon the stroke of noon the French storming parties flew at the Malakoff and drove out the Russian working-parties and gunners; the supports followed at once; and after very sharp fighting the Malakoff was captured. Simultaneously another French brigade seized the curtain to the north of it, and the Little Redan; and Pélissier thereupon gave the signal for Simpson to fall upon the Great Redan.

Part of the covering and ladder-parties and the whole of the storming party, in all about twelve hundred men, were crammed into a trench only nine hundred yards long.   The Light Division led the way, and it should seem that the storming party of the Nineteenth and Ninety-seventh, mistaking a cautionary word for the order to advance, sprang over the parapet before the ladder-parties, and rushed straight at the apex of the salient of the Redan.   They were received with heavy and destructive flanking fire from the Barrack battery; but the abatis had been so shattered by shell-fire that it presented no obstacle, and the slope of the

Redan had been so ruined that many men passed over
it without the help of ladders. The Russians, in small
force and taken by surprise, gave way at once; but the
greater number of the stormers never entered the work
at all, in spite of the efforts of their officers, preferring
to lie down behind the parapet and open fire. Those
actually within the Redan—not more than one hundred
—only filled the salient as far as the third or fourth gun
upon either face, and the Russians, recovering from
their panic and strengthened by reinforcements, took post
behind a breastwork in rear of the Redan and poured in
a hot fire. More than one attempt was made to charge
them, but the British leaders, both officers and men,
were at once shot down; and the desultory combat continued. Then the British supports ran across the open
in a solid column without flinching; but once again
most of the men dropped down behind the shelter of
the parapet to shoot, and would go no further, though
the fire from the guns flanking the Redan swept them
down by scores. General Windham, who was in command, sent three messengers to beg for reinforcements,
and since they were all killed, took the fatal step of going
back himself. There was, therefore, no directing head;
the various units were all mixed up; men did not know
their officers, nor officers their men; and no effort was
made by the stormers to establish themselves upon the
ground that they held. After a time five companies of
the Twenty-third, under Colonel Lysons, advanced in
line against the southern face of the Redan, so as to
avoid the crowd clustered round the salient. They
were riddled with fire from the front and both flanks,
but managed to reach the ditch, where Lysons was
badly wounded. Meanwhile the Russians, after the
British had been in the Redan about an hour, counter-
attacked in great force and charged with the bayonet.
Thereupon the British gave way in panic, and rushed
back, carrying their officers with them, while the
Russians showered hand-grenades and other missiles
upon the struggling crowd in the ditch until it was

1855.   choked with dead and wounded.   The assault, in plain
Sept. 8.   words, was repulsed with disaster and disgrace.
It is fair to add that the French, after hard fighting,
were beaten out of the Little Redan, and that every
one of their assaults upon the southern front likewise
failed.   In fact they could only hold the Malakoff
because it was a closed work; but in spite of heavy
losses, no effort of the Russians could drive them from
it.   Not until three o'clock in the afternoon were the
French finally left in possession, even then not without
prospect of being blown into the air by mines.   But
General Macmahon, whose division had carried the
Malakoff, was not in the least dismayed.   "If your
brigade is blown up," he said to General Vinoy,
" General Decaen's will replace you immediately."
Pélissier's subordinates were as resolute as himself that
there should be no second failure.   By good fortune
the wires leading to the mines were discovered, and the
Malakoff was held without further mishap.
For some weeks past it had been noticed that the
Russians had been constructing a bridge of rafts across
the harbour, and there had been much speculation as to
the tactical purpose for which it was intended.   On the
evening of the 8th, Pélissier observed large numbers of
the enemy passing over this bridge and had his suspicions that they were abandoning Sevastopol; but, as
there was no certainty, no steps were taken.   All night
the besieging forces were kept awake by a series of ex-
plosions.   Fires, already kindled by the shells of the
Allies on the night of the 7th, increased and multiplied,
until the entire city with its suburbs was one sheet of
flame.   It had been intended to renew the assault on
the 9th with the Highland brigade; and the British
Sept. 9.   approaches were pushing forward, when at about two
in the morning an officer of engineers, observing an
unusual silence, crept across the ditch of the Redan and
found the work deserted. It was now clear that the enemy
was retreating northward under cover of darkness; but
pursuit was hopeless owing to the conflagration.   At

daybreak it was seen that the whole of the Russian 1855.
fleet, with the exception of one ship, had been sunk, Sept. 8.
and that the last columns of the garrison were forming
up on the north side of the harbour.   The city and its
fortifications were one heap of ruins.

The losses of the French in the final assault amounted
to close upon six thousand killed and wounded, of whom
four hundred were officers.   Five generals were killed,
four, including Bosquet, were wounded, and six more
received contusions, which is clear evidence, though
none is needed, of the freedom with which they exposed
themselves.   General Macmahon, who, as marshal, was
wounded at Sedan and lived to be President of the
French Republic, was one of the first to mount the
scarp of the Malakoff; and his division, four thousand
seven hundred strong, lost half of its numbers.   Altogether the capture and retention of the Malakoff was a
fine feat of arms.   It may be added that the column
which attacked the Central bastion on the south front
suffered little less than Macmahon's, one regiment
losing thirty officers out of forty-five in a vain attempt
to achieve the impossible.

The fallen of the British amounted to close upon
two thousand four hundred and fifty, of whom one
hundred and fifty-four, or nearly one-sixteenth, were
officers.   Many of these last were mere schoolboys who
had not been a month in the Crimea, but they did their
duty as British officers always do.   It was their misfortune that most of their men were raw recruits, some
of whom apparently knew not even how to fire their
rifles.   It is always a question, however, whether the
Redan, even if captured, could have been held.   One
officer of considerable experience reckoned that it
would have cost seven or eight thousand men; [1] and
Simpson had two more divisions ready to make a stout
fight for it, if necessary.   But when once the Malakoff
was taken, the capture of the Redan, or indeed of any
other part of the enceinte, became unnecessary; and

[1] Campbell, *Letters from Sevastopol*, p. 321.

it is probable that Pélissier intended the attacks upon all other points to be simply diversions, if not feints, to distract the Russian garrison to many spheres of defence. For this purpose the attack on the Redan was effective enough; and it is possible to say, after seventy years have passed, that the sacrifice of another five thousand casualties, merely to save a point of honour, would have been simple waste. Nevertheless, both the army and the country felt acute mortification at the repulse of the British assault. There could be no doubt but that the affair was mismanaged, yet there was also no question that the men hung back. Various theories were put forward to account for the unpleasant fact, among others the dread lest the Redan had been mined; but the simple truth is that old soldiers cannot be made in six months.

The losses of the Russians on the 8th of September were thirteen thousand killed, wounded and prisoners, in addition to seventeen thousand casualties suffered between the 17th of August and the 7th of September. Never did the Russian soldier show his heroic powers of endurance more nobly than during the siege of Sevastopol. In one hospital alone on the day after the fall of the place there were found two thousand wounded men, five hundred of them still alive, who had lain for seven days without human aid or even water. How many Russian lives the Crimean campaign cost altogether seems to be uncertain, but the Russians speak of one hundred thousand dead. Whole battalions are said to have perished marching down to that remote corner of the empire; and though the besiegers grew uneasy over their own casualties, these were as nothing compared with the havoc wrought among the besieged. The ordnance employed by the Allies was very different from that of the Peninsular war. The cannon ranged from twenty-four pounders to sixty-eight pounders, all firing common shell or shrapnel, and there were many mortars of thirteen-inch calibre in use. Lastly, the Lancaster guns, rifled pieces of oval bore,[1] threw with great accuracy (according to the standard of the time) at a range of a mile and a half a conical shell which was very destructive. Though the projectiles were only of cast iron and the explosive only black powder, the bombardment of Sevastopol must still have been a very hideous thing.

1855.

The hero of the siege—for so it is convenient to call it—was of course the Russian engineer Colonel Todleben; and his adversaries were the foremost to praise his industry, his skill and his devotion. At the same time it must be remembered that his resources both in men and material were practically unlimited, and that the garrison of Sevastopol was not the only enemy that the Allies had to meet, for there was the Russian field-army in their rear as well as Todleben in their front. Looked at in this light, the prolonged defence of Sevastopol wears another aspect; and it seems discreditable to the Russian arms that, having survived the winter, the fortress should have fallen at all. The Russians suffered much from fatigue and exposure, though naturally far less than the Allies, and particularly than the British, who lay unsheltered on the plateau. It is difficult to understand why the British were left practically unmolested by even comparatively small sorties during December 1854 and January 1855, for they could not, from sheer weakness, have made long resistance. The lesson of Inkerman seems to have sunk deep into the Russian mind. They ought on the 5th of November 1854 to have made an end of the Allies; but, though they failed, they need not therefore have forsworn all further effort. The patience and heroism of the garrison of Sevastopol does not alter the fact that the Allies, though divided in command and thereby hindered from taking advantage of many opportunities, did very much what they liked with the Russian armies and, except within the fortification of

[1] The Lancaster guns had no grooves, but the oval bore made one turn in 360 inches, giving some rotatory movement to the projectile, which was of course oval and of elongated type.

1855. Sevastopol, held them, not without reason, in contempt.

As to the actual conduct of the siege by the Allies, the question is so highly technical that a civilian cannot lightly venture on criticism. But there is a point made by an acting-engineer officer which seems worth notice. The Malakoff was comparatively early recognised for what it proved to be, the key of the defences of Sevastopol. If the bulk of the Allies' resources had been concentrated against that point, they could almost have blown it into the air. It would no doubt have been necessary for the Allies to entrench themselves strongly along the whole length of the eastern and southern fronts; but there was no occasion to fight a duel of artillery along a line of eight miles.[1] The probable explanation is that the French engineers were reluctant, not without reason, to commit themselves to operations remote from their marine base at Kamiesch Bay. Canrobert was most unwilling to take over any part of the trenches on the northern and eastern fronts; and indeed, if he had remained in command, Sevastopol would never have been captured. When Pélissier succeeded Canrobert he had to spend much of his time repelling suggestions from Paris that the Allies should turn their main efforts against the Russian field-army; and it was difficult for him to carry on the siege at all, to say nothing of upsetting all the previous dispositions of his engineers. Ultimately, after the lesson of the 18th of June, he did devote his own exertions mainly to the Malakoff, and with complete success.

It remains only to deal with the reproach repeatedly launched against the allied commanders by the minutest and most verbose of the historians of the campaign, namely, that by marching round to the south side of Sevastopol they left open to the garrison its main communications with Russia. But supposing that St. Arnaud and Raglan had taken post on the Mackenzie Heights, what was to be their marine base? Eupatoria

[1] Campbell, *Letters from Sevastopol*, p. 297.

was only an open roadstead, forty miles away, and there 1855.
were difficulties of water-supply in any advance from
thence, to say nothing of the danger of exposing the
flank of the line of communications to the enemy. The
historian does not himself answer this question, possibly
because it had never occurred to him. If he expected
the Allies to depend upon the open beaches where they
had landed, the storm of the 14th of November 1854 is
a sufficient answer to such an absurdity. He is vehement
as to the insufficiency of Balaclava as a maritime base,
and shows clearly the evils and dangers that arose from
it; but he appears to contemplate with equanimity the
situation of the Allies without any maritime base at all.
It is unnecessary to waste more words on the subject.

Meanwhile the Russians, after the evacuation of
Sevastopol, took post on the heights on the north side
of the harbour and there entrenched themselves. Then
the question arose what should be done next. Direct
attack upon the Russians in so strong a position would
have been costly and doubtful of success. But it was
always possible to move them by threatening their communications; and there was some discussion whether
this should be effected by an advance from the allied
right, that is to say, from the southern end of their line,
against the Russian left, or by transporting the whole of
the troops bodily by sea to Eupatoria and manœuvring
against the enemy from that point. In either case it was
not considered advisable to follow them beyond a line
drawn east and west from Eupatoria to Simpheropol.
Sir John Burgoyne represented that it would be better
to wait for the winter, not very far distant, when difficulties of supply would force the Russians to evacuate
the Crimea. Amid many conflicting views it seemed
safest to do nothing, except to occupy Sevastopol, which
was accordingly portioned out among the Allies for
defence. The place was in strictness untenable until
the Russians had been driven from the forts on the
north side of the harbour, which commanded the south
side and took all the defences, so long maintained by

1855. Todleben, in reverse. But this fact seemed to cause no great anxiety to either party. A few troops were despatched to Eupatoria to make reconnaissances in case anything should be attempted on that side. An expedition was sent by sea to Kinburn in Taurida; the troops including four thousand five hundred British in addition to a contingent of French under command of General Bazaine. The fleets arrived before Kinburn Sept. 14. on the 14th of September; the disembarkation followed on the 15th; and after a heavy bombardment by the ships the Russian garrison, fourteen hundred strong, surrendered. There was a little engagement at Kertch Sept. 22. on the 22nd, in which a few French and British cavalry beat off some Cossacks with trifling loss. Lastly, the Allies and Russians exchanged occasional shots across the harbour of Sevastopol with the object, apparently, of showing each other that they were still at war.

But all life had gone out of the contest. Omar was allowed to take his army to Asia Minor to save Kars, which he failed to do. The English, having by this time got their army to respectable strength and into respectable order, were disposed for more active operations; but the French hung back. They had not, like ourselves, interests in India which were threatened by Russia. The campaign had been undertaken by Napoleon the Third chiefly to establish his new dynasty upon a foundation of glory. That object had been obtained by the capture of the Malakoff and the fall of Sevastopol, for which the French army was entitled to claim the chief share of credit; and there seemed to be no object to France in continuing a war which had proved most costly both in money and in lives. After a few weeks of apathy the imminent approach of winter sufficed as an excuse for longer inaction. Various plans were discussed for ousting the Russian army from its strong position on the Mackenzie Heights, and reconnaissances were made to test the possibility of turning its left flank. In January 1856 a British officer was sent to the south-eastern shore of the Black Sea to report

as to places of disembarkation and roads in Asia Minor. 1856.
But meanwhile the diplomatists had been busy; and Jan. 16.
on the 16th of January 1856, Russia accepted the good
offices of Austria towards the conclusion of peace.

In truth the French army, which had at the outset
been so far superior in the organisation of its auxiliary
services to the British, began to drop behind it in the
autumn of 1855. There was a great deal of sickness
among the French soldiers. Cholera had returned in
April; there had been five thousand cases in June, and
there had been over three thousand deaths in the six
months from May to October. But apart from this
extraordinary scourge, scurvy was more prevalent than
it should have been. That it should have raged during
the early months of 1855 was, in the circumstances,
not very extraordinary; but the number of cases grew
from six hundred in June to twelve hundred in July
and twenty-six hundred in August; not falling below
seven hundred at any time during the winter. This
points to bad feeding, or bad dieting, or both; and it
seems that after the fall of Sevastopol the French had
considerable difficulty in supplying some of their outlying troops, which were manœuvring towards the left
flank of the Russians, though at no greater distance than
of forty miles from their maritime base at Kamiesch.[1]
English officers noticed that these men looked thin and
dejected, having apparently neither huts nor winter
clothing; and it seems certain that they were ill-pro-
vided with food and other comforts. In April 1856,
after the conclusion of peace, the Russian General
Luders reviewed the French army, and three English
officers were told off to reckon up its numbers. It was
known that the French had turned out every man that
they could, and yet not one of the three computed them
at over thirty thousand, though their effective strength
in the previous November had been over one hundred
and forty thousand, and there had been no fighting since.[2]

[1] Campbell, *Letters from Sevastopol*, p. 331.
[2] Campbell, p. 379; Wolseley, i. 213-14.

1856. It may be reckoned that on this occasion there were from five to ten thousand men fewer on parade than there should have been; and the principal cause was the prevalence of typhoid or typhoidal fever. The returns attribute no fewer than six thousand deaths to this cause alone; and the vast majority of them appear to have occurred subsequently to November 1855. It seems, therefore, fairly clear that a new campaign would have tried the French army very severely. It must be remembered that France had made no common effort. First and last she sent out to the east over three hundred thousand men;[1] and of these there were killed or died of wounds rather more than eleven thousand, while diseases, chiefly cholera and typhus, claimed twenty-one thousand, making a total of thirty-two thousand deaths in all. The English Sanitary Commissioners complained loudly of the foulness of the French camps which adjoined the British, and the French authorities, as was natural, repelled the insinuation with something of contempt.[2] But for some strange reason the Latin races appear always to be more careless of sanitary matters than the Teutonic; and the returns of mortality tend to confirm the judgement of the Sanitary Commissioners. The most significant, perhaps, of all the figures is that of over four thousand deaths in the French army during the evacuation of the Crimea alone. It is hardly surprising that France should have been eager to withdraw from the conflict.

During the winter of 1855–56 the British, on the contrary, we're healthy and comfortable. The country had poured out money like water; and the men were well clothed, well housed in huts, and well fed. There were still some difficulties. The new Land Transport Corps, when the bad weather began, showed signs of breaking down, having been hastily

---

[1] 309,268 is the figure, which, however, included invalids who had recovered and returned to the front.

[2] *Archives de la Guerre*, Extract. Palmerston to Clarendon, July 2; Vaillant to Pélissier, July 6; James Newland to Panmure, July 13, 23, 1855.

formed of indifferent men who knew nothing of horses, 1856. and of rather doubtful officers. Many of the latter were drawn from the Indian army and, carrying the habits of Indian life with them, were lazy, luxurious and inclined to alcohol.[1] The discipline of the Corps was consequently bad and its work was inefficient until Colonel Wetherall, one of Airey's best officers, took it vigorously in hand and by the spring of 1856 reduced it to good organisation and order. Another undisciplined body which gave much trouble was the so-called Army Works Corps, a gang of about two thousand navvies. This was a creation of Panmure's, who brimmed over with unthinking energy and was fertile in unpractical expedients. Raglan did not smile upon this particular child of Panmure, suggesting that the navvies would be difficult to manage, and that he would rather not have them. " Believe me you are wrong," wrote the enthusiastic minister, " and you will do yourself great injustice to refuse them. They will not disgrace you, and they will do all sorts of work in advance of the army. They carry with them artificers of all kinds and will run you up an encampment and build you huts on a line of march in no time. They will fight if you let them, and armed with pikes will defend a trench." It seems not to have occurred to Panmure that a body of unarmed men sent in advance of the army would require first to be protected and next to be fed; but he insisted upon sending them out and giving them very high wages. The result was that they were always drunk, insubordinate and mutinous, gave a great deal of trouble and after all were of very little use, while their presence was bad for discipline at large and excited natural discontent among the soldiers,

[1] Kinglake, among many other comments on the breakdown of the British Commissariat in the winter of 1854–55, condemns the neglect to profit by the excellence of the Commissariat in our Indian armies. Possibly he may have aired the opinion at home and so encouraged resort to India for transport-officers. In this case, as in many others, he did not know what he was talking about. See the opinion of Lord Napier of Magdala on the Indian system of transport, *post*, p. 452.

1856. who did far more work, were punished for drunkenness, and received much lower pay. It is rather significant that the soldier at this very time received an additional field-allowance of sixpence a day; and altogether this crotchet of Panmure must have cost the country considerable sums which were absolutely wasted.[1]

Nevertheless, in spite of such drawbacks, the army improved steadily during the winter, and by the spring of 1856 was a really fine body of sixty thousand fighting men.[2]   In November 1855 Simpson, having

[1] *Raglan MSS.*, Panmure to Raglan, May 25, June 1; Raglan to Panmure, June 23, 1855; Campbell, *Letters from Sevastopol*, p. 376. I remember a past member of this " Army Works Corps " at Harrow in the eighteen-seventies—one of those " cads " who hang about public schools and are a thorn in the side of masters.   Physically he was the finest animal that I ever saw, and his muscular strength was so great that, when he chose to work (which was rarely), he could earn very high wages, and when he got drunk (which was frequently) needed four policemen to tackle him.   Had he been a man he might have died wealthy, but he was no more than a brute.

[2] I may give its final composition in tabular form.

CAVALRY DIVISION:
    1*st Brigade*: 1, 4, 5 D.G., 1, 2, 6 D.
    2*nd*   „   6 D.G., 4th L.D., 12 Lrs., 13th L.D.
    3*rd*   „   8, 10, 11 Hrs., 17th Lrs.
1ST INFANTRY DIVISION:
    1*st Brigade*: 3/G. Gds., 1/C. Gds., 1/S.F. Gds.
    2*nd*   „   9th, 13th, 31st, 56th.
2ND INFANTRY DIVISION:
    1*st Brigade*: 3rd, 30th, 55th, 95th.
    2*nd*   „   41st, 47th, 49th, 62nd, 82nd.
3RD INFANTRY DIVISION:
    1*st Brigade*: 4th, 14th, 39th, 50th, 89th.
    2*nd*   „   18th, 28th, 38th, 44th.
4TH INFANTRY DIVISION:
    1*st Brigade*: 17th, 20th, 21st, 57th, 63rd.
    2*nd*   „   46th, 48th, 68th, 1/R.B.
HIGHLAND DIVISION:
    1*st Brigade*: 42nd, 79th, 92nd, 93rd.
    2*nd*   „   1 and 2/1st, 71st, 72nd.
LIGHT DIVISION:
    1*st Brigade*: 7th, 23rd, 33rd, 34th, 2/R.B.
    2*nd*   „   19th, 77th, 88th, 90th, 97th.
    120 guns.

resigned the chief command, made way for Sir William 1856.
Codrington, with General Windham as chief of his
staff, and with a very capable body of divisional
generals. Latterly a better class of recruit had come
in, and the ranks were filled not with boys but with
men. Nearly seventy thousand recruits were enlisted
between January 1854 and March 1856, of which
nearly half were volunteers from the militia. But the
numbers were far short of the establishment voted by
Parliament—in March 1855 actually forty thousand
men short—and thereupon the Government decided to
raise a foreign legion of Swiss, Germans and Italians.
Recruiting for the first two began in May 1855, and
by the 31st of March close upon ten thousand men
had been engaged, of whom nearly four thousand
were actually sent to the east. Another recruiting
centre was opened in Turin, and by March 1856 three
thousand men had been raised and dispatched thence
to Malta. Yet another recruiting depôt was formed
at Niagara, and a certain number of Americans were
enlisted there. Lastly, twenty thousand Turkish
troops were taken into British pay, so that Codrington
had under his command in the spring of 1856 not far
short of ninety thousand men, while a reserve force of
eighteen thousand more had been collected at Aldershot.
The infantry also were armed with a new rifle, an
improvement on the Minié, called the Enfield rifle, so
that altogether after nineteen months of campaigning
the British had at last a really formidable force in
the field.

Unfortunately they were too late. The Austrian
mediation presently produced a Congress of the Great
Powers in Paris. On the 29th of February 1856, an
armistice brought even the semblance of hostilities to
an end, and on the 30th of March a definite treaty of Mar. 30.
peace was signed. Under a special article the Black
Sea was neutralised; "its waters and ports were formally interdicted to the flag of war"; the maintenance of
naval arsenals on its shores was forbidden, and ships of

1856. war were denied entrance into or passage through the Bosporus and the Dardanelles. Within three years, Austria and France being at war, Russia violated the treaty and, by blockading the Circassian coast, overcame the resistance of the tribes which had long impeded her progress eastward in Central Asia. In 1871 again, France and Germany being at war, she repudiated the article altogether; and thus all the results of the Crimean War to England were finally cancelled.

In truth the entire episode was far from flattering to us as a nation. Many years later an English Prime Minister declared openly that England in 1854 had followed a false policy in making war upon Russia. She had, as he phrased it, "put her money on the wrong horse." Ministers are not infallible, and indulgence should be extended to their mistakes. But the Crimean War was brought about less through active and consistent decision than through helplessness, improvidence and irresolution, and these are failings which are not so easily forgiven. As to the absurdity of the plan of campaign, the utter ignorance on the part of ministers of the nature and conduct of war, their panic fear of the Press and their consequent disloyalty to their generals, there is no need to say more. Their conduct was most discreditable to them alike as administrators and as the leaders to whom the public at large naturally look for guidance. The Press was undoubtedly more powerful in those days than in these, when the writers for it are so numerous that sheer sense of the ridiculous forbids them to claim infallibility. But a strong minister could, without alienating the Press, still have kept the supreme direction of public opinion in his own hands and inclined it towards calmness and sobriety. A nation, not less surely than a team of horses, instantly detects a weak hand upon the reins and becomes restless and ungovernable.

The false judgement of the ministry upon the whole situation was speedily revealed after the first clash of arms. The poor flow of recruits showed plainly

enough that the nation's heart was not in the war. 1856.
There was much foolish hysteria among the public
during the South African War of 1899–1902, and there
were many childish manifestations in London which it
is difficult to recall without shame.   Still, when matters
went wrong, recruits did at least turn out in tens of
thousands and set them right.   It was not so in the
years of the Crimean War.   After the stirring news of
Inkerman the monthly influx of recruits was for three
months doubled in volume, after which it rapidly sub-
sided.   There was no national interest in the struggle;
and ministers actually resorted to the condemned
methods of the eighteenth century, the levying of
mercenaries, to do the work which Englishmen should
have done for themselves.   Happily none of these
ever went into action, and many of the Germans were
turned to good account by the grant of lands to them
in South Africa, where they made excellent colonists.
But the bare fact that they were enlisted at all is a
reproach, if not a disgrace.

From a purely military standpoint, the division of
supreme command makes it extremely difficult to pass
any judgement upon the operations.   A difficulty which
even Marlborough could not wholly overcome may
well have been too great for lesser men.   But, passing
from the supreme to the subordinate commands, it
does not appear that officers had learned many useful
lessons from their previous campaigns in India or at
the Cape.   The circumstances were of course widely
different, but Pennefather, who had served under
Charles Napier in Sind, and Eyre, who had done
well under Harry Smith in South Africa, showed no
great intelligence, though boundless courage, before
Sevastopol.   Nor do the officers in command of battalions, as a rule, appear to have risen to the occasion.
The engineers made constant and just complaint of the
apathy and carelessness of the regimental officers in
charge of working parties; and this would not have
occurred had the commanding officers been imbued

1856. with the right spirit. It has always been difficult to induce the British soldier to dig, though he will do it for the right officers. On the whole, the campaign was profitable, perhaps, chiefly to intelligent young subalterns who, like Arthur Wellesley in Flanders in 1794, learned much of the way in which things should not be done. Two of these, Garnet Wolseley, the young acting-engineer of the Ninetieth, and Evelyn Wood, the midshipman, brought back from Sebastopol wounds from which they suffered to the end of their days, but lived to do great and lasting good work for the Army.

For the rest the Crimea is interesting as the last appearance of the old long-service soldier in the face of an European enemy. Never did he show himself greater than on the field of Inkerman, when he stood up for hours against odds of five to one, or on the bleak plateau above Sevastopol when he withstood cold and famine until death struck him off the roll of duty, patient and uncomplaining to the last. In any serious war it is always the fate of the existing British army to be destroyed within three months, but none has perished more tragically than this. The long-service soldier was by repute almost outside the pale of civilised society. So little was his real character known that it was a surprise to Miss Nightingale and her nurses to discover that, after all, he was a kindly creature, quickly responsive to gentle handling. The British nation had for generations treated him as an outcast, and done its utmost to make him all that they considered him to be. Yet they despised him chiefly because he was a disciplined man. The discipline of that day was certainly stern;[1]

---

[1] I give an instance, told to me by Major-General Sir Geoffrey Feilding, and by him derived from his father, who was a Coldstreamer and a general before him, and served with distinction in the Crimea. A private in the Coldstream Guards suffered from a physical infirmity which was interpreted as a symptom of fear on the prospect of action. His comrades made his life such a burden that he determined to justify himself. By chance his battalion occupied one of the advanced trenches before the Redan on the eve of the 8th of September. When it was

and yet soldiers brought up under that discipline were the model for the constabulary of the whole empire. Nevertheless, through sheer ignorance the public of that day preferred the navvy, who was quite as rough and quite as drunken, simply because he had not, to his great misfortune, been taught to obey.

We have yet to follow the long-service soldier through a few campaigns before he disappears, but the passing bell for him and for much more in the British Army began to sound in the Crimean War. This campaign taught the nation the urgent need for parting with the ways and the traditions that had governed the army with little essential change for two hundred years; and so far it did great good. Yet it is remembered, perhaps, chiefly for three things. The first is that for the first time in the history of war the surgeon's knife was disarmed of half of its terrors by the use of the anæsthetic, chloroform. The second is that reform of hospitals and of the nursing system, already mentioned, which is eternally associated with the name of Florence Nightingale. This was a great work, and has given rise to the legend that all nurses are angels, which is as true or as false as that all soldiers are heroes.[1]

The third is the institution by Queen Victoria of the Victoria Cross. Medals were becoming so common that they had ceased to be distinctive. Even the Order of the Bath had been scattered so widely as to fall into disesteem; so that there was room for a decoration which should really mean that a man had outdone his fellows in daring service. Nevertheless the older

---

withdrawn he secreted himself, joined the storming party next day, and was the first man inside the Redan. Escaping unhurt, he was tried by court-martial for desertion and found guilty, but was pardoned by the Commander-in-Chief and selected as a recipient of a present of clothing sent out by the Queen herself.

[1] See Evelyn Wood's account of two brutal female nurses in the Crimean hospitals, *From Midshipman to Field-Marshal*, i. 308.

1856. officers did not smile upon it. They remembered the days when Englishmen were content to do their duty without hope of outward adornment to their garments; and they recalled with pride Talleyrand's comment when Castlereagh alone of the plenipotentiaries at a congress of all Europe had appeared in a coat unsullied by cordon, star or badge—*Ma foi! c'est tres distingué.* A red ribbon for a few of the most eminent and a blue ribbon for the very highest were the utmost to which any aspired. Charles Stuart took the offer of the knighthood of the Bath as an insult and could hardly be persuaded to accept it. Wellington wished to throw it off when he received the Garter, on the ground that the Sovereign alone could belong to more than one Order. Still, Queen Victoria persevered with impatient eagerness, as her letters show, in the establishment of her new decoration, and the first distribution of it took place on the 26th of June 1857. The material, bronze, was wisely chosen as being of no intrinsic value, and the design was very simple—a Maltese cross, with the Royal crest superimposed, hung from a bar by a link shaped as the letter "V,"[1] with the inscription, "For Valour." Old officers continued to sneer at it, telling how men in the ranks, when directed to select one of their comrades for the honour of the Victoria Cross, by no means made valour the ground for their choice. Nor is there the slightest doubt that they spoke the truth.[2] It is, however, long since the Victoria Cross was thus misbestowed. Many a man has earned it who for want of witnesses has never received it; and men have received it in one campaign for deeds that would have passed unnoticed in another and greater. Such accidents are inevitable; but none the less a man who wears the Victoria Cross is now justly sure of the respect

---

[1] The " V " was an afterthought and does not appear in the first cross submitted to the Queen for approval. This cross, when last I saw it, was in the Royal Library at Windsor Castle.

[2] Evelyn Wood, *The Crimea in 1854 and 1894*, pp. 359-360. I could myself mention another parallel instance.

and admiration of his fellows; and the decoration is 1856. perhaps the most coveted in the world.[1]

[1] The holders of the Maria Theresa order—the corresponding order to the Victoria Cross in Austria—have (or had) a chapel where their crosses are (or were) hung up after their death with their names and the dates inscribed alongside it. It is a pity that no such regulation was laid down for the Victoria Cross, for it is not a pretty sight to see one (as I have seen myself) hung up in a pawn-shop. Collectors now acquire them; and many crosses happily find their way back to the holder's regiment.

Authorities: The principal printed authorities for the Crimean War are Kinglake's *Invasion of the Crimea*, the French history by Bazancourt, and Todleben's *Défense de Sebastopol* (St. Petersburg, 1863–70). Kinglake's work, insufferably wordy, prolix and ill arranged —journalism, not history—is not the less valuable, since it is based mainly on Raglan's papers. These papers have been carefully perused independently of Kinglake, as have also the French records of the campaign in the Archives de la Guerre at Paris. Of minor works Hamley's *Campaign of Sebastopol*, Wolseley's *Story of a Soldier's Life*, Wood's *Crimea in 1854 and 1894* and Campbell's *Letters from Sevastopol* are the most valuable. Hamilton's *History of the Grenadier Guards* and Ross's *History of the Coldstream Guards* are the best regimental histories of the campaign.

CHAPTER XLVIII

1856. THE last of the troops had not long left the Crimea before England found herself involved in a quarrel with Persia. Relations between the two countries had, as we have seen, been seriously strained upon the Persian siege of Herat in 1838; but friendship had been restored to remain unbroken until 1851, when Persia again threatened to occupy that city. The British resident at Tehran protested strongly but in vain; and in the spring of 1852 a Persian force invaded and occupied Herat, formally annexing it in October. In January 1853, in consequence of the representations of the British, Persia agreed to withdraw her troops and not again to interfere with Herat unless it were threatened from Afghanistan; but new difficulties soon arose owing to the arrogance and trickiness of the Persian government, and the dispute culminated in the withdrawal of the British mission from Tehran in December 1855. In that same month a second Persian expedition threatened to advance upon Herat. The scene of negotiation was now transferred to Constantinople; but little progress was made; and in July 1856 the British Foreign Office ordered the Governor-general of India to prepare an adequate force for the occupation of the island of Kharak and of the city and district of Bushire in the Persian Gulf. Instructions followed at the end of September for this force to proceed to its destination, and on the 1st of November the government of India definitely declared war against Persia.

Accordingly on the 29th of November a British naval 1856.
squadron bombarded and captured Bushire, which was
occupied by a force of about four thousand men,[1] under
Major-general Stalker. In January 1857 a second 1857.
division of about the same strength was dispatched
from Bombay with Major-general Sir James Outram
as Commander-in-Chief.[2] By the 1st of February all Feb. 1.
had been disembarked at Bushire. No enemy was in
the vicinity, but the Persians were reported to be entrenched in force at Brazjun, nearly fifty-five miles
distant, and on the night of the 3rd Outram marched Feb. 3.
out to attack them. By one o'clock on the afternoon
of the 5th he was before Brazjun, which, however, the Feb. 5.
enemy abandoned almost without firing a shot, leaving
large quantities of grain and vast stores of ammunition
behind them. These last were destroyed; the grain
was brought away on captured horses; and after two
days' halt Outram, on the evening of the 7th, started Feb. 7.
on his return march. At midnight his column was
suddenly surrounded by a wild mob of galloping horsemen, shouting, trumpeting, firing and making a great
deal of noise but doing very little damage. The
column halted with perfect coolness and order. The
enemy brought up guns, and the action resolved itself
into a duel of artillery, which lasted till daylight and
caused a few casualties.

Dawn revealed the Persians drawn up in line, about Feb. 8.
eight thousand foot and three thousand horse, with
their right resting on the village of Kush-ab, and their

---

[1] FIRST DIVISION :
   Cavalry: 3rd Bombay L.C., Poona Irreg. Horse.
   Infantry: 1*st Brigade*, 64th Foot; 20th Bombay N.I.
        2*nd* „   103rd Foot; 4th Bombay Rifles N.I.;
                  2nd Baluchi Battn.

[2] SECOND DIVISION:
   Cavalry: 14th L.D., Jacob's Irreg. (Sind) Horse.
   Artillery: 1 Horse battery, 2 Field-batteries.
   Infantry: 1*st Brigade*, 78th Highlanders; 26th Bombay N.I.
        2*nd* „   23rd N.I.; Light Battn. (10 light
                  cos. N.I.).

1856. left on a group of houses and a native fort.   Outram
Feb. 8. marched straight at them, with four battalions in first
and three in second line.   His guns soon reduced those
of the enemy nearly to silence, and his cavalry by a
sweeping charge drove the Persian horse from the
ground.   Then the Persian infantry wavered and broke.
Two or three regular battalions on their extreme right
showed some steadiness, and through one of them the
3rd Light Cavalry charged headlong, rallied, and
charged back again.   The rout was complete, and the
chase was pressed by the cavalry till the troopers were
weary of hewing.   Over seven hundred of the enemy
lay dead on the field, besides those slain in the pursuit,
whereas Outram's casualties did not exceed eighty-
three killed and wounded.   Heavy rain delayed the
return of the troops to Bushire until the night of the
Feb. 9. 9th, when they tramped into camp exhausted but happy.
On the march out they had traversed forty-four miles
in forty-one hours, and the same distance back in thirty
hours, a good performance for men of whom many
had not been long released from the cramping life on
a transport.

Outram then employed his men in strengthening
his entrenched camp outside Bushire; and meanwhile
reinforcements arrived in the shape of the 23rd Bombay
Native Light Infantry, additional light companies, some
mountain-guns and another horse-battery.   On the
Feb. 22. 22nd distant fires again indicated the presence of the
enemy, but patrols failed to discover his outposts.   On
Mar. 6. the 6th of March, Outram, leaving three thousand men
under Stalker to hold Bushire, embarked the remainder,
about four thousand strong, for the delta of the
Mar. 16. Euphrates.   By the 16th the transports were at anchor
in Shat-el-Arab.   A week was spent in preparing rafts
Mar. 24. for a disembarkation, and on the 24th the ships moved
up the river towards the enemy's batteries on the eastern
bank, at the junction of the Karun with the Euphrates.
These batteries, after three hours' cannonade by the
Mar. 26. squadron, were silenced on the 26th, and the first troops,

being landed with practically no molestation, advanced 1856. immediately against large masses of the enemy which were drawn up near the town of Mohumra.   At the first fire of the British guns the enemy fled precipitately, and Outram, finding that it was hopeless to try to overtake them, returned to Mohumra.   The casualties of the squadron in the action did not exceed forty.

The main body of the Persians having retreated to Akwaz, a hundred miles up the Karun, Outram, after landing supplies and stores, sent three hundred men of the Sixty-fourth and Seventy-eighth up the river in three steamers on the 29th.   On the 1st of April these April 1. came before Akwaz, which stands on the left bank of the river, and the enemy was seen in force upon the right bank.   The troops were therefore landed on the left bank, while the steamers opened fire upon the defences of the town, which was surrendered without resistance.   Thereupon the Persian forces, from nine to ten thousand strong, retreated up the river, leaving quantities of ammunition and huge stores of grain behind them.   The British detachment returned on the 4th to Mohumra; and shortly afterwards came the news April 4. that peace with Persia had been signed at Paris on the 4th of March, Persia surrendering all claims to Herat and binding herself not to interfere in the internal affairs of Afghanistan.   On the 15th of May the troops May 15. re-embarked at Mohumra for India, where, as shall presently be told, bad news and stern work awaited Outram, Havelock, who was one of his brigadiers, and the three English battalions.

By a singular chance yet another little war was awaiting the army as soon as it should be free from the entanglements of the Crimea.   China, untaught by the lesson of 1842, still declined to recognise England on a basis of national equality, and all who knew anything of the country averred that the trouble could only be settled by another war.   An attack upon the British ship *Arrow* in October 1856 brought matters to a crisis, and the British government determined to send

1856. Lord Elgin on a special mission to Peking and to strengthen his hands by reinforcing the naval force in Chinese waters and sending several battalions to Hongkong. The murder of a French missionary gave France a pretext for continuing the alliance already begun in the Crimea, and the two countries resolved to act together. But the troops from England were deflected from their destination by the sudden outbreak of military mutiny in India.

Allusion has been made in more than one of the foregoing chapters to the steady decline of discipline in the Bengal army. The causes that contributed to this result were many; and the evil system which tempted the best British officers to exchange a military for a political career has been recorded as one of them. Another was the growing centralisation of military authority at headquarters, which weakened the powers of commanding officers for reward and punishment, and deprived them of their old status as kings and fathers of their regiments. But this was perhaps inevitable, unless the Indian army were to be, like the British, a mere collection of small semi-independent corps. Petty parsimony on the part of the supreme government in the matter of allowances to sepoys provoked a number of small mutinies in 1843 and 1844; and the same cause, amounting to positive injustice, brought a number of Bengal regiments to the verge of revolt in 1849, when Sir Charles Napier disbanded one insubordinate regiment on the one hand, and redressed the grievance on the other by conceding, on his own authority, the pecuniary allowances which the sepoys demanded. For this exercise of authority he was publicly reprimanded by Lord Dalhousie. Napier thereupon resigned; and the sepoys thus saw the chief, who had observed equity on their behalf, rewarded by public disgrace. Dalhousie was certainly a strong man, but he was not always a wise one, and he evidently had very little conception of discipline beyond obedience to his own decrees.

Beyond all these minor though very serious troubles, 1856. the discipline of the Bengal army had been under- mined by the practice, long established, of enlisting by preference men of high caste.   Under this system a native captain, when off parade, was often to be seen cowering abjectly before the Brahmin recruit who was supposed to be under his command; and it was in- conceivable that their relative positions could be really reversed by the mere delegation to the captain of military authority.   In Bombay and Madras there was no such truckling to the prejudices of caste; and indeed, when British officers had the courage to defy them, they were not obtruded even in Bengal.   But military and civil opinion alike differed very greatly upon these and, indeed, many other points of discipline; and it was not easy for a Governor-general, fresh from England, to decide between them.   What was needed was a man of transcendent common sense, whose insight could pierce to the core of the matter, through all the husks of wordy controversy, and who should possess resolution to act firmly in the light of his vision.   In brief, an Arthur Wellesley was wanted, and there was no one better to hand than a Dalhousie.

Apart from military discontent there was also civil unrest in many quarters; nor is this surprising when account is taken of the vast extension of the Indian Empire in the half-century following the year 1803. This had been the outcome, not of rapacity, but of the experience forced upon all imperial nations, that order cannot exist side by side with anarchy.   Dalhousie, as it chanced, had to decide in several important cases how anarchy was not only to be ended for the time but exterminated for ever; and he solved the problem by the annexation of sundry minor principalities, which had lapsed in default of heirs, of the Punjab, which had been reduced to chaos by the Sikh Khalsa, and finally of Oudh, which was a sink of misgovernment and oppression.   His aim was to clear away every relic of what he conceived—and often rightly conceived—to

1856. be Oriental barbarism, and to rear up in its stead a stabler building on the basis of Western civilisation. He declared it with frankness and set about it with courage; but he did not realise that his intentions, however excellent and honourable, might be misconstrued, and that the foundations of a new civilisation are generally laid in blood.

He was, perhaps, unfortunate in the period of his lifetime, when there were much talk of the greatest happiness of the greatest number, a strong idea that happiness consists principally in material prosperity, and a firm faith that men require only liberty and education—to which some added Christianity—in order to make them good. We have seen how aspirations after the fulfilment of this ideal wrought upon even such able and accomplished men as Macnaghten and some of his subordinates, when they conjured up visions of a Central Asia governed by the wisdom and integrity of British administrators. In the light of all that has happened in the past seventy years, and of the many disillusions which they have brought with them, the dreams of that time seem somewhat pitiful; yet they must not be lightly sneered away. Enthusiasm is better for men than cynical indifference or apathetic despair. All alike tend in the first instance towards the same immediate though undesired end—bloodshed; but enthusiasm at least cannot be sterile and may be fruitful, at any rate for a time, of good.

It was, as must inevitably happen, in the first details of his reforms that Dalhousie and his subordinates went wrong. They were bound to deal with the very thorny problem of land-tenure and land-ownership, which had not been very happily handled in the north-west provinces by their predecessors between 1833 and 1842. It was not more felicitously treated in Oudh, and the mistake made in both cases seems to have been the same. It was assumed that the occupants of the soil, whatever their tenure, must always be protected, and that the territorial aristocracy, no matter what its precise status, must be hounded out as op- 1856. pressors. No doubt it was the peasant who most sorely needed protection; but the aristocracy could also claim certain rights which should not have been ignored. There seems here to have been an echo of the wild denunciations of the English landlords by the agitators of what was called the Manchester school. But there were a few men in India who thought for themselves, who were possessed of a little imagination, and who doubted alike the wisdom and the justice of humbling the aristocracy so roughly. Outram had quarrelled bitterly with Charles Napier because, while fully aware of all their shortcomings, he had stood up as champion of the Amirs of Sind. So too Henry Lawrence was the zealous advocate, even against his brother John, of the Sikh Sirdars, pleading the inexpediency of abasing them unduly, no matter what their past crimes. But imagination seems not to have been Dalhousie's strong point. He forgot that even in rural England the country squire, whose ancestors had lived in his manor house for generations, commanded, however backward and narrow-minded, a respect and attachment from his humbler neighbours which was denied to the rich manufacturer who bought him out. He did not realise that though he might ruin the territorial aristocracy in parts of India, he could not prevent the peasant from looking up to him as formerly; and that by alienating the aristocrat he alienated also the worker on the soil.

To south of the Ganges also, in Bundelkhand, arbitrary interference with native land-laws and land-customs had caused deep discontent; and Dalhousie had made for himself also two dangerous personal enemies. The last of the Peshwas, old Baji Rao, had been relegated after the Pindari war to ceremonious obscurity at Bithur, close to Cawnpore. He had adopted as his heir Dhundu Pant, and prayed that his own pension might be continued to him. After his death in 1851, Dhundu Pant, better known as Nana

1856. Sahib, preferred the same petition on his own account and was seconded by two British Commissioners on the spot. Dalhousie, however, rudely rejected the request, and the Directors of the East India Company, being appealed to, confirmed the rejection with equal discourtesy. Nana Sahib submitted with outward patience, but inwardly with rage and bitterness sought opportunity for revenge. Again, the Rani of Jhansi, a princess of great ability and influence, had lost her husband in 1854. Being childless, she claimed her right, under Hindu law, to adopt an heir. Dalhousie denied her this right, and declared that Jhansi had lapsed to the paramount power. The rulers of Jhansi had in the past done good service to the British at critical times, and of this the Rani reminded Dalhousie, but to no purpose. He was determined to make her subjects happy in his own way, with the result that he turned them into violent enemies, and the Rani herself not merely into an enemy but into a fury.

To these foes, thus unnecessarily made, there was added inevitably the Brahmin priesthood, which saw its power threatened by Dalhousie's measures for introducing Western civilisation, and not least by his project for the education of Indian women. Finally, the very establishment of law and order tended of itself to provoke discontent in many quarters. The peasant, it is true, could reap where he had sown, but he did not greatly trouble himself to ask how this happy circumstance had come about nor to whom he owed it. India, even before the decay of the Mogul dynasty, had been a paradise for adventurers; and now there was no longer an opening for a daring, reckless leader and for the swarms of the idle, dissolute and worthless who would cheerfully have joined him in the plunder of any unwary neighbour. In the course of a century—no more—a handful of strangers from Europe had imposed their will upon hundreds of millions by sheer fighting power. For long they had seemed invincible, but they had been worsted by the Afghans. They were there-

fore after all but men and, except in the estimation 1856.
of perhaps one native of India in half a million, only
a handful of men. In the late war with Russia the
British government had been unable to carry on the
contest without drawing regiments from India, so that
its power was evidently limited. There was no want
of combustible material should the fire be kindled.

In the face of these dangers, clearly perceived by a
few but ignored by the many, the number of the British
troops was small and their distribution to the last degree
faulty. In all there were some thirty-six thousand
British soldiers scattered over the vast territory of the
Indian Empire from the Indus to the Irrawaddy. The
cavalry comprised two Queen's and three Company's
regiments, the infantry twenty Queen's and nine
Company's battalions, and the artillery was all of the
Company's service. Of the twenty-nine battalions
three were for the moment in Persia with Outram;
one, the Eighty-sixth, had a wing at Aden; twelve
were in the Punjab, and three were in Burma; leaving
little more than ten battalions to look to the rest of
India. On the immense line of communication between Calcutta and Peshawar the first British troops
to be found were a single battalion at Dinapore, two
hundred miles up the Ganges from its mouth. Following up the river, there were none at Benares, none at
Mirzapore, and actually none at Allahabad—the point
of confluence between the Jumna and the Ganges, the
key of the north-western provinces, and a great arsenal.
Ascending the Jumna, there were only a depôt of infantry and a weak reserve company of artillery at Cawnpore, one weak battalion at Agra and actually none
at Delhi, the strategic point between mountains and
desert, near which most of the decisive battles of India
had been fought. Delhi's importance was so far recognised that it held an immense magazine, yet it had
no British troops to guard it. Turning north-eastward
from Allahabad towards Oudh, there was no British
garrison at Fyzabad, none at Bareilly, only a single

1856. weak battalion at Lucknow, and no semblance of a force of all three arms until at Meerut, forty miles north of Delhi, there were to be found a regiment of cavalry—the Carabiniers—the first battalion of the Sixtieth, two batteries and a company of artillery, all of them British. It was very obvious that, in case of any rising, the overwhelming of the little body at Meerut would signify the loss of Delhi, the isolation of the petty garrisons at Agra, Cawnpore and Lucknow, and the severance of all communication between the capital and the Punjab.

It was not less evident that, should such an insurrection at the outset meet with some success, only the troops in the Punjab would be at hand to deal with it, if—and the condition was extremely doubtful—they could be spared for the purpose. Happily the administration of the Punjab since the annexation had been such that an Englishman can always recall it with pride. The wreck of Ranjit Singh's dynasty and the crushing of the Khalsa had left behind them chaos indeed for the moment, but such chaos as yielded a plastic surface for British order to imprint its mark upon. A body of picked officers under the guidance, mainly, of the two Lawrences, John and Henry, took the work in hand, and by timely severity, unwearied industry and sheer force of character, not only calmed the unruly elements but attached the Sikhs firmly to their rule. The warriors who had fought so hard against us took service with the conquerors and were formed into regiments, which were to prove themselves great and faithful fighters. Still, this British domination was as yet barely seven years old, and it was impossible to divine how far the Sikh allegiance could be reckoned upon in the event of a great disaster, and whether it would be safe to withdraw the British troops. Even at best these were considerably dispersed. The line from Peshawar through Lahore to Ambala—north-west to south-east —measures four hundred miles as the crow flies, while that from Sialkot south-eastward to Multan is three hundred miles; and fifteen thousand men were not 1856. many to secure so large an area. Moreover, though the men in charge of the Punjab could certainly not be described as fools, they none the less kept not a single British soldier in the large and important magazines of Phillaur and Ferozepore.

It must be said for Dalhousie that he protested vigorously against the removal of any of his British troops either for the Crimean or the Persian war, and represented with all possible earnestness the need for increase of the British garrison in India. He had himself watched, not without grave anxiety, the course of the second Sikh war, and, when that had been happily ended, he had gone in person to Burma to examine for himself the progress of the operations there. These two theatres of war were roughly two thousand miles apart; and having travelled himself between them, he could realise the meaning of the distance, which may be compared to the interval that lies between the Thames and the Volga. His remonstrances, however, met with no response. The Directors of the East India Company had never loved military expenditure, and the British government, with War Office, army and the entire military system in a state of flux and confusion, was in no position to meet demands for more garrisons oversea. The most that Dalhousie could do was to conciliate a dangerous and justly embittered enemy. In 1853 Colonel Mackeson, Commissioner of Peshawar, whose name will be remembered in connection with the Afghan war, was assassinated by a fanatic, at the instance, as was supposed, of an Afghan priest. His successor, Herbert Edwardes, begged permission to open negotiations for a treaty of friendship with Dost Mohamed. Dalhousie, against the advice of John Lawrence, approved the idea; and the treaty was finally signed in March 1855. Eleven months later, in February 1856, Dalhousie resigned, and with health utterly shattered, returned home to die.

His successor, Lord Canning, was an amiable, pains-

1856. taking, unambitious man who had risen in the world of British politics to minor office. He lacked neither capacity nor courage, but excessive conscientiousness made him slow of resolution; and at critical times to delay the right decision is as bad as to make the wrong. His colleagues in Council were not calculated to give him much help, being capable officials and no more, content to carry on the regular routine and quite blind to the undisciplined state of the Bengal army. One of Canning's first duties was to find a successor as Chief Commissioner of Oudh to Outram, who wished to return to England on sick leave. Henry Lawrence volunteered to take Outram's place; but meanwhile the authorities in England had appointed a candidate of their own, a man of violent temper, who spent much of his time quarrelling with his principal colleague, an individual of equal self-importance. This person made his rule so odious that Canning was obliged to supersede him and in January 1857 to replace him by Henry Lawrence. But by that time the mischief had been done, and all classes in Oudh had been alienated.

Outram, meanwhile, hearing of the Persian war, delayed his return to England and took command, as has been told, in the Persian Gulf. Herbert Edwardes, observing the opportunity offered by this war to strengthen the friendly feeling of Dost Mohamed, urged Canning to grant him substantial help against the Persians; and Canning consented to give a subsidy to any Afghan force that should march against the Shah. Accordingly, in January 1857 it was agreed by treaty that the British should furnish a certain quantity of arms and a payment of £10,000 a month, and that the Amir should admit a British mission to Afghanistan to superintend the expenditure of the money. " I have made an alliance with the British Government," said Dost Mohamed, " and I will keep it till death." He was as good as his word.

During this time a change in the conditions of enlistment in the Bengal army exasperated its mutinous spirit. Six regiments only of that army were enlisted for 1856. general service and could be transported across the sea. Three of these were already serving in Burma, and the time for their relief was come. No one of the remaining three could be spared for this purpose; and, the road to Burma being at the time impassable, it was impossible to march regiments thither by land, and so to avoid the injury to their caste involved in crossing the sea. Canning thereupon, in July 1856, issued a General Order that all native recruits should in future be enlisted for service in any quarter; and therewith men of high caste, formerly eager to join the army, shrank from entering themselves as recruits. At a less critical time the change, which in any case would have needed some years to find peaceful acceptance, might have been accomplished safely, but, coming when it did, it provoked suspicion and discontent.

Another reform, fully justified in itself, added to the unrest of the sepoy at this juncture. Under the old regulations of the Bengal army privates after fifteen years' service, if certified as invalids, could return to their homes on a small pension. So great was the attraction of this pittance, added to the certainty of return home, that men would starve themselves for months till they were weak and emaciated in order to obtain the coveted status of invalids.[1] In England such a practice would be called by some such ugly name as malingering or fraudulent retirement; and, looking to the cost of granting pensions to men who were still young and fit for work, and of obtaining new recruits in their place, the government of India began at this very time to take the same view. It was therefore ordained that invalids in future should receive no pensions, but should do duty in cantonments, though exempt from active service. A further regulation, abridging privileges of the sepoys in respect of postal service, equally trifling in itself, aggravated the irritation of the native soldiers and disposed them to believe any story that

[1] Gubbins, *Mutinies in Oudh*, pp. 108-9.

1856. pointed them out as victims of deliberate oppression by the white man for the white man's own sinister ends.

1857. The climax came in January 1857, when greased cartridges for the new Enfield rifle began to be manufactured in Dum Dum. It was rumoured that this grease was the fat of cows or of swine, an abomination, the former to all Hindus, the latter to all Mohammedans. The biting of such a cartridge would pollute them for ever; and the report ran that the British were planning to deprive all alike of their caste—of all that made life worth living—with the ultimate object of converting them into Christians. By the end of the month the four native regiments at Barrackpore, close outside Calcutta, were setting fire to their officers' bungalows and showing other symptoms of insubordination. From them the infection spread to another regiment, the 19th, at Burhampore, which refused to accept their percussion-caps on the ground that they suspected the grease on the cartridges. This was open mutiny, but it was passed over for the time because there was no British regiment—incredible as it may sound—within reach to coerce them. Canning summoned the Eighty-fourth from Burma—a distance of eight hundred miles —and meanwhile General Hearsey, a good officer who spoke the sepoy's language as well as themselves, on the

March. 17th of March addressed the regiments at Barrackpore and did his utmost to soothe and reassure them. Twelve days later a private in the 34th regiment, named Mangal Pandi, fired at the adjutant, killed his horse, and then attacked him with a sword. Not a native officer nor sepoy would move to help the adjutant, and the guard, though under the command of a native lieutenant, actually struck the fallen British officer with the butts of their muskets. At last Hearsey himself came up with a revolver and threatened to shoot the first man who refused to move when ordered, when the guard at last came forward to arrest Mangal Pandi. The desperate man then tried to shoot himself, and fell

wounded, though not fatally; and a week later, he was 1857.
tried and put to death.

On the day following this outbreak the 19th Native Mar. 30.
Infantry were disbanded. The native lieutenant and
the guard of the 34th ought to have been tried and
summarily dealt with on the same day. But the
lieutenant was not sentenced until the 11th of April, April.
nor executed until the 21st, and the guard was allowed
to escape unpunished; Canning being apprehensive
lest such prompt severity should heighten rather than
repress the bad feeling in the army. The Governor-
general was evidently quite unfit by temperament and
training to cope with a mutiny.

Simultaneously with the disturbances near the capital
trouble revealed itself in the north-west provinces. Ever
since January the authorities had been perplexed by the
distribution of flat cakes—the ordinary loaf of the Indian
peasant—far and wide from village to village; and no one
could say what it might portend. The story of the cartridges had reached Ambala, and there too in April the
sepoys, declining to accept the explanations of the Commander-in-chief, began to burn down public buildings
and the officers' bungalows. There was excitement at
Delhi, where Bahadur Shah, the titular emperor of the
Mogul dynasty, was still suffered to hold his pageant of
a court. In Oudh, though Henry Lawrence had ended
the quarrels of his British subordinates, a Mohammedan fanatic was preaching a holy war against the
infidels and stirring up sedition. He was known as
the Maulavi, or learned doctor, and was a very remarkable man, of great ability, courage and determination. Furthermore, there was flitting between Lucknow
and Delhi, seemingly harmless but with singular
activity, the figure of Nana Sahib; while at Jhansi,
only a hundred miles from Bithur, the Rani was
watching events with rage in her heart. It may be
said that for a hundred miles on either bank of the
Ganges from Allahabad to Delhi there was one solid
block of enmity, with three dangerous leaders, two of

1857.
April.
them certainly, and the Rani probably, acting in concert.

Yet, except by Sir Henry Lawrence, no alarm was felt. The month of April passed off quietly, and the Supreme Government actually took up transports with the idea of sending the Eighty-fourth back to Rangoon. Meanwhile the disbanded men of the 19th Native Infantry had made their way to Oudh, and at the end of April Lawrence reported that he had discovered signs of disaffection in the 48th Native Infantry, one of his regiments at Lucknow. Canning answered, granting permission for the regiment to be moved to Meerut. Lawrence represented the futility of such a course; and learning that another of his regiments, the 7th Irregular Infantry, stationed seven miles from Lucknow, was showing symptoms of mutiny, he marched against them with the whole strength of his
May.
garrison on the night of the 3rd of May, disarmed them, arrested forty of the ringleaders, reduced or dismissed all the native officers and pardoned the men, keeping them at duty without arms. The whole affair, thus swiftly and resolutely dealt with, was over in a few hours.

Canning, on receipt of Lawrence's report, decided at last to disband the 34th Native Infantry, which was duly done on the 6th of May. This, being no punishment, was interpreted—not incorrectly—by the sepoys as a sign of weakness. A few days later a native lieutenant of the 70th Native Infantry at Barrackpore was arrested in the act of suborning his men to revolt. He was tried by a court of native officers and sentenced to dismissal, which ridiculous penalty was confirmed by the Commander-in-chief, and was naturally construed as an encouragement to mutiny.

Meanwhile the trouble had spread to Meerut, where some troopers of the 3rd Light Cavalry, on the 23rd of April, refused to receive the new cartridges, though permitted to tear instead to bite off the ends. The Commander-in-chief ordered them to be tried by court-martial; they were sentenced to ten years' im-

prisonment; and on the 9th of May they were stripped 1857
of their uniforms and fettered ceremoniously in the May 9.
presence of the whole brigade. In the afternoon a
native officer of the regiment warned Lieutenant Hugh
Gough, who commanded his troop, that the sepoys
were resolved to rescue their comrades. Gough
reported the matter to his colonel, who laughed at the
story, and later informed the Brigadier-general, Archdale Wilson, who likewise ridiculed it. The next day May 10.
was Sunday, when it was usual for the British troops to
attend divine service with their side-arms only. It
chanced that, owing to the lengthening days and the
increasing heat, the time fixed for service was half an
hour later than on the previous Sunday; and, when the
chaplain started to drive to the church, he saw clouds
of smoke rising from the native lines, and heard the
sound of musketry and of bugles sounding the alarm.
The cantonment at Meerut was, as was then the rule,
faulty in design. The quarters of the European troops
were far distant from those of the sepoys, and separated
from them by a wilderness of native bazaars. It
seems that the 3rd Light Cavalry had hoped to surprise
the British garrison in church, where they would be
practically defenceless, to cut them off from their arms
in barracks, and then to destroy them. Galloping
down upon the British lines they found that the troops
were assembled in the parade-ground; whereupon they
hastily galloped back to the gaol, and released their
comrades and the rest of the prisoners, some twelve
hundred all told. Meanwhile the two native infantry
regiments, the 11th and 20th, in a state of wild excitement assembled on the parade-ground, setting fire to
their own huts and firing their muskets at anything or
nothing. Their officers hastened to them, but found
themselves powerless. The colonel of the 11th was
shot dead, not by his own men but by those of the 20th;
and then, having hopelessly committed themselves, the
sepoys broke loose to massacre and plunder, seconded
by all the neighbouring villagers and the many ruffians

1857.
May 10.
that hung about the cantonment. Eight British officers in all were killed, besides two officers' wives, three children, and every luckless European of any age or sex who chanced to catch the eye of the rioters.

The British troops at Meerut consisted of the Carabiniers, a young regiment newly arrived in India, with half-trained men and half-broken horses; the first battalion of the Sixtieth, than which there was no finer in the army; a battery of horse-artillery; another of field-artillery and a company of foot-artillery; perhaps two thousand men in all. The commander of the Meerut division was General Hewett, an infirm old Indian officer of fifty years' service; the Brigadier-general was Archdale Wilson. The British troops were under arms in an incredibly short time, but it seems to have been long before they could find anyone to give them orders. Wilson, the first to arrive on the spot, detached two companies of the Sixtieth to guard the treasury and the barracks. Hewett arrived later, perfectly helpless; and then at last the British troops advanced to the lines of the native regiments. Night had fallen before they reached them, and on their arrival they found that the sepoys were gone, no man could say whither. Wilson, suspecting that they had moved round to assail the quarters of the Europeans, advised Hewett to return for the protection of the women, the children and the barracks. The troops accordingly marched back to the European parade-ground and there bivouacked for the night.

Few incidents in the history of the mutiny have been more unsparingly condemned than the apathy of the British garrison on the day of the outbreak at Meerut, nor is it easy to find excuse for it. The authorities had received warning of its coming, so, however they may have sneered at it before the event, the shock should not have found them wholly unprepared. The delay in moving upon the native lines is, and was at the time,[1] the circumstance most difficult to account for.

[1] Rotton, *Chaplain's Narrative of the Siege of Delhi*, p. 4.

Colonel Custance of the Carbiniers had turned out his 1857.
regiment promptly and asked for orders. He could May 10.
have trotted to the scene of action in a few minutes;
the horse-artillery battery, if it had not accompanied
him, could have followed very shortly. Their very
appearance would have created panic and confusion
among the mutineers, and diverted them from any set
purpose. The Sixtieth would have joined them in
half an hour, and the united force, dealing out unsparing
punishment, would have taught a salutary lesson to all
mutineers. Burning buildings gave plenty of light
after midnight, and there was later a moon which would
have enabled the troops to do their work thoroughly.
It is useless to plead the blind trust which, as a hundred
examples can prove, was mistakenly reposed in the
native troops by British officers. That is beside the
point. A military riot may break out unexpectedly
among any troops, and a commanding officer's first
duty is to put it down with a strong hand.

As a matter of fact the mutineers looked anxiously
for the wrath to come, and after a little destruction and
plunder thought only of saving themselves. Whither
should they fly? The cry rose, "To Delhi," and to
Delhi, thirty-six miles to south, they made their way,
the 3rd Cavalry leading. Emissaries had gone before
them to prepare their comrades of the 38th, 54th and
74th Native Infantry, which formed the garrison of
the city; but these regiments showed nothing unusual in their demeanour. The approach of a body
of horse on the morning of the 11th, however, put May 11.
the handful of British officials and officers in Delhi
on the alert, and every man hurried to his post. The
leading mutineers entered the city unmolested, released
the prisoners from the gaol, and then beset the palace
of the aged representative of the Moguls, Bahadur
Shah, crying out to him to lead them in their fight for
the faith. The guard, a party of the 38th, treacherously
admitted them, and they speedily made an end of the
few British, men and women, within the walls. Other

1857.   parties of mutineers assailed the European quarter,
May 11. killed every European or Eurasian, and gutted the
buildings.   Two young telegraphists, sticking to their
posts to the last, sent warning of the outbreak to every
important post in India, and were fortunate enough to
escape.   Lieutenant Willoughby, who was in charge
of the magazine, raised such hasty barricades as he
could contrive, placed two field-guns at salient points,
and with his little garrison of eight men prepared to
defend his charge to the last, laying a train to explode
the powder in case the worst should come.

Meanwhile the alarm had been given in the cantonments on the ridge to the north-west of Delhi; and
Brigadier-general Graves, with perfect confidence in
his troops, had ordered them to march down to the
city.   The leading regiment, the 54th Native Infantry,
reached the Kashmir Gate, when it was obstructed by
the mutineers of the 3rd Cavalry.   The officer on
guard at the gate ordered his men—some of the 38th—
to fire.   They refused, and the 54th then fired, some
into the air, some at their own officers, of whom four
were shot dead.   The 74th were now ordered forward
and remained halted before the main-guard, when at
about half-past three in the afternoon there came the
roar of a terrific explosion.   Willoughby and his eight
men, after a gallant defence of three hours, had realised
that they could save the magazine no longer and had
blown it up.   Not one of them had looked for anything
but death, yet by some miracle five of them survived,
and Willoughby himself escaped unhurt, though only
to be murdered on his way to Meerut.   One and all
had nobly done their duty.[1]   Therewith the sepoys
before the Kashmir Gate hesitated no longer.   Those
of the 38th fired a volley into the group of officers before

---

[1] Their names are worth recording.   The survivors, Lieutenants
Forrest and Raynor, Conductors Buckley and Shaw, and Sergeant Shaw,
received the Victoria Cross.   Conductors Scully (who fired the train)
and Crow, and Sergeant Edwards perished.   All belonged to the
Commissariat Ordnance Department.

them, killing three on the spot; and the remainder, 1857. seeing the certain fate that awaited them, turned and fled. With great difficulty they lowered the women and children, who had taken refuge in the main-guard, into the ditch, and the whole concealed themselves for the moment in the jungle. Thence they made their way as best they could through the terrible heat, some to Meerut, some to Karnal, nearly a hundred miles away, some even to Ambala, fifty miles beyond Karnal. Their sufferings from hunger, thirst, fatigue and mal-treatment by passing villagers were frightful. Some fell by the way through exhaustion and disease, or were murdered by stray ruffians; but the greater number, thanks to the compassion of friendly Indians, came in to some haven of refuge. Women equally with men sustained this trial with unflinching courage.

Meanwhile the fact remained that such few British as were in Delhi had been shamefully hounded out; that the East India Company had ceased to rule in the capital of the Moguls, and that Bahadur Shah of the house of Timour now reigned in its stead.

CHAPTER XLIX

1857.
May.
THE news of the outbreak at Meerut reached Canning at Calcutta by telegram on the 12th of May, and of the fall of Delhi two days later. He at once ordered the British troops from Persia to be sent without delay to Calcutta, and the Forty-third and the Hundred and Second to prepare for embarkation at Madras. He further dispatched a steamer to fetch the Thirty-fifth from Burma, asked the Governor of Ceylon to embark to him every soldier that he could afford to send, and directed the interception of all British troops that were on their way to China. He also requested John Lawrence to send down to Delhi every man that could be spared, gave him and his brother Henry a free hand in the Punjab and in Oudh, and published a proclamation to reassure the sepoys as to their religion and their caste. But he evidently failed to realise the full gravity of the situation, for he rejected an offer from Lord Elphinstone, the Governor of Bombay, to send a fast steamer with despatches to England; he took no measure to disarm the native regiments at Barrackpore; and he made no attempt to utilise such British troops as lay ready to his hand. These, it is true, were but two battalions, the Fifty-third and the Eighty-fourth; yet he could certainly have spared one of them, and, by enrolling as volunteers all the Europeans in Calcutta, as later he did when his eyes were opened, he could have assured the free service of both. One would have thought that the revolt of seven or eight battalions would have made any man suspicious of the rest; but

every commanding officer was confident that, whatever 1857. might occur in other regiments, his own would remain faithful; and Canning's advisers were not men of the stamp to enlighten him. The great majority of the Indian officials, both civil and military, were hide-bound by the deadly routine which in a hot climate too easily passes for activity.

On the 12th of May the Commander-in-chief, May 12. General George Anson, received at Simla a clear though incomplete statement of what had passed at Meerut and at Delhi. It came to him as a surprise, for he was in bad health and was contemplating a shooting excursion in the hills. On the 13th he ordered the May 13. Seventy-fifth to move down from Kasaoli to Ambala, and warned the Hundred and First and Hundred and Fourth to be ready to proceed to the same place. At the same time he took measures for securing the magazines at Ferozepore, Jallandar and Phillaur. On the 14th he definitely ordered the Hundred and First and May 14. Hundred and Fourth to march to Ambala, and the Sirmur battalion of Gurkhas to move to Meerut; directed the preparation of a siege-train at Phillaur, and appointed the Nasiri regiment of Gurkhas to escort it. On the same morning he set out for Ambala, fifty miles as the crow flies from Simla, and arrived there early on the 15th. He found matters in no very May 15. promising state. The troops quartered there were the Ninth Lancers, two batteries of horse-artillery, and three native regiments, all of which last were alike untrustworthy. The Hundred and First had come in with only seventy cartridges a man, the Seventy-fifth with only thirty, and there was no ammunition nearer than Phillaur, eighty miles away. Neither regiment had tents or baggage from want of carriage. Dalhousie, with the habitual improvidence of British administrators both at home and abroad, had abolished the permanent transport-service, and there was no means of mobilising the troops for the field. Commissariat and Medical Department were alike helpless. There were no

1857. stretchers for the sick and wounded; the bazaars were
May. disorganised by the general unrest; provisions were
difficult to collect; and contractors, upon whom the
Indian army had always chiefly depended for transport
and supply, were not easily to be found.

Anson fully appreciated that his first and most
important object was the recovery of Delhi; and he
had not been at Ambala forty-eight hours before he
received a letter from John Lawrence urgently pressing
this duty upon him. Anson replied that he had no
tents for his Europeans and no siege-artillery; that at
least sixteen days would be needed to collect the necessary transport; and that an advance to Delhi with the
few troops that he had at Ambala would be extremely
hazardous. Lawrence, adopting the tone typical of
the political officer when dealing with military operations, answered that " with good management on the
part of the civil officers, Delhi would open its gates on
the approach of our troops." But Anson was not to
be misled by specious representations of this kind. He
was thoroughly at one with Lawrence as to the expediency of the earliest possible advance upon Delhi,
but he would not lead his troops to certain destruction.
Upon another point Anson was less happy in his
resistance to Lawrence. The latter had urged the
immediate disarmament of the native regiments at
Ambala. Anson preferred to yield to the remonstrances of their commanding officers, who protested
that such action would amount to a breach of faith.
He was guilty of a blunder no greater than that of the
Governor-general himself, who shared his ignorance of
India, nor of scores of Englishmen in authority who
professed to understand the Indians; but it was a pity
that he did not allow his own common sense free play
as well in following as in resisting Lawrence.

This, then, was the situation in the two chief centres
of British power in the days immediately following the
outbreak. Canning had one battalion ready to his
hand, and would not employ it. Anson had a fairly

large though still insufficient force, and, owing to no 1857.
fault of his own, could not move it.   Meanwhile the May.
mischief spread rapidly.   At Ferozepore a new brigadier-general, Innes, had arrived on the 11th, to hear
on the next day of what had passed at Meerut.   He
paraded the garrison—the Sixty-first, one hundred and
fifty British gunners and three native regiments—forth-
with, and being dissatisfied with the demeanour of the
last named, ordered that the sepoys on guard at the
magazine should be relieved by Europeans.   His
directions were neglected or misunderstood, for, though
the Europeans were introduced into the entrenchment
around the magazine, the sepoys were not removed.
In the evening the two native infantry regiments
mutinied and attempted to storm the entrenchment.
They were driven out, but not pursued; and only after
they had burned down several buildings did Innes at
last turn upon them, disarming one regiment and
pursuing and dispersing the other.   A great number of
the mutineers none the less found their way to Delhi,
whereas they ought to have been shot down to a man.

At Agra the Lieutenant-governor, Mr. John Colvin,
though he had a British regiment, the Hundred and
Seventh, and a British battery at his command, did
not disarm his two native regiments but made them a
speech.   He did, however, apply to the Maharaja of
Gwalior and the Rajah of Bhurtpore for some of their
troops, which they loyally provided, though with a
warning that they could not be reckoned upon.   Thereupon Colvin sent reassuring reports to Calcutta.   On
the 20th of May four companies of the 9th Native In- May 20.
fantry at Aligarh, midway between Agra and Delhi,
broke into open mutiny, and, without injuring their
officers, seized the treasury, broke open the gaol, and
made for Delhi.   In the course of the next two days
detachments of the same regiment at Itawah, Bulandshahr and Mainpuri followed this example, though the
treasury at Mainpuri was saved by the extraordinary
courage of Lieutenant de Kantzow.   On the 30th a

1857. mutiny of three companies of sepoys at Muttra, thirty
May 30. miles north-west of Agra, at last brought Colvin to resolve on the disarmament of the two native regiments
at Agra, which was effected on the 31st.   He further
decided to raise volunteers, both horse and foot, from
all classes of Europeans in the city and district.

He had acted, however, a fortnight too late, for from
the 30th of May outbreak succeeded outbreak so rapidly
as to give the impression of concerted action.   On the
31st May the regiments at Shahjahanpur and Bareilly
mutinied, not without murder and massacre, and were
June. followed on the 1st and 3rd of June by those at Budaon
and Moradabad.   Therewith Rohilkhand was lost;
and with a mutiny at Farakhabad on the 18th of June
the hold of the British upon the space between the
Jumna and the Ganges was seriously imperilled.   On
the 4th of June the two regiments at Jhansi rose and,
with the connivance of the Rani, massacred every English
man, woman and child.   On the 14th, mutiny spread
to the contingent at Gwalior, but without alienating the
loyalty of the Maharaja Sindia.   In Rajputana the
native troops broke out at the two principal military
stations, Nasirabad on the 28th of May, and Nimach
on the 3rd of June; but the Agent, Colonel George
Lawrence, though with few resources, succeeded in
reasserting his authority.   Thus the British hold upon
the north-west provinces was practically reduced to
Agra; and it was a question for how long its line of
communication with Calcutta could be kept open.

Not less to Oudh and to Lucknow than to the north-
west provinces and to Agra was this maintenance of
communication of vital importance.   The two stations
nearest to both were first Allahabad and, eighty miles
beyond it, Cawnpore.   The garrison of Allahabad consisted of a regiment of native infantry and a battery of
native artillery, to which were added in May half a
battalion of Sikhs and sixty-five invalid British soldiers.
On the 6th of June the sepoys mutinied, shot down
seventeen British officers and seized the guns; but

Lieutenant Brasyer, who was in command of the Sikhs, 1857. kept them faithful to him and drove the sepoys from June. the fort. The mutineers then plundered the town, torturing and slaying any Europeans that they found; but the fort itself, the point of real importance, was secured. At Cawnpore there were two regiments of native infantry and one of cavalry, besides sixty-one British gunners with six guns, under the command of Sir Hugh Wheeler, whose name will be remembered as distinguished in the Sikh wars. Wheeler was one of the few Indian officers who had taken from the first a very serious view of the mutiny. He did not trust his native troops in the least, but he was practically at their mercy. His only resource was to fortify some position which would serve as a refuge for his few Europeans, victual it, take every precaution, and hope for the best. The cantonments, straggling over a length of seven miles, offered no stronghold except on the side towards Delhi. There was in that quarter a magazine well fitted for defence; but Wheeler, knowing that help must come from the opposite direction—that is to say, from Allahabad—selected two barracks in an open plain at the eastern end of the cantonments and proceeded to throw up earthworks around them. The ground being baked hard by months of burning sun, the work made but slow progress; but a rampart some four feet high was raised, and on the 21st the women and children were moved within this fortification. On the 22nd a detachment of two officers and eighty-six men of the Thirty-second, sent by Sir Henry Lawrence, came in from Lucknow; and Wheeler felt himself less insecure.

At Lucknow, since the news of the mutiny at Meerut, Henry Lawrence had received command of all the British troops in Oudh, and had begun to make every preparation against the worst. The women and children were removed into the Residency; an old fort called the Machchi Bhawan was repaired and turned into a magazine and store-house; and the trustworthy men were distributed among four strong fortified posts.

1857. Lawrence did not disarm his four native regiments, fearing that such action might precipitate mutiny in the outlying posts of Oudh, and above all at Cawnpore. The last-named post was a source of peculiar anxiety to him, for he believed that, so long as it was held, Lucknow was safe.   Hence his readiness to send a reinforcement to Wheeler, which, small though it was, amounted to a fifth of his European force.   We shall presently see that Wheeler showed himself as anxious and unselfish for the safety of Lucknow.

May.   Let us now glance at the Punjab, where there was a strong man in command, with a fair number of British soldiers besides loyal Sikhs and Gurkhas.   There were in all sixty-five thousand native troops; and it was resolved to disperse them as far as possible and to organise a movable column of British or loyal men which should be ready to deal with any emergency. Mention of the mutiny at Ferozepore on the 12th of May has already been made, and it must be added that on the 13th of May four native regiments were disarmed at Mian Mir, the headquarters of the Lahore division, and five miles from Lahore.   A few days later the revolt of a detachment at Naoshera brought about the instant disarmament of four regiments at Peshawar on the 22nd of May.   Two more regiments, one of foot and one of horse, which had broken out on the 23rd of May, were promptly pursued, and on the 25th utterly dispersed.   At Jallandar, where Lawrence's orders for disarmament were disregarded by a sentimental brigadier, there was as disgraceful and humiliating a scene as at Meerut; but for the most part the danger was dealt with quietly and peremptorily, whereby more and more of the British were set free for the operations against Delhi.

Meanwhile the events of May and early June had begun slowly to open Canning's eyes.   He at last pushed up detachments of the Eighty-fourth towards Cawnpore; and on the 25th of May the first of these arrived at Benares, whence they were forwarded in

carriages.   The announcement of their approach was 1857.
an immense relief to Wheeler,[1] who conceived that the
mere threat of reinforcements from Calcutta would
avert a rising in Cawnpore; and he was confirmed in
his confidence by the arrival on the 31st of May and May 31.
the two succeeding days of the first relays of the Eighty-
fourth.   In his generous way he at once passed on fifty
of them to Henry Lawrence at Lucknow.   Still, there
was then only one railway in India, which ran from the
capital some fifty miles to Raniganj; and Canning
reckoned that even half a battalion could not be moved
from Calcutta to Cawnpore in less than twenty-five
days.   However, a start had at least been made, and,
moreover, on the 24th of May the first reinforcement
had arrived at Calcutta from Madras.

This consisted of a wing of the Hundred and Second
under Colonel Neill, a great battalion under a great
commander.   On the same evening the men received
Enfield rifles, which had not yet been issued to them,
and on the following day Neill started for the front,
taking four companies with him by train and sending
the fifth up the river in flats towed by steamers.   So
little was the common danger understood that Neill
could only break through the stupid routine which
reigned at the railway station by putting station-master,
driver and fireman under a guard.   At Raniganj Neill
impressed every vehicle that he could find, and on the
30th of May, being dissatisfied with his progress, he
marched for Benares with twenty-five men and reached
it on the 3rd of June.   There he found a company of June 3.
the Tenth Foot which had been lately sent up from
Dinapore, a battery of artillery under Major Olpherts,
and three native regiments, one of them Sikhs.   On
the 4th came news that a native battalion at Azamgarh, June 4.
twenty miles to northward, had mutinied; and it was
resolved to disarm the native troops at Benares immediately.   Two hundred more of the Hundred and
Second had arrived, but even so there were none too

[1] Gubbins, *Mutinies in Oudh*, p. 43.

1857. many Europeans to overawe three regiments; one of which, on being ordered to pile arms, fired a volley at the Tenth. They were promptly mowed down by grape from Olpherts's guns; and the survivors taking to their heels, were sternly pursued by Neill, who was not the man to deal mildly with mutiny.

Being detained by the necessity of preserving order June 6-7. in the city, he on the 6th and 7th sent forward two detachments, each of fifty men, to Allahabad. The first of these, arriving on the day after the mutiny at that place, found the bridge of boats in the hands of the rebels; but though exhausted to extremity by an arduous march in the height of the Indian summer, these troops succeeded late at night in crossing the river lower down and in joining Brasyer within the June 9. fort. Neill himself, leaving Benares on the 9th with forty men in carriages, traversed the seventy miles to Allahabad in two night marches. He too had to cross the river below the bridge of boats, and reached the fort with his men nearly prostrate through the heat, being himself so faint that he could hardly move. He came none too soon, for both Sikhs and European volunteers had found liquor, and there was great dis- June 12. order in the fort. Neill's first action on the 12th was to attack the rebels and recover the bridge of boats, after which he restored discipline in the fort, and then sending out small parties in every direction he succeeded June 18. by the 18th in reducing all the neighbouring districts to trembling submission.

But whatever Neill might do during his advance he could not also look to his rear. Canning still hesitated to disarm the native regiments below Benares. The Commissioner on the spot was anxious to be safely quit of the three that formed the garrison of Dinapore, but he was denied authority to do so from Calcutta. Moreover, Canning declined to take decisive measures even against those at Barrackpore; and not until the 14th of June, after receiving certain intelligence of their intentions to rise, did he finally permit General

Hearsey to disarm them. But indeed Canning, 1857. though not wanting in courage, seems to have lacked June. all imagination as to the meaning of an armed insurrection in such a country as India, and hence to have been very unsteady of resolution. Thus on the 12th of June he revoked a previous decision, and permitted the enrolment of volunteers at Calcutta, though in the meantime the Thirty-fifth had arrived from Burma and the Seventy-eighth from Persia. Then on the 17th he declined the help of Gurkha regiments offered by the ruler of Nepal, and on the 23rd accepted it. One outcome of all this vacillation was a rather disgraceful panic at Calcutta on the 14th of June, which would never have occurred had confidence been felt in him as a strong man.

And if Canning did not shine in the matter of safeguarding his line of communication with the northwest, he was not more distinguished in his handling of the operations against Delhi. John Lawrence, as we have seen, pressed Anson to march thither at once with such troops as he had, leaving tents, transport and supply to chance. Canning supplemented this on the 31st of May by a telegram ordering Anson not only to deal with Delhi—" Your force of artillery will enable you (he said) to dispose of Delhi with certainty "[1] —but to detach a British battalion and a small force of British cavalry to the south of Delhi, so as to recover Aligarh and relieve Cawnpore immediately. It was really insufferable that a Governor-general should write such childish nonsense, evincing equal ignorance of the actual situation and of military operations at large. However, Canning and Lawrence between them succeeded in irritating Anson, against his better judgement, into immediate action. Anson's own wish was to move by Meerut upon Agra and to take a sufficient siege-train from the magazine there before approaching Delhi, but he was unfortunately overborne by his civil superiors.[2] He had at Ambala the Ninth Lancers,

[1] Malleson, p. 96.   [2] Greathed, p. 123.

1857. two troops of horse-artillery, the Seventy-fifth, the
May. Hundred and First, six companies of the Hundred and
Fourth, and the 60th Native Infantry. With these he
marched on the 25th of May, having ordered the troops
at Meerut and a small siege-train from Ludhiana to
join him at Baghpat, within one march of Delhi. On
the 26th he reached Karnal, where he was attacked by
cholera and died in a few hours. He was succeeded
by Sir Henry Barnard, who arrived on the spot just
before Anson breathed his last.

On the 27th Barnard, before continuing his march,
sent away the 60th Native Infantry, which shortly
afterwards mutinied;[1] and on the same day Archdale
Wilson led his troops out of Meerut—two squadrons
of the Carabiniers, a wing of the Sixtieth, Tombs's
troop of horse-artillery, Scott's field-battery, two
eighteen-pounder guns, some native sappers and a few
native irregular cavalry. Three days' march brought
them to the village of Ghazi-ud-din Nagar, about a
mile from the river Hindan, then spanned by a suspension bridge. On the opposite bank and in the
dry bed of the stream mutineers from Delhi were
May 30. awaiting them in position; and here at 4 P.M. Wilson
engaged them at odds of about one against seven and
drove them back with the loss of five guns. The
intense heat forbade the success to be followed up, and
May 31. on the morrow the mutineers returned to the same
fighting ground, but after a two hours' duel of artillery
fell back before the advance of the Sixtieth. The British
casualties in the two actions did not exceed thirty-one.[2]
On the 1st of June Wilson was joined by the 2nd
(the Sirmur) Gurkhas, five hundred strong, and after

[1] This was a very shameful proceeding, for the regiment was
known to be disaffected, and the British officers belonging to it were,
to all appearances, condemned to have their throats cut. However,
by good fortune they escaped. See Seaton, *From Cadet to Colonel*,
ii. 91-123.

[2] Half of them were due to the explosion of a captured ammunition
waggon by a pardoned mutineer of the Meerut garrison. Greathed,
Letters Written during the Siege of Delhi, pp. 6, 14.

some days' halt he marched on to Alipur, where on the 7th his own troops, the siege-train and Barnard's were safely united. 1857.
June 7.

The entire force thus assembled comprised three and a half British battalions, one weak Gurkha battalion, one and a half regiments of British cavalry, three horse-batteries, one field-battery, and one hundred and fifty gunners, mostly recruits, with the siege-train.[1] The whole seem to have numbered about thirty-five hundred fighting men.[2] The siege-train consisted of eight eighteen-pounders and sixteen mortars, the largest of these latter being of eight-inch calibre—half obsolete pieces and quite inadequate for attack on a strongly fortified city. In the terrific heat the men marched in their shirt-sleeves with a white cover and curtain over their forage-caps, which gave no too good protection against the sun. There were already many sick and prostrate soldiers on the 7th of June; but when Barnard issued his orders for advance at midnight, the invalids, feeling sure of an action, left the hospital and insisted on accompanying the column. Many of them could hardly walk; but the spirit of vengeance was upon them and they would not be left behind.[3]

Lieutenant Hodson, a very daring officer of irregular horse, had already reconnoitred the road to Delhi and found the enemy in force in a strong position at Badli-ki-Serai, about half-way to the city, so Barnard sent his cavalry forward to turn their left, and advanced

---

[1] The force was brigaded as follows:
    Cavalry: Colonel Hope Grant. 6th D. (2 squadrons),
        9th Lancers, Hodson's Jhind Horse.
    Infantry: 1*st Brigade*: Colonel Showers. 75th, 101st.
        2*nd*   „   Colonel Graves. 1/60th, 104th.

[2] Roberts, *Forty-one Years in India*, 1 vol. 1921, p. 84, gives the number at 600 cavalry and 2400 infantry with 22 field-guns. This, I imagine, includes the European troops only. Taking four batteries at 60 men apiece and adding the gunners of the siege-train, the artillery would be 390, say 400.

[3] *History of the Siege of Delhi*, by an Officer, p. 73.

1857. with the infantry against their front. As day broke
June. the mutineers opened fire from heavy pieces with
considerable effect, and Barnard having no guns large
enough to retaliate effectively, launched Showers's
brigade against the enemy's batteries, and sent Graves's
brigade round their right. The Seventy-fifth, which
led the frontal attack, carried all before them, and after
sharp fighting the mutineers retired hastily, leaving
twelve guns behind them. By that time the sun was
high and the men were much exhausted; but Barnard
pushed on to the ridge to north-west of Delhi and reached
the parade-ground at its northern extremity without encountering further opposition. The enemy then again
opened fire, and Barnard, dividing his force into two
columns, sent one to the southern and the other to the
northern extremity of the ridge so as to sweep it from
end to end. This was successfully done, and the day's
work was satisfactorily accomplished. The enemy's
loss was reckoned at a thousand killed or permanently
disabled. Barnard's casualties amounted to one
hundred and eighty-two, a third of which fell upon the
Seventy-fifth.

The famous Delhi ridge is to the ordinary observer
a very insignificant feature, rising not more than sixty
feet above the plain, little more than two miles in
extreme length, and varying in breadth from two
hundred yards in the north to eight hundred in the
south. But it lay right across the line of communication
with the Punjab, which was the base of the force, and it
presented a natural rampart for defence against the city
and a natural post of vantage for attack upon it. Its
left or northern end rested on the Jumna, which was
unfordable except during the winter, and was wide
enough to render the position safe from enfilading fire
of field-guns, so that this flank was secure. The northern half of it was also beyond range of the guns on the
walls of Delhi; and accordingly the camp was pitched
in rear, or to westward, of this quarter of it. The
right or southern end was more vulnerable, the ground

below it being covered with buildings and garden
walls in front and flank, with an inconveniently placed
suburb called the Sabzi Mandi, or vegetable market,
in the right rear.   But these, though offering cover to
the enemy, made organised and concerted attack upon
the British right flank and rear a difficult matter.
The flank itself was more or less covered by the western
Jumna canal, if the bridge over it were broken down;
and, moreover, the flat land at the southern extremity
was during the rainy season submerged.   The worst
defect of the position was that a great part of the front—
that is to say, of the ground to east of it—was covered
with old buildings, enclosures and clumps of trees,
which obscured the vision and broke up the field of
fire.

On this ridge accordingly Barnard took up his
position.   The main picquet was established at a
building called Hindu Rao's House, about half a mile
from the southern extremity; two hundred yards to
left or north of it was erected a battery of heavy guns;
five hundred yards to left of this was installed in an old
mosque a second infantry-picquet with two guns, and
half a mile to the left of the mosque, in a building
known as the Flagstaff Tower, was yet another infantry-
picquet with two more field-guns.   On the right, the
most dangerous part of the position, were an infantry-
picquet and three heavy guns above, and a cavalry-
picquet and two horse-artillery guns immediately below.
From the right of the position to the Flagstaff Tower
the distance was, as nearly as may be, twenty-six
hundred yards, so that, after making allowance for
casualties, for the sick, for camp-guards and the like,
it may be reckoned that Barnard had a defensive force
of one man a yard with which to encounter at the height
of the hot season an enemy, well provided with arms
and guns, which outnumbered him by at least twenty
and possibly by forty to one.

But Barnard was not supposed by John Lawrence and
Canning to stand on the defensive.   On the contrary,

1857.
June. he was expected to attack and conquer Delhi. Now, Delhi may be described as a fairly regular quadrilateral, with sides, roughly speaking, a mile and a half long, and with a total perimeter of seven miles. The eastern side, being washed by the Jumna, was inaccessible to the besiegers, but was open to the mutineers to introduce by ferries and a bridge of boats as many men, supplies and stores, as might please them. The main wall, broken by bastions at rather long intervals, was sixteen feet high and tapered in thickness from fifteen feet at the bottom to eleven feet at the top. Above it was a loopholed parapet, eight feet high and two feet thick. Outside the wall was a faussebraye from sixteen to thirty feet wide, with a vertical scarp wall eight feet high; and outside this again was a dry ditch twenty-five feet wide. The whole had been some years before strengthened and improved by an English engineer, the future Lord Napier of Magdala; and this was the trifling stronghold which Lawrence and Canning were quite prepared to attack with a battalion and a few heavy guns.

June 8.
June 9. On the very afternoon of the 8th the mutineers sallied out from Delhi and attacked Hindu Rao's house, but were driven off. On the 9th the Corps of Guides, perhaps the most renowned of all Indian soldiers, entered the camp after an extraordinary march of nearly six hundred miles in twenty-two days, went into action almost immediately to repulse another attack of the mutineers and lost an officer, Quintin Battye, of a famous fighting family. On this same day the enemy opened a cannonade from the walls, when Barnard found not only that his own guns were powerless to silence the enemy's, from the greater range and calibre of the latter, but that his small stock of ammunition was rapidly dwindling. In fact, he was fain to offer a reward for every twenty-four pound shot fired by the mutineers that should be brought to the artillery-park.[1] Meanwhile Hindu Rao's house was

[1] Roberts, p. 90.

riddled with shot and shell, and on the 10th and 11th 1857.
determined attacks were made upon it, the enemy being June
fully aware that it was the key of the British position. 10–11.
They were repulsed.   On the 12th, under cover of a June 12.
heavy fog, the mutineers fell upon the Flagstaff Tower,
and narrowly missed capturing it; and hardly had they
been driven back at this point when they advanced upon
Hindu Rao's house from the Sabzi Mandi, and were
only with an effort repelled.   After this experience the
defences towards the Sabzi Mandi were strengthened
and an advanced picquet was placed in a house, known
as Metcalfe's House, some twelve hundred yards east
of the mosque, so as to hold the enemy, if possible, at a
greater distance.   The need for these measures had
long been seen, but they had not been carried out from
want of men.

The British had now been before Delhi for five days,
and on every day they had been formidably threatened,
more than once having much ado to hold their own.
Every action signified from ten to forty casualties, and
the sun, the heat, divers diseases and overwork were
rapidly thinning their strength.   In the circumstances
Barnard decided on the 13th to make an assault by June 13.
surprise upon the city, according to a plan worked out
by three junior officers of engineers; but, owing to a
defect in the arrangements, the attack was never
delivered, which was fortunate, for it must have ended
in disaster.   The enemy, having caught wind of what
was going forward, were comparatively quiet for two
days, but on the 15th the mutineers fell upon the June 15.
picquets in force and kept them engaged for some eight
hours.   They then resorted to the more scientific
device of erecting a battery on a hill on the British right
flank so as to enfilade the position on the ridge, wherefore on the 17th Barnard ordered a sortie in two small June 17.
columns, which destroyed the battery and drove out
the mutineers with heavy loss.   On the other hand,
a single shot striking Hindu Rao's house on this very
day killed or mortally wounded nine officers and men.

1857. This, but a small incident in the ordinary routine of war, was serious in so small a force, for there was grave reason to believe that the losses of the mutineers in these countless little engagements by no means always exceeded those of the British.[1]

June 19.   On the afternoon of the 19th the enemy again attacked in great force, threatening the front of the position and, as darkness fell, turning their main strength upon the right flank and rear. The British infantry being nearly all engaged, the cavalry and horse-artillery alone were at disposal to repel this onslaught. They did so only with considerable difficulty. There was much confusion in the darkness; the British fired upon their own people; Tombs's troop of horse-artillery was in grave danger of capture, and the guns were only saved by an opportune charge of a party of the Sixtieth. In fact, the affair narrowly missed a disastrous issue; the casualties just exceeded one hundred; and the troops were sensibly depressed. The defences to the right rear were now further improved; the bridge over the canal was, rather late in the day, destroyed; but meanwhile the enemy had been strongly reinforced, and Barnard had been warned to expect a heavy attack on the 23rd—the hundredth anniversary of Plassey— when it had been predicted that the rule of the British

June 22.   should end. On the 22nd news came in that a small party of some eight hundred[2] British and Sikhs had arrived within twenty-two miles of Delhi; and orders were sent to hurry them forward. At 5 A.M. on the

June 23.   23rd the enemy turned out, some six thousand strong, and developed their attack with science and determination. The heavy guns on the walls maintained a violent cannonade upon Hindu Rao's house and the front of the ridge; other guns mounted in the western suburbs enfiladed it from the right; and a series of resolute assaults were launched against the right flank

---

[1] Rotton, pp. 75, 86.

[2] 100 of the 75th, 4 Coys. of the 104th, 1 squadron 2nd Punjab Cavalry, Headquarters of the 4th Sikhs, 6 Horse-artillery guns.

and rear. The mutineers fought bravely, charging 1857.
the Sixtieth, Guides and Gurkhas again and again. June 23.
Every man of the British was engaged; the situation
became most critical; and only by calling in the newly
arrived reinforcements, weary and unrefreshed though
they were, was the enemy finally repulsed after twelve
hours' fighting with the loss of a thousand men. The
casualties of the British numbered one hundred and
sixty; and the men were utterly exhausted by the
terrific heat. Still the success was sufficiently decisive
to restore great elation to the British.

It was now decided to occupy the Sabzi Mandi
rather than run the risk of such another onslaught,
though this threw a serious strain upon the strength
of the force. The enemy remained comparatively
quiet on the ensuing days, but on the 27th the mutineers June 27.
again attacked at the Sabzi Mandi and Metcalfe's
House, and were repulsed with a loss of sixty-two killed
and wounded to the British. On that same day the
monsoon burst; the camp became a pool of water;
cholera began to claim its victims at once; and it may
be said that the first phase of the siege of Delhi, so-
called, came to an end.

It must now be asked what in the world, apart from
doubtful moral effects, was the use of it. As Anson,
with wise prescience, had foreseen, the force was far too
weak to effect anything except, possibly, its own destruction. Barnard was fresh from the Crimea and must
have reflected on the similarity of his own position on
the ridge before Delhi to Raglan's on the plateau above
Sevastopol, nominally the besieger, really the besieged.
Indeed, he was even worse off than Raglan, for he had
to do with an enterprising enemy which left him no
rest; the mutineers knowing well that they had the sun
on their side, and that they had only to keep the British
incessantly alarmed and on the alert to wear them down
into their graves without taking the trouble to kill.
More than once, as is very plain from the narratives
of the British, the fate of this handful of men hung

1857. trembling in the balance; and all felt very grave misgiving as to the future.   They were saved by their own indomitable spirit amid perils and hardships such as have rarely found a parallel even in the eventful history of the British Army.

On the whole, Canning's action—and John Lawrence must bear his share of the blame—in thus pushing this tiny and inadequate column before Delhi seems to me open to very grave censure.   Too weak and too imperfectly equipped to produce the slightest effect upon the defences of the fortress, or even upon the spirit of the defenders, its little strength was simply frittered away in desperate efforts to maintain its bare existence and to stave off dangers which need never have been incurred.   Not less wasteful was the system of feeding it with tiny driblets of reinforcements which barely sufficed to make good casualties and left it just as powerless as before.   And was Delhi, after all, the point at that moment of primary importance?   Anson, it is true, agreed with Lawrence that it was, but with the vital provision that the column dispatched against it should be at least of sufficient strength to capture the fortress.   But Canning himself, as we have seen, wished Anson to operate to the south as well as to the north of Delhi so that Cawnpore might be relieved immediately. " It is impossible," he wrote, " to overrate the importance of showing European troops between Delhi and Cawnpore.   Lucknow and Allahabad depend upon it." Now, it would not have been a more dangerous operation to direct Anson's force first against Agra than against Delhi.   The distance of the objective was, it is true, far greater—three hundred miles as against one hundred.   But supposing that Anson had marched on the 27th of May for Agra, two hundred miles, he should have reached it in thirty days, that is to say, on the 25th of June; and though a hundred miles still lay between him and Cawnpore, the mere knowledge of his approach would have daunted the mutineers and gone far to keep open communication between Agra and

Allahabad, possibly even to avert serious attack upon 1857. Lucknow.   As will be seen in due time, nothing that could be called a serious attack on Delhi was under-taken until the 6th of September, nor was the city stormed until the 20th.   Perhaps it would be too much to say that the efforts of the troops before Delhi were a waste of power until that date; but it is difficult to see what advantage commensurate with their heavy losses was gained by their presence there at least during June, July and the first half of August.   On the other hand, reaching Agra on the 25th of June, they might have accomplished much, and they could have been steadily reinforced from Calcutta.   Wisdom after the event is, of course, easy.   Most of the ablest men in India misjudged the situation at the time.   But there is one principle in warfare which, though constantly transgressed by the British from the year 1775 (to go back no further) to the year 1915, remains eternally true; namely, that to send forth a weak army and reinforce it by driblets is to ensure for it the greatest possible wastage and the least possible power.

CHAPTER L

1857. LET us now turn back to the line of communication on
June. the Ganges, where we have seen Neill push the first of
his detachments as far as Allahabad on the 7th of June,
and reduce the neighbourhood to submission by the
18th.   Eighty miles still lay between him and Cawnpore, but there mutiny, so long dreaded by Wheeler,
had already broken out on the 4th.   Against the advice
of Henry Lawrence, Wheeler had given his confidence
to Nana Sahib, who indeed had always been on friendly
terms with the British residents in the city; and
Wheeler had on the 22nd of May entrusted the treasury
to the Nana's protection.   Such a chance of plunder
must have so stirred the cupidity of the disloyal sepoys
as to cause wonder that they did not rise earlier.   On
the night of the 4th of June the cavalry first threw off
discipline and galloped away to the treasury, and on the
next day they were joined by the three regiments of
native infantry, excepting some eighty faithful men
who were true to their masters until the end.   The
Nana accepted the offer of the mutineers to become
their commander and to lead them to Delhi.   They
actually started on their march, and it seems that
Wheeler, counting upon this movement, thought himself safe.   The Nana, however, persuaded his followers
first to attack and overwhelm Wheeler's handful of men
within the feeble rampart which they had thrown up.
June 6. They returned accordingly; and thus on the 6th of
June began the siege of Cawnpore.
Within the rampart were pent in some nine hundred
souls, nearly four hundred of them women and children.
Of the remainder some two hundred were European

soldiers, about one hundred officers, as many European 1857.
civilians, with about one hundred loyal native officers,
sepoys and servants.   The assailants numbered three
thousand fighting men, and had, moreover, all the
resources of the magazine, with its heavy cannon and
ammunition, at their disposal.   Two guns began to play
upon the flimsy entrenchment on the 7th; three more
opened fire on the 8th; and by the 11th the mutineers had June 11.
brought up in all fifteen pieces, twelve of them of large
calibre.   With these and with musketry they swept the
little fortified space continuously day and night.   The
garrison was crowded together; the heat was intense;
the only water-supply was a well on which the mutineers
kept up a constant fire; and the sufferings of all were
terrible.   Yet not a man nor woman uttered a complaint; and with one heavy howitzer, two field-guns
and small arms, the defenders bade their assailants an
effective defiance.   On the first day there arose the
difficulty of disposing of the dead; and a disused well
was made into a burying-place.   On the fourth day one
of the barracks, used as a hospital and a refuge for
women and children, was kindled by a shell and burned
to the ground, and on the 12th of June the enemy June 12.
attempted a general assault, which was ignominiously
repulsed.   Two days later a party of the garrison made June 14.
a sortie, spiked several guns and bayoneted many of
the besiegers.   The supplies of food within the entrenchment were already failing, and the daily ration
was reduced to a handful of flour and a handful of split
peas; but still the defenders, though sadly thinned
by sunstroke and disease as well as by shot and shell,
remained unshaken.   On the 23rd the mutineers June 23.
attempted a second assault, and were again repulsed.
Then Nana Sahib fell back upon treachery, and sent
in a letter promising safe-conduct to Allahabad to all
" who had not been connected with the acts of Lord
Dalhousie."   Wheeler strongly opposed the idea of a
capitulation and was seconded by the younger officers,
who were proud, with justice, of the defence that they

1857. had made.   But the older men pointed out that not
June 23. only were food and ammunition alike well-nigh exhausted, but that there were women and children who could not die sword in hand, fighting to the last.   For their sake Wheeler consented, not without misgivings,
June 26. to treat; and on the 26th the terms were agreed upon. The British were to march out with their arms and sixty rounds of ammunition, and were to be escorted to boats, duly laden with provisions, on which they should drop down the river to Allahabad.
June 27.   On the morning of the 27th accordingly they set out for the place of embarkation, and the boats were just shoving off when, at the signal of Tantia Topi, Nana Sahib's military adviser, the mutineers poured on them a shower of grape and musketry.   The men were shot down; the women were dragged ashore; out of forty boats only one was uncaptured, and of her passengers three officers and two privates, after many vicissitudes, escaped.   The women and children were huddled together in a small building, fed with the coarsest food, and forced to grind corn for their conquerors.   Nana Sahib had already shot down some scores of European refugees, chiefly women, being always valiant against the defenceless; and, thinking
July 1. that he had vanquished all his enemies, he on the 1st of July, with great pomp and circumstance, proclaimed himself Peshwa.   His action showed the blind vanity and vindictiveness of the petty megolamaniac, the most contemptible type of criminal; and his littleness is thrown into strong relief by the behaviour of the handful of British who, under all the torment of burning sun, thirst, hunger and an unceasing fire, held their paltry entrenchment against him and his cowardly levies for twenty days.   There is no space in this history for details of the story, nor is there need for it, since it has been told long ago by an admirable writer.[1]   Suffice

---

[1] In a little volume entitled *Cawnpore*, by Sir George Trevelyan. On the day that I wrote these words, July 20, 1928, he celebrated his ninetieth birthday.   He is since dead, but the book lives.

it that there are few episodes of which Englishmen can 1857.
feel prouder than the defence of Cawnpore.   June.
The loss of Cawnpore reacted immediately upon
the situation at Lucknow. There on the night of the
30th of May a great proportion of the four native regiments in garrison had mutinied, but found themselves
helpless in the face of Sir Henry Lawrence's dispositions, and withdrew. Mutinies in the outlying districts of Oudh followed in rapid succession, and the
revolted troops began to close around Lucknow until,
on the 28th of June, heartened by the fall of Cawnpore, June 28.
they approached the village of Chinhat, eight miles
from the Residency. On the 30th Lawrence sallied June 30.
out to meet them with about seven hundred men, including three hundred of the Thirty-second Foot, fifty
European volunteers and eleven guns. Lawrence was
failing in health and had little or no experience of
handling troops in the field, but none the less he took
personal command. The hostile leader, whoever he may
have been, knew his business. Having great superiority
of numbers, he completely out-manœuvred Lawrence
and drove him back into Lucknow with a loss of three
guns captured and of over three hundred and fifty
officers and men; the casualties of the Thirty-second
alone amounting to one hundred and fifteen killed and
thirty-nine wounded. The whole affair was sadly mismanaged. The troops were weary when they started;
they did not march until the sun was up; and they
were fidgeted backwards and forwards to no purpose.
This was the fault of Lawrence, and it was supplemented
by the neglect of the military officers to throw out
picquets from a village which they had occupied, and to
see that their men's rifles were properly loaded.[1]   In
principle Lawrence was no doubt right to take the
offensive, but he should have left the business of commanding in the field to his officers.
    This was a serious misadventure, at a time when
every British soldier was precious. Such native troops

[1] Gubbins, *Mutinies in Oudh*, p. 212.

1857. as had hitherto refrained from mutiny now naturally
June. joined their victorious comrades, though nearly eight
hundred of them still remained faithful. The mutineers
bore hard upon Lawrence's retreating British; and by
sunset they had invested the Residency on all sides.
The defences, or what passed for such, were still
imperfect, for no one had expected a siege so soon.
There was much confusion and some panic; and, had
the mutineers possessed the courage to press their advantage, things might have gone ill with the garrison.
But they were content to fire their guns and muskets
from a distance, and so missed their opportunity. On the
July 1. 1st of July Sir Henry Lawrence ordered the withdrawal
of the garrison from the fort of Machchi Bhawan,
which was then destroyed by blowing up the stores of
ammunition contained therein. On the following day,
July 2. the 2nd of July, Sir Henry Lawrence was dangerously
wounded by the fragment of a shell, and after lingering
in extreme agony for some hours he expired on the
July 4. morning of the 4th. In him died a very able man and
a public servant of the noblest type. If he had blundered
in fighting the action of Chinhat, he atoned for any
mistake by the preparations which he had made for the
protection of Lucknow, and by the spirit which he had
infused into all about him.

The civil command after his death devolved upon
Major Banks, a strong and capable man, and the
military upon Colonel Inglis of the Thirty-second, a
resolute and sensible officer, who had been distinguished
for personal gallantry in the second Sikh War. Lawrence's dying charge to both had been never to
surrender; but the Residency was, from a military
point of view, indefensible, the only fortifications being
slight and uncompleted earthworks. The general con-
figuration of these earthworks was, roughly speaking, a
diamond, about seven hundred yards from north to
south and four hundred from east to west, with a total
content of about thirty-seven acres (nearly twice the
size of Windsor Castle) and a total perimeter of about

a mile. This space was filled with private houses and 1857.
their gardens, which were combined at different points July.
into ten principal sections of defence, whereon were
mounted some fifteen guns and seven mortars. The
whole was surrounded on three sides by native houses,
which, while forbidding the formation of columns for
assault, gave ample cover for sharpshooters. In fact,
the enemy was, so to speak, on the other side of the
street upon all sides. Only over against the salient
of the northern angle was there open ground for the
building of batteries and the massing of troops. The
total strength of the garrison was about seventeen
hundred, of which five hundred belonged to the Thirty-
second, nearly two hundred and fifty more were officers
of the mutinied regiments and soldiers of other descriptions, and one hundred and fifty were civilians, making
altogether nine hundred Europeans and eight hundred
natives. The enemy without numbered some six
thousand, and were constantly reinforced by other
mutineers and malcontents. But their most formidable
ally was the sun.

The garrison daily strengthened and improved their
defences; and the besiegers made no scientific use of
their cannon, though their sharpshooters during the
first week of the siege caused from fifteen to twenty
casualties daily. In fact, after the initial terror had
passed away, it was with the greatest difficulty that
either civilians or soldiers could be persuaded to keep
themselves under cover. At last, on the 19th of July July 19.
the enemy, after springing a harmless mine off the
northern angle, attempted an assault, but were beaten
back after four hours' fighting with very heavy loss.
On the following day Major Banks, exposing his head July 20.
to watch the besiegers' operations, was shot dead, and
Inglis assumed civil as well as military command. On
the 21st a spy in British pay came in and announced July 21.
the assurance of speedy relief; and the garrison was
doubly heartened to resistance.

The besiegers now worked hard at the erection of

1857.
July.

new batteries, but devoted themselves chiefly to the digging of mines, wherein they showed not only energy but considerable skill. They were foiled, however, by the activity of the chief engineer, Captain Fulton, who, choosing a select body of old Cornish miners from the Thirty-second, brought all hostile projects to naught by ingenious counter-mining. Meanwhile the weeks passed and no relief came. The garrison made constant little sallies, but the casualties were heavy. The Thirty-second alone had one hundred and seventy killed and wounded in the month of July. Every man dead or disabled threw heavier duty on the survivors, and the heavier duty, by weakening men against disease, signified yet more casualties— a deadly circle which military commanders dread to see in full turn. Smallpox and cholera were at work, for it was impossible to clear away foul matter or to drain the stagnant pools left by the rains; and, as at Delhi, there was a plague of flies. Wounded and sick men pined away in the overcrowded hospitals for want of proper food and air;[1] every case of amputation was fatal, and children withered away like plucked flowers. Still Inglis was ubiquitous, cheerful and indefatigable; and, though often so weary that he could hardly speak, he never for nearly three months took his clothes off to sleep.

Aug. 10.

Aug. 18.

At length on the 10th of August the enemy, having sprung a mine which opened a breach of ten yards on the southern front, attempted a second assault, which was easily repulsed. On the 18th they exploded a second and more dangerous mine which had escaped the vigilance of Fulton, killing eight men outright. Again they assaulted and were repulsed, but they occupied an outhouse on the flank of the breach; and it was necessary by a resolute sortie to blow up this and

[1] Yet marvellous to say, an officer of the Thirty-second recovered completely from the wound of a bullet which fractured his skull and lodged in his brain, from which it was extracted nine months later in England.—Gubbins, pp. 268-269.

adjoining buildings in order to restore security. On 1857.
the 29th a letter came in from General Havelock, who Aug. 29.
was known to be on march to the relief of Lucknow,
containing the words, " Do not negotiate, but rather
perish sword in hand." This was not quite encouraging, and many of the natives now deserted the
garrison. The numbers of the able-bodied shrank
lower and lower. By the end of the month the five
hundred and fifty men of the Thirty-second and Eighty-
fourth had lost one hundred and twenty-five killed or
dead of wounds, to say nothing of other casualties from
hurts or sickness. The end seemed to be drawing near.

On the 5th of September the enemy sprang two Sept. 5.
more mines, happily without doing serious damage,
and again attempted an assault, which was repulsed with
heavy loss to them and practically none to the garrison.
It was evident that the besiegers of themselves would
never storm Lucknow; but the provisions of the
defenders were thought to be failing. There was, as
a matter of fact, an ample store of grain for several
months, but the Chief of the Commissariat had been
disabled and Inglis had been left with a false impression of the true state of affairs. He reduced the daily
rations, which naturally led to more exhaustion and more
sickness. Despondency began to overcome the defenders. They had no idea of surrendering, but their
hopes of relief sank low; and on the 16th a devoted Sept. 16.
native spy, who had for the second time made his way into
the city, was sent forth with an urgent appeal for help.

As a matter of fact there had been no want of energy
on the part of those who were advancing up the river
to their assistance. Neill's force at Allahabad had been
slowly and steadily growing. He had laboured inde-
fatigably to provide it with transport and victuals, and
to such purpose that he felt confident of starting upon
his advance to Cawnpore by the end of June. On the
24th he was superseded by the appointment of General June 24.
Havelock to the command of his column; but, though
bitterly disappointed, he continued his preparations

1857.
June 30.
with unrelaxed diligence, and on the 30th sent forward an advanced force of eight hundred men, half of them Europeans,[1] under Major Renaud, upon the road to Cawnpore. On that same day Havelock arrived at Allahabad. After forty-one years' service he was at last to attain the object which had always excited his keenest ambition, the chief command of a force in the field. On the 3rd of July he sent, pursuant to Neill's arrangements, a hundred men of the Hundred and Second with two guns up the Ganges to cover Renaud's flank; but, though the news of the massacre of Wheeler's garrison reached him soon after his arrival, it was a full week before he could complete his preparations for movement. Even then there were several deficiencies. Many of the men had only their winter clothing, though Neill had clad the Hundred and Second in suitable attire of a white smock and trousers, with a curtain over their forage caps. His regiment also was the only one completely armed with Enfield rifles. Finally the entire column, barely two thousand strong, was composed of ten different units, comprising British soldiers, civilian volunteers and two or three varieties of Indian troops, with six guns.[2]

July 3.

July 7.
In pouring rain the column started on the afternoon of the 7th along the grand trunk road on the south bank of the Ganges, making at first only short marches, for there were many young soldiers in the ranks. On the 12th Havelock received intelligence from Renaud that the mutineers from Cawnpore were advancing to meet him at Fatehpur, wherefore pushing on he joined forces with Renaud and moved to within four miles of that place. The troops were just cooking their breakfasts when the enemy appeared and made a half-hearted semblance of attack. They were easily driven off by

July 12.

---

[1] 200 of the 84th and 200 of the 102nd.
[2] Havelock's own force (exclusive of the parties sent in advance) was : Royal Artillery, 76; 64th, 435; 78th, 284; 84th, 190; 102nd, 376; Volunteer Cavalry (civilians), 20; Bengal Artillery, 22; Sikhs, 448; Irregular Cavalry, 95; Indian Gunners, 18. *Total*, 1964.

the fire of rifles and of Maude's battery, and fled, 1857.
abandoning all their baggage and twelve guns. Havelock's column suffered twelve casualties from sunstroke,
not one from lead or steel; but his native cavalry had
shown itself untrustworthy in the action and was therefore dismounted and disarmed. There was consequently no possibility of following up the success.

After a day's halt Havelock resumed his advance,
and, gaining information on the evening of the 14th of
rebel forces six miles ahead of him, marched early on the
15th to attack them. The mutineers made not quite July 15.
so bad a fight as on the 12th, but presently retired to a
second position, where they used a heavy siege-gun to
some purpose. But once again they soon gave way,
abandoning four cannon of large calibre, after suffering
some loss from the Enfield rifles; while Havelock's
casualties did not exceed twenty-five killed and wounded.
On that night Nana Sahib gave orders for the destruction of the British captives, nearly two hundred women
and children, whom he still held imprisoned. His
sepoys shrank from the ignoble duty of shooting them
down, whereupon he sent in five ruffians with knives to
hack them to pieces, though not all of them to death;
and in the morning the living with the dead were cast
into a well hard by. There is no need to dwell on this
insensate cruelty of a terrified degenerate; it is more
relevant to dilate on the extreme folly of a crime which
stirred every British soldier to incredible effort for the
avenging of his murdered countrywomen. The geo-
graphical situation of Cawnpore ensured that the greater
number of British troops should pass through it, and
not a man left the blood-stained scene of the massacre
without blind fury in his heart. " Had any Christian
bishop visited that scene of butchery when I saw it,"
wrote Lord Wolseley, nearly fifty years later, " I verily
believe that he would have buckled on the sword."

Havelock's troops bivouacked where they lay,
twenty-two miles from Cawnpore. The night was of
such intolerable heat that they had enjoyed little rest

1857. when at dawn they moved off once more.   The sun
July 16. was unusually fierce, and men fell out right and left
through sunstroke and exhaustion; but the survivors
tramped on doggedly for sixteen miles, when they
halted under the shade of a grove of trees.   News came
in that Nana Sahib, at the head of five thousand men,
was in position astride the road to block the way to
Cawnpore.   Advancing, Havelock observed the enemy
drawn up in the form of a crescent, with a fortified
village upon either horn; and naturally decided to
attack his flanks.   Some loss was incurred from the
rebel artillery during the preliminary movements,
Havelock's field-guns being too light to silence the
enemy's heavier pieces; but Nana Sahib's line gave
way at once before the turning movement and some
of his batteries were stormed by the Seventy-eighth.
After retreating for some distance the Nana faced about,
and brought a reserve gun into action, but, in spite of
their exhaustion, Havelock's men drove him off by a
final charge.   The Nana himself galloped off in terror
July 17. to Bithur; and on the morrow Havelock entered Cawnpore, to find that he had arrived too late.   The late
action had cost him just over one hundred casualties,
of which six only were killed; but cholera and the sun
had been far more deadly than the enemy, and he had
little more than fifteen hundred men fit for duty.

His position was not of the pleasantest.   He was
bound to occupy Cawnpore, which would still further
weaken his field-force.   The mutineers of the Gwalior
contingent were gathering as one body at Kalpi, forty-
five miles to south-west; the Nana's forces were reported to be at Bithur, twenty miles to north; and
Lucknow was crying out for his help, forty miles to
north-east, so that, if he marched thither, he would be
threatened not only in front, but on his left flank and
left rear.   He summoned Neill to Cawnpore with such
men as he could bring with him, a mere two hundred
and twenty, and committed the defence of the city to
him.   He then made his preparations for the passage

of the Ganges—no easy matter over a rushing flood a 1857.
mile wide—and on the 26th the troops, having crossed July 26.
in boats without mishap, bivouacked on the left bank
of the river.   Three days were employed in collecting
transport and provisions; and then, mounting a few
picked men of the infantry to supplement his meagre
force of cavalry, Havelock moved on the morning of
the 29th towards Lucknow with a force of unknown July 29.
strength in his front and an impassable river in his rear.
After a short march he came upon the enemy in a strong
position near the town of Unao, with their right resting
on a swamp and their left upon flooded meadows.   A
frontal attack was inevitable, and the enemy resisted
obstinately for some time in enclosures and loopholed
houses before their fifteen guns were captured, when
they finally gave way.   As they did so, intelligence was
brought that another body of the rebels, some six thousand strong, was advancing from Lucknow; and Havelock hastened to take up a position beyond the ground
that he had won, whence the enemy, blundering upon
him in disorder, were easily driven back.   Moving forward again about six miles, after a short halt, Havelock
came upon another party of the rebels in the walled
town of Bashirat-ganj, and laid his plans to assail them
with his artillery and the Seventy-eighth in front, while
the Sixty-fourth should fetch a compass to cut off their
retreat.   The attack was successful, but, as so often
happens, was delivered before the turning movement
had been completed; and hence the bulk of the enemy
escaped.   The loss of the rebels in the two actions of
the day was reckoned at about four hundred, while
Havelock's did not exceed eighty-eight killed and
wounded.

Such a casualty-list sounds trifling in these days, but
it was doubled by the number of men dead or disabled
through sickness and fatigue; and, if the first advance
of fifteen miles had cost already so much hard marching
and hard fighting, Havelock might well ask himself
where he should find the strength to carry him through

1857.
July.
the thirty miles that still lay between him and Lucknow. He had already fired away a third of his ammunition; and he was greatly embarrassed by the disposal of his sick and wounded. He had no means of carrying them with him, and he could not leave them, because he could spare no force to protect them. He was already hesitating as to the expediency of further advance when news came in of the mutiny, presently to be related, of the native troops at Dinapore, and of the consequent interception of reinforcements upon which he had counted. In the circumstances he felt that he had no alternative, and on the 31st he fell back to Mangalwar.

July 31.
Thence he sent his sick and wounded into Cawnpore, and wrote to Neill that without another thousand infantry and an additional battery of artillery he could not hope to reach Lucknow.

This was sound sense, and Havelock showed great moral courage in facing unwelcome facts, for no man was more bitterly disappointed than he over his enforced retirement. But Neill, in great excitement, wrote a most insubordinate reply, urging that, while Havelock waited for reinforcements, Lucknow would be lost, and that he ought to advance immediately to its relief. Havelock answered sharply that the critical state of affairs alone prevented him from placing Neill under arrest; but, like Anson before him, he was stung by unmerited reproach into acting against his better judgement. With no further reinforcement than a company of the Eighty-fourth and a half battery, he, on the 4th of August, again advanced, found the mutineers again in position at Bashirat-ganj and drove them off, but failed to capture their guns. His casualties amounted only to two killed and twenty-three wounded, whereas those of the enemy were reckoned to be ten times as great; but after all, he had accomplished nothing; wherefore once again facing facts he retired to Mangalwar, where he busied himself with establishing the equivalent of a permanent bridge across the Ganges.

Aug. 4.

Aug. 11.
On the 11th, Neill, who had been striking out all round

him to preserve order, so far as his strength permitted,
reported the assembly of four thousand rebels at Bithur
and his doubt whether he could hold Cawnpore against
them.   Havelock realised the danger, and resolved to
join him, but decided first to make another sally upon
the enemy in his front as a movement of defiance.   On
the 12th accordingly he moved rapidly forward, and,
coming upon the rebels in an entrenched position
before Bashirat-ganj, attacked them in front and flank
and captured three guns.   On the next day he retired
across the river to Cawnpore; but he was not disposed
to leave the enemy at Bithur unmolested, and on the
morning of the 16th he led against them the remnant
of his force, a mere handful of seven hundred and fifty
gaunt, careworn, overworked British and two hundred
and fifty Sikhs.   The rebels, as usual, were well posted
and ensconced, the approach to them being covered by
two unfordable streams, each of which could be passed
only by a single bridge, while in rear were entrenchments and the town of Bithur, well prepared for defence
—" one of the strongest positions I have ever seen,"
wrote Havelock.   It was carried within a short hour,
with the loss to the enemy of two hundred and fifty
killed and wounded and of two guns.   But Havelock
also lost forty-nine killed and wounded and twelve dead
of sunstroke.   The men, from some mistake, did not
start until half an hour before sunrise; they were so
feeble that it took them eight hours to traverse fifteen
miles, and on the return march the rain was sometimes
so heavy that the whole force was obliged to halt and
turn about.   They reached Cawnpore drenched to the
skin, and the men who were then detailed for the outlying picquet were practically doomed to death from
cholera.[1]
    In fact this little column of Havelock's was literally

---

[1] Wylly, *Neill's Blue-Caps*, ii. 68.   " Chisholm was detailed for
outlying picquet and said to me (Second Lieutenant Dale), ' I am wet
through.   I know I shall get cholera before I am relieved.'   He was
seized with cholera next day and died two days later."

1857. marched and fought to a standstill. On the 14th of
Aug. August Havelock's surgeon reported that, at the reign-
ing rate of mortality from cholera, the force would be
annihilated in six weeks. On the 15th there were
fourteen hundred and fifteen British of the Sixty-
fourth, Seventy-eighth, Eighty-fourth, Hundred and
Second and gunners with Havelock, of whom three
hundred and thirty-five were disabled by wounds or
sickness. On that day there were ten deaths from
cholera in one regiment alone,[1] and on the 16th, as we
have seen, there were twelve deaths from sunstroke in
the field, apart from any that may have taken place in
hospital. Seventy men—not absolutely a great number,
but relatively one-twentieth of the whole—were reported, without any specific disorder, to be " too much
exhausted to do anything," or in plain words they were
worn out and were left in charge of a surgeon.   " They
are called invalids," wrote an officer at this time, " but
the whole force might be classed in the same category.
Such a lot of ragged, woebegone, bearded ruffians
you never saw." [2]   And what had Havelock's column
accomplished at the cost of so much effort?   The
occupation of Cawnpore and the restoration at least of
that stage on the line of communication.   They had
incidentally killed a few thousand rebels, but they had
achieved nothing more solid towards the restoration of
order and of British rule.   It was no fault of theirs nor
of their leader's.   Havelock, at the age of sixty-two,
shared all their hardships, and would sleep, if need
were, on the ground with his horse saddled beside him
and the bridle over his arm.   But his force was not
strong enough for the task assigned to them; and there
is no surer method of swelling casualty-lists than
overwork.

The truth is that Canning and his advisers would
not realise that the mutineers were not a mere rabble
of insurgents but men disciplined and trained by the

[1] Marshman, *Life of Havelock*, p. 357.
[2] Wylly, *Neill's Blue-Caps*, p. 70.

British themselves, with plenty of arms, of ammunition 1857. and, thanks to the general carelessness of the Indian administration, of guns.   They were not good fighters, as the story of Havelock's actions sufficiently shows; but they could choose strong positions—every Indian seems to possess that gift—they could inflict loss before they ran away, and they understood the advantage of having the climate on their side.   The times were desperate; there were garrisons in sore straits to be relieved; there were distractions in a score of places; there were confusion and panic enough to upset all but the calmest heads.   One is passing judgement long after the event; and yet it seems doubtful whether the government at Calcutta, when it hurried Anson's and Havelock's columns independently into the field at the height of the hot season, did not play into the rebels' hands.   The question is not one of apportioning praise or blame to individuals, but of the principle which should govern those who direct operations if, in India or in any other British possession, a similar situation should arise in future.   Here we have independent columns sent off hurriedly, the one to the capture of Delhi, the other to the relief of Lucknow.   Both are overmatched; both work themselves heroically to death; and neither accomplish anything until they have been reinforced, re-equipped, and to all intent re-created.   There are times, no doubt, when all rules must be thrown to the winds.   Was the opening of the Indian Mutiny a time for dispersion or concentration of military force?   Were political exigencies and moral requirements best met by setting impossible tasks to mere handfuls of men, or would it have been wiser to keep, at the outset, those handfuls collected in one body which might have accomplished some solid work?   To one who has studied the methods of Indian "politicals" in the past, it seems that all of their old faults were repeated in the early stages of the Indian Mutiny.

CHAPTER LI

1857. MEANWHILE the government at Calcutta had, through no error of judgement but through sheer foolishness thrown up for itself a fresh crop of very serious difficulties. Allusion has already been made to the tardiness of Canning in disbanding the native regiments at Barrackpore, and to his abstention, in the face of the local Commissioner's entreaties, from disarming and dismissing the three native battalions at Dinapore. The dearth of British regiments may perhaps be pleaded as an excuse for delay in dealing with those at Dinapore; but that excuse vanished with the arrival of British regiments from oversea. The first of these, the Thirty-seventh from Ceylon, reached the Hugli in June, and the Fifth Fusiliers, summoned from Mauritius to China and diverted to India, landed on the 5th. Both regiments, as soon as they could be equipped, were sent up the Ganges by detachments to reinforce Havelock; and, since they would pass Dinapore on their way, the leading residents there and at Patna waited upon Canning and begged that they might stop at Dinapore for a few hours and disarm the three native battalions before they proceeded on their journey. Canning curtly refused to give any such order, but agreed to leave the treatment of the three native battalions to the discretion of the commanding officer at Dinapore, an effete and unnerved old man named General Lloyd. Thereby Canning showed his utter unfitness for high command. He was, as a matter of judgement, wrong in his decision not to disband the

regiments, and, though any man may err, he should by 1857.
the middle of July have learned better than to make such July.
a blunder.   But to shift the responsibility for correcting
that decision upon a subordinate was not only wrong,
it was contemptible.

General Lloyd under this trial showed pitiable
irresolution.   On the 22nd of July the two leading
companies of the Fifth reached Dinapore and were
allowed to proceed on their way.   On the 24th arrived July 24.
two companies of the Thirty-seventh.   Lloyd ordered
them to land, and next day decided to compromise in
the matter of disarmament by depriving the sepoys of
their percussion-caps.   He succeeded in securing the
percussion-caps in the magazine, and then sent the
Thirty-seventh on towards their destination, leaving it
to the officers to get hold of the percussion-caps already
served out to the men.   Thereupon the sepoys broke
into open mutiny and marched off westward to the
river Son, pointing towards Arah, where they had a
friend in a large native landowner, Kunwar Singh, who
nursed a grievance against the law courts of Calcutta.
Reaching the river on the 26th they crossed it in boats July 26.
provided by Kunwar Singh; and, having reached Arah,
they released all prisoners from the gaol, plundered the
treasury, and proceeded in search of the British residents.
These, however, had been warned by Commissioner
Tayler, who had further sent them fifty Sikh police;
and the whole body of them, fifteen British and
Eurasians, one native gentleman and the native servants,
making with the Sikhs sixty-eight souls in all, had
fortified a house and determined to defend themselves.
On the evening of the 27th the mutineers moved upon July 27.
this house without misgiving, but were met by so sharp
and deadly a fire that they were fain to keep themselves
under cover and turn the assault into a blockade.

Meanwhile it had never occurred to Lloyd to send
troops in pursuit of the rebel soldiers; and it was not
until he heard of the danger of the British at Arah that,
yielding at last to the entreaties of Commissioner

1857.
July 27.
July 29.

Tayler, he on the evening of the 27th sent off a party to rescue them. After some delay, owing to the stranding of the steamer that conveyed them, this detachment disembarked on the afternoon of the 29th— a composite force of the Tenth, Thirty-seventh, and volunteers, in all rather over four hundred strong, under Captain Dunbar. Eager to save his countrymen, Dunbar pushed on through the night, refusing to halt when the moon went down, but stumbling on without precaution through the darkness. As his troops reached the suburbs of Arah they fell into an ambush, and there was a panic. Dunbar and many others were killed, and the survivors were harassed and pursued for fifteen miles until the remnant reached the steamer which was waiting to convey them back. The unwounded did not exceed three officers and fifty men. In the circumstances, at that particular moment, the mishap was little less than a disaster, the more exasperating because it was wholly unnecessary. Dunbar no doubt had blundered tactically; Lloyd had blundered because he was incapable of anything but blundering; but the real responsibility lay upon Canning.

Meanwhile the little garrison in the house held out gallantly, with equal resolution, ingenuity and resource; yet it should seem that, but for a happy chance, they would have been left to their fate. It happened that on the 25th of July Major Vincent Eyre, whom we have already seen as a subaltern of artillery at Kabul, touched at Dinapore when moving by river with his battery from Calcutta to Allahabad. Arriving at Baksar, one hundred and twenty miles further up the river, he took one hundred and fifty men of the Fifth Fusiliers, which had reached that point on the way up the river, col-
July 30. lected supplies and transport, and on the 30th marched to the relief of Arah, some fifty miles distant. His whole force, including forty gunners and a dozen mounted volunteers, numbered two hundred and sixteen of all ranks, with three guns. On the 1st of August he heard of Dunbar's defeat, and on the follow-

ing morning he came upon the enemy, twenty-five 1857.
hundred strong, drawn up in a belt of jungle to Aug. 2.
oppose his advance. With the fire of his guns and of
Enfield rifles he drove them back for a couple of miles,
when the rebels turned in a second belt of jungle
and manœuvred to surround him. Thereupon Eyre
ordered the men of the Fifth to charge, and the
mutineers fled in a panic before the bayonet. Another
four miles' march brought the party to the beleaguered
house, where the gallant little garrison of civilians still
held their own; and Arah was made safe. Eyre's
casualties in the action did not exceed two killed and
fifteen wounded, besides one man dead of cholera on
the march. The numbers furnish an eloquent com-
mentary on the mismanagement of Dunbar.

Having accomplished so much on his own responsibility, Eyre determined to follow up Kunwar Singh, and
asked for reinforcements. By the 9th these had reached Aug. 9.
him—two hundred men of the Tenth and a hundred
Sikh police from Dinapore—and with these he advanced upon Kunwar Singh's castle. On the 12th he Aug. 12.
came upon the enemy strongly posted, as usual, behind
a maze of jungle. The rifle-fire of skirmishers soon
compelled them to show themselves; Eyre's guns then
played upon them; and a charge with the bayonet sufficed to disperse them. The whole affair did not cost
Eyre more than six men wounded. By evening he was
in possession of Kunwar Singh's stronghold, where he
found large stores of ammunition and six months'
supplies of grain for twenty thousand men. After
blowing up the principal buildings he marched in pursuit of Kunwar Singh until recalled by instructions to
Baksar, which he reached on the 23rd. He had done Aug. 23.
invaluable service by restoring fear of the British around
Patna; and his rapid success with a handful of men
shows how contemptible the enemy really was in the
face of common energy and resolution. But it was no
thanks to the Supreme Government at Calcutta that
there was not a serious rupture in the line of communi-

1857. cation about Patna. Meanwhile the reinforcements which were on their way to Havelock were of course delayed, and his column, as we have seen, was reduced to impotence. The operations for restoring order north and west of Cawnpore had come to a stand.[1]

June 23. Let us now return to Delhi, where we left the British hard beset, but heartened by the timely arrival of reinforcements during the critical action of the 23rd of June. On the 28th a wing of the Eighth Foot and on

July 1-2. the 1st of July a wing of the Sixty-first joined them, together rather fewer than eight hundred men; and these were followed on the 2nd by the First Punjab infantry, slightly over eight hundred strong, one hundred Punjab cavalry, and two hundred irregular cavalry, these last of doubtful fidelity. Lastly, on the

July 6. 6th there arrived sixty-two European artillerymen and eighty Sikh gunners. These accessions little more than made good previous casualties through action and sickness; but the coming of Lieutenant-colonèl Baird Smith as chief engineer was a real addition to the strength and energy of the force. On the other hand, the hostile troops in Delhi were strengthened by large bodies of mutineers from Rohilkhand. Meanwhile, on the 3rd the enemy, after a demonstration in force against the British right, had slipped round under cover of darkness to their left or northern flank, as if to threaten the British communications with the Punjab. Hitherto they had not thought of so obvious and formidable a movement; and it was imperative to send a detachment to deal with them at once. As it happened, the menace proved not to be serious, and, after a short skirmish, both parties returned to their own place. The troops, however, were on foot ten hours in great heat, and, though their casualties in action were trifling, they were, as usual, doubled by the sun. On the 5th July Sir Henry Barnard was smitten with cholera and died

---

[1] Eyre's account of his operations is printed in Appendix X. of Gubbins's *Mutinies in Oudh*. The best account of the defence of Arah is that of Sir George Trevelyan.

within a few hours. He was succeeded by General 1857.
Reed, who, though senior to Barnard, had, owing to
ill-health, made over the command to him.

The next affair with the enemy was brought about July 9.
on the 9th of July through the treachery of some of the
native cavalry, lately arrived, whereby a party of hostile
horse was quietly brought into the British lines, and
was only driven back by the extraordinary gallantry
and presence of mind of two artillery officers, Major
Tombs and Lieutenant Hills. Then the enemy, following their usual sound tactics, assembled in the
southern suburbs to threaten the British right flank
and rear; and a detachment of about eight hundred
infantry with six guns under Brigadier-general Neville
Chamberlain was ordered to dislodge them. In a
maze of gardens and walled enclosures the rebel sepoys
fought well; and, though they were finally driven out
with an estimated loss of a thousand killed and wounded,
the casualties of the British exceeded two hundred.
And these losses were absolutely unprofitable, for no
effort was made to blow up the suburbs and make an
end of so favourable a fighting ground for the enemy.
General Reed, after the action, determined to disarm
all Hindustani soldiers and turn them out of the camp.
Altogether the result of the day's work was a serious
diminution in the strength of the British force.

On the 14th the enemy again occupied the southern July 14.
suburbs, and it was necessary again to drive them out.
On this occasion the British pursued them too far, and,
coming under fire of the heavy guns on the walls of
Delhi, suffered heavily. They were fiercely assailed
as they retired, and but for their steadiness would have
been in great peril. Once more the casualties exceeded
two hundred, though the number actually slain was
small, and among the severely wounded was Neville
Chamberlain, in himself a great loss. On the 18th July 18.
the enemy again fell upon the southern suburbs, and
were again driven out. Lieutenant-colonel Jones of
the Sixtieth, who was in charge of the troops, wisely

1857.
July.
forbore to approach too near to the walls; yet even so, the casualties numbered over eighty; and it is difficult to see how the capture of Delhi had been advanced in the slightest degree by the sacrifice of five hundred men in nine days.

On the 17th General Reed, his health being broken down, handed over the command to Brigadier-general Archdale Wilson. This latter was not a great genius, but he was at least alive to certain shortcomings in the force which he set out to remedy at once. Discipline had grown very lax among the men, who had been allowed to become slovenly and to turn themselves out very much as they pleased. Officers again had grown very negligent about ordinary precautions when in charge of the picquets, true to the carelessness which had always been characteristic of Indian military operations. Lastly, Wilson introduced order and method in the distribution of the various duties, arranging for systematic reliefs, which gave the men far more rest.[1] The neglect of these matters by his predecessors reflects credit neither on them nor on their staff, and seems to indicate that Barnard, fresh from the Crimea, had not realised the casual ways of Indian officers. Next, as a more practical measure, Wilson swept away many of the buildings and enclosures in the Sabzi Mandi, so as to give the British picquets a better field of fire. None of these measures demanded any extraordinary military ability, but Wilson was the first to undertake them. As to general military policy he seems to have had some doubt whether it would not be wiser to quit Delhi altogether and to employ his troops to better purpose elsewhere; but, looking to the political effect of such a step upon the Punjab, he decided to prosecute the siege, and to make it such in something more than name by ordering a siege-train to join him from Ferozepore.

Meanwhile the enemy, finding the defences on the British right flank to be improved, moved out on the

[1] Roberts, ch. xvi., beginning; Rotton, pp. 155-156.

23rd against the left, and occupied a building, known as 1857.
Ludlow Castle, about half a mile to north-west of the July.
Kashmir gate. They were driven out with little difficulty,
at a cost of fifty casualties. After this they remained
quiet until the 31st, when they made an attempt upon
the British right, followed on the 1st of August by a Aug. 1.
more determined assault upon the same quarter. Both
attacks were repulsed at small cost to the defenders; and
the rebels, who had from the first been torn by dissensions, quarrelled the more bitterly among themselves
owing to discouragement. They persisted, however,
in their endeavours to enfilade the British position by
batteries erected on the right flank, and guns were
mounted by them also on Ludlow Castle. Accord-
ingly on the 12th, Wilson made a sortie against Ludlow Aug. 12.
Castle, which resulted in the capture of the guns, four
in number, and in the infliction of heavy loss upon
the rebels, at a cost of little more than a hundred
casualties.

Two days later, on the 14th, there marched in from Aug. 14.
the Punjab, under command of Brigadier-general John
Nicholson, the movable column with which he had
maintained order in that province—the last reinforcements that John Lawrence could spare. They were
but a few, namely, the Fifty-second and the remaining
wing of the Sixty-first, together eleven hundred strong,
a field-battery, the 2nd Punjab infantry, two hundred
newly raised Multani cavalry, fine men but totally
undisciplined, and four hundred native military police.
Some days earlier the Kumaon battalion of Sikhs had
also come in; and now for the first time the force
before Delhi began to assume a reasonable strength.
The siege-train, however, had not yet come in, and
it was known that the enemy would move out in force
to intercept it as it approached. A large body of them
was seen to leave Delhi in the night of the 23rd-24th;
and accordingly, before sunrise of the 25th, Nicholson
marched with about two thousand men, one-fifth of
them cavalry, and sixteen horse-artillery guns, to foil

1857. them.[1] The rain was falling in torrents, and the
Aug. 25. country was one great quagmire. After traversing
nine miles Nicholson ascertained that the enemy was
still ten or twelve miles ahead of him; wherefore pushing on, always through water, he came at four o'clock
in the afternoon upon the enemy, some six thousand
strong, in a formidable position, with a broad flooded
drain covering their right and rear. The day being
far spent he attacked at once, fording the water breast-
high to fall upon the enemy's right, and drove them off
with a loss of eight hundred men, thirteen guns, and of
the whole of their baggage and transport. Nicholson's
casualties were just under one hundred killed and
wounded. Since, however, his force, after a most
exhausting march, bivouacked on the wet ground
without food or covering, the sick list must have been
a long one. On the next day he marched back safely
to the ridge before Delhi.

This was really a profitable action, and the more so
since the mutineers in Delhi seized the opportunity
of Nicholson's absence to attack the ridge in great
Aug. 26. force on the following morning, and were repulsed
with trifling loss to the British. Meanwhile the
British engineers had been considering the sites for
Sept. 4. batteries; and on the 4th of September the siege-train
at last came in, thirty-two pieces, making up the heavy
artillery to fifteen twenty - four pounders, twenty
eighteen-pounders, and twenty-five mortars and howitzers of various calibres. The escort included over two
hundred men of the Eighth Foot and a Baluch battalion,
Sept. 6. and on the 6th there came in also the remainder of the
first battalion of the Sixtieth. The entire force before
Delhi now amounted to nearly nine thousand soldiers,[2]
more than a third of them British, exclusive of some

---

[1] Guide Cavalry, 120; 2nd Punjab Cavalry, 80; 61st, 420; 101st,
380; 1st and 2nd Punjab Infantry, 400 each; Sappers and Miners,
30; Multani Horse, 200.

[2] 8748; of which 3217 British, viz. 580 artillery, 443 cavalry,
2294 infantry.

three thousand men from the friendly rulers of Kashmir
and Jhind.   Not another man could be spared from
the Punjab, and the prospect of reinforcements from
the east was very remote.   The troops were falling
down fast from sickness, the Fifty-second having been
reduced in three weeks from six hundred to two
hundred and forty-five fit for duty.   Now, if ever, a
decisive blow must be struck; yet Wilson shrank from
running the risk of an assault.   It should seem that
he dreaded not so much the danger of a repulse as
the possible dissolution of his army in the event of
success.   Here was an Oriental city more than two
miles square in extent, with narrow tortuous streets
and endless buildings where a mutinous sepoy, from
his local knowledge, might prove as good a man as the
British soldier.   The precedents of Rosetta and Buenos
Ayres suggested a very good chance of failure, while
that of Badajoz was a painful reminder that pillage and
liquor could reduce a British army to an ungovernable
mob.   Poor Wilson, ill and worn out by heat, anxiety
and hard work, had some excuse for hesitation.

His superiors and subordinates alike, however,
insisted that the hazard must be taken.   Lawrence
wrote from the Punjab that every day's delay signified
increasing peril in that province.   Baird-Smith, himself worn down by disease and a painful wound, was
resolute in supporting Lawrence's opinion.   Chamberlain, Henry Norman, who had taken Chamberlain's
place as Adjutant-general after his wound, Henry Daly
of the Guides, Alexander Taylor, who had acted as chief
engineer until Baird-Smith's arrival, were all of the
same mind; while John Nicholson went so far as to
resolve that, if Wilson hesitated longer, he would move
in council of war that Wilson should be superseded.
No such drastic measure proved to be necessary, for
Wilson, yielding to his advisers, agreed to an assault,
and on the 7th in a general order announced his
intention to his troops.

Ground was broken on that same evening.   Baird-

1857. Smith had resolved to push the main attack from the
Sept. British left, where the walls of the city could be more
nearly approached under cover, and where the river
gave protection to the left flank—in fact, practically
to throw the whole of his strength against the northern
front of the fortress.   In order to deceive the enemy,
however, he had thrown up a battery on the extreme
right, by a building known as the Sami House, which
would serve at once to play upon the Mori bastion, at
the north-western angle, and to check any sorties from
the western front.   The batteries against the northern
front were five in all.   The first was thrown up seven
yards to north of the Mori bastion and armed with
ten pieces, six of which were designed to play upon
that bastion, and four twenty-four pounders upon the
Kashmir bastion.   It was completed shortly after sun-
Sept. 8. rise of the 8th, and by the afternoon had silenced the
Mori bastion and reduced it to a heap of ruins.

On the evening of the 8th the British occupied
Ludlow Castle and began to throw up a second battery
in advance of it, five hundred yards from the Kashmir
gate.   The enemy now realised what was going forward, and did their utmost by heavy firing to prevent
Sept. 11. it; but by the morning of the 11th the second battery
was completed and armed with sixteen heavy pieces,
and the sites for the third and fourth were marked out
a little to east of it.   The third, which was the most
easterly within close range of the Water bastion, was
the most costly to erect, forty native pioneers being
killed and wounded on the first night of its construction.
It was finished none the less, and armed with six
guns and twelve mortars, as was the fourth battery
likewise with twelve heavy mortars.   From the moment
when the pieces were in position they opened and
maintained a continuous fire which soon knocked the
Kashmir and Water bastions to pieces.   Nor did the
enemy fail to reply, bringing guns into the open and
keeping up an incessant rain of musketry from the
walls, to such purpose that between the 7th and the

14th of September the British casualties exceeded three 1857.
hundred.

By the evening of the 13th practicable breaches had Sept. 13.
been made in the Kashmir and Water bastions, and
Baird-Smith advised an immediate assault.   Since the
cannonade had opened, practically every man had been
on unintermitted duty.   Even the Ninth Lancers and
Carabiniers had been called upon to furnish gunners
for the batteries.   It was evident that such a state of
things could not be prolonged; and orders were issued
for the delivery of the assault before daybreak.   Three
columns and a reserve column were told off to the
northern front.[1]   The first, under command of Nicholson in person, was to storm the breach in the Kashmir
bastion; the second, under Brigadier-general Jones of
the Sixty-first, was to fall on the breach in the Water
bastion on Nicholson's left; the third, under Colonel
Campbell of the Fifty-second, was to enter the Kashmir
gate as soon as it should be blown open; and the
reserve, under Brigadier-general Longfield of the
Eighth Foot, was to act as required.   A fourth
column, under Colonel Reid, was to attack the suburbs
of Kisenganj and Paharipur at the southern end of the
ridge, and force an entrance at the Kabul gate, immediately to south of the Mori bastion.   Each column
was about a thousand strong, with a proportion of from
one-third to one-half of Europeans; but they were
only made up even to this poor strength by employing
every man who could bear arms.   The picquets were

[1] 1st *Column*: Nicholson. H.M. 75th, 300; 101st, 250; 2nd
Punjab Inf., 450 = 1000.
2nd   „   Jones. H.M. 8th, 250; 104th, 250; 4th Sikhs,
350 = 850.
3rd   „   Campbell. H.M. 52nd, 200; Kumaon Battn., 250;
1st Punjab Inf., 500 = 950.
Reserve: Longfield. H.M. 61st, 250; 4th Punjab Inf., 450;
Baluch Battn., 300 = 1000. Also 300 of the
Jhind Contingent.
4th *Column*: Reid. Sirmur Battn., Guides Inf., British and
Native piquets = 860. Also 1200 men of the
Kashmir Contingent.

1857. dangerously weakened; and sick and wounded men were called out of hospital for the protection of the camp.

Sept. 14. The sun was up when the batteries suddenly fell silent and Nicholson gave the order to advance. Two hundred of the Sixtieth from the reserve ran out in skirmishing order to cover the storming party, and the ramparts were instantly ablaze with musketry. So fierce was the fire that most of the men carrying ladders were killed; but after a short delay the ladders were brought forward and the breach in the Kashmir bastion was carried. Simultaneously Jones's column mastered the breach in the Water bastion; and meanwhile Lieutenants Home and Salkeld of the Engineers, with a few followers to carry powder-bags, had rushed forward to blow in the Kashmir gate. Half of this party were killed or wounded, but the wicket was successfully destroyed; and, crossing the ditch by a narrow plank, Campbell's column likewise entered the fortress. Reid's column was less fortunate. By some mistake there was delay in sending him his guns, and meanwhile some of his irregular troops became prematurely engaged. He therefore advanced into Kisenganj without them, and presently was disabled by a wound. His Gurkhas thereupon hung back; there was uncertainty as to who had succeeded him in command; the irregulars succumbed to panic, increasing the confusion, and at last the officers drew off such few British troops as were present and fell back to Hindu Rao's house. The enemy, encouraged by success, pressed on and seemed likely to break into the British position, when Hope Grant brought up his cavalry brigade and, together with Tombs's battery, resolutely barred the way.

Meanwhile the three assaulting columns had made good their lodgements within the walls. The first and second were to all purposes united into one, and the whole set off to follow the ramparts and clear them along the eastern and western fronts. Nicholson, separated from his own people for a time, accompanied Campbell's column eastward, and then southward

through the heart of the city to the mosque of the Jama 1857.
Masjid.   The amalgamated columns meanwhile struck Sept. 14.
southward along the western front, mastering it as far as
the Kabul gate, and beyond it, until they were checked
at the Burn bastion.   At this point the mutineers
brought up a gun, and, occupying the buildings on the
east side of the narrow way with infantry, compelled
the assailants to fall back to the Kabul gate.   Here
presently Nicholson appeared and, chafing over even
the semblance of a reverse, ordered a fresh advance
upon the Burn bastion.   The approach to it was along
a narrow lane between the ramparts and wall on one
hand, and flat-roofed, parapeted houses on the other,
all affording safe and commanding positions for the
enemy's sharpshooters.   Torn by grapeshot from the
front and overwhelmed by bullets, cold shot and other
missiles from above, the troops ran forward and carried
and spiked one gun, but were driven back again and
could not face the storm.   Then Nicholson came
forward himself to lead the men to a second attack, and
was instantly brought down by a bullet through the
chest.   Therewith all further attempts were abandoned,
and the column fell back to the Kabul gate.   Campbell
upon reaching the Chandni Chauk—the " Silver
Street " which traverses Delhi from east to west—
and finding himself unsupported, fell back slowly and
in good order to the church at the north-eastern angle
of the city, where the reserve-column had secured the
gains of their comrades.

Meanwhile the safety of the ridge and of the
British camp had only been ensured by the staunchness
and endurance of the Cavalry Brigade, which stood for
two hours patient and passive, never moving a step nor
firing a shot under the fire of a heavy gun from the
Lahore bastion.   Tombs's battery and two guns of
Campbell's stood with them, but they at least had their
guns in action.   Tombs lost twenty-seven men out of
forty-eight; Campbell as large a proportion; and the
Ninth Lancers, who numbered a bare two hundred

1857.
Sept. 14.

men, had forty-two men and sixty-one horses killed or wounded. They were at last relieved by a party of infantry and another battery, having nobly played their thankless part in the work of the day.

Wilson had ridden in at the Kashmir gate as soon as he was satisfied that the attack had been successful, and taken up his station at the church. As report after report of mishap came in he grew seriously disquieted, and even spoke of withdrawing again from the city to the ridge. He held, as a matter of fact, only an external fringe of Delhi from the Water bastion to the Kabul gate—perhaps one-fourth of the whole perimeter—and his right flank was dangerously exposed. He had lost sixty-six officers and eleven hundred men killed and wounded, and he could not feel too certain as to the discipline of the survivors. It was not a pleasant position, but it must be faced. Chamberlain and Baird-Smith again insisted that such part of Delhi as had been taken must be held to the last extremity; and Wilson decided to take the strong man's line.

Sept. 15.

The next day was spent in consolidating the captured position and getting the troops together. The mutineers had been cunning enough to sow the deserted streets and dwellings with bottles of wine and spirits, and it was not surprising that a good number of men, in the reaction after great excitement and prolonged fatigue, succumbed to the temptation. Indiscriminate plunder likewise led men astray; and if the mutineers had attempted a counter-attack [1] they might have made things extremely unpleasant. But the Oriental, when once a footing has been secured in his stronghold, invariably loses heart. Wilson had every full bottle of liquor broken; the men were collected; and artillery was mounted to shell the enemy's strong-

---

[1] According to Lord Roberts they gave signs of a counter-attack on the evening of the 15th, but a band struck up " Cheer, boys, cheer " (a popular song unknown to the present generation); the troops all began to cheer, and the enemy thought better of their intention. —*Forty-one Years in India*, ch. xviii. *ad finem*.

holds within the city.   It was very soon decided that 1857.
the British were not strong enough to capture the place
by street-fighting; and the men were kept under cover
while the engineers sapped from house to house.   On
the 16th the magazine, close to the church, and on Sept. 16.
the 17th the bank a little to south of it, were mastered.
On the 20th, after two days' sapping, the Burn Sept. 20.
bastion and the Lahore gate were taken in rear and
captured.   On the same day the Jama Masjid and the
King's Palace were taken after trifling resistance; and
Wilson made the hall of audience his head-quarters.
On the 21st the unfortunate Emperor, who had fled Sept. 21.
to the tomb of Humayun, seven miles north of Delhi,
was taken and brought in by Captain Hodson, who
later in the day returned and shot dead with his own
hand two sons and a grandson of the dethroned
monarch.   A royal salute proclaimed that the British
again ruled in the capital of the Moguls.

The capture of Delhi was a feat of arms most creditable to the courage and endurance of the troops.   For
twelve weeks they had lain on the ridge in the height
of the hot season and of the monsoon, perpetually
harassed and perpetually engaged.   In the course of
that time they fought thirty actions of greater or less
importance and, as has been told, were for long the
besieged rather than the besiegers.   Happily they
had to do with an enemy which was divided by dissensions and which possessed no guiding head and no
strategic instinct.   Tactically, the mutineers showed
some skill.   They hit the weak point of the British—
the right flank—immediately; and, when the breaching
batteries were raised, they at once brought out guns to
enfilade them.   Among buildings and enclosures too,
the rebels showed considerable stubbornness as fighters,
though they always gave way when the white man closed
with them.   But the want of strategic insight on
their side was lamentable.   They hardly threatened the
communications with the Punjab.   On the one occasion
when they ventured on a menace, they were easily dis-

1857. persed by a handful of irregular cavalry under one who
Sept. delighted in fighting against odds, that strange and seemingly doubtful character, William Hodson.   The British siege-train with its ammunition occupied eight miles of road, and its escort was of paltry strength, yet no serious attempt was made to intercept it.   It is small wonder that the British took liberties with such an enemy.

But on the British side also there was lack of a leader.   To judge from the orders issued by Wilson when he took over command, the most elementary details of order and method had been neglected; and yet there were many complaints of Wilson's irresolution and incompetence.   When Nicholson came upon the scene, then indeed there was a leader before Delhi. With his iron physical frame, his dominant personality and his fierce resolution, he made his presence felt immediately.   But he was not the chief, and his rather arrogant bearing did not commend itself to all of his brother officers.   It is remarkable that he seems to have been the first general officer who went everywhere and looked into everything with his own eyes; but even he wanted a guide, and he found one in Alexander Taylor, the engineer.   Indeed, it should seem that it was Taylor who by action and unseen, almost unconscious, influence was the main link that held the force together.   Arriving early in June he made it his first task to throw up a continuous line of breast-works and intermediate defences so as to bind the principal posts together, thereby incidentally saving the lives of hundreds of soldiers as they passed to and fro.   Of inexhaustible physical strength, he was everywhere and always at work, never resting and, apparently, never sleeping.   He did all the detail of the engineers' work, his senior, Baird-Smith, disabled by wounds and sickness, having other tasks on his hands and being content to give his approval.   It was Taylor who, with some of his subalterns, went time after time at great personal risk into the enemy's ground to choose the sites for breaching batteries; and it was Taylor who was responsible for the plans both of the preliminary 1857. bombardment and of the assault. As Nicholson himself prophetically said, it was Taylor who captured Delhi. The whole story of the siege from first to last is characteristically English. Here we see a tiny column despatched by impatient politicians upon an impossible task against the advice and better judgement of its commander. It arrives on the scene; and chief after chief, overweighted with responsibility, succumbs or despairs. Yet, though the higher leadership is wanting, the force goes cheerfully on. It is full of daring spirits who know each other and trust each other, and who, in default of higher direction, are ready to fight against any odds with their own unit, summoning their friends when they need help. If there be trouble there are always Tombs and Hills of the Artillery, Probyn and Hodson of the native cavalry, Reid of the Gurkhas, Daly of the Guides, to mention but a few names out of many. And these junior leaders, happily very numerous, infect with their spirit the men, who, moreover, are stimulated by the insult to their superiority of race, and by a deep call to vengeance. And thus in spite of burning sun, and hot wind, and drenching rain, and flooded camp, and unspeakable stench, and unendurable flies, and dysentery and cholera, and a hundred other clogging miseries, the machine, quite merrily, if rather crazily, goes clanking on. It was not Taylor alone but the whole body of British regimental officers who captured Delhi.

The casualties from the 30th of May to the 21st of September numbered close upon one thousand killed and twenty-eight hundred wounded and missing[1]

---

[1] The actual figures are:

Killed:	European officers,	46;	other ranks,	516
	Indian ,,	25	,,	416
Wounded:	European officers,	140	,,	1426
	Indian ,,	49	,,	1180
Missing:	Europeans	12		
	Indians	18		

Total casualties: Europeans, 2140; Indians, 1688.

1857. —the proportion of the British to the Indian fallen being about five to four. A very large number of the severely wounded died, for, in spite of anæsthetics, amputation was generally fatal. But the tale of the slain and the maimed represents only a portion of the total loss of the British through cholera, dysentery and the sun. The Eighth, Fifty-second and Sixty-first in particular were terribly thinned by cholera, from which few recovered. The Sixtieth, which by general consent was the finest battalion at Delhi, suffered less. Of the dead the most notable was John Nicholson, who expired after nine days of lingering agony. Even his astounding vitality could not save him. On the march down from the Punjab, when the column halted and other men lay down exhausted in the shade, Nicholson remained in the sun, impatient to go on. When he received his death-wound, and his liver was shot through by a heavy bullet at a few yards' range, he did not immediately fall. One of his staff, hearing the ball strike him, said, " You are hit, sir." " Yes, yes," answered Nicholson, with some irritation at the irrelevance of the remark. Then his knees gave way under him, and he propped himself against the wall, grinding his teeth with rage, until he collapsed.[1] If ever man fought valiantly against death, it was John Nicholson. Hearing a rumour that General Wilson was contemplating withdrawal from Delhi after the assault, Nicholson gasped out fiercely that he had still the strength to shoot him if he attempted it. Born to command, he was one of those Englishmen who could find full scope for his powers in the still rather anarchic India of the earlier decades of the nineteenth century; and he is worshipped there dead, as he was worshipped when living, by the men over whom he bore rule, not as mortal but as divine.

[1] These details were told to me by Sir Seymour Blake, who was with Nicholson at the time.

CHAPTER LII

Let us now return to Havelock, whom we left with his spent and discouraged column at Cawnpore, powerless for further action until reinforced. At the beginning of September fresh troops, set in motion by General Outram, began to move up from Allahabad, and on the 16th Outram arrived with the last of them in person, having brushed away some small opposition on the march. His first act was to issue an order waiving his superior rank, so that Havelock might complete the work which he had begun, and announcing that he would accompany the force as a volunteer in his civil capacity only. This generosity was characteristic of the man, but, though willing to concede to Havelock all credit for any success, he did not wholly abstain from interference with his operations. The Fifth Fusiliers and the Ninetieth, neither of them complete, together with Eyre's battery, brought Havelock's force to a total strength of rather over three thousand men,[1] including a few irregular cavalry and three batteries of artillery. The infantry was distributed into two brigades, of which the first was commanded by Neill and the second by Colonel Hamilton of the Seventy-eighth.[2] Havelock's preparations were already complete, and on the night of the 18th he began the passage of the Ganges by a floating bridge, leaving four hundred convalescents to hold Cawnpore.

1857.

Sept. 16.

Sept. 18.

----

[1] British volunteer cavalry, 109; artillery, 282; infantry, 2388; Sikh infantry, 341 ; Native cavalry, 50; total, 3170.

[2] *Neill's Brigade*: 5th, 2 cos.; 64th, 84th, 102nd.
 Hamilton's Brigade: 78th, 90th, Brasyer's Sikhs.

1857.   The enemy offered but trifling opposition to the
Sept. 21. crossing of the river, and on the 21st Havelock fairly
entered upon his advance, easily pushing away the
rebels that attempted resistance at Mangalwar and
Sept. 22. halting for the night at Bashirat-ganj. On the 22nd
the column reached Bani Bridge, which was un-
defended; and, being now within sixteen miles of
Lucknow, Havelock fired a royal salute to apprise the
beleaguered garrison of his coming. So far rain had
fallen continuously ever since daybreak of the 21st;
Sept. 23. but the morning of the 23rd was fine and, after a march
of ten miles, the column came in sight of the Alam
Bagh, a large garden surrounded by a wall, which
flanked the road about two miles to south of Lucknow.
Reconnaissance showed that the enemy was here in
position in force, their left on the Alam Bagh, and their
right on rising ground astride the road. The whole
country up to a short distance from their front was
under water; but Havelock's batteries came into action
in despite of all obstacles and held the rebels in front,
while Hamilton's brigade, wading knee-deep, moved
round to turn their right flank The enemy soon gave
way, and Neill, advancing, captured the Alam Bagh in
a few minutes. Outram pursued with his handful of
cavalry until checked by hostile reinforcements at the
canal which runs round the south side of the city, and
captured five guns. As he returned, a message was
put into his hands which reported the fall of Delhi; and
with this news to hearten them, the troops bivouacked
for the night, wet and hungry, for the supplies had
not come up, but in the best of heart.
Sept. 24.   On the following day Havelock gave his men a rest
while he worked out his plans for the decisive action.
The direct road to the Residency crossed the canal at
the Charbagh bridge and thence passed through nearly
two miles of the city; but deep trenches had been cut
across the roadway, and Havelock dreaded the loss and
confusion that must ensue from forcing his advance
along a lane of loopholed houses. He proposed there-

fore to bear to his right to the Dilkusha, a palace about 1857.
four miles to north-east of the Alam Bagh, cross the Sept. 24.
Gumti, bear northward till he struck the Fyzabad road,
about three miles distant from the river, then turn
westward along that road to a building known as the
Badshah Bagh, occupy it and then recross the Gumti at
the iron bridge a mile further to westward, which would
bring him into the city five hundred yards to north of
the Residency.   Outram objected that in the flooded
state of the country it would be impossible to move
the heavy artillery along Havelock's proposed route.
He advised that the passage of the Charbagh bridge
should be forced, and that the column should then turn
to its right along a lane leading to the palace of the
Sikandar Bagh, strike westward from that point and
penetrate through a maze of fortified palaces and
bazaars to the eastern front of the Residency.   Outram
only offered advice as a volunteer, but he none the less
did not look for it to be rejected; and Havelock,
whatever his inward feelings, was fain to accept it.
Outram, as he acknowledged later, was wrong to
abdicate his command for one moment.

Accordingly a guard of some three hundred footsore
men was left at the Alam Bagh, and shortly after eight
o'clock in the morning of the 25th the column advanced Sept. 25.
upon the Charbagh bridge, under a heavy fire of
artillery in front and of musketry from the high grass
which flanked both sides of the road.   The bridge
was barred on the side of Lucknow by a breastwork
mounting five guns, and was further commanded by
scores of sharpshooters ensconced in the adjacent
houses.   Two guns of Maude's battery—there was
no space in the road for more—engaged the enemy's
artillery, while a party of the Hundred and Second
tried to silence the musketry from the houses.   But
the odds against Maude's gunners were too great; and
Lieutenant Havelock, son of the general and a member
of his staff, urged Neill to carry the bridge with the
bayonet.   Neill refused to take the responsibility,

whereupon young Havelock turned and galloped away
out of sight, as if in search of his father, and coming
back at full speed saluted Neill and ordered him to
attack the bridge at once.   A small party of skirmishers,
which made the first attempt, was shot down almost
to a man, but the main body of the Hundred and
Second coming up swept away all resistance by a single
charge, bayoneted the gunners and captured the guns.
Thus entry was gained into the city of Lucknow.

Leaving the Seventy-eighth to hold the head of
the bridge and cover the passage of the heavy guns,
Havelock pushed on along the appointed lane.   His
men met with little resistance until they came within
thirteen hundred yards of the Residency, when they
were checked by a ravine, over which there was but a
single narrow bridge, near the Kaisar Bagh, while a
very heavy fire was poured on them from that building
itself.   Meanwhile the Seventy-eighth also had been
desperately attacked, and had been obliged to storm a
building for their protection and to hold it against
repeated assaults.   At last, after nearly three hours'
fighting, they moved off by a shorter route to join their
comrades and came in the nick of time in rear of the
hostile batteries in the Kaisar Bagh, which they captured
out of hand.   The passage of the ravine was then
forced, and the column, reuniting, halted under cover
of the walls of some deserted buildings over against
the north front of the Residency.

It was now nearly dark, and Outram was for giving
the men a few hours' rest; but Havelock, anxious
lest the enemy should occupy the courtyards of the
palaces and mosques that were yet to be passed, urged
immediate advance, and Outram gave way.   As the
column filed out of an archway Neill was shot dead by
a hidden rebel a few yards from him, but the men
rushed on under a storm of bullets from the buildings
on either side, nor faltered till they had reached the gate
of the north-eastern angle of the Residency's defences.
This had been too securely barricaded to be easily

opened, so Outram, Havelock and their staff entered
by an embrasure.   Then the gate was opened and the
column marched in, smothered in sweat and dust,
weary, but triumphant.   Considering the nature of
the fighting, they had not suffered very heavily, the
full number of the killed, wounded and missing in the
six days between the 21st and 26th of September being
five hundred and thirty-five.

Not all of the troops came in to the Residency that
night.   The extreme rearguard, with two heavy guns,
had been forced to take refuge in a palace where the
enemy held them closely invested; and it was necessary
to send a detachment on the 26th to bring them in.
One party of about forty wounded, its escort having
mistaken its way, was cut off and massacred to a man.
Another tiny party of nine men of the Ninetieth took
refuge in a building and defended themselves successfully against repeated attacks until they were finally
rescued on the 27th.   Thus, though Havelock had
forced his way to the Residency, he was by no means
master of Lucknow; and gradually it dawned upon
Outram, who now assumed command, that the whole
of his operations had been undertaken upon a false
impression of the circumstances.   For this he was not
to blame.   The commandant of the garrison, Brigadier-
general Inglis, had contrived to inform him that his
supplies were rapidly failing.   This was not the fact,
though Inglis believed it and had shown his sincerity,
as has been seen, by reducing the rations.   It seems
that, both of the commissaries having been early disabled, no one rightly knew what quantity of grain still
remained in Lucknow.   Upon the assumption that the
garrison was starving, therefore, Havelock had hastened
his advance; and his troops, having left all baggage at
the Alam Bagh, had brought nothing with them except
that which they carried on their backs.   Both Outram
and Havelock, when they first entered the Residency,
took it as a matter of course that they would retire
almost immediately, carrying the beleaguered garrison

1857.
Sept.
with them.   Outram requested Mr. Martin Gubbins, the Financial Commissioner, who was one of the besieged, to negotiate at once with the people in Lucknow in order to obtain the necessary transport; and apparently it took him some time to realise that for nearly four months the garrison had been entirely cut off from the world, and that not a bullock nor a cart could be procured from without.[1] It seems strange, many years after the event, that a man of Outram's experience should have entered upon a military enterprise under such an absolute misconception of the true state of affairs, still stranger that none of his contemporaries should have considered it anything out of the common.   The incident throws light on the habit of mind which governed officials in India.

There, however, the matter was.   He had led three thousand men to Lucknow, and there seemed no prospect that he would be able either to keep them there or to bring away the sick and wounded and some hundreds of women and children who were with the garrison.   A more painful and perilous situation can hardly be imagined.   It was relieved by the discovery that there was grain enough in store, thanks to the foresight of Sir Henry Lawrence, not only for the original garrison but actually to supply the force brought by Outram also for two months.   This made a decision easy; and Outram resolved to stand fast.   His operation is wrongly called the first relief of Lucknow.   It was nothing of the kind.   It was simply a reinforcement of the defenders; and though these were not, as their commandant had reported, in danger of starvation, yet help came to them none too soon.   For sixteen weeks they had been under incessant fire of cannon and of musketry at close range, and in constant danger from mines.   They had repelled many attacks, some of them formidable, and made many successful sorties; but of nine hundred and twenty-seven Europeans three hundred and fifty had fallen, while the mortality among

[1] Gubbins, p. 368.

the children during the trials of the hot weather had 1857.
been terrible. Captain Fulton of the Engineers, who
had been the soul and brain of the defence, had been
killed on the 14th of September. Heavier work and
less food had naturally increased sickness. Desertion
among the few natives who still clung to their old
masters became more frequent. The number of their
enemies was multiplied by the arrival of reinforcements from Delhi; and, though the resolution of
the defenders never faltered, their faith in deliverance was beginning to fade when it was revived by
the sound of Havelock's guns. Another fortnight
would have brought their endurance very nearly to
an end.

Having made his resolution, Outram, by a series of
petty operations, at once extended his line of defence to
the Gumti on the north and for about a thousand yards
to east, taking in a range of lofty and well-built palaces
which gave ample accommodation for the men. An
enemy which had not the courage to overwhelm the
original garrison in the Residency was not difficult to
keep at a distance; but the most dangerous foe was
within. Having intended to evacuate Lucknow immediately, Outram had brought with him nothing. He
had no bakers, and the flour was necessarily made up
into native cakes, which induced diarrhœa. He had no
spirits, wine, tea, coffee, nor sugar, no medical comforts
and few medicines, while the stock of chloroform was
exhausted. There was abundance of these things at
the Alam Bagh, but they could not be brought in to
Lucknow; and indeed Outram was justly nervous as
to the safety of the Alam Bagh itself, with its tiny
garrison of enfeebled men. The general result was
that the sick were multiplied and that most of the
wounded died from gangrene or from sheer lack of
nourishment, for even milk was scarce.[1] The reinforcement of Lucknow, therefore, signified indeed the
rescue of the survivors of the original garrison and of

[1] Gubbins, pp. 369, 400-401.

1857. the women and children with it, but at the cost of lock-
Sept. ing up, under strict blockade, some twenty-five hundred fighting men in an isolated entrenchment under
conditions of extreme hardship and unhealthiness.
Such a result had not been foreseen, much less intended;
yet such the situation was.   The relief of Lucknow had
not been effected and was now more urgent than
ever.

Aug. 13.   Meanwhile on the 13th of August Sir Colin Campbell had arrived at Calcutta to assume supreme command in India.   Having taken the overland route he
had outstripped the reinforcements which were sailing
or ordered to sail from England, and was much in the
position of a general without an army.   At Calcutta
he found helplessness and stagnation.   No preparations had been made for the equipment, transport and
supply of an army in the field; no one, in fact, seemed
to have any idea of the thousand necessities which must
be made good in order to carry on war; and he was
obliged to look into every description of detail himself.
The line of communication with Cawnpore was still
insecure, as it was bound to be owing to the past
neglect and mismanagement of the Indian administration; while the few troops between Calcutta and Cawnpore were dispersed in small detachments.   Few complete battalions were, in fact, to be found anywhere;
odd companies having been hurried to the front, owing
to the urgency of the danger, as fast as they arrived, with
scores of unhappy civilians clamouring for their aid at
every stage of the journey.   To collect these detachments alone would take weeks; yet somehow a force
of some kind must be assembled to bring away the
garrison of Lucknow for work in the field.   A few days
before him, Captain Peel of the Royal Navy, fresh from
high distinction won before Sevastopol, had brought
the *Shannon* into the Hugli, and had organised a naval
brigade of extreme efficiency, with eight heavy guns.
In the *Shannon* and in the Queen's ship *Pearl* had
come three companies of the Ninetieth which had been

wrecked in the China Seas on a Queen's transport 1857.
during the outward voyage. Few more troops were
to be expected before October; and Campbell could
do nothing but push all that he had upon Cawnpore
without delay.

General Wilson, however, at Delhi was not un-
mindful of the general situation, and on the 24th of Sept. 24.
September had ordered a detachment of his force under
Brigadier-general Greathed to march for Cawnpore.
The full strength of this column amounted to rather
fewer than three thousand men,[1] one-third of them
Europeans, with fifteen guns.   On the 28th Greathed Sept. 28.
encountered a force of the enemy at Bulandshahr and
drove them off with a loss of three hundred killed and
wounded, capturing two guns and much ammunition
and baggage at a cost of fewer than fifty casualties.
On the 10th of October the column, after some more Oct. 10.
petty affairs, reached Agra, and crossing the Jumna encamped on the parade-ground.   There it was, through
sheer neglect and carelessness, surprised by an attack
of this enemy which, notwithstanding some confusion,
was easily beaten off; and pursuit of the rebel force
resulted in the capture of thirteen guns, the casualties,
in spite of all mishaps, not amounting to seventy.
Colonel Hope Grant shortly afterwards took command
of this force, which eventually reached Cawnpore on

---

[1] Remington's and Blunt's troops of horse-artillery.   (say) 120
    9th Lancers   300
    8th and 75th Foot   450
    Bourchier's field-battery   .   .   .   .   (say) 60
                                                   ——
    Total Europeans   930
    Detachments of native cavalry   500
    2 Punjab battalions   1200
    Sappers and miners   200
                                                   ——
                                                   2830

Roberts, *Forty-one Years in India* (1 vol. edn.), p. 141 *n.*, gives
the total at 2650, but does not include the artillery in his reckoning.
Greathed's report states the units under his command but not their
numbers.

1857.   the 26th of October.   There it found four companies
Oct. 26. of the Ninety-third Highlanders which, diverted from
China at the Cape, had reached the Hugli on the 20th
of September and were moving up country by detachments with all possible speed.   The Twenty-third,
likewise diverted from China, had also landed and was
on its way to the front; and the advanced parties of
Oct. 30. the Naval Brigade were close at hand.   On the 30th
Grant, by telegraphic order from Campbell, crossed
the Ganges into Oudh, and halting a little to north of
the Sai river sent forward a convoy of supplies and
ammunition to the Alam Bagh.   On the 9th of
Nov. 9.   November Sir Colin Campbell with his chief of staff,
Brigadier-general Mansfield, joined the column in
person.

Passing by Cawnpore on the 3rd, Campbell had
taken a very important decision.   It was now known
that Sindia's revolted troops from Gwalior had joined
the other mutineers, and were concentrating at Kalpi
under command of Tantia Topi for an attack upon
Cawnpore.   It was therefore a question for Campbell
whether he should not deal first with this menace
before marching upon Lucknow.   Outram urged this
course, undertaking to make his supplies last until the
end of November, for, as he wrote, it was obviously
to the advantage of the State that the rebels of Gwalior
should be destroyed before Lucknow was relieved.
Campbell, however, stuck to his original resolution,
and leaving General Windham with about five hundred
British and a few Sikhs to hold Cawnpore, went on his
way.   He left orders with Windham to improve the
defences of the entrenchment, which had been thrown
up for protection of the reserves of supplies and stores
and for covering the bridge of boats, and to make every
possible display of strength, but on no account to
move out to the offensive unless the entrenchment
were threatened with bombardment.

By the 9th of November the strength of the force
at Alam Bagh had risen to some forty-five hundred

men,[1] drawn from at least sixteen different units, with 1857.
forty-two guns of various calibres, Hope Grant being
in executive command.   On the 10th Mr. Kavanagh, Nov. 10.
a clerk in an office at Lucknow, appeared with a
message from Outram, having made his way, dis-
guised as a native, at extreme risk through the enemy's
lines.   Outram, mindful of past experience, recommended that Campbell should take the route originally
advocated by Havelock; namely, to turn from the
Alam Bagh north-eastward to the Dilkusha palace,
wheel thence northward to the building called the
Martinière, cross the canal by the bridge nearest to
the Gumti and, covering his right flank with the river,
to advance on the Sikandar Bagh.   Accordingly on the
12th Campbell moved upon the Alam Bagh, brushed Nov. 12.
away a party of the enemy that hindered his march,
and there stowed his camp-equipment and reserve-
stores, leaving the remnant of the Seventy-fifth to
replace three companies of the Ninetieth, which were
added to Adrian Hope's brigade.   On the 14th Nov. 14.
Campbell was joined by two hundred of the Military
Train, equipped as dragoons, two more light guns
and another company of native sappers, which raised
his strength to about five thousand men; and on the
same day he occupied the Dilkusha and the Martinière
after a trifling resistance.   The enemy later in the day
made two distinct sallies against the British centre and
left, threatening the long train of vehicles which were
conveying Campbell's supplies; but they were beaten
off with little difficulty or loss.   The 15th was spent in Nov. 15.
fortifying the Dilkusha as a general depôt, the Eighth

---

[1] The troops additional to those brought from Delhi were Peel's
Naval Brigade, 1 co. R.E., 2 cos. native Sappers, 1 field-battery and
2 cos. R.A., detachments of the 5th, 64th, 78th, 84th and 90th,
a wing each of the 23rd and of the 53rd, 2 cos. of the 82nd, and
the 93rd Highlanders.   The infantry was brigaded thus:
Adrian Hope's Brigade: Wing of 53rd, 93rd, battn. of detachments,
                    4th Punjab Infantry.
Greathed's   „   8th, battn. of detachments, 2nd Punjab Inf.
Russell's   „   Wing of 23rd, 2 cos. 82nd.

1857. Foot and the cavalry remaining there for its defence, and in making a demonstration against the western
Nov. 16. side of the city. On the 16th the main body advanced northward, forded the canal unopposed—the rebels having been deceived by the feint of the previous day; and, having passed through a village, the advanced guard plunged into a deep narrow cutting which led to the north-eastern corner of the Sikandar Bagh.

A squadron of native cavalry led the way, followed in succession by a wing of the Fifty-third and Blunt's troop of horse-artillery; and the rebels seem to have allowed the whole of these to enter the defile before they suddenly opened fire upon them from the front and both flanks. For a time there was wild confusion. The cavalry, quite helpless under such conditions, naturally turned back, to find the way choked by the infantry and artillery in rear. After a time, with much difficulty the horsemen were withdrawn; the Fifty-third, mounting the banks on both sides, drove the enemy's sharpshooters from the adjoining enclosures; while Blunt, by amazing efforts of horses and men, actually took his guns also up the bank on the right-hand side, galloped over a short intervening space and unlimbered sixty yards from the eastern wall of the Sikandar Bagh, with his guns pointing in three different directions against a heavy fire from three sides. The Fifty-third and Ninety-third presently cleared the enemy out of the nearest buildings; but it was evident that no further progress could be made until the Sikandar Bagh should be carried.

This was no easy matter. The place was enclosed by a strong wall, one hundred and thirty yards square, carefully loopholed, and flanked at the angles by circular bastions. The only gateway on the south side was protected by a traverse of earth and masonry, with a double-storied guard-room above. Over against the north side was a flat-roofed pavilion, prepared for defence; and it was plain from the violence of the fire from within that the whole place was strongly held.

Campbell, in order to see the position for himself, rode 1857. up to Blunt's guns, and was there struck, though not Nov. 16. disabled, by a spent bullet which had passed through and killed a gunner.   He decided to breach the wall at the south-eastern angle; and meanwhile a heavy gun had already been brought into the cutting.   By main force of many hands this was forced up the bank, the enemy's bullets pattering heavily all the while on the piece itself and on the tires of the wheels, and at a range of eighty yards it presently opened fire.   In half an hour a breach, three feet square, had been battered a yard above the ground, and Campbell gave the order to assault.   Highlanders, Fifty-third and Sikhs raced for the opening, which was soon choked by the crowd of men struggling to enter; and other ingress was sought at a barred window and at the gateway.   The traverse before the latter was carried with a rush by the 4th Punjab infantry, and, before the gate could be shut, one of the men thrust his arm, protected by a shield, between the closing leaves.   His hand was badly gashed, whereupon he withdrew it and thrust in the other arm, which was immediately almost severed at the wrist.   But he had hindered the meeting of the leaves long enough. The gate was forced.   British and loyal Indians dashed into the enclosure; and then followed a slaughter grim and great.   Two thousand mutinous sepoys had stationed themselves within the enclosure, hoping to fall on the flank of their assailants as they passed westward towards Outram's entrenchments.   They were caught in a trap from which there was no escape. They fought desperately, but they were driven back, foot by foot, against the north wall, where at last they lay, a ghastly heap of dead and dying, as high as a man's head.   A few, taking refuge in the upper rooms of the towers at the angles, were followed by the Sikhs and bayoneted or hurled down.   Three or four managed to scramble over the wall; the rest were cut off to a man.

The afternoon was by this time advanced, but about half a mile beyond the Sikandar Bagh stood a large mosque, the Shah Mujif, which Campbell was anxious to master before nightfall. Peel brought up his heavy guns before it, but could not silence the biting fire from the loopholed walls, while the enemy's artillery, concentrating upon Peel's battery, caused heavy loss. After three hours' firing Campbell decided to assault with infantry, and led the Ninety-third to the wall of the mosque; but it was too high to be scaled; no ladders were at hand, and Peel's heavy guns produced no impression upon it. Campbell had actually given the order to retire, when one of his staff, having found a gap in the wall, discovered that the enemy, terrified by Peel's rockets, were evacuating the building in all haste. It was, therefore, occupied without further trouble or loss; and the troops bivouacked for the night in a semicircle extending from the Shah Mujif through the Sikandar Bagh to the former barracks of the Thirty-second, half a mile to the south.

On the 17th Campbell judged it prudent first to secure the line of the canal on his left as far as the Dilkusha bridge, after which he brought up Peel's heavy guns against the former mess-house of the Thirty-second, which lay half a mile to west of the barracks in his front. It was a two-storied building surrounded by a ditch of revetted masonry, with a loopholed wall within, from which the rebels kept up a heavy fire of musketry. About 3 P.M. this fire slackened, and Campbell ordered three companies of the Ninetieth, under Captain Garnet Wolseley, to assault. The storming party entered the building unresisted, the defenders being in full retreat; and Wolseley, being joined by a number of the Fifty-third, proceeded, without orders, to the attack of the Moti Mahal, or Pearl Palace, three hundred yards beyond the mess-house, while one of his brother officers took in hand the Tara Kothi, another large building a little to south of the mess-house. The wall of the Moti

Mahal was twenty feet high, and the gateways were 1857.
protected by an outer wall which had been loopholed Nov. 17.
and prepared for defence.   With some difficulty a hole
was made in this outer wall.   Ensign Haig of the
Ninetieth wriggled through it on his belly.   The rest
of his company followed, as the hole was enlarged,
forced the main gate, and, making their way into the
courtyard, found the rebels flying to refuge in the
adjoining buildings on the eastern side.   These the
Ninetieth cleared one after another with the bayonet,
and were still busily engaged in the work when there
was a sudden explosion on the western wall.   Then
out of the dust emerged another company of the
Ninetieth, part of Outram's garrison, which had sprung
a mine under the wall in order to make a sortie in aid of
the relieving force.   Thus the relief of Lucknow was
finally accomplished.   Outram and Havelock presently
came down through a storm of fire which wounded
four out of five of their staff, and passing on towards
the mess-house, met and greeted Campbell.   The first
part of Sir Colin's task was done.

There remained the difficult business of withdrawing
the garrison with its encumbrance of some fifteen
hundred women, children, sick and wounded. Campbell
had indeed made his way to Outram's line of defence,
but he was by no means master of Lucknow, the
rebels having still a large and important stronghold
in the Kaisar Bagh palace, a vast building a quarter of
a mile south-west of the mess-house.   It was therefore
necessary for him to secure his left flank carefully before
his retreat by the occupation of buildings to south of
the Sikandar Bagh.   These posts were attacked by the
rebels on the 18th with some persistence, but were Nov. 18.
successfully held.   Screens of canvas were thrown up
across the open ground, under cover of which the sick
and the women were on the 19th withdrawn along the Nov. 19.
line of Campbell's advance; the enemy's fire from the
other side of the Gumti being kept down by guns about
the Moti Mahal and by sharpshooters posted in the

1857. Shah Mujif. In successive stages the whole were gradually brought from the Residency into the Dil-

Nov. 20. kusha; and meanwhile on the 20th and the two following days Peel's heavy guns played unceasingly upon the Kaisar Bagh, in order to lead the mutineers to expect

Nov. 22. an assault. At midnight of the 22nd the garrison was at last brought away in dead silence, and marched off; detachments of the relieving force guarding every yard of the way, and falling in successively in rear of the column as it passed. It was a very difficult and delicate operation, well thought out by Campbell's staff to the minutest detail, and admirably executed.

Nov. 23. Before dawn of the 23rd every soul was safely in the Dilkusha camp.[1]

The casualties in the various actions between the 14th and the 23rd of November amounted to five hundred and thirty-six killed and wounded, the heaviest of the loss falling upon the Ninety-third and upon the artillery, naval and military. The fallen of each of these latter corps numbered just over one hundred, and those of the Punjab infantry were nearly as great. In all the circumstances the casualties cannot be considered severe; and it is noteworthy that those of the Ninety-third, who on the 16th bore some of the hardest of a hard day's fighting, did not exceed one hundred. Yet Campbell's opponents were trained soldiers who outnumbered his troops by about eight to one, holding a succession of fortified buildings from which they should not easily have been dislodged. But they were disconcerted first by Campbell's line of advance, which was not what they expected; and the moral effect of anything like a surprise is very potent among Orientals. Next, they were cowed by their moral inferiority to the British, who were ready to do and dare anything against them. Had there been any sign of irresolution on the

---

[1] One officer of the original garrison was left behind. He had fallen asleep and his friends had not roused him. He woke to find himself alone in the Residency, but overtook the rearguard before it reached camp.—Gubbins, p. 456.

part of the British; had any misfortune brought 1857. about a serious mishap; had the mutineers even detected Campbell's movement of retreat; they would instantly have gathered confidence. Then the struggle must have been desperate and the consequences possibly disastrous. British commanders have always taken great liberties and great risks against an Indian enemy, but the fortune of war has sometimes turned against them, and Campbell must have been thankful when the rearmost rearguard came safely into Dilkusha.

Among the sick who were carried thither was Havelock, frayed to a thread by hard work, and reduced to a shadow by dysentery. Early on the morning of the 24th he died, and was buried near the Alam Nov. 24. Bagh, which was Campbell's halting-place on that day. Havelock was an officer who, apart from much service in the field, had studied his profession exhaustively in preparation for the tenure of high command. An echo of Napoleon's style may be heard in the general order which he issued to his little column after his action before Cawnpore on the 16th of July. "Soldiers, your general is satisfied and more than satisfied with you." But, unfortunately for him, his chance as an independent commander came too late, when he was nearly worn out by many campaigns in India. He died in harness, but it is doubtful whether he would have enjoyed the fame which for long made his name sacred in many households, had he not been a very earnestly religious man of the sect of Baptists. This type of low churchman or dissenter was very dear to a large section of the British public, as was seen later in their idolisation of General Charles Gordon. Havelock lived up to the highest ideals of his religious creed, but this made him hard and exacting; and, though he was as stern to himself as to those under him, he was not on that account the better beloved by his men. On the whole, there is little more to be said of him than of hundreds of other officers, that he was a good man and a good soldier.

1857.   On the 25th Campbell reached the Alam Bagh,
Nov. 25. where he left Outram with about four thousand men,
twenty-five guns and ten mortars to overawe Lucknow.
Two days were consumed in making the necessary
Nov. 27. arrangements, and on the 27th Campbell proceeded
with three thousand men and his huge unwieldy
convoy, twelve miles in length, towards Cawnpore.
He was uneasy, because for some days no message had
come in from Windham.   On the march he heard
heavy firing, and on reaching Bani Bridge, learned that
the like sound had been heard from the direction of
Cawnpore on the 25th and 26th also.   He, therefore,
Nov. 28. marched early on the 28th, and was met by a succession
of unfavourable messages.   Their purport was that
Windham had been driven from the city and cantonments of Cawnpore into the entrenchments at the head
of the bridge of boats over the Ganges, and that the
bridge itself, on which communication with Oudh depended, might be in the enemy's possession, if it were
not actually destroyed.   Campbell, in deep anxiety, sent
a staff-officer forward at once, and presently followed
himself.   He found the bridge intact and Windham
perfectly calm and collected, but his troops much
shaken and demoralised.

What had happened was briefly this.   No sooner
had Campbell fairly started for Lucknow than Tantia
Topi with some twenty thousand men moved from
Kalpi upon Cawnpore and crossed the Jumna, leaving
posts to cut off Windham's communication with the
country.   Windham thereupon sought and obtained
permission from Campbell to intercept certain reinforcements which were on their way to join the
Commander-in-chief, and having thus raised his force
to some seventeen hundred men, encamped osten-
tatiously, in pursuance of Campbell's orders, on the
Nov. 17. west side of Cawnpore.   On the 17th two detachments
of the rebels arrived at two villages fifteen miles apart
and the same distance from the city; and Windham
asked Campbell's leave to advance and surprise one

or the other of them. Receiving no answer after 1857.
waiting for a week, he, on the 24th, moved out six Nov. 24.
miles on the road to Kalpi; and on the 25th Tantia Nov. 25.
Topi advanced with twenty-five thousand men and
forty guns to Pandu Nadi, within three miles of
Windham's camp. Windham had with him only
twelve hundred infantry and ten light guns, his force
being made up in great measure of detachments of
battalions which had just arrived in India from
England;[1] but he decided to attack on the 26th, Nov. 26.
and without difficulty drove back the enemy in his
immediate front, capturing three guns.   Having, however, no cavalry, and being too weak to prosecute his
success, he was fain to fall back, followed and insulted
all the way by Tantia Topi's Mahratta force.

On the morrow at noon Tantia's artillery opened Nov. 27.
a heavy fire, and shortly afterwards he developed a
general attack against the northern and western sides
of Cawnpore from the Ganges to the Ganges canal, on
a curved front of some four to five miles.   Windham,
not having sent his baggage to the rear, engaged the
enemy along the whole length of the curve and for an
hour held his own, the detachment (called a brigade)
on the northern front maintaining its position stoutly.
But the heaviest attack was directed against the western
front, and here the weight of Tantia's artillery made
itself felt.   The misbehaviour of an officer, who retreated from a village without orders and without resistance, was decisive on this side; and the bulk of the
troops gave way in confusion.   They were covered by
three companies of the Rifle Brigade, which, though
ammunition failed, contrived by sheer good marksmanship to check for a time the enemy's advance, and to
drag away two abandoned guns with their rifle-slings.
Windham now gave the order to fall back upon a line of
brick-kilns immediately in rear of his camp.   Colonel
Carthew, on the northern front, at first refused to obey,

---

[1] 34th, detachments of 82nd, 88th and 2/ R.B.   The last-named,
350 strong, only reached Cawnpore on the evening of the 25th.

being confident of maintaining his ground, but, the command being repeated, he was fain to retire. Meanwhile the rebels passed round the southern flank of the brick-kilns and threatened the entrenchment itself; whereupon Windham directed Carthew to occupy a building, covering the road to Bithur, about three-quarters of a mile to west of the entrenchment, and ordered the remainder of his troops to retreat within the entrenchment itself. The bulk of them did so as a disorderly rabble; and, on reaching the security of the earthworks, some of them broke open the stores and drank themselves drunk. It must be said for them that many were raw recruits, only just landed in India; but the incident was not a creditable one.

Carthew, on the other hand, fought his way calmly to his assigned position, inflicting severe loss on the rebels, and there established himself. To remedy the disorder in the entrenchments, moreover, there had happily come in the nick of time four companies of the third battalion of the Rifle Brigade. One of these, moving in advance of the rest, had already replenished the ammunition of the second battalion, and had joined with them in covering the retreat. The other three, which had started from Fatipur as escort to a convoy, had hastened their march in response to Windham's urgent summons, and actually traversed close upon forty-nine miles in twenty-six hours. Windham met them and led them into the entrenchment, from which they speedily beat off the enemy's attack. When nightfall came, these newly arrived riflemen took up the line of outposts, a fact which is a sufficient comment on the condition of the majority, though not of the whole, of Windham's troops.

During the night Windham, anticipating further attack, made fresh dispositions. Carthew, with the Thirty-fourth and four guns, was left in the building which he was already occupying as an advanced post on the right, with a detachment of the Sixty-fourth stationed between him and the Ganges to cover his

right flank; while the Rifles, two companies of the 1857.
Eighty-second and four guns, under Colonel Walpole,
were pushed out as an advanced post on the left to
north of the Ganges canal.   The troops in the entrenchment marched to their places under heavy fire
soon after daybreak of the 28th, but the enemy's on- Nov. 28.
slaught did not come until some hours later.   On the
left Walpole maintained himself successfully, the riflemen picking off the enemy's gunners with unerring
aim; and two heavy guns were captured and brought
in.   On the right Carthew took up a position astride
a bridge over a ravine, and for two hours and a half
defied all efforts of the mutineers to dislodge him.   At
noon he received orders to attack the enemy's battery
in his front; but the fire both of musketry and artillery
was too severe, and the Thirty-fourth was forced to
abandon the attempt after suffering heavy casualties.
A detachment of the Sixty-fourth, which had been sent
to protect his right, took by chance a wrong turning
which led them away from ground where they could
have assailed the enemy effectively.   As things fell out,
this party found itself faced by four guns, against which
they advanced for half a mile, but were then driven
back with severe loss.   The enemy then worked gradually round the left flank of Carthew, who retired slowly,
contesting every inch of ground; and by nightfall
Windham's whole force had been pressed back within
the entrenchment.   The enemy then occupied the entire city of Cawnpore, and prepared to bring forward
their artillery against the bridge of boats.   They had
inflicted on Windham a loss of over three hundred
killed and wounded, captured the whole of his baggage,
his camp-equipment, and most of his transport, and
destroyed further most of the baggage and camp-equipment of Campbell's own troops, as well as the stores and
clothing accumulated for the benefit of the refugees
from Lucknow.

Such was the state of things in Cawnpore when on
the night of the 28th of November Campbell rode back

1857. across the bridge of boats to rejoin his own column.
Nov. 28. Windham was much blamed for not taking the offensive on the 17th, as he had planned, without awaiting Campbell's permission; for, as was pointed out, since he did take the offensive upon his own responsibility on the 26th, he might as well have done so a few days earlier as a few days later.   There is force in this contention; but it may be questioned whether Campbell himself did not deserve the greater condemnation.   If Windham had been left in an entrenched position, with all the mass of stores entrusted to him safely inside it, a garrison of five hundred men would have been none too strong to secure it.   But he was supposed, somehow, with this quite inadequate force to protect the whole city of Cawnpore, or at any rate certain buildings situated half a mile distant from the bridge-head, which was his only stronghold.   In such circumstances Campbell might well have imparted to Windham certain general principles for his guidance; but it was surely unwise and unfair to fetter Windham's discretion in any way.   As a matter of fact Windham, as has been seen, received reinforcements, otherwise it is hard to see how his garrison could have escaped annihilation. Campbell seems entirely to have ignored the fact that Tantia Topi had heavy guns which hopelessly outranged Windham's few light pieces, and that he had left Windham in the same situation as Gough at the opening of the first Sikh war, unable to silence his enemy's batteries except with the bayonets of his infantry.

And this raises the whole question whether Campbell was not guilty of a grave error in judgement when he rejected Outram's counsel to deal first with Tantia Topi's army before advancing to the relief of Lucknow. It is easy to understand Campbell's impatience to be quit of Lucknow.   The blockade of the garrison there hampered his movements and kept a relatively large number of troops, which were badly needed for the field, in unprofitable inactivity.   Moreover, that number was daily shrinking, not from starvation, for

Outram had reassured him on that point and had, as 1857.
he afterwards discovered, provisions enough to last him Nov. 28.
to the end of December, but from lack of the commonest
medical remedies and comforts.   Yet, on the other
hand, the whole of Campbell's operations depended on
the safety of Cawnpore and of the bridge of boats over
the Ganges.   He had to choose between risking the
loss of the whole of his communications, and perhaps a
fortnight's delay in securing them.   If the bridge over
the Ganges had been destroyed, Campbell would have
found himself between the Lucknow mutineers on one
side and Tantia Topi's army on the other, utterly
isolated in a country where no supplies were procurable.
No limit can be placed on the disastrous consequences
which might then have ensued.   On the other hand,
during the fortnight's delay possibly three hundred
men, at a liberal estimate, might have died at Lucknow;
but as against this, Tantia Topi's force might have been
dispersed, at any rate for the time; Cawnpore might
have been made safe; the reinforcements which joined
Windham would have been at hand to make good any
casualties; the return from Lucknow need not have
been so much hastened; Windham's losses would have
been saved, and much anxiety might have been spared.
Nor, in the face of Outram's counsel, can this be called
wholly wisdom after the event.   The choice between
risks is always, indeed, a hard one; but Campbell's
choice in this instance rather suggests preference for
spectacular over sound operations.

In this case his sin had found him out; though
fortunately he had to deal with a timorous enemy.
Owing to the length and disorder [1] of his march on the
28th his heavy guns did not come in until early on the
29th.   Tantia Topi had already brought forward his Nov. 29.
own artillery in the course of the forenoon and opened
fire upon the bridge, though without doing much
damage; but Campbell, retorting with Peel's naval
guns and other pieces from the opposite bank of the

[1] Gubbins, pp. 462-464.

1857. Ganges, soon compelled it to withdraw.   In the forenoon the passage of the river began, and by six o'clock
Nov. 30. on the evening of the 30th the last cart had crossed
the bridge and the rearguard had come in without the
slightest molestation—sufficient testimony to the
enemy's lack of enterprise.   Adrian Hope's brigade,
which, with two batteries and a squadron or two, was
the first to traverse the bridge, took up a position to
south-east of the city to re-open communications with
Calcutta; and then the force, facing to west, remained
Dec. 3. perforce inactive until the night of the 3rd of December,
when the sick, wounded, women and children, making
a convoy five miles in length, were sent off to Allahabad
under escort of six companies of the Thirty-fourth.
Campbell gave them two clear days to move to a safe
Dec. 6. distance, and at last on the 6th felt himself free to act.
There had been several little affairs of outposts in the
interval; the enemy's artillery had also fired inter-
mittently; and two unsuccessful attempts had been
made to destroy the bridge of boats with fire-rafts;
but the mutineers, as usual, had shown no real spirit of
adventure.   The head-quarters of the Eighty-eighth,
five more companies of the third battalion of the
Rifle Brigade and a battery came up in two separate
parties during the course of the 5th, after making
extraordinary marches, and thus Campbell's force was
increased to five thousand infantry, six hundred cavalry[1]
and thirty-five guns.   The enemy's position was
strong, their left resting on the Ganges, their centre
occupying the narrow streets of the city, and their right,
which consisted of the Gwalior Contingent, extending
some two miles into the open plain to south of the city.
These last being the most vulnerable as well as the

[1] *Cavalry Brigade*: 9th Lancers, detachments 1st, 2nd, 5th Punjab
Cavalry, Hodson's Horse.
Greathed's „   8th, 64th; 2nd Punjab Infantry.
4th Infantry Brigade, 42nd, 53rd, 93rd, 4th Punjab Rifles.
5th   „   „   23rd, 32nd, 82nd.
6th   „   „   2/ and 3/ Rifle Brigade, detachment of
38th.

most formidable of his foes, Campbell decided to make 1857.
feint attacks against the rebels' centre and left, and to Dec. 6.
turn his full strength against their right.

Accordingly at nine o'clock on the morning of the
6th the guns in the entrenchment opened upon
Tantia's centre and left; and two hours later three
brigades began their advance across the plain, Walpole's
Riflemen on the right, nearest to the city, and on their
left, in succession, the brigades of Inglis and Hope,
with the cavalry and horse-artillery pushed out wide to
the extreme left, ready to intercept the enemy's retreat
along the road to Kalpi. The British met with little
resistance, the mutineers making no stand except at
the brick-kilns, from which they were driven by Peel's
naval guns; and very soon the enemy was in full flight.
The cavalry not appearing, Campbell pursued with his
own escort and a battery of horse-artillery until at last
the missing horse, which had been misled by their
guide, took up the chase, which they pressed until long
after dark. On the other hand, General Mansfield,
to whom Campbell had entrusted a detachment for the
purpose of cutting off the retreat of the enemy's centre
and left upon Bithur, allowed them to escape, behaving
with a feebleness comparable only to that of John
Stuart at Wellington's passage of the Douro. Thus
the success of the day was marred; but none the less
Campbell had inflicted on the rebels considerable loss
at a cost to himself of no more than ninety-eight
casualties.

On the 8th he sent Hope Grant with a detachment Dec. 8.
in pursuit of the fugitives, whom Mansfield had let go,
in the direction of Bithur. Grant overtook some of
them and captured fifteen guns, but was prevented
from punishing them heavily by marshy ground.
Grant was next pushed on to Bithur to destroy Nana
Sahib's property; and Campbell now set himself to
clear the Doab, between the Jumna and the Ganges,
from Delhi to Allahabad, so as to restore the security
of the communications between the North-west

1857. Provinces and Calcutta. Colonel Seaton, with an enormous convoy, was to advance from Delhi south-eastward upon Mainpuri; Colonel Walpole with another column was to make a semicircular sweep from Cawnpore, first southward and then north-east-ward, upon the same spot, and finally Campbell by a more direct march north-eastward was to work his way towards both. Seaton, with a convoy which covered nineteen miles of road and with only nineteen hundred men to escort it, started from Delhi on the 9th of December, parked his encumbrances at Aligarh, cleared his front by a series of successful little actions, and by the 31st had brought his clumsy charge safely to Mainpuri. Campbell, having started on the 24th, reached Gursahaigang on the 31st; and on the 2nd
1858. of January 1858 he attacked and dispersed a body of rebels between that place and Fatehgarh, driving them headlong into Rohilkhand. On the following day Walpole joined Seaton close to Mainpuri, and on the
Jan. 6. 6th their united columns came up with Campbell's at Fatehgarh.

Then arose the question what should be done next. Campbell was anxious to complete the pacification of Rohilkhand; but Lord Canning, for political reasons, insisted that Oudh, which represented a dynasty in defiance of British sovereignty, should be dealt with first. Canning, however, conceded that sufficient troops should be left to keep open the communications through the Doab, and that the recapture of Lucknow might for the present suffice, without the immediate sequel of the subjugation of Oudh. The Doab itself, despite of the recent operations, was still full of mutineers, who might at any moment give trouble; and at Aliganj, no more than seven miles from Fatehgarh, there were as many as fifteen thousand infantry with guns, besides some of the best of the revolted cavalry. Campbell, however, did not trouble himself to disturb them, simply leaving Seaton with two weak British battalions, a Sikh battalion, a field-battery and a body

of raw native horse to hold Fatehgarh and do his best. 1858.
Meanwhile he ordered Walpole with a small column
to manœuvre as if for the invasion of Rohilkhand so as
to deceive the enemy as to his intentions; and he himself remained until the 1st of February at Fatehgarh. Feb. 1.
Throughout this time preparations for the re-conquest
of Lucknow were going forward at Unao, over against
Cawnpore on the left bank of the Ganges. Reinforcements continued to arrive from England, and a Gurkha
contingent under Jung Bahadur was on its way from
Nipal, working in concert with a small flying column
under General Franks, and dispersing bodies of rebels
as it marched southward. On the 31st of January Campbell ordered Hope Grant with the main body to march
from Fatehgarh upon Cawnpore, and on the 8th of Feb. 8.
February Grant took command of all the troops at Unao.

Thereupon Ahmad Alla, the ablest of the native
leaders, perceiving that the day of reckoning for
Lucknow was at hand, became active in aggression
against Outram's garrison at the Alam Bagh. Few
incidents in the course of the mutiny show the
mutineers in a more contemptible light than the
immunity of this isolated little body of men. The
rebels could, it was reckoned, call into action about
Lucknow one hundred and twenty thousand fighting
men, perhaps one-fifth of them trained sepoys. The
troops in and about the Alam Bagh did not amount to
five thousand, three-fourths of them British. These
last consisted of six battalions,[1] all much exhausted by
previous service, some three hundred gunners with
twenty-five field-pieces, and some of the Military
Train which had been hastily converted into cavalry.
The various picquets absorbed eight hundred men by
day and over a thousand by night, so that the duty was
heavy; and the little force, having no transport, must
in case of disaster have fought its way back to Cawnpore as best it could. Yet the rebels, though they

---

[1] 5th, 75th, 78th, 84th, 90th, 102nd. The 75th being quite worn
out, was withdrawn and sent to the hills before Campbell's advance.

1858. had heavy guns, left them comparatively unmolested. They did indeed deliver four half-hearted attacks in the course of December and January, and on the 16th, 21st and 25th of February they made more serious efforts; but all alike were repelled with heavy loss; and they then realised that they had let slip the golden opportunity.

While awaiting the arrival of Sir Colin Campbell, Hope Grant beat round his neighbourhood with a small compact column, breaking up bodies of rebels, and on one day inflicting on them a loss of a thousand
Feb. 28. killed and taken.   On the 28th Campbell finally left Cawnpore and made for Banthira, on the road between Unao and Lucknow, where he had ordered his army to assemble.   He could reckon for the approaching operations on a total force of some thirty thousand men of one kind and another, including Jung Bahadur's nine thousand Gurkhas, and one hundred and sixty-four guns.[1]   On the 2nd of March he moved forward

---

[1] CAVALRY DIVISION: Hope Grant.
    1st Brigade: 9th Lancers; 2nd Punjab Cav.; det. 5th Punjab
        Cav.; 1st Sikh Irregular Cav.
    2nd   „   2nd D.G.; 7th Hussars; Hodson's Horse; Pathan
        Horse.
NAVAL BRIGADE.
    ARTILLERY. 1 troop R.H.A.; 2 troops Bengal H.A.; 6 cos.
        R.A.; 1 co. Bengal Artillery.
        164 guns.
INFANTRY:
    First Division: 1st Brigade—Russell. 5th, 84th, 102nd.
              2nd   „   Franklyn. 78th, 90th, Fero-
                      zepore Regt.
    Second „   3rd   „   Guy. 34th, 38th, 53rd.
            „   4th   „   Hope. 42nd, 93rd, 4th Punjab
                      Inf.
    Third „   5th   „   Douglas. 23rd, 79th, 101st.
              6th   „   Horsford. 2 and 3/R.B.; 2nd
                      Punjab Inf.
    Fourth „   (Franks's Force)
              7th Brigade—Evelegh. 10th, 20th, 97th.
              Gurkha troops.
On the 14th of February the force, including the Naval Brigade, but exclusive of the 4th Division, was stated at 18,277 of all ranks, viz. cavalry, 3169; artillery, 1745; engineers, 865; infantry, 12,498.

towards Lucknow, drove the rebels with little difficulty 1858.
from the Dilkusha and occupied it. On the 4th Mar. 4.
General Franks came in with his own troops and
three thousand Gurkhas, and on the 5th Campbell Mar. 5.
threw two bridges of casks across the Gumti, half
a mile below the Dilkusha palace. Therewith his
preparations for the first stage of the attack were
complete.

The rebels, if they had given little trouble to Outram
at the Alam Bagh, had at least bestowed much labour
on the defences of Lucknow. Anticipating, from
previous experience, an onslaught from the east, they
had made the canal on the east side of the city their
first line of defence, extending it northward till it met
the river, and backing it with a rampart from the point
of junction with the Gumti for some two miles southward. The second line, half a mile in rear of the first,
stretched from the river southward to the principal
street, which it joined by the great building called the
Imambara. In rear of this the vast structure of the
Kaisar Bagh formed a citadel. Between these lines
the principal streets were blocked by barricades and
field-works, and most of the houses were loopholed
and prepared for resistance. Altogether the task of
driving over one hundred thousand men from such a
stronghold did not promise to be easy. Colonel
Robert Napier, however, had pointed out that a flanking column, moving on the north bank of the Gumti,
would take in reverse the enemy's first and second line
of defence; and Sir Colin regulated his plans accordingly. Such a division of force on both banks of a
great river was, of course, a violation of all sound
tactical rule; but any liberty could be taken against
such an enemy.

The engineers, through some blunder, had laid
their bridges over the river within range of the enemy's
nearest batteries in La Martinière,[1] wherefore it was
necessary to hurry Outram's division, which formed

[1] Hope Grant, p. 247.

1858. the flanking column, over the water before daylight.[1]
Mar. 6. But this was successfully accomplished, and just as the
first dawn appeared the last of the troops had moved
off.   A short advance parallel to the Gumti brought
the advanced guard in contact with the rebel cavalry,
which was driven off; and the division encamped for
the night by the Fyzabad road, some four miles from
the city.   There it was attacked next morning by
Mar. 7. twelve thousand men with twelve guns.   The enemy's
round-shot were falling into the camp almost as soon
as the alarm was given, which does not point to great
vigilance on the British side; but the assailants were
Mar. 8. easily repelled.   The 8th was spent in choosing a site
for batteries and bringing up heavy guns; and on the
Mar. 9. 9th Outram with little difficulty cleared the enemy out
of a position on the north bank which guarded the
flank of their first line of defence.   Thereupon, before
the British heavy guns could be brought into position,
the rebels evacuated the first line.   Campbell had
meanwhile sent a force to attack the rebel outpost at
La Martinière, which was yielded up almost without
resistance; and the troops, pressing on, occupied the
abandoned works along the canal.
Mar. 10.   On the 10th Outram shifted his camp close to the
river and threw up batteries for the bombardment of
what was now the second line of defence, the Kaisar
Bagh; Hope Grant meanwhile manœuvring the cavalry
and horse-artillery to cover the operation.   Campbell on
his side drove the enemy from Banks's House, a post at
the southern extremity of their first line of defence, and
then erected batteries against the Begum's palace.   On
Mar. 11. the 11th Outram continued his advance up the northern
bank, clearing the enemy out of the houses as he went,

---

[1] Outram's force consisted of:
Cavalry: 2 D.G., 9th Lancers, detachments of 1st, 2nd, 5th Punjab
    Cavalry.
Artillery: 5th Brigade—Douglas.   3 troops horse-artillery, 2 field-
    batteries.
Infantry: 3rd Division—Walpole.   23rd, 79th, 101st.
    6th Brigade—Horsford.   2 and 3/R.B., 2nd Punjab Inf.

took possession of the iron bridge over against the Resi- 1858.
dency, and pushed on as far as the stone bridge about Mar. 11.
half a mile above it; but finding the troops exposed to
a heavy fire, he contented himself with the iron bridge
only.   Simultaneously Campbell's batteries opened
fire on the Begum's palace; and at four o'clock in the
afternoon General Lugard ordered Adrian Hope's
brigade [1] to the assault.   The Ninety-third led the way,[2]
and for two hours hunted the defenders through barricaded ways, narrow passages and every kind of obstruction, with bullet and bayonet.   Brasyer's Sikhs
followed them in support, and, when at last the
buildings were cleared, over eight hundred corpses of
mutineers were carried from them.   The numbers of
the rebel garrison were reckoned at five thousand.
The Ninety-third went into action eight hundred
strong, and their casualties little exceeded sixty,[3] from
which the inevitable inference is that the mutinied
sepoy, if boldly attacked, was not a very formidable
foe.

One notable soldier, however, met his death in the
Begum's palace, namely, William Hodson of Hodson's
Horse.   Why he should have been there at all it is
difficult to explain,[4] but there he was and there he fell.
Whatever his failings, he had rendered incomparable
service.   On the 19th of May 1857 he had received
orders to raise a body of irregular horse.   Friends in
the Punjab enlisted for him recruits while he did duty
with the Guides before Delhi.   The first batch of three
hundred, untrained, unequipped, undisciplined, arrived
on the 12th of July.   On the 14th they went into action,
and at the end of six weeks Hodson's Horse was chosen
for all dangerous duties of reconnaissance and observa-

---

[1] 93rd, 4th Punjab Infantry, 1000 Gurkhas.
[2] Sir Colin Campbell himself had chosen them for this honour.
[3] 2 officers and 13 men killed; 2 officers and 45 men wounded.
Burgoyne, *Records of the 93rd Highlanders*, pp. 253-256.
[4] He was not killed in the act of looting, as Lord Roberts (*Forty-one
Years in India*, ch. xxix. *note*) has shown.

1858. tion, which were accomplished with exceeding skill, enterprise and audacity. His regiment outlived him, and still survives with heightened reputation. His own fame has been bandied to and fro between admirers who would exalt him to be an angel, and detractors who would abase him to be a fiend. He was neither the one nor the other; but he was a really fine soldier who, at a most critical time, wrought great things for his country.

Mar. 12.   On the 12th Bahadur Jung arrived with the main body of the Gurkhas, who were at once employed in clearing the way to the Imambara, which still barred the way to the Kaisar Bagh. Between the enfilading fire of Outram's guns and the direct fire of Campbell's, progress was fairly rapid, and on the morning of the

Mar. 14.   14th the Imambara was stormed by the Tenth and Brasyer's Sikhs. The men, inflamed by their success, were eager to go on. Reinforcements of the Tenth and Ninetieth were brought up, and the citadel of the Kaisar Bagh was assaulted in turn. Outram, fully informed by signal of the progress of the attack, begged permission to force the passage of the iron bridge and strike in to cut off the enemy's retreat. Campbell returned the astounding answer that he might do so provided that he would undertake not to lose a single man.[1] Though with the help of his heavy guns Outram could probably have secured the passage of the bridge at a cost of, at most, fifty casualties, he unfortunately would not venture to disobey. The Kaisar Bagh was stormed with little difficulty, and the troops broke loose in a mad search for plunder, of which too much lay ready to their hands. The mass of the rebels escaped with comparatively slight loss, and Campbell's ill-judged parsimony of lives was destined to prolong the struggle for a year, and to sentence thousands of British soldiers to death from sunstroke and heat-apoplexy.

Mar. 15.   On the 15th Campbell continued his preparations to clear the city on his side of the river, and meanwhile

[1] Rice Holmes, p. 444 *n.*

sent Hope Grant with eleven hundred cavalry and two 1858.
horse-batteries northward in the direction of Sitapur; Mar. 15.
the rest of the cavalry, under Brigadier-general Campbell of the Bays, being moved north-westward towards
Sandila.   This was an effort to retrieve the mistake of
the previous day, but it was utterly futile, for the
fugitives had dispersed and for the present had disappeared.   Grant had only accomplished his first
march towards Sitapur when, on the 16th, he received Mar. 16.
orders to return, Sir Colin having discovered that there
were still fifteen hundred rebels in the city.[1]   On this
day Outram crossed the river, leaving Walpole's
brigade to watch the bridges, and moved to the attack
of the Residency.   The enemy would not await his
assault at close quarters, but fled towards the river,
followed up by Outram, who mastered in succession the
fortress of Machchi Bhawan and the building called the
great Imambara near the head of the stone bridge.
The fugitives from the Residency, who numbered not
fifteen hundred but twenty thousand, then adroitly detached a party across the stone bridge to occupy Walpole's attention, while the mass of them, crossing the
Gumti higher up, fetched a compass round his rear,
gained the road to Fyzabad, where they were joined by
the party which had crossed the stone bridge, and were
free to continue the war.   One strong detachment of
all three arms was shrewd enough to attempt a counter-
stroke against the British post, reduced to fewer than
one thousand men, at the Alam Bagh, and was only
driven off after four hours' fighting.

On the 17th Campbell's cavalry returned, having Mar. 17.
been sent, so to speak, into the air just when they were
most wanted; and Outram continued his advance on
this day and on the 18th, clearing the buildings on the Mar. 18.
left bank of the Gumti above the stone bridge.   There
still remained a vast building, called the Musa Bagh,
about four miles above the Residency, where nine thousand rebels had taken refuge; and Sir Colin resolved

[1] Hope Grant, p. 257.

1858. that he would at least secure this party. He therefore
Mar. 19. directed Outram to attack them with two divisions of infantry, posted Brigadier-general Campbell with a brigade of infantry, artillery and fifteen hundred cavalry to cut off their retreat, and stationed Hope Grant on the left bank to intercept any fugitives that might cross the river. Grant was in position for two hours before there was any sign of Outram, but in due time the latter appeared and opened fire with his artillery upon the Musa Bagh. Therewith the enemy at once took to their heels, and Brigadier-general Campbell made practically no attempt to molest them. A single squadron of the Ninth Lancers charged and captured twelve guns,[1] but, being checked by artillery-fire from a village, could do no more. A party of some fifty fanatics, maddened with drugs, fell upon one small detachment of the Seventh Hussars, and were cut down to a man, though not before they had wounded three
Mar. 22. officers, one of them mortally. On the 22nd Grant continued the pursuit eastward, along the road to Fyzabad, when two squadrons of Sikhs, under Captain Samuel Browne, and a party of irregular horse rode through them five times, killed about two hundred of them and took fourteen guns. This was a brilliant little affair; but, with these exceptions, the insurgents from the Musa Bagh escaped practically unscathed. On the 21st a few rebels who still remained in the city were dislodged, and therewith the operations at Lucknow came to an end.

The twenty days' fighting had cost Sir Colin no more than seven hundred and twenty-two casualties,[2] about one-sixth of them killed. This would have been a trifling loss if any solid advantage had been gained; but, as a matter of fact, there was little to show for it except a much battered city of palaces, and a good deal of plunder acquired by individuals to the detriment alike of military discipline and efficiency. The entire conduct of the operations that followed upon the first

[1] Hope Grant, p. 258.   [2] 127 killed, 595 wounded.

relief of Lucknow in November has been severely 1858. criticised, and Sir Colin has been accused of wasting many valuable weeks of the cool season. This, however, was no fault of his. He and the Governor-general, as has been told, differed as to the enterprise that should be next undertaken; and the discussion of these differences necessarily took time. Again, the task set to Sir Colin at Lucknow was not only to force powerfully entrenched lines but to clear several square miles of fortified buildings. His only means of averting great sacrifice of British lives was to take with him plenty of heavy artillery; but the collection of draught-cattle and the transport of siege-cannon from the arsenal at Agra was a matter of time, and in fact the first of them did not leave Agra for Cawnpore until the 21st of January. A different question arises when we come to the actual employment of the troops. Sir Colin, after more than forty years' service, must have been fully alive to the fact that the British Parliament had always steadily refused to maintain an army large enough for the Empire's needs. He cannot have been ignorant of the huge losses of the army in the Crimea from sickness, nor of the difficulty in raising recruits to make them good. Moreover, his function was, not like Archdale Wilson's or Henry Havelock's, to carry a single operation to a successful issue, but to put down the rebellion on all sides and in all quarters; and it was very difficult for him or for anyone else to predict when and where that function would end. It was only certain that any failure on the part of the British in the field would certainly prolong the struggle. In the circumstances, therefore, it seems that he cannot be blamed for assembling an unusually large force for the final expedition to Lucknow, and, as a general principle, for husbanding the lives of his soldiers to the utmost.

But the surest means of attaining this latter object was to avoid another campaign in the hot weather. It was the sun and not the enemy that had wrought such havoc in Havelock's column and before Delhi. The

1858. rebels, as a body, had proved themselves contemptible foes in the field, and less formidable even in street-fighting than the Spaniards of Buenos Ayres or the Arabs of Rosetta.   It was, therefore, Campbell's imperative duty to inflict the greatest possible punishment upon them, even at the sacrifice of a few hundreds more or less of killed and wounded, while the cool season lasted.   But this neither he nor Mansfield, his chief of staff, seem to have apprehended.   It has been seen how Mansfield allowed numbers of mutineers to escape from Cawnpore; and he is said to have asked what was the use of intercepting a desperate soldiery whose only wish was to escape.[1]   In any case the language of his despatch suggests that he acted deliberately, not thinking the military gain worth the loss even of a single life; and, since Campbell passed no censure upon him, it seems to be a just inference that he was governed by what he knew to be Campbell's wishes.   Nor is this inference impugned by subsequent events.   During the operations against Lucknow in November 1857, Colonel Ewart of the Ninety-third asked permission to sally out of the buildings where his regiment was covered, and to drive off a party of mutineers which was maintaining an incessant fire.   Campbell's answer was that Ewart might do so if he would guarantee that he would not lose a single man.[2]   The same phrase, as has been told, was repeated to Outram in March 1858; whence it should seem that it sprang too readily to Sir Colin's lips.   So old a soldier should have known that there are occasions in war when ill-considered thrift costs more dearly than timely profusion.

As it chanced, the mischief wrought through Campbell's blunders at Lucknow was heightened to the utmost by a proclamation issued by the Governor-general immediately after its fall.   Herein Lord Canning declared that, inasmuch as the mutineers had received great assistance both from the citizens of

---

[1] Sherer, p. 143.
[2] Ewart, *Events of a Soldier's Life*, ii. 88.

Lucknow and the inhabitants of Oudh, the lands of the 1858. province were confiscate by the British Government. Six persons who had shown conspicuous loyalty were exempted by name from this sweeping penalty, and reservations were made in favour of such as could subsequently prove that their conduct had been equally irreproachable. But, with these exceptions, the inhabitants of Oudh were told that life and immunity from disgrace were the utmost that they could expect. Canning regarded this manifesto as erring, if anything, on the side of lenience. Outram, on the other hand, considered it dangerously severe, urging that it would drive the people of Oudh to despair and lead them to engage in a guerilla warfare which would mean death to thousands of British soldiers. John Lawrence likewise advised Canning in the same sense. No mutineer had surrendered, because surrender had meant certain death; and therefore the time was ripe for an amnesty to all who had not actually committed murder. But Canning, a typical weak, violent man, would consent only to modify his proclamation by a vague and meaningless clause. Thus on the one side there was a general who thought it useless to intercept a desperate soldiery that only wished to escape, and on the other a civilian who insisted on maintaining the desperation not only of that same soldiery but of every man in Oudh. Between the two it is small wonder that the suppression of the mutiny was prolonged, and that thousands of lives were sacrificed to no purpose on both sides. It will be a relief to turn to another sphere of operations and to a commander very different from Sir Colin Campbell.

CHAPTER LIII

1857. So far our survey of the mutiny has been limited, broadly speaking, to the line of communication between Calcutta and the north-west. It is now time to examine its ramifications in Western and Central India. At Bombay, fortunately, there was a Governor, Lord Elphinstone, of cool judgement and rare courage, who, while not hesitating to send every man that he could spare to the principal scene of disorder, made the most by swift and resolute action of such slender reserves as were left to him. There were Mahrattas, countrymen of Nana Sahib, to north of him at Baroda, to north-east at Indore, and to south about Poona and Kolhapur; while to north-east lay Central India and to east the great territory of the Nizam. The problem set to him was to maintain communication between Bombay and Agra, and to prevent the insurrection from spreading to south of the Narbada. To fulfil these duties he equipped a movable column under Major-general Woodburn and ordered it to proceed to Mau, within less than ten miles of Indore and less than twenty of the Narbada. Its strength, or rather its weakness, throws a curious light upon the history of the times, for it consisted of three troops of the Fourteenth Light Dragoons, a battery of European artillery and a single battalion of Bombay Native Infantry. On the 8th of June it marched from Poona for Mau.

Trouble was not slow in coming. The British Agent responsible for Holkar's territory and, among other adjacent states, for Bhopal and Dhar, was Colonel

Henry Marion Durand, whom we last saw in the act of 1857. blowing in the gate of Ghazni. His residence was in Holkar's capital, Indore, and, though the Maharaja himself, a mere youth, was not ill-affected, Holkar's troops rose in mutiny on the 1st of July, when Durand, being defenceless, was fain to fly. On the same day the native troops at Mau revolted, and nothing was left of the garrison but a single battery of British artillery, whose commander none the less threw himself into the fort at Mau and resolved to hold it to the last.

There was for a moment danger in Bombay itself, which was, however, averted by the energy of Mr. Forjett, the Superintendent of Police; and though there were sporadic mutinies at one or two isolated stations, the native army of Bombay as a whole remained loyal. In the Mahratta countries danger was averted by the admirable firmness of the civil officers, Sir Richmond Shakespear to north at Baroda, Mr. George Seton-Karr to south, and others of not less merit. An outbreak at Kolhapur was quelled by the amazing vigour of Lieutenant Kerr, who with fifty troopers of the Southern Mahratta Irregular Cavalry marched from Satara and covered the eighty miles to Kolhapur, after swimming three deep and rapid rivers on the way, in twenty-four hours. He was followed by a stronger column, which included the Hundred and Sixth, under Colonel Jacob; but trouble and unrest still lingered about Kolhapur until Jacob, by the instant suppression of a second mutiny in December, restored a surer order.

In Hyderabad the loyalty of the Nizam and of his chief minister, Salar Jang, backed by the influence of the British Resident, Captain Cuthbert Davidson, promised to be of immense service in preserving the peace of Southern India. The Hyderabad contingent, trained by British officers, were troops little, if at all, less efficient than the Bombay Government's own native regiments; and in June they were placed at that Government's disposal for active service. On the

1857.
June. 12th of June there were ugly signs of mutiny in a small column of all three arms of the contingent which had been moved to Aurangabad. The officers contrived to stave off anything like a general rising until the arrival of Woodburn's column, which had been hastily summoned to Aurangabad, on the 23rd. A few executions then sufficed to stamp out all disaffection, and the contingent became once more an efficient weapon. There was, indeed, no lack of malcontents in Hydera-

July. bad itself; and on the 17th of July a mob of these, led by five hundred Rohillas, made a determined attack upon the British Residency. The onslaught was successfully repulsed; and the behaviour of a party of the contingent's cavalry in the defence was so admir-able as to discourage all further attempts of the kind, contributing in fact materially to overawe all unruly elements to south of the Narbada.

August.   On the 2nd of August Woodburn's column, now under the command of Brigadier-general Stuart, marched into Mau, having been joined on the march by Durand, who assumed the general direction of opera-tions. The troops had suffered some loss from cholera and fever while crossing the valley of the Tapti, but had shaken off the plague after passing the Vindya hills; and the arrival on the 5th of August of four companies of the Eighty-sixth, which had lain within the Bombay command since 1842, gave a welcome addition of a few hundred British infantry. All move-ment, however, was for the present forbidden by the rains, and Durand had to content himself with the collection of a siege-train. Every information indi-cated that some fifteen thousand insurgents, formed round a nucleus of mutinous cavalry of the Gwalior contingent, were assembled under command of Prince Firoz Shah, of the royal house of Delhi, at Mandsaur, one hundred and twenty miles north of Indore; but it was hopeless to think of approaching them until the

Oct. monsoon was past. At length, on the 20th of October, Durand set a column of fourteen hundred men in

motion [1] towards Dhar, some forty miles to westward. 1857.
On the 22nd the enemy tried to meet them in the open, Oct. 22.
but were easily routed and driven back into the fort.
Batteries were then erected, for the fort was formidable
and well built; but after a week's cannonade the garrison stole away by night without awaiting an assault,
and left treasure of considerable value behind them.

Having thus cleared his left flank and dismantled
the fort of Dhar, Stuart on the 8th of November struck Nov.
northward upon Nimach, having meanwhile been reinforced by two regiments of cavalry, the equivalent of a
battalion of infantry and fourteen guns of the Hyderabad contingent, under Captain Orr. On the 10th
two British officers of Holkar's contingent at Mehid-
pur, fifty miles north of Indore, came in with news
that they had been attacked and defeated by the rebels
on the 8th, and that the main body of the contingent
had joined their attackers and were moving upon
Mandsaur. Captain Orr was at once sent forward to
intercept them. He overtook them, cut down about a
hundred, and captured over seventy more with every
one of their guns. On the 19th Stuart crossed the
Chambal, and on the morning of the 21st approached
Mandsaur. In the afternoon the enemy attacked a
small advanced force of Stuart's cavalry, which charged
them at once and drove them off with heavy loss. On
the 22nd Stuart advanced to within three-quarters of a
mile west of Mandsaur, when his cavalry came upon
the advanced guard of a rebel force moving southward
from Nimach. On the next day he fell upon them,
capturing all their guns, and following up his success
on the 24th, dispersed them with great slaughter.[2]
The country people turned upon the fugitives; and

---

[1] His force at Mau consisted of:
Europeans: 5 troops 14th L.D.; 4 cos. 86th; Woolcombe's Bombay
battery, Hungerford's Bengal battery.
Indians: 3rd Hyderabad Cavalry; 25th Bombay N.I.; detachment
of Madras Sappers and Miners.
[2] His casualties were 7 killed and 69 wounded.

1857. Durand, leaving Orr for the present at Mandsaur,
Dec. returned to Indore, which he reached on the 15th of
December. He had effectually suppressed Holkar's
revolted troops, confirmed the loyalty of Holkar him-
self and prepared the way for a decisive campaign in
Central India.

Dec. 17.   On the 17th of December a new General, Sir Hugh
Rose, assumed command of what was now termed the
Central India Field Force. Sir Hugh was now in his
fifty-sixth year. His career had been almost more that
of a diplomatist than of a soldier, and he had filled
admirably the very difficult post of British representative at the French head-quarters in the Crimea. To
India he was an absolute stranger, and his appointment
was received with some derision by officers of the old
Indian school; nor can it be denied that his methods
were different from theirs. The force placed at his
disposal was not great, consisting of two brigades, each
composed of all three arms, and including one regiment—the Fourteenth Light Dragoons—of British
cavalry, two battalions, the Eighty-sixth and Hundred
and Ninth, of British infantry, and two batteries of
British artillery, besides Indian troops of all three
arms.[1] The whole may have numbered some six
thousand fighting men, perhaps five-twelfths of them
British; and they very soon discovered, by the way in
which the new commander pushed preparations forward, that behind the most charming manners he veiled
extreme energy and a very strong will.

The general idea for the operations for the restora-

---

[1] 1st Brigade: Brigadier-general Stuart, Bombay Army.
   1 squadron 14th L.D., 1 troop 3rd Bombay Cavalry, 86th Foot,
   25th Bombay Infantry.
   2 European batteries.   Indian Sappers.
   2nd Brigade: Brigadier-general Steuart, 14th L.D.
   H.M. 14th L.D., 3rd Bombay Cavalry, 109th Foot (3rd
   Bombay Europeans), 24th Bombay N.I.
   1 Field battery, 1 Horse battery, Madras and Bombay Sappers.
   Siege-train.
   Detachment of all arms Hyderabad contingent.

tion of order in Central India was that a column of the 1858. Bombay Army under Rose should march from Mau north-eastward upon Kalpi by way of Jhansi; and that another of the Madras Army, under General Whitlock, should move from Jabalpur northward upon Banda, each supporting the other and relieving Sir Colin Campbell's rear from the pressure of the revolted Gwalior contingent and of the insurgents who had attached themselves to it. Whitlock, however, was behindhand, and Rose was not the man to wait for the unready. It had been arranged that his two brigades should move separately on a more or less parallel course; the First Brigade to northward, following and clearing the Grand Trunk Road, and the Second, under Rose himself, upon Sagar, where a tiny British garrison had for eight months been beleaguered by the rebels. Both columns were then to unite before Jhansi and proceed further as circumstances might dictate. The work promised to be severe, for the distance from Mau to Jhansi as the crow flies is not much less than three hundred miles; and Rose gave immense pains to the improvement of his transport, and to the provision of ambulances for the sick, depending for carriage chiefly upon camels.[1] Officers were ordered to leave their heavy baggage behind, and no effort was spared to make the columns travel light. On the 6th of January Jan. 1858, Rose started from Mau for Sihor, about ninety miles east and north of Indore, where the Second Brigade was assembled, leaving Stuart to follow as soon as the Eighty-sixth, of which only two companies as yet were present, should have arrived in full strength.

On the 16th of January Rose moved off from Sihor Jan. 16. with the Second Brigade, and proceeding by Bhopal and Bhilsa came on the morning of the 24th before the Jan. 24. fortress of Rahatgarh, about ten miles west of Sagar. The place was of great extent and very strong, but Rose

[1] Rowe, *Central India during the Campaign of* 1857–58, p. 162; Sylvester, *Recollections of the Campaign in Malwa and Central India,* p. 54.

1858. promptly invested it and erected heavy batteries, with the result that after a few days' firing the enemy stole
Jan. 28. away in the night of the 28th, passing through the midst of some raw levies lent by the Begum of Bhopal. This cleared the way to Sagar, which Rose, after dis-
Feb. 3. mantling Rahatgarh, relieved on the 3rd of February. The villagers around were all starving owing to the depredations of the rebels, and the distribution of grain to these poor people was Rose's next care.   He then,
Feb. 9. on the 9th, turned against another rebel stronghold, the fort of Garhakota, about twenty-five miles east of Sagar; but once again the garrison escaped him, his force being insufficient to invest the place completely. However, the Hyderabad Cavalry pursued them vigorously for five and twenty miles, inflicting some loss. The dismantling of the fort detained him for some
Feb. 17. days, but on the 17th the column returned to Sagar, where Rose was fain to halt for some days, both to allow Whitlock, who had left Jabalpur on the 17th, to come up and take charge of the station, and to make further preparations for his own column.   The serious business of the campaign was now about to begin.   The heat was daily increasing; and one of Rose's first measures was to provide the Hundred and Sixth with loose khaki clothing.[1]   Experience at Sagar, moreover, gave warning that the country between that place and Kalpi would afford little in the way of grain and forage, so that it was necessary to collect very large supplies. The siege-train was likewise replenished with ammunition and increased with heavy pieces from the arsenal at Sagar.   But these precautions signified necessarily more transport-animals, particularly elephants;

---

[1] Rowe, p. 200, calls it "stone-coloured."   Sherer, *Daily Life in the Indian Mutiny*, pp. 58, 93, speaks of Neill as dressed in "khakee," and defines *khakee* as "ash-coloured."   Sylvester, p. 126, speaks of "khakee dye," but does not define the colour.   Both stone and ashes vary in hue, but the impression left upon me by the above extracts is that khaki was originally less yellow and more grey than at present; though I have always been told that the original khaki dye was curry-powder.

and the collection of these inevitably took time. It 1858.
was not until the 27th of February that Rose was able Feb. 27.
to resume his march.

The courage of the rebels was restored by this
respite; and they took up strong positions to bar the
three passes of the mountainous ranges which shut off
the Sagar district from Bandelkhand. The main road
to Jhansi led through the pass of Marhat; and this
was occupied by the Raja of Banpur, who had thrown
up strong parapets and abatis and held the defile with
ten thousand men. Advancing to a central position
from which he threatened equally all of the passes,
Rose made a feint against Marhat, and on the 3rd of Mar. 3.
March forced another pass, which was held by the
Raja of Shahgarh, further to the east, thus effectually
turning the enemy's defences at and in rear of Marhat.
By the 7th he had reached the fort of Moraora, which
was abandoned by the rebels; and there the British
flag was hoisted and the territory of the Raja of Shahgarh was formally annexed to the British Crown. Rose
had meanwhile sent orders to Stuart to strike eastward
from Goona and attack the fort of Chanderi, which lay
on the left flank of Sir Hugh's line of advance to
Jhansi. Stuart, who had been detained at Mau until
the 6th of February, arrived within six miles of
Chanderi on the 5th of March and, driving scattered Mar. 5.
parties of rebels before him, sat down before it. The
fort was exceedingly strong, and some days were consumed in bringing up heavy guns and battering a
breach. On the 15th the main body of the Eighty- Mar. 15.
sixth was still twenty-eight miles distant from Stuart's
headquarters, when he sent them a message to announce
that he was about to assault. They had just completed
a march of thirteen miles, but at ten o'clock next
forenoon they strode into camp; and at three o'clock
on the morning of the 17th, St. Patrick's Day, they Mar. 17.
were at the head of two storming parties. The place
was carried with little difficulty or loss, but, as usual,
the bulk of the enemy escaped, though some were

1858. pursued and cut up by the cavalry.   It was not possible
Mar. 17. either for Stuart or for Rose to seal up with their small
numbers all avenues of egress from forts with a perimeter of four or more miles, generally veiled on one
side or another by a belt of jungle.   Nevertheless, the
irresistible advance of both, the activity of the cavalry,
chiefly of the Hyderabad contingent, and the execution
of all captured mutineers had carried fear into all ranks
of the rebels, and the name of Rose was already a name
of dread.

Meanwhile Sir Hugh had pushed on, and on the
night of the 19th/20th a march of fifteen miles brought
the Second Brigade within eight miles of Jhansi.   On
Mar. 20. that same day, the 20th, a despatch arrived from Sir
Colin Campbell, ordering Rose to move at once to
the aid of the Raja of Charkari, who was besieged in
his fort by the mutineers of the Gwalior contingent.
This would have meant a march of eighty miles to the
eastward, giving the impression that the British were
afraid to attack Jhansi, and encouraging the ten
thousand men within it either to fall upon their rear,
as they moved, or to assail their line of operations.
Sir Robert Hamilton, the Civil Commissioner with
Rose, had received instructions of similar purport from
Lord Canning; but he and Rose agreed that both
Governor-general and the Commander-in-chief must
be ignored, and that the operations against Jhansi
must proceed.

Cavalry and horse-artillery were sent forward to invest
Mar. 21. the place; and on the 21st the main body encamped
before the city.   It was surrounded by a high and
massive wall with numerous flanking bastions, its total
perimeter being of four and a half miles; and it was
dominated by the fort, of equal strength, at its western
end, the western face of which was steep inaccessible
rock.   The garrison numbered some twelve thousand,
with thirty or forty guns under a skilled artilleryman;
and to the outward eye the stronghold might well have
seemed impregnable.   Rose established seven flying

cavalry-camps so as to make the investment as complete as possible, and then constructed his batteries for an attack upon the southern face.   On the 25th the first of these opened fire, and, upon the arrival of the First Brigade on the 26th, fresh works were thrown up to bring its siege-artillery also into play.   By the 30th the defences of Jhansi had been in great degree dismantled; most of the guns had been dismounted by the cannonade; and a practicable breach had been made.   The besieged worked desperately to close it by a stockade, which the besiegers destroyed by means of red-hot shot; and the two were still in fierce contention on the 31st when one of Rose's outlying posts reported by signal that the enemy was advancing in great force from the north.

Sir Hugh received the tidings with perfect equanimity.   He had on the 30th heard that Tantia Topi, with five or six regiments of the Gwalior contingent and other troops amounting in all to some twenty thousand men, was moving down, having captured Charkari, to the relief of Jhansi.   Rose had even led troops on that night to the fords of the Betwa in the hope of fighting these new enemies with the river in their rear, but had drawn them off at daybreak.   On the evening of the 31st, without relaxing the investment of Jhansi in the least, he again marched eastward towards the nearest ford; and this time the rebels did cross the water and took up a position in order of battle over against the camp of the Second Brigade.   In all Rose could spare from the siege for the field about nineteen hundred of all ranks, drawn from all units of both brigades; but, in order to deceive the enemy, he struck the tents of the First Brigade, and sent the troops to the appointed place by a circuitous route so that they should not be observed.   The two brigades bivouacked in two lines after dark; but at midnight Rose received intelligence that the enemy was crossing a ford eight miles down the river in great force. Without hesitation Rose sent Stuart off with the First

1858. Brigade [1] to look to them, and remained with his own tiny force to stand the shock alone.

All night the enemy taunted Sir Hugh's outposts with threats and jeers, while the besieged within Jhansi kept up a continual riot of drumming and bugling and yelling and matchlock firing.   Day had barely dawned

April 1. on the 1st of April when Rose's vedettes fell back, and the enemy came on, with their twenty-eight guns backed by infantry in the centre, and six to seven hundred horse. Rose was ready for them with heavy guns and infantry in his centre, and a squadron and a light battery on either wing, his entire force numbering perhaps nine hundred and fifty.[2]   The enemy advanced to within six hundred yards and opened a heavy and well-aimed fire. Rose replied with his artillery, bidding his infantry lie down, and advanced his light batteries so as to enfilade the enemy on either flank.   In the course of this movement one British horse-artillery gun was disabled; and Rose cut matters short by charging the enemy's line upon both flanks.   He himself rode at the head of a troop of the Fourteenth Light Dragoons into the enemy's left.   In a moment the hostile line was crumpled up; and the advance of Rose's infantry speedily dissolved it into groups of fugitives, amid which Rose's handful of cavalry—three troops of the Fourteenth and one of Hyderabad horse—broke in irresistibly with the sabre.   Steadily as the pursuit continued these groups shrank first into tiny squares and then into individual men, all streaming towards the Betwa. After a chase of two miles a second line of the enemy came into sight, the reserve commanded by Tantia in person, who at once opened fire from his guns.   The two British batteries galloped up, unlimbered and replied;

---

[1] Stuart's force was, 14th L.D., 40; 86th, 208; Hyderabad Cav., 107; 25th Bombay N.I., 500; total, 855 rank and file—say 1000 of all ranks, with 8 guns.

[2] 14th L.D., 203; Hyderabad Cavalry, 100; 109th, 226; 24th Bombay N.I., 298; total, 827 rank and file, or say 950 of all ranks.

and now it was, apparently, that Stuart's brigade began
to play its part in the day's work.

On arriving at the lower ford assigned to him Stuart
could see no sign of an enemy, and, when Rose's guns
opened, he promptly marched to the sound of them.
On the way he met a band of rebels flying to the ford,
and promptly turned them back, his cavalry—two
troops only—cutting up as many as they could.   Next
he came upon a party of about three thousand with six
guns.   These had occupied a village, which after a few
rounds of shrapnel was carried with the bayonet.   The
enemy retired fighting, and Stuart's solitary troop of
the Fourteenth, reduced from thirty mounted men to
ten, could produce little effect on them.   The ground
was impracticable for artillery, and the infantry was too
much exhausted to follow rapidly.   It should seem,
however, that this body of defeated rebels came across
Tantia Topi's front or down upon his flank, for his
reserve gave way almost immediately before the fire of
Rose's batteries.   These and the cavalry hunted it on to
the Betwa, where they made large captures.   Beyond
the river was jungle which had been set on fire, either
by Tantia's orders or by the British shells.   It mattered
not.   The cavalry galloped through it, not a few men
being badly burned, and desisted not till they could
gallop no longer.   Had Rose been able to dispose of
the whole of his force, few of the enemy would have
escaped.   As things were, fifteen hundred of them lay
dead on the ground and every one of their twenty-eight
guns was captured.

Meanwhile the garrison of Jhansi, overawed by a
false attack delivered by Rose's orders, had not dared to
sally out against the besiegers during the day, and
showed no more courage during the night, when Rose's
field-force must have been utterly exhausted by its
exertions.   On the following day Sir Hugh gave his
men a day of comparative rest, and at three o'clock on
the morning of the 3rd he assaulted Jhansi with three
columns, one of which was launched against the breach

1858.
April 3. and the remainder against other points, all alike mounting the walls by escalade.   Notwithstanding a slight check to one column, all three effected their entrance after a sharp struggle and fought their way to the Rani's palace, which Rose, knowing nothing of the interior of the city, had assigned as the principal objective.   There was grim slaughter on that day, for the massacre of British at Jhansi had been less savage only than that at

April 4. Cawnpore.   Street-fighting continued on the 4th, but in the night the Rani fled; and her followers, losing heart, began to fly likewise.   On the 5th the fort was found

April 6. to be deserted, and on the 6th, when a last body of desperate men had been destroyed, Jhansi passed finally into Rose's hands.   The enemy's dead in the four days' fighting were reckoned at from three to five thousand.   Rose's casualties from lead and steel in the action of the 1st of April and in the assault were three hundred and forty-three.

Not for the first time in the course of the Mutiny this light casualty-list brings home the fact that the rebels were really not a very formidable enemy.   As usual the bulk of them gave way as soon as the storming parties had gained a footing upon the ramparts; but many British officers fell while leading the way, and among them those of the Engineers were conspicuous, only two out of seven escaping unhurt.[1]   But at Jhansi, as at Delhi and Lucknow, it is difficult to reconcile the perfectly sincere accounts, written by those present, of desperate combat, with the low proportion of killed and wounded on the British side.   We have the testimony of doctors that some British soldiers staggered out of action disabled by fearful sword-cuts received in close combat hand to hand;[2] and yet the bayonet of the conquering race proved to be irresistible.   The men, of course, had the memory of a massacre to goad them to vengeance, and Rose himself went with them through the hottest fire in the streets.   Yet there was no mad fury of slaughter.   The British soldiers slew only those

[1] Sylvester, p. 268.   [2] Rowe, p. 258.

who had arms in their hands, sparing the aged and the 1858.
helpless, and even sharing their rations, on the evening April 6.
of the storm, with the distraught and terrified native
women.[1]   There was abundance of spoil, yet there was
no plundering; though it must be added that there was
no liquor.   Altogether Rose seems to have infused a
tone into his force which was peculiar to his personality.
Other writers have lauded with justice the amazing
nerve with which, while maintaining the investment of
Jhansi, he sallied out with a mere remnant to meet
Tantia Topi; and indeed no praise can be too high
for it.   And it should seem that, but for his own individual interposition, the action of the 1st of April
might have been disastrous.   The leader even of no
more than nine hundred men does not take personal command of thirty or forty British dragoons
and charge at their head, unless the issue of the combat for the moment trembles in the balance.   But
Rose evidently had a very quick tactical instinct, and
his men would follow him anywhere, knowing him
not only as a leader of singular personal bravery but
as a friend.[2]

After the fall of Jhansi Sir Hugh remained perforce
stationary for nearly three weeks while he replenished
his supplies and ammunition.   The arrangements
made at Bombay for the transport and supply of his
army were very unsatisfactory, adding greatly to his
difficulties.   However, his cavalry during this halt did
useful and effective work in scouring the country and
breaking up small parties of rebels.   But there was
still a centre of rebellion at Kotah on his western flank,
while the garrison of Charkari was active in mischief
to east of him.   Not until he was assured of a column
marching from Rajputana to protect his conquests did
he venture to quit Jhansi.   Even then he was obliged
to leave behind him a wing of the Hundred and Ninth
and four companies of his Bombay infantry, which made

---

[1] Sylvester, p. 115; Rowe, pp. 262-263.
[2] Rowe, p. 252.

1858 a very serious subtraction from his already weakened
April 25. force.   At midnight of the 24th/25th April he marched
with the First Brigade from Jhansi on the road to Kalpi,
the Second Brigade following on the 2nd of May.   It
should seem that it was physically impossible for the
two to move in one body.   Not only was the heat now
terrific, the hot wind blowing day and night, but with
every stage passed the flat arid country yielded less and
less water.   The dust lay so thick that the men were
caked, choked and blinded with it; and thus every march,
though invariably conducted by night, signified utter
exhaustion.   Then, when the day came, sleep was impossible, or, if men were fairly overcome by it, they
never woke again, having succumbed to heat-apoplexy.[1]
All this had been the experience of Havelock's men and
of the troops before Delhi, but they had at least been
spared a dearth of water.   However, the columns
tramped on, and Tantia Topi steadily withdrew from
before them, hoping that the sun would destroy them
before they could reach Kalpi.

May 1.   On the 1st of May Rose arrived at Punch, about fifty
miles north-east of Jhansi, where he learned that Tantia
Topi had taken up a strong entrenched position at
Kunch, fourteen miles ahead.   Here he halted, and was
May 3. joined on the 3rd by the headquarters wing of the
Seventy-first, dressed in khaki blouse and overalls, with
a head-dress which gave good protection from the sun.[2]
On the 5th the Second Brigade came up, and on the
night of the 6th, Rose marched to turn the position of
Kunch by the north-west.   Something seems to have
May 7. gone wrong with the action that followed on the 7th
for, though the First Brigade easily drove the enemy
off, the Second remained halted in the sun inactive, its
cavalry and horse-artillery alone doing some execution
on the rebel infantry as they retreated.   But it was past
noon before the rebels gave way, and the pursuit ended

---

[1] Sylvester, pp. 124-125.
[2] They had come from Malta by the overland route to Bombay
and had reached Mau in March.

only just before dark, with a loss to the enemy of five 1858.
hundred slain and nine guns captured.   Rose's casu- May 7.
alties in action did not exceed twenty-four; but the
heat had been appalling.   Ten horses in one single
battery had perished of exhaustion and thirst; twelve
men of the Seventy-first had died outright, and over
thirty more had been prostrated.   Rose himself had
fallen down thrice from sunstroke, but, thanks chiefly
to his indomitable will, had never for long left his duty.
A new and disquieting effect of the sun was that it
rendered useless the Enfield rifles which hitherto had
given vast advantage to the British soldiers.   Through
some defect in the ammunition, the men could not with
all their strength drive the bullet down into the breech.
Thus to all of Rose's trials was added his soldiers' distrust of their weapons.[1]

The hot wind blew hard all night and many of the
troops could find no water, so Rose was fain to grant
them a rest.   At two o'clock in the morning of the
8th he moved on with the First Brigade to a strong fort May 8.
which was found to be evacuated by the enemy.   Once
again he was obliged to halt.   The Second Brigade
was to have followed him on the 9th but was detained
by a dust-storm, which went near to suffocate both
men and beasts, with a high wind which left scarcely
a tent standing.   After an hour the rain fell heavily,
and the temperature suddenly cooled down, giving
much refreshment to the exhausted troops.   On the
other hand the tents, soaked with rain, were so heavy
that the march was inevitably postponed until the 10th. May 10.
Meanwhile the rebels, who had at first been greatly
disheartened by their defeat at Kunch, had been joined
by reinforcements from the Nawab of Banda;   and,
thus encouraged, Tantia Topi determined to fight
resolutely for Kalpi.   The main road to that place was
barred by strong entrenchments and breastworks, and
every preparation was made for a desperate resistance.
Rose on the 10th marched with the First Brigade to

[1] Sylvester, pp. 128-129, 134-135; Rowe, p. 275.

1858.
May 10.
move round the enemy's left and to turn their defences by the east, leaving orders for the Second Brigade to follow the main road upon Kalpi. A force detached by Sir Colin Campbell under Colonel Maxwell[1] was waiting on the north bank of the Jumna to co-operate with him; and, by a feint against the enemy's front, Rose hoped to gain communication with it and to replenish his supply of ammunition, which was running very low. His order for the march of the Second Brigade reached it at Orai, about twenty miles south-west of Kalpi, soon after sunrise. The thermometer then marked one hundred degrees Fahrenheit, and the men were already exhausted. When, however, they were asked if they would make a further effort, they responded readily and marched on. Rose, however, had required too much of them, and they had undertaken more than they could fulfil. They began to fall out first by twos and threes, and presently to drop down by dozens and by scores. There was neither shade nor water to restore them. The carriage set apart for the sick was already overcrowded, and the wretched bearers themselves could not carry the litters. Every soul was prostrated by the heat. The staff succumbed with the rest; and the column, with no one to guide it, wandered off on the track of the First Brigade, and knew not what it had done till the tents were perceived in the distance. When the camping ground was reached there was no water there, and only after painful search was there found at last a deep well. The few strong men who had survived the march barely provided sentries enough to maintain order while the water was distributed. Stragglers were coming in all night, but there were many of the fallen who rose no more.[2]

For three full days the Second Brigade seems to have been paralysed, and the First Brigade dared not move far from it. No doubt also Rose calculated, by

[1] *Maxwell's Force*: Camel Corps, 682; 88th, 578; Tawana Horse, 266; Sikh Police, 458; 48 guns, Blunt's battery, 8 heavy mortars.

[2] Sylvester, pp. 138-140.

his inaction, to lull the enemy into a false security; but 1858.
on the 13th the First Brigade advanced nearer to the May 13.
Jumna at Etora, and, sending back its hospital-transport,
enabled the Second Brigade to join it on the 14th.
Water was still scarce in the new encampment, and on
the 15th the First Brigade, together with the Hydera- May 15.
bad contingent, made its decisive movement to the
village of Golaoli, six miles east of Kalpi and within
one mile of the Jumna.   Thence Rose dispatched
orders to Maxwell, who was thirty miles distant, to
move up to the bank of the Jumna immediately; and
he launched upon the river two pontoon-rafts, which
he had brought with him from Poona, to establish
communication between the two forces.

Then at last Tantia Topi perceived that he had been
outwitted, and became active immediately.   Though
his elaborate entrenchments on the main road had been
turned to naught, he had still some twenty thousand
men in Kalpi, which was the principal arsenal of the
insurgents, with the Rani of Jhansi, the Nawab of
Banda and Rao Sahib, Nana Sahib's nephew, all of
them present to instil energy and inspire confidence.
On the 16th at three o'clock the Second Brigade May 16.
marched for Golaoli; and the long column of baggage
was at once threatened by the appearance of the enemy
in great strength upon its left flank.   The main body
reached the village of Diapura and effected its junction
with the First Brigade unmolested; but the rearguard
was assailed by about six thousand men of all three
arms, and was at one moment so hardly pressed that
Rose himself started with a small detachment to extri-
cate it.   So ably, however, was the rearguard handled
by Major Forbes of the Bombay cavalry that he brought
it into Diapura unaided, with the loss indeed of some
bullock-carts but with few other casualties.   The
enemy then summoned reinforcements from Kalpi
and attacked a position which dominated Diapura.
Colonel Campbell of the Seventy-first, who had succeeded to the command of the Second Brigade upon

1858.
May 16. the disability of Colonel Stuart through sickness, was about to withdraw from it, when Rose arrived in person and, summoning reinforcements, drove the rebels off. Tantia, rightly judging that other points must have been weakened for this purpose, thereupon attacked Golaoli, on the British right, and another village in their centre. Being in each case repulsed,

May 17. he made another attempt upon Diapura on the 17th. He knew well that the heat had reduced Rose's troops to a shadow of their former strength, and was shrewd enough to leave them no rest. But he had missed his great opportunity when the Second Brigade was on the march. His cavalry outnumbered Forbes's parched and exhausted troopers by twenty to one, yet, though the rebels once or twice showed feeble signs of attacking, they never had the courage to charge when they might have swept all before them.

May 18. On the 18th Maxwell's force reached the Jumna and took up a position to bombard the town and fort of Kalpi on the eastern side, and to play upon some batteries erected by the enemy on the ground between

May 19. Golaoli and the walls. On the 19th Rose drew in his centre and left, encamping them in rear of Golaoli and within reach of the Jumna. A network of ravines still separated them from the river, but the mere sight of the sheet of blue water was refreshing; and the animals wandered down to it in herds, though many

May 20. reached it only to die. On the 20th the enemy attacked a mortar-battery which covered Rose's front, but were easily repulsed, and on that night reinforcements from Maxwell's force crossed from the north to the south bank of the Jumna. These consisted of a Camel Corps, formed early in April at Lucknow of two hundred men of the Rifle Brigade and as many Sikhs, and of two companies of the Eighty-eighth, which was Maxwell's own regiment. The whole forded the Jumna on camels and all were in camp by

May 21. 9 A.M.; yet eight men of the Eighty-eighth were prostrated and two died of sunstroke on this short

march.[1]   It is hardly surprising that with the sun for 1858.
their ally, the rebels had appointed the next day for a May 21.
great attack, and had sworn by the sacred waters of
the Jumna to make an end of the British.

Fully apprised of this, Rose made his dispositions
on the morning of the 22nd.   The mortar-battery on May 22.
his right was strengthened by three field-guns; and
the Eighty-sixth, a wing of the 25th Native Infantry
and the Hundred and Sixth were extended in succession from right to left as a line of skirmishers along
the network of ravines to the river; the remainder
of the infantry and artillery were drawn up on their
left, with the Camel Corps on the left of all; and the
bulk of the cavalry was stationed beyond the Camel
Corps, the ground being there more open and favourable for the action of horse.   At nine o'clock the enemy
advanced in great force and with confidence, and their
batteries opened fire, but were quickly silenced by the
British guns.   Their cavalry then threatened to out-
flank Rose's left, but Sir Hugh was not deceived by
this manœuvre, being convinced that the main attack
was designed upon his right.   There the ravines
afforded such good shelter for the concentration of
overwhelming masses of infantry, that the enemy bore
back the thin line of British foot, contesting every inch
of ground, upon the mortar-battery.   The peril was
so urgent that the brigadier joined the gunners and
called upon them to fight for their pieces to the last.
Then, as usual, Rose appeared in the nick of time.   He
had already summoned the Camel Corps from the left.
The riflemen and Eighty-eighth dismounted, and with
Rose at their head ran to the threatened battery and
charged straight at the rebels.   The latter awaited
them until they were within eighty yards, then turned
and fled.   The infantry of the right wing at once
followed in pursuit.   The British cavalry and artillery
on the left promptly advanced, and the whole mass of
the enemy gave way.   Maxwell's guns on the north

[1] Sylvester, p. 153; Cope, *History of the Rifle Brigade*, p. 433.

1858.
May 22.
side of the Jumna enfiladed the fugitives on that side, and showered shot and shell upon Kalpi itself; and the chase was only ended when the men, utterly exhausted by the heat,[1] could move no more.

May 23.
At three o'clock on the 23rd the force resumed its advance in two bodies, one column following the road on the left, the other clearing the ravines on the right. The resistance was trifling. The fort and city were abandoned, and the rebels fled along the road towards Jalaon, where the cavalry and horse-artillery overtook them and did real havoc, until men and horses were so much parched with thirst that they could advance no further. For once the enemy was not only defeated, but routed and heavily punished. Kalpi itself was deserted, and vast masses of military stores, including over two hundred and fifty tons of gunpowder, within it were abandoned. On the evening of the 23rd Rose, who on that day had suffered for the fifth time from sunstroke, pushed out a column of observation towards Jalaon, and then turned to the heavy task of transporting his many sick officers and men to Cawnpore. He himself was almost worn out; his chief staff officer, Colonel Wetherall, was raving in delirium; his quartermaster-general was utterly exhausted. All ranks in fact had reached the end of their strength. The Central India Field Force had accomplished its work to all appearance, and was to be broken up. On the 1st of
June 1.
June Rose issued a farewell order, thanking his troops for their devotion and good discipline. They had, he said, marched more than a thousand miles, through mountain-passes and jungle and over rivers, had taken a hundred guns, mastered the strongest forts and never sustained a check.

There was still, as it chanced, a fortnight's hard work to be done, which, though it prolonged the march and added to the tale of captured guns, left the general record unchanged. But the full significance of Rose's

---

[1] As an example, the casualties of the 200 riflemen may be cited. Killed, 0; wounded, 3; prostrated by the sun, 1 officer and 25 men.

final effort can be appreciated best after following the 1858.
movements of Sir Colin Campbell in Oudh and
Rohilkhand.[1]

---

[1] The best accounts of Sir Hugh Rose's operations are those of the
two doctors, Rowe, *Central India during the Rebellion of* 1857 *and*
1858, and Sylvester, *Recollections of the Campaign in Malwa and Central
India.*   Burton's *History of the Hyderabad Contingent* is an useful
supplement.   Rose's despatches, which are very full, are printed in
the *London Gazette.*

CHAPTER LIV

1858. THE final capture of Lucknow was accomplished, as will be remembered, on the 21st of March, the very day upon which Sir Hugh Rose's force came before Jhansi. Sir Hugh's advance delivered Sir Colin Campbell from the menace of the mutineers of the Gwalior contingent and the rebels of Bandelkhand against his rear; but Sir Colin's communications with Calcutta were not yet secure. North of Benares Kunwar Singh, with a mixed force of mutineers and feudal levies, seized Azamgarh at the end of March, and Lord Canning was seriously alarmed lest he should descend upon Benares itself. It chanced that a part of the Thirteenth Light Infantry, under Colonel Lord Mark Kerr, was at Allahabad; and Lord Canning at once sent them off, with a troop of the Bays and four pieces of artillery, to recover Azamgarh. Lord Mark, a most eccentric individual[1] but a good soldier, fulfilled

---

[1] I may perhaps be allowed to give a few details about this officer, whom I remember well myself, since he was of a type which is long since extinct. Lord Mark was a very able, well-read man, with, among other gifts, some skill with his pencil. His regiment (an earlier Lord Mark Kerr had commanded it during the second siege of Gibraltar in 1727–28) was in first-rate order, but he regarded it as his own, and resented any interference with it by superior officers. Later on in the course of the Mutiny he was placed under a feeble, incompetent old Indian officer, whose orders he positively declined to obey; and he ended by asking leave to put him under arrest (Wolseley, *Story of a Soldier's Life*, i. 387). One of his peculiarities was that, whether in England or in India, he carried his hat in his hand and not on his head, shading his head from the sun with an umbrella. He was a fine horseman, and in India rode without stirrups. He persisted in

his task resolutely and well; though Sir Colin refused 1858.
him leave to take the offensive, sending some three April.
thousand men under Brigadier-general Lugard from
Lucknow for this purpose.   Kunwar Singh was soon
hunted across the Ganges, and shortly afterwards died;
but his brother, Ammar Singh, who succeeded him,
kept seven thousand men engaged in the country between the Ganges and the Son for the next six months
until his bands were finally dispersed.   However, the
menace to the communications had disappeared by the
end of April, and Campbell was free to consider his
general measures of pacification.

His own wish was to complete the subjugation of
Oudh, where, with the important exception of the
peasants, all classes were still in rebellion, which signified that the garrison of Lucknow might be again
blockaded and might require a fourth expedition to
relieve it.   Lord Canning, however, decided that for
political reasons Rohilkhand should first be taken in
hand.   There, though the bulk of the population was
friendly, a Mohammedan usurper, Khan Bahadur
Khan, was exerting a merciless tyranny; and Canning
feared lest the loyalty of the Hindus might be strained
beyond endurance, unless they were speedily delivered.
Campbell, therefore, arranged that three columns
should invade Rohilkhand, one under Walpole from
the south-east, the second under Penny from the south-
west, and the third under Jones from the north-west,
all converging upon Bareilly.   They were to be further
supported by Seaton who, with the Eighty-second, a
battalion of Sikhs and some irregular troops, was watching the Doab at Fatehgarh.   Early in April three
strong bodies of rebels threatened an invasion of the
Doab above Fatehgarh and a renewal of disorder, which

---

riding about London long after the traffic had driven all other horsemen
(with the exception of one contemporary) off the streets.   He was very
thin and spare, faultlessly turned out, and rode an Arab with flowing
mane and tail.   His stirrups were very long; he sat, when long past
seventy, very erect, and occasionally wore his hat on his head.

1858. might close for a time the Grand Trunk Road and all communications with the north-west.   Seaton averted this peril by a swift raid on the 6th of April upon the central body of the three, which he struck so hard that the two other parties made haste to withdraw.

April 7.   On the following day Walpole left Lucknow with the Highland Brigade, a Sikh battalion, the Ninth Lancers, a Sikh cavalry regiment and eighteen guns —as fine a little force as Campbell could give him— and lost no time in proving his unfitness to command them.   Marching north-west he came upon a party of rebels in a fort two miles from the Ganges, assaulted it upon its only unassailable face, and was repulsed with a loss of a hundred killed and wounded, among the slain being Brigadier-general Adrian Hope, one of the most promising officers in the Army.   This done, Walpole allowed the enemy to escape in the night, and then, crossing the Ramganga and the Ganges, he, on the

April 22.   22nd, fought a more successful action near Aliganj. Penny, meanwhile, had moved down from Bulandshahr to Fatehgarh, where he met Campbell on the 24th, crossed the Ganges and struck north-west upon Budaun. While approaching that place during a night march, he fell into an ambush and was killed, though his column successfully defeated the enemy.   Jones, starting from Rurki, crossed the Ganges a little to east of it at Hardwar, whence, striking south, he twice defeated the rebels on the 17th and 21st and by the 26th was near Murada-

April 27.   bad.   On the 27th Campbell with his own column joined Walpole, and on the 30th entered Shahjehanpur, which he left in the occupation of a small detachment under Colonel Hale.   On the 3rd of May he picked

May 4.   up Penny's column, and on the 4th advanced within a single march of Bareilly, his total force now amounting to close upon eight thousand men.[1]

Khan Bahadur Khan awaited him in front of a deep stream a little to the south of Bareilly, where Campbell

[1] 42nd, 7 cos. 64th, 78th, 79th, 4 cos. 82nd, 93rd, 4th Punjab Rifles, 2nd and 22nd Punjab Infantry, Baluch Battn.

engaged him at seven o'clock in the morning of the 5th. 1858.
The enemy being very strong in cavalry, Campbell May 5.
advanced with the Highland Brigade [1] and two Indian
battalions only, leaving the remainder of his infantry as
baggage-guard; but after a brief duel of artillery the
enemy fled back across the one bridge over the stream,
and the British, crossing likewise, followed them up.
There was a slight check for a moment when a party of
Mohammedan fanatics by an impetuous charge drove
back the Sikhs; but these bold assailants were annihilated by the Forty-second with the bayonet; and the
British line advancing swept all before it.   Meanwhile
the hostile cavalry, having fetched a compass, came
down like a whirlwind upon the baggage-train and made
some havoc among the unarmed camp-followers, but
were scattered instantly by a few rounds from Tombs's
horse-artillery guns and a charge of dragoons. Throughout the Indian Mutiny the rebel horse had shown miser-
able cowardice, as Campbell must have known; and his
baggage-guard was at least thrice as strong as that with
which Major Forbes had foiled quite as formidable an
onslaught on the march to Kalpi.   Nevertheless Campbell halted his first line, and, by the time that he had
been reassured, his men had wilted like plucked flowers
under the blast of the hot wind, and were too much
parched and exhausted to do more.   Khan Bahadur
Khan, of course, with the greater part of his force,
slipped away; and, when Campbell entered Bareilly April 5.
next day from the south, he met Jones's column coming down upon it from the north; hammer thus meeting anvil truly, but with no metal between them. The
action, however, put an end to the rule of Khan Bahadur
Khan; and Campbell flattered himself that he had done
with Rohilkhand.

Before starting on this expedition Campbell had
directed Hope Grant to march from Lucknow northward against the Maulavi, who had been active in promoting sedition before the Mutiny and still more

[1] 42nd, 79th, 93rd.

1858. malignant since the outbreak.   Grant moved out accordingly on the road to Sitapur with about three

April 13. thousand men.[1]   On the 13th his advanced guard struck against the enemy, who began to work round his left flank in order to attack the baggage in rear. The rebel horse were in the act of charging the baggage when they were themselves charged and dispersed by a single troop of the Seventh Hussars.   A second onslaught was repelled by two companies of the Hundred and First, and the rebels then took to their heels. Grant continued his advance without meeting any foe

April 20. until the 20th, when he was recalled by Campbell to Lucknow and diverted, before he reached that place, to Cawnpore.   The chief civil commissioner of Oudh, a nervous individual, sent a succession of alarming messages to Grant requiring his presence to meet large forces of imaginary foes in many directions; but the General went calmly about his own business, visiting forts which were in possession of suspicious owners, and

May 12. dispersing, on the 12th of May, one small body which made a show of resistance.   On this occasion he, as Rose had once done, asked too much of his troops, requiring his infantry to march in line of quarter-column at deploying distance in the full heat of the sun, with the result that the men, choked by dust, fell out by dozens.   Some of them died of heat-apoplexy; some were murdered by small parties of the enemy's horse; and altogether it was a disastrous march.[2]   Soon afterwards, noticing that even hardened and acclimatised regiments could not stand the heat,[3] Grant resolved to renounce further operations for the present, and returned to the vicinity of Lucknow.

Campbell, after his defeat of Khan Bahadur Khan, was about to return to Fatehpur, when he learned that the Maulavi had rallied his force after his defeat by Hope Grant and held Colonel Hale's little garrison

---

[1] 7th Hussars, 1 squadron Bays, 5 squadrons of irregular horse, 38th, 101st, 500 Sikh Infantry.

[2] Wolseley, i. 364-366.   [3] Hope Grant, p. 285.

besieged in Shahjehanpur. On the 8th of May, 1858.
therefore, he detached Brigadier-general John Jones May 8.
with three and a half battalions and a proportion of
cavalry and artillery [1] to Shahjehanpur, where Jones
safely joined Hale on the 12th. The Maulavi had May 12.
been reinforced by large bodies of insurgents and was
particularly strong in horse; and Jones reported to
Campbell that he was too weak in cavalry to attack
him. On the 15th the Maulavi actually ventured to May 15.
assail Jones, but was easily repulsed; and Campbell,
who on that same day had marched from Fatehpur,
turned aside to the help of Jones and joined him at
Shahjehanpur on the 18th. There was a skirmish on May 18.
the same afternoon; but Campbell judged himself too
weak in cavalry to take the offensive and sent for reinforcements, which arrived on the 23rd. On that same May 23.
evening the Maulavi fell back into Oudh, and Campbell,
leaving Jones to deal with him, marched finally for
Fatehpur. Once again it seems strange that a few
hundreds of rebel horse, which had always shown
themselves most dastardly foes, should have inspired
Sir Colin with so much respect; but the fact remains
that the troops were kept marching for some days in
the hottest of the weather to no purpose whatever.
Fortune, however, came to Campbell's aid. The
Maulavi slipped away from Jones, but a few days
later was shot dead while trying to force the gateway June 5.
of a loyal raja. A very dangerous and persistent
enemy was thus removed.

It was just at this time of distraction between
Rohilkhand and Oudh that news came in which, for
the moment, upset all Sir Colin's plans. Tantia
Topi, with Rao Sahib and the Rani of Jhansi, had made
for Gwalior after their defeat at Kalpi, and arrived
before it on the 30th of May. On the 1st of June June 1.
Sindia marched out to attack them; and, evidently
by preconcerted arrangement, his army, after firing

[1] 2 squadrons 6th D.G., Multan Horse; 1/60th, 79th, wing of
82nd, 22nd Punjab Infantry.

1858. one gun, went over to the enemy and forced their master to fly for his life, afterwards proclaiming Nana Sahib to be Peishwa. So there were the most formidable of the rebel leaders in possession of the strongest place in India, with a large treasure and abundance of military material, threatening the communications between Bombay and the north-western provinces, and in a position, if they would, to leave a garrison in Gwalior and carry the standard of Nana Sahib, the Mahratta, across the Narbada into the southern Mahratta territory.

Sir Hugh Rose saw the danger at once. Ill and exhausted as he was, he resumed command of his troops on his own responsibility and made ready to march to Gwalior. Already, on the first rumour of that which had happened, he had sent Brigadier-general Stuart with part of the First Brigade [1] to reinforce the corps of observation which had followed up Tantia Topi's retreat. He now summoned the garrison which he had left at Jhansi; while the Hyderabad contingent, which had been sent towards its own place a few days before, turned back, without orders, to rejoin him. Sir Colin Campbell directed a brigade under Brigadier-general Smith, from the Rajputana Field Force, and a column under Colonel May 6. Riddell to march to him; and on the 6th of May, within forty-eight hours of receiving the tidings of the fall of Gwalior, Rose left Kalpi with such few troops as could be spared. Moving by night to spare his men as far as possible, he overtook Stuart's advanced May 16. corps on the 12th at Indurkhi, and on the 16th arrived at Bahadapur, five miles east of Morar and three miles east of Gwalior. The troops had had a long and fatiguing march, but Rose decided to attack at once, in order to secure some good buildings which would afford shelter to his men. Manœuvring to turn the

[1] 2 troops 14th L.D.; wing of 71st; wing of 86th; 4 cos. 25th Bombay N.I.; ½ co. Bombay Sappers and Miners; 1 field-battery and 3 heavy guns.

enemy's left, Rose drove him off with little difficulty, 1858.
though a few brave men offered a desperate resistance. May 16.
He thus gained the great road leading northward from
Jhansi to Agra, which was the line of Smith's advance,
and opened communication with him.

On the following day Smith[1] attacked a force of May 17.
rebels which was trying to bar his passage in the hilly
country of Kotah-ki-sarai, four miles south of Gwalior,
and drove it back, a squadron of the Eighth Hussars
pursuing almost to the walls of the city and capturing
two guns.   In this affair the Rani of Jhansi, who was
riding as a horseman with the rebel cavalry, was
mortally wounded by a bullet; and the fall of this
woman, "the best and bravest military leader of the
rebels," to use Sir Hugh Rose's own words, was perhaps the most important result of the action.   The
troops indeed were fit for little when the fighting ended
at sundown, for the heat had been excessive.   The
Hussars, after the excitement of their charge, were
utterly exhausted, and could hardly sit in their saddles.
The Ninety-fifth had ninety cases of sunstroke, of
which eight proved fatal.   The enemy, recovering
from their panic, rallied on all sides, and Smith encamped for the night on the hilly ground.

On the 18th the remnant of the Second Brigade, May 18.
which had been left at Kalpi, marched into Morar,
and Rose, entrusting it to the command of Colonel
Robert Napier, who had joined him on the 16th,
moved off with the First Brigade[2] to unite with Smith
at Kotah-ki-sarai.   The heat was so terrific that one
hundred of the Eighty-sixth fell out, overpowered by
the sun.   The rebels cannonaded Smith's camp at
long range throughout the day, and early in the morning of the 19th their infantry was observed moving May 19.
forward from Gwalior to the attack.   Rose, who had

---

[1] Smith's force included the 95th, the 10th Bombay Infantry,
and a detachment of the 8th Hussars.

[2] 2 troops 14th L.D.; wing of 71st; wing of 86th; wing of
5th Hyderabad Infantry; 1 field-battery and 3 heavy guns.

1858. already laid his plans to fall upon the enemy's advanced troops about Kotah-ki-sarai before the main body could join them, set his force in motion at once to turn their left flank.   Very soon the rebels were driven off with the loss of five guns; and Rose, at once following up his advantage, easily gained possession of the city and the palace.   The fort still held out, but was taken next day by two officers of the 25th Bombay Infantry, Lieutenants Waller and Rose, who calmly broke down the gates with the help of a blacksmith, and rushed in with the few soldiers under their immediate command. They met with some resistance from a handful of brave men, and Lieutenant Rose received a mortal wound; but, when these few had been overcome, the fort of Gwalior passed tamely into British hands.

Meanwhile Napier had taken up on the 20th the pursuit of the fugitives, and by nightfall had already May 22. followed them twenty-five miles.   On the 22nd he overtook them at Jaora Alipur, about thirty miles north and west of Gwalior.   The enemy were in position about four thousand strong, with artillery and infantry in the centre and cavalry on both flanks.   Napier had with him five hundred and sixty sabres and Lightfoot's troop of Bombay horse-artillery.   The battery, with an escort of three hundred sabres, opened the attack by firing on the enemy's left flank.   The enemy soon wavered, and then guns and escort came down upon them at the gallop; the rest of Napier's force spontaneously followed the movement; and in a few minutes the rebels were in full flight, abandoning their cannon. Wherever a group of them tried to rally, Lightfoot's guns broke them up, and the chase was pressed for full six miles until men and horses were worn out.   Twenty-five pieces were taken, and three to four hundred of the rebels were cut down at a cost of four killed and eight wounded.   Tantia Topi, always the first to fly, and the Rao Sahib escaped across the Chambal into Rajputana.   The former was destined still, as shall be seen, to give much trouble; but the immediate peril

threatened by his capture of Gwalior was banished for- 1858.
ever.   Then Sir Hugh Rose granted himself his well-
earned rest.

With his rear thus finally secured, Campbell was
able to turn once more to the final subjugation of
Oudh.   Tantia Topi's seizure of Gwalior had encouraged the rebels to assemble once more; and Hope
Grant found himself obliged, on the 13th of June, to June 13.
sally out with about thirty-five hundred men [1] against a
strong party of rebels which was assembled at Nawab-
ganj, about eighteen miles east of Lucknow.   The
enemy, some fifteen thousand in number, were strongly
posted and fought better than usual, but were dispersed after three hours' fighting with a loss of six
hundred killed.   Hope Grant's casualties amounted to
sixty-seven, which was higher than usual, but they were
trifling compared with the number of victims prostrated
by the sun, for thirty-three men died outright from
sunstroke and two hundred and fifty more went into
hospital.[2]   Indeed it was high time that the campaign
should end, and no one felt this more strongly than
Grant himself.   Though twice called into the field in
July and August to prevent reassembly of rebels,
therefore, he gave his troops rest for the most part
until October, against which time Campbell had prepared his plans for trampling out the last embers of
rebellion.

The suppression of Tantia Topi was a far more
difficult matter.   Central India was subdivided into
nearly one hundred and fifty chieftainships, great and
small, Bhopal and Jaora alone of them being Mohammedan, and the remainder Hindu.   Bhopal from first
to last was steadily loyal, but the only Hindu ruler who
worked actively for the British was Sindia, who was

---

[1] 2 squadrons 2nd D.G., 7th Hussars, 500 Hodson's Horse.
    400 police and irregular horse.
    1 horse-battery, 2 field-batteries.
    2nd and 3rd R.B., 5th Punjab Infantry.
[2] Hope Grant, p. 292.

1858. hampered, as has been seen, by the defection of his own troops. Many others were outwardly faithful, but inwardly vacillating or indifferent, and at best could exert no great control over their own folk. It was only natural, too, that the bulk of the people should favour one of their own religion and a fellow-countryman, and hence Tantia Topi was operating in a friendly country. He could depend on it for supplies, for recruits, for remounts, and above all for information; and what was not freely given he hesitated not to take, when he could, by force. He was, in fact, practically the leader of a gang of banditti among a sympathetic population. And the range open to his wanderings was wide. Roughly speaking, it was the quadrilateral enclosed between a line drawn from Gwalior in the east to Ajmir on the west, and from those two places southward to the Narbada—a parallelogram whose sides measured each of them three hundred and fifty miles, with a total area about equivalent to that of England proper. Actually he wandered outside the northern and southern limits above indicated; and the distance that separates the extreme points which he touched from north-east to south-west is not much less than five hundred miles as the crow flies, or rather more than the interval which separates London from Stirling. Let it be added that during the rains there were not only flooded rivers to contend with, but that much of the country became for days together impassable, that at various points there was dense jungle, and towards the south-west a whole district of forest which afforded a safe refuge in time of need. Finally—and this was the crowning difficulty—Tantia Topi on principle put flight before combat. His outposts were always alert, and, if overtaken, he threw out a line of skirmishers to parry the impending blow while the main body decamped. If hard pressed, his followers dispersed, but only to reassemble in a few hours and begin mischief once more. Fresh men and horses were for long steadily forthcoming to serve his purpose;

so that his army or bands or gangs seemed to be im- 1858.
mortal. Troubling himself little about sick and
wounded, he was burdened with few encumbrances;
and the population, whether through sympathy or
terror—for he was quite ruthless—gave him all that
he asked. No one can refuse him the fame of a great
guerilla-leader; but all the advantages were upon his
side. If we consider the parallel case of Mina and
other guerilla-leaders who, far more formidable and
aggressive as fighting men than Tantia Topi, so long
defied all the power of France in Spain, the success of
this Mahratta appears far less astonishing.

To attempt to follow him at length through his
wanderings of three thousand or more miles during
the weary months from June 1858 to April 1859
would be tedious. It would serve no useful purpose
even to enumerate the columns which at various times
joined in the chase of him nor to state their composition,
which was generally a medley of detachments from
various regiments and was frequently changed. Such
details belong more rightly to regimental history than
to a general history of the Army. The utmost that
can be done is to give a general sketch of the campaign,
or chase, and record the most remarkable efforts of
endurance which were made by the British troops.

After his flight from Gwalior Tantia made for
Jaipur, one hundred and fifty miles to west, where he
could count upon a number of adherents. He was,
however, headed off by a column under Colonel Roberts,
which had been restoring order in Kotah, and he then
turned south. The intense heat forbade Roberts to
press him, and Tantia marched straight for the Narbada,
hoping to raise insurrection in the southern Mahratta
country; but the rains forbade him to cross the Chambal
and he wheeled west over the Bundi hills. Roberts, on
the 8th of August, overtook him, or rather grazed his Aug. 8.
rear, at Bhilwara, about seven miles west and south
of Bundi, and again on the 14th at Kankraoli, sixty Aug. 14.
miles further to south-west. Another column, under

1858.   Brigadier-general Parke, which Roberts met at Poona,
Aug.–   fifteen miles south of Bhilwara, then took up the
Sept.   pursuit, but to no purpose, and now there was an alarm
lest Tantia should swoop down to the plunder of Ujjain
in Holkar's territory.   A column was sent from Mau
to foil any such movement; and meanwhile Tantia,
instead of striking south, as had been expected, doubled
back eastward upon Jhalra Patan, fifty miles to south-
east of Kotah, helped himself to one hundred thousand
pounds of treasure and thirty guns, enlisted a number
of recruits, and with a strength of some nine thousand
men proceeded south with some hope of reaching
Indore.   If he should succeed, Holkar's troops would
probably join him, and he would be able to rekindle
rebellion with renewed strength.

The column from Mau was joined at Nalkhera, about
seventy miles north of Ujjain, by Major-general Michel,
who was presently appointed to command in Malwa
and Rajputana.   His information was that the enemy
was somewhere to north-east; and with great difficulty,
for the heat was intense and the black cotton soil turned
into a sea of mud by the rain, his advanced guard came
within sight of Tantia Topi's force at Rajgarh on the
Sept. 14.   evening of the 14th of September.   The infantry, however, was long in coming up, and in fact only arrived
in the last stage of exhaustion.   Of Michel's two British
battalions, the Seventy-second and Ninety-second, one-
third of the men had fallen out and several had died.
By the next morning the enemy had vanished, though
Michel pursuing with his cavalry captured twenty-
seven guns; but the heat was once again overpowering,
and a detachment of native cavalry, two hundred strong,
lost more than half of their horses.   Michel was fain
to give his men rest for a day, and then followed Tantia,
who had fled away eastward through a district of dense
jungle upon Sironj.   Both parties were presently
stopped by heavy rains, at the close of which Tantia
moved north-west upon Isan-garh, where, being resisted by the chief, he killed all the adult males, burned

all the clothing of the females, and sacked the town, as 1858.
a warning to all friends of the British.   Here Brigadier-
general Smith's column threatened him from Sipri,
some forty miles to north, and Tantia turned south-
eastward to Mangraoli, arriving before it on the 9th
of October just as Michel, who had marched up from Oct. 9.
Sironj, was pitching his camp.   The rebels of course
made off at once, but a few were caught by the cavalry,
forty-three men of the Seventeenth Lancers accounting
for ninety of them.   The rebels, or some part of them,
then turned south-east, and on the 18th at Narhat Oct. 18.
Michel obtained information of their whereabouts.
Moving north-east he came upon them after a march
of sixteen miles at Sindwaha, where Tantia actually
drew up his infantry in position.   They were swept
away by a charge of cavalry;[1] but the British troopers,
having been in the saddle for fifteen hours, were too
weary to pursue; and though some execution was done
among the rebels, the bulk of them escaped.

They fled away north-westward, and Michel after
a few days followed them on the 21st to Lalitpur. Oct. 21.
Tantia was headed back by a British column on the
Betwa, and at this moment was probably in greater peril
than at any other.   The jungle, however, helped him.
He doubled back, unobserved, within four miles of
Michel's camp, and struck southward with the intention
of passing the Narbada at all hazards.   Michel, hearing
of this movement, sent word to Colonel Parke, whose
duty it was to cover Indore, and started southward himself in all haste.   On the three ensuing days his infantry
traversed seventy-four miles, and his column reached
its camping-ground at Kurai, about fifty miles due
south of Lalitpur, just as the tail of Tantia's force was
leaving it.   These were overtaken by Michel's cavalry,
many of them were dispatched and the remainder dispersed, some of them to northward, though the bulk

---

[1] 1½ squadrons 8th Hussars, 1 squadron 17th Lancers, 4 squadrons
of Native Cavalry.   The rest of Michel's force included detachments
of the 71st, 92nd, 95th and 19th N.I.

1858.
Oct.-
Nov.
followed Tantia towards the Narbada.   He inclined at first south-westward, hoping to plunder the loyal Begum of Bhopal, but was headed off, and finally crossed the Narbada about forty miles north-east of Hoshangabad. Michel had been obliged to halt at Bhilsa for three days to rest and recruit his troops, and Tantia seems for the moment to have evaded all pursuers.

The alarm in the presidencies both of Bombay and Madras at his appearance in the Dekhan was very great; but Sir Hugh Rose, who was now Commander-in-chief at Bombay, had taken full precautions. Tantia pointed first for Nagpur, but found the way barred, and turned westward some seventy miles upon Melghat. This again was closed to him, and he bent himself irresolutely first some thirty miles northward to Charwa and then westward to Kargun, about seventy miles due south of Indore, where having far outstripped every relay of the chase, he halted for a time to rest.   Mean-while Michel's column, or at least the mounted portion

Nov. 9.
of it, had, on the 9th of November, reached Hoshanga-bad, where a new column was formed under Colonel Benson of the Seventeenth Lancers, comprising seven squadrons of his own regiment and of native horse and a battery of horse-artillery.   This force went south almost to Ellichpur, being much straitened for forage; and meanwhile detachments were sent from Mau to watch the two main passages of the Narbada immediately to south of that place.   One of these— two hundred of the Ninety-second mounted on camels, and as many native infantry—on news of Tantia's departure from Kargun, tried to intercept him, but succeeded only in taking his abandoned guns; for the cunning chief had recrossed the river at Burwani and was again flying to westward.   However, Colonel Parke, who had been sent down to Charwa on the

Nov. 21.
21st, renewed the pursuit with fresh men and horses,[1] marched two hundred and forty miles in nine days,

---

[1] His force was 8th Hussars, 47; 2nd Bombay L.C., 51; 72nd High-landers, 94; ½ battery Bombay Artillery; about 700 native irregulars.

overtook Tantia at Chota Edepur, about fifty miles 1858.
east of Barode, on the 1st of December, and sent him Dec. 1.
speeding north in discomfiture.   On that same day
Benson, suddenly recalled by an alarm that Tantia was
threatening Indore, arrived at Mau, having marched
fifty miles, including the passage of the Narbada, in
twenty-six hours; the elusive enemy being at the
moment in full flight over a hundred miles away.

Tantia now plunged into the jungles of Banswara,
apparently at the end of his resources.   The passes to
east and west were beset against him, and Benson was
ready to cut off his retreat to the south.   At this
moment, however, there came to him a stroke of luck.
Prince Firoz Shah, defeated, as has been seen, in Oudh,
was marching to join him; wherefore throwing himself suddenly against one of the little parties that kept
him hemmed in in the east, Tantia contrived to force
his way through it near Partabgarh and made away to
eastward.   Brigadier-general Somerset had meanwhile
taken over Benson's command and moved up slowly,
owing to uncertain information, to Jaora, where he
arrived on the 14th of December.   On the 23rd Dec.
Somerset was called away to assume the direction of
another column; and Benson, pressing on at the rate
of thirty-five miles a day, overtook Tantia's rear on the
29th and inflicted some loss, but exhausted his men and
horses in the effort.   On the 30th Somerset rejoined
him and, though he had himself been marching with a
handful of Highlanders on camels with little inter-
mission since the 27th, he added a squadron of the
Seventeenth Lancers and four guns to these and pushed
on.   By the evening of the 31st he had covered forty
miles more, and on the morning of the 1st of January 1859.
1859, on emerging from the village of Barode, he came Jan. 1.
upon Tantia's horse, about two thousand strong, drawn
up in one long line, seven hundred yards away.   At the
moment he had nothing under his hand but his guns,[1]

---

[1] The force with him was 100 of the 17th Lancers, 150 of the 92nd
and 4 guns.

1859. which had followed a track, for the Lancers, wide on each flank, had been checked by high crops, and the Highlanders had not come up.   The enemy actually advanced at a slow trot, and Somerset promptly gave the word for the guns to gallop to the front.   They did so at once, unlimbering and opening fire when the enemy had closed to within four hundred yards.   Three shots into the middle of the rebels caused them to halt, and then the two troops of Lancers charged independently, half a mile apart, and dispersed them to the four winds. The pursuit was pressed for another ten miles, and in the evening Somerset returned to Barode.   The village lies about one hundred and ten miles east of Partabgarh; and between three in the morning of the 27th of December and five in the evening of the 1st of January, Somerset's column had traversed over one hundred and seventy miles.

Tantia Topi fled northward, and at Indagarh, about forty-five miles south-east of Tonk, was joined by the scanty following of Firoz Shah.   His numbers were thus again raised to about two thousand, with which he hurried into Rajputana, fetching a compass from east to west, round Jaipur.   Colonel Holmes, with a few infantry and artillery,[1] thereupon sallied northward from Nasirabad.   He traversed two hundred and ninety miles in thirteen days without a halt and, after a march of fifty-four miles in little more than twenty-four hours across a sandy desert, surprised the rebel camp

Jan. 21. at Sikar and set them running once more.   Six hundred of them a few days later surrendered to the Raja of Bikanir, and Tantia himself, with a handful of followers, fled across the Chambal and took refuge in the jungle of Sironj, the territory of Man Sing, an outlawed feudatory of Sindia.   The remainder of his party struck south, and then turned eastward upon the Aravalli hills; whereupon Michel, who had moved to Nasirabad,

---

[1] His force was made up thus: Native gunners, 103; 83rd, 247; 12th N.I., 291; R.E., 16; Bombay Sappers and Miners, 27; Irregular Horse, 262.

ordered troops southward in all haste to beset the passes. Brigadier-general Honner, with detachments of the Eighth Hussars, Eighty-third, 1st Bombay Lancers and 12th Native Infantry, marching one hundred and thirty miles in four days over deep sand, overtook one party of them on the 11th of February. General Somerset's column,[1] starting on the 13th of February, marched day and night for nine days upon Kankraoli, but was unfortunately diverted from that place by false intelligence exactly when, if it had pursued its way, it would have caught the rebels. Following them up Somerset received the surrender of a certain number whose horses' hooves were worn down to the quick, or who could no longer sit in the saddle.   The rest, about two hundred strong, struggled on eastward by Partabgarh to Runiya, where they surrendered.   Tantia Topi, weary of the life of a hunted beast, remained hidden in the jungle until his hiding-place was betrayed by Man Sing, and he was surprised in his sleep and captured on the 7th of April.   He was tried by court-martial a week later and hanged.   Although he gave, first and last, much trouble, and brought about the only semblance to a reverse sustained by a British force in the whole course of the rebellion, he possessed no real military talent.   But he had a perfect genius for running away.

Meanwhile Sir Colin Campbell, having so far as possible given rest to his troops during the hot months, had taken the field in October for the final subjugation of Oudh.   Very timely to his purpose was a royal proclamation, dated the 1st of November, whereby the Crown announced its purpose of taking over the direct government of the British possessions in India, and added that full pardon would be granted to rebels (saving those convicted of murder of British subjects) upon their submission before the 1st of January 1859. It would be tedious to enter into the details of the

1859.
Jan.–Feb.

April 7.

1858.

---

[1] D battery R.H.A.; 17th Lancers, 2 squadrons Bombay Cavalry; 130 of 92nd and 140 of Bombay Rifles.

1858. operations, which may be briefly summed up as the sweeping by a number of columns of the Baiswarra District, between the Ganges and the Gumti, so as to drive the rebels north-eastward across the Gogra, and to force them back across the Rapti against the frontier of Nipal. Since Oudh was flat and offered no commanding positions, the great feudal lords had in the past thrown up strong and very extensive fortresses which compelled Campbell to attach siege-artillery to many columns. The movements were conducted according to a careful time-table and were completely successful; and Campbell had taken care to secure his conquests by forming a body of five thousand native police, which took charge of the various districts as they were cleared. By the end of 1858 Campbell's task had been accomplished at the negligible cost of eighteen killed and eighty-four wounded. Such of the rebels as had not surrendered fled to Nipal, with the result that Jung Bahadur begged that they might be hunted out again. Hope Grant fulfilled this duty with little difficulty in the spring of 1859. 1859. He failed, however, to catch Nana Sahib, whose fate remains a mystery to this day. It was reported that he had perished of fever in the pestilent jungles of the Terai; but no man knows, and no man need care, for he has long since gone to his account.

Another year was needed before the last dying embers of the rebellion were finally trampled out; but no further account need be taken of it. There are many narratives of the Indian Mutiny, some of them filling many volumes, but not one can afford the space to tell the whole story at large. Indeed, the recounting of endless petty details would in any case be unprofitable; and in the present history it is impossible to do more than summarise the principal events. As a study of war the Indian Mutiny is naught. Every strategical and tactical principle was disregarded, and rightly disregarded, by the British commanders with, practically, perfect impunity. The enemy beyond question included many brave men, but they lacked a leader, and they lacked cohesion.   The mutinous sepoys and those who 1859. joined them in rebellion no doubt were anxious to rid themselves of British rule, but, when that end should have been accomplished, the desire of the great majority was to gather up all the plunder that they could, and go home. Others, more ambitious, doubtless looked forward to a glorious period of anarchy, when they should shine as leaders of banditti and gain wealth and power.   But to fight hard and strenuously for their ascendancy was more than they could compass.   They had not even the wit nor the courage to hamper the communications of the British nor to harass them on the march. Occasionally a pack of horsemen would make a raid on the transport at the tail of a column, cut the throats of a few defenceless camp-followers and carry off a few wagons; but they would never stand up against even the weakest escort.   So the British, in the great majority of cases, trailed about the country with huge clumsy trains of baggage, every officer having a ridiculous number of servants and animals, in the old and evil Indian fashion.   It should seem that even in Sir Hugh Rose's force, though he tried to cut down encumbrances to the lowest limit, the number of baggage-wagons soon became extravagant.[1]   Again, the ordinary precautions, which every army in the field should observe, were neglected in the most casual way.   Thus, as has been seen, Greathed's force was most discreditably surprised outside Agra on the 10th of October 1857, though it paid very cheaply for its carelessness.   Sir Colin Campbell plumed himself upon the exact performance of outpost-duties by all troops under his immediate command; yet in November 1858, Hope Grant, with a squadron of cavalry, rode into Campbell's camp and straight to his tent without encountering a picquet of any kind.[2]   All this was wrong and, moreover, thoroughly bad training for the troops; and viewed in this aspect, the Indian Mutiny sometimes ceases to appear a serious campaign.   This impression, more-

[1] Wolseley, i. 349; Sylvester, p. 125.   [2] Wolseley, i. 385.

1859. over, is heightened by the accounts of the hundreds of engagements with various forces of the rebels. Their numbers were always superior, they had plenty of guns, they had the climate in their favour, and they frequently fortified positions or buildings for a resolute defence. Yet, a commander had only to attack them otherwise than as they desired to be attacked (which was not very difficult), and they invariably gave way without inflicting any great loss. We hear frequently of their stubborn resistance, yet the lists of the British casualties rarely, if ever, suggest any very severe struggle. A generation, which has fresh in its memory a far more desperate contest against an European foe, may feel disposed to smile at the fervour of enthusiasm displayed by their ancestors over the suppression of the Indian Mutiny.

Not the less does it abide as one of the great achievements of the Anglo-Saxon race and of the British Army. It is true that the episode does not show the Governor-general, still less his Council, in a very favourable light; but Lord Canning, perforce, took over a bad system as he found it, and, if he were not the right man as supreme ruler at so critical a juncture, he at least worked with an energy which prematurely ended his life. But the greater is the honour of his many subordinate civil administrators who, with a very few exceptions, faced the danger with a courage, firmness, resolution and resource which were beyond all praise. Not one of them could say how far the peril might extend. We know that there was trouble at Karachi in the west and at Dhaka in the east—in the valley of the Indus and in the valley of the Brahmaputra, fifteen hundred miles apart—while the range of mischief from north to south, if we take it as from Meerut to Hyderabad, measures a thousand miles. There were, of course, native princes who were loyal and, if supported, would remain so; but at the outset the servants of the East India Company were confronted with a vast and appalling uncertainty, which might well have tried the nerves of the hardiest. Yet, with

a very few exceptions, all retained their self-possession, 1859.
all preserved the proud and confident bearing of a
dominant race.   Some kept disorder within bounds by
sheer force of character; a great many, finding their
civil occupation gone, fought most gallantly as combatant soldiers.   Whether they prevailed against rebellion; whether they fled, unable to do more, from
one place to assert themselves in another; whether they
fell at their posts, or whether they shared in some
desperate defence of a beleaguered garrison; they
strove nobly to do their duty, and left a lasting heritage
of honour.

The two most famous among these civil administrators are the two Lawrences, John and Henry.
Both, being human, made bad mistakes; but the
salvation of India seems to have been due in great
measure to the moral courage of the one and to the
wisdom and foresight of the other.   The mere prosaic
business of gathering a vast store of provisions into
Lucknow was in itself an inestimable service.   Without it the defence of Lucknow would have been
impossible; and it is that defence against overwhelming
numbers within pistol-shot of the garrison, which will
probably, of all incidents in the Mutiny, be longest
remembered.   Marvellous as it was, it seems to me a
less extraordinary feat than that of the little garrison at
Cawnpore, which, with no shelter against the sun and
very little against bullet or cannon-shot, held a formidable host, armed with a powerful artillery, at bay
for three weeks, and though slain by treachery was
never conquered.

And now we come to the work of the British soldier;
and of him, too, it can be said that he excelled himself.
Never, I think, before 1858, had there been a British
army of equal strength in any one country—a vast
country, it is true—as in India during the Mutiny.
Excluding the British troops in the East India Company's service, there were in India at the end of 1858
eight regiments of British cavalry and sixty-eight

1859. battalions of British infantry.   The brunt of the work, as has been seen, fell upon the few that were on the spot in May 1857, and went through the first campaign during the hot season and the rains of that year. They had not only the heat but cholera as their enemies; and it was well for the column which marched to Cawnpore, and thence, after a pause, to Lucknow, that it had such resolute leaders as Havelock, Neill and Outram.   But the force which lay so long before Delhi had no commander comparable to anyone of these three at its head, and, until Nicholson came upon the scene, no senior officer of real inspiration among them.   Yet, though wasted by constant action, fatigue and disease, the troops never lost heart nor energy. Pride of race and regimental feeling seem to have sufficed to maintain in them unbounded confidence and moral strength.   The only parallel that I can think of for this intense consciousness of superiority is the case of the garrison of Quebec in 1760, when Murray, without hesitation, led out three thousand men to fight twice their number of French at Ste. Foy, and could hardly persuade them to retreat even after one thousand had fallen.   There are other nations of Europe with traditions of military achievement and a heritage of military glory far transcending our own; yet it may be doubted whether any men except British soldiers could have endured the trial of Delhi and passed through it with success.   It may, of course, be justly urged that no military nation would have entered upon such an operation in such a fashion; but I am speaking of affairs as they actually occurred, and not as, by the light of wisdom after the event, they might conceivably have been conducted.   To face such a conjunction of adversities without flinching needs that close touch between officer and soldier which is only to be found in the British Army.

It is difficult and invidious to institute comparisons between different detachments of the same force; and it is not always a simple matter to weigh the evidence

as to their various performances. Thus the two 1859.
principal chroniclers of Sir Hugh Rose's march through
Central India were both of them doctors, who had the
best opportunity of all to observe the havoc wrought
by the sun. They have left us most pitiful accounts of
litter after litter passing to the rear with officers and men
prostrated by sunstroke, some dead, some laughing or
sobbing hysterically in delirium. " Men," writes one
in an awful picture of one of Rose's marches, "begin to
talk of home and cool shady places and brooks as the
hot wind begins to blow over them, parching up every
drop of moisture in the body; and dogs rush past with
great raw wounds like sabre-cuts, caused by the sun,
howling for water and shade."[1]   The hot wind spared
none in any part of India, so that all alike suffered
from it; but, except in the case of Rose's troops, I can
recall no constant and repeated dearth of water, not
merely on the march but in camp or bivouac, for days
together.   The details recorded by those who were with
this force are beyond measure distressing—the thermometer bursting its bulb as it marked one hundred and
thirty degrees Fahrenheit; men falling down by scores
and perishing for want of shade and water; others
staggering on with drooped head like drunkards;
patient elephants trying to rest the raw soles of their
feet; emaciated thirsting bullocks dragging their
weary legs forward at the rate of a mile an hour; dogs
fairly dropping dead; the track paved with the bodies of
camels, bullocks and ponies, not putrefying but dried
up into mummies by the sun.[2]   One wonders that the
entire force was not annihilated; but it was not, thanks
to their own good courage and the indomitable will
of their commander. The men's work might end
when, more dead than alive, they came into bivouac,
but Hugh Rose galloped out into the sun to reconnoitre
and prepare for the next move. He had practically
no maps, and there were no plans of the fortresses

[1] Lowe, pp. 273-276.
[2] Lowe, *loc. cit.* and p. 281.

1859. which barred his way, so that he was obliged to base all his plans upon personal observation.

On the whole Rose's march of a thousand miles to Kalpi and thence to Gwalior strikes me as the most remarkable achievement in the history of the Indian Mutiny. In the first place, it was one long sustained effort, interrupted, indeed, necessarily by halts of one, two or three weeks, for the replenishing of stores and supplies, but not the less one continued strain from the beginning of January to the end of June, with constant fighting and such fatigue and exhaustion as the mere reader can but faintly imagine. No hostile army, though inspired by the bravest of the rebel leaders, the Rani of Jhansi, could stop Hugh Rose; no fortress, never so renowned or formidable, could long delay him. Lead, steel and, above all, disease might thin his ranks but could not discourage the remnant, nor intimidate their leader. He marched on irresistible, not to be turned from his purpose even by the orders of the Governor-general; and he prevailed. It was a great feat of arms, whose difficulties have been masked by the apparent ease of its performance not only to the public eye but, seemingly, to Sir Colin Campbell himself. The Commander-in-chief actually censured him for resuming command and marching upon Gwalior without orders; and, while mentioning his name with laudation, coupled it with those of Roberts and Whitlock, whose achievements were not comparable with Rose's. In fact his services were at the time very imperfectly appreciated, not a little through his own delay—intelligible in all the circumstances—in submitting his reports and despatches. The force which served under him was likewise scurvily treated. No special clasp was granted to them on their medal, and they were debarred from sharing in certain prize-money which had been taken, bloodlessly, by Whitlock's column. Their claim to this last was acknowledged by the Governor-general and the Commander-in-chief in India, and by the military

authorities and the Prime Minister in England, but 1859.
was set aside by the lawyers upon some ruling of the
Admiralty respecting naval blockades.   This was a
gross injustice to all ranks.   Rose had been stern in
repressing all plunder and placing all captured property
in the charge of prize-agents, so that his men had
no such windfall as Campbell's enjoyed in Lucknow.
By this decision Rose himself, who was a poor man,
lost thirty thousand pounds; but the hardship to his
officers and men was even more severe, for he at least
was not married.   However, it is idle to revive dead
grievances.   The great point is that Sir Hugh Rose
and his soldiers should at least receive due credit for all
that they did.   All wrought well.   Among the native
troops the Hyderabad contingent, led by excellent
British officers, was most efficient; among the British
the Fourteenth Hussars and the Eighty-sixth were
unsurpassed in good service by any regiments that
shared in the repression of the mutiny.   Sir Hugh
Rose himself seems to me beyond dispute the ablest
commander who appeared in that field.

Long though Tantia Topi evaded capture, it would
be unjust to omit special mention of the efforts made
by the columns employed in the pursuit.   Some hint
of this has already been given in the record of certain
of their marches; but these afford only a faint idea of
the fatigue and hardship endured by officers and men.
All baggage, of course, was discarded when it was
necessary to move with extreme rapidity, and frequently men and horses had little to eat.   A great
disadvantage to the British cavalry was the weight of
the men and of the saddlery, which forbade them to
compete with Tantia's light horsemen lightly equipped.
After every sharp burst (to borrow the language of the
chase) the British mounted troops were obliged to rest
for two or three weeks to enable the horses to recover;
and indeed the hunting of Tantia Topi reduced itself
in great measure to a question of horse-mastership.
Marching incessantly day and night, officers and men

1859. could with difficulty keep themselves awake. Indeed so
weary were the men that, during the rains, they fell off
their horses rather than dismounted when they came to
a halt, were asleep before they reached the ground, and
lay where they dropped in the mud of the black cotton
soil till roused.[1]   The inevitable result was that they
slept in the saddle, which, as is well known, is a sure
way of giving sore backs to the horses.   Under great
exertion, often combined with insufficient food, the
animals naturally lost condition, which, without great
care, brought about more sore backs.   Thus pursuing
columns, if provided with Cape or Australian horses,
which could not stand this excessively severe work,
dwindled away to nothing.   Those which had Arab
horses did better.   It is difficult to decide which unit
of the British cavalry travelled the longest distance.
Captain Clowes's troop of the Eighth Hussars with
Brigadier-general Parke's column is reputed to have
marched two thousand miles; but it is doubtful whether
his travels were not equalled by Sir William Gordon's
squadron of the Seventeenth Lancers, which left Kirki
on the 25th of May 1858, marched through the rains
to Mau, and, after much arduous work, took part in
Somerset's final great effort to intercept Tantia Topi
in the Aravalli Hills in February 1859.   This squadron
was mounted on Arabs, and Sir William was not only
a superb horseman but a great horse-master.   It was
one of his rules that if a horse had a sore back, the rider
must walk and lead him until it was healed.   But over
and above this salutary regulation, he personally looked
to every horse's back himself, and with his own hand
adjusted the stuffing of the saddle to spare any tender
place.   Thus he accomplished the amazing feat of
bringing back at the end of a long and most distressing

[1] This detail was told to me by Lieutenant-Colonel John Brown,
who began life as a trumpeter in the 17th Lancers, and went through
this campaign with them.   See also Evelyn Wood's account of his
waking and finding every soul in his column, including sentries, fast
asleep.   *From Midshipman to Field-Marshal*, i. 150.

campaign every horse with which he had started, 1859. sound and whole, excepting only those which had been killed or disabled in action.   But it must be repeated that these horses were Arabs, which sometimes showed leg-weariness but were never " off their feed."   Cape horses and walers lay down, refused their food and died.

More than one commentator upon the later phases of the campaign has lamented the fact that infantry mounted on ponies were not employed for hunting down the fugitive bands which gave so much trouble, not only in Central India but in Western Behar.   As we have seen, a small camel-corps was formed comparatively early and did useful service, but the general idea of mounted infantry did not commend itself to Sir Colin Campbell.   Sir Henry Havelock the younger, however, did actually form a tiny body of mounted infantry in Western Behar during the autumn of 1858, and showed how valuable such a force might have proved itself.   The great advantage would have been that it would have substituted missile for shock action in dealing with these evasive bands.   Cavalry, whether British or native, of course swept them away like chaff, but their horses, being exhausted by long marches, could never maintain high speed for long nor sustain a continued pursuit.   Again the sword, effective enough in Indian hands, was not equally so in those of the British dragoons, though the lance was always deadly;   and in fact British cavalry officers adopted the hog-spear as the favourite weapon for their own use.[1]   But one steady man with an Enfield rifle could have done more

---

[1] I learned this fact directly from Sir William Gordon and from Sir Dighton Probyn.   Sir William, a fine horseman well mounted, distanced all his men in a charge and generally accounted for more of the enemy than any one of them.   Few who knew Sir Dighton in his later years—he lived to past ninety—realised that that mild, courteous old gentleman had killed more men with his own hand than any living Englishman.   His rule, as he told me, in attacking a man who carried fire-arms was always to let him fire first (those were the days of muzzle-loaders, it must be remembered), and, he went on, " if he missed me I reckoned that I had got him."

1859. execution in the same time with much less exertion and risk, if only he could have been carried to the spot more swiftly than upon his own legs.   Apart from the gain of speed, moreover, the mounting of infantry would have saved the men much fatigue.   Experiments in later years show that the British soldier can generally manage to preserve some kind of a seat in a saddle, though it may not be very comely, nor, at first, very secure.   But in those days, when recruits were still drawn in preponderant numbers from the rural districts, there must have been a great many men who, though not finished horsemen, were accustomed to ride.

And this rejection of mounted infantry by Sir Colin Campbell leads us finally to some estimate of his merits as a commander.   Not many generals, it must be acknowledged at the outset, could have found themselves in a more embarrassing position than did he upon his first arrival in India.   There were few troops, a thousand calls for them in all directions, insecurity of communication along the valley of the Ganges, and a well-meaning but rather slow Governor-general with an useless Council at Calcutta.   Happily the date of his arrival at the capital coincided almost exactly with the advent of Nicholson to Delhi.   Before Campbell had been in command for a month Delhi had fallen, and his first operation was clearly defined for him to be the relief of Lucknow.   The military departments at Calcutta had made no preparations for an active campaign, and it was only by indomitable patience and persistence that he succeeded in overcoming their inert helplessness, and fairly driving them to equip his force for the field.   This arduous task, however, he achieved while maintaining always the most cordial relations with Lord Canning.   Nothing, in fact, does Campbell greater honour than his loyalty to the Governor-general and to his chiefs in England from beginning to end.   But it may be questioned whether he were the man to deal with the rebellion in India in 1857.   In the first place, he completed his fiftieth year of service while in India, and, though he was active and energetic enough, his was a mind that stagnated rather than ripened with age. He had always been rather irascible, rather excitable,[1] and at the same time very cautious. He was ever at heart a regimental officer, with all the excellencies and all the limitations which are connoted by that term. He had very strong prejudices, notably in favour of soldiers of long service, of Highland regiments and of officers who had served in India over officers, no matter how highly gifted, who had not. In fact he was a steady, sober, methodical, plodding old soldier, without the slightest pretension to genius and with a not very bright intellect. Mansfield, his chief of staff, on the other hand, possessed a very remarkable intellect but not the instincts of a soldier. There have been commanders—Blücher, for example—who could turn such a combination of their own and their chief adviser's qualities to the very best account, but Campbell was not one of them. Mansfield's superior ability seems to have overawed rather than stimulated him, principally, perhaps, because it was his own instinct always to put safety first. This does not mean that he was not always foremost under fire at any critical moment, for he thought nothing of his own personal security, and delighted to become again a regimental officer at such moments. There was no more intrepid soldier in action. But he seems to have lacked the higher intrepidity which will accept great risks for a great object.

Indeed, despite of all his preference for officers who had served, as had he himself, in India, he seems not to have grasped the essence of Oriental fighting, which is never to strike one blow without following it up with a succession of blows. Moral, not less than strategic considerations, should have prompted him to deal a buffet to Tantia Topi from Cawnpore before

---

[1] Raglan during the Crimean war wrote to Newcastle that Campbell's excitability unfitted him for high command. I have unfortunately mislaid the reference, but am sure of the fact.

1859. marching upon Lucknow, as was urged upon him by
Outram.   The relief of Lucknow would then have been
the second stroke of a series, whereas it became in actual
fact a mere raid followed by a retreat.   Many have
blamed him, no doubt upon the same principle, for
evacuating Lucknow at all in November 1858; and,
whether on the whole he were right or wrong in taking
that course—a matter upon which it is more easy than
just to pronounce after the event—there can, I think,
be no doubt that the moral effect was bad.   Even his
most favourable critics have condemned the blunder
which allowed the bulk of the rebels to escape after the
final capture of Lucknow; and this lapse on Campbell's
part is the more extraordinary because he felt very
deeply that his mission was not merely to win victories
in the field but to restore order in India at large.   That
the responsibility should have weighed very heavily
upon him is no matter for surprise; but he seems to
have been bewildered by guerilla warfare, though it was
certainly no new thing in India.   " The mere march of
troops," he wrote in July 1858, " is unattended by any
real and substantial results.   We beat the enemy in
the open field with the utmost ease—we take his guns;
he appears utterly routed.   A fortnight afterwards we
again hear of the reassemblage of rebels at another point
—perhaps at three or four points—while our movable
columns have marched away to meet danger in another
quarter." [1]   The British Army has had to deal with
these exasperating conditions many times in many countries, and against far more formidable enemies than
the Indian rebels; but it has prevailed, as, to do him
justice, Campbell himself in due time prevailed.   For
the final subjugation of Oudh he employed four columns
of three thousand men and upwards, and as many of
two thousand and upwards, besides sundry more of
lesser strength.   One wonders how long he would have
taken to complete the whole of his task if there had been
no Sir Hugh Rose in Central India.   It is true that

[1] Shadwell, ii. 274.

Rose's campaign in some respects fell into the category 1859 of Campbell's " mere marches." Many months were to pass before the last gangs of banditti were extirpated in that quarter; and in fact the condition of Central India called into being the famous corps known as the Central India Horse. But Rose, small though his column was, kept open his communications; and the terror of his name—of that irresistible warrior whom nothing could stop—is perhaps even now not wholly extinct. Rose understood Oriental warfare.

However, Campbell did get through his work in his own rather heavy and methodical fashion, though he might have finished it sooner had he been less impervious to new ideas. His task was a very arduous one, and, for all his shortcomings, he did at any rate parts of it well. He seems to have been popular with his troops, always saving his predilection for Highlanders, having all the regimental officer's zeal for the welfare of his men. Whether they looked up to him as to a great and inspiring leader may be doubted. A commander-in-chief who " executes a war dance in public round an erring major," [1] may sometimes fail to gain the respect of his soldiers; and this seems to have been the case with Campbell. In December 1857, the Fifty-third, composed chiefly of Irishmen who were more remarkable for fighting spirit than for discipline, once broke away to an attack without a word of orders from their officers or from anyone else, and suffered some loss. Campbell, furious, rode up to them with angry words of reproof, only to be interrupted, whenever he opened his mouth, by cries of " Three cheers for the Commander-in-chief, boys," until he abandoned his purpose and rode away laughing.[2] This does not give the impression of a man who was feared by the insubordinate. Hope Grant, a few days later, dealt with a manifestation of general indiscipline in this same regiment in a very summary fashion.[3] On the whole Sir Colin

[1] See Wolseley, i. 296.   [2] Hope Grant, *The Sepoy War*, p. 216.
[3] Hope Grant, p. 231.

1859. Campbell, who was ennobled in 1858 with the title of Lord Clyde, does not stand very eminent among successful British commanders.

For the rest the Indian Mutiny first gave a real value to the Victoria Cross.   It was earned by many men, among others by such as Samuel Browne and Frederick Roberts, who later rose to very high command.   As in the Crimean war, certain regiments were called upon to elect a limited number of their members to receive the honour, and the story goes that the Ninth Lancers could think of none so worthy as their faithful *bhisti*, or water-carrier, who had brought water to them a hundred times under heavy fire.   Whether true or false the tale is characteristic of the British soldier.   For throughout the Indian Mutiny he preserved that merciful gentleness which has at all times been peculiar to him.   When he met the mutinous sepoys hand to hand he gave no quarter and expected and received none. Nor did he spare the mounted rabble which followed them, when they fell into his hands, for they would not face him in the field, and, when they occasionally broke into the lagging tail of a column, would cut the throats of soldiers, helpless through wounds or sunstroke, as they lay in their litters.   Beyond question, too, in their first fury over the massacre of Cawnpore the British troops held all men with coloured faces to be accessory to that crime, and did not a few innocent persons to death.[1] But there was no wanton slaughter nor outrage even after the storm of a fortress.   " In hardships, in temptation and danger," wrote Sir Hugh Rose in his farewell order, " you have never left your ranks.   You have fought against the strong and you have protected the rights of the weak and defenceless, of foes as well as of friends. I have seen you in the ardour of the combat preserve and place children out of harm's way.   This is the

---

[1] There is a curious entry in the defaulter-sheet of the Hundred and Second (Madras Fusiliers). " Pte. ——. Hanging a native without permission—two days' C.B." Wylly, *Neill's Blue Caps*, ii. 70.

discipline of Christian soldiers, and it is this that has 1859. brought you triumphant from the shores of Western India to the waters of the Jumna." And this was no cant that flowed from Rose's pen. He was in the truest sense of the word himself a Christian soldier. As with his men, it was training that had taught him obedience, but it was nature that had inspired him with mercy.

CHAPTER LV

1859. WHILE Sir Hope Grant was resting, after his labours in Nipal, at Lucknow during the autumn of 1859, he was informed that he had been appointed to the command of a force which was to repair to China and there co-operate with a small detachment of French troops in compelling the Court of Pekin to observe the treaties made with France and England at Tientsin in 1858. Under those treaties those two powers were entitled to keep a minister resident in China, and in the summer of 1859, Mr. Bruce and Monsieur de Bourbolon, the representatives of England and France, had prepared to take up their duties. The British fleet, numbering in all nineteen vessels of all kinds under the command of Admiral Hope, was assembled in the Gulf of Pechili; and the Admiral himself, with a single ship, proceeded to the anchorage off Taku on the 17th of June 1859, and sent a boat ashore with a messenger to announce the coming of the two residents. An armed rabble met the boat on the beach and forbade any landing, announcing also that obstacles had been placed to close the navigation of the Pei-ho. On the 20th the residents arrived and, after consultation with Hope, left him to take his own measures for opening the river. After three days spent in vain wrangles with the Chinese

June 25. authorities, Hope, on the 25th, attacked the Taku forts with gun-boats, landing also a detachment of sailors and marines to assault the defences by land. The result was disastrous. Four gun-boats were sunk or disabled by the accurate fire of the Chinese guns; and

the storming party, hardly able to move on the mud 1859.
flats on which they had disembarked, was helplessly June 25.
mown down. Out of eleven hundred men disembarked four hundred and thirty-four were killed or
wounded. The gun-boat on which Hope had hoisted
his flag had only nine men left standing out of a crew of
forty, and the Admiral himself was twice severely
wounded. But for the help of Commodore Tatnall
of the American Navy, who brought his barge himself
through the hottest of the fire to the rescue of Hope,
matters would have been even worse than they were.
In any case, however, the action made war inevitable.

Thus it was that certain of the troops in India found
themselves bound for a new campaign under one of the
most successful and popular of the subordinate leaders
who had come to the front during the mutiny. Sir
Hope Grant was one of those officers who, in theory,
should have been unfit for high command, but in
practice showed himself more capable than his fellows.
He had little education except in music, which he knew
thoroughly, being not only a skilful player on the
violoncello but a composer for that instrument. To
this accomplishment he owed, curiously enough, his
first opportunity of distinction. Lord Saltoun, who,
it will be remembered, commanded a brigade in China
in 1842, was a violinist and wished for a violoncellist
to play with him. The published compositions of
Captain Hope Grant of the Ninth Lancers were remembered, and, with no other qualification, he was
appointed brigade-major. He was a very fine horseman and he had been a good rider to hounds, yet
singularly enough possessed not what is called an eye
for country. He read, and had read, little except his
Bible, for he was a sincerely religious man; he was by no
means at home in the perusal of maps or topographical
sketches; and he was so inarticulate that he found
great difficulty in putting thoughts and plans into
words. On the other hand, he had a military instinct
which, quickened by active service, led him unerringly

1859. in the right path, and an intuition, sobered by common sense, which guided him to original ideas. He had very good eyesight, and could take in an enemy's dispositions accurately at a glance; he was a master of outpost-duties; and he handled cavalry, his own arm, with sureness and rapidity. He was tall and spare, with power to endure much fatigue; brave and daring almost to a fault in action; and in all his doings the soul of integrity, honour and uprightness. It is hardly surprising, therefore, that, though stern in discipline, he was immensely popular with all ranks.

1860.   Embarking at Calcutta, Sir Hope landed at Hong-
March. kong on the 13th of March 1860, and formed a camp at Kaolun to receive his troops as they arrived, the French having their rendezvous at Shanghai. On the 8th of March an ultimatum had been sent to the Court of Pekin, demanding an apology for the firing upon the fleet, an indemnity for the damage done, and the ratification of the treaty of Tientsin; and threatening hostilities unless an answer were returned within thirty days. The interval was spent in preparation, particularly of land-transport, which as usual promised to be the great difficulty. The British cavalry and artillery had brought their horses with them, which was fortunate, for few ponies or horses could be obtained in Japan or Manila, and not a great many in China itself. Moreover, as every scrap of forage had to be imported, it was not desirable to use more animals than were absolutely necessary. It was therefore decided to raise a large corps of Chinese coolie-bearers, which duty was entrusted to an officer of the Indian army. A battalion of the Military Train had arrived from England and was broken up into three divisions, denominated the Horse Transport Service, one of which was sent to Japan for the purchase of horses and cattle there. By right, of course, the officers of the Military Train should have made all arrangements for transport, but this duty they were incompetent to fulfil. They had been employed as dragoons in India, and aspired

to be treated as cavalry. Eventually the transport, 1860. apart from the coolies, was composed of horses, asses, pack-mules, bullocks and every conceivable beast that could be laid hold of, with drivers from Manila, China, Bombay and Madras—such a heterogeneous and polyglot assembly as must have tried to the utmost the patience of those who directed them.[1]

The Chinese Government returned its answer two days before the thirty days of grace had expired, and, since it was on all points unsatisfactory, the two commanders proceeded to land troops upon the island of Chusan. This utterly futile action was dictated from home, under the idea that a blockade of the northern Chinese ports would bring about a scarcity of food at Pekin, and thus in some mysterious fashion put pressure upon the Imperial authorities. The experience of the war of 1842 had shown this notion to be absurd; and, even if it had been otherwise, it was not politic to starve the population when our quarrel was with the Emperor. However, the occupation of Chusan made no great difference one way or the other; and meanwhile the troops were gradually assembling, in all about fourteen thousand British, organised into two infantry divisions and a cavalry brigade, and half that number of French.[2] In the middle of May these embarked for

[1] Report of Deputy Assistant Commissary Bailey, Jan. 24, 1861.

[2] *Cavalry Brigade*: Brigadier-general Pattle.
    1 D.G., Probyn's Horse, Fane's Horse, Stirling's battery.
  1st Division: Major-general Sir John Michel.
    1st Brigade: Staveley. 1st, 31st, Ludhiana Regiment.
    2nd ,,   Sutton. 2nd, 2/60th, 15th Punjab N.I., 1 co.
              R.E., Barry's and Desborough's batteries R.A.
  2nd Division: Major-general Sir Robert Napier.
    3rd Brigade: 3rd, 44th, 8th Punjab N.I.
    4th ,,   67th, 99th, 19th Punjab N.I.
A small siege-train accompanied the force. In addition to the above the 21st Madras N.I. was left to garrison Hong-kong; and the 87th, with the 3rd and 5th Bombay N.I., to garrison Canton. A battalion of marines was also placed in Shanghai to protect it against the Taiping rebels, who were in arms against the Imperial house; and to these were later added the 11th Punjab N.I. and (June 15) the Ludhiana Regiment of Sikhs.

1860. the Gulf of Pechili, where the British landed at Talien-wan and the French at Chifu, laying up in these places their depots of stores for the coming campaign.

There was now long delay while the French completed their preparations. Having come from France, they had naturally brought no horses with them, so were obliged to procure them from Japan and, having obtained them, to break them. They had three field-batteries and one mountain-battery, but no cavalry excepting an escort of fifty men for the General, so that fortunately their requirements were not excessive. But in truth the French were not happy in this campaign. They had no experience of little expeditions, such as had been familiar to the British for a century and a half. They were consequently rather helpless, and for that reason all the more jealous of their Allies, constantly raising petty questions of precedence and yet rendering little service. "They act," wrote Mr. Harry Parkes, British Commissioner at Canton, in July, "in every respect like a drag on the coach. They use our stores, get in our way at all points and retard all our movements." After the battle of Inkerman the French might for a time have said much the same of the British in the Crimea.

July. At last, however, all was ready. The troops were re-embarked, and on the 20th of July they sailed; the British vessels of all kinds numbering one hundred and seventy-three and the French thirty-three. By the 28th all had arrived at the appointed anchorage off the July 30. Pei-tang-ho, and by the evening of the 30th Sutton's brigade, with one nine-pounder gun and a rocket-battery, and a party of French soldiers, had been towed to the shore. The scene on landing was inexpressibly ludicrous. The disembarkation took place on a bank of deep mud, and the general led the way, with his trousers, boots and socks slung over his sword, which he carried over his shoulder, and nothing left on him but a large white helmet, a dirty red serge jacket and a very narrow margin of grey flannel shirt below it.

The example thus sensibly set in high places was 1860.
naturally followed by the staff and, apparently, by the July 30.
entire brigade, which, hung about with its nether
garments, toiled painfully through a mile of mire knee
deep, with their little bandy-legged brigadier swearing
volubly at their head.[1] Eventually they bivouacked
for the night on a muddy road without fuel and without
water, every soul having drained his water-bottle in
the course of the struggle through the mud.

In the course of the evening a staff officer, with Mr.
Parkes as interpreter, made his way to Pei-tang and
learned that the town held no garrison. The two
therefore broke open the gate, and at daybreak the
troops entered and took possession. A heavy storm
on the 31st forbade further attempt at disembarkation,
but on the 1st of August the remainder of the force was Aug. 1.
landed, and Sir Hope Grant and his French colleague,
General Montauban, took up their quarters in the
town. Any disposition to plunder on the part of the
British was instantly and sternly put down; but the
French soldiers appropriated such Chinese silks and
satins as they could find and flaunted them openly
abroad. For ten days every man of Sir Hope Grant's
force was busily employed, repairing roads, building
wharves and landing supplies and stores, which were
towed up by steam gun-boats. The French, having
few gun-boats, were slow in throwing their men and
material ashore, and their soldiers spent much of their
time in idleness except in the matter of hunting for
food, which was rendered necessary by the methods of
their commissariat.[2]

Meanwhile, on the 3rd a small reconnoitring force Aug. 3.
made its way for a short distance along the causeway
which led to the Taku Forts, about ten miles distant,

[1] Lord Wolseley tells the story (*Story of a Soldier's Life*, ii.
23-24). But I had it at first hand from General Sir Frederick
Stephenson, who was also an eye-witness. He could not tell it, even
thirty years later, without choking with laughter.
[2] Wolseley, *The War with China*, pp. 94-98.

1860.
Aug. 9.

Aug. 12.

found the way barred by entrenchments and exchanged a few shots with the enemy; and on the 9th a second and smaller party fetching a compass to north of the causeway, discovered that the country was traversable by all arms. On the 12th, the French being at last ready to move, the First Division and the French marched out along the causeway south-westward against the front of the enemy's position, while the Second Division and Cavalry Brigade, following the track of the reconnaissance of the 9th, turned its left, or northern flank. The cavalry was at once confronted by a large body of Tartar horse, which advanced in irregular order with great steadiness. With the British force were two batteries of breech-loading twelve-pounder rifled Armstrong guns —the very latest development of artillery—one of which opened fire with great accuracy but little effect, for the Tartar horsemen continued to advance until charged by Probyn's and Fane's cavalry, when they turned and made off, easily distancing their pursuers through the superior condition of their ponies. The First Division meanwhile advanced to within a thousand yards of the Chinese entrenchments astride the causeway, soon cleared them by the fire of British and French rifled guns, and pushed on to the village of Sin-ho immediately in rear of them. Two miles and a half to south-east of Sin-ho another entrenched position was seen about the village of Tang-ku, the approach to it being a narrow causeway with a ditch on either side. North of this causeway lay an impassable swamp; south of it, over about a mile of space between the causeway and the Pei-ho, the ground was fairly firm. Montauban pressed urgently for an immediate attack on Tang-ku. Grant demurred, objecting that, until the canals which separated the causeway from the firm ground had been bridged, the only possible access lay along a single narrow road which was commanded by the enemy's guns. In other words, he had no intention of moving by the way which an Oriental foe expected and wished him to take. Montauban, therefore,

advanced with his own infantry and artillery and opened 1860.
fire from his guns at long range.   The Chinese replied, Aug. 12.
gun for gun, and after a couple of hours Montauban
thought better of the matter and returned.   The
entire force halted for the night at Sin-ho.

On the 13th Grant bridged the various canals, as Aug. 13.
he had purposed, and ascertained by reconnaissance
that the enemy's cavalry had all retired to the other
bank of the Pei-ho, leaving no troops on the north bank
except those that actually held the entrenchments at
Tang-ku and the Taku Forts to south-east of them.
During the night a trench extending for two hundred
yards northward from the Pei-ho was thrown up at a
distance of five hundred yards from the enemy's works
at Tang-ku, and at daybreak the First Division on the
right and the French on the left advanced across the
space between the causeway and the Pei-ho.   They
opened fire from thirty-six guns at a range of nine
hundred yards, under cover of which the skirmishers
of the Sixtieth advanced to harass the enemy's gunners.
The Chinese artillery was soon silenced, and a party of
the Sixtieth, finding a dam across the ditch close to the
Pei-ho, entered the works to find the enemy in full
retreat.   The French, further to the left, had greater
trouble in passing the ditch but met with little resistance.
Thus with slight difficulty and trifling loss the Allies
had made their way to within two miles of the Taku
Forts.

There was now a halt of six days while ten days'
supplies were accumulated at Sin-ho, and the heavy
guns and ammunition were brought up to the front.
A bridge of boats was thrown across the Pei-ho at
Tang-ku, and the two commanders made close reconnaissance of the Taku Forts.   Upon each bank of the
river there was a detached fort, lying to westward of a
larger and principal fort.   On the northern bank this
detached fort lay only two miles from Tang-ku, and
could be approached, by making a detour as far as
possible from the river, without risk of coming under

a cross-fire from the southern bank.   The capture of
this detached fort, moreover, would mean not only the
enfilading of the whole length of the more important
fort to east of it on the northern bank, but the overlooking of the corresponding detached fort on the
southern bank.   Grant, therefore, considered the detached fort on the north bank to be the key of the
position and resolved to attack it first.   Montauban
vigorously protested.   All military science, according
to him, demanded an advance against the southern
forts—demanded, that is to say, that the Allies should
divide their small force and throw the greater part of it
across an unfordable tidal river, leaving the remainder
to maintain, if it could, the communication between it
and Pei-tang, or rather with the fleet off Pei-tang,
which was the true base of operations.   So far did
Montauban carry his predilection for the southern forts
that, even before the bridge of boats had been constructed over the Pei-ho, he passed two thousand men
across the river; only to find the road to the forts so
much cut up that he could not advance without
throwing bridges across the breaches.   Grant, far too
sensible to be moved by such demonstrations, insisted
resolutely upon following his own plans; and Montauban, after finally abjuring, on behalf of himself and
his Government, all military responsibility for the
result, was fain to give way.

By the night of the 20th Grant's preparations were
complete.   A road had been so constructed over the
two remaining miles of intervening ground as to take
every possible advantage of the shelter afforded by the
numerous canals that intersected it; the canals themselves had been bridged; batteries had been thrown up
before the northern face of the detached fort; and
twenty-three pieces, four of them French, had been
mounted in them.   The Chinese likewise had not
been idle.   Finding themselves practically unthreatened
from the side of the river (for the Admiral had not yet
brought up his gun-boats even to make a feint attack

at long range) they had reversed the guns on their 1860. elevated cavaliers so that they now pointed to landward. For the rest the defences were by no means contemptible.   The first obstacle to be cleared was a deep dry ditch; beyond that came an open space blocked by an abatis; then a wet ditch; then twenty feet of ground covered with pointed bamboo stakes planted as thickly as stalks on a stubble-field; then a second wet ditch; then another staked space; and finally a thick wall of unburnt brick, with loopholes for wall-pieces.[1]   A causeway led through all these obstacles to the gate, but the bridge over the first wet ditch had been destroyed, and the drawbridge over the second wet ditch had naturally been raised.

At daybreak on the 21st the batteries opened fire Aug. 21. and were vigorously answered by the Chinese, who had mounted among other ordnance two English thirty-two pounders, recovered from the gun-boats which they had sunk during Hope's abortive attack.   At about six o'clock a magazine blew up within the fort, and the Allies reckoned that the affair was ended; but after only a minute or two of silence the enemy gallantly reopened fire.   Half an hour later another magazine, in the larger fort beyond that under attack, was exploded, apparently by a shell from one of the four gun-boats which had now appeared in the river.   By seven o'clock every gun in the detached fort had been dismounted.   The two batteries of field-guns were pushed forward and the storming parties advanced. The British, consisting of the Forty-fourth and Sixty-seventh, moved straight to their front upon the gate, and the French to their right upon the western angle, close to the river.   The British stormers were preceded by a party of engineers carrying pontoons for the purpose of crossing the ditches; and these pontoons proved to be a serious impediment.   They blocked up the causeway leading to the gate, keeping a number of

---

[1] I follow the description given by Rennie, who examined the works carefully (*British Arms in North China and Japan*, p. 116).

1860. men under heavy fire, and after all proved to be useless.
Aug. 21. The stormers, therefore, swam across the ditches under a storm of missiles from the walls and an enfilading fire from the detached fort on the south bank; and it was some time before a sufficient number of them could be assembled at the foot of the wall to attempt to surmount it.   Meanwhile Major Anson of Sir Hope Grant's staff had reached the post over which hung the ropes of the drawbridge, and, hacking at the rope, brought the bridge down with a crash.   The bridge had been so much damaged that it would bear little weight, but the men managed to cross.   The French, who had wisely carried only scaling ladders with them, were the first to enter the fort, but the British were only a few seconds behind them, having either climbed the walls or broken through the barriers of the gate.   The garrison still resisted bravely, but were overcome and annihilated with the bayonet.   After three hours and a half of fighting the fort was finally taken.

The heavy guns were then brought forward for attack on the main fort, a thousand yards away, and a staff officer advanced to examine the ground before it. The Chinese fired heavily upon him and his party; but suddenly a white flag was hoisted upon the main fort on the southern bank, and a messenger appeared with letters for the Allied Commissioners, Lord Elgin and Baron Gros.   The answer was that, unless the forts were surrendered within two hours, the Allies would reopen fire; and towards the end of that period the troops advanced.   The enemy discharged not a shot upon them, so they walked quietly into the main fort and took possession.   The garrison, two thousand strong, had thrown away their arms and military garments and bore the appearance of meek and submissive citizens.   They were bidden to go their way in peace; and before nightfall Mr. Parkes, after much persuasion, persuaded the Chinese Governor-general to sign a capitulation yielding up all the country and strong places on the river as far as Tientsin, including

that city itself.   Sir Hope Grant's plan of action was
thus triumphantly justified, and the cost of success
had not been high, for the casualties of the British
were only two hundred and one, and of the French only
one hundred and fifty-eight, the number of the killed
in each force being no more than seventeen.

After a day had been spent in the removal of the
obstacles in the river, the Admiral and Mr. Parkes
steamed up the Pei-ho to Tientsin, and on the 25th
the troops followed, two battalions and a battery by
water, and the remainder marching by land.   The Buffs
were left to hold the Taku forts and the Sixtieth to
guard the bridge of boats at Sin-ho.   By the 5th of
September all had reached Tientsin except the Forty-
fourth, which had been hurried back to Shanghai to
avert a threatened attack by Taiping rebels.   Thus the
little force was depleted by three battalions; but this
was regarded as of no importance since everyone
expected the immediate conclusion of peace.   Commissioners from the Imperial Court had indeed reached
Tientsin on the 31st of August, and after much talk
it was agreed that they and Lord Elgin should sign a
convention on the 7th of September.   Then, rather
late, it occurred to the British diplomatists that the
Chinese Commissioners had produced no written
powers authorising them to sign any convention at all.
Since no such powers were actually forthcoming, the
negotiations were broken off; and on the 8th the army
began its march upon Tang-chao, some sixty miles up
the river, and twenty miles below Pekin.   Meanwhile
the astute Chinese had defrauded the British out of a
full week of time, and had further contrived that every
driver and every beast, which had been laboriously
collected in Tientsin by the Allies for transport, should
vanish in the night of the 9th.   British diplomatic
agents are sometimes strangely gullible.

Means of conveyance being thus scarce, the force
marched on by small detachments, leaving the Second
Division behind at Tientsin, while the siege-train and

1860. part of the supplies were brought on by water.   On
Sept. 13. the 13th the troops reached Ho-si-wu, about half-way
to Tang-chao, where fresh emissaries arrived from the
Imperial Court.   Some days were gained by the
Chinese in preliminary haggling, after which it was
agreed that the Allied forces should advance to within
two miles of Chang-kia-wan, that Lord Elgin should
advance thence to Tang-chao with a thousand men for
escort, that the terms of peace should then be finally
arranged, and that Lord Elgin should thereafter enter
Pekin with a thousand men for the ratification of the treaty
of 1858.   This business was, of course, conducted solely
by Lord Elgin, Mr. Parkes and the other " political "
gentlemen who, in accordance with our evil custom in
the East, accompanied the army with independent
powers.   Sir Hope Grant was not consulted, nor was
any other military authority; otherwise they might
have pointed out that the diplomatists had already been
once deceived by specious talk, and that the isolation
of a thousand men in a vast city such as Pekin was, to
say the least, an extremely hazardous measure.

However, these guileless gentlemen went their way,
Sept. 17. and on the 17th the British troops, with a thousand
French, reached Matao.   Here most satisfactory as-
surances were received from Mr. Parkes at Tang-chao
that all was going well; and orders were issued for a
further advance on the morrow to Chang-kia-wan,
where a camping ground had been chosen for the troops
Sept. 18. by agreement with the Chinese.   The force marched
accordingly, but after traversing a few miles found itself confronted by a very large army, covering a front
of about five miles.   Sir Hope Grant instantly halted;
and presently Mr. Henry Loch,[1] a member of the diplomatic mission, who had formerly been an officer in the
East India Company's army, galloped in with an escort
of three Sikh sowars, bearing a letter from Mr. Parkes.

[1] He became later Lord Loch, having held more than one high
colonial government. He had served in the second Sikh War, and
commanded a squadron of native cavalry in action at the age of eighteen.

This missive announced that all had been satisfactorily
arranged; but Loch, on the contrary, reported that he
had passed large bodies of troops and many batteries
of guns where there had been none on the previous day.
Mr. Parkes had also noticed this and ridden back, with
a single dragoon for guard, to demand an explanation.
The rest of the party, which included Colonel Walker
and another staff-officer, who had gone forward to mark
out the camp, two civilians and an escort of rather more
than twenty dragoons and Indian troopers, had remained behind to watch the enemy's movements, sending Loch ahead to give warning to Sir Hope Grant.
The General was much embarrassed. He had advanced with a very small force, relying on the assurance
of the diplomatic agents that peace was certain; and yet
here was a Chinese army drawn up before him, with
every indication of hostile intent; while, worst of all, some
thirty officials and soldiers, British or French, were behind
the Chinese lines, virtual hostages on whom the Chinese
authorities could wreak their revenge if he should take
the initiative in attack. Mr. Loch volunteered to return to Tang-chao with orders for all persons attached
to the Allies to return at once; and Sir Hope Grant
accordingly dispatched him and one of his staff, Captain Brabazon, for this purpose. He then pushed his
cavalry out towards his flanks to watch the enemy's
movements, though with directions to avoid any collision with them. This done, he awaited events.

First came a flag of truce with a Chinese commissioner, who asked to see Lord Elgin, but returned on
learning that he was at Ho-si-wu. Then a Chinese
officer appeared, saying that he had come to lead the
Allies to their appointed camp. Next, after Sir Hope
had waited two hours and a half, a commotion was visible
among the Chinese troops. Their artillery and infantry
opened fire, and Colonel Walker with his party was seen
galloping through the midst of the enemy. He reported that the Chinese had at first been civil, but had
presently changed their tone, hustled him and his

1860.
Sept. 18.
escort, and finally attacked and cut down a French officer, wounding also Walker himself.   Thereupon Walker had called to his people to ride for their lives, and had brought them through a fusillade of the entire Chinese army with no greater loss than two men wounded.   Since the enemy continued their fire, Hope Grant promptly made his dispositions for attack. General Montauban advanced on the right; while, under cover of artillery-fire, the Ninety-ninth and 15th Punjab Infantry marched forward in the centre, and the Queen's, with the cavalry and the horse-artillery, began a wide flanking movement on the left. The Tartar cavalry, manœuvring round Grant's left flank and rear, was checked by the shells of the Armstrong guns and dispersed by a charge of Probyn's Horse.   The Punjabis captured a troublesome battery with little effort; and Montauban, having pushed away the enemy from his front, let loose upon them his own escort and a squadron of Fane's Horse.   In every quarter the Chinese were dispersed, and an attack of their cavalry on the baggage-guard was repulsed with heavy loss to them.   The Chinese, who were reckoned to be twenty thousand strong, suffered severely, and left eighty guns on the field.   The casualties of the British numbered twenty and of the French fifteen, so that the combat was evidently not very strenuous.

But unfortunately there were still in the hands of the Chinese two British military officers; Mr. Parkes, Mr. Loch, and two more civilians; also one dragoon, eighteen Indian troopers and twelve French subjects; and everyone was apprehensive as to their fate.   Grant, after the action, advanced to Chang-kia-wan, which was given over to plunder in reprisal for the treachery of the

Sept. 19.
Chinese; and on the 19th the allied Commanders-in-chief sent a flag of truce demanding instant restoration of the prisoners on pain of an attack upon Pekin.   The messenger returned, being unable to pass the Chinese

Sept. 20.
outposts, and the 20th was occupied with reconnaissance of the enemy's position, which was found to be

in front of the Yang-Liang canal, the waterway between the Pei-ho and Pekin.   It was spanned by two
bridges, one of marble called Pa-li-chao, and the other
of wood, a mile further to the westward.   It was
arranged that the French, now reinforced to a strength
of three thousand, should advance on the right upon
Pa-li-chao, and the British infantry on the left upon the
wooden bridge; while the cavalry was to make a wide
sweep to the left, driving the enemy's right upon his
centre, so as to make havoc of his troops, when crowded
between the two bridges.   The action opened with a wild
fire from the Chinese guns, which was answered by the
British artillery; and then the Tartar horse manœuvred
to turn Grant's left flank.   They were charged by the
King's Dragoon Guards and Fane's Horse in first line,
with Probyn's Horse in support, and were fairly shivered
to pieces.   Grant followed up their success, when the
ground became too difficult for cavalry, with two battalions and three Armstrong guns, breaking up camps,
capturing guns and inflicting considerable loss.   The
chase finally ended within six miles of Pekin, the entire
action having cost the British no more than thirty-one
casualties, and the French a like trifling proportion.

The Chinese now again made overtures to Lord
Elgin who, however, declined any further parley until
the prisoners should have been released; and meanwhile Sir Hope Grant hurried his siege-train and the
Second Division to the front.   The rapid approach of
winter made delay very hazardous; but these mishaps
are always liable to occur when military operations are
hampered by the dictatorship of " politicals."   But for
their sanguine promises of immediate peace, Sir Hope
would never have advanced to Pekin except in full force.
However, by the 2nd of October both siege-train and
troops had arrived; and, after two days more of waiting for a large French convoy, he was at last able to advance upon the 5th.   The march was only a short one,
the French having a greater distance to traverse than the
British; but on the 6th the forward movement was

1860. resumed, when it was found that the enemy had retreated.

Oct. 6. The ground was extremely difficult, being a tangle of ruined fortifications, and, when Sir Hope halted for the night, the French were nowhere to be seen.   It was

Oct. 7. ascertained on the morning of the 7th that they had found their way to the Emperor's summer palace, and were busy plundering it of its priceless treasures.   On the same day a letter arrived from the Chinese authorities promising the restoration of the prisoners on the following day.   Mr. Parkes, Mr. Loch and certain

Oct. 8. others duly came in on the 8th, and the remainder a few days later.   All had been hideously tortured, and out of thirty-nine souls only nineteen survived.   Among those that perished was Private Phipps of the Seventh Dragoon Guards who, knowing a little Hindustani, kept up the spirits of the Indian sowars with indomitable patience and fortitude until he became unconscious.   The condition of the prisoners was not calculated to incline Grant to leniency, and, while negotiations were conducting for the surrender of Pekin, he was active in throwing up his breaching batteries.

Oct. 13. Noon of the 13th of October was the time appointed for opening fire unless the British terms were complied with; and the guns were actually loaded, run out and laid when, at the last moment, the north-eastern gate was swung open, and the Allies were admitted peaceably into Pekin.   On the 18th what was left of the royal palace plundered by the French was destroyed

Oct. 24. by fire; and on the 24th a convention settling the indemnity to be paid by China and the ratification of the treaty of 1858, was signed.   The war was over, and on

Nov. 8. the 8th of November the main body of the troops began their march back to their transports, leaving three battalions, a battery and Fane's Horse in temporary occupation of Tientsin and the Taku forts.

This, but for the interference of the diplomatic agents, was a well-managed little expedition, the chief lesson of which, for the British, was that transport and supply could not be conducted under two different

heads.   There was constant friction between the Commissariat, which was responsible for supply, and the
Navy and the Military Train, which were responsible for
transport afloat and ashore, but declined to take the
orders or respect the wishes of the Commissariat.[1]
The British force would have fulfilled its task far more
rapidly but for the presence of the French, who did not
understand that description of work, and were, therefore, except on the actual field of action, an encumbrance.   Meanwhile the French indemnified themselves
by the ruthless pillaging of the summer palace, though
after plundering and destroying, they deprecated its final
destruction as an act of barbarism.   Altogether they
were rather difficult and trying.   It must be added that
British officers went to the palace, before it was burned,
to glean where the French had reaped; but Sir Hope
Grant ordered everything taken by them to be handed
over to prize-agents and sold by auction, so that the
proceeds might be thrown into a general prize-fund.
He renounced his own share, as likewise did his divisional commanders, Michel and Napier, with the result
that nearly every private received nearly four pounds
sterling there and then.   As a rule British armies,
owing to official delay, had had to wait years for their
prize-money; and this timely distribution comforted
the men for the sight of French soldiers with their
pockets full of silver, and their shoulders laden with
costly silks.   The whole transaction betrays one secret
of Sir Hope Grant's popularity with his troops.   No
man was more merciless to plundering at large, as he
had shown during the Indian Mutiny, but he shrank
from allowing his men to suffer for their good behaviour.
He had a fine force of hardened, seasoned men, and he
so contrived matters that there should be little sickness
and no discontent, or, in other words, that there should
be no avoidable privation, hardship and fatigue.   Knowing that their general would never call upon them for any

[1] Memos. of Commry.-gen. Power and Major-gen. Sir John
Michel on Transport and Supply in the China War.

1860. unusual effort without good cause, the men always responded readily and heartily to any such summons and, in fact, would do anything for him.   No man ever more thoroughly understood the British soldier, and, for all that he had read no books, not many men have better understood war than this gentle, kindly, pious, daring lancer who could play as skilfully on the hearts of his men as on the strings of his beloved violoncello.

The principal authorities for the China War of 1860 are: Wolseley, *Narrative of the China War*, 1860; *Story of a Soldier's Life*; Rennie, *The British Arms in North China and Japan*; and the despatches printed in the *London Gazette*.   There are interesting details on the Transport Service in the report of Lord Strathnairn's Committee on Transport and Supply, 1867.

CHAPTER LVI

A<small>BOUT</small> the year 1824, one Syad Ahmad Shah of Bareilly, having spent a stormy youth in free-booting under the famous Pindari, Amir Khan, turned religious adventurer and came a year later to preach his doctrine among the Yusafzai tribes of the frontier about Peshawar. With him he brought some forty Hindustani disciples, for he had made the pilgrimage to Mecca by way of Calcutta, and during the journey had gained influence over the Mohammedans of Bengal. He stood for the original tenets of Islam in all their purity; he claimed to be a man of peculiar saintliness; and he declared himself to be commissioned by Allah himself to wage war against the infidels to extermination. Such pestilent, self-seeking rogues have never failed to impose upon the simple Pathan tribesmen; and Syad Ahmad came at a happy moment, for they were smarting under defeat at the hands of the hated Sikh, Ranjit Sing. He easily gathered recruits; and meanwhile his own following had been swelled to some nine hundred by malcontents and fanatics from Bengal. In 1827 he sallied out to lay siege to Attock, but after a slight preliminary success was utterly defeated by the Sikhs; and he then fled with a few companions to Swat, and gradually worked his way back through Buner to Yusafzai. With full faith in his miraculous powers the Pathans again assembled round him, and in a two years' career of conquest he gathered the whole of Yusafzai under his control. Unfortunately the holy man's love of money made his rule so

1863. oppressive that the Pathans rose against him and drove him across the Indus, where, after a stubborn battle against the Sikhs, he was overpowered and slain.

Such of his disciples as survived betook themselves to Sittana, on the Mahaban mountain some fifty miles above Attock on the right bank of the Indus. There they settled down to the depredation of the lower lands and the kidnapping and murder of peaceable traders on the highways, receiving occasional recruits and even subsidies from the great reservoir of rogues in Lower Bengal. The first collision of the British with them had been in 1853, when the fanatics had abetted an offending tribe in hostilities against us, boasting loudly of their prowess, but had fled precipitately before two Sikh regiments. Being then left alone they returned to their evil ways and brought upon themselves a second punitive expedition under General Sir Sydney Cotton in 1858. Cotton attacked Sittana itself, inflicting severe loss on the troublesome Hindustanis, who fought doggedly and well; but it was felt at the time that the penalty exacted was insufficient. Two neighbouring tribes had engaged themselves to prevent the fanatics from reoccupying Sittana; so the latter built themselves a new village at Malka, some eleven miles to north-west of their old settlement and on the northern slope of the Mahaban. By 1862 they had recovered themselves, thanks to money and reinforcements received from Bengal, had moved back to Sittana and had renewed their old nefarious activity of thieving and murder. Once again the lawless colony called upon all good Mohammedans to fight the infidel; and one tribe, responding, went the length of attacking peaceable friends of the British. By September the majority of the tribes on the border of Hazara were defying the Indian Government, and a military expedition became inevitable.

In 1863 there still continued in India the system of maintaining local forces—or as they were called "contingents"—which were commanded by British officers but were not under control of the Commander-in-chief. The object was, or seems to have been, that civil lieutenant-governors or commissioners should have a military force at their disposal without inconvenient superintendence from the higher military authorities; and the practice helps to account for the readiness with which "politicals" interfered with the military operations of British armies also in the field. One of these contingents was the Punjab Irregular Force, horse, foot and artillery, some ten thousand strong, recruited from the Pathan tribes, led by British officers and in the highest degree efficient. They were distributed in little parties for hundreds of miles along the north-west frontier, all of them with means of transport, so as to be ready for immediate action; and they were under the orders of the lieutenant-governor of the Punjab. In the middle of them, however, at Peshawar was a strong garrison of the regular army, under the orders of the Commander-in-chief. There were thus two military authorities on the frontier; and, though the sanction of the Supreme Government was necessary before any military operations could be undertaken, it was always possible that a lieutenant-governor, in urgent cases, might initiate operations first and obtain sanction for them afterwards. In such a case if the enterprise proved to be more formidable than had been expected—and we have seen in the course of the Afghan War how incapable the "politicals" were of judging of such things—then one of two things happened. Either the frontier was denuded by the concentration of scattered posts at one spot, or the regular army was called in hastily to redress the miscalculations of the civilians.

In the expedition which now lies before us all of the proceedings were characteristically Indian. First, the lieutenant-governor of the Punjab decided, very reasonably, that the Hindustani fanatics were a root of mischief and turbulence which could not be extirpated too soon. He, therefore, on the 15th of

1863. September put the case before the Viceroy, Lord Elgin, and asked permission to send a force of five thousand men into the mountains for this purpose without delay. He reckoned that the operations would last three weeks; and since winter, intensely cold in those regions, was at hand, with the possibility of heavy snow before the end of November, it was advisable that the expedition should begin work early in October at latest. As to the plan of campaign, there was to be an entire change from that of 1858. The mountainous mass known as the Mahaban is, roughly speaking, of triangular shape with its apex to north-east, the Indus forming one side, the valley of Chamla a second, and the Yusafzai the base. Hitherto the attacks had been directed from the Yusafzai in the south, and the fanatics had been simply pushed back into the hills. It was now proposed to enter the Chamla valley, get into their rear and drive them towards the plains, thus improving the chances of annihilating them by death or capture.

The operation was put forward as very simple. One column would be based on Hazara to watch the line of the Indus. The other moving from Peshawar to the Yusafzai would assemble, as had Cotton's force, at Manairi and Nawakila, as if to follow Cotton's route, but would then strike northward to the Ambela Pass and thence pass eastward into the Chamla valley. The first day's march would be by camel-road, stated to be "easy in the extreme," through the pass to Kogah; the second day's march would be sixteen miles down the valley to Cherorai; and the third from Cherorai to Malka, six miles as the crow flies, over the hills. There remained the question of the attitude of the tribes. The Chamla valley was bounded on the north by the Guru mountain, six thousand feet high, which with the district to north of it was the home of the Bunerwals. No trouble was anticipated from them, for they had no sympathy with the fanatics and held different religious opinions. Moreover, they formed part of the flock of the Akhund of Swat, 1863. rather a remarkable man, who was a kind of pontiff of Islam in those quarters and had denounced the fanatics as actual infidels.   Both the Bunerwals and the Swats, who lay to north-west of them, were expected to look with approval on the coming campaign; and the valley of Chamla itself belonged to a mixture of unimportant tribes, some friendly, some hostile.   It was considered imprudent to sound any of the clans as to their feelings lest the plan of campaign should thereby be revealed, which was likely enough.   Still on the whole the entire affair should be ended in three weeks. Such was the forecast of Sir Robert Montgomery, lieutenant-governor of the Punjab.

The Viceroy answered, agreeing that the expedition was necessary and approving the proposed numbers— five thousand infantry, besides cavalry and guns. Having taken his decision he communicated it to Sir Hugh Rose, the Commander-in-chief.   The actual plan of operations was not laid before Sir Hugh, for it was not finally determined upon by the lieutenant-governor until the last moment; but none the less Rose lost no time in giving his opinion.   He pointed out, first, the danger of denuding Peshawar and other stations of troops and transport at the very moment when, by entering the mountains at one point, we should arouse excitement along the whole line.   Next, he remarked that the proper equipment of even five thousand men, as regards supplies, ammunition and transport, for so difficult and arduous a duty would need far more time than had been allowed, and that the period allotted for active operations was too short. Finally he urged that hasty flying marches through the mountains had produced no satisfactory results in the past, and were not likely to produce them at present. He therefore advised a strict blockade of the district during the winter and the despatch of a carefully prepared and equipped expedition in the spring.

This sound common sense was disregarded. Nothing

1863. could wean the Indian civilian or "political" from his belief in "demonstrations." Every soul of them, even men of such capacity as the Lawrences, was, as we have seen, infected by this distressing delusion. The troops [1] were hastily collected from the northern stations, which were dangerously weakened; and there was no reserve nearer than Lahore, over two hundred miles as the crow flies from Peshawar, with, of course, no railway yet to connect them. The transport was hastily collected of bad animals and worse drivers; and the only redeeming feature in the whole arrangement was the appointment of Sir Neville Chamberlain to the chief command. His great reputation and experience, won in many campaigns, his striking personal bravery and his chivalrous character warranted the assurance of ultimate success. But his service had all been in the East, and he had never had a chance of shaking himself free from the essential faults of the Indian army.

There were early miscarriages in the concentration of the force—insufficient boats for the passage of the Indus, backwardness in the preparations of the commissariat and ordnance departments—and it was not Oct. 18. until the 18th of October that the leading troops marched to the mouth of the Daran pass, by which Cotton had entered the mountains in 1858. On the Oct. 19. night of the 19th these joined the advanced party of the main body from Nawakila at Parmali; and the whole,[2]

---

[1] *Punjab Irregular Force*:
>   2 mountain batteries.
>   Guides, cavalry and infantry.
>   1st, 3rd, 5th, 6th regiments N.I., 5th Gurkhas.
> *Regular Troops*:
>   11th Bengal Cavalry (Probyn's Horse).
>   ½ battery R.A.
>   71st and 101st, 20th and 23rd N.I.
>   2 cos. native Sappers.

[2] *Cavalry*: 100 Guide Cavalry, 100 11th Bengal Lancers (Probyn's Horse).
> *Artillery*: 2 mountain batteries.
> *Infantry*: Guide Infantry, 1st, 5th, 20th Punjab N.I., 5th Gurkhas.

under Colonel Wilde of the Guides, moved north- 1863.
ward upon the Ambela pass.   Colonel Reynell Taylor,
the commissioner, accompanied this column, and sent
forward a proclamation to the Bunerwals and other
tribes, setting forth that no hostility was intended
against them, but only against the Hindustani fanatics.
At sunrise on the 20th the force reached the entrance Oct. 20.
to the pass, where the baggage was parked; and the
advance was then continued through the defile, flanking
parties being duly thrown out upon the hills on either
hand.   About two-thirds of the distance had been
traversed when at noon shots were fired by straggling
parties of tribesmen.   These were dislodged with
little difficulty, one prisoner being captured; and by
2 P.M. the top of the pass had been secured.   Wilde
then encamped his men there and on the space beyond,
on fairly open and level ground, leaving room for the
main body to bivouac in rear.

The main body,[1] meanwhile, was in difficulties.
It had started from Nawakila at one o'clock in the
morning, reached Rustam, some twelve miles to north-
west, at seven, and moved off eastward upon Surkhawai
—another four miles—at nine.   As far as Surkhawai
the track had been tolerably good, but just beyond it
came the pass, and then the troubles began.   The
way lay, as usual, up the bed of a stream, obstructed
by boulders and large masses of rock, and overgrown
with low trees and scrub.   It was necessary to load
the guns on to the backs of elephants; and in many
places even the men could move only in single file.
Late in the afternoon the column closed in upon the
rear of Wilde, but the guns did not get in until ten
o'clock at night, while the rearguard was still at
Surkhawai.   The ammunition-mules had with great
difficulty accompanied their battalions, but not a single
baggage-animal came in that night.   On the 21st the Oct. 21.

---

[1] 3 guns C Battery, 19th Brigade R.A.
   500 71st H.L.I.; 550 101st; 3rd, 6th, and 32nd Punjab N.I.
   1 co. Sappers and Miners.

1863.
Oct. 21.
baggage began to struggle through the pass. The mules and ponies broke down in all directions; and their drivers were helpless and intractable. Loads were thrown by the hapless beasts and knocked off by overhanging branches, and the road became choked. A great effort to push on stores for the European troops before nightfall increased the confusion and the obstacles at narrow points in the track. The whole line came to a dead stop. Very little baggage reached Chamberlain on the 21st, and the rearguard was still far in rear. According to the programme, the column should have been at least at Kogah in the Chamla valley by the 21st, but it was not yet even clear of the pass.

Still the outlook was not so far very serious. Taylor had dispatched his prisoner with a friendly message to the Chamla tribes, and had received an answer that they would give him assistance with supplies and so forth. The Bunerwals likewise had sent an intimation that the British were at liberty to follow their enemies, and that the Bunerwals would offer no resistance unless Oct. 22. attacked. In the morning of the 22nd, the rearguard being at no great distance, Chamberlain sent forward parties to improve the two miles of road downward from the crest towards the egress from the pass, and found them unoccupied by the enemy. A party of cavalry advanced to Kogah, four miles from camp, keeping as far as possible from the territory of the Bunerwals on the north side of the valley, and Lieutenant-colonel A. Taylor of the Royal Engineers, with a small escort, finding the valley level and clear, pushed seven miles further on to Kuria. Large bodies of Bunerwals had been observed watching the proceedings from their own territory on the Guru mountain; and when Taylor, having returned to Kogah late in the afternoon, was making his way back to camp, great numbers of them were seen descending to occupy some broken ground at the very head of the valley and thus to intercept the return of the reconnoitring party. To

prevent this and to gain time for infantry to come 1863.
forward, the cavalry charged and cut down half a dozen Oct. 22.
tribesmen, while two companies, taking up their position
on the broken ground, ensured the safe retreat of Taylor's
men.   These companies were, however, themselves
followed up closely by the enemy, who several times
broke in upon them sword in hand; and they were obliged
to fight for every yard of their way back.   Even after they
had come in, the tribesmen made general attacks on the
front and flanks of the camp, not desisting until midnight.   They were beaten off with no great difficulty
and with, apparently, some loss to themselves, whereas
the British casualties did not exceed six and twenty.

    It was now discovered that the Hindustani fanatics
had been too cunning for the British agents.   Before
the issue of Reynell Taylor's proclamation they had
by some means learned its purport and, setting forth
its terms almost word for word, warned the Bunerwals
that these professions were merely a cloak for the real
purpose of the British, which was to devastate and
annex Chamla, Buner and Swat.   Had Chamberlain's
column been able to pursue the scheme originally laid
down for it and to march rapidly through the Chamla
valley upon Malka, the insinuations of the fanatics
might have been belied.   But there his troops stood,
halted in the pass, and there they had been for three days,
which was sufficient to lend colour to the imputation of
sinister designs.   In any case, the mischief was done.
The Bunerwals had already taken up arms, and that
fact had at a stroke wrecked the original plan of the
British operations; for an advance up the Chamla
valley, with a strong and warlike tribe in a practically
unassailable position flanking the line of march along a
length of seventeen miles, was out of the question.   If
other tribes should join the Bunerwals, the situation
would be still more serious. Chamberlain's sick already
numbered nearly one in ten of his effective men,[1]

---

[1] 430 sick, 4896 effectives (*Record of Expeditions against the
North-Western Frontier Tribes*, p. 166).

1863. the native soldiers evidently feeling the effect of the climate; and the proportion was not likely to be lessened as the weather grew colder. He summoned to him the 14th Native Infantry, which he had left to protect his advanced base at Rustam, and begged for another native battalion to be dispatched from Oct. 24. Peshawar. On the 24th he sent back to Rustam all his sick and wounded, with every scrap of baggage which could be in any possibility spared; detaching fatigue parties to improve the road and remove the worst of the obstacles upon it. The enemy meanwhile remained quietly at the mouth of the pass; and it was observed that among them, besides the Hindustani fanatics, who were distinguishable by their dress, there were three tribes from the Northern Indus.

Ordinary precaution demanded that strong picquets should be maintained in the rocky hills, patched with forest, which flanked either hand of the camp in the pass. These posts, three upon either flank, were fortified by loopholed stone walls, abatis and sometimes by stockades; but the ground was so much broken and, in places, so blind that it was not difficult for an enemy to creep up close to the defences in large numbers. The approach to the camp was barred by a breast-work with guns in position, and the rear was likewise secured; but the posts were so numerous as to lay a constant strain upon the strength of Chamberlain's force. The enemy were quite cunning enough to understand that his flanks were his most vulnerable points; and on Oct. 25. the 25th they delivered the first of a series of attacks upon them. It was repulsed with little difficulty, owing to a misunderstanding among the tribes themselves; for it had been arranged that the fanatics and others should assail the northern picquets and the Bunerwals the southern; and the Bunerwals failed to Oct. 26. perform their part. On the 26th, however, the Bunerwals made two resolute attempts to storm the outermost of the northern posts—a very steep rocky knoll called the Eagle's Nest—at the same time attacking the other

British positions on the same side and making a
demonstration against the front. They went to work
scientifically, employing matchlockmen, in well-chosen
cover, to maintain a constant fire which should keep
the defenders' heads below the parapet, while the
swordsmen ran boldly down to the assault. They
were repulsed after some hours of hard fighting, some
two hundred and fifty of them being killed; but the
loss of the British also was appreciable, numbering one
hundred and twenty-four killed and wounded. The
casualties in action and through sickness were hardly
made good by the arrival on the following day of the Oct. 27.
14th Native Infantry.

And meanwhile new enemies had come upon the
scene. First and foremost was the Akhund of Swat,
who, heretofore a counsellor of peace and a bitter
religious opponent of the Hindustani fanatics, now
suddenly laid all sectarian prejudice aside and took
them to his arms. Next and less important were a
few hundred bigots and malcontents from the Afridi
and other tribes under British sovereignty, attracted
by the delight of any disturbance and the prospect of
plunder. These last infested Chamberlain's communications, while the main concourse of the tribesmen threatened his front and flanks. His position had
never been pleasant. The duty of keeping the pass
open behind him and of escorting convoys through it
had fallen very heavily upon his few troops. But now
it became almost impossible. To advance into the
valley, according to the original plan, would be sheer
madness, the protection of a long line of laden animals
against vastly superior numbers in front, flanks and
rear being out of the question. Nor could he even
move from his present position into the open ground,
for that would mean giving up the pass, and retaking it
at serious cost of life every time that he wished to send
out a convoy. In fact he had no choice but to sit still
and ask for reinforcements, which were none too close
at hand. On the 28th he sent away another convoy of Oct. 28.

1863.
Oct. 29.
sick, and on the 29th he was joined by the 4th Gurkhas and two guns of a light field-battery. But this reinforcement made him no stronger than before; and, having information that he would be attacked on the morrow, he was obliged to hold the whole of his extensive position in strength, which signified that half of his native infantry were on duty.

Oct. 30.
Before daybreak of the 30th the enemy delivered their assault simultaneously upon the front and both flanks. The most formidable onslaught was directed against a point called the Crag picquet, which was the key of the defences upon Chamberlain's right or southern flank. This post was a high rocky hill, the summit of which commanded all of its lower defences but would hold no more than twelve men. Within half an hour the tribesmen were masters of the summit, though the lower parts of the hill were still held. The officer in command, Major Keyes, promptly counter-attacked, and, though the path was so steep as to admit only one or two men abreast, the enemy was driven out with the bayonet and the summit was recovered. Thereupon the tribesmen in that quarter were seized with panic and fled. Meanwhile the onslaught upon the centre had been repelled with considerable loss to the enemy, and that upon the northern picquets, which was little more than a demonstration, likewise failed of its purpose. The men of Swat, who left forty-five corpses in front of the central defences, were so much dismayed by their defeat that they ran off, carrying the Akhund with them, far into the Buner country, before they were stopped by the entreaties of the Bunerwals and induced to return. Chamberlain's casualties on this day amounted to fifty-five.

There was now a lull in the operations of which Chamberlain took advantage to strengthen his defences and to change his line of communications, shifting his base from Rustam to Parmali, and making a road south-westward over the hills by the villages of Khanpur and Sherdara to Parmali, so as to avoid the

difficulties and dangers of the pass.   He also began the
construction of a rough way down from the slopes of
the hills to north of the pass into the Chamla valley,
with a view to his ultimate advance.   These were wise
and sound measures, but naturally they did not diminish
the fatigue of the troops, for the enemy was careful to
keep up a constant fire upon all exposed breastworks
and to make demonstrations of intended attack.   Meanwhile the lieutenant-governor of the Punjab began to
realise that his little military promenade had developed
into a frontier war.   For long he had refused to face
facts, and had clung to his original design that Chamberlain should march to Malka.   But unpleasant warnings
were coming in from every side.   The general commanding at Peshawar reported that there was unrest
along the whole of the frontier, and that he had been
obliged to equip a flying column to deal with possible
incursions;   wherefore he asked for reinforcements.
The Viceroy was expected shortly at Lahore, and three
regiments had been told off for duty with his camp.
Without awaiting the sanction of the Commander-
in-chief the lieutenant-governor ordered all three of
these,[1] as well as the Ninety-third Highlanders from
Sialkot, to reinforce Chamberlain, and gave directions
for the collection of over six thousand camels and mules
at Naoshera.   Here at least was some appearance of
vigour;   but constancy was, as shall presently be seen,
not an attribute of Sir Robert Montgomery.

All remained quiet in the pass until the 6th of
November, when there was an unpleasant mishap.
One of the parties which was covering the men at
work on the road into the Chamla valley was cut off
by the enemy, and, before it could be extricated, three
British officers had been killed, two more wounded, and
altogether seventy-eight of all ranks had fallen.   There
was no hint of any misconduct;   but a very capable
officer, in his anxiety to carry off his wounded men,
had made the mistake of delaying his retirement a

[1] 7th Fusiliers, 23rd and 24th Punjab N.I.

1863. little too long.   The enemy had evidently suffered
severely, for they would not meet the troops which
came down next day to recover the bodies of the slain;
but none the less their success was calculated to en-
Nov. 11. courage them; and on the 11th the gathering of
large bodies on the northern slopes above the pass
portended a fresh attack upon the defences upon that
side.   The posts were therefore reinforced, and in
particular the Crag picquet, the defences of which had
been improved so as to admit a garrison of one hundred
and sixty picked marksmen.   At ten o'clock at night
about two thousand tribesmen fell upon this stronghold
with fury, clambering up the steep ascent, pulling down
the breastwork and hurling the stones at the defenders.
At one moment they were nearly masters of the summit,
but were driven back in turn by a hail of stones.   For
six hours they launched assault after assault, each
weaker than the last, till at last they fell back foiled.
The garrison of the Crag picquet was then withdrawn,
worn out by forty-eight hours of watching, working
and fighting, and with muskets so foul that they could
scarcely load them.   They were relieved on the morning
Nov. 13. of the 13th by one hundred and twenty Punjabis, the
enemy meanwhile menacing the adjacent posts of the
Standard picquet in such strength that more men
could not at the moment be spared, and at the same
time holding the British front and left flank in check
by steady demonstration of attack.

Heavy firing, however, continued about the Crag
picquet, and after a time its garrison came rushing
down headlong past the breastwork of the Standard
picquet.   Major Keyes, who was in command there,
tried in vain to stop them.   They ran down into the
camp upon which the enemy was firing heavily from
the Crag picquet; the camp-followers caught the infection of panic and fled; and there was wild confusion
of scared animals and men.   Keyes, observing that his
own soldiers wavered, with great promptitude ordered a
counter-attack, which was most gallantly led by two of

his young officers; but all the troops on the spot were
shaken, and it was not possible to form them for an
assault to recapture the lost fort. Fortunately the
Hundred and First was ready under arms for some
other duty; and Chamberlain, judging that there had
been some mishap, ordered them to retake the position
of the Crag, which they did without halting or pausing
from the moment when they stepped off from the camp.
This ended the day's work. The enemy had lost over
two hundred killed and wounded. The losses of the
British amounted to one hundred and fifty-eight, full
half of them falling upon the garrison of the Crag
picquet.

For the next few days the enemy remained comparatively quiet, and Chamberlain seized the opportunity to press forward a change in his dispositions for
which he had long been preparing, namely the evacuation of the posts on the hills to north of the pass, and
the concentration of his entire force upon the heights on
the southern side. The enemy was said to be much
discouraged and inclined to disperse; and on the 16th
the Akhund of Swat actually took his station on the
Bunerwal pass to prevent his followers from going
home. But meanwhile other tribesmen had set themselves to harass Chamberlain's new line of communications, and it was necessary to move strong parties in
that direction. On the morning of the 18th the
picquets on the north of the pass were successfully withdrawn without any molestation, and the camp and the
whole of the troops were transferred to the south side.
The enemy did not at first notice this movement, but,
finding certain positions to be vacated, concluded that
the British were retreating. Thereupon, pouring down
in great numbers into the gorge, they attacked the left
front of the new position; and after some of the foremost defences had twice changed hands, they compelled
the defenders to fall back to the inner posts nearer to
the camp. The fighting lasted from eleven in the
forenoon until dark, and cost the British one hundred

1863.
Nov. 18.
and eighteen casualties.   A detachment meanwhile went out to clear the enemy away from a position where they threatened the supply of water, which was duly accomplished with trifling loss; but it is noteworthy that Chamberlain took command of this small body of troops in person.   The truth is that the men's hearts were beginning to fail them.   For a month they had been working and watching day and night, standing on the defensive against a wary and dangerous enemy who could choose their own moment for attack, could always concentrate superior numbers and, through their agility and hill-craft, held them, in so difficult a country, always at a disadvantage.   The nights, too, were growing steadily colder, which told upon the health of the troops; and the sick-list increased ominously.   Nor could the sick and wounded, numbering at the moment four hundred and fifty, be sent to the rear without strong escorts, which was not only a harassing duty in itself but weakened the defensive strength of the garrison and threw yet more work upon those that were left within the defences.

Nov. 20.
About nine o'clock in the morning of the 20th the tribesmen were observed to be gathering in strength before the Crag picquet and the Water picquet, which were only four hundred and fifty yards apart and could therefore support each other by cross-fire.   Each had a garrison of two hundred men, half British and half sepoys.   The enemy's standards could be seen gathering thicker and thicker under the breastworks of the summit, and they must have timed the moment for a rush upon it in great force with skill and accuracy. Be that as it may, at three o'clock in the afternoon the garrison, both British and native, came pouring down in panic from the summit, and the parties lower down the hill, after a desperate effort to stem the tide of fugitives and pursuers, were swept away.   Chamberlain at once turned his guns upon the Crag to prevent the captors from holding it in serious strength, and then in person led the Seventy-first and 5th Gurkhas

to a counter-attack. The Crag was stormed and re- 1863.
covered without great loss, but Chamberlain was Nov. 20.
struck by a bullet near the crest, and though he staggered on with undaunted spirit to the summit, he was
so severely hurt that he soon found himself unable to
retain the command. The enemy's loss was reported
to exceed three hundred, but that of the British reached
the figure of one hundred and thirty-seven, including
seven British officers killed and wounded.

Chamberlain's report by telegram of these oc-
currences threw the lieutenant-governor of the Punjab
into a panic. The situation was certainly very unpleasant. The tribes in all quarters were greatly
excited. Even from Kabul emissaries came to encourage the Akhund; and there was dangerous unrest
on the frontier of Peshawar. In the circumstances
Sir Robert Montgomery decided that Chamberlain's
column should be withdrawn to the plains; and he
telegraphed on his own responsibility to Major James,
who had taken the place of Colonel Reynell Taylor as
civil commissioner, authorising, though not ordering,
the General to act accordingly. Evidently he looked
for a repetition of disaster as at Kabul in 1841, not
perhaps unreasonably, since there had been much in
common between the inception of both adventures.
Chamberlain, suffering grievously from his wound,
could only say that military considerations did not
justify such a step; and James represented that its
political consequences would be calamitous. Most
unfortunately the Governor-general, who had been
lying desperately ill for some days in the hills, died on
the actual day of the last action about the Crag picquet,
and, until his temporary successor, Sir William Denison,
should arrive from Madras, there was no authority to
whom an ultimate decision could be referred. But Sir
Hugh Rose, seeing that matters were becoming hopelessly entangled, had hurried from Lord Elgin's bed-
side to Lahore, and had arrived there on the 14th of
November, so that the lieutenant-governor had the

1863. best advice ready to his hand if he had chosen to seek it.   However, he preferred to rely upon the plenitude of his own wisdom; and Rose could only write a strong remonstrance to the Council at Calcutta against the impolicy, upon every ground, of abandoning the expedition.   As Commander-in-chief, however, he could issue orders to the troops, whatever the lieutenant-governor might say, and he directed large reinforcements to move by forced marches to the frontier. Finally he dispatched two officers, who were later to rise to great eminence, Colonel John Adye and Major Frederick Roberts, both of the artillery, to proceed at once to the scene of action and report to him the actual state of affairs.

As it happened, the attack of the 20th of November was almost the expiring effort of the tribesmen.   They had suffered heavily and gained nothing; and Major James took advantage of their depression to induce clan after clan to return to their homes.   The Akhund fulminated curses upon the deserters, and the leader of the Hindustanis seconded him with exhortation and entreaty, but to little purpose.   Even the Bunerwals were wavering; and, though these defections were countervailed in some measure by the arrival of some three thousand men from Bajaur and Kunar, mistrust had sprung up among the tribesmen and their short-lived unity was steadily dissolving.   On the 25th Adye

Nov. 25. and Roberts arrived, and without hesitation advised Sir Hugh Rose that the operations should be prosecuted to the end.   The enemy was disheartened; a newer and better road of communication had been opened over the hills; and reinforcements were daily coming

Nov. 30. in.   On the 30th Major-general Garvock arrived and took over the command, the force gradually increasing, until by the middle of December it numbered about nine thousand men.[1]   Meanwhile Sir William Denison

[1] *First Brigade*: Colonel Turner, 97th Foot.
   Half battery C, 19th R.A.
   Peshawar Mountain battery.

had arrived at Calcutta on the 2nd of December to find 1863. that the Council favoured the withdrawal of the force Dec. from the Ambela pass, and had even given orders to this effect. Denison, after reviewing the circumstances, decided to overrule them; and Garvock, with sufficient troops under his hand, was free to take the offensive.

Before any advance could be made into the Chamla valley it was necessary first to clear away from the right flank a body of some four thousand tribesmen which was established at Lalu, a village in the hills about a mile and a half east and south of the Crag picquet. Lalu in its turn was covered about sixteen hundred yards to westward by a remarkable eminence called the Conical Hill, whose sides were by nature rocky and precipitous, while the summit had been fortified by stone breastworks and was strongly occupied. Accordingly, on the morning of the 15th of December, Dec. 15. Garvock sallied out with two columns, jointly nearly five thousand strong, against the Conical Hill, which was stormed in spite of the difficulties of the ascent by the Hundred and First and the Guides Infantry; the enemy, about two thousand strong, flying away to eastward. Turner with the right hand column then pressed on and captured Lalu; whereupon the enemy, thinking that Wilde had been left in isolation, boldly attacked his left flank. Simultaneously they threatened the front and left flank of the camp, where their sharpshooters caused some annoyance. But they were repelled and counter-attacked at all points, and by two o'clock in the afternoon were in full retreat, having suffered considerable loss. The British then halted on

---

7th Fusiliers, 71st H.L.I., 1st, 3rd, 5th, 20th, 32nd Punjab N.I., 5th Gurkhas.
Second Brigade: Lieut.-Col. Wilde, Guides.
Half 3rd Punjab Light Field battery.
Hazara Mountain battery.
93rd Highlanders, 101st Foot, 14th N.I., Guides Infantry, 6th, 23rd Punjab N.I., 4th Gurkhas.

1863.   the ground that they had gained, and Probyn's Horse
was ordered to join in the advance over the open valley
Dec. 16. next day.   On the 16th Garvock found the enemy in
a very strong position on a ridge covering the village of
Ambela. He decided to turn their right and, if possible,
to cut them off from the Bunerwal pass through the
mountains to northward.   The movement was in progress when a body of two hundred Mohammedan
fanatics suddenly broke in upon the left flank of the
23rd and 32nd Native Infantry and, for the moment, sent
them staggering back. The assailants were checked,
however, by two companies of the Seventh Fusiliers,
which Turner had disposed to meet any such attack, and
were slain to a man. The two native regiments, having
rallied, drove the enemy headlong before them up the
pass, when Garvock halted, respecting the promise
made to the Bunerwals that their country should not
be invaded; and the force bivouacked for the night in
the neighbourhood of Ambela. Its casualties in the
two days' fighting were twenty-four killed and one
hundred and fifty-seven wounded.

This day's work was decisive. The enemy encountered on the 15th and 16th had numbered some
fifteen thousand, chiefly Hindustanis and men from
Bajaur, Swat and Dir; the Bunerwals, in their desire
for peace, having taken no share in the fight. On the
night of the 16th all, except the Akhund of Swat and
the Bunerwals, fled to their homes; and the Akhund
was ready to fly at the first moment, while the Bunerwals
Dec. 17. in the morning of the 17th came to Major James and,
without even speaking of terms, asked for his orders.
Now came up the question of the advance to Malka,
which had been the primary object of the expedition.
The obvious course seemed to be that the force, or a
sufficient detachment, should march upon this home
of the Hindustani fanatics. But this was not so simple
a matter as it seemed to be. It would necessitate, in the
first place, the renewal of supplies and stores from the
base at Parmali, which, it was calculated, would take

seven days.   Thus the operations would be broken
off just when it was most essential to press them; the
Akhund would have breathing space to rally his disheartened men;   and the tribes about and around
Malka—Amazais, Mada Khels and Hassanzais—who
certainly would not welcome a British force, would
have time to prepare and organise resistance.   Lastly,
if Malka were reached and burned in despite of them,
they would not be likely to encourage the return of the
Hindustani fanatics, who were hostile to the British.
It was, therefore, resolved to commit the destruction of
Malka to the Bunerwals, whereby the recent successes
could be immediately followed up, further fighting
would be avoided, and the tribes about Malka, above
mentioned, working with the Bunerwals instead of
against the British, would prevent any return of the
Hindustani fanatics to that quarter.   Since, however,
it was essential that the destruction of Malka should be
complete, it was necessary that a body of British officers,
with a small escort, should accompany the Bunerwals
and see the work done with their own eyes.   This
was a very serious matter.   If any collision should
arise with the tribes on the line of march, then beyond
question not a man of the officers, nor of their escort,
would escape.   In the event of such a calamity a new
expedition and prolonged warfare against the tribes,
with all its attendant danger and expense, were inevitable.   The choice between the two courses was very
nice and delicate, but to Garvock and his advisers it
appeared preferable that the campaign should be
completed by the Bunerwals.

Accordingly, Colonel Reynell Taylor, who had
returned to the scene, with six other officers and an
escort of about two hundred of the Guides under a
lieutenant, set out on the afternoon of the 19th from
Ambela and reached Kuria, at the eastern end of the
Chamla valley, on the same evening.   It had been
expected that two thousand Bunerwals would accompany them, but only seventy appeared;   and it was

evident that they were aiming to conciliate rather than intimidate the Amazais.   Heavy rain caused a day's
delay, but the mission started again on the 21st and, after a very difficult march, traversed the twelve miles to Malka amid the undisguised disgust of the Amazais, groups of whom, of course fully armed, were en-
countered at every step.   On the 22nd the burning of the village attracted many thousands of angry and menacing tribesmen, but Reynell Taylor, with a placid courage beyond all praise, simply informed the headmen that, the work being done, the mission would at once return. This excited the Amazais even more; but Taylor stood alone in the midst of the raving, gesticulating crowd without moving a muscle.   Then a grey-haired, one-armed leader of the Bunerwals forced his way to Taylor's side, and told the headmen plainly that, if they meant to murder the British, they must first murder the Bunerwals who had sworn to protect them. Therewith the storm for the moment was lulled, and the little column began its homeward journey.   The hills on either flank of them were covered with armed men, and progress was frequently stopped during angry debates whether the infidels should be allowed to proceed further.   In one narrow defile an armed man waving a standard actually started to rush down at the little party; and the accidental firing of a single shot at any time would have ensured a massacre.   All the way to Kuria the Amazais followed the mission, and then at last they fell off and went back to their own place.   The danger was over, but it had been very great.   Sir Hugh Rose, on hearing what Taylor had done, declared his action to be madness, and gave up the whole mission for lost.   Beyond all doubt it was saved only by Taylor's coolness, seconded by great good fortune.

So ended the expedition to Malka, which was to have been a military promenade of three weeks, but lasted through three perilous months and cost over nine hundred casualties.   It may be compared with the Afghan War, though on a much smaller scale, as 1863. an instance of the heedless fashion in which Indian civilians set military forces in motion without the slightest appreciation of the difficulty of all military operations. It seems to have been impossible to bring home to them in those days—not so very far distant—the elementary fact that soldiers must eat before they can fight, and that in a mountain-campaign above all the first requisite is a well-organised system of transport and supply. So far as the purely military side of the operations is considered, the work seems to have been done well. The enemy was daring, wary and formidable, with a tactical instinct which seems to have been unerringly true. Against them the British officers matched their own tactical ability with marked success, and more than once with extreme personal gallantry. At all critical moments there was one—whether field-officer or subaltern—who knew what was the right thing to do and did it; and full advantage was taken of the superior range and accuracy of the Enfield rifle. A counter-attack was indeed once pushed too far, and a small rearguard once lingered too long. The garrison of the Crag picquet, too, not only sepoys but British soldiers, was twice driven out headlong; but the post was promptly recovered, and allowance must be made for men, worn out with toiling and waking, when they suddenly find themselves surrounded by savage faces and gleaming swords. These are the ordinary incidents of war. But there was no serious blundering, no discreditable mishap due to negligence or ignorance; and it is very clear that the army in India had made notable progress in the conduct of a mountain-campaign since the operations in Nipal in 1814 and the war in Afghanistan thirty years later.

Authorities: *Record of the Expeditions against the North-West Frontier Tribes* (Edition of 1884), very full and detailed. *Sitana*, by Colonel John Adye. *Forty-one Years in India*, by Lord Roberts. *Journal of the United Service Institution*, vol. xi. No. 47, by Major Fosbery, V.C.

CHAPTER LVII

1863. ONCE again the course of our history leads us to a land hitherto untrodden by the British soldier. Abyssinia in the eighteenth century was known to the British best as the home of that Queen of Sheba who travelled from Axum in Tyre to the court of King Solomon, and returning, bore him a son from whom, as legendary tradition maintains, the royal house of modern Ethiopia traces its descent to this day. Probably the very name was unfamiliar except to readers of Samuel Johnson's *Rasselas*. There was good reason for the obscurity which hung over Abyssinia. Containing as it did the sources of the Nile, it had in early days been in close touch with European civilisation. From the third century of our era it had been Christian, and its first primate had been consecrated by St. Athanasius. Then the conquest of Egypt by the Arabs shut off the Ethiopians from the valley of the Nile, and the growing power of Islam threw them back for the best part of ten centuries upon themselves. In the fifteenth century the Portuguese revived the touch of Ethiopia with Europe; but the Turks meanwhile were spreading themselves along the shore of the Red Sea. Moreover, as if that were not enough, there came in the middle of the sixteenth century an invasion of Gallas from the south, who embraced the creed of Islam and drove a wedge of Mohammedanism into the midst of the country, severing the Christians of the north from those of Shoa in the south. Missions of Franciscans and Jesuits were as rudely repelled by the followers of

Christ as by those of Mohammed; and Abyssinia 1863. remained in its isolation, hostile to all progress, a prey to disputed successions and intestine war.

It was the Egyptian campaign of 1801 which first attracted British attention to the Red Sea and its bordering lands. English travellers early in the nine-teenth century penetrated for some little way into the country; and the chiefs who were contending for pre-eminence within it sought alliance with England. Hence it came about that in 1849 a treaty of commerce was negotiated with one of them at Adowa and ratified in 1852. In that very year there rose into prominence a young noble named Kassa, then about thirty-five years of age, who, after an unsuccessful encounter with dis-ciplined Turks, made himself master of all rivals within the country, and in 1855 assumed the title of Theodore, King of Ethiopia. Then a great mis-fortune fell upon him in the death of his wife, who had been his good genius, a faithful companion and a wise counsellor. He married another, the daughter of a chief whom he had overthrown, but quickly tiring of her, betook himself to drink and debauchery. Never-theless he was not as yet unfriendly to Europeans. Captain Cameron, who arrived as British Consul in 1862, bearing presents from Queen Victoria, found a tiny colony of Germans and French round him, some of them missionaries, some adventurers, nearly all, apparently, of some value for the manufacture of munitions and the making of roads. Theodore sent Cameron away with a friendly letter to the Queen, but, being prostrated by sickness on the upper Nile, Cameron returned to the highlands of Abyssinia to recover. Meanwhile Theodore, taking offence at some supposed affront from the French Government, had first put the French consul in irons and then un-ceremoniously dismissed him. In January 1864, he imprisoned Cameron upon the ground that he had brought no answer from Queen Victoria, and, laying hands also upon others of the European colony,

1864. tortured all of them brutally.   Cameron had contrived
to communicate the fact of his arrest to a British agent
at Massaua; and a mission was sent to Theodore,
who released Cameron, and received the new envoy
at first with friendliness, but in April 1865 imprisoned him likewise.   It seems that he had some
idea of holding him as a hostage in order to obtain
artillery from Europe, for he sent a letter by a member
of the mission to the Foreign Office in London, asking
for workmen and machinery for the manufacture of
munitions.   In fact his power was slipping from him,
for he was utterly demoralised.   His former friends
rose up against him in all directions, driven to desperation by cruelty and oppression, and he turned upon
them savagely, slaying and laying waste.   Until June
1865 the European prisoners were not unkindly
treated, but they were then removed to Magdala and
loaded with chains.   In December 1866, Theodore's
messenger to England returned, saying that the
machinery for which the King had asked was lying at
Massaua, ready to be handed over to him as soon as
he should release the European prisoners.   Theodore
took no notice.   By the spring of 1867 the rebellion
against his rule was almost general, but he still struck
out fiercely, and in a single month killed or burned alive
more than three thousand people.   Though his army
was rapidly deserting him, he resolved to establish
himself in his stronghold at Magdala and fight to the
end.   It was very clear that he would never set free
his prisoners nor atone for his insults to England unless
compelled by force.

1867.   Accordingly, in July 1867, the Secretary of State
for India telegraphed to the Governor of Bombay to
ask how soon an expedition could be dispatched, if it
should be necessary, to Abyssinia, and followed up
this message by a letter requesting all particulars as to
its strength, its transport, its place of disembarkation
and so forth.   The question was one of peculiar
difficulty.   In the first place the western shore of the

Red Sea belonged to Egypt, and it would be necessary 1867.
to obtain the permission of the Egyptian Government
before a force could be disembarked at all.   This was
an obstacle which could be, and in fact was, easily
removed by diplomatic intervention; but the grant of
a port was only the raising of a veil which revealed
the troubles that lay behind.   The lofty plateau of
Abyssinia does not abut upon the Red Sea.   It is
divided from it by a salt and waterless plain which at
its broadest is two hundred and fifty miles wide, and at
its narrowest twelve.   The first thing to be provided,
therefore, at the base and for at least twelve miles
beyond it, was water, the natural supply being wholly
insufficient.   Then came the ascent of the plateau
through, roughly speaking, fifty miles of passes to a
height of over seven thousand feet; and then an advance
of over three hundred and fifty miles of rugged mountain and valley to the fortress of Magdala, nearly ten
thousand feet above the sea.   Little was known of the
country except that, though not trackless, it was
roadless, and had been devastated by long civil war.
Popular clamour, finding a voice for its silliness in the
English newspapers, declared it to be beset by deadly
insects, both winged and reptile, as well as by devouring
hippopotami, and predicted that no army sent to
Abyssinia would ever return.   But setting this childish
nonsense aside, the enterprise was most formidable and
hazardous.   To fix the numbers of the force must
be pure guess-work.   Theodore's subjects, it is true,
were in general rebellion against him; but they might
none the less fight against an invasion.   Or again, they
might help the invaders forward until Theodore had
been overthrown, and then turn upon them on their
return march.   The troops must needs take with them
artillery, for Magdala was a powerful fortress; and
numbers of men would be required to clear the way
for guns over the mountains.   The force, again, must
keep open its communications over a length of four
hundred miles, and still muster sufficient strength to

1867. strike a blow at the end.   Moreover, they must not
only advance to Magdala but retire from it as they
had come.   The men would be subjected to the heat
of a tropical sun on the salt plains and, by day, even on
the mountains; but at an altitude of seven thousand
feet they would require warm clothing by night.
Therefore they must be provided with raiment for two
different seasons, and a part of that raiment must be
carried for them.   Lastly and principally the men must
be fed; and it seemed no more than prudent that their
numbers should be as great as it was possible to feed.
This possibility in its turn would depend upon the
amount of supplies which could be carried by a given
number of animals, which would also need to be fed.
The whole problem, therefore, resolved itself into one
of transport and supply, complicated by the fact that
not only forage but also water must be provided at the
base and for twelve miles beyond it.

Sir Robert Napier, who was in command at Bombay, after due weighing of all considerations, pronounced that the force should be twelve thousand men,
and that it would require at least that number of
Aug. 13. animals for its transport.   On the 13th of August the
British Government decided that the expedition must
be dispatched, and appointed Sir Robert Napier to
command it; and therewith preparations were pressed
forward both in India and in England.   Orders had
been issued a fortnight earlier for the purchase of
mules along all the shores of the Mediterranean from
Valencia to Beyrout and for the collection of them at
Suez; for the campaign could only be conducted
during the dry season, that is to say, between January
and June, and there was therefore no time to be lost.
Sept. 15. On the 15th of September a reconnoitring party of ten
officers under command of Colonel Merewether, with
a small escort, was sent to choose a landing-place.
They fixed upon Malkatta in Annesley Bay, about
thirty miles south of Massaua, as, upon the whole, the
most suitable, with the village of Zula, a mile to west

of it, as the site for a camp of assembly. After exploring various routes to the foot of the plateau, they
finally entered the pass of Kumayli, and followed the
track southward as far as Senafe. They then tried an
alternative route from Hadoda, six miles to north-west
of Kumayli, up the river Hadas; but after pursuing it
for thirty miles southward, they came back on the 21st
of November with a decided preference for the former.
Water was none too plentiful even there; grass was
very scarce; and only wood was abundant. However,
the chiefs of the country along the line of both routes
had come in, and agreed to give safe passage to troops
and to convoys. So far, therefore, matters were fairly
satisfactory. There was a vast deal of work to be done
in sinking wells, improving tracks, building piers,
establishing depôts and so forth, but, if all went well at
the base, this might be pushed forward.

The first requisite at the base was of course the
speedy landing and distribution of supplies and stores.
The landing was a matter of difficulty, for the sea
shoaled abruptly two hundred yards from the shore,
forbidding the nearer approach of laden boats. Until,
therefore, a pier could be constructed of that length,
everything must be carried through the water by wading
men; and neither timber nor stone were obtainable
except from a distance of from ten to twelve miles.
Another complication was that there was very little
water and practically no forage on the spot. The
formation of the base, therefore, presented most intricate and difficult problems, the solution of which in
their proper order demanded peculiar forethought.
The first men landed must obviously be skilled workmen, and their first duty must be to provide a good
water-supply. They could not at the outset be many,
nor, though they would need the help of beasts of
burden from the beginning, would they be able to
provide for more than a certain number of these. The
base must in fact be built up gradually, the force
landing in driblets, both of men and beasts, until due

1867. arrangement could be made for their reception on the
Sept.– barren plain of the foreshore, and for their rapid transfer
Nov. to posts on the plateau.   The difficulties were so great
that much hardship and fatigue and considerable waste
were almost unavoidable, and to reduce these to the
lowest possible degree demanded hard thinking even
by the best and most skilful brains.

Ancillary to these preliminary preparations was
the organisation of transport and supply, generally
comprehended within the term commissariat-duties.
The Indian Commissariat enjoyed a great reputation,
seemingly in all three presidencies.   When the transport broke down in the Crimea, people pointed to
India to provide a model for restoring it; and Indian
officers to the very end of the nineteenth century firmly
believed in its excellence.   Yet the Indian system was,
as had been abundantly proved in the Afghan war, no
system at all, except possibly on the plains of India.
" The Commissariat," wrote Sir Robert Napier on
the 9th of September 1867, " have had but a small
quantity of their own carriage to manage; the greater
portion has been hired carriage, managed under a kind
of social organisation peculiar to itself, which has
existed from time immemorial, and which goes on
somehow, one hardly knows how." [1]   Only in the
Punjab contingent was there any approach to a
properly organised transport, the troops being liable
to be called at any moment to active service on the
frontier; and therefore there were both at Lahore and
at Rawal Pindi mule-trains under military control, the
muleteers being armed and disciplined men.   It was
very obvious that a system of transport " which goes
on somehow, one hardly knows how," would break
down hopelessly in an Abyssinian expedition; and
accordingly Major Warden, the officer selected to
organise the transport, did not condescend even to
notice it.   He had served in the Land Transport Corps,
since converted into the Military Train, in the Crimea;

[1] *Official History*, pp. 245-246.

and, with that experience strong upon him, he urged
that native non-commissioned officers and men should
take charge of the smaller units of the transport.
Hired superintendents, as he represented, could not be
trusted to obey orders nor to enforce them on their
subordinates; whereas disciplined men would maintain discipline and thus place the entire organisation
upon a military basis.   To this proposal the Governor
of Bombay, from the fulness of his wisdom and the
wealth of his military knowledge, raised objection,
having evidently prepossessions in favour of the old
chaos.   Thereupon Sir Robert Napier pointed out
that transport-animals were gathering in from many
quarters, and that a gang of drivers of various races
and tongues—Egyptians, Arabs, Persians and Hindustanis—unless very completely organised so as to secure
order and discipline, must inevitably produce nothing
but confusion.   The Bombay Government, however,
with sublime conceit set Major Warden's proposals
airily aside; and during the month of September the
formation of the Transport Corps went forward upon
the old chaotic lines.   Then Sir Robert Napier
inspected it, pronounced that " in its present dis-
jointed state it would utterly fail of its purpose," and
pressed for the adoption of Warden's suggestions.
After ten days' delay the Bombay Government yielded,
and volunteers were called for from both native and
British regiments to take command of the transport-
drivers.   But meanwhile six or seven precious weeks
had been lost; and at the end of October the Land
Transport Corps was still in the making.[1]

During this interval work upon the base had already
begun.   The reconnoitring party had brought with
them one hundred and forty mules with trained and
disciplined drivers, which made the nucleus of the
Transport Corps on the spot.   From three to five
hundred Shohos (the tribesmen about Zula) were
hired to land supplies and stores; and on the 5th of

[1] *Official History*, i. pp. 231-254.

1867.
Oct. 5.

October a temporary Commissariat depôt was opened about three-quarters of a mile from the shore.   The water-supply at Zula was for the moment sufficient, thanks to the sinking of wells; but it very soon began to fail; and the few troops with the reconnoitring party were moved to the Hadas river, where again wells had been sunk, though the supply of water was limited.   On

Oct. 13.

the 13th of October the first ship-load of camels came in from Aden with their drivers and one hundred coolies; and these were followed a few days later by a company of Sappers and Miners from Aden and a steamer for condensing water.   This was all well

Oct. 21.

enough; but on the 21st there came in to the anchorage transports carrying what was called the advanced brigade, which consisted of a regiment of native cavalry, a battalion of native infantry,[1] two companies of Sappers and Miners, a mountain battery, and detachments of the Commissariat, Land Transport and Ordnance Corps, in all about fourteen hundred combatants, as many followers, nearly five hundred horses and about the same number of mules.   This force had been designed by Sir Robert Napier to guard the depôts on shore; but the dispatch of it was premature and, in fact, a curiously clumsy blunder.   The officer in command, Colonel Field, found that no preparations nor arrangements had been made for landing the troops and stores; and indeed there had in fact been no time to make them.   The construction both of a pier and of a tramway to the camp had been begun, so that there had evidently been no lack of energy; but these were not works which could be completed in a day under the sun of the Red Sea.   The reconnoitring party, with all of its senior officers, was exploring the mountains, and the senior officer in camp was the head of the Commissariat, Major Mignon, who had no staff with him except seven men for the issue of supplies.   To him Field made application, and was answered that Mignon could do nothing to help him.   On the contrary, Mignon

[1] 3rd Light Cavalry, 10th N.I.

gave him to understand that he had neither food nor 1867
water for the advanced brigade, and that, if they disem- Oct.
barked, they must land food and water for themselves
daily from the transports. Merewether had, indeed,
left behind him advice that the advanced brigade should
move up at once to the Hadas and to Kumayli, where
there was plenty of water, but how they were to be fed
and watered until they had travelled thither across the
desert he had apparently omitted to consider.

So nearly three thousand men and a thousand
animals remained mewed up in their stifling ships for
nine whole days, during which thirty-two tanks were
landed high up on the beach, and filled with water from
smaller casks rolled or carried up by manual labour.
As the daily drinking-ration of the men and animals of
the advanced brigade amounted to eight thousand
gallons, and no boat could draw nearer than one hundred and fifty yards from the shore, the effort to keep
abreast of the water-supply alone was terribly severe.
But, besides supplies, stores and camp-equipment were
all alike landed by wading men; and it speaks most
highly for the troops, both officers and soldiers, that
they threw themselves into this arduous work with unquenchable zeal. Then at last they could land, when
the cavalry and artillery were gradually passed across
the desert to the Hadas and the 10th Native Infantry
to Kumayli. There the first companies of the 10th
found no open space even for one of them to encamp, and for thirty days the battalion laboured strenuously first to clear and level the ground, and next to
make roads backwards towards Zula and forward up
the pass of Suru. The defile was simply the bed of a
mountain torrent, so much encumbered with huge
boulders and masses of rock that even a mule could
hardly scramble through it, and the toil of making it
passable under the fierce sun was exacting and incessant. Yet all ranks bent themselves to it with a
spirit beyond all praise.[1]

[1] *Official History*, pp. 328-329.

In the meanwhile two men-of-war had arrived, the
Star on the 22nd and the *Satellite* on the 28th of October,
which had given help in the general work of disembarkation; but on the 29th the first batch of mules began to
come in from Suez, and then trouble began. Owing to
the interference of the Bombay Government, the Transport Corps was still in course of formation.   Major
Warden had not been able to choose his officers and
non-commissioned officers; the whole was in a state of
anarchy; and there was practically no staff on the spot to
receive the animals and organise them into serviceable
detachments.   The Persian and Egyptian muleteers,
who accompanied the mules, were a pestilent nuisance.
The Persians refused to work unless they received
double the pay which they had agreed to accept, and
though enlisted to take charge of five mules apiece,
would only look after three.   The Egyptians were even
worse, for, if any animal lagged or broke down, they
simply threw the load on the ground and left it to be
plundered by the Shohos while they rode comfortably
on.   Both Egyptians and Persians insisted upon riding
every third mule, and if prevented from doing so when
they started, would cast off a load and ride as soon as
they were out of sight.   As many mules as possible
were sent to the foot of the passes about Hadas, for
facility of watering, but it was necessary to carry their
forage there for them, and this made a frightful complication.   There was water at Hadas but no forage;
there was forage at Zula, but practically no water except
that produced by condensing.   More tanks, to the
total number of sixty, were landed at Zula, but it was
impossible to keep more than half of them full, and the
scenes around them were appalling.   As many as a
thousand mules could be seen in one dense mass
struggling for a place at the drinking-troughs, and the
followers scrambling to share it with them.   Later,
when the arrangements had been somewhat improved,
the followers were still fighting for water. When one of
them reached the tank, he mounted himself on the top

of it, and began to dole out water to all and sundry, 1867.
regardless of the allowance which each was supposed Nov.
to receive.   Then others climbed up, spilling the water
over their dirty feet, and so filling the tank with mud
and sand that the water became foul and undrinkable.
There was no order, no discipline; only waste and
destruction.

While things were in this state there arrived from
India on the 4th of December another brigade—the Dec. 4.
Thirty-third Foot, a battalion of Baluchi Sepoys, the
Sind Horse and a mountain-battery; roughly speaking,
fifteen hundred combatants, a thousand followers and
about as many animals.   Two days after there came one
of the divisional commanders, Sir Charles Staveley, and
found utter chaos.   However, there was now for the
first time a responsible commandant at the base, for the
military authorities—and herein Napier and his staff
seem to have been grievously to blame—had never
thought of appointing such an officer, with a duly
qualified assistant, to organise the base upon a stable
and orderly foundation.   Hundreds of animals had
already been lost, some strayed away, some stolen by
the Shohos, many dead of hunger and thirst.   The
neglect of beasts by their drivers was an old defect in
the Indian transport-service.   Arthur Wellesley and
Charles Napier had laboured effectually to remedy it,
but they found no imitators among Indian officers.
Moreover, in the present instance, the muleteers had
some excuse for not looking after their animals.   In the
first place, instead of tethering chains only ropes had
been provided, which the mules gnawed asunder in a
few hours; and having thus broken loose they wandered
away for miles.[1]   In the second, some thousands of
mules had been disembarked before a saddle had been
landed to place on their backs.   With no transport-
officers to take command of them and no means of
setting their mules to work, it is hardly surprising that
these worthless drivers allowed them to take care of

[1] *Official History*, i. 311.

1867. themselves.   Moreover, as if there were not troubles
Nov.- enough already, a kind of spurious glanders, un-
Dec. pleasantly near akin to the genuine disease, was
epidemic in the belt of desert between the mountains
and the sea, which promptly attacked horses and
mules, weakened as they were by lack of forage and
overwork.   Lastly, there was no sanitary system at Zula.
Latrines were neglected, the offal at the slaughter-
places was not cleared away, and the air was poisoned
by the unburied bodies of dead horses, mules and
camels.   The authorities, civil and military, at Bombay
had not shown themselves very competent to deal with
the preparations for an expedition oversea.

For a month Staveley battled with the general disorder before he could make any great impression upon
it; but by the end of the year matters were greatly
improving.   One pier had been finished and a tramway from the camp had been laid to its head.   Meanwhile the 10th Native Infantry was assiduously levelling
its way through the passes to the upland so that at
least they could be traversed by pack-mules.   Slowly
and steadily it ascended first ten miles from Kumayli
to Upper Suru, twenty-six hundred feet up; then ten
miles on to Undwul Wells—nearly four thousand feet;
then ten miles more to Rahagedi—over six thousand feet;
and finally eight miles to their temporary goal at Senafe
—seven thousand eight hundred feet.   Moreover, since
reports gave warning that their advance would be
opposed by a powerful chief, all labour was necessarily conducted with due military precautions.   How-
Dec. 7. ever, by the 7th of December the Advanced Brigade,
cavalry, infantry and artillery, was assembled at Senafe;
the powerful chief was conciliated; and the inhabitants
showed friendliness and were ready to bring in such
provisions as they could spare.   But even so, it was
with the greatest difficulty that starvation was averted
from the garrison at Senafe.   It was an effort to take a
convoy of mules even from Zula to the Hadas and
back, a journey of sixteen miles.   Leaving Zula as soon

as they had been watered at daybreak, they did not 1867.
reach Hadas until evening. Then they had to be fed Dec.
and watered; and, since it took from ten to twelve
hours to water the whole of them, drivers and beasts
frequently did not return to Zula until dawn of the
following day. Thus both alike were overworked.
The weaklier broke down; a greater strain was thrown
upon the stronger, which in their turn succumbed;[1]
and so the vicious circle was completed.

Nevertheless by the end of the year important progress had been made. The troops and animals at the
base were still living from hand to mouth, but one pier
had been completed. Moreover, one condenser had
been set up at the end of it, and a second upon an arti-
ficial island, which, with the vessels in harbour, ensured an ample supply of water for all. Wells had been
successfully sunk at Kumayli and at other posts on the
upland. Large quantities of supplies had already been
landed, and the construction of a second pier promised
greater facilities for the landing of more. The laying
of a railway from Zula to Kumayli was projected; one
locomotive engine had already arrived, and a corps of
men for the work was shortly expected. The epidemic
among the horses and mules was dying out; and the
troops were remarkably healthy. There were by this
time some nineteen hundred British and over six
thousand native troops at different points between
Zula and Senafe, and not one hundred of them on the
sick list. In the passes by intense labour a road fit for
wheeled traffic had been carried through the Suru pass,
and was being pushed forward, with great relief to the
transport, since a mule can draw twice the weight
that he can carry. The arrival of Sir Robert Napier
on the 2nd of January 1868 gave a vigorous impulse 1868.
to the exertions of all. The disciplined and organised Jan. 2.
mule-trains of the Punjab contingent from Lahore and
Rawal Pindi, following shortly after him, gave a model
of efficiency for the rest. Every soldier worked

[1] *Official History*, i. 339.

1868.
Jan. 18.
infinitely harder under that burning sun than ever he had worked at home.   By the 18th of January a detachment had been pushed forward twelve miles beyond Senafe to Gunaguna.   By the end of the month the railway had been carried half-way to Kumayli, and a telegraphic line erected from Zula to Suru.   The allowance of camp-equipage was reduced, and all baggage was cut down to the lowest figure, with the ready compliance of all ranks.   The veterinary surgeon had issued instructions as to the care of animals in case of sickness and exhaustion in the rarefied atmosphere of the mountains. Fresh beast of all kinds, including elephants, came pouring in to make good casualties.   The filtering of supplies, stores and troops through the passes into the upland never ceased; yet still it remained to be seen whether even a small force could reach Magdala before the breaking of the rains.

Jan. 25.
Jan. 29.
Jan. 31.
Feb. 15.
By the 25th of January, Napier, though there were many troops still waiting in India to join him,[1] thought that he might begin his advance; and leaving Zula on that day he reached Senafe on the 29th, having minutely inspected every post and pass on the way.   On the 31st the entire length of the road from Kumayli to Senafe was open for wheeled traffic, and the work of converting Senafe into an advanced base was progressing.   Meanwhile detachments had crept forward thence by stages of about ten miles, forming a new post at Adigrat, about thirty miles to south of it, and reaching Antalo, some seventy miles further to the south, on the 15th of February.   Some forage was found upon the way, but few supplies; and Napier decided to reorganise his transport-train in two separate divisions, the highland train for the upland from Adigrat southward, and the lowland for the distance between Zula and Adigrat.   Of the former he made the two Punjab trains the nucleus and the model, and with eight

---

[1] 3rd D.G., 10th and 12th Bengal N.C.
H.M. 26th and 45th, 21st Punjab Pioneers, 2nd, 8th, 5th, 18th Bombay N.I.

thousand mules and muleteers armed and disciplined, 1868.
it soon became very efficient.   A telegraphic line was   Feb.
set up from the base to Senafe, but want of poles delayed its prolongation to Adigrat, which was the centre,
for the time, of Napier's exertions.   While there he
still further reduced the allowances of camp-equipment,
as also the allowance of spirits; for the troops and the
followers on the upland were consuming ten thousand
rations daily, and not more than twenty thousand were
delivered daily at Senafe.   Thus the accumulation of a
large reserve of provisions at Senafe promised to take
an interminable time.

Leaving Adigrat on the 18th of February, Napier   Feb. 18.
was obliged to spend three days on his journey southward in the entertainment of a friendly prince, and
after a most toilsome march over most difficult and
dangerous paths he reached Antalo on the 2nd of   Mar. 2.
March.   With the help of two elephants and large
parties of men he actually brought with him a battery
of Armstrong guns; and he had assembled at this post,
half-way to Magdala, two regiments of native cavalry,
a light battery, a native battalion, a wing of the Thirty-
third and two companies of Engineers, altogether
about two thousand men.   Here he halted for ten days,
for the reconnoitring party before him had chosen the
wrong route and wasted much labour in trying to
render it passable.   Local transport, brought in by the
people of the highlands, had eased the strain upon his
own animals; and the Lowland Transport Train now
took charge of the line of communications as far as
Adigrat, to which place the telegraph line had been
extended from Suru.   But the railway had not yet been
carried more than half-way from Zula to Kumayli, the
Bombay Government having sent out rails which were
not uniform in size or preparation, and therefore
could not be readily put together.   It may be pleaded
that railways were a comparative novelty in India, but
Arthur Wellesley had had experience of much the
same kind of inefficiency more than sixty years earlier.

1868. In any case the defects in the railway were calculated to give grave anxiety to Napier.

Mar. 12. On the 12th Napier continued to advance due south by stages of about ten miles, the troops in the posts behind him moving forward as fresh parties came up from the rear to relieve them. On the third day the pass of Amba Alaji, ten thousand feet high,

Mar. 18. was traversed; and on the 18th Napier, taking personal command of the advanced party and (as it was called) the pioneer-force, arrived with it at Ashangi, forty-five miles from Antalo and rather over one hundred and twenty from Magdala. The army had by this time become half of it an armed working party and the other half an armed transport-corps; for it had been found a great economy in time and labour to place every mule in charge of a fighting man. On the

Mar. 20. 20th Napier resumed his advance over terrible precipitous tracks, where some mules with their loads slipped down to destruction, and on the 22nd reached Lat. Here a final reduction of the baggage and camp-equipage was made; the baggage being in fact left behind, and the luxury of a tent to himself being allowed to no one under the rank of a divisional commander. No private baggage-animals were permitted upon any pretext whatever. From Lat Napier purposed to move more swiftly, and it was imperative that not one superfluous ounce should burden his much-tried transport-animals.

Mar. 23. The first day's march proved the wisdom of Napier, for though the distance to the next stage, Marawah, did not exceed nine miles, and the General had with him barely a thousand troops of all three arms, it was with great difficulty that the mules of the transport-train were brought in before dark. The

Mar. 24. next day's march of fifteen miles to Dildi was terrible. Parts of the track were as difficult as had been the Suru pass before the engineers had taken it in hand, that is to say, hardly to be traversed even by mules. By sunset the transport-train had barely covered half

the distance, and the rear of the column was surprised 1868.
towards evening by a terrific storm.   Night came upon Mar. 24.
them, black as pitch, but they could not halt, and were
fain to grope their way onward.   The last of them came
in long after sundown.   Every soul was drenched to
the skin; not one, whether officers or men, had a
change of clothes; and they had to make the best of a
dreary bivouac in a sea of mud.   The Commissariat
train did not reach camp till the following morning,
and after so exhausting a day Napier granted the men a Mar. 25.
day's rest.   On the 26th he pushed on again, and now Mar. 26.
the advance became regular, Napier himself leading
the way with what was called the First Brigade, and
Staveley following with the Second Brigade, one march
in rear.[1]   A Third Brigade, so called, had been organised to make the road passable for elephants.   This advanced at a short interval in rear of Staveley, and was to
be fused into the First and Second as soon as its work
had been accomplished.   The arrival of the remainder
of the force from India at Zula enabled the rearward
posts to be filled up as they were vacated by the forward
movement of their garrisons.

The march of the 26th brought the First Brigade
to Wandach, a distance of no more than eight miles but
including a continuous ascent of three thousand feet.
A heavy thunderstorm burst over them as they reached
their destination and turned the camping ground into
a quagmire.   The Fourth, who had made a double
march on being transferred from the Second to the
First Brigade, only with the greatest difficulty brought
in their mules through torrents of rain after dark, when
they settled down for the night on the swampy ground,

---

[1] *First Brigade*: Detachment Sind Horse, 10th co. R.E., A Battery
    21st Brigade (6 steel seven-pounder mountain guns),
    H.M. 1/4th, 6 cos. 23rd Punjab Pioneers, wing of 27th N.I.
  Second Brigade: Detachment 3rd Bombay L.C., B battery
    21st Brigade, H.M. 33rd, Naval Rocket Brigade.
  Third Brigade: Armstrong battery, two 8-inch mortars, 2 cos. of
    Madras and 1 co. of Bombay Sappers and Miners, 1 co.
    H.M. 4th, 1 co. H.M. 33rd, 2 cos. Punjab Pioneers.

1868. wet through, with the thermometer below freezing point at an altitude of nearly eleven thousand feet.

Mar. 27. None the less the First Brigade advanced on the 27th to Muja, and on the 28th, crossing the river Takazze, toiled up a steep ascent of three thousand feet to Santara, where Napier halted for two days to replenish supplies and to concentrate his three brigades. They were now amalgamated into two, with a total strength of not quite four thousand men, while fourteen hundred more, strung out along the posts from Antalo to Dildi, were on march to join them.[1] Of the entire force of about eleven thousand fighting men about one half had, after five months of incessant exertion, been brought within striking distance of Magdala.

Mar. 31. On the 31st Napier again advanced with the First Brigade by Gahso and Abdikum to Sindi, Staveley following, as before, one march in rear, and closing up to within two miles of him at Abdikum on April 2. the 2nd of April. The force at Santara had entered upon a plateau over ten thousand feet high, where the temperature ranged from one hundred and ten degrees Fahrenheit at noon to twenty degrees at midnight, April 3. which was extremely trying to the men. On the 3rd a party was sent ahead to secure a defile leading from the ravine of the river Jedda to the next lofty plateau of Talanta, Napier following this party closely on the April 4. 4th, while Staveley's brigade came forward to Bethor. The sudden descent into the ravine and the re-ascent from it, both being of three thousand feet, were very

---

[1] *First Brigade*: 3rd Sind Horse; wing of 12th Bengal Cav.; 10th co. R.E.; A-21 R.A.; Naval rocket batteries; H.M. 1/4th, 23rd Punjab Pioneers; wing of 27th Baluchis.

2123

Second Brigade: 4 troops 4th Bombay L.C.; Armstrong battery (four 12-prs.); B-21 battery R.A.; detachment R.A. with 2 8-inch mortars; H.M. 33rd; wing 10th Bombay N.I.

1749

Advancing Troops: Wing 3rd D.G.; 1 troop 3rd L.C.; 1 squadron 10th Bengal Cavalry; 6 cos. H.M. 45th; wing 3rd Bombay N.I.; wing 27th Baluchis.

1404

difficult, but at Bethor Napier struck a road which had 1868.
been constructed by King Theodore to bring his heavy April 4.
guns to Magdala, and this, though very steep, was at
least broad and clear.   On the 5th Napier reached April 5.
the summit of the Talanta plateau and halted, while
Staveley on the same day closed up to him.   From
Bethor onward the country had been a desert of burned
hay and stubble, dotted with ruined heaps of blackened
stones which had once been dwellings.   There was no
sign of flocks or herds, and scarcely a single human being
was to be seen, for here King Theodore had passed by
in his wrath and left as his mark a blasted trail of
desolation.

For four days the force was detained on the Talanta
plateau by the old difficulty, want of supplies, but
happily the peasantry after a time came forward with
the grain which they had buried to conceal it from
Theodore's marauders.   In the course of this halt the
column was strengthened by the arrival of six companies of the Forty-fifth and of the Armstrong battery,
which had gone through a terrible struggle over the
ascent to the Talanta plateau.   Everything in such
difficult ground had been carried by the elephants, but
the patience even of the elephants gave way.   Some
threw their loads, and at one slimy spot on a wet
incline an elephant slid back fifty yards, threatening
death and destruction to men and beasts in rear.   She
stopped herself but could not be induced to proceed,
and eleven more elephants, which had witnessed her
mishap, declined likewise to move until the track was
dry.   However, after the gunners had been out twenty-
eight hours the battery was at last brought in by noon April 7.
of the 7th.[1]   On the 9th Napier advanced five miles April 9.
to the brink of the descent into the valley of the
Bashilo, and there encamped, four thousand feet lower
than at his last halting-place.   Beneath him ran the
river; beyond it to southward a long ridge between
two shallow valleys rose higher and higher until it

[1] *Official History*, ii. 40-41.

1868. broke into a mass of wild rugged ground culminating in two tall peaks, over eight thousand feet high, around which Theodore's soldiers could be seen in swarms. Magdala, on a peak yet a thousand feet higher, lay behind these twain; and the goal, though unseen, had been reached.   Napier sent forward a messenger to demand the release of the prisoners.   No answer was returned, and Napier dispatched an emissary to the Gallas in the south, begging them to cut off King Theodore's retreat in that direction.   Five days were spent in making scaling-ladders of the litter-poles and in preparing sandbags; and on the 9th Napier gave his orders for the final advance.

April 10.   The approach to Magdala from the Bashilo ran for some four miles due south along the comb of the ridge already mentioned, then turned east and, after about another mile of more or less open ground, passed along the northern slope of a savage and precipitous fortified peak called Fahla. Thence it wound under the guns of another peak, Selassie, over against it, and then turned again south over a kind of plateau, to the sternest and ruggedest peak of all, whereon stood the fortress of Magdala. The only source of water between the Bashilo and Magdala lay under the enemy's fire; the day was intensely hot; and the organisation of the water-carriers for the supply of the troops in action became, therefore, a matter of urgent importance. For the rest, it was obvious that the peak of Fahla was the key to the defence of Magdala, for a force advancing into the defile between it and Selassie would be simply thrusting its neck into a halter. Napier made his dispositions accordingly, ordering the infantry of the First Brigade to advance along the comb of the ridge, and the mules with the mountain-guns to move parallel with them up the ravine to east of it. The ridge was so steep and rough that many men fell out, exhausted by fatigue; and the mules in the hollow arrived at the head of the ravine before the main body had had time to deploy and protect them. Theodore, who was in person at

Fahla, directed his guns to open fire, and, thinking 1868.
that the mules were carrying baggage, let loose his April 10.
warriors to the welcome prospect of plunder.   Some
seven thousand of them sprang joyfully down to the
spoil, but when they swarmed over to the plateau they
were met by the Fourth, in skirmishing order, shattered
to fragments by the fire of their breech-loading rifles
and, despite of many efforts to rally, were driven into
flight.   One party which attempted to assail Staveley's
right flank was as easily driven back by rockets and by
the fire of two mountain-guns.   A third body, which
bore down upon the guns and their escort at the head
of the ravine, actually closed with the Punjab Pioneers,
who had smooth-bored muskets, and were hurled back
with the bayonet.   A fourth, pressing against the
baggage-guard, was stopped by them and, while
checked, found themselves under enfilading fire of
two companies which Staveley had wheeled up against
their flank, and were severely punished.   The action
lasted from four o'clock in the afternoon until seven,
the Abyssinians returning again and again to the fight
and being very unwilling to confess themselves beaten.
Their casualties were reckoned at seven hundred killed
and thrice that number wounded.   Those of the British
did not exceed twenty wounded, of whom only two died.

Theodore had watched the fight from Fahla and had
been greatly dismayed by the rockets, which had killed
a horse close to him; but it was not until evening that
he realised the destruction of his army.   Soon after
dawn of the 11th he sent down two of his prisoners April 11.
with a message intimating his wish to be reconciled to
the British Government.   Napier, whose force had
halted for the night in its position, returned a courteous
answer, but insisted on submission.   Theodore at first
sent back an insulting rejoinder, and Napier trembled
for the fate of the prisoners; but the astute General had
been careful to show his Armstrong guns to the King's
emissary, and before evening most of the European
prisoners had been freed and had come into Napier's

camp.   On the 12th Theodore sent an apologetic
letter, released the rest of the prisoners and tendered a
peace-offering of cattle; but, finding that Napier would
not be satisfied without his personal surrender, he resolved to fight to the last.   Accordingly on the 13th,
Napier prepared to attack with his infantry and
artillery, having already sent off his cavalry to intercept
Theodore's retreat.   By half-past eight the artillery
was in position, and the infantry advanced with scaling-
ladders upon Fahla, but met with no resistance.
Selassie likewise was occupied without the firing of a
shot, the Abyssinians laying down their arms and moving away immediately when bidden.   There remained
Magdala, to which the approach was along one thousand yards of plateau from Selassie.   Above this plateau
the rock rose steeply to a height of three hundred feet,
seamed by a single narrow rugged path which led to a
strait gate in a double line of defences.   It was a for-
bidding-looking stronghold enough, if defended, and
Theodore actually moved a couple of guns down to the
plateau to check the British advance.   These were captured after a slight skirmish, and at 1 P.M. Napier opened
fire from his guns upon the gate.   There was no answering discharge from the Abyssinian cannon; and Staveley made his dispositions for an assault.   The Thirty-
third led the way under a continuous fire of musketry
from the walls, and, the gate having been built up,
there was some little delay until a point was found
where the wall was low enough to be escaladed.   Here
the stormers broke in and, taking the defenders of the
gate in flank, were soon masters of the fortress.   As
the entrance of the gate was carried, Theodore put the
muzzle of a pistol into his mouth, fired, and fell dead.
The casualties of the British were fifteen injured, most
of them so slightly that they would not acknowledge
themselves to be wounded.

Theodore's artillery was found to number thirty-
eight pieces, many of large calibre, and all, with one
exception, serviceable. The group of strongholds, Fahla,

Selassie and Magdala, was most formidable and, if 1868
resolutely defended, might have cost many lives to an
attacking force. Napier, therefore, was fully justified
in refusing to approach it without his battery of Armstrong guns and two heavy mortars, though the labour
of bringing them forward was, as has been seen, excessive. But Theodore had degenerated into a mere
debauchee and a fiend of cruelty. On their way from
Fahla to Magdala some troops passed at the foot of a
precipice a heap of mangled bodies, men, women and
children of the Gallas, who had been massacred and
cast out less than a fortnight before. He had at least
the pride and the dignity to take his own life rather than
surrender. Very wisely Napier appointed three officers
to hold a kind of inquest on the body of Theodore, so
as to establish the fact of his suicide beyond all cavil,
after which the body was decently, though without
military pomp, interred in the church of Magdala.

The occupation of Magdala was a matter of some
difficulty owing to the numbers of people within it, and
to the aggression of the Gallas, who not only sought
every opportunity to plunder and destroy their Christian
neighbours of Abyssinia, but were equally ready to rob
the followers of the British force—any man, indeed,
who was unarmed—and to carry off their mules. They
were, in fact, mere gangs of thieves, and were only
held under restraint by bullet and bayonet. But this
method of keeping the peace could not endure for long,
and Napier was greatly puzzled as to the disposal of
Magdala, for one powerful chief declined to have anything to do with it, and two rival queens of the Gallas
were quite ready to fight for it. He solved the problem by blowing up the fortifications and the guns on
the 17th, and on the 19th began his return march to April 19.
Zula.

Then all the tribes in Abyssinia showed themselves
in their true character. Christians and Mohammedans
alike hung about the flanks and rear of the columns,
making with increasing boldness attacks upon the

1868. muleteers and followers in hopes of plunder, and even
April– venturing sometimes to assail armed men.   They suc-
May. ceeded in slaying a few followers, but suffered themselves considerable loss in killed and wounded, and
paid dearly for such little spoil as they gained.   As a
matter of fact, the transport-animals were weak, for at
Magdala they had to travel to the Bashilo—eight miles
—for water; and the ground in and about the city was
littered with their corpses.   The retirement was, therefore, more trying even than the advance.   Not only
were the animals exhausted, but the men, overworked,
insufficiently fed and deprived of all stimulants for five
weeks past, began in the reaction after great strain to
break down.   Frequent storms of rain were added to
all other trials, and the rearguard was again and again
benighted.   When Dildi was reached, the troops
gained the comfort of the tents and clothing that had
been left there; but, on the other hand, these encumbrances now required to be carried back, and the mules
were dropping down with alarming rapidity.   Finally
May 2. at Marawah, on the 2nd of May, Lieutenant-colonel
Bray of the Fourth, a veteran of the Afghan campaign,
was placed permanently in command of the rear-guard.
He dealt with the situation ruthlessly, firing on all
marauders and destroying all loads thrown by exhausted
animals; and then the tribesmen, finding that there was
little to expect except a Snider bullet, became less
troublesome.   But no one could help reflecting that, if
the force had retreated after failure instead of after success, its fate would have been in the highest degree
precarious.

So the troops wended their dreary way back, the
garrisons of the various posts retiring before them.
On the 15th of May the rear, always accompanied by
Napier in person, evacuated Antalo, reaching Adigrat
on the 18th and Senafe on the 24th.   Here a review
was held on the 25th in presence of a friendly native
chief, to whom were made over as a gift the muskets of
two regiments of Indian infantry and vast quantities of

supplies and stores which had been accumulated in the 1868.
depôt. A quantity of reserve-ammunition, which May.
could not be carried away, was destroyed. The spring
rains, of extraordinary severity, made the retreat a
burden to the very end. The road in the Suru pass
was constantly damaged by floods during May, and on
the 19th a rise of water, so sudden that it baffled all
precautions for warning, swept away and drowned
seven camp-followers and some cattle. To the last,
too, the danger from marauders continued; an incautious
civilian, who had given much help to the Intelligence
Department, being murdered on the 28th of May in
the Kumayli pass. On the 29th the last of the troops
left Senafe; by the 1st of June all stations, except June.
Kumayli and Zula, had been evacuated; and on the 9th
only Zula was still occupied. Ever since the 11th of
May transports had been carrying troops back to India,
and on the 18th of June the last of them sailed from
Annesley Bay. The Abyssinian expedition was over.

Upon the whole this was perhaps the most difficult
and dangerous enterprise in which a British army was
ever engaged; and it is worth while to recapitulate the
conditions which made it so. In the first place the
base was on the scorching shore of the Red Sea, and
the objective four hundred miles away, approachable
only by the rudest tracks over rugged mountains that
rose to eleven thousand feet, and across chasms where
men and beasts could hardly keep their footing. It
was imperative to conduct the campaign in the dry
season, otherwise floods made the rivers and tracks
impassable. But this signified that there was no water
obtainable at the base, and but little even after holes had
been digged and wells had been sunk at the foot of the
mountain-ranges. Forage was everywhere very scarce,
and provisions were only occasionally procurable owing to
the poverty of the country and its desolation by intestine
war. At the base even water had to be supplied and,
practically from the base to the objective, the force had
to carry with it all food for man and beast and, as a

1868. first means to that end, to make tracks more or less into roads.   It was impossible to employ only a few troops, for the line of communication must be kept open; it was impossible to employ many because they would have starved.   Then, apart from all difficulties of food and water, a sickness, very fatal to horses and mules, was epidemic on the flat shore of the Red Sea. Lastly, the force must not only advance from its base to its objective but, which was equally difficult, to return from its objective to its base.

Yet the problem was solved, partly by the strong will of the commander, partly by the extraordinarily fine spirit shown by the troops, both British and native.   Never were men more severely worked nor subjected to greater privation and hardship; and it must be remembered that all exertion was the more exhausting to them owing to the rarefaction of the air on the upland.   Yet though heavily loaded and traversing terrible ground, they never failed and never complained, accepting cold, wet and hunger with equal cheerfulness.   Not upon even one single occasion did they take by force from the inhabitants one mouthful of food or forage.   Their discipline was as fine as their spirit, and both were wholly admirable. If any be singled out for special praise it must be the 10th Native Infantry, who were the first to land and wrestle with the fearful task of making roads through the Suru pass, and the handful of gunners who took the Armstrong battery to Magdala and back.   The task of these last was to load their guns and carriages on the elephants when it was impossible for the horses to draw them, and to unload them again when the road admitted wheeled traffic.   On the return journey there were only twenty-six men for twenty-nine elephants; and, as it required eighteen men to load or unload any one elephant, they were worn out with fatigue.   But they accomplished their task, though when they at last reached Zula, on the 28th of May, they had marched one hundred and seventy-seven miles over the mountains in thirteen days without a 1868. halt, and had not had a regular night's rest since the 23rd.   The Royal Regiment has never done finer service than this.[1]

Altogether there were landed in Annesley Bay, from first to last, nearly twelve thousand troops [2] of all branches of both armies; and though the admissions to hospital were many, especially on the flat land, there died of disease not more than forty-six British of all ranks, and two hundred and eighty-four Indian soldiers.   Looking to the extremely doubtful character of the water-supply at the outset, these figures do credit to the medical department, and testify to the excellence of the three hospital ships fitted out in England and sent thence to the Red Sea.   The animals fared worse.   At their greatest strength they amounted to nearly twenty-seven thousand in all—elephants, camels, mules, ponies and bullocks—and the tale of casualties amounted to close upon seven thousand. Much of this loss might have been avoided if the Land-Transport had been properly organised from the first; but the hard work in the mountains destroyed many mules; and even elephants fell exhausted on the return march, and were shot where they lay, as if they had been mules.   It remains only to mention the admirable work of the Royal Navy in the arduous and thankless business of loading and unloading transports and store-ships.   The senior naval officer was

---

[1] *Official History*, ii. 99-101.
[2] *Cavalry*:   3rd D.G. (203), 3rd Bombay L.C., 10th, 12th Bengal Cav., Sind Horse, 1735.

  Engineers: 10th co. R.E., 82; Indian Sappers and Miners, 807.

  Artillery: Batteries C-14, A-21, B-21, 5-25, 452; one Indian battery, 86; Naval Rocket battery, 100.

British Infantry: 4th, 26th, 33rd, 45th, 3027.
Indian Infantry: 3rd, 10th, 18th, 21st, 25th Bombay N.I., Punjab N.I., 23rd Punjab Pioneers, 27th Baluchis, 5469.

  Total, 11,961.

1868. Commodore Heath, but the man who was in charge of the shipping in Annesley Bay was the very able and indefatigable Captain George Tryon, who rose to be pre-eminent among British admirals of his time, and was drowned by the sinking of his flagship owing to a false signal of his own—a mystery which has never been explained.

For the rest the Abyssinian expedition marks an era in the history of the Army through the first appliance of certain mechanical and scientific discoveries to the business of war. The railway from Zula to Kumayli had been anticipated in the Crimea. The telegraph-line, though not what is now called a field-telegraph, was a novelty, as also was the employment of a small body of expert photographers. The corps of signallers marks the inception of a service in which the British seem always to have taken the lead. Lastly, the appearance of what may be called the first[1] British breech-loading rifle in the field, is a fact of significance. Napier, an engineer, was not the man to despise such improvements, though he had begun life amid flint-locks and smooth bores. This was his last campaign, which gained for him the title of Lord Napier of Magdala.

Authorities: The *Official History*, which is very full and crammed with detail, furnishes all that is necessary for a campaign in which the principal difficulty was not to beat the enemy but to reach him.

---

[1] Some of the Eighth Hussars had the Westley Richards carbine in the Indian Mutiny. In this weapon, however, the cap was not part of the cartridge, but required to be fixed on a nipple.

CHAPTER LVIII

ONCE again the scene is shifted to New Zealand, where 1860. many changes had been wrought since the first petty struggle with the Maoris. The white population had swelled to some eighty thousand, which were scattered about in six principal settlements, three in the South Island, and as many at Auckland, Wellington and Taranaki in the North Island. Each had its petty provincial legislature, and there was, moreover, a General Legislature, which in those days was assembled at Auckland. This latter met for the first time in May 1854, under a Constitution Act passed by the Imperial Parliament in 1852, and marked the intro-duction of what is called responsible government in the Colony. What appears to have been ill-defined in it was the assertion of the Crown's position, long upheld throughout the Empire, as the mediator between the British colonists and the original native inhabitants, the Maoris. Hitherto the Governor, as representative of the Crown, had held the balance between the two. Now the colonial ministers were disposed to claim that the Governor must act by their advice in native as in all other affairs. This was not unnatural. The first grant of self-government can hardly fail, especially if it be a novelty, to make some heads giddy in any com-munity, since it offers men, apart from the opportunity of hearing their own voices, the supreme prize of power. To the mediocre, who are least to be trusted with power, nothing is so galling as any limitation set upon it. If they have not wisdom, they have at least

1860. self-confidence, and if they lack sagacity they can make it good, as they suppose, with impatience. In New Zealand, moreover, there was an element of terror in the native question. The Maoris were not numerous, not exceeding fifty-six thousand in all, or at the extreme estimate twenty thousand fighting men; but practically all of them were in the North Island and in the centre of it, whereas the British settlements were dispersed around its fringes. They could thus act, strategically speaking, on interior lines and, though themselves also much scattered, could concentrate in a relatively short time a force strong enough to sweep away outlying settlers and annihilate their petty towns. Moreover, they were not fools but highly intelligent, and capable of rising, as many contended, to the level of the civilisation which the English had brought with them. Missionaries had long worked among them with striking success, and they had many friends, admirers and champions among the colonists themselves. But they had begun to realise that their country was likely to pass from them, and they had bethought them that they might unite and keep at any rate some part of it for themselves, governing it upon the English model. They would cease to fight each other, and would become one people, with their own king, their own assemblies and their own courts to deal with their own disputes. Eloquence had long been dear to them, adorned by a dignity of presence and a felicity of gesture which no Englishman could approach. As yet the "King-movement" (as it was called) was not fully developed, but it was alive and, though the colonists professed to despise it, none could wholly put it out of sight, while some certainly held it in dread. For the rest there was no lack of rogues both among colonists and Maoris. There were English who coveted the native land and looked upon the Maori owners as mere obstructions to their own greed; and there were low English scoundrels who lived among the Maoris, teaching them every kind of evil and making mischief impartially against all parties. There were 1860. likewise Maoris who welcomed these scoundrels, and would take any advantage of any shift that trickery and savagery might suggest, for their own profit. Lastly, the Maori, after his experience of past encounters with the English, had conceived a high opinion of the British soldier's valour but a very low estimate of his intelligence, and on the whole held him in decided contempt. He was not, therefore, without confidence in the result if events should at any time bring about an appeal to arms; and the colonists were quite aware of it.

The Governor, who after a brief interregnum took over the administration of New Zealand under the new order, was Colonel Gore-Browne, an officer who had served in the Afghan campaign of 1842, a good and conscientious man, but not one who could hold his own in the direction of native affairs as could his predecessor, Grey. In 1859 a dispute arose over the sale of certain land on the Waitara river, a little to north of New Plymouth, the principal settlement in Taranaki on the west coast of the North Island. One chief offered to sell it to the Government, chiefly, it should seem, with the object of annoying another chief who had rights over it. That other chief, Te Rangitake, not himself an estimable character, with perfect justice objected to the sale, vowed that he would never permit it and drove off the party that came to survey the land. Thereupon the Governor, on the 29th of January 1860, declared martial law in the province of Taranaki and declared that the survey should be made, if necessary, by force. He had passed by this time wholly into the hands of his ministers as regards Maori business; and it was a remarkable coincidence, though it may have been no more, that the minister for native affairs was member of Assembly for Taranaki, and that his constituents had openly advocated coercion to compel the Maoris to part with their land. Be that as it may—and the question is now of small importance

1860. —it is at least certain that the purchase of the land in question by the Government of New Zealand was a breach of faith and a wrongful act.

There were at that time about a thousand British troops in the Colony, namely, the Sixty-fifth and detachments of artillery and engineers. These, according to the pernicious practice of the place, were scattered over five different stations, Auckland in the north, where were the headquarters and four hundred men, Wellington in the south, Napier on the east coast, Wanganui and New Plymouth on the west. At New Plymouth, which was within twelve miles of the scene of action, there were slightly over two hundred men, and, since these were judged to be insufficient, Colonel Gold of the Sixty-fifth sailed from Auckland with a small reinforcement. Then landing at New Plymouth he took the field with something over four hundred of all ranks, a few rockets and two heavy howitzers. Te Rangitake had built a *pa*, or fortification, on the Mar. 6. disputed land. On the 6th of March the troops came up before it, and the Maori chief was bidden to destroy it, otherwise fire would be opened within twenty minutes. Thereupon he evacuated it, but on the 15th he built another *pa*, pulled up all the surveyors' pegs, retired within this stronghold and declined to receive a summons to surrender. Gold opened fire upon him with howitzers and rockets on the 17th, continued his Mar. 18. bombardment on the 18th and, advancing to the assault, found the *pa* empty. The works were none the less exceedingly strong, and the Governor, when he faced the facts, could not but feel ruefully ashamed. A fortification, thrown up in one night and garrisoned by only seventy Maoris, had kept four hundred men and artillery fully employed for two days; the bombardment had done little damage; and the Maoris had escaped with trifling loss.

The British had struck the first blow in the quarrel, and the Maoris naturally retaliated by killing some outlying settlers. This roused the people of New

Plymouth. The local militia and volunteers, some of
the Sixty-fifth, and a party of bluejackets and marines,
landed from H.M. ship *Niger*, sallied forth; and after
some confused skirmishing, the bluejackets, under
cover of dusk, stormed a *pa*, inflicting on the Maoris a
loss of some thirty killed.   This trifling encounter
took place on the 30th of March, after which all operations, excepting small raids for the destruction of crops,
were suspended pending the arrival of reinforcements,
which had been urgently requested from Australia.
By the end of April detachments of the Twelfth and
Fortieth, with a few artillery, together about six hundred strong, had landed at New Plymouth, and were
moved up to an entrenched camp formed by Colonel
Gold at the mouth of the Waitara river.   Within
sight of it was a double *pa*, each with its defences of
ditches, stockades and rifle-pits, the whole known by
the name of Puke Tauere.   The position had, as usual,
been chosen with admirable skill, on a ridge encom-
passed by deep gullies full of brambles and thick, tall
bracken;[1] but, in spite of all past warnings, Captain
Seymour[2] of the Royal Navy, who commanded a
small naval brigade, and Major Nelson of the Fortieth,
determined to attack. On the 27th of June accordingly
they opened a preliminary bombardment with two
heavy howitzers, and then launched three hundred and
fifty men in three small columns at different points of
the *pa*. The Maoris could have desired nothing better.
In addition to all other difficulties the soil was heavy
clay and soaked with rain, and the troops had not a
chance from the first.   They were beaten back, leaving

---

[1] The New Zealand bracken is rather finer, but tougher and more
wiry than the English, and, growing taller than the height of a man's
head, makes good cover for a defender and a most wearying obstacle
to an attacker. The New Zealand bramble is far more formidable
than the English, its thorns being hooked, so that a man cannot tear
his way through them. Thousands of sheep have perished by becoming
entangled in them.

[2] Beauchamp Seymour, later Lord Alcester, nicknamed " The Swell
of the Ocean."

1860.
June 27.

on the field some of their wounded, who were promptly despatched by the Maoris, and retired with a total loss of thirty killed and thirty-four wounded, five-sixths of the casualties falling upon the Fortieth. The whole proceeding was one of almost criminal folly. The Maoris were naturally much elated. Tribes which were wavering took courage to join the fighting party; and marauding bands burned and destroyed the settlers' houses in all directions, venturing even up to the outskirts of New Plymouth.

Upon hearing of this mishap Major-general Pratt, who commanded in Australia, determined to assume the direction of the operations himself. Landing at

Aug. 3.

New Plymouth on the 3rd of August he found that he had a force, on paper, of about three thousand five hundred of all ranks, including sick. Of these, however, nearly nine hundred were militia or volunteers who, though ill-armed and undisciplined, might be counted on for defence of New Plymouth but, constituting in fact the male population of the town, could not spare above a tenth of their number for service in the field. As to the theatre of operations, the first drawback was that the coast was most dangerous. There was no safe harbour on the whole of the western seaboard; [1] gales were frequent; and a nasty surf made landing at the best of times difficult and hazardous. No sailing ship would ever stay off New Plymouth a moment longer than she could help, and even steamers were constantly obliged to put to sea and remain at sea for days together. Next, the country near the coast was seamed by the network of ravines which carry off the melting snow and the heavy rain from Mount Egmont, [2] and which were sometimes dry and smothered in fern and brambles, and at other times rushing torrents. Even this difficult tract was but a belt running inland for

[1] All the good harbours in the whole of New Zealand are on the east coast. Those on the west coast have at the best bad bars.
[2] Mount Egmont, a most beautiful volcanic cone abutting on the sea, is over 8000 feet high.

three or four miles, when it gave place to a continuous 1860.
mass of forest, penetrable only by Maoris. Information respecting the enemy's movements was practically
not to be obtained. A missionary had made his way to
a *pa* in the forest, and his report showed that it was inaccessible and unassailable. Lastly, the inhabitants of
New Plymouth were alike helpless, obstructive and
self-seeking. Though the little town was overcrowded
by refugees, they would not take the most elementary
sanitary precautions, and made great difficulties over
the removal of women and children to a place of safety.
They objected to the contraction of their line of defence, and persisted in straying beyond it; but, while
looking always to the regular troops for protection and
welcoming their arrival for the money that they brought
with them, they were quite sure that they understood
how to carry on a Maori war better than they. The
General, fully appreciating the value of local knowledge, gave one ambitious party of volunteers permission to carry on operations on their own account and
in their own way; but when it came to the point, the
men did not approve the plans of their officers, and
the enterprise came to naught. All this was characteristically English, but it did not endear the settlers
to their compatriots who wore the Queen's uniform.[1]

Having dealt with New Plymouth as best he could,
Pratt paid a short visit to Auckland, where the Governor
pressed him to wipe out the reverse at Puke Tauere as
soon as possible by a decided success. This was not
so easy, for the enemy must be found before they could
be beaten. Of course the Maoris built *pas* in abundance, but these had no strategic purpose whatever
either for them or for the British. Their only object
was to keep hostilities as remote from the Maori homes
and crops as possible; and in fact they were so many
red rags flaunted in the face of any military bull that
might be foolish enough to rush at them. They were
always placed in the strongest possible position from

[1] Carey, pp. 71-84.

1860. which retreat could be secured; and it was almost impracticable to surround them, for a naked Maori could creep away through ravine and fern under the very nose of a British soldier.   On the other hand, they were practically the only place in which a Maori force might be found; and the only expedient was to drive the Maoris from them, with greater loss to the defence than to the attack, if possible, and to force them back thus from *pa* to *pa* into the forest.   The Maoris were quite content to evacuate them if they had inflicted heavy loss on a blundering assailant, but it was no part of their tactics to yield them up not only without exacting toll of lives from their enemy, but possibly paying the cost of that toll themselves.

Before Pratt returned from Auckland the Maoris had quitted the Puke Tauere *pa*, wherefore, having called in many useless outlying posts, he prepared to seek them

Sept. 8. elsewhere.   Not until the 8th of September did he gain intelligence of Maoris assembled in three *pas* on the south bank of the Waitara about seven miles from its mouth, when he set a thousand men in motion against them in three columns.   The march lay over most difficult ground where a really enterprising enemy might have given much trouble; but such was not the way of the Maoris.   They lay fast in their entrenchments while the columns were reaching their appointed places, and then, after a trifling skirmish, withdrew into the forest, whither Pratt was too wise to follow them. Leaving his fortified posts in the valley of the Waitara, he turned next, by wish of the Government, to another group of three *pas* on the Kahihi river.   Arrived within reach of them he, on the 11th of October, opened a trench within two hundred and fifty yards of the nearest of them under cover of a flying sap, and dug his way methodically towards it, while an eight-inch gun, brought up by the naval brigade, maintained a steady bombardment.   The Maoris kept up a constant and well-aimed fire against the sap, but did little damage; and after twenty-four hours, observing the trench to be

close to their outer stockade, they evacuated all three 1860.
pas and retired, abandoning a considerable quantity of Oct.
provisions.   Pools of blood showed that they had
suffered some loss, though probably their casualties
did not greatly exceed those of the British, which
numbered only five.   But they had been compelled
to withdraw from laboriously built strongholds without
inflicting greater loss than they had suffered; and in
their eyes this signified failure.   It was found that
many hours' bombardment had failed to make a practicable breach, the palisades of the stockade being
bound together by supplejacks, which kept the fragments of timber swinging, so that Pratt was wise not
to attempt an assault.   The local politicians in Auckland
sneered because he had suffered the garrison to escape,
but how any commander was to prevent a few hundred
naked savages from slipping away singly at night through
a wilderness of ravines, bracken and brushwood, they did
not explain.   Such idle prattle would be unworthy of
notice but that it increased the bitter feeling of the
British soldiers against the British settlers, thereby
causing mischief in the present, and laying up more
trouble for the future.[1]

Further prosecution of operations to south of New
Plymouth was arrested by intelligence that the
Waikato tribes, the finest of all the Maoris, who
occupied most of the space between Auckland and ·
New Plymouth, were moving southward upon the
Waitara river.   Pratt, therefore, moved thither, converted the captured *pa* at Puke Tauere into a fortified
post, established a signalling station there, and prepared
to convert another abandoned *pa* at Mahoetahi into an
intermediate post between it and New Plymouth.   To
his astonishment he learned early in November that
the Waikatos, supposed to be seventeen hundred strong,
had actually anticipated him in the occupation of
Mahoetahi; and he laid his plans to move upon it with
two columns simultaneously from the Waitara in the

[1] Carey, pp. 116-118.

1860.
Nov.
north and from New Plymouth in the south. He himself took command of the latter column, which was rather more than six hundred strong, and Colonel Mould of the Engineers of the former, which numbered rather less than three hundred. Both were composed principally of detachments of the Twelfth, Fortieth

Nov. 6.
and Sixty-fifth; and both marched at dawn of the 6th of November. Pratt, having only eight miles of good road to traverse, was the first to arrive, Mould having to make his way through four miles of thicket and ravine. The site of the *pa* was strong, but its defences were out of repair; yet the Maoris made no attempt to resist Pratt's advance over the very difficult ground by which it was approached. At eight o'clock Pratt's heavy howitzers opened fire, and presently the troops attacked. They entered the *pa* with little difficulty, but the Maoris fought hard in the swamp and thicket at its foot, unseen themselves and betraying their presence only by puffs of smoke. At last they gave way and were hunted for three miles into the forest, leaving forty-nine dead behind them, and a number of good double-barrelled guns and rifles. Their total loss was reckoned at about one hundred, whereas that of the British amounted only to nineteen killed and wounded.

Trifling as the affair sounds, it was the most important success thitherto gained by the British against the Maoris. The Waikatos, magnificent fighting men, had come down boasting of the great things that they would do, yet within twelve hours of their arrival they had been beaten, and many notable chiefs among them had fallen. But Pratt was not allowed to follow up his success. Reports reached the Governor that the tribes about the Waikato district were marching upon Auckland to take their revenge, and Pratt was ordered to bring back troops for the defence of the capital. The few hundred men that he could spare after providing garrisons for his posts in Taranaki were therefore embarked on a steam-sloop, which had been lent from Australia, and were carried up to Manukau, which may

be described as the western port of Auckland. And, 1860.
though this may sound a small matter, let it be re- Nov.
membered that the troops had to embark through surf,
that they must have been much overcrowded, that the
passage, though not above one hundred and fifty miles,
probably occupied the best part of twenty-four hours
and that it was almost certainly a rough one.[1] Then,
after they had disembarked, the alarm proved to be
false; and, five companies of the Fourteenth having
arrived at Auckland from Cork on the 29th of November, the detachments were sent back over the same
rough sea to New Plymouth. Pratt thereupon fixed Dec.
upon the Waitara as the base of his future operations,
and there concentrated twelve hundred men, all of them
regular troops; for the Taranaki militia and volunteers,
though called upon for further service in the field, preferred, for their own reasons, to stay at home. This
was a pity, for five or six score of them had shared in
the attack on Mahoetahi and had done well; and their
evasion did not pass unnoticed by the regular troops.

The Maoris were known to be in some force in a
group of three *pas* about five miles up the Waitara from
the river's mouth, and to be building a fourth post,
named Matarorikoriko, in advance of them. Leaving
three hundred men to hold his base, Pratt moved
forward early on the 29th of December with the Dec. 29.
remainder to within eight hundred yards of Matarorikoriko, threw up a redoubt, left a garrison of half his
force there and returned with the rest to camp. The
Maoris, unseen in their rifle-pits, kept up a heavy
fire on the working parties all day and crept up to the
ditch of it during the night, but would not venture to
attack. On the next day, being Sunday, they hoisted Dec. 30.
a white flag to indicate that fighting would cease until

---

[1] During a four years' residence in New Zealand I made many
passages about the New Zealand coast—perhaps thirty—but I remember only one that can be called smooth, and even then there was
sea-sickness aboard. Manukau has a nasty bar, where H.M.S. *Orpheus*
was wrecked with heavy loss of life in these very years.

1860. Monday, and in the night evacuated the *pa* in haste. Since they left twelve buried corpses behind them, it was reckoned that their loss must have exceeded Pratt's, which was three killed and twenty-two wounded. They had, however, only retired to other *pas* a little way in rear, about Huirangi on the edge of the forest. The position was exceedingly strong. Its right rested on the Waitara river; its centre was covered by marshes and an impassable ravine; and there was for fifteen hundred yards along the length of the forest one continuous chain of rifle-pits. The remainder of the Fourteenth having by this time reached Auckland, Pratt

1861. had now fifteen hundred men at his disposal; and on
Jan. 14. the 14th of January 1861 he commenced his operations by throwing up a second small redoubt six hundred yards in advance of that already built before Matarorikoriko. On the next day he began to build another and larger redoubt, Number Three, five hundred yards closer to the Maori position, keeping down their fire
Jan. 20. by steady bombardment of the forest. By the 20th Number Three, large enough to hold four hundred
Jan. 22. and fifty men, was completed; and on the 22nd the garrison began to sap forward to the site of yet another redoubt within the forest. This was more than the
Jan. 23. Maoris could endure, and at dawn of the 23rd they made a furious attack upon Number Three. Their plan of action was good. The assaulting force crept into the ditch unperceived in the dark; sharpshooters were posted all round to keep down the British fire; and with the first shots the stormers dashed up the sides of the parapets, even seizing the bayonets of the men within and trying to wrest them away. So determined was their onslaught that the commanding officer signalled for help to Number One redoubt, when two companies came up and, charging the Maoris in flank, drove them from the ditch. Then the assailants broke and fled, the British chasing them back to the forest. Pratt's loss in this little affair was sixteen killed and wounded. That of the Maoris was never

ascertained, but they left behind them thirty-four 1861.
killed and six wounded; and more dead bodies, buried
and unburied, were found as the British advanced, so
that there cannot have fallen fewer than one hundred.

On the 24th the sap was resumed under heavy fire; Jan. 24.
and other Maori tribes now threatened attack south of
New Plymouth to make a diversion. But Pratt was
not to be turned from his purpose. Steadily he dug
his way on, throwing up Redoubt Number Four on the
27th, Redoubt Number Five on the 29th, and Redoubt
Number Six, level with the first line of the enemy's
rifle-pits, on the 3rd of February. As he advanced, Feb. 3.
the Maoris retired, until they were driven to the rearmost of their group of *pas*, Pukerangioria. They had,
however, taken care to honeycomb the intervening
space with rifle-pits, and Pratt's next movement was
more difficult. On the 10th of February he turned out Feb. 10.
every man that he could, some nine hundred in all, and
moved through a bewildering sea of bracken and
bramble, ridge and ravine, to within eight hundred
yards of the enemy's position. There skirmishers
were thrown out to keep down the incessant fire of
unseen Maori sharpshooters, while the rest worked
strenuously to complete Redoubt Number Seven before dark. The work was done and the garrison was
installed at a cost of twelve casualties. Some of the
smaller redoubts in rear were evacuated, Pratt's numbers being very small, and on the 14th the work of
sapping forward began. On the night of the 26th the Feb. 26.
Maoris, eluding the vigilance of the sentries, stole up
in the darkness and destroyed a portion of the works;
after which a live shell was attached to the sap-roller
at the head of the sap, with a contrivance to make it
explode if the roller were moved. But the work was
steadily pursued in spite of incessant petty attacks;
Redoubt Number Eight arose within two hundred
yards of the *pa*, and the sap was pushed forward in-
exorably. On the 11th of March a leading Maori chief Mar. 11.
sent a message to Pratt asking for a truce that he might

1861. consult his peers with a view to peace.   Armstrong
guns had just arrived in Auckland, and Pratt willingly
granted a cessation of hostilities until the 14th.   By
that day the guns had arrived and had been placed in
position and, as the negotiations had made no progress,
Pratt resumed his operations.   On the night of the
16th the Maoris again tried to destroy part of the sap,
with the result that three of them were blown to pieces;
Mar. 19. and on the 19th hostilities came to an end pending the
conclusion of peace.   On the 31st Lieutenant-general
Duncan Cameron arrived from England to assume
chief command, and Pratt returned to Australia, having
finished his work.

Petty in scale though his operations were, they are
not without interest as a study of savage warfare.   The
Maoris erected their *pas* upon much the same principle
as the Gurkhas made their stockades.   They lacked,
it is true, the keener tactical intelligence of the Gurkhas,
but in both the dominant motive was the same, to provoke an attack which must cost the assailant dear in any
case and would not profit him greatly even if successful.
Then the problem arose how to turn the tables upon
them and force them to attack instead of waiting to be
attacked.   In Nipal this was accomplished principally
by outdoing the Gurkhas in the seizure of tactical
positions; in New Zealand by sapping the way up to
the *pas* of the Maoris and compelling them either to
attack the sapping parties, or to abandon their stronghold without exacting the loss which they considered a
fair price for it.   The truth is that the Maoris were as yet
pedants in the matter of warfare.   They had no ideas
beyond digging themselves into a strong position, stay-
ing there until seriously threatened, and then dispersing
to reassemble again.   Had they really understood their
business they might have harassed the British to death
in nearly every march that they made, firing into the
column from all sides, under shelter of scrub and fern,
in which they could move like their own wingless birds,
invisible and undiscoverable.   There were hundreds

of places àt the crossing of ravines and of streams where 1861. they could have arrested advance for an hour or many hours and worn the troops out with bewilderment and fatigue, for the sun is hot in the north island of New Zealand.[1]   But beyond the occasional cutting off of unwary stragglers they attempted nothing of the kind; and Pratt, by following a sound and simple principle, easily got the better of them.   That principle was, broadly speaking, never to do what he knew his enemy wanted him to do, which had long been honoured in India by the simple rule of never making a frontal attack upon a native enemy.   But Pratt was the first commander who applied it to the Maoris; and if it be objected that this was, after all, only common sense, he deserves the greater credit for it.   For the rest, the operations were excellent training for the troops.   The erection of the redoubts signified a daily skirmish from dawn until dark, exercising the men well in vigilance, in the use of their eyes, ears and brains, in woodcraft, marksmanship and work with the spade.

The casualties of the British in this little campaign of Taranaki were two hundred and eleven.   To these the Taranaki militia added twenty-seven, many of them incurred through straggling, in defiance of all orders, beyond the zone of safety about New Plymouth.   There were fine fellows among them, but the settlers in general —and the militia were only armed settlers—did not commend themselves to the troops, nor the troops to the settlers.   Disciplined and undisciplined men, among the British at any rate, are inclined to feel a certain contempt for each other, and this tendency is strongest where soldiers from an old country and colonists in a new country are thrown together.   The colonist has crossed the sea generally to escape the trammels of an old society; or, if he has not, he quickly becomes conscious that he has escaped them.   He is independent and self-helpful; he acknowledges no

---

[1] The winter months of England are, of course, the summer months of New Zealand, January corresponding with July.

1861. superior and takes no orders from anyone; and though on good terms with his neighbours, and, in case of misfortune, ready to give his utmost help to them, he works chiefly for himself. Cut off from the comforts of the old country, he not only dispenses with them cheerfully but frequently affects a roughness that is excessive. With no one to criticise his habits or appearance, he is apt to become slovenly and untidy, sometimes even dirty, both in his person and in his dwelling. Above all he is firmly convinced of the fallacy, so dear to the mediocre, that one man is as good as another, and, lest he should be thought subservient, often loses hold of the habit of courtesy. To such a man the soldier of 1860 presented little that was attractive. He seemed, not without reason at first, a helpless creature without initiative and unable to do the least thing without orders. He had, it is true, discarded the scarlet tunic and the shako for a blue serge jumper worn over his belts, and a forage-cap;[1] but none the less, his neat appearance, the rigidity of his movements, above all his obedient bearing and his practice of saluting his officers, jarred upon the notions of the free and independent settlers. They could not endure the recognition of one man as superior to another, and deliberately slighted all requests of military officers, not because these requests were unreasonable, but because they themselves delighted to disobey.

The soldiers, on the other hand, were not favourably impressed by the settlers, not least because their own discipline had taught them to work each man not for himself but for all. They could not but contrast their own method and order with the confusion that prevailed among the colonists at New Plymouth, the cleanliness and healthiness of their own quarters with the foulness and filth of the township, where fever and diphtheria were rampant because, in defiance of all warnings, the settlers and refugees refused to recognise or observe any sanitary regulations. They, the soldiers,

[1] Carey, p. 95.

had been trained above all things to work as a team; 1861. but nothing could induce these settlers to make any sacrifice for their common good. The soldiers again had a suspicion that the settlers, despite of all their grumbling, intended many of them to make money out of the war, and were not ill content to see it continue. Another cause of difference, as the operations progressed, was the estimation in which settlers and soldiers held the Maoris. To the settlers the Maoris were mere noxious pests, who had ruined the homesteads of many and had done to death not a few. They maltreated them, when they found opportunity, and yet they feared them. The soldiers, on the other hand, respected the Maoris, despite of occasional outbursts of savagery, as a most gallant and even chivalrous foe. They tended their wounded as carefully as their own stricken comrades; they buried their dead with decency and fenced in their graves; above all they sent strong escorts to guard prisoners against insult and attack from the settlers. That the rank and file troubled themselves greatly about the cause of the quarrel is unlikely; their business was to obey orders. But it would have been strange if some of the officers had not suspected, rightly or wrongly, that greed of Maori land was at the bottom of the whole dispute, and that they and their men were being used as instruments in a contest which had been precipitated, not by Maori aggression but by unjust dealing on the part of the New Zealand Government.[1]

Both sides, no doubt, could adduce arguments to support their own contention; and it is not the present writer's desire to reopen bitter controversies which are best forgotten, nor to decide between the contending parties. Still there remains the fact, which cannot be passed over, that bitter feeling arose early between the troops and the settlers, and that it grew continually until it overtook the highest authorities, both civil and military, and affected seriously not only the operations

[1] For the last two paragraphs see Carey, pp. 71-80, 86, 189.

1861. in the field but even high questions of imperial policy.

The truce that had been patched up over the land at the Waitara was but hollow. Governor Gore-Browne and his advisers, indeed, were for treating it but as an incident, and for meting out summary punishment to the Waikato tribes, who had dared to intervene in a quarrel which was not their own. The Fifty-seventh and the Seventieth had reached Auckland from India, the former in January, the latter in May 1861, so that he had now six British battalions at his disposal; and the opportunity may have seemed to him propitious for the settlement of differences with the Maoris once for all. He was, however, recalled before he could carry out his intention, and was succeeded in September by Sir George Grey, who had administered the government of New Zealand already with signal success.

Grey, who had much influence with the Maoris, reversed his predecessor's policy, preferring one of conciliation; but the Waikatos held aloof. The wrong done at Waitara rankled deeply in their minds, and its general effect had been to strengthen the movement in favour of a Maori king. Grey was in a difficult position. The House of Assembly had, in June 1861, passed a resolution condemning the establishment of any authority in New Zealand independent of the British Crown, which defined pretty clearly their attitude toward the " King-movement." Grey undoubtedly wished to preserve peace, but he not unreasonably wished also to be prepared for war; and he set the troops to work at the construction of a road due south from Auckland to the Waikato river. This increased the suspicions of the Maoris. A proposal to introduce a steamer upon the Waikato was also deeply resented. Grey, however, after looking into the question of the land at Waitara, which had been the cause of war in 1860, decided that the New Zealand Government had been wrong, that an injustice had been committed and

that the land should be restored. His ministers, after 1863.
a fortnight's delay, signified their agreement with him,
but it was then too late. The misgivings of the Maoris
had been quickened by the military reoccupation of
other land, called the Tataraimaka block, near New
Plymouth, which had been rightfully purchased but
temporarily abandoned. Remembering the occur-
rences at the Waitara, they thought that they saw a
cunning design of the British to take their land piece-
meal. On the 4th of May 1863, the very day before May.
Grey's ministers consented to give back the land at
Waitara, a party of two officers and six men of the
Fifty-seventh, who were moving in the routine of
peaceful business to Taranaki, was fired upon from an
ambush and every one of them was killed. The concession of the 5th of May was naturally ascribed by
the Maoris to the terror inspired by their attack on the
4th. There could be little doubt but that war must
follow, and Grey wrote home begging for reinforcements.

Meanwhile the British Government had been growing dissatisfied with the progress of affairs in New
Zealand. They could not have been ignorant that the
justice of the British aggression in 1860 was questionable, nor could they have failed to learn from private
letters that some at least of the officers thought of themselves and their troops as mere catspaws used by
settlers to pull Maori land out of the fire. General
Cameron also reported that the Colonial local forces
were not playing their due part, being neither organised nor equipped.[1] Thereupon the Colonial Office
wrote sharply that, unless these defects were speedily
remedied, the greater number of the troops would be
withdrawn. As it happened, the discovery of gold in
1861 had attracted numbers of emigrants from Australia
and other quarters to New Zealand; and the white
population actually doubled itself between December
1860 and December 1863. It is true that many of

[1] Rusden, ii. 192.

1863. these newcomers were of the restless and unprofitable type which rushes headlong from place to place in the passion to grow rich quickly; it is true also that most of them were attracted to Otago, in the south of the South Island, and knew or cared as little concerning Maori wars about Auckland, six hundred miles away, as concerning the raids of the Hindustani fanatics in the Ambela valley. Yet none the less the Imperial Government might urge with some force that one hundred and sixty thousand colonists should need little help in dealing with a few thousand hostile savages, and that, if the mother-country provided men to fight New Zealand's battles, she had a right to a voice in the conduct of native affairs. It seemed not quite reasonable that the Colony should pick the quarrel and that England should bear the brunt of it. However, though the British Government had none too many regiments at disposal after the recent troubles in India, they had already ordered the Eighteenth to embark for New Zealand in April 1863, and, as events were to show, did not prove themselves inexorable to Grey's further appeal.

The main difficulty in the coming contest, as in the war of 1860, was that the Maoris from their central position could strike out in any direction, and that Cameron was therefore obliged to divide his force. There was little danger in the south towards Wellington; but eastward towards Hawke's Bay, westward and south-westward towards Taranaki and Wanganui, and above all northward towards Auckland, attack might with reason be apprehended. The British battalions had been weakened by sickness; and yet Cameron was obliged to keep a thousand men on the west coast, over five hundred more divided between the east coast and Wellington, and actually one hundred in remote Otago to preserve order among the gold-diggers. The Colonial authorities, however, now took their local forces more seriously in hand, and before autumn had raised in the North Island close upon ten thousand militia and volunteers, nearly a third of them 1863. in and about Auckland. For the rest, the New Zealand Government, in the course of 1863, committed itself to the dangerous principle of confiscating the land of Maoris who had risen in insurrection and offering it as a reward to volunteers, militia and others who should undertake military service against them. Over two thousand men were thus raised in Australia.[1] Grey had evidently in his mind the military settlements which had been formed in South Africa as a bulwark against the Kaffirs; and, regarded as a mere question of local defence, the principle was sound enough. On the other hand, the war which had just broken out was the result of the forced purchase of the Maori land at Waitara in 1860, which had now been acknowledged to be wrongful. The justice, therefore, of punishing the Maoris for distrusting and resisting further extension of British authority over themselves was at least questionable; and, even if this difficulty could be set aside, the expediency of such a course was more questionable still. The Maoris were a fighting race; and, being threatened with the loss of their land in any case, those who took up arms were likely, having nothing more to lose thereby, to fight desperately to the end.

Meanwhile there had been constant bickerings between the British and the Maoris on the Tataraimaka block; and on the 4th of June, under cover of the fire June 4. of a man-of-war and a battery of Armstrong guns, Cameron attacked their principal stronghold on the Katikara river. After a stout resistance it was carried with the bayonet, the loss of the Maoris being relatively heavy and that of the British trifling.[2] This done, Cameron withdrew the troops from the Tataraimaka block and embarked with most of them for Auckland. The main scene of operations would ultimately be the

[1] Rusden, ii. 230, 248, 254.
[2] 800 men of the 57th, 65th and 70th were engaged. The casualties were 12.

1863. Waikato, forty miles to south of Auckland, towards which river Grey, as has been told, had already completed his military road, with a chain of posts for its protection.   Cameron took the first step on the 12th of July 1863 by crossing the creek, which formed the boundary between the Imperial troops to north and the Maori insurgents to south, with four hundred men. These he established in a redoubt on the Koheroa hills, at a point close to the great curve where the Waikato river alters its course from north to west, and overlooking the stream itself.   Then he bent himself to the accumulation of supplies, all of which were brought overland for want, as yet, of the necessary ships to carry them from Manukau to the Waikato river.   The Maoris, meanwhile, forsook their usual tactics and advanced northward, constantly attacking convoys and harassing his line of communications.   A number of petty encounters inevitably followed during the next three months, with disadvantage to the Maoris; and

Oct. at the end of October Cameron, having at last two small steamers at disposal, took the offensive.   The Maoris were assembled in a strongly fortified position within three miles of Cameron's most advanced post, but they evacuated it before he could develop his attack, and retired twelve miles further up the Waikato to Rangiriri.   Here they threw up very strong entrenchments, the main line of them being traced across an isthmus which divided Lake Waikare from the river, with a square earthwork within for citadel.   Cameron, who had with him thirteen hundred men, laid his plans to attack with eight hundred of these and to intercept retreat with the remainder.

Oct. 19.   After a long and heavy bombardment from gunboats and Armstrong field-guns, Cameron ordered the assault; and the outer works were carried despite of a sharp resistance.   But the central redoubt, which had a ditch twelve feet wide and a parapet eighteen feet high, defied two separate attacks by seamen and artillery men armed with revolvers.   Many fell,

among them Captain Mercer of the Artillery, who 1863.
lay mortally stricken exposed to the fire both of Oct. 19.
British and Maoris, until one of the hostile Maori
chiefs, Te Oriori, with magnificent courage and
chivalry, leaped down and carried him to a place of
safety.   While doing so Te Oriori received a wound,
which the more commended him to the enthusiastic
admiration of his foes.   Since the day was far spent
and the enemy was almost completely surrounded,
Cameron decided to throw away no more lives, but to
sap up to the parapet during the night and to blow it
up.   At dawn next day a Maori came forward with a Oct. 20.
white flag, and the soldiers sprang forward to shake
hands with the brave men who had so gallantly repelled them.   Cameron likewise addressed them with
sympathy and appreciation, promised them good
treatment while with him, and entreated the Colonial
authorities to be generous with them all, and particularly with Te Oriori.   In truth the Maoris had
suffered heavily.   Thirty-six dead only were found
within the *pa*, and, since the wounded had been removed, some of the defenders had certainly escaped.
But several had been shot or drowned while swimming
across the swamps in rear of the position, and the
prisoners numbered one hundred and eighty-three.
It was the heaviest blow that the Maoris had ever
suffered.   Of the British forty, including five officers,
were killed or mortally hurt, and ninety-five were
wounded, most of which loss might have been saved by
abstaining from the unnecessary assault of the central
redoubt.

The Maoris were not a little discouraged by this
action, the effect of which was the greater since it
followed closely upon their failure to interrupt
Cameron's communications.   To neutralise their efforts
in this latter direction Cameron had, in November, Nov.
detached a small force to throw up a chain of posts
between the estuary of the Thames and the Waikato,
thus drawing a defensive line across the island from

1863. east to west, with stations that permitted the rapid
transmission of signals from end to end of it.   Ad-
Dec. vancing on the 8th of December he occupied Ngaru-
wahia, the nominal capital of the Maori king, at the
junction of the Waipa and Waikato rivers, and there
1864. halted until the 24th of January 1864, to replenish
supplies.   By this time, in addition to the Eighteenth,
which arrived in July, there had joined him also the
Forty-third and the Fiftieth from India; but the Maoris
were not yet beaten, and withdrew forty miles up the
Waipa to Paterangi, where they threw up four or five
pas of great strength.   Cameron followed them, but
found the works at Paterangi so formidable that, having
tried to no purpose the effect of bombardment, he
decided not to assault.   After a successful skirmish,
Feb. 11. brought on by accident, on the 11th of February, he
left six hundred men before Paterangi and, making a
flanking movement, pushed on to Rangiaohia, where the
Maoris had established a depôt of provisions.   This
Feb. 21. was taken with little difficulty, and the Maoris thereupon withdrew from Paterangi and began to entrench
themselves near Rangiaohia.   Before they could en-
Feb. 22. sconce themselves, Cameron attacked them on the 22nd
and, despite of a sharp resistance, drove them south-
eastward towards Mauntatari with a loss of forty
killed.   The two actions had not cost the British[1]
thirty casualties.

The Waikato tribes were by this time almost at
their last gasp, and Cameron, gathering that they would
make their final stand in the Mauntatari range, shifted
his headquarters eastward to a point near the site of
the modern Cambridge, for the convenience of obtaining supplies up the stream of the Waikato.   A strong
detachment under Colonel Carey was left at Te
Awamutu, meanwhile, to cover the ground—rich open
country—already mastered.   By the merest chance a
band of roving Maoris decided for sentimental reasons
to throw up a *pa* at Orakau, three miles to south-east

[1] Detachments of 50th, 65th and 70th.

of Te Awamutu. A party of colonial troops, which 1864.
had stumbled against them, brought information of March.
this on the 30th of March to Carey, who decided to
surround the position before it could be strongly
fortified. He therefore set about eight hundred
regular troops of the Fortieth and Sixty-fifth and about
five hundred militia in motion to close in upon Orakau
from three sides; and by dawn of the 31st of March Mar. 31.
the whole were in position around it. The Maoris,
however, had already made their entrenchments
very strong, and had contrived an ingenious defence
against the round shot of Carey's heavy gun, in the
shape of huge bundles of fern bound with flax. Three
attempts to assault having been repulsed, Carey,
knowing that the Maoris had little food and no water,
decided to proceed by way of sapping, and called up
additional troops to make his encompassing cordon
the surer.

So matters went on until the 2nd of April, when April 2.
hand-grenades thrown from the sap wrought havoc
in the Maori rifle-pits, and an Armstrong gun made
two breaches in the defences. Carey sent in a messenger promising to spare the lives of the defenders
if they would surrender. They answered that they
would fight for ever. They were urged to send out
their women and children; they answered that the
women would fight too. Very reluctantly Carey
ordered an assault, and the outer works were carried;
but the stormers, who had already lost heavily, recoiled
before the fire of the inner entrenchment. Unwilling
to sacrifice more lives, Carey was debating what he
should do next when the Maoris resolved his doubts
for him. Finding that his ammunition was almost
spent, their chief, Rewi, formed the survivors into a
solid column and started in broad daylight to fight his
way out. To make a diversion, another chief coolly
walked out and surrendered. No one seems to know
exactly what occurred, for the investing cordon, at the
point where the Maoris broke out, was supposed to be

1864.
April 2.
safely closed by two lines of the Fortieth. One story is that the Maoris made a rush and jumped over these two lines. Another account is that at one point the Fortieth had been thrown back right and left to make space for the Armstrong gun, and that the Maoris made for the gap. However that may be, it seems that the sheer audacity of the movement prevented its purport from being immediately realised. Then troops were hurried forward to fire into both flanks of the column, and a small body of cavalry was ordered to head them off; but from one-third to one-half of the Maoris made good their escape to a stronghold forty miles up the Waipa. It seems that the original garrison numbered about three hundred fighting men; and Cameron, who had come up to watch the operations, did not disguise his admiration of their "heroic courage and devotion." The losses of the British were sixteen killed and fifty-six wounded, less than half of the enemy's; but the honours of the combat rested certainly with the Maoris.

April 5.
Cameron then returned to prosecute his operations against Maungatatari, but on reconnoitring the enemy's *pa* there on the 5th of April, found it evacuated. The final stroke at Orakau had broken the spirit of the Waikato tribes, and the campaign in that quarter was over. In Taranaki, too, Colonel Warre of the Fifty-seventh, after months of petty skirmishes, had practically overcome all resistance. There remained the east coast about Tauranga, not more than forty miles east of Cameron's headquarters, which Cameron had already decided must be the next field of operations. Tauranga was in fact the seaport of the Waikato tribes, whereby warriors from other parts of the island were able to join them. The Maoris in that quarter were believed to have assisted the Waikato tribes and, even if they had not done so, were strongly in sympathy with them and were prepared to fight elsewhere. Believing that their turn for invasion would shortly come, they had built a *pa* at Pukehinahina, about three miles from

Tauranga, which became known as the "Gate *Pa*," 1864. because it was situated upon a ridge between two swamps which served as a passage into the Maori lands. There were already detachments of British troops in and about Tauranga itself; and on the 21st April 21. of April Cameron shifted his headquarters thither, bringing with him reinforcements. On the 27th he April 27. reconnoitred the *pa*, which was situated on the highest eminence of the ridge—at that point about a quarter of a mile wide between the two swamps. It was of oblong shape, about seventy yards by thirty, well palisaded and surrounded by a strong fence of timber, while the slopes leading down to the swamps on either hand were honeycombed with rifle-pits. Having at his disposal about seventeen hundred of all ranks and three heavy guns besides lighter pieces,[1] Cameron decided to attack without delay.

On the evening of the 27th half of his force encamped within twelve hundred yards of the *pa*, and on that day and on the morrow the guns were brought up and placed in position. After dusk on the 28th April 28. a feigned attack was made, under cover of which the Sixty-eighth, taking advantage of low tide, passed along the beach outside the swamp on the enemy's right and extended itself across their rear to cut off their retreat. Soon after daybreak of the 29th the guns April 29. opened fire and continued with short intermissions until four o'clock in the afternoon, by which time part of the exterior fence and palisading had been destroyed and a practicable breach had been made. Three hundred men of the Naval Brigade and as many of the Forty-third were appointed for the assault, half of each of them as the storming column, and as many for the reserve. The breach was gained with little loss, and hardly an enemy was to be seen within the inner trench; but the column was met by a hail of bullets from

---

[1] The force consisted of a Naval Brigade (429), 5 cos. 43rd (293), 68th (732), detachments of several regiments (181), one 110-pounder and two 40-pounders.

1864.   concealed passages and rifle-pits.   Almost immediately
April 29.   nearly every officer was shot down, and the men
wavered; the reserve rushed in, overcrowding the
already confined space and increasing confusion; and
then the whole mass of the assailants rushed back in
panic.   The whole affair had lasted only a few minutes,
during which there had fallen one hundred and twelve
officers and men.[1]

This mishap of the Gate *Pa* is the only incident
that is remembered (if indeed it be remembered still)
of all our little fights in New Zealand, and that chiefly
because it brought misfortune upon one of the most
famous regiments of the Light Division.   Much
ridiculous nonsense was talked about it,[2] as if there had
not been panics, with more or less of shame and loss,
in every war.   The facts seem to be these.   It is
certain that the Maoris, comfortably sheltered under-
ground, suffered little if at all from the bombardment,
and that they were still unseen when they checked the
first rush of the assault with their murderous fire.
Then seeing the British waver, they sprang out of their
cover suddenly to the counter-attack; and the sight of
some scores of fierce heads, taking the assailants by
surprise, overwhelmed them with the imagination of a
countless host and so caused them to turn.[3]   As a
matter of fact, the Maoris in the Gate *Pa* numbered
at most two hundred; and, as they had no water, there
was no occasion to assault at all.   Indeed friendly
Maoris with Cameron pressed him not to do so.   The
enemy, three-quarters of an hour after the attack had
been repulsed, endeavoured to retire, but were driven

[1]   43rd, 9 officers and 72 men; Naval Brigade, 4 officers and 40 men
killed and wounded.

[2]   " It was said that no English regiment at Waterloo lost so many
officers as the 43rd at the Gate *Pa* " (Rusden, ii. 298).   The truth
is that most of the regiments at Waterloo lost more and very few less.

[3]   I talked over the subject of the Gate *Pa* with many men in
New Zealand, some of whom had been present, though not of the
storming party.   The best opinion favoured the explanation in the
text; though who can account for a panic?

back by the Sixty-eighth. Cameron threw up a line 1864.
of entrenchments within a hundred yards of the *pa*, and April 30.
deferred further operations till next day. The Maoris
stole away in the night, however, in their mysterious
fashion; one of them first making his way through the
British sentries to fetch water, and placing some small
allowance of it alongside each one of the British
wounded. They left behind them twenty killed and
six wounded of their own, hardly one of them touched
by round-shot or shell.

This success was the ruin of the Maoris at Tauranga.
In their arrogance they threatened attack on the British,
now left under command of Colonel Greer of the Sixty-
eighth; and at last they began to entrench themselves
at Te Ranga, about four miles from the Gate *Pa*.
Greer, hastening to attack them before they could
complete their palisades and subterranean defences,
marched against them on the 21st of June with six June 21.
hundred men, chiefly of the Forty-third and Sixty-
eighth. He found that they had thrown up a chain of
rifle-pits, wherefore he kept them engaged for two hours
until he could bring up two hundred and thirty more
men, which were all that could be spared from camp.
When these had approached within supporting distance
Greer sounded the advance, and the troops dashed at
the hostile entrenchments with the bayonet. The
Maoris stood firm and for a few minutes fought
savagely, but presently gave way. Sixty-eight were
killed in the rifle-pits; the remainder rose up and
walked away, disdaining to run, under an unrelenting
fire. The British pursued for some miles but, the
country being intricate and full of ravines, the Maoris
escaped absolute annihilation. One hundred and eight
of their dead were buried by the victors, and twenty-
seven wounded, besides ten unwounded, were taken
prisoners, whereas the British casualties were but ten
killed and forty wounded. The blow, in fact, was
crushing. Those that survived it shortly afterwards
gave up their arms, and in August surrendered their Aug.

1864. lands, of which Grey retained one-fourth in punishment for rebellion.   Therewith the last hope of the Waikato tribes was swept away.

Meanwhile in Taranaki Colonel Warre by means of small flying columns had prevented any serious mischief by the tribes in that quarter, and to all appearance there remained little more for the troops to do. In the spring of 1864, however, a new disturbing influence sprang up among the Maoris in a form common among the Mohammedan clans on the northwest frontier of India, but a novelty in New Zealand. A false prophet arose who, mixing together strange doctrines gathered from the Pentateuch, from observation of the Roman Catholic rites and from primeval superstition, proclaimed his mission to extirpate the British by the sword.   He soon gathered a following, and the sect from the use of the sound Hau Hau [1] in their ritual, became known as the Hau Haus.   They were simply disreputable banditti with whom decent Maoris would have nothing to do; but they formed a rallying point for the desperate and the discontented, of whom the war had made many.   Their first warlike encounter was against a party of the Fifty-seventh, which shot down some forty of them, including a leader who claimed to be, through his sanctity, invulnerable.   They then tried to advance upon Wanganui, but were stopped by loyal Maoris, who met them in open

May. battle on the 14th of May and defeated them.   Thus further trouble on the west coast was for the present averted, though the mere existence of the Hau Haus constituted an element of danger.

But of even more serious consequence were the measures of confiscation proposed, in the flush of victory, by the ministers at Auckland to the Governor

June. in June 1864.[2]   They were combated by Sir George Grey, who understood the Maoris far better than his

---

[1] Written Maori words are pronounced in the Italian fashion, so Hau Hau would rhyme with the English " now, now."
[2] Rusden, ii. 325.

advisers, and there ensued a long controversy between 1864. them.   Among other points upon which the ministers laid stress was the drawing of a frontier-line from the west coast at Kawhia to the east coast at Tauranga, to which General Cameron, being consulted by the Governor in August, took strong objection, since it would probably draw him into further operations in that quarter.   The scheme of confiscation in Taranaki seemed to him likely also to involve further work for the troops in the field; and the month of August in New Zealand, it must be remembered, corresponds to February in England, which is not the most favourable time for a campaign.   Then in September there Sept. arrived from the Colonial Office, bearing date the 26th of April, a despatch in which Mr. Cardwell recommended—it may be said enjoined—that the policy of confiscation should be abandoned, and that the Maoris should be called upon rather to make voluntary cession of land in return for clement treatment at the hands of their conquerors.   " To confiscate for European use the most valuable land, and drive the original owners to forest and morass, would convert the Maoris into desperate banditti."   Such   were   Mr.   Cardwell's words; and they were justified by the recent experience of Lord Canning's plan of wholesale confiscation in Oudh.

Grey thereupon submitted to his advisers a draft proclamation, drawn up in the spirit of Cardwell's despatch, to give the Maoris an opportunity of submission before resorting further to arms.   The ministers demurred, being strongly intent upon their own designs and very resentful against any interference from England.   For some reason they were disposed to be very hard on the Maoris; and it seems likely that, having been at first frightened, they had become vindictive.   Though the General and Governor had pleaded hard for generous treatment of the Maori prisoners captured at Rangiriri, the ministers had kept them for months mewed up in a hulk in Auckland

1864. harbour, with nothing but bare boards to sleep upon. For long they refused even to release the heroic Te Oriori on parole.   Naturally the captives suffered in health; and, what was worse, other Maoris, who were willing to surrender, were deterred from doing so by the prospect of the like hardship for themselves.   At last Grey persuaded his advisers to yield up the prisoners to his care; and in August 1864 they were transferred to Sir George's own island of Kawau, about thirty miles from Auckland; the ministers, however, insisting that he should be responsible for the cost of their maintenance.   There they were allowed to cultivate land, and apparently settled down in peace.   It had been arranged that a written promise not to escape should be exacted from them, but this detail was from sheer

Sept. 9. carelessness omitted.   On the 9th of September a man-of-war came into Auckland and there was some firing practice.   Whether the prisoners thought that this portended doom for themselves or were inspired by some vaguer fear is uncertain, but on the 11th the

Sept. 10. ministers were terrified by the news that on the 10th the whole of the two hundred prisoners had escaped to the mainland.   A day or two later they were found. They received all visitors kindly and were perfectly quiet and harmless.   They declared that they would not go back to Kawau and that they would interfere with no one unless soldiers were sent against them, in which case they would plunder and kill.   In the circumstances it was thought advisable to let them go quietly to their homes, which they did, and gave no further trouble.   It was thus proved that the harshness shown towards them by Grey's ministers had been not merely inhuman but unwise.[1]

This incident would have been unworthy of narration had it not coincided in time more or less with the arrival not only of Mr. Cardwell's despatch, but of other signs that in England people were looking askance at this Maori war.   They were beginning to

[1] Rusden, ii. 270, 272, 284, 306-308, 314.

inquire whether it had not been provoked by the 1864.
settlers for the sake of seizing Maori land for their own
purposes at the cost of British soldiers' lives and, to a
considerable extent, of British taxpayers' money. And
there was certainly something to support this view.
In the first place, the purchase of the land at Waitara
had been admitted to be wrongful; and this, beyond
question, had been the direct cause not only of the war
of 1860, but, indirectly, through the distrust which
it bred in the Maoris of the New Zealand Government's good faith, of the war of 1863. In the second
place, there were the threatened confiscations, which
were finally proclaimed in December 1864. It has
been seen that there was no good feeling between the
settlers and the British troops in 1860; and their relations had not improved in 1863 and 1864. All
ranks of the army in New Zealand were full of admiration for their Maori enemies, and probably thought
much more highly of them than of the settlers. They
cannot but have been indignant at the ignoble maltreatment of the Maori prisoners, with whom they had
hastened to shake hands, by politicians at Auckland.
Lastly, they had begun to suspect that they were mere
tools placed by mistake in the hands of those same
politicians and by them used for their own selfish ends.
They had done their work in Waikato, Tauranga, and
partly in Taranaki; and now the politicians proposed to
employ them about Wanganui in making a road between
that place and New Plymouth, and in securing the purchase of a block of native land a little to north of it, at Waitotara. In fact, as it seemed to them, they were called
upon with hardship and peril to minister to the appetite
of the settlers for land; and that appetite was insatiable.[1]

The General made himself the mouthpiece of this 1865.
discontent, which he himself felt as bitterly as any.
On the 20th of January 1865 he arrived at Wanganui, his mission being to open the country between
that place and New Plymouth. To this end he had

[1] Rusden, ii. 325, 327, 335, 337, 339, 347, 350.

1865. arranged that a force from New Plymouth under Colonel Warre should advance simultaneously with him and meet him half-way, the total distance being one hundred and sixty-eight miles. Before he left Auckland for Wanganui he had warned Grey that, if the new scheme of confiscation were carried out, he must apply for reinforcements; and on the day after his arrival he wrote to Grey expressing his conviction that it was wrong to bring war into so quiet a settlement. This was not a very happy spirit in which to enter upon a Jan. 24. campaign; but none the less on the 24th a force of about eleven hundred men of the Eighteenth, Fiftieth and Fifty-seventh advanced westward to Nukumaru and encamped there within two miles of a Maori *pa* at Wereroa. On the next day the Maoris attacked one of the picquets in such strength and with such persistence that they forced it back upon the main body, and were not repulsed without a lively little skirmish, in which eleven of the Fiftieth were killed and twenty wounded. As the Maoris left eleven dead behind them, they gained little by their temerity. But Cameron was not disposed to punish them. He wrote on the 28th that his force, eleven hundred men, was insufficient for an attack on Wereroa, and he added in a private letter of the same day that he believed the purchase of the Waitotara land to be an even more iniquitous job than that of the Waitara land in 1860. He urged Grey once again to ask for reinforcements, and then, collecting a few more men from Wellington and Taranaki, Feb. 5. he on the 5th of February crossed the Waitotara river, leaving a strong detachment under Colonel Weare at Nukumaru. The Maoris shortly afterwards killed a settler and a straggling militiaman; and a panic at once set in among the settlers, which compelled Cameron to reinforce the garrison of Wanganui. At the same time fifty Hau Haus invaded Tauranga; and, though the party was promptly captured by a tribe of friendly Maoris, the incident showed that these fanatics had gained ground. This caused new terror and

distraction. On the 14th of February a detachment 1865.
under Colonel Waddy was pushed on to the Patea Feb.
river, where it stayed for a month throwing up redoubts upon both banks, while Weare's column took its
place on the Waitotara. Cameron himself repaired to
Wanganui and asked Grey to meet him there to discuss the situation.

General and Governor were by this time on bad
terms. Cameron's imputations of malpractice and evil
motive against the Government of New Zealand were
naturally resented by Grey and by his ministers, and the
more because Cameron had not confined them to the
colony but, without informing Grey, had repeated them
also to the War Office. The General in fact actually
wrote home in February to resign his command, and,
having taken this step, was perhaps the less inclined to
be conciliatory. News of fresh adherents gathered by the
Hau Haus on the east coast, and of the savage murder
of a missionary by a party of them, did not help matters.
Fresh pressure laid upon Cameron to attack and have
done with the Wereroa *pa* drew from him an angry
private letter to Grey, to the effect that, though the
colonial ministers might not care how many men and
officers were lost in the operations that they might re-
commend, he, the General, felt very differently.[1] The
colonial ministers took a high tone and declared, not
for the first time, that they would prefer to dispense
with imperial troops and rely on their own resources
rather than receive imperial aid and be hampered by
such interference as Cameron's. But these were mere
words, for they still wished to use the imperial troops,
having no other force upon which they could confi-
dently rely; and their finances were in such disorder
that they were sadly in need also of imperial credit.
Moreover, though some of Cameron's insinuations seem
to have been founded, in detail, upon quite insufficient
authority, there was in the general purport of them a
very disagreeable sting of truth.

[1] Rusden, ii. 365.

1865.   Meanwhile on the 9th of March Weare's party
from Nukumaru joined Waddy's column on the Patea,
and the whole, nearly fourteen hundred strong, ad-
Mar. 13. vanced on the 13th up the right bank of the river.
Before they had marched three miles they found
Maoris strongly posted on their right flank about
Kakaramea, drove them off with a loss of forty killed
into the forest, and proceeded on their way. On the
14th they found at Manutaki a large depôt of food
which had been abandoned by the Maoris, but saw
nothing of the enemy to the close of their march,
April 9. which ended at Waimate on the 9th of April. Since
winter was approaching, Cameron halted the column
at that point and sent it back to Patea, whence a
June 2. detachment moved forward on the 2nd of June to
meet Warre's column marching down from Taranaki, effected its junction successfully, and returned.
Cameron himself went back, at the end of April, to
Auckland, where he busied himself with writing despatches concerning his quarrel with Grey. Throughout this time the Maori *pa* at Wereroa remained unmolested, and the officers in command of the British
troops declined to concern themselves with it unless
ordered by Cameron. Grey, therefore, in July took
the business in hand himself. Collecting a force of
nearly five hundred men, half of them Maoris, he
induced the officers of two hundred British troops to
encamp in front of the *pa*, and sent his own force by a
circuitous path through the forest to a height that
commanded the *pa* from the rear. With great difficulty and fatigue they reached this height; and after
they had fired a few dropping shots into the *pa*, the Maori
July 21. garrison abandoned it. Since these Maoris escaped
unharmed, no object whatever was gained; and it may
be suspected that Grey's principal object was either to
show that he could do work in the field as well as a
general, or to bring contempt upon the Commander-in-
chief. He certainly succeeded in irritating Cameron,
who referred the matter to the authorities at home.

They decided that a Governor, albeit by his commis- 1865.
sion Commander-in-chief, was not thereby entitled to
take immediate direction of any military operations;
and so this silly incident ended.

This decision was announced, however, long after
Cameron, who left New Zealand in August, had re- Aug.
turned home. Having quarrelled bitterly with the
Governor and ministers, he naturally left no very great
reputation behind him; but his task was most difficult
and unthankful. Transport and supply in a rough and
roadless country were a very serious problem, and it
was puzzling to know how to subdue an enemy who
had no wealth of cattle, as had the Kaffirs, no property,
no towns and no lines of communication, and who
could always evade pursuit by retirement into impenetrable forest. He may be pardoned, too, if he sometimes found it distasteful to hazard the lives of his
troops for behoof of men for whom he felt no respect.
Other British commanders have felt as he did in other
colonies. But he had no right whatever to bring against
the New Zealand Government charges which he could
not substantiate, least of all to insinuate them to the
War Office, without sending copies of his letters to
Sir George Grey. Thereby he enabled the colonists to
insinuate on their side that British officers complained
of them simply because they were anxious to return
home to ease and comfort.[1] In a contest of calumny
those who are the more sensitive upon points of honour
are sure to come off the worse.

In September Sir George Grey proclaimed, by ad- Sept.
vice of his ministers, the confiscation of large blocks of
land in Taranaki, and, of his own motion, declared likewise that formal war was at an end. At about the same
time arrived a dispatch from the Imperial Government
pressing once more for the return of five of the ten
British regiments from the Colony. Grey, after the
capture of Wereroa, had signified his readiness to do
this;[2] but, despite of his proclamation of peace, the

[1] Fox, *The War in New Zealand*, p. 15.   [2] Rusden, ii. 373.

1865. Hau Haus were still giving trouble between New Plymouth and Wanganui, and the work of the imperial troops was not yet done. On the 25th of August, Sir Trevor Chute arrived to succeed Cameron in command, and, waiting for broad midsummer before commencing operations, moved out from Wanganui to Wereroa on

1866. the 30th of December. He took with him detachments of the Fourteenth, Eighteenth, Fiftieth and Fifty-seventh, a few colonial troops and a native contingent of three hundred friendly Maoris. It would be tedious to give an account of his operations, his bloodless attacks upon *pas* and the like. It must suffice that after most fatiguing marches over most difficult country he entered New Plymouth on the 27th of January

Jan.-Feb. 1866, and doubling back by a different route reached Patea on the 7th of February, when he could report that he had left not one village nor fortified position in possession of the rebels. His loss during these movements was trifling. Therewith all systematic operations ceased, and the withdrawal of the troops began. The casualties of the British in action between the 1st of January 1863 and the 15th of February 1866 amounted to six hundred and twelve, and those of the colonial troops to seventy-six. Five regiments[1] embarked from New Zealand in the course of 1866, and the Imperial Government urged the return of the rest, for Chute had taken up the general quarrel of the troops with Grey, and all ministers in Downing Street were weary of the eternal wrangles between the representatives of the Colony and of the Army. Four more

1867. regiments quitted New Zealand in the course of 1867, and only the Eighteenth was left, to be scattered about the Colony in small detachments, after the fashion so dear to nervous civilians but so detestable to commanding officers. Early in 1869 they too were warned to take their departure; but in the meanwhile events had occurred which opened yet another Maori war.

[1] 70th (Jan.), 43rd (Feb.), 68th (Mar.), 40th (May), 14th and half of 50th (Oct.).

On the 4th of July 1868 some four hundred Maori 1868.
prisoners, one hundred and sixty of them men who had
been without any warrant or authority deported to the
Chatham Islands,[1] rose, overpowered their colonial
guards, took thirty rifles from them, seized a ship and
compelled the master to carry them to Poverty Bay,
where they landed. Their leader was one Te Kooti, who
had been harshly and unjustly treated and, though
humane to his guards and to the crew of the ship, was
not disposed to spare the settlers in New Zealand. He
proved to be a military genius—a Tantia Topi afoot,
except that he could fight as well as run away. He established a reputation at once by outwitting and dispersing
some local levies which tried to arrest him, and, renouncing the old Maori tactics, he took to active guerilla
warfare, not less bold in attack than cunning in evasion.
He worsted more than one little colonial force, spreading terror wherever he went, and finally, by the massacre of thirty settlers and a large number of friendly Nov. 10.
Maoris at Poverty Bay, he inspired panic along the whole
length and breadth of the North Island. He had already gained adherents; he might—who could tell?—
rally to him not only the Hau Haus but every man of
the Maori king's party. The Governor, a pusillani-
mous old pedant, who had succeeded Grey in 1867,
shrieked to England for help, and the whole Colony
cried out against the removal of the Eighteenth. The
Colonial Minister answered calmly that the population
of New Zealand, now two hundred and twenty thousand strong, could surely deal with a few hundred
rebels, and refused to counter-order the withdrawal of
the Eighteenth. The outcry and alarm then became
frankly pitiful, and General Chute, who had come
over from Australia, through sheer compassion consented on his own responsibility to detain the
Eighteenth, which did not finally leave New Zealand
until 1870.

[1] The Chatham Islands lie about 400 miles east and south of
Wellington.

1868.   A great deal of blame, in the writer's opinion, attached to the Governor on this occasion. The Sovereign's representative in the Colonies is generally a man who has seen something of the world, and can view events in truer proportion than men belonging to a small society who have naturally no vision beyond their own limited horizon. But this Governor was more frightened than anyone. He actually descended to write foreboding of horrors that would compare with those at Delhi and Cawnpore, and to forward extracts from colonial newspapers which advocated annexation of New Zealand to the United States. But no pathetic periods of His quaking Excellency, no eloquent remonstrances of his terrified ministers could move the hard heart of the Imperial Government. New Zealand must fight her own battles, and the British troops must be withdrawn. At this distance of time it is easy to pronounce that the Imperial Government was right. The colonial ministers who, consciously or unconsciously, had steered their young community straight for war in 1860 and 1863 had blundered seriously. " I believe," wrote one of the New Zealand cabinet in 1869, " that the members of the cabinet are agreed that the confiscation-policy, as a whole, has been an expensive mistake." [1]   With this frank confession we may dismiss the controversies which fill the pages of the historian of New Zealand. Other administrators in all parts of the Empire have made and continue to make mistakes; but not all of them learn wisdom from experience.

The probability is that it was a misfortune for New Zealand that she received the gift of self-government so early. Sir George Grey would have managed the delicate business of the Maoris far better if left with absolute powers and unhampered by advisers, for he knew and understood the tribes and though, if provoked, a most formidable enemy, would have been a sympathetic friend. He felt his position keenly. He

---

[1] Rusden, ii. 563, 585-586, 596-597, 600.

complained in 1864 that, out of his Cabinet of five, 1868.
three were frequently absent from Auckland, and the
remaining two were partners of a legal firm in town.
Practically, therefore, he had to act upon the dictates of
two petty provincial attorneys, which, for a man of his
ability and experience, could not but have been humiliating.[1] As things fell out, he spent a lamentable amount
of his time and energy in fighting with his ministers or
with the generals, and came home at last a man with a
grievance, seeking in vain for the righting of personal
wrongs, and for the settlement of personal quarrels upon
the merits of which all wise men steadily refused to pronounce.   He had his defects, for he was inclined to be
rancorous and unforgiving, but he was not the least of
the many great civil administrators who have been
drawn from the junior officers of the Army.   He was,
in fact, in his day the man whom the Colonial Office
chose for all places of difficulty, and his statue at Capetown shows that he was not chosen in vain.   While in
Cape Colony, too, he hurried, unbidden, all troops
that were passing or could be spared to India upon the
outbreak of the Mutiny.   He was in fact (as I believe)
always at heart a soldier,[2] as became one whose father
had fallen at Badajoz.   His memory, despite of his
wrangles with Cameron and Chute, is worthy of honour
by the Army.
   As to Grey's advisers, it cannot be said that they
were incapable men.   Indeed for so small a community
they were rather remarkably able, but their single-
heartedness was ruined by factious quarrels.   Englishmen are the most contentious of mortals, but the first
Englishmen in New Zealand were, I think, even among
their own countrymen exceptional.   Little groups were

---

[1] Grey to Sec. of State, Aug. 26, 1864. I knew one of these two
individuals as an old man. No one could have trusted a person with
such a face.
[2] I knew Sir George Grey only in New Zealand forty years ago,
when he was an old man verging on eighty and somewhat bowed, but
I should never have taken him for anything but a soldier.

1868. constantly thrusting each other in and out of power; and the subordinate officials, who had the task of executing their orders, were, as generally happens in a new country, careless and inefficient. It is fair to add that all the settlers seem to have regarded the contest with the Maoris, however brought about, as the mother country's business. One unblushing Scot, the Superintendent of Otago province, hundreds of miles from the scene of action and resolute to have nothing to do with war there nor anywhere else, proclaimed his sentiments with conviction. " The Colonists regard the wars with the Maoris as matters of Imperial concern; they did not come to New Zealand to fight the Maoris." [1] But too much must not be made of such things in the early days of a young colony. The fact remains that it fell to the lot of the long-suffering British soldier to break the power of the Maoris, and that he found them on the whole the grandest native enemy that he had ever encountered. Gurkhas and Sikhs were formidable before them; Zulus were formidable after them; but all of these had copied the European discipline. The Maori had his own code of war, the essence of which was a fair fight on a day and in a place fixed by appointment, when the best and bravest men should win. The British soldier upset his traditions, but could not touch his proud courage nor degrade his honour. A Maori was capable of slaughtering wounded and prisoners and perhaps of eating them afterwards, but he could also leap down into the fire of both sides to save the life of a fallen foe. The British soldier, therefore, held him in deep respect, not resenting his own little defeats, but recognising the noble side of the Maori and forgetting his savagery.

The story of these petty campaigns in New Zealand would not be complete without reference to the men who really did the hardest of the work—the obscure

---

[1] Rusden, ii. 548. I remember this individual well and, officially, attended his funeral. His record, though he had been Superintendent of the Province, was not of the cleanest.

but devoted officers of the Commissariat Staff Corps 1868.
who fed the troops in the field.   Their difficulties were
stupendous.   There were no roads, and the country
furnished no food nor forage—nothing in fact except
fuel.   The Commissariat had literally to carry everything to the mouths of all ranks—not only bread and
meat, but groceries and vegetables.   From the base
the operations extended to a distance of one hundred
and eighty miles, which was traversed partly by land
and partly by water.   The rivers were shallow,
changeable and treacherous, often running over submerged forests, which made navigation both difficult
and dangerous.   Not the least of the embarrassments
was that, in the course of the one hundred and eighty
miles, there were ten changes from water-carriage to
land-carriage, and from land-carriage back to water-
carriage, involving great labour and incidentally sad
waste.   For the bluejackets, who were necessarily
much employed in this work, thought themselves
entitled to some compensation and plundered freely,
especially when their cargo happened to be rum.   So
hard was it to prevent this abuse that the naval
authorities declined to give receipts or to accept
responsibility for supplies that were under the charge
of their boats' crews.   Too much must not be made of
this weakness of the thirsty and overworked sailor, set
down to a thankless and uncongenial task; but it added
to the trials of the Commissariat Staff.

At the outbreak of hostilities in 1861 the operations
were so trifling that the Commissariat Staff, whose real
business was supply, undertook the duties of transport
also. They began by forming two companies, with something over three hundred pack-animals and draught-
animals.   When matters became more serious in 1864,
some of the Military Train came out and proposed to
take over the transport.   The Commissariat officers
protested that, in this case, they could not supply the
troops in the field; and Cameron, wisely listening to
them, declined to upset existing arrangements, using

1868. the Military Train, as it had been used in India, for the work of cavalry. The Commissariat officers gradually took the whole business into their own hands. They designed and built their own boats and trained their own crews, so as to dispense with the services of the Royal Navy; and they ended with a total strength of thirteen companies, afloat and ashore, comprising fifteen hundred officers and men and over twenty-two hundred horses and draught-bullocks, besides the boats on the rivers. When it is remembered that all supplies, excepting occasionally a few slaughter-cattle, had to be brought from other countries, that none of the harbours on the west coast of New Zealand were safe, and that the whole of the organisation for storing the supplies and sending them inland had to be improvised, but that even so the Commissariat managed to feed the troops in the field, not merely with biscuit and salt meat but frequently with fresh bread baked in field-ovens, the ability and industry of its officers deserves the highest praise.[1]

With the long and weary work done by the colonial forces before they finally ended the trouble with the Maoris, this history has no concern. The very memory of it must be growing dim, and all bitterness of feeling between the British born and the Maori has long since died away. The petty combats of the remote past have been blotted out by the astonishing prowess of all New Zealanders alike against the sternest warriors of eastern and western Europe during the bitter struggle which raged against Germany and her allies between 1914 and 1918. An Englishman, who was for four years a resident in their enchanting country, may be allowed to say so much with gratitude, admiration and pride.

[1] There are many interesting reports of the work of the Commissariat in New Zealand attached to the report of Lord Strathnairn's Committee on Transport and Supply, 1867. They are the source from which the above particulars are drawn.

Authorities. For the first period Carey's *Narrative of the Late War* 1868. *in New Zealand* is clear and concise. For the second period Fox's *War in New Zealand* is an *apologia* setting forth the colonial view for behoof of the British public. It requires to be carefully watched and checked. Rusden, *History of New Zealand,* vol. ii., is the antidote to Fox. His work shows how an able, cultivated and upright man, full of industry and shrinking from no labour, may none the less lack all idea how to write a book. The masses of printed Parliamentary Papers on the subject of New Zealand at this period are serviceable; and the regimental histories of the 12th, 14th, 18th, 40th, 43rd, 50th, 57th, 68th and 70th contain useful details.

CHAPTER LIX

1854–
1870.

FOR the last time we return to affairs at home, to a Parliament and a nation shame-faced, shaken and bewildered. The Crimean war had given the public a rude shock, and the revolt of the mercenary troops in Bengal had followed as a staggering blow. Not only had the War Department been found wanting, but the whole administration of India had proved to be utterly rotten. This was disquieting enough, but it was not all. Troubles had succeeded troubles in all parts of the Empire. Those in the East have already been traced in the account of the expeditions to China, on the north-west frontier of India and on the Red Sea. But these were not the only centres of anxiety. In South Africa, only a short time before the Crimean war, there had been, as has been told, a menace nearly as formidable, on its own scale, as in India. There had been not only a Kaffir invasion but an insurrection, which might easily have become general, of the native races; the native mercenaries—only a single regiment, it is true—had mutinied; and, worst of all, such of the Dutch settlers as had not migrated northward had refused to come forward for their own defence. In 1861 some of these Dutch migrants formed themselves into an independent republic in the Transvaal, thus erecting a separate white state in rivalry to the British in South Africa. For a time this rivalry portended nothing very serious. There was a great military native power, that of the Zulus, which could be counted upon to hold

any small communities of Dutch in awe; but the time 1854–
might come when Zulus and Dutch would come to 1870.
blows, and then it would be a question which of these
two parties England should support against the other,
and whether she might not find herself compelled to
extinguish each of them in succession.   The situation
certainly promised work sooner or later for the British
Army.

Next, there was another quarter in which recent
changes had wrought a transformation.   The abolition
of the old commercial code following upon the emanci-
pation of the slaves had hurled the West Indies from
their high estate, and was in process of reducing them
from the most to the least valuable of our possessions.
The little assemblies of the various islands, no longer
sustained by great wealth, were becoming ridiculous;
and, since the Reform Bill of 1832, the West Indian
interest, once so potent in the House of Commons, was
fading rapidly away.   An insurrection of negroes in
Jamaica in 1865 brought the new situation in that
quarter home to the Imperial Government in an unpleasant fashion.   There was only one weak white
battalion in the island at the time, but the rising was
quelled without difficulty.   The persecution of Mr.
Eyre, the Governor, for enforcing order at a moment
of great danger, is not a question which concerns us,
for he was a civilian; though it is worth noting as a
reminder that any Englishman in authority, be he
civil or military, who dares to save many lives by
taking a few, does his duty at his peril.   The immediate
point, however, is that, though the glory of the West
Indies was departing, and the islands were no longer,
commercially speaking, worth the cost of a white
garrison, one central fact remained.   The whites were
but a handful at the mercy of a multitude of negroes,
and in any time of alarm would cry out for the protection of the Army.

Next, there arose in 1861 a wholly novel and unexpected complication in the west.   Certain of the

1854–
1870.
southern states of America seceded from the Union, and the northern states girded themselves to prevent such secession by force. They adopted, in fact, precisely the policy which the British Government had followed, unsuccessfully, in 1776 when the American Colonies themselves seceded from the British Empire. The southern states sent two emissaries to Europe in a British steamer, the *Trent*, to negotiate for the recognition of their independence, precisely as the revolted American Colonies had sent Benjamin Franklin and Silas Deane to Paris for the same purpose in 1777. The *Trent* was stopped by an American man-of-war whose captain claimed the right of search and, finding the two emissaries on board, removed them in spite of all protests and carried them off. The like high-handed action, when exerted by British men-of-war towards American ships, had been the pretext for the American declaration of war against England in 1812. But, as the entire story of the American Civil war sufficiently proves, circumstances alter cases. The British Government promptly claimed the restitution of the captives taken from under the protection of the British flag, and, to strengthen their diplomacy, decided to strengthen the battalions in Canada and to send out at once, among other reinforcements, a brigade of Guards. In fact by February 1862, there were eighteen thousand British troops in Canada. And this was a costly matter; for all of them, quite apart from the expense of transporting them across the Atlantic, required special clothing, at the price of nearly three pounds a head, to protect them against the Canadian winter. Meanwhile the American President had wisely given way and released the two emissaries; and the whole matter was peaceably arranged. But Sir George Cornewall Lewis, a very able and wholly unsentimental man, who was then Secretary of State for War, added a comment upon the whole affair which was singularly apt and pithy. " During the American war Parliament passed an Act

by which it was declared illegal to tax the Colonies. 1854–
I believe it would be very difficult to pass an Act 1870.
declaring it illegal for the Colonies to tax us." [1]

Three weeks later, on the 4th of March 1862, the
House of Commons carried a resolution that " this
House, while fully recognising the claims of all portions
of the British Empire to Imperial aid in their protection
arising from the consequences of Imperial policy, is of
opinion that Colonies exercising the right of self-
government ought to undertake the main responsibility
for providing for their own order and security, and
ought to assist in their own external defence."   The
hint, for it can hardly be called more, was in the
circumstances justified; and, as we have already seen,
it was turned five years later in New Zealand into
something like a principle.   There was, of course,
always room for controversy over the signification of
the words " consequences of Imperial policy "; but in
the matter at any rate of internal police it was time for
the Dominions, as we now call them, to provide for
themselves.   At any moment of extraordinary urgency
they could always call upon the King's ships on their
particular station, towards the maintenance of which
they contributed nothing.   The new policy, as it
seemed to be in 1862, was after all only a return to the
old system of the seventeenth century, when all British
settlements had been supposed to look to their own
defence, and had done so.   As a matter of fact, since
1862 only one of the Colonies then existing has
received military aid for the furtherance of Imperial
policy, namely, South Africa.

But, apart from Imperial defence, affairs in Europe
caused anxiety as to security at home.   England had
hardly suppressed the rising in India when the bellicose
utterances of some French officers caused her misgivings as to the intentions of her late ally in the
Crimea.   She was presently reassured by the turning
of the French arms not against herself but, in alliance

[1] *H.D.*, Debate on Supplementary Army Estimates, Feb. 14, 1862.

1854–
1870.
with Sardinia, against Austria. France appropriated Savoy and Nice for her pains, but she drove the Austrians from Italy, of which the sovereign of Sardinia was in 1861 declared to be King. Next, in 1865 Austria and Prussia wrested Schleswig and Holstein from Denmark, the British Ministry protesting with much indignation but, from want of an effective armed force, with absolutely no effect. In the following year, 1866, Prussia turned upon Austria and certain of the German states in alliance with her, and within six weeks, by a succession of victories, assured to herself the hegemony of an united North Germany. The swiftness with which the Prussians put their armies into the field, the excellent organisation manifested thereby and, above all, the superiority of the new rifle—the needle gun—with which their infantry was armed, caused much searching of heart. The prevailing disquietude was heightened in 1870 by the ease with which those same Prussians utterly overthrew the armies of France.

The years from 1854 to 1870 were therefore unusually full of anxious changes. The balance of power in Europe was shifting with startling suddenness; and, though there was as yet no actual addition to the Empire, yet the completion of the Suez Canal in 1869 opened a new route to India, China and Australasia, and drew the eyes of British statesmen inevitably to Egypt. The cession of the Ionian Islands to Greece in 1863 did indeed relieve England of one garrison in the Mediterranean, but this was countervailed by the taking over of the Straits Settlements from the East India Company. The institution of police for counties and boroughs in 1856 lightened the Army's burden of maintaining order at home, but, in another respect, as shall presently be seen, depleted the Army of some of the best men in the ranks. The formation of a permanent establishment of men for the Navy was another valuable reform which set at rest all apprehensions lest the Army should again

be called upon, as throughout the eighteenth century, 1854–
to man the fleet.   Yet none the less the Army seemed 1870.
to be slowly perishing of sheer overwork.   It is not
too much to aver that, but for the exertions of the
officers, it might to all intent have perished before
1854.   For two hundred years it may be said that the
officers had, from sheer regimental pride, averted the
extinction of their regiments by a Parliament animated
by unquenchable hostility and unutterable meanness.
It was they who, by easing the strangulation of the
halter which Parliament kept ever about the Army's
neck, had enabled it with difficulty to breathe and to
remain alive.   But they had almost reached the limit
alike of their patience and of their endurance.

The Army Estimates of 1856, before the conclusion of peace, provided for an establishment of two
hundred and forty-five thousand men, of whom
twenty-two thousand were foreign mercenaries.   These
figures, however, were purely documentary, for the
actual number of men on the muster-rolls fell forty-
nine thousand short of this establishment.   At that
moment the Queen's troops in India, owing to the
calls of the Crimean war, had sunk to twenty-six
thousand.   The militia at this same time had reached
the figure of sixty-six thousand, as against thirty-eight
thousand in 1855.   The militia had played their part
well.   Eleven regiments had, with their own consent,
taken over much of the duty of the Mediterranean
garrisons, and thirty-eight more had offered themselves for the same service.   Furthermore, the militia
had furnished the regular Army with thirty-three
thousand recruits.   But it is very evident that one and
the same force, recruited by voluntary enlistment,
cannot at one and the same time make good the
casualties of another and yet continue to exist.   By
transfusion of blood from a sound man to a sick man
you may save the sick man, but continual transfusion
will kill the sound man.   Castlereagh, as has been
told in its place, had used the Old Militia only for

1854–
1870.
transfusion of blood, and had set up the Local Militia as a sound man in its place.   But the Ministry of 1855 was content with makeshifts.[1]

After the conclusion of peace with Russia the establishment was promptly reduced to one hundred and fifty-seven thousand men.   A new departure was made by providing that men should enlist for ten years only, with the option of re-engagement within six months to complete twenty-one years' service; but as a matter of fact recruiting was entirely suspended.   Still no men were discharged, for the excess of them only amounted to nine thousand, and it was thought prudent to keep these as "a kind of reserve."[2]   Three months later came the Indian Mutiny.   Twenty-five thousand militia were embodied to make good any garrisons depleted by the withdrawal of troops to India; and in 1858 up went the establishment of the Army again to two hundred and twenty-three thousand.   The regiments of the Line from the Second to the Twenty-fifth were augmented by a second battalion apiece; and yet another battalion, raised by the patriotism of volunteers in Canada, came into existence as the Hundredth, Royal Canadians.   It seems that in September 1857, there was actually a recurrence of Pitt's vile and pernicious system of raising men for rank,[3] an accursed thing which should never have been permitted, no matter under what safeguards and restrictions.   Happily the evil was of short duration.   Enthusiasm had been kindled by the stories of Cawnpore, Lucknow and Delhi; and recruits poured in during the winter of 1857 and spring of 1858 at the rate of six thousand a month.[4]   The total number of recruits gathered in for the year was forty-seven thousand, of which nearly eight thousand were volunteers from the militia.

[1] *H.D.*, Speeches of Mr. Monsell, Feb. 21 and 22, and of Lord Panmure, May 8, June 16, 1856.
[2] *H.D.*, Speech of Mr. F. Peel, Mar. 12, 1857.
[3] *H.D.*, Speech of General Peel, Mar. 19, 1858.
[4] *H.D.*, Speeches of Panmure, Feb. 4, 18, and of General Peel, Mar. 12, 1858.

In 1859 the establishment again rose by seven thousand to a total of two hundred and thirty-seven thousand
men; and General Peel laid down the principle which
he had taken for the guidance of the War Department
in future, namely, that the battalions of the Line at home
must always be half as numerous as those in garrison
abroad.   Thus India would henceforward require fifty
battalions and the Colonies thirty-seven, making eighty-
seven in all, wherefore there must be forty-four battalions in the British Isles.   It was not a very liberal
allowance, but it signified adherence to the old rule
that every battalion must spend two-thirds of its life
abroad and one-third, if it were lucky, at home.   In
this year began what was called the " Volunteer Movement," a patriotic answer to the challenge, unpleasant
though unofficial, of our neighbours on the other side
of the Channel.   In its inception it was altogether good,
its promoters being ready to give much and to take
very little.   Yet it should not have been countenanced
by the Government.   The system had been tried and
found wanting in the great war against revolutionary
and imperial France.   The volunteers of 1859, beginning with a nucleus of sixty or seventy thousand
genuine enthusiasts who cost very little, soon swelled
to twice and thrice that number, demanding and, because they had votes, obtaining a great deal more than
they were worth.   The whole principle of the volunteers was wrong.   It was inequitable to allow a small
fraction of the citizens to undertake a duty which
should have fallen upon all alike; and it was very un-
wholesome for the petty tradesmen, who then composed the electorate, to see their more enlightened and
patriotic fellows come forward to relieve them of the
trouble and expense of defending their country.   However, those same petty tradesmen were masters of the
situation; and, in the circumstances, the volunteers
were perhaps the best expedient that could be devised
for evading their wishes.   The volunteers endured for
the best part of half a century, maintaining always a very

1854– few choice corps which were creditably efficient, and
1870. a very great many which served no purpose except to
inspire the negligent and ignorant with a false feeling of
security.

At this same time, owing to the extinction of the
East India Company and the Queen's assumption of
sovereignty over India, there came up the question of
the Indian garrison.   It was taken as a matter of course
that, under the Act of Parliament which erected that
sovereignty, the Company's European troops would
pass without further ado into the service of the Queen.
The men thought otherwise.   They had enlisted into
the Company's army, and maintained that no number
of Acts of Parliament could transfer them against their
will to the Queen's.   They claimed that they must be
re-enlisted, receiving, as usual, a bounty.   Lord Clyde
advocated concession on this point, knowing intimately
the soldier's mind and his sensitiveness as to his
rights.   " Enlistment," he wrote, going straight to
the heart of the question, " is a personal matter."
The Indian Government, with a lack of imagination
which amounted to stupidity, declined to listen to
him; and the result was a movement among some of
the Bengal European regiments which came dangerously near to a mutiny.   One of these, newly raised,
actually made overtures to the Sikhs to join them in
driving the Queen's troops out of India; and it was a
very bad sign that the non-commissioned officers gave
no hint of what was going forward to their officers.
The feeling of disaffection spread rapidly, and the
Indian Government, becoming frightened, appealed to
Lord Clyde.   Upon his advice a court of inquiry was
set up; and every man was invited freely to come
forward and state his grievance before it.   After some
days of intense anxiety, the men became quiet; and
contentment was restored by an intimation that any
soldier who desired his discharge should receive it.
In other words, the Indian Government having by
sheer folly put itself in the wrong was obliged ignomini-

ously to give way. There had been some very serious 1854–
instances of insubordination, but the Government 1870.
dared not punish them. Eventually some thousands
of the Company's European troops took their discharge; and those that entered the Queen's army
received an allowance of two years' service towards
their pension. There was still some trouble with the
newly formed Bengal European regiments. Discipline
had become relaxed among all the British troops engaged in the late campaigns, most notably among
those of the Company; and Sir Hugh Rose, who in
June 1860 had become Commander-in-chief in
India, was determined not to suffer such a thing. In
November he confirmed a sentence of death passed on
a private of the Fifth Bengal European regiment for
mutinous conduct, and disbanded the regiment itself.
Therewith all trouble came to an end.[1]

The " white mutiny," as it was called, decided a
question which had been agitated ever since the rule
of the East India Company had ended, namely, whether
the European garrison of India should be a local force
or should be supplied by the British Army. The
possibility that a local force might mutiny, thus
practically demonstrated, inclined the balance to the
latter side; and it was determined that a Staff Corps
should be formed of the officers of the three Presiden-
tial armies to provide for the wants of the native army.
For the rest, there passed into the Queen's service nine
battalions, which were numbered the Hundred and
First to the Hundred and Ninth, and three regiments
of cavalry which became the Nineteenth, Twentieth
and Twenty-first Hussars. The Indian artillery disappeared and was replaced by the equivalent of two

---

[1] Shadwell, *Life of Lord Clyde*, ii. 326-332, 408-416, 418-420.
H.D., Debates on East Indian Army Bill, June 12, 1860; speech of Sir
C. Wood, June 21, speeches of Col. Sykes and Mr. Peacocke, June 28,
1860; speeches of Sidney Herbert, Col. Dunne and Sir de Lacy
Evans, Aug. 7; speech of Mr. Baring, Aug. 20. Sir C. Wood's
answer to a question. Burne, *Clyde and Strathnairn*, pp. 163-164.

battalions [1] of the Royal Regiment. Altogether, after
the addition of a battalion and a half to the Royal
Engineers, the estimates of 1860 fixed the establishment of the Army, including embodied militia, at
two hundred and forty thousand men. Mr. Sidney
Herbert, in commending these estimates to the House
of Commons, brought forward many figures to prove
that this number was not, relatively speaking, a large
one. It was certainly a triumph to have made Parliament accept permanently the twenty-five new battalions raised in 1858; and to this end the war between
France and Austria gave valuable furtherance.

In this same year Sidney Herbert introduced a new
Bill for regulating the militia. He explained that a
good many changes had already been wrought in the
past few months. It had been ordained that militia
must serve in any part of the United Kingdom, and
might serve, if they consented of their own will, in the
Channel Islands; that the Secretary of State might
fix the time and place of training; that the militia of
small counties might be amalgamated and trained in
two wings to conciliate local jealousies; that only men
of known habits and fixed residence should be enlisted;
that trained serjeants should be attached to the
battalions to give instruction in musketry, and that
subaltern officers should pass an examination before
they were promoted. The new Bill was designed with
two principal objects: first, to unite maritime counties together with a view to the formation of militia-
artillery; second, to provide for an increase of the
Scottish and Irish militia in case of invasion. The
English militia would thus be raised from eighty to
one hundred and twenty thousand, the Scottish from
five thousand to ten thousand, and the Irish from
fifteen thousand to thirty thousand. Another Bill,
which, together with the first, was passed into an Act,
fixed a higher rate of pay for the permanent staff.

---

[1] A brigade of field-artillery and a brigade of garrison-artillery,
each equivalent to a battalion.

Altogether this signified an effort to improve the status of the militia.

It was indeed high time, for the double function of providing recruits for the Army and garrisons for foreign possessions was breaking the force down. Embodiment, as Mr. Herbert said, had benefited the infantry of the Line but was ruining the militia. The agricultural labouring class looked upon embodiment almost as a breach of faith. They had not reckoned upon being withdrawn from their homes and families for months together. The employment of the force abroad had driven from it many of its officers, who could not afford to let their land look after itself for an indefinite period. Thus the old connection of the militia regiments with their counties was weakened, and they were losing their territorial character. In the eighteenth century, as has been told, the country gentlemen looked upon the militia as their peculiar property. They paid the land-tax by which it was supported; they and their sons provided it with officers, and their labourers filled the ranks with men. But the new militia of 1852, recruited by voluntary enlistment, was a very different matter. The control of it was rapidly and inevitably passing away from the Lords Lieutenant. It was now subject to the War Office, instead of to the Home Office, in itself a most significant change. Moreover, the conversion of the militia into a recruiting ground for the Army had led to an extraordinary amount of fraudulent enlistment. Men went from a regiment of militia, offered themselves to the regular army, received a bounty, deserted, became militiamen in another regiment, received another bounty for enlisting into the Army, again deserted and continued the process indefinitely. One man, from whom it is difficult to withhold the homage that is due to genius, had thus re-enlisted forty-seven times and received forty-seven bounties; and, among the forty-seven thousand men enlisted in 1858, over nine thousand deserted, of whom fewer than two thousand

1854–
1870.

were recovered.[1] It was to check this evil that the rules above mentioned were introduced, namely, that none but men of known residence should be recruited as militiamen, and that the Secretary of State should have power to fix the dates of training so that, the same date being appointed for several regiments simultaneously, men might be prevented from serving in more than one regiment. These expedients were not without good effect; but the old militia, thanks to forty years of neglect, was gone for ever. The policy of free imports had not yet ruined British agriculture. The final crash, delayed apparently by the discoveries of gold in 1848 and 1849, did not come until 1879. But the agricultural population was being steadily attracted into the towns by the prospect of industrial employment, and the transformation of the people into a horde of mechanical workers, uninterested and therefore discontented, was rapidly proceeding. Looking back seventy years it should seem that the reconstitution of the militia upon a voluntary basis was, both from an economical and a military point of view, a very grave mistake.[2]

However, the mischief had been done; and it remained to be seen how the country could make shift to protect itself and the Empire with the resources grudgingly doled out by Parliament. In 1861 the establishment showed the round figure of two hundred and fifteen thousand men for the Army, of which the garrison for India claimed, with its depôts at home, sixty-nine thousand. The actual net decrease, on comparison with the numbers of the previous year, amounted to nine thousand men; but the threatened rupture with the United States raised the establishment for 1862 to two hundred and twenty-nine thousand. The alarm passed away, and the numbers were cut down by four thousand in 1863, and by

---

[1] *H.D.*, Speeches of General Peel and Sidney Herbert, Mar. 4, 1859.
[2] For this Militia Bill *see H.D.*, Speech of Sidney Herbert, June 26, 1860.

another fifteen hundred in 1864. In this year the 1854–
Secretary for War examined the results of allowing 1870.
men to take their discharge after ten years' service, and
made some rather curious discoveries. Up to 1860
something over seven thousand men completed their
terms, of whom rather more than half re-engaged themselves at once, and rather fewer than half took their
discharge. Of these latter six hundred and fifty re-
enlisted within six months. But among the provisions of
the Act was one which permitted men on completion
of their ten years with the colours to join an Army of
Reserve, counting twenty-two years' service therein
(that is to say twice the eleven years required with the
colours) to gain a pension. The scheme was a hopeless failure. Commanding officers, not wishing to lose
their men, gave no encouragement to the Army of Reserve, with the result that the reservists counted only
the ludicrous number of sixteen hundred. Meanwhile the net loss to the Army through limited service
amounted to over two thousand men, which must
somehow be made good. The Army of Reserve was,
therefore, dismissed as hopeless; and it was decided to
offer an additional bounty of £1 to every man who would
re-enlist, and to allow men to re-enlist within twelve
months, instead of within seven months, after taking
their discharge, reckoning all their past service towards
the twenty-one years which would ensure them a pension.[1]

The years 1865 and 1866 each witnessed a further
reduction of the establishment, but no reductions could
keep pace with the steady shrinking in the flow of
recruits. The additional bounty, offered to men who
re-enlisted, had failed of its object. As one member
put it, the Government tendered to them £1 for bounty,
£2 in lieu of a free kit, and one shilling a day for twenty
days, or £4 in all, all of which was spent in a few days,
after which the old soldier found himself drawing the
pay of a recruit.[2] The deficiency in the appointed

---

[1] *H.D.*, Speeches of Lord Hartington, April 7, 12, May 5, 1864.
[2] *H.D.*, Speech of Colonel North, Mar. 5, 1860.

1854–
1870.
strength of the Army swelled steadily from under six
hundred in 1862 to over six thousand in 1866; and in
May 1866 the Secretary for War was fain to commit
the recruiting problem to a Royal Commission, and
meanwhile to resort to the old pernicious habit of
asking militiamen to volunteer for the Line.[1] It
was suggested at this time that native Indian troops
might be employed in Colonial garrisons,[2] and it is
curious that the Government of New Zealand two
years later asked for Sikhs or Gurkhas to fight the
Maoris. Any idea was welcome which might enable
the country to pursue its time-hallowed policy of
striving to purchase a good Army for the price of a
bad one.

In 1867 a Conservative Government came for a short
time into power and found itself confronted with a very
critical state of affairs. Over twenty-one thousand men
would become entitled to their discharge in the course
of the year; death, desertion and sickness would add
another ten thousand casualties; so that altogether over
thirty-two thousand recruits would be needed within
the ensuing twelve months. Against this was to be
set the fact that the average number of recruits enlisted
annually during the previous three years barely
amounted to fourteen thousand. However, curiously
enough, the bare appointment of the Royal Commission to investigate this question had sufficed to improve recruiting; and for the first time since 1862,
the enlistments during the last quarter of 1866 exceeded the casualties. Meanwhile the Commission
had made its report, its principal recommendations
being as follows:

First. That enlistments should be for general service
and not for particular regiments.

This was accepted, because under this system the
maturer men could be sent to India and the youths
kept in England until ripened.

---

[1] *H.D.*, Answer of Lord Hartington, June 14, 1866.
[2] *H.D.*, Speech of Major Anson, Feb. 26, 1867.

Second. That military training schools for boys should be established, akin to the training ships of the Navy.

This was rejected as too expensive, the cost of each boy being reckoned at £30.

Third. " Localisation," meaning what is now called the territorial system.

It was remarked that local sentiment could not be improvised, and must therefore be allowed to grow up with time.

Fourth, Fifth and *Sixth.* That recruits should receive a greater reward on enlistment, that the soldier should get a free supply of necessaries and that his ration of meat should be increased.

The first of these was accepted, and in lieu of the two last the soldier's daily pay was increased by twopence.

Seventh. That men should receive an additional twopence a day upon re-engaging for a second term of service.

One penny only was conceded.

Eighth. That the first period of service should be raised from ten years to twelve.

This was accepted.

Then arose the question of a Reserve. It was pointed out that the militia was a Reserve; but that two Reserves were required, the first ready to fill the ranks at any moment and to serve abroad, and the second for home-defence. How was the First Reserve to be formed? The experiment of 1857 had failed completely. The enlistment of men for twelve years, of which part was to be spent with the colours and part in the Reserve—the system, in fact, which has obtained from 1870 up to the present time—was deliberately rejected. It was thought that the reservists would not easily find employment nor be readily discovered when wanted. It was therefore proposed, first, to give men long furloughs when their regiments returned from abroad, and, if they found employment, to allow them,

1854–
1870.
as a favour, to serve the remainder of their time in the militia; and, next, to permit men to take their discharge after serving five years abroad, or two-thirds of their service at home, and make them liable to general service for war only. " I am told," said General Peel, in putting these proposals forward, " that wars are unlikely now to last more than one campaign "— a hasty generalisation which was far too readily accepted for fifty years after the Austro-Prussian war of 1866. It was further proposed to increase the militia to one hundred and twenty thousand men, and to call upon one-fourth of them to engage themselves for the First Reserve. The inducements were to be a bounty of £12, spread over five years, to the men, and permission to every commanding officer who furnished a certain quota to recruit his regiment up to its full strength. For the rest, soldiers who had enlisted in the Army for ten years and re-enlisted for a second term of ten years were to be relegated for the last two or three years of their service to the enrolled pensioners, as a Second Reserve.

It is unnecessary to dwell upon the weakness of these expedients, which, if they came to anything at all, were of no long duration. But the most important point of these reforms of 1867 was the twopence added to the soldier's daily pay. In 1865 the pay of a private of infantry of the Line was thirteen pence a day, namely, one shilling for wages and one penny for beer-money. From this was deducted eightpence halfpenny for rations, groceries and vegetables. From the balance of threepence halfpenny he had to pay for barrack-damages, washing, and the renewal of his forage-cap, shell jacket, three shirts, razor, brushes, mits, soap, sponge and haversack. Moreover, owing to the American Civil war and what was called the cotton famine, the price of cotton shirts had risen, between 1862 and 1865, by thirty per cent.[1] Additional pay had been granted both to the Navy and to the police

[1] H.D., Speech of Colonel North, Mar. 20, 1865.

on this account, but in the Army, owing to the long 1854–
tradition of neglect and maltreatment, it was withheld 1870.
for three years.   With the tardy grant of this act of
justice the situation was transformed.   Recruiting improved at once.   The deficiency in the establishment,
which in 1865 had been nearly seven thousand, fell
by March 1868 to a little over nine hundred.   The
recruits gathered in during the last quarter of 1867
exceeded by one-fourth those of the corresponding
quarter of 1866.   Lastly, the re-engagements for a
second term of service, which from 1860 to 1866 had
averaged annually little over three thousand, rose in
the last nine months of 1867 to over twenty-six
thousand.[1]   Thus at last amid all the talk of re-
organising the Army there was some assurance that
there would be an army to reorganise.

Let us now glance at the condition of the private
soldier during these years; and first let us see how he
was housed.   As recorded in a previous volume of this
work, attention had already been called to the bad
condition of the barracks and of the military hospitals;
and the work of Miss Nightingale and of the Sanitary
Commission in the Crimea had given some impulse
towards improvement.   But many of the buildings
were still in a shocking state, and there were constant
complaints of them in Parliament.   Sir Joseph Paxton
in 1856 contrasted bitterly the sums spent on housing
convicts in new prisons—£150 to each convict—with
the scanty allowance allotted for housing the soldier.[2]
The Duke of Somerset two years later pointed to the
huge sums lavished on new Houses of Parliament and
new public offices, while good barracks were grudged
to the soldier.[3]   But a more practical member was
Lord Ebrington, an enthusiast for sanitary science,
who went the round of many barracks and of nearly
all the military hospitals, caught ophthalmia in one of

[1] *H.D.*, Speech of Sir John Pakington, Mar. 23, 1868.
[2] *H.D.*, Speech of Sir Joseph Paxton, June 19, 1856.
[3] *H.D.*, Speech of Duke of Somerset, Mar. 26, 1868.

1854– them, and came down to the House of Commons
1870. blinded in one eye and primed with unpleasant statistics.
First he called attention to the overcrowding. On an
average the allowance of space to every soldier was
four hundred cubic feet; in ten hospitals it was less
than four hundred, in many barracks and actually in
five hospitals it was less than three hundred cubic feet.[1]
The Guards' barracks in Portman Street were among
the worst, but those at Woolwich were unspeakable.
The buildings were so ruinous that they were shored
up to prevent them from falling, and the state of the
latrines below was such as to breed pestilence.   For
nine years the authorities had complained of them to
no purpose.   The general result was that, whereas the
general rate of mortality among the population of
military age varied between seven and a half and nine
in a thousand, that of the Guards was twenty, that of
the Line eighteen, and that of the Cavalry eleven in
the thousand.   So also the deaths from consumption,
due principally to overcrowding, in the Army were
eighteen in a thousand, while among the rest of the
population they were but three and a half.   Could
there be worse economy, Lord Ebrington asked, than
to give bounties to recruits in order to kill them off
prematurely twice as fast as the rest of the population?[2]
He concluded by a long motion, which was unanimously
passed, to the effect that the excessive mortality in the
Army was due to the bad sanitary condition of the
barracks.

It was very characteristic of Parliament, in which
perhaps at that time the sickly sentimental side of the
English character was excessively represented, to take

---

[1] General Sir William Codrington pointed out in Parliament that
the allowance for convicts was 1000 cubic feet.

[2] *H.D.*, Speeches of Lord Ebrington, May 10, 11, 1858. I shall
not, I hope, be accused of unduly magnifying my father's share in
this work.   He never magnified it to me, but it was well known in
the House of Commons (*see* Mr. Stafford's speech, *H.D.*, June 19,
1856); and, if it had been the work of one unknown to me, I could
not have refrained from mentioning it as fully.

better care of convicts, who were public enemies, than 1854–
of soldiers who were a public safeguard. However, 1870.
from this time forward the improvement of barracks
began, both at home and abroad, though the process
was necessarily long, if indeed it may be said yet to be
completed.   Meanwhile an entirely new quarter for
the soldier had sprung up in the form of Aldershot
camp.   Aldershot was originally purchased by Lord
Hardinge as an exercising ground in 1853, and was
opened as a camp, for militia, during the Crimean war
in 1855.[1]   The idea of an exercising ground was
excellent, for in time of peace there was only one
quarter in the British Isles—Dublin—where troops
enough could be collected even for the drilling of a
brigade.   Furthermore the situation of Aldershot,
strategically, was well chosen.   But there seems to
have been some halting between the two opinions
whether Aldershot should be merely a training ground
or a permanent station; and apparently the Crimean
war decided that it should be more or less permanent.
As a kind of compromise wooden huts were erected
instead of stable buildings, and thousands of pounds
were wasted in throwing up these shelters of green
timber, which were cramped, uncomfortable and, in
the matter of married quarters, not too respectful of
decency.[2]   In fact, as one member of Parliament truly
described it, Aldershot became a kind of squatters'
village;[3] and, through extreme bad management,[4] the
undesirable population, which invariably haunts a

[1] *H.D.*, Speech of Sir F. Smith, Mar. 16, 1865.
[2] *H.D.*, Lord Hartington's answer to question in Commons,
June 10, 1864.
[3] *H.D.*, Speech of Captain Vivian, June 18, 1857.
[4] This mismanagement was due, so far as I can ascertain, to the
military and not to the civil authorities.   My father (who had gone
pretty closely into the question of Aldershot and was careful of his
statements) told me that the Queen and Prince Consort rode over the
newly acquired ground with Lord Hardinge, and that the Prince,
pointing to a portion of it, observed that it would be a pretty site for
a camp.   Thereupon Hardinge complaisantly placed the camp there
without asking further questions.

camp, was able to settle down close to it and yet beyond the reach of control. For the camp was placed on the edge of the Government's property; and the Government, having raised the value of the adjacent land, so to speak, against itself, was obliged later to buy it up at an excessive price. Altogether Aldershot at the outset was very far from an attractive place.[1]

Nevertheless the mere concentration of a comparatively large body of troops was productive of good to the soldier. At Aldershot crime diminished, while the general health of the men was bettered beyond precedent;[2] and thus it was proved that with a little care the lives of thousands of men could be saved.[3] Moreover, provisions could be bought in greater bulk and so retailed more cheaply to the rank and file. The soldiers were very suspicious of this latter change at first, but presently became reconciled to it, and then welcomed the improvement. The Commissariat, of which more shall be said later, was learning its business, and the bread which it issued at Aldershot was far superior to that baked in London. Gradually these benefits were extended to foreign stations; and in 1861 the stoppages had been so far adjusted to conditions oversea that, for the first time in his history, the net pay of the soldier was the same all over the Empire.[4]

[1] *H.D.*, Mar. 16, 1865. Sir H. Verney declared that Aldershot was detested by the Army; the huts were verminous, and there were no amusements for the men except in the vile places which had sprung up alongside. The women who haunted the camp were known until well into my own lifetime as the " wrens."

[2] *H.D.*, Speeches of Mr. Peel, Mar. 4, and of Sidney Herbert, July 14, 1859.

[3] The average annual mortality in England between 1841 and 1856 fell, by 1859, in the Household Cavalry from 10 to 8 per 1000; in the Line Cavalry from 13 to 8; in the Artillery from 11 to 7; in the Guards from 19 to 7·7; and in the Line Infantry from 17 to 8. At Aldershot the rate was only 5 per 1000. *H.D.*, Speech of Sidney Herbert, Feb. 17, 1860.

[4] *H.D.*, Speeches of Mr. Peel, Mar. 4, Sidney Herbert, July 14, 1859; of Sidney Herbert, Feb. 17, 1860; of Mr. Baring, Mar. 14, 1861.

It must not, however, be supposed that the neglect, 1854–
the abuses and the prejudices of two centuries could be 1870.
banished in a day.   There were still constant complaints of the lack of recreation-rooms, and above all
of the want of light in barracks, the Government only
allowing two wretched candles for one large room.
Small grants were from time to time made towards
curing these evils.   Thus in 1862 the sum of seven
thousand pounds was allotted by Parliament to supply
reading-rooms and gymnasia; but Sir George Cornewall
Lewis did not feel justified in asking for more, since he
was actually demanding thirty thousand pounds—no
less—for sanitary improvements.   Again in 1864 five
thousand pounds—the salary of a Secretary of State
—was grudgingly vouchsafed for the provision of
recreation-rooms.[1]   The old evils of the canteens had,
moreover, again cropped up.   Some at least of the
canteens had again fallen into the hands of contractors,
one of whom made £10,000 a year out of them; and a
member brought the matter up in the House of Commons. Sir George Lewis answered that it was no doubt
a pity that soldiers drank beer and spirits, but that he
saw no preferable way of supplying them.[2]   This was
no more than could be expected of an overworked civil
administrator;   but, as usual, regimental officers had
stepped in to do the work which the higher authorities
could not or would not touch.   At Gibraltar a Captain
Jackson had established a regimental institute—a kind
of club—which numbered two thousand five hundred
subscribers, and proved to be a great success.   It had
not, however, been based upon sound principles, for it
declined upon Captain Jackson's departure from the
Rock.   In 1862 Sir George Lewis granted a small
sum for setting up a like institute at Portsmouth; and
meanwhile in one or two stations in India and the

[1] *H.D.*, Speeches of Sir G. Lewis, Mar. 13, 1862, and of Col.
North, May 9, 1864.
[2] Speeches of Mr. Wyld, Mar. 6, 1862, Mar. 16, 1863, and of
Sir G. Lewis, Mar. 16, 1863.

Colonies the experiment had been tried of taking
canteens away from tenants altogether, and of placing
them in the hands of a committee of officers, who made
the best bargains that they could for the purchase of
goods and applied any profit that might arise to the
benefit of the men.   The principle was extended to
the United Kingdom in 1864, with the provision, at
that time wise and sound, that the canteens should
thenceforward be a regimental affair.   " These things,"
said Lord Hartington, " are not a success except as
regimental institutions."   So in every regiment there
was appointed by the commanding officer a committee
of three officers to manage the canteen; and by 1865
the system had proved itself to be thoroughly successful.
Regimental officers had thrown themselves eagerly into
the work and had in some cases saved their men a
penny a day, while at the same time supplying them
with better goods than they could ever have obtained
before.   And this, as Lord Hartington said in the
House of Commons, they had done " without hope of
reward."   He doubtless wished to do them justice;
but he might have added that every amelioration of the
private soldier's lot had been wrought by regimental
officers without hope of reward, except the welfare of
their men and the consequent superiority of their regiment.   This new and improved regulation for canteens
lasted for forty years, growing steadily more insufficient.   Then, after some struggles, it was superseded by a superior system, once again devised, as
shall presently be seen, by regimental officers.[1]

In the matter of clothing the soldier decidedly
profited by the abolition of the old system of " clothing
colonels," the material provided by the Army Clothing
Factory, which had been set up in Pimlico, being better
than had ever been provided before.   In respect of
design, the tunic had been substituted for the old

[1] H.D., Speeches of Sir G. Lewis, May 12, 1862; Lord Hartington
and Mr. Childers, Mar. 3, 1864; Lord Hartington and Sir H. Verney,
May 5, 1864.

coatee, and the fashion of the shako had been changed 1854–
—all in imitation of the French.   But it was only after 1870.
the defeat of France in 1870 that the spiked helmet of
the Prussian infantry came into fashion.   Such foolish
fopperies were destined to endure for another generation; but common sense was beginning to prevail in
the matter of raiment.   Every man who sailed for
India during the Mutiny received some light clothing
upon landing;[1] and attention has already been drawn
to the use of khaki in India, and of other sensible
material in New Zealand for actual work in the field.
A smart uniform was of course an encouragement towards recruiting, and any attempt to do away with it in
the nineteenth century would have raised violent outcry.
Only after the lapse of two generations is it perhaps per-
missible to hint that the money saved in clothing might
have been better spent in raising the soldier's pay.

For the rest, the chances that a soldier could rise
from the ranks to a commission were small, for an
officer's expenses were so great that a promoted non-
commissioned officer could not afford to incur them.
Moreover, the abolition of the old system of clothing
brought unexpected hardship upon regimental quartermasters, whose places had been one of the few refuges
for deserving non-commissioned officers.   Under the
old system the quartermaster, as the Colonel's em-
ployee, had bought regimental necessaries wholesale,
and sold them retail; and the profits thereby accruing
had enabled him to maintain himself as became an
officer.   This practice was one of the many shifts
whereby Parliament had saddled the men with expenses which should have been borne by the country.
In 1865 this grievance of the quartermasters was
redressed by an allowance of thirty pounds a year and
through the payment of their mess-bills by the public.[2]

[1] *H.D.*, Speech of Sir J. Ramsden, Aug. 6, 1857.   The men
received each 4 white jackets, and 6 pairs of trousers.
[2] *H.D.*, Speeches of Sir F. Smith, June 16, 1864, and of Lord
Hartington, Mar. 16, 1865.

1854–
1870. Another regulation, which had caused much discontent among non-commissioned officers, was that men on promotion to serjeant's rank necessarily forfeited their good-conduct pay; which amounted to inflicting a penalty upon serjeants for previous good behaviour. This monstrous absurdity, due of course to the niggardliness of Parliament, was abolished by the grant to serjeants of an additional twopence to their daily pay.[1] Upon the whole, therefore, the condition of the private soldier at home was decidedly improved.

But unfortunately the private of infantry still spent very little time at home. Lord Hartington announced triumphantly in 1865 that for the first time one-third of the battalions of the Line were actually to be in the British Isles.[2] The rule was that they should have five years at home for every ten abroad; but the country had never kept faith with the soldier since Waterloo in granting even this scanty allowance. It was, in fact, only by the steady reduction of the garrisons of the tropical colonies that the battalions of the Line gained any respite from foreign service at all; and, even so, the situation, both in South Africa and in India, threatened them with constant abridgement of their short periods at home. It was always assumed, and no doubt with correctness, that the conditions of housing, food and amusement were worse abroad than in the British Isles, though in foreign stations, too, improvement was going forward. But there is one point which has generally been ignored in consideration of the soldier's life, and that is the time which he actually spent on passage between England and the different parts of the Empire. We occasionally hear of the wreck of a transport, as, for instance, of the *Birkenhead*; but there happen at this period to be rather curious examples of the soldier's life at sea which are worth a few brief remarks.

Those were, of course, the early days of steamships,

[1] *H.D.*, Speech of Lord Panmure, Mar. 26, 1858.
[2] *H.D.*, Speech of Lord Hartington, Mar. 16, 1865.

when every one of them was rigged to carry sail and was not thought safe at sea without it.   Whether the majority of them were really ill-built and provided with bad machinery, or whether the Admiralty was very unfortunate in the vessels which it bought or hired, it is not easy now to say; but the number of mishaps among the transport-ships was very discreditable. There was a Queen's ship called the *Megaera*, which took the Rifle Brigade out to the Kaffir war in 1852. She started from the Downs on the 3rd of January, encountered a gale in the Channel, caught fire twice, and put into Plymouth on the 5th utterly disabled. Hastily refitted, she put to sea again on the 7th, and after catching fire again more than once at last reached Capetown on the 24th of March.[1]   This wretched ship was run ashore by her captain twenty years later to save her from sinking, and so happily was got rid of, being a disgrace to the Navy.

Another ship purchased by Government was the *Transit*, of two thousand six hundred tons, which was appointed to carry the Ninetieth to India in 1857. Meeting with rough weather in the Channel she was obliged to put into Coruña to refit.   Later in the voyage she encountered a cyclone in the Indian Ocean, which so loosened her iron plates that she leaked dangerously.   By a fortunate mishap she ran ashore in the Straits of Banca, and there became a total wreck; otherwise she would have foundered before she reached her destination.[2]   Yet another ship, the *Urgent*, was purchased at the same time as the *Transit*.   She sailed with troops from England for Barbados; broke down and put into Coruña on the 3rd of March; broke down again and put into Madeira on the 9th; and finally, leaking all the way, reached Barbados, where it was found that the screw had displaced a large sheet of iron in the stern.[3]

---

[1] Cope, *History of the Rifle Brigade*, pp. 269-270.
[2] Wolseley, *Story of a Soldier's Life*, i. 234-241.
[3] *H.D.*, Speech of Mr. Lindsay, May 8, 1857.

The most memorable voyage of the time, however, was that of the *Sarah Sands*, a hired iron screw-steamer of eleven hundred tons, which sailed from Portsmouth for India on the 15th of August 1857, with about three hundred and fifty officers and men of the Fifty-fourth. She was manned, owing to the dearth of seamen, by a rabble of worthless foreigners; and it is supposed that it was owing to their carelessness that the ship caught fire on the 11th of November between the Cape and Ceylon. The crew at once took to the boats and made off. The soldiers, preserving perfect discipline, fought the flames with indomitable courage and persistence. The vessel was divided by three transverse water-tight bulkheads; and her safety depended on confining the conflagration to the aftermost compartment. The men were formed up in small columns, and as the foremost were carried away, asphyxiated by smoke and half-roasted by heat, those in rear came forward in succession to take their place. After fourteen hours of desperate work the fire was subdued; but by that time the after-compartment was a mere wreck of buckled girders, with a big hole on the port quarter where the explosion of a barrel of gunpowder, which no efforts had availed to remove, had blown away the iron plates. The leak was stopped as best it could be; a jury-rudder was rigged up; and the ship made sail for Mauritius. All the provisions had been destroyed except a barrel or two of salt-beef and one or two barrels of flour, and the only water was a filthy liquid produced by damaged condensers. For a fortnight the *Sarah Sands* crawled along, surrounded by sharks all the way, and in danger of foundering at any moment, until at last she crept safely into Port Louis. The behaviour of all ranks of the Fifty-fourth was superb. A General Order issued from the Horse Guards made special mention by name of four officers and twenty-five non-commissioned officers and soldiers; and the story of the *Sarah Sands* has ever since been rightly held up as a grand example of discipline.

These examples avouch that the perils of the sea in the early days of steam-vessels were appreciable, and that they were aggravated by what can only be described as criminal neglect.[1]   It must, however, in justice to the Government, be added that they took up the largest ship afloat to convey troops to Canada in 1861, and that the *Great Eastern* actually carried in a single voyage across the Atlantic two battalions of infantry and a battery of artillery, counting over two thousand officers and men, with the usual proportion of women and children and one hundred and twenty-two horses.   The number may not in these days of gigantic ships sound very great, but seventy years ago it was positively startling.   Indeed the *Great Eastern*, for years the largest ship afloat, was then esteemed one of the wonders of the world.[2]   There were then many officers living who had crossed the Atlantic with detachments of their regiments in sailing vessels of two or three hundred tons.

From the domestic life of the soldier at home and abroad, afloat and ashore, I turn next to his training. The most important reform here was the formation of camps of instruction for all arms not only at Aldershot, as has already been mentioned, but at Shorncliffe and Colchester in England and at the Curragh in Ireland. All of these were duly established by the year 1862. This policy of concentration, made possible by the institution of the constabulary of boroughs and counties, has long been accepted as a matter of course; but at the time it was nothing less than revolutionary.   Another startling novelty, induced by the introduction of the rifle, was the establishment of schools of musketry at Hythe and Fleetwood.   It will be remembered that, when the Army sailed for the Crimea, small-arms were in a state of transition, certain divisions only being

---

[1] See Lord Wolseley's account of his voyage in an infamous old tub called the *Melbourne* in December 1861.   She took twenty-three days to steam from Cork to Halifax.

[2] I still keep my childish vision of her at sea off the Isle of Wight, with her six masts and her four funnels, about the year 1865.

provided with the Minié rifle; and that there was attached to Raglan's staff an officer specially chosen to train officers and men to the use of the new weapon. The Minié, as we have seen, was superseded by the Enfield rifle, also a muzzle-loader; but in 1858 the seamen and marines of the American navy were already armed with breech-loading rifles, and the British Navy, spurred to emulation, was making trial of experimental breech-loading weapons for itself. Many private firms were busying themselves with the improvement of rifled barrels and the devising of expanding bullets to take full advantage of the grooves; and already some of them were reducing the bore with the object of obtaining greater accuracy. Though, therefore, it was decided in 1864 to give the Army a breech-loading rifle, there was much difficulty in deciding as to the choice of a weapon. Meanwhile an attempted Fenian invasion of Canada in 1866 had caused the Canadian Government to beg for an immediate supply of breech-loaders for the troops there; and four thousand were accordingly purchased in America. The events of the war between Prussia and Austria in the same year showed that the need for a breech-loading rifle was urgent; and it was decided to convert the existing Enfield rifles into breech-loaders according to the designs of Mr. Snider.[1] The work proceeded night and day, both on weekdays and Sundays; and as has been seen, the British troops in the Abyssinian expedition were armed with Snider rifles. By 1869 this rifle had been issued not only to all the regular troops but also to sixteen thousand of the militia; and its great significance was that for the first time the percussion-cap formed part and parcel of the cartridge.[2]

---

[1] H.D., Speeches of General Peel, Mar. 7, 1867; of Mr. Cardwell, Mar. 11, 1869; of Captain Vivian, Aug. 6, 1869.

[2] In these days the Snider might be condemned as inhuman. The bullet was made hollow, with a base of clay, so that it might expand and take the grooves. And it did expand. I have seen a fallow-deer shot with a service Snider carbine, and the hole at the bullet's point of exit would have held my two open hands.

This change pointed to the early disappearance of the external hammer in fire-arms; and, in fact, in this same year (1869) a new hammerless rifle—the Martini-Henry[1] —of smaller bore, far greater range, lower trajectory and superior accuracy, had already been distributed for trial in the various climates wherein the British Army may at any moment be called upon for service.

The changes in the drill and tactics of infantry, which followed upon the introduction of the breech-loader, fall outside the limits of time by which the present work is bounded.   It was by chance rather than design that they coincided with an alteration of some importance in the drill of cavalry.   For more than a century the ranks of mounted men had been told off, for purposes of manœuvre, by threes; an arrangement which made the movements particularly neat, for the breadth of three horses was just the length of one horse. It was found, however, on active service that, if two men out of the three were struck down, the moral effect upon the third was too severe to be borne by ordinary soldiers; so the ranks were now told off by fours.   Thus the word "Fours right" took the place of the old word "Threes right," and the taunt of "Threes about" which, if addressed to members of one or two regiments, almost sufficed at one time to cause a military riot, became obsolete and meaningless. The change usefully anticipated the time when cavalry should be largely employed on foot; for under the old system it was possible only to dismount two men in three, whereas, under the new, there were dismounted three out of every four, the fourth man sufficing to hold three horses.   For the rest no serious effort was made to reduce the weight upon the troop-horse's back, in spite of the lessons taught during the Indian Mutiny, and the saddlery continued to be heavy.   As a mere picturesque detail, it may be mentioned that in 1861

---

[1] This rifle was duly issued shortly afterwards, and was a favourite weapon with the men, as we know from Mr. Kipling's early military tales.

1854–
1870.
Light Dragoons disappeared from the British Army with the conversion of the Third, Fourth, Thirteenth and Fourteenth into Hussars.   Since the new designation affected practically nothing except the dress of officers and men, it is unnecessary to say more of it.

In the Ordnance Corps, as the Royal Artillery and Royal Engineers used to be called, their transfer from the control of the Board of Ordnance to that of the Horse Guards was bound to bring with it far-reaching changes.   In the Artillery and Engineers promotion went by seniority, one result of which arrangement was that officers who attained to field-rank were generally very old.   Moreover, since their promotion to general rank depended upon their standing in the regiment and not in the Army, few of them reached general rank at all, and practically none were ever to be found on the Staff of the Army.   Another serious consequence was discovered in the Crimea when all the Colonels of Engineers broke down, being too old to withstand the hardship and fatigue.   This grievance was brought forward more than once by a former officer of Engineers in the House of Commons, and it was evident that it must be faced sooner or later; but the only answer for the present was a disquisition on the difficulty of promoting officers by selection.[1]   Meanwhile both Artillery and Engineers had increased very greatly in numbers and importance.   The abolition of all native artillery and of the East India Company's batteries in India had led inevitably to considerable augmentation of the Royal Regiment; and, after the Crimea, the whole status of the Engineers had been altered by the incorporation with them of the Royal Sappers and Miners. The Artillery and Engineers had always been the best educated corps of the Army; and it had further been ordained in 1855 that cadetships at the Royal Academy at Woolwich, which had heretofore been granted by nomination of the Master-General of the

[1] *H.D.*, Speeches of Captain Leicester Vernon, June 19, 1856, Mar. 6, 1860.

Ordnance, should thenceforward be gained only by competitive examination.   Now that the Artillery and Engineers stood on the same footing, save in the matter of the purchase of commissions, with the Cavalry and Infantry, it was impossible that, looking to their superiority in numbers and intelligence, they should be shut out of high command.

It so happened, too, that just at this time circumstances lifted the officers of Artillery and Engineers into peculiar prominence.   In the first place, a great scheme was going forward for the defence and fortification of the Royal Dockyards both at home and abroad, demanding not only great professional skill, but good administration, good husbandry, and, above all, patience under the provocation of political critics who, with a jealousy that had its laudable side, watched keenly over the expenditure of millions.   The officer mainly concerned in this task was Colonel Jervois of the Royal Engineers, and it seems to have been mainly owing to his moral courage, tact and good sense that the work went forward at all.   The rapid development in the range and power of artillery have long since rendered most, if not all, of his fortifications obsolete, but that does not detract from the merit of his service at the time.[1]

Then in the Artillery the traditions of ages were overset by the introduction of rifled and breech-loading ordnance.   The whole science of the artillerist was entering upon a new phase; and the fact was recognised in 1859 by the establishment of a school of gunnery at Shoeburyness.   Both within and without the Royal Regiment great intellects were busily at work.   Armstrong's field-pieces had hardly emerged from their first trial in active service in China before

---

[1] See Clode, *Military Forces of the Crown*, ii. 407 *n*.   Sir William Jervois, as he became later, finished his career as a most successful Colonial Governor.   I was his private secretary in New Zealand, and heard much of his difficulties at the time mentioned in the text.   But he was far too modest to speak of his conquest of them.

1854– they were superseded by an improved pattern of the
1870. same gun; and Armstrong contracted with the Government to supply in the course of 1861 over one thousand
rifled cannon of various calibres.[1] Whitworth produced rival guns which were also tried, but not pronounced superior to Armstrong's.[2] Major Palliser of
the Royal Artillery came forward with a new projectile
of chilled iron.[3] But all of these details brought up
the large question of the Royal Arsenal at Woolwich.
There, only brass cannon had hitherto been cast, and
for all iron pieces the Government had resorted to
private firms.[4] Now all cannon were to be of iron;
before long they were to be all of steel. Was the
country to depend wholly upon Elswick and other
great private arsenals, or was Woolwich to throw off
its old traditions and be foremost in the manufacture
of the country's ordnance? Looking to the fact that
England had shaken off the trammels of Birmingham
by the erection of the small-arms factory at Enfield, and
could produce rifles at a cheaper rate for herself than
by purchase from Birmingham, there could be little
doubt of the ultimate answer.[5]

Next, there was a new service, something more than
a rival of the old Waggon Train, which had been called
into being by the Crimean war—the Land Transport
Corps. We have seen that at the close of that war this
new corps had attained to a notable strength both in men
and horses. With the return of peace it was at once
cut down to twelve hundred men and rechristened the
Military Train. Sir William Codrington, who had

[1] 330 100-prs.; 280 40-prs.; 197 25-prs.; 200 12-prs.
H.D., Speech of Mr. Baring, Mar. 14, 1860.
[2] H.D., Speech of Sir G. Lewis, Mar. 6, 1862.
[3] H.D., General Peel (answer to question), Feb. 14, 1866. Palliser
shells were at one time well known in the Royal Navy.
[4] H.D., Speeches of Captain Boldero, Mr. Monsell and Sir C.
Napier, Mar. 7, 1856; Clode, Military Forces of the Crown, ii. 226-227.
[5] The extraordinary, almost insane, reversion to muzzle-loading
ordnance which was hastily corrected in 1885–1886 does not come
within the scope of this history.

returned to the House of Commons at the conclusion 1854–
of his command in the Crimea, protested vigorously 1870.
against this reduction, saying truly enough that twelve
hundred men were only enough for a single division,
and that no expedition, whatever its size, should leave
England without its own transport-corps.   He urged
meanwhile that the Military Train should be exercised
in its duty of carrying tents and ammunition and providing ambulances.[1]   Meanwhile some trouble arose
out of the reduction itself, for more than one hundred
of the officers of the Land Transport Corps had been
non-commissioned officers promoted from the Artillery
and from the Line.   It was cruel to turn any of these
adrift without a special retiring allowance, and yet the
Government dared not grant it, lest other officers, who
lacked private means, should claim the same indulgence.[2]   Again the status of the officers was uncertain.
The Land Transport Corps, when originally formed,
had been excluded from the operation of purchase;
but the system, as was almost inevitable, had crept
into the Military Train, and no one could say positively
whether it were what was called a " purchase-corps "
or not.[3]   Such anomalies were unfavourable to a new
organisation which in its infancy needed fostering with
all possible encouragement.

It is hardly surprising, therefore, that the Military
Train, when dispatched to India for the suppression
of the Mutiny, should have embraced the chance of
becoming combatant soldiers and doing duty, gallantly
enough, as dragoons.   In the discharge of their legitimate business, Lord Strathnairn complained of their
incompetence, and the like shortcomings were observed
in New Zealand.   Meanwhile the Military Train in
1858 had been further reduced to eleven hundred men;

---

[1] *H.D.*, Speech of Sir William Codrington, Mar. 12, 1857.

[2] *H.D.*, Second speech of Mr. Peel, Mar. 12, 1857.   Speeches of
Lord A. Vane-Tempest, and of the Under-Sec. for War, April 23, 1858.

[3] *H.D.*, Sir G. Lewis (answers to questions), Mar. 25, 1862; Lord
Hartington, May 22, 1865 (answers to questions).

1854– and Codrington again spoke in remonstrance, not against
1870. the policy only but against the general use to which
the corps was turned. " It should not be kept as a
matter of economy," he said, " to do a variety of
dirty things," from which we may gather that from
this period dates the unworthy and opprobrious title of
the " Muck-Train." [1] Altogether the condition of the
corps was not satisfactory, and it seems to have been
too much the practice for Ministers, if they decided to
augment any branch of the service, to make good the
expense by reduction of the Military Train.[2]

On the other hand, the Commissariat Corps, which
was concerned entirely with supply only and not with
transport, made great advances, and by buying in
bulk was able, as has been told, to provide the troops
not only with good food but with groceries at a very
low rate. Mention has also been made of the excellent
work which it did in New Zealand. If the Commissariat had been united to the Military Train and the
whole had been placed on a military basis, as in the
present Army Service Corps, the benefits conferred
by each might have helped forward the popularity of
the other. But the trouble was that the Commissariat
remained a civilians' service, while the Military Train
were soldiers. Unfortunately a Committee had in
1859 recommended the continuance of this system,
though the representatives both of the Commissariat
and of the Military Train dissented from this decision.
In fact the most prominent members of both services
repeatedly emphasised the imperative need for placing
transport and supply, whether on a military or a civil
basis, under a single head. It was, as they consistently
urged, unsound in principle to make one authority
responsible for the waggon and another for its load.[3]

This evil was remedied under a far-reaching scheme

---

[1] *H.D.*, Speech of Sir William Codrington, May 10, 1858.
[2] *H.D.*, Speech of Mr. Baring, Mar. 14, 1861.
[3] See the report of Lord Strathnairn's Committee on Transport
and Supply, 1867. Evidence of Commr.-Gen. Drake; Dep. Com.

which, so to speak, covered the reorganisation of the 1854–
War Office from top to bottom.   The hasty transfer 1870.
of all work done in connection with the Army by the
Treasury, the Home Office, the Board of Ordnance and
sundry minor departments to the War Office, had produced for the time absolute chaos.   The Secretary of
State for War was cruelly overworked; and no remedy
for the confusion seemed to be discoverable except the
appointment of endless committees of inquiry and the
issue of endless reports.   Within twelve years seventeen Royal Commissions, eighteen select committees
of the House of Commons, nineteen committees of
officers within the War Office and thirty-five committees of military officers had considered sundry points
of policy in the administration of the War Department;
and still the clumsy machinery groaned and creaked,
while the wheels, when they revolved at all, turned
slowly with much friction.   Among the committees of
military officers was one appointed in 1866 under the
presidency of Lord Strathnairn to inquire as to the
organisation of transport and supply for an army in the
field.   They presented their report in 1867, and recommended the junction of the principal departments
of military supply, including treasure, under a single
functionary to be styled the Controller.   The five departments mainly concerned were the Commissariat,
Transport, Stores, Hospitals and Barracks.   The idea
was an imitation of the French *Intendance*, and did not
commend itself to some English administrators; [1] but
it was none the less adopted.   In 1868 the Chief Controller was appointed in the person of Sir Henry
Storks, a very able officer, and within twelve months
his sub-controllers were established over most of the
military commands in the Empire.   The Duke of Cambridge at the outset expressed apprehensions lest the

Fonblanque; Maj.-gen. Balfour, and Memos. of D.A. Commr.-Gen.
Bailey and Commr.-Gen. Power; letter of Colonel Clarke Kennedy,
Dec. 18, 1860.

[1] See the scathing comments of Clode, ii. 413 *seq.*

1854–
1870.
Controller might override the authority of a Commander-in-chief in the field; but the " control system," as it was called, was short-lived, because even in time of peace it divided responsibility between controller and general officer.   The story, however, falls outside the bounds of this history; and our chief concern with the system of control in this place lies in the junction of transport and supply under a single authority.

The Medical Service, after the experience of the Crimean war, became naturally the subject of inquiry by a Royal Commission in 1857, with the result that in 1859 a medical school was opened at Chatham for special study of the diseases incident to armies in the field and of gun-shot wounds.[1]   Soon afterwards this was superseded by the building of two model hospitals, one at Netley and one at Woolwich.   The former of these became in 1863 the Army Medical School, to which candidates between the ages of twenty-one and twenty-six, possessing diplomas in medicine and surgery, were admitted after passing an examination.   The erection of two good military hospitals in itself was a great step in advance; but the regimental organisation for medical officers was still retained until 1873.   Moreover, the real problem, which was not solved until many years later, was how to prevent the medical service from being clogged by the accumulation of a number of elderly men, mostly of mediocre attainments, who from want of varied practice had no opportunity of keeping abreast of the progress of medical science, and yet through mere seniority attained to high rank.

The Crimean war revealed also a dearth of chaplains, there being in 1854 no more than seven for the whole Army.   These Lord Panmure supplemented with twenty-two more chaplains and thirty-five assistants,[2] all of the Church of England.   But in 1858 Roman Catholics and Presbyterians were added, and the whole, of whatever denomination, were divided into

---

[1] *H.D.*, Speech of Mr. Sidney Herbert, July 14, 1859.
[2] Speech of Lord Panmure, Mar. 26, 1858.

four classes, those of the first class ranking as colonels 1854–
and of the fourth as captains.   There was at first some 1870.
difference in the rates of pay, ludicrously suggestive of
bigotry, for, while Anglicans received ten shillings a
day, only three-quarters of that sum were accorded to
Presbyterians and no more than half to Roman Catholics.   These monstrous distinctions were abolished in
1859 by General Peel, who placed all chaplains alike
upon the same footing.[1]

Last, there remains for review the condition of the
officers of the Army at large.   In 1856 George, Duke of
Cambridge, was appointed Commander-in-chief, a post
which he held for over thirty years.   In the course of that
period the Army was utterly transformed from top to
bottom, not always in accordance with his own opinions;
and only when those transformations can be viewed
from some distance of time in their due perspective can
justice be done to the unfailing loyalty and tact with
which the Duke discharged his most difficult and trying
duties.   One of the earliest changes in the Horse
Guards came in 1860, when it was ordained that the
Staff at Head Quarters should hold office in future for
five years only.   In the past one Quartermaster-general
had retained his post for forty years, and one Adjutant-
general for twenty years.   It had already been laid
down that after the 1st of January 1860 no officer was
to be eligible for the Staff until he had gone through
the Staff College and passed the final examination there;
but this rule of course could not yet be applied to the
senior posts at Head Quarters, which were still filled by
men who had graduated in the more searching school
of active service.   Prominent among these was Sir
Richard Airey, later Lord Airey, the wisest and ablest
officer in the Army.[2]

[1] *H.D.*, Third speech of General Peel, Mar. 4, 1859.

[2] " The wisest and ablest soldier it was ever my lot to do business
with," Wolseley, *Story of a Soldier's Life*, ii. 242.   It must be remembered that Wolseley when brought into contact with Airey was
the most brilliant, pushing and impatient of the younger school of
officers.

1854–
1870.

But the more important question agitated at this time was the future of the man upon whom the existence of the Army had for two centuries depended and was still dependent—the regimental officer. He had suffered no less than the men from incessant exile, and like them was chafing under it. " No officer," said one of his champions in Parliament, " who goes to India can say when he will return. He must either leave his bones or his regiment in India—a species of cruelty practised by no other Government in the world."[1] He, no less than the private, was underpaid. A subaltern's expenses were reckoned at £157 annually and his pay at £95, leaving a deficit of £61.[2] There was an instance of a promoted non-commissioned officer struggling to keep a wife and children upon his pay of six shillings and fourpence a day—the wages, at that time, of a first-class mason, less than the wages of a first-class carpenter and considerably less than the salary of a clerk in a bank.[3] But there seemed to be less anxiety as to the supply of officers then as to their manner of entering the Army. A Commission had been appointed to inquire into the whole subject of the purchase of commissions. Sir de Lacy Evans continued to move persistently in the Commons that purchase should be abolished; and Mr. Sidney Herbert had worked towards that end by cutting down the price of commissions by one-third, and endeavouring to limit purchase to the grades junior to that of lieutenant-colonel.[4] Purchase was likewise forbidden in the regiments transferred from the East India Company's to the Queen's service;[5] but it had also been excluded from the Land Transport Corps, yet by stealth had crept into its successor, the Military Train. It was evidently not easy to check purchase in one or two corps unless it were prohibited in all.

[1] H.D., Speech of Mr. H. Baillie, Mar. 3, 1862.
[2] H.D., Speech of Colonel Freeston, July 28, 1858.
[3] H.D., Speech of Major Jervois, April 13, 1867.
[4] H.D., Speech of Mr. Sidney Herbert and of Sir de Lacy Evans, Mar. 6, 1860.
[5] H.D., Speech of Sir Charles Wood, Feb. 22, 1861.

Meanwhile for a short time purchase remained half 1854–
alive and half dead.   A Committee on military organ- 1870.
isation had recommended that there should be only one
gate of entrance to the Army—through a military
college—and the Duke of Cambridge strongly upheld
this recommendation.   A Military College existed at
Sandhurst, which, as already told, had been founded
for the benefit of officers' sons.   The original system
at Sandhurst had been that the Commander-in-chief
nominated the cadets, of whom there were about four
hundred in all, that they were admitted at the age of
thirteen, and that, after passing out at sixteen, they
received a commission without purchase.   Later these
rules had been changed.   The Commander-in-chief
still nominated the cadets, who had to pass an examination to enter the College and a second competitive
examination after twelve months' stay in it, after which,
on payment of £100 for a year's residence, they once
more received their commissions without purchase.
In 1861 it was decided that every aspirant to a commission must pass through Sandhurst; but by the
spring of 1862 this resolution had been reversed, and
Sandhurst was open only to cadets whose commissions
were not to be purchased.   The truth was that there
was no excess of space in the College, and that into each
room measuring twenty-one feet by nineteen there
were packed five cadets.[1]   The immediate result was
that officers who purchased their commissions were
exempted from passing any examination at Sandhurst
or elsewhere;[2] and the only method of abolishing such
exemption seemed to be to enlarge the buildings.
But enlargement would have signified expense; and
Parliament had always considered overcrowding a
condition inseparable from the military profession.
In this difficulty the Universities of Cambridge, Oxford
and Dublin proposed to give candidates for the Army

[1] *H.D.*, Speeches of Sir G. Lewis and Colonel W. Stuart, Mar. 13,
1862.
[2] *H.D.*, Speech of Mr. Bruce, Mar. 6, 1862.

1854–
1870.
a course of training, including drill, for six terms—to graft, in effect, the education given at Sandhurst upon their own curriculum.   Sir George Lewis was a man of clear and sober thought; and possibly he may have considered the atmosphere of Oxford and Cambridge, with their short terms, their lax discipline and the too ready credit granted by tradesmen, not too favourable for young officers.   In any case he rejected the offer of the Universities, and there was an end of it.[1]

Thus affairs staggered on for yet a few years, but there could be only one conclusion to the matter. Since 1854 the entire military system had been turned upside-down.   Not only was the War Office in sole control, but every department had been reformed; and the State had set up its own factories for the making of small-arms, of guns and of clothing—revolutionary changes which provoked one member in the Commons to the criticism that the Government was becoming " a gigantic Moses and Son."[2]   Two relics of the old system alone remained, long service for soldiers and purchase for officers.   The former was swept away in 1870, the latter in 1871; and therewith the knell of the old British Army was rung.

---

[1] *H.D.*, Speeches of Mr. Selwyn and Sir G. Lewis, Mar. 6, 1862.
[2] *H.D.*, Speech of Mr. Bernal Osborne, Mar. 6, 1862. This individual had a reputation for wit, and even more for matchless impudence.

CHAPTER LX

Some other hand must record the vicissitudes of the New Army which grew up after the abolition of purchase for officers and the institution of short service for soldiers. It remains for me only to trace the influence which was wrought upon it by the traditions of its predecessor, and to show very briefly how little in its essential character the New Army differs from the old. To do so within reasonable compass I must necessarily select only such details as seem to be most important and deal with them in succession, thus gathering up the ravelled threads of my long story, and plaiting them, as I trust, into a seemly end.

First, let me deal with the most salient feature of the Old Army, regimental feeling. The troops had hardly accommodated themselves to the shock of the great changes of 1870 and 1871, when in 1881 they were shaken to their foundations by the introduction of what is called the territorial system. Such regiments of infantry as had but one battalion were grouped together in pairs. The old numbers were swept away. Territorial designations took their place. The facings, excepting in royal regiments, which retained their original blue, were made uniformly white for English regiments, yellow for Scottish and green for Irish. The outcry against this reform was loud and prolonged. It was proclaimed to be death to all regimental pride. In some official quarters it was hoped that the territorial system would put an end to the regimental exclusiveness which hindered the reorganisation of the

Army. The ordinary soldier, of whatever rank, perceived this, but did not realise that the change would be ultimately for his own benefit, and that it signified a return to the principle initiated by the Duke of York during the last great war with France, namely, that every regiment should consist of two battalions, whereof one should serve abroad and the other at home. Since Waterloo, from two-thirds to four-fifths of the infantry had been simultaneously oversea. It was hoped now that the proportion could be reduced to one-half.

For the best part of a generation the discontent continued. Who could recognise the old "Slashers" —the regiment which had given a name to "Slashers Reef" in Torres Straits—as the first battalion of the Gloucestershire? What was the significance of the "Pompadours" when they could no longer show their unique purple facings? Moreover, at first not all of the battalions took kindly to their yoke-fellows, though infinite pains had been taken to find some historic or sentimental connection between them. But gradually the newly assorted regiments settled down, and became as proud of their territorial titles as of their old numbers. A new regimental spirit sprang up which, aided by the interest of the counties in their military children, became as strong as the old. So powerful were the traditions of the old proprietary system that soldiers still thought of themselves as belonging to this or that regiment rather than to the Army at large. Regimental pride, far from being weakened, may almost be said to have gathered new strength.

I turn next to the bond of union, most precious relic of old days, between officers and men. This again, far from being loosened, became closer than ever. Apart from work in the field—frequent enough between 1870 and 1900—which always draws all ranks nearer to each other, the disappearance of the old soldier imperceptibly altered the relations between officers and men. The youthfulness in the ranks made the position of the officer, so to speak, more paternal. Gradually, too, the training of the men, which under the old order had been chiefly the business of the adjutant, was transferred to the captains and subalterns of each company, according to the system imposed by Sir John Moore upon his light brigade at Shorncliffe in 1803. Moreover, drunkenness began to diminish all over England and, with the elimination of the old soldier, very greatly decreased in the Army. The new recruits, being all of them young, took a boyish delight in games. Sixty years ago, if not longer, officers and men were playing in the same regimental team at cricket, but football was confined to schools and universities. Since then football has grown into a national pastime, in which the Army eagerly takes part; and the officers, not content with working with their men, have steadily played with them. In other armies such an association of all ranks on a common footing might be regarded as dangerous to discipline. In the British Army an officer who has led his men to victory in a football match will be the more devotedly followed by them in a sterner field.

Moreover, regimental officers continued to work for the general welfare of their men as they had worked in less favourable days. The State was beginning to treat the soldier less shabbily, and the attitude of the nation towards him became very slowly less hostile. There were still thirty years ago—there may be yet—respectable wage-earning families which wept if one of their numbers "went for a soldier," and thought it a disgrace to themselves. The first reservists which were thrown upon the country were not too kindly received, so deeply rooted was the old suspicion of the military calling. But as more and more of them spread over the country, employers woke to the value of steady men who had learned discipline; and the old prejudice was at least weakened. As usual, too, the regimental officer came to the help of the men, and regiment after regiment formed organisations to help forward reservists of good character in their civil career. The example had, it is true, been given to them in the Corps of Commissionaires established for discharged soldiers of the Old Army by Captain Walter in 1859. But these organisations were and are regimental; and the regimental officer needs no example to lead him to take care of his men. It is always the officer, not the State, who thinks of the soldier.

The most remarkable instance of this truth is to be found in a small institution founded by a little group of officers in the year 1894. Three captains, Harry Craufurd of the Grenadier Guards, Lionel Fortescue of the Seventeenth Lancers and Herbert Ramsay of the Army Medical Corps, being dissatisfied with the conduct of their regimental canteens under the regulations of the War Office, set themselves to improve it. Craufurd originated the idea of forming a co-operative society on co-operative principles for the supply of canteens. They themselves with a few friends raised four hundred pounds, founded the Canteen and Mess Co-operative Society, registered it under the Industrial and Provident Societies Act and affiliated it to the Co-operative Union. No individual was allowed to hold shares to a greater value than £200; the interest thereon was limited to five per cent; and all profits in excess of that figure were returned to the canteens for the benefit of the soldier. The Society, though frowned upon at headquarters, prospered steadily; and Fortescue, going further than Craufurd, declared that he should not be satisfied until the regiments which dealt with the Society had bought out the shareholders and made it their own—indeed, until he had gathered every regiment into the co-operative fold. His very associates in the venture were, most of them, startled at the audacity of the idea. The contracting firms, which hitherto had supplied canteens, were of course bitterly hostile and uneasily contemptuous. The authorities at the War Office were suspicious and

discouraging. Through many vicissitudes the Canteens and Mess Co-operative Society held steadily on
its way. We shall very shortly see it again under a
new name, and shall be better able to estimate the
service done by these three officers.

I turn now to a matter of deep import to the service,
the establishment of the Transport and Supply Service
of the Army upon a sure and worthy footing. Since
the days of William the Third, the commissary in the
Army, even as the purser in the Navy, had been regarded as the natural enemy of the combatant branches.
Sherbrooke in the Peninsula had threatened to hang a
commissary, and Wellington's dry comment had been
that Sherbrooke was likely to be as good as his word.
We have seen how Sir Robert Kennedy brought the
Commissariat to a high pitch of excellence in that same
Peninsula. We have seen how it was allowed to decay
by successive Governments until the Crimean war
revealed its hopeless collapse. We have seen the rise
of the Land Transport Corps and of the Military Train;
we have watched the excellent work of the Commissariat, in charge both of Transport and Supply in New
Zealand, and have followed the struggle of the man in
charge of the load for control of the waggon also. One
principle cause of contention, as has been told, was that
combatant officers wished the Transport to be under
military organisation and command, but the Supply
department to be, as heretofore, civil and of no military
status. In 1875, upon the fall of the system of Control,
the Commissariat and Transport, united, were formed
into a separate corps which languished under discouraging conditions until 1880. Its status was then
improved, and its name was changed to the Commissariat and Transport Staff, with a provision that its
officers should have served not less than five years in
the Line. This was the first step towards placing this
vital service on the footing of respect which it deserves.
Finally, in 1888, through the fostering care of Sir
Redvers Buller, was formed the present Army Service

Corps, on a purely military footing; its officers being taken from other branches of the Army, specially trained in the theory and practice of their business, and distinguished by combatant rank. Its organisation for active service at the time, being adapted to animal traction only, has long been superseded in detail and need not be stated here. But the great point was that the officers, having served for a time in a combatant branch, could not be looked down upon by those who were still combatant; while, having been themselves in charge of fighting men who required feeding, they could the better understand their wants and sympathise with their requirements. The corps was of course small, for the army which it served was small; but there is good reason to believe that it had not its equal in any army in the world.

Next, I come to what is perhaps the most remarkable of the achievements of the Army, the building up of the police of the Empire. The training of other races to soldiership began, as we have seen, in India in the eighteenth century, and was continued in the West Indies, on the West Coast of Africa and in Ceylon. In the nineteenth century, during the period under review, it was extended further to Eastern Africa; but this was a small matter to the silent change which was going forward all over the Empire. We have seen the establishment of the Metropolitan Police and of the Royal Irish Constabulary, both children of the British Army and endued with its peculiar spirit. It was not at first sight easy to provide men who should be suddenly lifted in London to a situation of authority, and could yet be trusted to exercise that authority in a spirit not of mastership but of service. Yet such men were readily found among the veterans of Wellington's army. The Duke himself did not complain, because he was powerless to move a corporal's guard from London to Hounslow without authority from a civil minister. Should his soldiers not serve in the same spirit? Throughout the latter part of the nineteenth century more and more troops were withdrawn from the Colonies, and their place was taken by constabulary raised and trained upon the spot.   Every corps of these countless peoples, nations and languages is a child of the British Army, either directly or through the Metropolitan Police or the Irish Constabulary.   Probably there is not one that was not originally formed by a British officer, and some proportion of them are commanded by British officers to this day.   Certain of them, such as the Canadian Mounted Police, are of unsurpassed excellence, vying with the Royal Irish Constabulary and the old Australian Mounted Police in their best days.   But even in petty West Indian islands there are police, some of them armed, composed of African negroes, and in the highest degree smart and efficient.   All alike inherit throughout the Empire the traditions not of arrogance, but of dutiful and disciplined service.

We speak of *pax Brittannica*, peace within the Empire.   Peace is as indefinable as war, so let us speak rather of the King's peace, signifying that where the British flag flies there the citizen may go about his lawful business unarmed.   The statement is not, of course, literally true.   One need wander no further than to some districts of London to find dangerous quarters which belie it.   Nevertheless, as a broad fact the King's peace reigns within the Empire.   We take it as a matter of course, but it is not the least of the achievements begun by the Old Army and completed by the New.   In truth the new soldier differs nothing in essential character from the old.   Like him he can be terrible in combat, but it is not in his nature to hate his enemies in the field.   The old soldier could break out into wild orgies of drunkenness and pillage which, in these more humane times, would be hardly possible.   But both the old and the new have rarely entered a country as a conqueror which they have not quitted as a friend.   The troops which sacked San Sebastian marched from the Garonne to the Channel without provoking a single complaint from the inhabitants. The Burmese sorrowed at the departure of the rough, war-hardened veterans who had survived the terrible campaign of 1824–26. "We are Englishmen," Wellington wrote during the occupation of France after Waterloo, "and pride ourselves upon our deportment," and he thanked his British troops for "the example which they have given to others"—others of other nations who prided themselves not on their deportment but on their triumph. To the new soldier as to the old the idea of military arrogance is utterly strange. Both alike were and are endowed with an amazing gift of making themselves intelligible to all races of whatever origin, colour or speech. It is a gift not of tongues, but of good nature and kindness of heart.

Before the New Army had endured for a generation a change came over the general feeling of the public towards the service. One soldier in particular, General Charles Gordon, that strange compound of pugnacity, religious fanaticism, contempt of fame and riches and vast ambition of power, exerted a strange fascination over the popular mind. A writer of genius, Mr Rudyard Kipling, moreover, revealed the private soldier, with all his faults and all his virtues, as never before to the public eye. His heroes, it is true, suggested sometimes rather the last relics of the Old Army than the first pioneers of the New; but his readers, numbered by hundreds of thousands, assumed a kind of sentimental liking, not wholly devoid of patronage, towards "Tommy," as they thought fit to call him.[1] The popular admiration thus generated was not very intelligent, nor was it very helpfully guided by the press. Neither the one nor the other, pardonably enough,

---

[1] Thomas Atkins was the name of a fictitious private in the book (showing his age, enlistment and state of accounts) which was first issued to every private soldier as part of his kit by order of Nov. 29, 1829. It was the book and not the man which was first called "Tommy Atkins." See Clode, *Military Forces of the Crown*, ii. 59.

knew anything of the history of the Army. They therefore fastened their attention principally upon regiments whose uniforms were easily distinguishable; and, Queen Victoria having a predilection for kilted regiments, the Highlanders of all denominations became great favourites. Occasionally when a battalion of the Line mounted guard at St. James's, Londoners became conscious that such battalions existed; and, if it happened to wear a green jacket, it became so much the more an object of curiosity. So too the campaigns in the Sudan aroused, for Gordon's sake, insatiable interest; while other little less arduous adventures in Burma passed unnoticed. Few realised that the period of transition, while the Old Army was dying out and the New had not yet come into being, was one of great peril; but it was passed without serious mishap, and the first grave test of the New Army came in South Africa in 1899.

That campaign, the most inglorious and yet the most difficult since the American War of Independence, opened ill, and was chequered by petty reverses from the beginning to the end. The Government, fearing to incur the guilt of aggression, gave every initial advantage to the enemy. The force originally sent out was far too small; and in a very few weeks it became evident that the enterprise was beyond the strength of the Army which Parliament maintained for the safety of the Empire. All difficulties were in due time overcome; but sundry little mishaps, which were called by the dire name of disasters, provoked an outburst of hysteria from the public similar to that which had followed upon the Crimean war. There were committees of inquiry which took reams of evidence and issued lengthy reports; but they could tell little that was new. There was no fault to find with the system of short service. The reservists had come up in a force exceeding all expectations; and there was no doubt about their quality as fighters. The auxiliary services had done well, though the Army

Service Corps had been hampered by the fact that Lord Kitchener, who was first Chief of the Staff and later Commander-in-chief in South Africa, knew nothing whatever about its organisation and functions, and tried to subject it to alterations of his own.[1]   In fact the chief defects of the Army were that it was too small, and that the machinery for expanding it was very imperfect.   These were an evil inheritance from the improvident politicians who had placed the militia upon a voluntary basis and revived the obsolete expedient of volunteers.

All men with eyes to see could perceive danger looming ahead.   Those who best appreciated it urged the adoption of some form of national service, and an increase of the Army.   But the Government was already spending vast sums upon the Navy, and, rightly attaching most importance to the fleet, would spare little money for the military service.   Very many among the nation blinded their eyes to the peril and pinned their faith to international tribunals and the like expedients.   For four years there was unprofitable discussion; and then the task of setting the nation's military house in order was taken in hand by Richard Burdon Haldane.   A jurist of eminence and a deep student of philosophy, he seemed to be the least fitted of men to wrestle with military problems; but he was an admirable administrator, and was careful to learn from others before he began himself to teach.   When once he had grasped the essential details of the situation he brought a great intellect to bear upon them; and the readiness of sympathy and understanding which he showed towards his military colleagues called from them their best and most strenuous work.   First he built up on the German model a striking force of the Regular Army, small indeed but perfect to the last detail. Next, he treated the militia avowedly as what it had always been since its revival—a training depôt to feed

[1] Hence the biting epigram: " K. of Chaos."   Lord Kitchener of Khartoum was familiarly spoken of as K. of K.

the Regular Army.   Lastly, he abolished the volunteers
and converted them into a territorial force, of which
he threw the administration in great part upon the
authorities of the counties.   The political party to
which he belonged had for many decades heaped abuse
upon the country gentlemen and done their utmost to
ruin them both in wealth and influence.   Yet Haldane
turned to them in the hour of need; and they, as he
gratefully acknowledged, did all that they could to
help him.   Without their loyal and unselfish co-
operation, indeed, the whole scheme would have failed.
Haldane's work was still incomplete when, most unfortunately, he was called away from the War Office;
but the service which he wrought was of untold value
to the country.   He was called by Lord Haig the
greatest Minister for War that has ever been in
England.   This was an exaggeration.   Haldane was
not greater than Castlereagh; but he was at least the
only man who could bear comparison with Castlereagh.
    Then in 1914 came war; and the striking force—
the Expeditionary Force, as it was called—was sent to
France to gain time for England to make the preparations which should have been made before.   Small
though it was in comparison with the hosts of other
nations, it was incomparably the finest army which
this country had ever put into the field and, alike in
the quality of its troops and the efficiency of its auxiliary
services, it had not its equal among any of the belli-
gerents.   It perished, as have all other British armies at
the outset of a great war, in fulfilling the task assigned
to it, having set a noble standard for all the other
forces of the Empire.   To the present writer not the
least interesting point in its brief career was to observe
how the noble old regiments of the Line, which had
fought under William and Marlborough and Cumber-
land and Ferdinand of Brunswick, at once stepped
forward into their former prominence.   If a moment's
egoism may be forgiven me, I think that not even their
own veterans rejoiced with greater exultation over their

prowess than did I who had been privileged to follow them from their cradles.

But I must address myself to my purpose, which is to show how the achievements and influence of the Old Army reacted upon the New, or rather the Newer, which was called into being between 1914 and 1918, and what were the differences which they brought about in the conduct of this as compared with former wars.

First, owing to the existence of the police and constabulary all over the Empire, there was little anxiety over internal order in any part of it,[1] and no occasion to distract troops from active work to a weary and thankless duty. We take all this as a matter of course; but it must be repeated once more that it was the Army that made the original police and gave them its own high tone. It is possible, without any extravagant stretch of imagination, to conceive of the first efforts in that direction as failures. The Metropolitan Police and the Royal Irish Constabulary might very well have proved themselves uncertain experiments, at any rate for a time. But, thanks to the fine spirit of the veterans of the great war with France, both officers and men, they were an immediate and striking success, and they begat offspring like unto themselves.

Secondly, in the war of 1914, for the first time in British military history, practically no new combatant regiments were raised. Instead, countless battalions were added to the old regiments.[2] This was of course due to the scheme for territorial expansion of the Army, though Lord Haldane's original plan for the same was unfortunately departed from. But one result of it was to propagate the old regimental spirit, inherited from the Old Army, to the widest extent. Every new

---

[1] I shall be reminded of the insurrection in Ireland in 1916; but this was due to culpable neglect and mismanagement.

[2] The colonel of the Manchester Regiment wrote to me at this time that he was the titular commander of 50,000 men; and he cannot have stood alone.

battalion had its standard set for it by its regimental history in the past and, more nearly, by the achievements of its own regular battalions in the present. Commanding officers who knew their business rightly made a great point of this; and the old regimental pride counted for much during the war.

Thirdly, there was the old tradition of close attachment between officers and men. Thanks to the South African War we had at first a larger number of officers, professional and unprofessional, who had seen active service than the established numbers of our military force could in theory warrant. But the dearth of officers soon made itself felt, in our own as in all the belligerent armies. Nevertheless, it is a very striking fact that, whereas there were in the course of the war serious mutinies in the armies of all the great powers engaged—Germany, Austria, France, Italy, Russia— there was none in the British Army. The people which was sneered at by its Continental neighbours as unmilitary, proved that it could outdo them all in military spirit and military discipline. It was not for nothing that the Old Army, the despised, the maligned, the persecuted, had handed down its traditions of duty and long-suffering; not for nothing that the old regiments, each jealously isolated for its own protection, had set the regimental honour before all things; not for nothing that the bond between officers and men has for generations been nowhere so fast as in the British Army.

Last, let us glance to a contribution of obscure regimental officers to the general welfare of the Army in the field and at home during the German war. Ever since its foundation the Canteen and Mess Co-operative Society had been quietly at work, uniformly discouraged by the War Office and hated by the firms of canteen-contractors. In 1914 it was suddenly lifted into prominence. Evil dealing was revealed in one of the commercial firms selected by the War Office itself for the supply of canteens; the matter became a public scandal;

and attention was naturally turned upon the Society. Very shortly afterwards the German war broke out. The Commander-in-chief on the Western Front begged for a field-canteen. The War Office summoned the representatives of the Canteen and Mess Co-operative Society and of one leading firm of contractors and entrusted the task to them, insisting, however, that the canteen should be managed upon co-operative principles. Since only the Society understood those principles, it took the entire matter into its own hands, appointed the whole of the staff and conducted the whole of the business. Thus came into being what was known as the Expeditionary Force Canteen, better known by its initials as the E.F.C.

Its story cannot here be even briefly set down, but it has the air of a romance rather than of sober fact.[1] The Expeditionary Force Canteen on the Western Front began life with a single motor car and ended with a fleet of four hundred and fifty. " It spread the table for the entire British Expeditionary Force from the mess at General Headquarters to the private soldiers' billets." And, not content with France, it followed the Army to Italy, to Gallipoli, to Salonica, to Palestine, to Mesopotamia, even to the Arctic Circle. The range of its activities was too wide and its volume of business too colossal to allow of detailed mention here. Every commander in the field testified to its efficiency and to its value in maintaining the cheerfulness and contentment of the troops. It bore its share in keeping mutiny at a distance. Yet it cost the country practically nothing, and returned huge revenues to officers and men.

Nor was even this the limit of its usefulness. Its success was so great that its principles were applied at home as well as abroad; and thus there grew up a gigantic organisation which reckoned its volume of

---

[1] I have sketched the story briefly, if anyone chances to be interested in it, in a tiny volume entitled *A Short Account of Canteens in the British Army*.

trade by tens of millions sterling.   The Navy and Air Force begged to be admitted to its privileges; and, when the war was ended, this organisation was permanently established as the Navy, Army and Air Force Institute.   Wherever men of these three forces are to be found, there is a branch of the Institute to minister to their comfort, charging the lowest possible prices and returning the revenues to them.   Be it specially noted that the Institute is not a department of the State. It is managed by the men who controlled the Expeditionary Force Canteen, that is to say, by the staff of the Canteen and Mess Co-operative Society.   It has grown up in spite of the State, and is untainted by the hand of the politician.   In its origin it was built up by a few humble regimental officers for the benefit of the soldier, and in its development it fulfils, and more than fulfils, their own declared purpose.   The Institute belongs to the officers and men of the Navy, Army and Air Force, and to them alone.   They are responsible for its management and for the disposal of its revenues.   It is their very own.   There is nothing like it to be found in any country in the world.   It is the crowning work of the regimental officer for the Army.

EPILOGUE

My task is done.   My story, however imperfectly, is
told.   We see the first really organised military force
in English history created for civil strife in 1645.   We
watch its immediate triumph, and see it first rise to
sovereign power, making constitutions and trying political experiments, then fall amid universal execration and
disappear, leaving behind it a national dread of military
government and a national loathing of standing armies.
Yet some kind of organised force was imperatively
necessary for the preservation of order and for defence
at home, and for the protection of the growing Empire
abroad.   So a certain number of regiments was called
into being, and the system of purchase, inherited from
the old mercenary bands, was adopted to provide them
with officers.   It was cheap, for an officer's pay little
exceeded the interest on the cost of his commission;
and it was secure, for, since an officer, if cashiered, forfeited the price of his commission to the King, he was
practically bound over in a substantial sum to good
behaviour.

But it was another incident of the purchase-system
which really kept the Army in existence and gave to it
its peculiar character.   The regiment became the property of the colonel, and its troops or companies the
property of the captains.   It was in fact a possession,
carrying with it all the pride and delight of ownership,
and a peculiarly interesting possession, since it consisted of disciplined men.   It was also a little close
society—a kind of military congregation—bound by

the implicit vows of obedience and sacrifice, with its colours as the emblem of its corporate unity, and its colonel for president or high priest. It was absolutely self-contained, for all of its incidental expenses were defrayed by an allowance of fictitious men on the muster-rolls. The financial business was discharged by the colonel's own clerk, known as the agent; and the physical and spiritual needs of all ranks were under the care of two of the colonel's servants, called the doctor and the chaplain. A regiment, in fact, at the outset was more of a private than of a national affair. No emblem of royalty or nationality was at first necessarily borne on the colours. The colonel as proprietor was all in all. If the King himself had a regiment he ruled it rather as colonel than as King.

It was in virtue of this independence that the little group of regiments, which was called the Standing Army, was able to withstand for two centuries the hatred, malignity and stinginess of Parliament, and the contempt and scorn of every citizen. The behaviour both of Parliament and citizens was nothing short of imbecile. Without the soldiers the law could not be enforced; the fleet could not be manned; the British Isles and the British Empire could not be defended by land or sea. Yet the persecution of the soldier continued unrelentingly. Against such an Army as that of Cromwell it might have succeeded. Against a collection of proprietary regiments it failed. The officers might not possess greater humanity than other men, but the soldiers of their regiments were their own men, and therefore must be protected. Marlborough's troops marched from victory to victory, and returned to be cursed as the plagues of the nation. Thousands of officers and tens of thousands of men were turned adrift. The only result was to make the survivors cling more closely together. Maltreated and despised sects—and such were the regiments of the eighteenth century—are likely, especially if they be English, to gain vitality rather than to lose it.

Regiments were sent abroad to foreign garrisons in vile climates, ill-housed and ill-fed, to perish from cold in one quarter, to drop dead of heat in another. The officers only became the more assiduous in lightening the heavy burden of their men, and the men, as a natural consequence, became the more attached to them. At home soldiers were vilified, bullied and oppressed; and the officers, though they did what they could, were often powerless to shield them. With complaint, though not the less with good discipline, they endured with patience, for the honour of their regiments.

And, no matter how Parliament might rage, nothing could prevent the regiments from increasing. There was always fresh work for them at home or abroad. The feeble ministers who governed England at the opening of the Seven Years' War tried to carry on that war—and indeed to defend the realm—with German mercenaries. They were obliged after all to call in British soldiers, who conquered for England an Empire. Her only gratitude for the gift was loud reiteration of the cry " Down with the Standing Army." An attempt—quite legitimate though not very wise—to induce the Colonies to contribute towards the cost of it, brought on the general quarrel with the American Provinces and the loss of the Western Empire. There were high hopes that the Army might be greatly reduced; but the extension of sovereignty in India forbade this. However, if the Army could not be diminished, it might at any rate be starved. The officers, indeed, represented at this time that the men were so ill paid that they had no alternative, literally, but to desert or to starve. The Government was quite content that it should be so. It was paying a retaining fee for German mercenaries after the manner of its predecessors. The British soldier might go hungry and make the best of his hunger.

Then came the war of the French Revolution, and after four years the crash. The Navy mutinied, with very good reason. The Army, which had suffered no less provocation, remained staunch; and the politicians, under the stress not of justice but of fear, hastened to grant the increase of pay which the officers had for years been vainly entreating for their men. The Duke of York rescued the force from the mischievous hands of the civilians, and after many vicissitudes it emerged under Wellington as great as it had been under Marlborough. In 1815 as in 1714 it was cursed for its pains as the plague of the nation.

But meanwhile it had won a new Empire; and, since it could not therefore be destroyed, the politicians decided that it should be banished. However, a long course of combined maltreatment and active service had drawn officers and men closer than ever together. In regiment after regiment officers had thought out the means of bettering the soldiers' lot, and thereby were making good the meanness of the State. They could not, of course, sweep away insanitary barracks. There could be no arguing with legislators who provided a thousand cubic feet of space for each convict and thought three hundred sufficient for each soldier. There could be no reasoning with economists who complained of the cost of recruits and laid themselves out to kill them as rapidly as possible. But the officers could at least show the way towards improvement of the soldier's condition, and compel the sordid, sluggish, sulky State from very shame to follow them. But, though the State, thanks to the officers, could not destroy the regiments, they could and did destroy every auxiliary department and allowed all stores of war to sink well below the margin of safety. Then it sent an army out to the Crimea and was somewhat shocked to see it perish of cold and hunger—still more surprised to find that this was its own fault. For the moment Parliament softened towards the Army. It turned it upside down and inside out to discover what could be the matter. But it soon relapsed into its old niggardly ways, until it suddenly awoke to the prospect that the Army was rapidly dissolving before its eyes. Then at last under sheer compulsion, as in 1797, it granted the one thing needful, an increase of pay for the private soldier.

In the generation that followed 1870 there was some change for the better in the nation's attitude towards the soldier, but no real change of heart. The old prejudice against a sufficient army still continued, and the people steadily shirked their duty to make adequate preparation for war. The inevitable result followed. They were obliged ultimately not only to submit to compulsory national service, but to pay for their blindness and sloth with a heavy toll of blood and treasure. And now the nation has returned to its ancient ways; and there is pathetic effort to make an end of war by making first an end of armaments. If unreadiness for hostilities be any furtherance of the cause of peace, then assuredly the English cannot be blamed for leaving the experiment untried in the past. Yet the result has not been encouraging. For war does not depend either always or wholly upon armaments. Even if external wars could cease, there remains always civil war, which is not the less war because internal. Human envy, hatred and malice will always find weapons. Human enthusiasm or wickedness will always find pretexts. In 1926 there was a movement called a General Strike, which was an effort to gain political advantage by paralysing the internal communications of the country and inducing, among other things, a scarcity of food. The methods of war were employed for what was, ostensibly, a peaceful end, and among them one of the deadliest weapons of war—famine—which is a sure means of setting men at each other's throats. Practically, therefore, the General Strike was a declaration of a kind of civil war, though many who abetted it were loudest in denunciation of war in the abstract. So idly do men use words, and so little do they think of their meaning.

There is talk of universal brotherhood, yet the quarrels of brethren are proverbial for their bitter-

ness. There has been talk of a reign of the saints, yet
in the earliest days of Christianity St. Paul contended
against St. Peter. There are those who maintain
that human nature can be changed; and there can
be no question of their sincerity and good intent. But
there can also be no question that, notwithstanding
all their efforts, a month's starvation—always possible
through some catastrophe in nature—would turn not
a few members of the most highly civilised community
into something akin to savages. There is so much that
is hidden even from the most steadfast view; there are
so many human reactions which, if not called into play,
are forgotten. With an eye and a heart fixed aloft
upon the known good, yet with a wasting downward
tendency to evil, this human nature of ours, if viewed
in all its latent powers, its possibilities and its activities,
remains for ever unchanging and perhaps unchange-
able. To our imperfect understanding war may well
seem horrible, lamentable, an accursed thing to be
utterly abolished; yet there it is—perhaps, if we are to
judge from history, the oldest and most persistent of
human institutions. We trust that it has its high
purpose in the divine scheme which passes our intelligence, but we may not end it. Man cannot alter his
essential nature, nor can he load the balances of God.

Wars, therefore, will never cease, grievous though
the thought may be. Yet, to descend again to lowly
mundane things, its former outward manifestations
seem likely to be transformed. It may well be that by
new methods of scientific destruction the whole nature
of armies may be changed. Infantry and cavalry may
vanish away, and regiments and even armies, in the
old and honoured sense, may cease to be. Then shall
the British Army likewise perish; and its place shall
know it no more. It matters not. Were the Army
to be swept to-morrow into nothingness, it has already
done enough to give it rank with the legions of ancient
Rome. And it will be remembered best not for its
surpassing valour and endurance, not for its countless

deeds of daring and its invincible stubbornness in battle, but for its lenience in conquest and its gentleness in domination. Let Wellington's phrase be repeated once more, "We are English and pride ourselves on our deportment."

Empires decay and fall, and the British Empire cannot escape the common lot. Already the Dominions are virtually independent. They will forget, as the Americans have already forgotten, what they owe to the British soldier; but not the less will his work for them remain. In India the rule of the British will fade in due time into a legend of stolid white men, very terrible in fight, who swept the land from end to end, enforcing for a brief space strange maxims of equity and government. The age may be hereafter mournfully recalled by the Indian peasant as that wherein his forefathers reaped what they had sown under the protection of the British soldier. When the Empire shall have passed away, it is the British soldier's figure that will loom out eminent above all, the calm upholder of the King's peace.

And the historian of the dim future, summing up the whole story, may conclude it in some such words as these. "The builders of this Empire despised and derided the stone which became the headstone of the corner. They were not worthy of such an army. Two centuries of persecution could not wear out its patience; two centuries of thankless toil could not abate its ardour; two centuries of conquest could not awake it to insolence. Dutiful to its masters, merciful to its enemies, it clung steadfastly to its old simple ideals—obedience, service, sacrifice."

INDEX

INDEX

THE END

FORTESCUE'S HISTORY OF THE BRTISH ARMY
IN 14 VOLUMES OF TEXT AND 1 MAP VOLUME

Vol. I – First Part–to the close of the Seven Years' War
ISBN: 1 84574 500 0   £36.00

Vol. II – First Part–to the close of the Seven Years' War
ISBN: 1 84574 501 9   £36.00

Vol. III – Second Part–from the close of the Seven Years' War
to the Second Peace of Paris   ISBN: 1 84574 502 7   £36.00

Vol. IV – Part I – Second Part continued – from the Fall of the Bastille
to the Peace of Amiens   ISBN: 1 84574 503 5   £36.00

Vol. IV – Part II – Second Part continued – from the Fall of the Bastille
to the Peace of Amiens   ISBN: 1 84574 504 3   £36.00

Vol. V – Second Part continued – from the Renewal of the War
to the Evacuation of Rio de la Plata   ISBN: 1 84574 505 1   £36.00

Vol. VI – from the Expedition to Egypt, 1807,
to the Battle of Coruna, January 1809   ISBN: 1 84574 506 X   £36.00

Vol. VII – 1809-1810   ISBN: 1 84574 507 8   £36.00

Vol. VIII – 1811-1812   ISBN: 1 84574 508 6   £36.00

Vol. IX – 1813-1814   ISBN: 1 84574 509 4   £36.00

Vol. X – 1814-1815   ISBN: 1 84574 510 8   £36.00

Vol. XI – 1815-1838   ISBN: 1 84574 511 6   £36.00

Vol. XII – 1839-1852   ISBN: 1 84574 512 4   £36.00

Vol. XIII – 1852-1870   ISBN: 1 84574 513 2   £36.00

Maps - originally published in 6 volumes ISBN: 1 84574 514 0   £98.00

The Naval & Military Press Ltd

Unit 10, Ridgewood Industrial Park,
Uckfield, East Sussex, TN22 5QE, England
Tel: 01825 749494   Fax: 01825 765701
email: order.dept@naval–military–press.com

Order online:
www.naval–military–press.com

Online genealogy research:
www.military-genealogy.com

Printed in the United Kingdom
by Lightning Source UK Ltd.
134933UK00002B/28/A